A History of the Pachinko Industry

JAPANESE SOCIETY SERIES
General Editor: Yoshio Sugimoto

Lives of Young Koreans in Japan
Yasunori Fukuoka

Globalization and Social Change in Contemporary Japan
J.S. Eades, Tom Gill and Harumi Befu

Coming Out in Japan: The Story of Satoru and Ryuta
Satoru Ito and Ryuta Yanase

Japan and Its Others:
Globalization, Difference and the Critique of Modernity
John Clammer

Hegemony of Homogeneity: An Anthropological Analysis of Nihonjinron
Harumi Befu

Foreign Migrants in Contemporary Japan
Hiroshi Komai

A Social History of Science and Technology in Contemporary Japan, Volume 1
Shigeru Nakayama

Farewell to Nippon: Japanese Lifestyle Migrants in Australia
Machiko Sato

The Peripheral Centre:
Essays on Japanese History and Civilization
Johann P. Arnason

A Genealogy of 'Japanese' Self-images
Eiji Oguma

Class Structure in Contemporary Japan
Kenji Hashimoto

An Ecological View of History
Tadao Umesao

Nationalism and Gender
Chizuko Ueno

Native Anthropology: The Japanese Challenge to Western Academic Hegemony
Takami Kuwayama

Youth Deviance in Japan: Class Reproduction of Non-Conformity
Robert Stuart Yoder

Japanese Companies: Theories and Realities
Masami Nomura and Yoshihiko Kamii

From Salvation to Spirituality: Popular Religious Movements in Modern Japan
Susumu Shimazono

The 'Big Bang' in Japanese Higher Education:
The 2004 Reforms and the Dynamics of Change
J.S. Eades, Roger Goodman and Yumiko Hada

Japanese Politics: An Introduction
Takashi Inoguchi

A Social History of Science and Technology in Contemporary Japan, Volume 2
Shigeru Nakayama

Gender and Japanese Management
Kimiko Kimoto

Philosophy of Agricultural Science: A Japanese Perspective
Osamu Soda

A Social History of Science and Technology in Contemporary Japan, Volume 3
Shigeru Nakayama and Kunio Goto

Japan's Underclass: Day Laborers and the Homeless
Hideo Aoki

A Social History of Science and Technology in Contemporary Japan, Volume 4
Shigeru Nakayama and Hitoshi Yoshioka

Scams and Sweeteners: A Sociology of Fraud
Masahiro Ogino

Toyota's Assembly Line: A View from the Factory Floor
Ryoji Ihara

Village Life in Modern Japan: An Environmental Perspective
Akira Furukawa

Social Welfare in Japan: Principles and Applications
Kojun Furukawa

Escape from Work: Freelancing Youth and the Challenge to Corporate Japan
Reiko Kosugi

Japan's Whaling: The Politics of Culture in Historical Perspective
Hiroyuki Watanabe

Gender Gymnastics: Performing and Consuming Japan's Takarazuka Revue
Leonie R. Stickland

Poverty and Social Welfare in Japan
Masami Iwata and Akihiko Nishizawa

The Modern Japanese Family: Its Rise and Fall
Chizuko Ueno

Widows of Japan: An Anthropological Perspective
Deborah McDowell Aoki

In Pursuit of the Seikatsusha:
A Genealogy of the Autonomous Citizen in Japan
Masako Amano

Demographic Change and Inequality in Japan
Sawako Shirahase

The Origins of Japanese Credentialism
Ikuo Amano

Pop Culture and the Everyday in Japan: Sociological Perspectives
Katsuya Minamida and Izumi Tsuji

Japanese Perceptions of Foreigners
Shunsuke Tanabe

Migrant Workers in Contemporary Japan:
An Institutional Perspective on Transnational Employment
Kiyoto Tanno

The Boundaries of 'the Japanese', Volume 1:
Okinawa 1868–1972 – Inclusion and Exclusion
Eiji Oguma

International Migrants in Japan: Contributions in an Era of Population Decline
Yoshitaka Ishikawa

Globalizing Japan: Striving to Engage the World
Ross Mouer

Beyond Fukushima: Toward a Post-Nuclear Society
Koichi Hasegawa

Japan's Ultra Right
Naoto Higuchi

The Boundaries of 'the Japanese', Volume 2:
Korea, Taiwan and the Ainu 1868–1945
Eiji Oguma

Creating Subaltern Counterpublics: Korean Women
in Japan and Their Struggles for Night School
Akwi Seo

A History of the Pachinko Industry

From a Peripheral Economy to a Huge Market

By

Jaehyang Han

TRANS PACIFIC PRESS

Originally published in Japan by THE UNIVERSITY OF NAGOYA PRESS, Aichi.
English translation rights arranged with THE UNIVERSITY OF NAGOYA PRESS, Japan through THE SAKAI AGENCY.

This English edition published in 2022 by:
Trans Pacific Press Co., Ltd.
2nd Floor, Hamamatsu-cho Daiya Building
2-2-15 Hamamatsu-cho, Minato-ku,
Tokyo 105-0013, Japan
Telephone: +81-(0)50-5371-9475
Email: info@transpacificpress.com
Web: http://www.transpacificpress.com

Edited by Miriam Riley, Armidale, Australia.
Designed and set by Ryo Kuroda, Tsukuba, Japan.

Distributors

USA, Canada and India
Independent Publishers Group (IPG)
814 N. Franklin Street
Chicago, IL 60610, USA
Telephone inquiries: +1-312-337-0747
Order placement: 800-888-4741 (domestic only)
Fax: +1-312-337-5985
Email: frontdesk@ipgbook.com
Web: http://www.ipgbook.com

Europe, Oceania, Middle East and Africa
EUROSPAN
Gray's Inn House,
127 Clerkenwell Road
London, EC1R 5DB
United Kingdom
Telephone: +44-(0)20-7240-0856
Email: info@eurospan.co.uk
Web: https://www.eurospangroup.com

Japan
MHM Limited
3-2-3F, Kanda-Ogawamachi, Chiyoda-ku,
Tokyo 101-0052
Tel: +81-3-3518-9181
Fax: +81-3-3518-9523
Email: sales@mhmlimited.co.jp
Web: http://www.mhmlimited.co.jp

China
China Publishers Services Ltd.
718, 7/F., Fortune Commercial Building,
362 Sha Tsui Road, Tsuen Wan, N.T.
Hong Kong
Telephone: +852-2491-1436
Email: edwin@cps-hk.com

Southeast Asia
Alkem Company Pte Ltd.
1, Sunview Road #01-27, Eco-Tech@Sunview
Singapore 627615
Telephone: +65 6265 6666
Email: enquiry@alkem.com.sg

ISBN 978-1-925608-39-7 (hardback)
ISBN 978-1-925608-46-5 (paperback)
ISBN 978-1-925608-40-3 (ebook)

The publication of this book was supported by a Grant-in-Aid for the Publication of Scientific Research Results (Grant Number 20HP6002), provided by the Japan Society for the Promotion of Science.

Cover photo: Pachinko parlor in Tokyo, June 1953. Source: Mainichi Newspapers.

CONTENTS

LIST OF FIGURES

LIST OF TABLES

LIST OF PHOTOGRAPHS

ACKNOWLEDGEMENTS

I am fortunate in that my research into the pachinko industry, which began during my doctoral thesis and as part of my previous book, benefited from the resolute guidance of professors Takeo Kikkawa, Haruhito Takeda, Tomohiro Okada, Shigeru Matsushima, Kazuo Wada, Yoshitaka Suzuki and Asobu Yanagisawa, who offered their support despite my own concerns about the topic's significance. That support went further than sharing important viewpoints concerning the direction of this book. The interest shown by people who were like legends to me, and the rigorous discussions in which we engaged, helped me maintain a sense of constructive tension while providing opportunities for me to return to my roots as a researcher and realign my approach to my subject matter accordingly. I would like to express my heartfelt gratitude for that assistance.

My time at the Harvard-Yenching Institute and the Reischauer Institute of Japanese Studies at Harvard University from 2015 to 2016 offered a valuable opportunity to broaden my perspective. The ability to exchange views with those institutions' scholars – even as their questions' focus on gambling and relationships with organized crime surprised me – enabled me to examine the significance of pachinko and the relationship of ethnic minority Koreans in Japan to the industry from a different perspective. Each time I sought refuge in explanations of economic rationality, my discussions with professors Carter J. Eckert, Andrew Gordon, Hiroshi Ishida and Gavin H. Whitelaw drew me back to a perspective that focused on a structural understanding of the industries' chaotic relationships with society.

I also received valuable advice related to this work from Waka Aoyama, Tamaki Endo, Momoko Kawakami, Sun Huei-min and Hyuga Shoko. I was also fortunate to have the opportunity to participate in sessions at the seventeenth World Economic History Congress, Kyoto 2015, organized by Asuka Imaizumi, and the 2017 Association for Asian Studies Annual Conference in Toronto, organized by Holly Stephens. I received many suggestions regarding this work from the organizers and other participants. I am grateful for the encouragement I was given to pursue research on economic activities at the periphery of society.

I would also like to thank Associate Professor Hiroto Suzuki of Josai International University, Faculty of Management and Information Sciences, for the statistical analysis he conducted and Fei Carnes and Hongsu Henry Wang of Harvard University for the GIS analysis. Professor Yuichi Hashimoto of Hokkaido University's Graduate School of Humanities and Human Sciences also offered valuable advice about GIS. Professor Takahiro Sugita of Keio University Faculty of Law helped me understand laws related to the pachinko industry. I take this opportunity to express my gratitude for their contributions. I consulted Zhe Ren, a researcher at the Institute of Developing Economies, Japan External Trade Organization, concerning Chinese surnames and received valuable advice.

I am also very grateful to Shingo Miki of the University of Nagoya Press for suggesting that I consider publishing a history of the pachinko industry. I mentioned it in a book in which I explored the history of businesses run by ethnic minority Koreans in Japan. At the time I thought he was only joking, because so few people have conducted academic research on the pachinko industry. I then started to take his suggestion more seriously when I became interested in working in more detail on the history of the pachinko industry as a prime example of businesses run by ethnic minority Koreans in Japan.

The body of accumulated industrial history research, while being remarkable in both its quality and quantity, focuses primarily on the manufacturing industry. Hence, I could not apply their methodology directly to the pachinko industry, which is a service industry. It also does not have the voluminous historical materials we find in the manufacturing industries. However, the main challenge was personal. I had a hard time convincing myself that research on the pachinko industry was worth the effort. Furthermore, I was blindsided by the fixed ideas and stereotypes people have about the pachinko industry and thus had a hard time finding a new and worthwhile direction to take in conducting research on the industry. People mentioned above pointed me in the right direction and helped me realize the importance of the research. Without their involvement, I would never have been able to write this book. Of course, it goes without saying that I am responsible for its content.

Finally, I would also like to express my gratitude to everyone who provided materials for my research or cooperated with my requests for information and materials. I owe a debt of gratitude to those who agreed to be interviewed, including representatives of pachinko parlors, manufacturers and prize companies as well as pin adjusters and others. The willingness of Tatsuyuki Sasaki of Yūgi Tsūshinsha, the late Seiichi Yamada, the late Tokuji Kamiya, Yoichi Suzuki of the Tokyo Pachinko and Pachislot Associations, the Japan Amusement Machine Industry Association and the All-Japan Federation of Amusement Business Cooperative Associations, amongst others, to provide access to a variety of materials and information, and to make themselves available for interviews, was invaluable.

I also would like to express once more my deep gratitude to the people at Maruhan Co., Ltd. and Masamura Shōkai, who generously gave me access to their company materials. In addition, people at Maruhan Co., Ltd. participated in three separate interviews and answered questions by email.

This research would not have been possible without the cooperation of the late president, other Masamura Shōkai family members and Emiko Suzuki. They allowed me to see materials from the 1950s to 2010 when the company ended its sixty-year history in June of that year.

I am also grateful for the financial support that funded my research. I received two grants from the Japanese government's Grants-in-Aid for Scientific Research program. In addition, financial support from the University of Tokyo Management Education and Research Center, the School of Economics and Business of Hokkaido University and a scholarship from the Harvard-Yenching Institute allowed me to study materials and discuss my research with their scholars. I also received a 2020 Grant-in-Aid for the Publication of Scientific Research Results, the 2020 Support for Overseas Publication by the Suntory Foundation and the 2021 Rikkyo University Special Fund for Research.

While working on the project, I became increasingly aware of its challenges. Potential readers may not appreciate the value of an academic study on the pachinko industry, considering it as a local issue in Japan. On the other hand, those who are aware of the importance of the topic might avoid reading the book because they know of its politically sensitive nature. I would like to express my sincere gratitude to Trans Pacific Press and Yuko Uematsu, its director, as well as Ms. Miriam Cath Riley, the book's editor, for agreeing to publish the translated book and thereby taking on all the challenges involved. I would also like to sincerely thank Brian Douglas Rafter, who put in a great deal of effort in translating the book.

GLOSSARY

Terms

chūrippu: literally 'tulip'; a *yakumono* accessory that became extremely popular during the 1960s; a tulip-shaped catcher into which balls fell, signaling a win, at which point the tulip petals would open and close

Fībā: literally 'fever'; a pachinko machine developed by Sankyo in 1980 that was a game changer in the machines market

jinmitto: the first generation of pachinko machines to be equipped with a *yakumono* accessory with a bridge; passing by the bridge resulted in loss, while a win was achieved by hitting a ball into a back pocket; the name derived from the Jinmu economic boom between 1954 and 1957

komikku: abbereviation of '*komikku gēto*', literally 'comic gate', developed in 1957; these machines were the first generation of pachinko machines, along with '*jinmitto*', to be equipped with mechanisms that functioned to move *yakumono* accessories; a win was achieved by passing through a winning groove, while balls coming from the top interacted with the windmill in the middle of the bridge (of *jinmitto*) providing the players with visual entertainment

komono: literally 'small article'; a pachinko machine that used an arrangement of randomly placed pins

kugishi: pin adjuster

michi: paths along which balls travel between a pachinko machine's pins

pachinko musume: the female attendants who supplied and retrieved balls manually behind the machines in the 1950s

pachinko-ya: pachinko businesses

pachislot machines: pachinko-size Japanese slot machines

renpatsu-shiki kikai: successive-shot machines

sararīman: literally 'salarymen,' meaning office workers

sebun-ki: literally 'seven-machine'; a category of Fībā-type machine incorporating three rotating drums in the manner of a slot machine that yielded a jackpot when three sevens showed

shinkin banks: generally larger and serve a more varied range of businesses than credit unions

shinsōkaiten: renewal reopenings

shogi: a Japanese game similar to chess

yakumono accessories: objects affixed to the board to change balls' trajectories apart from catchers and pins

Zainichi: literally 'staying in Japan'; used to refer to Koreans who have lived in Japanese society over the long term following Japan's colonization

Organizations

Kenkyū Kyōkai: Japan Amusement Machine Research Association (Nihon Yūgiki Kenkyū Kyōkai)

Konwakai: Japan Amusement Machine Invention Group (Nihon Yūgiki Hatsumei Jisshi Konwakai)

Nikkōso: Japan Amusement Machine Industry Association (Nihon Yūgiki Kōgyō Kumiai)

Nittokuren: Japan Amusement Machine Patent Management Federation (Nihon Yūgiki Tokkyo Unei Renmei)

Toyūkyō: Tokyo Pachinko and Pachislot Cooperative Associations (Tokyo-to Yūgigyō Kyōdō Kumiai)

Zenkenkyō: National Amusement Machine Right-holders' Association (Zenkoku Yūgiki Tokkyo Kenrisha Kyōkai)
Zenkōren: National Confederation of Amusement Machine Manufacturing Industry Associations (Zenkoku Yūgiki Seizō Kōgyō Kumiai Rengōkai)
Zenshōren: National Confederation of Amusement Machine Merchant Associations (Zenkoku Yūgiki Shōgyō Kumiai Rengōkai)
Zen'yūkyō: National Confederation of Amusement Industry Cooperatives (Zenkoku Yūgigyō Kyōdō Kumiai Rengōkai)
Zen'yūren: National Confederation of Amusement Industry Associations (Zenkoku Yūgigyō Kumiai Rengōkai)

JPY-USD EXCHANGE RATE

Year	Value of US$1 (yen)	Year	Value of US$1 (yen)
1972	303.07	1996	108.78
1973	271.17	1997	120.99
1974	293.76	1998	130.91
1975	297.26	1999	113.91
1976	296.19	2000	107.77
1977	267.27	2001	121.53
1978	207.64	2002	125.39
1979	221.23	2003	115.93
1980	226.74	2004	108.19
1981	220.54	2005	110.22
1982	249.08	2006	116.30
1983	237.51	2007	117.75
1984	237.52	2008	103.36
1985	238.54	2009	93.57
1986	168.52	2010	87.78
1987	144.64	2011	79.81
1988	128.12	2012	79.79
1989	137.96	2013	97.60
1990	144.79	2014	105.94
1991	134.71	2015	121.04
1992	126.65	2016	108.79
1993	111.20	2017	112.17
1994	102.21	2018	110.42
1995	94.06		

Source: New Electronic Power Net (Shin Denryoku Net) *website managed by the Energy Information Center, https://pps-net.org/statistics/exchange#.*

MAP OF JAPAN

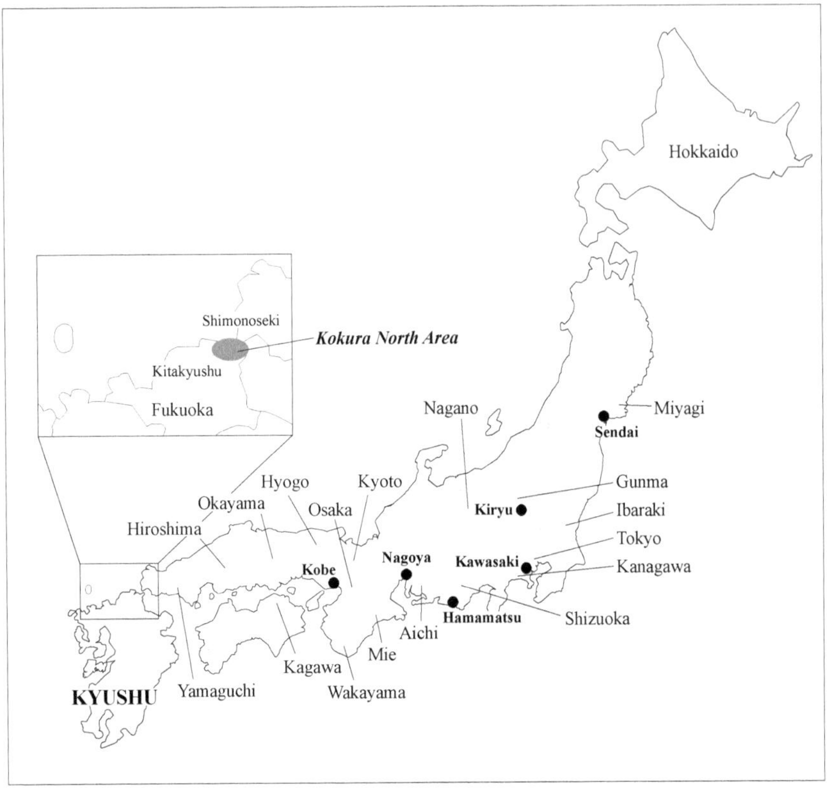
Hokkaido
Shimonoseki
Kokura North Area
Kitakyushu
Fukuoka
Nagano
Miyagi
Sendai
Hyogo
Kyoto
Gunma
Okayama
Osaka
Kiryu
Ibaraki
Hiroshima
Tokyo
Nagoya
Kawasaki
Kobe
Kanagawa
Hamamatsu
Shizuoka
Aichi
Mie
Kagawa
KYUSHU
Yamaguchi
Wakayama

Introduction: A Struggle for Survival

As its title implies, this book takes as its main subject the path along which pachinko, a pastime centered on an adult-oriented game machine, developed from an amusement fad into a full-fledged industry in Japan. Pachinko is defined as an amusement, but it satisfies the Japanese demand for gambling, which is strictly prohibited by law, through a system that effectively enables customers to turn their winnings into cash. My selection of such a prosaic title reflects the following fact: although numerous books have been published in Japanese on the subject of pachinko due to its popularity, many adopt highly distorted points of view. My goal is to address often-overlooked historical facts from a new perspective.

WHAT IS PACHINKO?

First, I should explain what pachinko is for readers of the English translation. Photo 0.1 shows people playing digital pachinko machines in a pachinko parlor in 2018. Photo 0.2 is an image dating from around 1950 of the type of pachinko machine that developed into postwar-style machines. Such machines are equipped with a flipper at the lower right and have a vertical pinball-like appearance consisting of a board with pins and holes. Players propel the balls with a flipper through a pinball-like maze on the pachinko machine. As the balls bounce through the maze of vertical pins, they

Photo 0.1: People sit inside a pachinko parlor in Tokyo
Source: AFP.

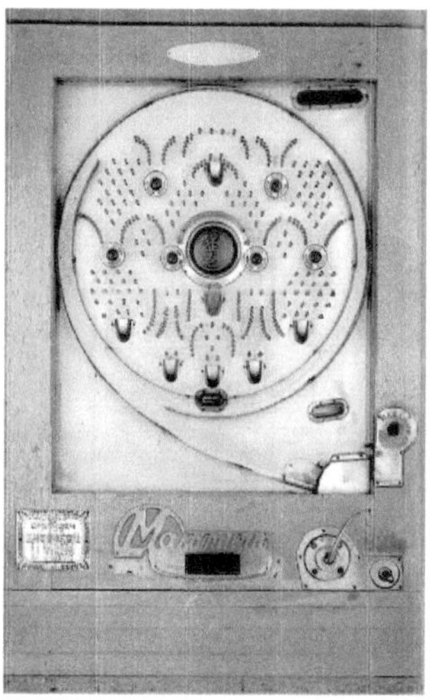

Photo 0.2: Pachinko machine in 1951
Source: Based on Hyakusu Henshūshitsu (1985: 7).

either hit the jackpot to produce more balls or fall into the gutter at the bottom of the machine. More detail on the mechanisms of pachinko machines is provided in Chapter 1 (see pp. 42–43).

Players at pachinko parlors purchase steel balls measuring about 11 millimeters in diameter. Balls cost a maximum of 4 yen (about US$0.04) at the time of writing (2021), as prescribed by the National Police Agency, so a player can purchase 5000 balls for 20,000 yen (about US$186), which is averaged using expense per day as of 2018. Players cannot redeem winning balls for cash as gambling is prohibited by law, but they can earn prizes such as cigarettes, chocolate and tokens (so-called special prizes) *within* the parlor.

Pachinko parlors are not in violation of the law as long as they do not allow customers to trade balls for cash. This arrangement is similar to the prizes people receive after winning at games at Japanese festivals such as fishing for goldfish or other stall games. Tokens, however, are exchanged for cash at independent shops *outside* the pachinko parlor. This reality has prompted discussion and controversy.[1]

The historical processes underlying the pachinko industry have been veiled over the years. To address the complex question of whether pachinko is properly considered an amusement and look at the manner in which it facilitates gambling, we must examine both the gray zone in which the industry operates and the arbitrary manner in which it is understood.

GANGSTERS, GAMBLING AND THE KOREAN COMMUNITY IN JAPAN:
Questioning the Economic History of the Pachinko Industry

COVID-19 exposed the negative image of pachinko that people have held for many years. On April 7, 2020, the Japanese government declared the first state of emergency in Tokyo, Osaka and five other COVID-19 hotspots before expanding it nationwide on April 24. Subsequently, the Osaka prefectural government publicly released the names of six pachinko parlors that had defied its request to close in the fight against the novel coronavirus under the Act on Special Measures for Pandemic Influenza and New Infectious Diseases Preparedness and Response.[2] The government explained that the infection could spread easily in pachinko parlors. Afterwards, many other prefectures took similar name-and-shame approaches.

Public opinion seemed to endorse that policy.[3] The media portrayed pachinko parlors as 'likely' the most dangerous places in terms of the potential spread of the virus.[4] Pachinko parlors came to represent businesses that were uncooperative with the government's policies in the nationwide fight against COVID-19.

The practice of publicly shaming businesses that did not comply with the government's requests reflected a historical trend in Japanese society of aversion toward public humiliation. It was also the only option available under the Act on Special Measures for Pandemic Influenza and New Infectious Diseases Preparedness and Response, which at the time did not contain penal provisions because Japan, unlike many other countries, did not implement a strict lockdown.[5] In fact, all of the named pachinko parlors shut down after being labeled as potential hotspots by the government.

However, pachinko was reportedly targeted without scientific evidence. Infectious disease specialists pointed out that the possibility of infection while playing pachinko was not high because mask-wearing prevented the disease from being easily spread by reducing exposure to airborne respiratory droplets.[6]

The above contextualizes pachinko's image among the Japanese public. Regardless of the actual occurrence – or rather, lack – of clusters, there is a public discourse that tries to link pachinko to increased likelihood of infection. This suspicion regarding pachinko reflects the industry's historically negative image, one that has been promoted by people's general lack of interest in historical fact.

Viewing pachinko negatively through suspicious eyes is not necessarily unique to Japanese society.

I had the opportunity to give a presentation entitled 'Gangsters, Gambling, and the Korean Community in Japan: Questioning the Economic History of the Pachinko Industry' in 2016 at the invitation of the Harvard-Yenching Institute. The presentation included material that was later included in my book, *The History of the Pachinko Industry* (in Japanese, published by the University of Nagoya Press in 2018). I had been nervous in the lead-up to the presentation because I worried that few people had heard of pachinko and thus would not be interested in this Japanese-specific topic. I was pleasantly surprised to find the hall overflowing with people, even though it was not a large space. My first point in the presentation was that pachinko parlors can be found in many cities and towns, making them part of *everyday life for Japanese people*. This differs from the less common practice of visiting a casino in the United States. Second, I outlined the importance of focusing on the innovative systems involved in the development of the industry rather than its connection to gangsters. Third, I posited that it is crucial to pay attention to the industry's changing relationship with the Korean minority historically, which I will explain later, rather than relying on fixed stereotypes.

The most surprising aspect of the questions was that some concentrated on the relationship between gangsters and the pachinko business. Several audience members seemed to imagine a strong connection between organized crime and pachinko. I used a still from the film *The Godfather* in the presentation in order to depict this imaginary linkage, which has been applied historically to the pachinko industry, yakuza and the ethnic minority Korean in Japan, sometimes called Zainichi Koreans. The film charts the story of the Sicilian mafia and the Corleone crime family of New York in the 1970s. Casinos appear as a symbolic business in which the crime family invested and with which it had a relationship. The questions from my audience might have been prompted by the title of the presentation and the film still, or by a mindset symbolized by the attitude that correlates suspicions regarding the image of ethnic minorities with suspicious business activities.

My explanation of why I do not focus on the relationship might not be acceptable. To be precise, before World War II in Japan, stall-keepers known as *tekiya* originally managed street pachinko shops at festivals, and gangsters were able to set up this type of business in the early stages of the pachinko industry. The realm of gangsters' involvement, however, has narrowed due to the growth of the industry, as this book describes. The point at issue is how this change happened and why. It is sufficient here to affirm that one line of thought links pachinko to a sort of black market dominated by organized crime, as the reader will have already noticed.

THE PACHINKO INDUSTRY IN HISTORICAL CONTEXT

Despite a well-known trend toward contraction in recent years, the pachinko industry remains undeniably vast, with a market valued at some 20 trillion yen (about US$18 billion) in 2018. Numerous authors have made note of this point and attempted to explain its principal causes. One all-too-typical point of view stresses the growth of the underground economy, which is held to dwarf the visible market, by touching on tax evasion, organized crime, ethnic minorities and their overseas cash remittances – to North Korea in this case. While the logic of reformers who seek to confront these issues from a perspective of concern about, and criticism of, social harms is persuasive, their argument is problematic in that it tends to show interest only in the current state of affairs. While admitting that pachinko has a number of issues, they never take into account the prevalence of pachinko parlors throughout Japan. That attitude, which inevitably focuses exclusively on negative aspects, leads one to conclude that the lives of the public are supported by an underground economy. While the purpose of this book does not lie in refuting the issues highlighted by such reformers in order to solve the problems, it will examine the growth and development process of the pachinko industry concentrating not on the underground economy, but rather on the changes that enabled the industry to break free from it.

Another tendency in distorted discussions of the industry runs in the opposite direction by extolling the tenacity of its leaders as they struggled against innumerable adversities. Sometimes this approach focuses on the indomitable spirit and perseverance of the ethnic minorities (many of them Koreans who had immigrated to Japan during the colonial period) considered important leaders in the industry. Many of the authors in this camp are involved with the industry and possess considerable knowledge about it, and they tend to emphasize efforts to improve the industry's image in the face of severe criticism, even while subject to strong police regulation. While this book too recognizes the value of such efforts, the fact remains that shadowy elements involving issues such as tax evasion and the funding of organized crime have accompanied the industry's growth and development. We should not disregard questions about who first recognized these elements as problematic, which aspects they chose to focus on, what reactions they provoked in doing so, how those interactions impacted the industry's growth and development, whether the elements in question remain problematic today and how ways of relating to them have changed over time.

In addition, academic studies tend to be interested in defining the meaning of pachinko as a cultural phenomenon that expresses Japanese particularity. The examination of pachinko – a cultural and leisure phenomenon not seen outside Japan – through the methodologies of folklore and leisure history has a productive and constructive place in the analysis of industrial history. That said, explanations grounded in economic theory are more essential when considering the process by which pachinko grew into a mass market. This book will attempt to fill the gaps in these academic studies by explaining the process from a new approach.

Studying pachinko is meaningful in connection with three phenomena: the pastime's ubiquity, by which I mean its status as a part of everyday life; its historical background; and its growth into a mass market. Regarding pachinko's ubiquity, other countries restrict similar businesses to specific locations, as seen in the example of casinos on Indian reservations in the United States. To gamble, members of the public must first travel to such locations. As exemplified by the business model widely adopted in Las Vegas, casinos offer an out-of-the-ordinary experience not found in everyday life, making a visit to one a special event like going on vacation. By contrast, in Japan, pachinko parlors are found near railway stations, in entertainment districts, in shopping districts and occasionally in the suburbs. They are accepted as natural background elements in the living space. In this way, pachinko has been incorporated into everyday life. What does this ubiquity mean when comparing Japan to other countries?

Considered in light of the history of leisure activities, such ubiquity is unusual. Figure 0.1 illustrates the form pachinko took during the prewar years. Unlike today, pachinko was enjoyed at mobile street stalls. During this period, pachinko was one of a number of out-of-the-ordinary, celebratory experiences, placing it outside the

Figure 0.1: People enjoying pachinko (prior to World War II)
Source: See Asahi Shimbun *(1938), 'ペンニュース　パチンコ詮義' (Pen news: Pachinko discussion), November 1.*

everyday world of the mundane. How did pachinko break out of this festive category to emerge into the everyday living space and develop into its current form?

In addition, an examination of market size shows that the pachinko industry has grown far beyond what might reasonably have been expected. Acts of gambling have, traditionally, been strictly regulated in Japan,[7] and they have been closely surveilled by the police since the prewar years. The pachinko industry, which began to thrive after World War II, is no exception. Why was it able to grow into a mass market despite such regulation? Any explanation of the industry's present ubiquity must provide an account of the dynamism that enabled it to thrive in the midst of regulation.

To facilitate a comprehensive understanding of the above points, this book will pay close attention to two features that have long distinguished the industry. The first is pachinko's status as a regulated industry. As used here, the term 'regulation' does not refer only to the unilateral control of economic activities by the state in the narrow sense, but also includes rules established by market players themselves to ensure discipline in the conduct of market participants. It is clear that as the actors and scope of such rules broadened, regulation had a positive effect on consumption and economic activity by building a basic foundation for growth.

The second point is the fact that, for various complicated reasons, the development of pachinko machines involves a very high degree of risk, and companies face severe restrictions. I will focus here on how this characteristic has shaped the actions of pachinko-machine manufacturers. While such development risk is hardly limited to the pachinko industry, studies of the subject have yet to sufficiently examine the industry's dynamism from the perspective of the relationships characterizing regulatory restrictions, severe swings in popularity and corporate activities. I will trace this aspect of the industry's development, which tends to be overlooked when approaching pachinko's growth into a mass market simply as the result of growth in demand, with particular care.

The course along which the pachinko industry reached its current state has been a chaotic one, with complex crossroads of light and shade linking one era to the next. In addition, under the bright conditions of economic growth during the postwar years, regulators (policymakers) came to see the pachinko industry as a peripheral domain. I will aim to chart the industry's history through an understanding, within a long-term context, of the buildup of choices made in response to excessive regulation or industry growth and the subsequent backlashes. To provide a point of departure, this Introduction examines the moment pachinko was born as an industry, identifying the first crisis in which the relationship between pachinko and regulation was brought into stark relief. In doing so, it will introduce the key theme of survival as a frame of reference for considering all of the periods covered in this book, while explaining the book's topics and analytical methods.

SURVIVAL

The argument for abolishing pachinko

While pachinko today has been assimilated into everyday living space, a look at the conditions around 1950 makes it apparent that it was not so readily accepted during that period. In a meeting of the Committee on Budget in the House of Councilors on November 15, 1951, an issue was raised that threatened pachinko's survival.[8] The discussion came at a time when pachinko had broken free from its prewar status as a form of entertainment for children on festival days and started to flourish. Although somewhat protracted, the following description is offered by way of background information.

During the postwar recovery period, local governments faced severe budgetary challenges and needed to expand their meager revenue sources in order to rebuild national infrastructure, which stood in ruin after Japan's defeat. State-controlled gambling on events such as bicycle, horse and boat racing were considered to constitute one effective means of doing so.[9] Even if it was initially accepted out of budgetary necessity, such gambling was considered by many as a merely temporary measure, and local assemblies debated its abolition numerous times thereafter.[10] Informing these arguments were critical views that believed that condoning gambling would promote bad habits, harm people's livelihoods by sapping motivation to work, drive growth in the number of criminals and adversely impact youth.[11] In the Diet, the arguments of Tamae Fukagawa of the Democratic Party of Japan, who held a similar point of view, inspired growing debate against the spread of pachinko. At the same time, in an answer to parliamentary questions, Minister of Finance Hayato Ikeda, who would become prime minister in 1960, had referred to pachinko, which was becoming increasingly popular, by including it in the category of gambling.

While remaining vague, Ikeda revealed his view that pachinko could no longer be ignored through statements such as 'the sound of pachinko is impossible to escape no matter where one goes in the city or in rural areas' and 'its effect is largely harmful, with very little benefits'. Although he accepted pachinko on an official level, his personal desire was to abolish it: he stated repeatedly, 'its harmful effects greatly outnumber the good' and commented, 'Personally, I would be in favor of getting rid of it'.[12]

These arguments had an impact, and people increasingly came to see pachinko as a social evil. For example, an opinion survey conducted by the *Mainichi Shimbun*, a national newspaper with a long history, on the public's views of Ikeda's comments found that approximately 60 percent of respondents were in favor of abolishing all forms of gambling.[13] However, the survey found that a greater percentage of respondents (although the exact figure was not identified in the newspaper's report) were in favor of maintaining the current status of pachinko, compared to only 10 percent who favored taking such an approach to bicycle racing, and this tendency was more pronounced in Japan's six largest cities and among respondents in their twenties. In this way, pachinko enjoyed a limited base of support among people who accepted it as a form of entertainment. A news magazine published an analysis that briefly summarized the arguments for and against pachinko at the time.[14] The 'Yoroku' column in the January 17 issue of the *Mainichi Shimbun* supported Ikeda's argument for the abolition of pachinko, seeing it, in accordance with the parliamentary debate, as a form of gambling similar to the lottery or horse racing and identifying the loss of motivation to work and negative effects on children as problematic.

Another powerful view, however, saw pachinko as differing from state-controlled gambling in that it did not cause any real harm and argued that it would be preferable to wait for it to disappear naturally, rather than abolishing it forcibly through the power of law. An editorial in the *Yomiuri Shimbun* argued against Ikeda's views by asserting 'It is preferable that the government refrain from interfering in the lives of the public using the power of the state'. The author argued that business operators had the right to continue to operate businesses that conformed with the law and that the abolition of pachinko would usurp their right to survival. The weekly magazine *Shūkan Asahi* considered pachinko to involve only a fringe element of gambling, describing the reasons for its explosive popularity as follows: 'When all is said and

Figure 0.2: People enjoying pachinko (1950s)
Source: See Mutsuura, Mitsuo (1951) 'パチンコ談義' (Pachinko narrative), Finance Digest, 5(16), p. 98.

done, with winnings [...] in trifling amounts, [...] the general public instead is able to forget its cares through the nonsensical activity of pachinko, [...] a solitary game [...] that is a form of self-consolation for the man on the street'.[15]

These are likely an expression of the fact that pachinko came to be partially accepted in society during the early 1950s. Figure 0.1 above shows a child, an older man and a family that seemed to consist of a young father and a mother with a baby on her back gathered around pachinko machines during the 1930s. While an illustration drawn in 1951 (Figure 0.2) resembles the prewar scene, in addition to a familiar middle-aged man in a suit it also depicts a wife and a young mother on the way home from shopping, indicating that pachinko had spread to a more diverse range of customers.[16]

As seen above, when pachinko first began to attract attention based on its nationwide popularity in the early 1950s, it drew strong condemnation from some sectors, backed by the historical fact that gambling had until then been strictly regulated as a social evil.[17] At the same time, diverse opinions were aired, including the view that pachinko was acceptable as a trifling type of gambling in the domain of public entertainment or 'self-consolation for the man on the street'. This connected with the state of society during the immediate postwar years and the expectation that pachinko was nothing more than a temporary fad that would eventually fade away. The small amounts of money used in pachinko was also used to justify the case for tolerance.

However, the understandings and expectations of that time would be undercut by the subsequent rise of pachinko brought about by the interaction between its popularity and the speculative nature of the machines. While some important side effects will be considered in Chapter 1 and later chapters, the conditions in which the pachinko industry operated became increasingly complex, to the extent that opposition strengthened and prospects for the industry's survival became unclear.

Under the Entertainment and Amusement Trades Control Act (passed in 1948), pachinko was subjected to regulation as 'an amusement business that involves the use of equipment to stimulate customers' speculative spirit'. Whether or not a given action was in violation of the law was determined based on the ambiguous standard of the degree of 'speculative spirit' involved. Actions considered entertainment rather than gambling fell within the scope of the law, and as such doing business was permitted. 'Speculative spirit' refers to the desire to secure gains by chance without working for them.[18] While today's pachinko machines are configured to limit the number of shots to no more than 100 per minute in order to keep this speculative element in check, the so-called *renpatsu-shiki kikai* (successive-shot machines) that drove the pachinko boom beginning in 1952 were able to shoot as many as 200 pachinko balls per minute. Such rates corresponded to gambling at stakes that made it difficult to claim players were wagering trifling amounts in return for their winnings. These machines were banned on November 16, 1954, when the Tokyo Public Safety Commission announced the Ordinance on Measures to Prohibit Self-feeding Pachinko Machines (enacted in April 1955).

In December 1954, after the Tokyo Public Safety Commission had announced its regulations, *Jiji Tsūshin* (a newsletter)[19] reported that public opinion tended to support such measures.[20] Since these machines led players to use three or more times the money they used on traditional machines, the evolution of pachinko into a form of gambling came to be seen as problematic by the general public. Hard-line arguments that called for the abolition of not only pachinko but also other forms of gambling such as horse racing and bicycle racing also appeared.

The position taken by government and the police in prohibiting machines that involved a conspicuous speculative element was based on the regulation of businesses permitted under the Entertainment and Amusement Trades Control Act. While this approach stopped short at the full abolition of pachinko, it nonetheless had a tremendous impact. Numerous *pachinko-ya* (pachinko businesses)[21] and pachinko-machine manufacturers were forced out of business, and the industry fell into a severe slump. An article from 1957, after the enactment of the successive-shot ban, described an area of the city of Nagoya that had thrived during the pachinko boom as follows: 'Just as the autumn leaves were starting to fall, here and there in the city only a few pachinko fanatics who have not yet given up on the game gathered to flick the pachinko levers with their fingers today'. The author described how the numbers of parlors and pachinko-machine manufacturers had decreased dramatically, to the point that 'today, the once prosperous pachinko center has a lonesome feel'.[22] The expression 'who have not yet given up on the game' suggests uncertain prospects for the future of pachinko.

The payback for this excessive speculative element appeared in the form of a downturn in business spurred by the 1955 regulations. Regulation and solid critical public opinion were enough to inspire a sense of crisis in stakeholders in the pachinko industry, who feared that their livelihood would disappear. It is doubtful that anybody at that time could have predicted future developments. Some even decided on their own to shut up shop out of fear that their livelihood was under threat and could disappear in the near future.[23] What kinds of choices were left to those businesses that remained?

The fact that the industry was so greatly influenced by regulation suggests the possibility that the business conditions characterizing pachinko parlors were liable to shift in response to changes in the form of regulation and the views of society that informed it. It also intimates that the positioning of pachinko could change amid the subsequent, bewildering upheaval that was to sweep through society and the economy.[24] However, pachinko would continue to be regulated under the Entertainment and Amusement Trades Control Act and would need to continue to comply with the law. Since decisions concerning types of regulation and the potential abolition of pachinko were left to the government, administrators, police and public opinion, consensus concerning the manner in which pachinko could survive and grow would emerge as those involved in the industry sought out appropriate degrees of speculation while remaining conscious of public opinion.[25]

From mere survival to mass market

On January 17, 1973, the *Asahi Shimbun*, another major newspaper, began publishing a series of articles entitled 'Yoka' (leisure). The first subject covered by the new series was pachinko, under the catchphrase 'Starting with the national pastime'. That a national newspaper would choose such language symbolizes the change in the public's consciousness regarding pachinko and suggests how far pachinko had permeated Japanese society.

Twenty years later in the 1990s, it was the vast size of the pachinko market that attracted society's attention. *Report on a 1994 Basic Survey of the Service Industry*, published by the Management and Coordination Agency in 1996, estimated the industry's business revenue at approximately 30 trillion yen (about US$275 billion), based on the going rate paid by customers of 4 yen (about US$0.04) per ball. The figure corresponded to just under 40 percent of the national budget, which was approximately 78 trillion yen at the time. A simple estimate derived by dividing this figure by the population of pachinko players at the time (approximately 30 million people who played at least once per year) suggests that the average player spent 1 million yen per year on pachinko. Naturally, the finding was widely reported in the mass media.[26] It even became a topic of discussion overseas, where the *Economist* ran an article entitled 'Pachinkoholism: Japan' in its July 6, 1996, issue, emphasizing the fact that pachinko's net sales of 30 trillion yen exceeded domestic sales in the automotive industry, known as one of Japan's most competitive industries.

As pointed out by Ichiro Tanioka[27] and various other commentators, there was room for criticizing the method used in the 30-trillion-yen[28] market valuation and the sales calculation based on the number of balls rented[29] as well as the degree of error. However, even when these factors are taken into consideration, it is clear that what had once been an insignificant form of public amusement had undergone quite a transformation.

The changes in the pachinko industry can be observed from another perspective as well. In the 1950s, most pachinko machines had been built by hand by small and medium-sized firms that were part of a cottage industry. Today's production structure, in which large numbers of machines are assembled from standardized parts, had yet to form. Heiwa, which was founded in 1949 in the city of Kiryū in Gunma Prefecture, also home to two other leading pachinko manufacturers, grew over roughly forty years to the point where its shares were listed on the Second Section of the Tokyo Stock Exchange in 1991 (and then on the First Section in 1997). Its founder, Kenkichi Nakajima, who had ethnic minority Korean roots, was ranked as the twenty-seventh richest person in the world in 1989 and attracted attention as the highest-ranked Japanese person on the list, published by *Fortune*.[30] Heiwa's IPO was the first in the pachinko industry, although other firms soon followed suit, for example Sankyo in 1995.

As of December 2019, the number of pachinko parlors nationwide stood at 9639,[31] and the number of companies in the industry at 2798.[32] Those numbers had fallen by about 22 percent and 15 percent, respectively, over the half-decade from 2015. Market size as estimated based on ball charges had also continued to fall after peaking in 2005 at 35 trillion yen (about US$311 billion), first falling below 30 trillion yen in 2008 and then continuing to slide to 18 trillion yen (about US$165 billion)[33] by 2019. In this way, the market shrank to about half of its previous size in the space of fourteen years. The number of people employed in the industry – averaged per establishment – stood at 271,066[34] in 2012, down about 10 percent from its 2006 level of 300,188.[35]

While the market has contracted considerably over the past two decades or so, it remains true that compared to the situation during the 1950s, when the very survival of the industry was an open question, the subsequent growth of the pachinko industry exceeded even the wildest expectations (see Table 0.3 below). In light of the fact that the transformations that swept the industry since the 1950s went beyond predictable catch-up growth, the trajectory of pachinko's development merits closer attention.

To fill in the gaps between pachinko's emergence as a part of everyday life and its development into a mass market, this book will trace developments in the industry from the 1950s through the 1990s. In doing so, it will throw into sharp relief the conditions under which people such as entrepreneurs in the industry struggled with challenges day in, day out during the 1950s merely to ensure survival in the face of uncertain prospects. The trail they blazed to forge their future (whether or not they were aware of doing so) was possible because they successfully found ways to stabilize the business. This book intends to examine that process, which I will call the '*search for long-term survival*'.

The birth, survival and growth of pachinko

Many studies, including Kazuo Sugiyama's detailed investigation,[36] have charted pachinko's origins. As early opinions that traced those origins to horizontal pinball games[37] have been abandoned due to problems with corroboration, the view that 'chance' machines ('*ah su* machines') and wall-mounted pinball machines were the forerunners of modern pachinko machines has become firmly established.[38] After horizontal bagatelle games, which got their start in Britain, were converted to vertical wall-mounted machines at the turn of the twentieth century, they took on a unique form as they spread throughout Europe, reaching Japan during the 1920s. According to Sugiyama's analysis, these machines came to be known as *pachinko* machines as they became popular nationwide during the 1930s. Authorities stopped issuing permits for the opening of new outlets in 1937, and then the manufacture of pachinko machines was prohibited due to the impact of World War II, along with the operation of amusement businesses.[39] During the postwar period, business resumed when the machines were installed at an amusement facility for the General Headquarters (GHQ) of the occupation forces.[40]

It is only natural that new products and services would be introduced over time. New products stimulate consumption, and then a market forms as they secure a stable position. The market then grows hand in hand with demand. Production methods also evolve, and specialization in the industry promotes the growth and progress of related fields. Product (industry) life-cycle theory[41] focuses on technology, modeling industrial history as a series of different stages based on the state of the market and competitive conditions and appropriately describing the process from the birth of an industry as various products are introduced to its ultimate decline. The process of the pachinko industry's emergence as an established industry and its growth into a mass market can also be understood in light of various studies[42] that have analyzed industries by classifying their development into the phases of introduction, growth, maturation and decline.[43]

Indeed, product life-cycle theory assumes the presence of a self-evident flow from each stage to the next, and for this reason it does not proactively discuss the causes and conditions of shifting stages; rather, it discusses individual stages in terms of strategy, marketing and policy as appropriate in light of the external environmental conditions that a firm faces. However, this book's analysis of the pachinko industry does not treat this series of stages as a given but instead acknowledges the need to explain the survival of the pachinko industry after its birth and its further development in a manner that takes into consideration the conditions of each individual era. The fact that this process was characterized by trial and error rather than direct linear change is significant here. While it is not wrong to say that technological change brings about industrial change, inadequacies in the conditions for realizing such change restricted sustained technological progress. To reiterate, there was no definite path along which the pachinko market moved inexorably towards long-term survival due to these factors as well as the special nature of the industry in terms of its relation to gambling and the severity of the boom-and-bust cycle in the amusement industry.

Accordingly, instead of a unilateral and restrictive relationship from which suitable corporate behavior could be identified for a specific stage, as in product (industry) life-cycle theory, it is essential to view the cyclical relationship as one that is explained by changes in the business environment, including external conditions, and advancement to the next stage as a result of the efforts companies make in response to such changes. From this perspective, it is essential to elucidate how the continued existence of the industry was secured by taking into account factors including the development of systems that permeate the industry.

Uncertainty about the pachinko industry's future was enhanced by issues related to society's evaluation of pachinko as a grey area as well as regulations and systemic deficiencies. In connection with society's view of the industry, at a time when state-controlled gambling too was subject to criticism, recognition of pachinko as a lawful industry was weak, and it was thought to be difficult to forge a social consensus regarding the industry's tendency to allow the speculative element to go too far. For these reasons, there was the possibility that strict regulations could be imposed at any time. The more popular pachinko grew, the stricter the supervision to which it was subjected would become, in terms of not only the types and unit prices of prizes and how balls were exchanged for such prizes, but also factors such as the design of pachinko machines and the numbers of balls they were permitted to use. Since it was impossible to predict how issues related to pachinko would develop, regulations on cash exchanges and prizes, in which public safety commissions and the police were involved, were handled more on an ex-post basis and were not necessarily appropriate from the outset.

Under such conditions, it took time for a prize exchange system to be developed that would resolve the issue of such transactions serving as a source of funding for organized crime, which dogged the industry during its initial stage, while simultaneously meeting customers' expectations. The distribution of authority among regulators such as public safety commissions and the police resulted in differences among prefectures, forcing manufacturers of pachinko machines to supply machines that had been designed with such regulatory differences in mind, and operators of pachinko parlors to respond to those differences when advancing into other prefectures. Development of the systems that would serve as the foundation of the industry's growth and development took the form of a series of trial-and-error starts and stops on the part of both regulators and the subjects of regulation.

Even aside from such issues, the uncertainties that accompanied the possibility of calculation and the scope and direction of technical progress, which were related to the sustainability of the industry and the companies in it, forced the individuals and companies involved with the industry to face numerous challenges. From a broader perspective of industrial development – not restricted to the pachinko industry alone – it was not self-evident that a new market would form in a manner that would encourage business growth and guarantee a stable business foundation. In addition, artificially low price levels were enforced that would make it difficult even for outstanding firms to survive in competition.[44] The path trodden by the pachinko industry shows that it is not easy for goods and services to become established as an industry as markets develop and then to grow with the support of market functions. It is possible, in examining the process of organization that drove business and market stability in the pachinko industry, to discover an answer to the question of how market functions are maintained and connected to industrial growth and development. This book will highlight a number of important points that will aid in explaining the formation, growth and progress of the industry in a broader context. From this point of view, it will depict the process by which pachinko developed from the circumstances it faced during the 1950s, widely permeated Japanese society during the 1970s and achieved mass-market status during the 1990s not as an accumulation of disconnected, random occurrences, but rather as the result of consistent, directed efforts.

A CLOSER LOOK AT PACHINKO

In order to shine a light on aspects of the industry that have remained in the shadows until now, this book will employ an approach in the analysis of pachinko that is somewhat removed from what might be generally expected, causing it to diverge from established views of pachinko and perspectives taken in attempts to explain it to date. For example, the fact that stereotypes such as those of pachinko serving as a funding source for organized crime or a means of tax evasion inevitably arise when the pachinko industry is discussed highlights how the industry is seen. A brief survey of the conventional view of pachinko will help elucidate how my approach differs.

Peripheral economic activity

Full-fledged, detailed investigation of and academic research on pachinko began around the 1980s. There was a considerable time lag between when journalists took an interest in pachinko, beginning with contemporaneous reports during the 1950s that focused on the scale of the industry's economic activity and its popularity among the general public, and when academics started to look at the subject. One well-known reason for this lag is the lack of highly reliable statistics on the industry. Their absence demonstrates the relatively low degree of importance given to pachinko-related policies by the governmental agencies tasked with statistics through collecting and compiling information.

Observers began to point out issues related to data on the leisure sector, including pachinko and other amusement industries, when the government and society started to pay attention to the leisure industry as a growth industry.[45] To address those issues so that government and industry could promote leisure activities, the Ministry of International Trade and Industry took the lead in the establishment of the Leisure Development Center,[46] with the participation of the Economic Planning Agency and the private sector.[47] This marked the start, at last, of comprehensive thinktank-style activities based on organized efforts, and in 1977 the center began publishing its *Leisure White Paper*.

Until the 1970s, only limited statistical studies were conducted on pachinko, which was not even included as a leisure industry in Yoshimitsu Asano's *System Industry Series: Leisure Industry* (Nikkei Business Publishing), which was published in 1970 (see Table 0.1). This omission came despite the fact that pachinko sales in 1967 as estimated by the Nomura Research Institute, a private-sector research institution, accounted for one-half of those of gambling and exceeded sales of 350.7 billion yen (about US$974 million) and 307.5 billion yen (about US$854 million), respectively, for the separate segments of horse racing and bicycle racing.[48] Even the report *Industries of the Future 5: Leisure Industry* (published by Tōyō Keizai Shinpōsha), which included these statistics and was published in that same year by the Industrial Research Association of the Long-Term Credit Bank of Japan, merely provided a summary of the actual state of the industry. In this way, the pachinko industry was a peripheral presence that lay beyond the economic activities on which attention was focused.

However, my use of the expression *peripheral* in this book reflects more than policymakers' dismissal of the industry as beneath what they recognized as important economic activities. The expression is also apt because the process by which pachinko came to establish itself as an industry began with its sense of existing in a peripheral domain. This point will be reconsidered later; for now, let us get back to reviewing another aspect of the conventional view of pachinko.

(Units: Hundreds of millions of Yen, %)

Segment	Japan Center for Economic Research (nominal)[b]				Nomura Research Institute	
	1955	1960	1965	vs. 65	1965	1967
Sports	363	711	2,132	5.2	2,963	
Gambling sports[c]	262	455	1,344	3.3	1,348	2,159
	(1,048)	(1,822)	(5,375)			(8,636)
Pachinko						4,140[d]
Published matter	1,552	2,587	4,781	11.6	3,064	
Visual entertainment and art	1,433	4,615	7,618	18.5	5,612	
Hobbies, toys and games	172	280	760	1.9	686	
Commercial entertainment	933	2,404	3,812	9.3	3,835	
Travel	1,329	2,582	6,169	15.0	4,213	
Alcohol and tabacco	6,009	9,474	15,795	38.5	13,312	
Total	11,792	22,654	41,068	100.0	33,685	

Table 0.1: Estimated sales (nominal) for gambling in leisure industries and pachinko parlors

Notes:

a. The exchange rate during the years in question was fixed to about US$1 = ¥360.

b. Original data drawn from 'Estimated or forecast sales in the leisure industry', published by the Japan Center for Economic Research.

c. Admission and wagers paid to horse race, bicycle race, boat race and car race operators. Remaining 25 percent after subtracting 5 percent payout to people holding winning betting tickets and other payouts from total sales (figures in parentheses indicate estimates by the author).

d. Estimated sales for the pachinko market were first announced in 1967. Original data drawn from four years of Comprehensive Research (SōgōKenkyū), as published by Nomura Research Institute (calculated by multiplying the number of pachinko machines nationwide as estimated by the Ministry of Home Affairs by sales per machine).

Source: Segment sales other than pachinko were drawn from Asano (1970: 214–15). Pachinko sales for 1967 were drawn from Kitahara and Nippon Chōki Shinyō Ginkō Sangyō Kenkyūkai (1970: 168–70).

Pachinko and ethnic minority Koreans in Japan

Another factor that led to the formation of a negative image of pachinko was its connection to ethnic minorities. This has become an established view of the subject. This strong connection can be considered to have determined the directions of academic interest in the subject and to have hindered its promotion as a domain of economic and industrial research. What is this generally accepted idea linking pachinko with ethnic minority Koreans in Japan?

The novel *Pachinko*,[49] an eagerly anticipated work by the novelist Min Jin Lee, known for her bestseller *Free Food for Millionaires*, was published in the United States in February 2017. Due in part to the popularity of its author, the novel attracted enthusiastic attention even before its publication.[50] The author's previous work, which took as its theme Korean immigrants living in New York, was praised for its penetrating insights into the complexities of life as an immigrant in America as seen through the difficulties faced in society by two generations of one family: the first-generation immigrant parents working at a dry cleaner – considered a typical occupation for Koreans – and their second-generation children, who graduated from Ivy League schools.

The tale of *Pachinko* begins in a fishing village on Yeongdo – now part of the greater Busan metropolitan area – before the Korean peninsula was annexed by Japan. The novel spans four generations of a Korean family that moved to Japan during the colonial years, remained there after World War II and then lived in Japan through the postwar period. While the story was based on the experiences of the author, who had lived in Tokyo, and interviews with ethnic minority Koreans in Japan, it is said to have taken approximately thirty years to finish because it took the author so long to understand their feelings.[51] Since the novel's American readers cannot be expected to be familiar with pachinko, one wonders what the author intended by, after much pain and effort, titling the work *Pachinko*. Surely the title was chosen for this novel, which was published overseas, because pachinko is symbolic of the lives of ethnic minority Koreans in Japan and because, through the role of pachinko in the story, one can perceive its position in Japanese society.

In an interview on American public radio, the author explained her choice of title as follows: 'The Korean Japanese could not find legal employment for [...] seven or eight decades. Even now they have great difficulty finding jobs in certain sectors. So, in pachinko they were able to find a kind of employment haven'.[52] In the novel, pachinko is identified as the employment of the main characters, a pair of third-generation brothers, who were born in 1931 and 1937, respectively. Primarily, pachinko is depicted as the lowest layer of Japanese society, an occupation frequented by ethnic minorities unable to assimilate into Japanese society. After being admitted to the School of Humanities and Social Sciences at Waseda University, a prestigious university, the elder son drops out. Posing as Japanese, he takes a job working at a pachinko parlor under Japanese management, and then later runs a parlor. The younger son, who had been forced to drop out of middle school, builds up experience working in pachinko parlors under ethnic minority Korean management and then eventually comes to operate several parlors, enjoying a middle-class lifestyle. It goes without saying that these two brothers' interactions with the world of pachinko crystallize the difficult social conditions of the ethnic minority Korean in Japan. While it served as a means of securing economic stability and success, pachinko did not serve as a way of being accepted as a member of Japanese society or increasing one's social standing. As the younger son confides to his closest Japanese friend, 'in Japan, I'm just another dirty Korean no matter how much money I make or how nice I am'.[53]

What should be noted here are the connections between ethnic minority Koreans in Japan and pachinko, and the fact that the author chose pachinko as a symbolic concept to depict the immigrant community in Japan for American readers. The novel opens with the memorable declaration, 'History has failed us, but no matter'.

These words foretell the immigrant community's attitude toward survival under conditions imposed by the host society as well as the complexity of the fate of the main characters and of the future they will build. Recognizing that one cannot predict in which direction the balls launched into the gauges in a pachinko machine will travel, Min Jin Lee may have projected onto the speculative element of pachinko the way of life of ethnic minority Koreans in Japan – one they were not free to choose on their own.

The ties depicted in *Pachinko* between pachinko and the economic activities of ethnic minority Koreans in Japan were formed under the social conditions of employment discrimination against the Korean minority and against pachinko as an occupation.[54] The generation of brothers survived the most trying time for ethnic minority Koreans in Japan. This comports well with a Western understanding, and this view also resonates with the way the phenomenon is described in Japan.[55] The long-recognized ties between ethnic minority Koreans in Japan and pachinko symbolize their status within Japanese society. Indeed, this symbolic connection has taken on a life of its own. Is there any discrepancy between the image and the industry's history as it has evolved?

Inconspicuous changes

The way in which the relationship between pachinko and ethnic minority Koreans in Japan is discussed is a product of the times, informed by historical facts.[56] Therefore, the way pachinko is seen may change. This possibility can be considered in the manner indicated in Table 0.2, which summarizes the results of a questionnaire survey[57] I conducted in 2012 and 2014 while teaching courses on ethnic minority businesses in Japan. The same questions were asked at a public college operated by Tokyo's Setagaya Ward and Hokkaido University, where I was employed, and the answers were totaled for the two. There are limits on the utility of this data, since the sample size was small and respondents were not selected randomly, among other concerns. Although the results should be taken with a grain of salt for these reasons, there was a considerable difference among generations between the two groups. As noted in the table, the average age of the former group was more than sixty-five years, while that of the latter was twenty, an age difference of nearly two generations. I would like to focus on a difference in awareness that cannot be overlooked.

First, answers to question (1), which was intended to gauge subjects' image of pachinko, indicate that only a relatively small percentage – less than 25 percent – of respondents in both groups voiced support for abolishing pachinko (A). Less than half answered disinterestedly that they did not have a particularly bad image of the subject (B), and the younger group was more likely to choose this response.

(Units: %)

Questions	Number of responses/size of sample		
	Setagaya Ward Citizens' University	Hokkaido University	
		First Survey (2012)	Second Survey (2014)
(1) Image of pachinko (multiple answers acceptable)			
A. Pachinko is gambling, and I'd like to see it banned.	24.5	17.6	24.5
B. Pachinko is gambling, but I don't think it's especially harmful.	52.8	72.5	66.0
C. Pachinko is intimately related to crime.	9.4	13.7	13.2
D. Pachinko is related to organized crime.	41.5	23.5	17.0
E. I have a darkly negative image of pachinko.	28.3	25.5	34.0
(2) If you were considering launching your own business and learned that pachinko parlors were a highly profitable business, which of the following would you choose?			
A. I would be OK with investing in pachinko.	9.4	45.1	54.7
B. I would choose another business.	73.6	52.9	45.3
(3) Do large numbers of ethnic minority Koreans in Japan own pachinko parlors?			
A. I've heard that they do.	77.4	19.6	39.6
B. No.	13.2	80.4	60.4
Size of sample	53	51	53

Table 0.2: Survey on the pachinko industry and ethnic minorities

Notes:

a. Dates of surveys: September 2012 at Setagaya City Citizens' University; October 2012 and September 2014 at Hokkaido University.

b. Age of respondents: all post-retirement (65 or older) at Setagaya Ward Citizens' University; first- and second-year undergraduate students (average age estimated as roughly 20) at Hokkaido University.

c. Gender distribution: unknown for both groups.

It is conceivable that given the diverse forms of amusement available to them, their interest in pachinko is low. The percentage in each group that continued to have a negative image of pachinko (E) amounted to around 30 percent. On the other hand, the percentage that saw pachinko as related to crime (C) was low overall, and the percentage of the younger group who viewed pachinko as being related to organized crime (D) was only about one-half of that of the older group. It is important to note here that while the negative image of pachinko that was typical in the past remains among the older population, the pachinko industry is recognized as a presence in society, and changes are apparent between the two generations, particularly in the weakening of the connection to organized crime that had served to strengthen pachinko's negative image.

From the difference in responses to question (2), which were somewhat related to (1), we can get an idea of what respondents would focus on if they were deciding on a field in which to invest, with regard to the economic consideration of growth rate under the assumption of no restrictions on investment funds. When asked if they would invest in the pachinko industry, more than 70 percent of the older generation answered no, regardless of the industry's growth. In contrast, about 50 percent of the younger group would be willing to start a business in the industry in light of its growth rate. This shows that the younger generation's behavioral decisions are more impacted by economic factors than other considerations. However, it remains a fact that about one-half said that they would not invest in the industry, and those who chose this response were concerned about pachinko's negative image in society as well as characteristics that are inherent to a gambling business. Even so, this result is interesting insofar as it highlights the large difference of opinion between the two generations.

Lastly, there was also a clear difference in perception between the generations on the subject of pachinko's relationship with ethnic minorities, as revealed in question (3). Among the younger generation, the link between the pachinko industry and ethnic minority Koreans is weakening.[58] Thus, it appears that the idea of the industry's connection to a particular ethnic group is not being passed down the generations.

We cannot draw general conclusions from the above results, and there are presumably multiple ways in which they can be interpreted. Still, we can safely judge that awareness of the pachinko industry, and its image, is changing over the generations, although there remain questions as to the extent of those changes. This judgment raises questions about changes in the economic facts of the pachinko industry, which are behind these shifts in perception.[59]

Past studies and reports have not properly considered the significance of these changes in people's levels of understanding concerning the industry. In them, the ties between pachinko and the underground have served as an established perspective. For example, on the topic of the growth of the pachinko industry and related businesses, authors have discussed how the industry adroitly carried out illegal activities such as tax evasion.[60] It is a fact that during the 1970s, pachinko was often cited in newspaper headlines as an example of an industry involved in tax evasion, and cases of tax evasion in the industry have long been reported.[61] However, how many people recall that hospitals were another industry that appeared on the list of tax evaders, and in fact that sector was ranked the highest among offending industries in terms of tax evasion, eclipsing pachinko, in 1976.[62] While the manner in which pachinko is discussed serves as one element in reproducing a certain image of the industry, its growth into a mass market has not yet been explained sufficiently in economic terms. This oversight suggests that we need to change the way we look at the industry.

THIS BOOK'S PERSPECTIVE: RETURNING TO THE SUPPLY SIDE

Pachinko's consumers and suppliers

While pachinko has grown into a mass market with a customer base that rose as high as 30 million, roughly equivalent to half of Japan's working population, it is a form of amusement that is unknown in other countries. Many observers have wondered why Japanese people play pachinko to such an extent. Various consumer-focused explanations of the phenomenon have been attempted not only in the world of journalism, but also via the approaches of cultural theory, sociology and psychology, and interdisciplinary discussions of the subject first appeared quite some time ago.[63] Indeed, it is not easy to answer this fundamental question.

In *Leisure and the Japanese people*, Michitaro Tada (1974), a scholar of French literature, considered pachinko in the context of Japan's rapid industrialization.[64] He saw pachinko machines as modern light-industrial products made of materials such as steel and glass, and the act of playing pachinko itself as one of the players adapting themselves to industrial society. While Tada's portrayal is a highly interesting interpretation considered from the standpoint of the relationship between amusement and broader social conditions, it probably needs to be reconsidered in light of the structural industrial changes that have occurred since the 1970s and the relationship of office workers and those in other occupations with pachinko.

Some works have approached the subject from the perspective of Japanese peculiarity. Hidetoshi Kato[65] describes playing pachinko as a means by which Japanese people, who do not like spare time, can fill such intervals, as moments of absorption in themselves. Naomichi Ishige[66] argues that pachinko is well suited to Japanese consumers because, unlike Western-style gambling, which depends largely on chance, it more closely resembles work in that rewards depend on the player's effort, exerted here through skill and judgment. In this way, he sees pachinko as a form of amusement that does not represent a complete release from work. Ichiro Tanioka[67] sees the popularity of pachinko as the result of internal motivations on numerous layers – including economic development and cultural diversification at the levels of society, community and the individual, ways in which gambling is accepted, and release from the subsumption of the individual in Japanese society – rather than external factors including its nature as a mechanical game and the levels of service provided in pachinko parlors.

The above studies explaining pachinko consumers' motivations are highly interesting in that they are attempts at structural analysis based on the distinguishing features of contemporary society while also focusing on individual preferences, seeking solutions in the form of group behavioral patterns. However, while they have presented various interpretations of the meaning of the act of playing pachinko itself, as exemplified by Tanioka, they have seen the business of providing pachinko machines and the service of offering pachinko as mere external inducements from a demand-side perspective.

In comparison to the degree of interest in consumers of pachinko, many aspects of the supply side, such as the fundamentals that enable the existence of the industry, remain unclear. Hiroshi Takeuchi, former general manager of the research division of the Long-term Credit Bank of Japan, was one of the first to take an interest in the economic significance of the pachinko industry. Takeuchi emphasized manufacturers' highly motivated development of pachinko machines, the various technical innovations that arose through the management of pachinko parlors and pachinko's contribution to employment opportunities that formed an economic base for those in the lower echelons of society.[68] However, his understanding of pachinko as a 'back-alley'[69] economic activity has its limits in light of subsequent changes to pachinko sites and employment.[70]

As pachinko attracted attention as a mass-market activity in the 1990s, a variety of new arguments appeared. One of the important questions raised concerned the need for analysis of an industry that remained relatively little understood, despite its having grown into a mass market. For example, one observer noted, 'We have a surprising lack of accurate information concerning this familiar industry [...]. There are surprisingly few studies that systematically and accurately describe the facts [of the amusement industry]'.[71] Various commentators, including Yoichi Mabe,[72] voiced expectations of the industry's future growth and agreed on the need for reforms to address its underground aspects in order to enable its further development. That numerous works attempting to analyze pachinko as an effective target for investment were published on the basis of such structural analysis suggests the high degree of interest in the pachinko industry at the time.[73]

The 2000s brought the vibrant studies of Hiroyuki Kaji, who offered historical context for noteworthy reforms and praiseworthy developments in the pachinko parlor business, which had embarked upon a new era of growth during the 1990s.[74] However, academic interest has subsided in recent years in the face of the contraction of the market and significant shrinkage of the pachinko-playing population.

The meaning of providing pachinko: this book's significance

The above can be summarized as follows: Leaving aside industrial analysis for the purpose of predicting the future, traditional discussion of pachinko has focused on aspects of the demand side, such as the reasons for pachinko's popularity, from perspectives such as those of cultural theory, leisure history, psychology and gambling history. From a point of view that sees demand as determining supply, this approach would not be particularly problematic if consumption factors could be understood to determine the actual state of the industry directly. However, there is a qualitative difference between demand and supply, as while the former is an abstract concept accompanied by ambiguity, the latter involves services and mechanical goods that change from day to day in line with actual circumstances. Pachinko parlors and manufacturers need to deal with ambiguous consumer psychology on a daily basis through practical services and machines.

In this book, I will pay special attention primarily to the supply side of the industry for a number of reasons, which I enumerate below. Consumption of pachinko on the demand side is a relatively inexpensive form of consumption and one on which the time spent may vary with a high degree of flexibility. Aside from the degree to which one is concerned about society's critical views of gambling, particularly in Japan,[75] there are not many restrictions on pachinko consumption. What is more, the fact that the speculative nature of pachinko had been restricted over a long period of time as incomes rose during Japan's postwar era of rapid economic growth can be considered to have amplified its drawcard as an inexpensive pursuit. With regard to playing time, the long working hours of Japanese workers may have accentuated the advantages of pachinko as a form of leisure that can be consumed at the player's discretion at short intervals during the day.

Compared to the demand side, the supply side acts in line with stricter restrictions, and the choices available to businesses have been more limited, not least because the pachinko industry is inseparably linked to regulation and because awareness of public opinion has been a constant concern. An approach stressing the 'dirty' elements of the industry proved unsuccessful at understanding these points in connection with growth. To understand the industry's growth into a mass market, one must elucidate the nature of the business actions chosen amid limited means of competition.

In connection with a historical consideration of the pachinko industry, Kazuo Sugiyama's argument, mentioned above, suggests several points at issue that require further exploration.[76] To chart the industry's beginnings, Sugiyama investigated the origins of pachinko machines themselves and the spread of the pachinko business. Drawing on Sugiyama's analysis, let us examine the relationship between the business of prewar *yashi* (street-stall vendors) and improvements in machines.

Sugiyama argues that pachinko-machine technologies as seen in patents involved designs that were highly similar to those of wall-mounted pinball machines, which were imported from the West for manufacture in Japan and which were in fact copied. He also notes that Japanese pachinko was connected to businesses run as street stalls, which he identifies as a decisive factor that shaped how pachinko machines were improved. Unlike Western wall-mounted machines, from which coins were ejected automatically, pachinko machines were designed to use a manual method instead. Improvements in the form of technological downgrades implemented to suit the business style of street-stall vendors were in fact very important in pachinko machines' development process. The development of Japanese versions of the machines also had the effect of reducing malfunctions and keeping costs to a minimum. In this way, design elements of wall-mounted machines were rearranged to suit the business style of street-stall vendors, enabling the spread of the machines and ultimately leading to the development of the pachinko machine unique to Japan. More specifically, Japanese designers narrowed down the wide range of designs imported from the West, as Figure 1.2 describes (see p. 42), settling on the so-called *komono* ('small article'), a machine that used an arrangement of randomly placed pins[77] that would serve as the established starting point of the industry in the postwar years. However, Sugiyama himself leaves unanswered the question of why this random pin arrangement was chosen. Other questions remain concerning the business of street-stall vendors, necessitating further empirical study to assess their role in propagating the game nationwide.

The trend toward a design based on random pin arrangement is a development that must not be overlooked because it can be considered to have laid the groundwork for the subsequent development of the Masamura Gauge, an innovative pin arrangement (see Chapter 1), and thus to have pushed the industry one step forward on its evolutionary path toward the stable pachinko parlor business while simultaneously capturing customers' attention. In this sense, the convergence on *komono*-style pin arrangement was a critical milestone in the process of realizing pachinko as a viable parlor business.

With regard to the spread of the industry, even if one accepts Sugiyama's view that pachinko spread nationwide during the 1930s through street-stall vendors, it is difficult to connect this prewar form of business, which was linked to special, out-of-the-ordinary events, directly to the business of permanent pachinko parlors that arose in the postwar years and still dominates today. If Sugiyama's view that a nationwide market formed during the 1930s were correct, the industry would have simply recovered with the resumption of machine manufacturing in the postwar period after its prohibition for a time during the war. In other words, an exclusive focus on the consumer aspects of the industry suggests that the postwar business would have been simply a continuation from the prewar period.

By contrast, this book considers the shift from a portable business to permanent pachinko parlors to be a dramatic advance that cannot be understood as simply a continuation of developments in a linear fashion because it involves a transformation that extended to such matters as profit sources, competition among businesses, forms of management and revenue. It would be possible for street-stall vendors to do business on a portable basis while managing low rates of winnings and high discount rates on prizes and avoiding direct competition. As a form of out-of-the-ordinary amusement available only on festival days, customers might accept the high discount rates, even though they could be described as somewhat predatory.

However, the customer base for a permanent store consists of repeat customers who work or live in the vicinity, and thus competition arises between parlors in the same area. A business with low win rates and high discounts, which would make it easy for it to earn profits, would be abandoned by customers through the process of competition. It goes without saying that in order to recover investment and depreciate fixed assets, prospects for stable earnings are essential. The conversion to an everyday form of amusement would probably require changes in not only the outward appearance of the business, but also the manner of its management, transforming the business into one with a focus on continuity.

In this way, the operation of a pachinko parlor requires a management approach that differs fundamentally from that involved in a prewar portable pachinko stall. What led pachinko operators to consider concepts such as return rates and machine updates in order to attract customers on a regular basis instead of on special days only?

TOPICS AND PERIODS

The peripheral economy and the pachinko industry's rise

As noted above, this book will consider the processes by which the pachinko industry was established, grew and developed as a business. The principal question asked by this book may, at first glance, seem to be a little behind the times. How can historical analysis be considered to have significance today, when the alarm is being raised about the market shifting away from pachinko?

The growth of the pachinko industry itself is not necessarily an important topic that demands explanation. However, the sector's development into a mass market was neither inevitable nor self-evident, and the factors that helped it grow to a size at which it could not be ignored as an industry in Japanese society have yet to be explained economically. The pachinko industry was able to grow over the long term even while facing dire threats such as a destructive slump following the introduction of regulations in 1955, and was even poised to achieve further growth in scale during the 1980s, when the decline of state-controlled gambling in rural areas became a cause of concern.[78] It could be said that this growth was driven by tireless efforts on the part of leaders at machine manufacturers and pachinko parlors to seek out ways to provide new services. While all forms of state-controlled gambling, including horse, bicycle and boat racing, are operated by publicly managed corporations, in the pachinko industry a large number of private-sector businesses offer a gambling-like service. Therefore, the provision of goods and services in the industry is basically governed by market mechanisms and competitive principles, under pressure to provide new services tailored to customer needs within the scope permitted under the regulations imposed by the Entertainment and Amusement Trades Control Act. The sustained growth of the pachinko industry must be seen in light of this perspective of competition to capture customers' business.

To understand the above dynamics, this book will employ a perspective from the peripheral economy. Generally, an industry is thought of as a collection of similar economic activities providing goods or services, and in fact the suppliers of these are grouped and categorized as individual businesses. Just as cooking meals at home is not considered an industry, calling an economic activity an industry does not simply mean that it provides us with goods and services. Rather, such production and exchange must be conducted in a sustained manner at or above a certain level, via the market.

Since its establishment in 1949 to facilitate accurate description of the country's industrial structure, the Japan Standard Industrial Classification has been revised to reflect the appearance and decline of industries.[79] In the first set of classifications introduced in 1949, a *pachinko-ya* was simply a service listed under 'other leisure or amusement facility' at the lowest subcategory level. In the 1957 revision (the fourth), the business was moved to the subcategory of 'billiard halls and shooting galleries', and then in 1967 (the sixth revision), *pachinko-ya*[80] was established as its own industry sub-classification. This reclassification process illustrates how the pachinko-parlor business grew to the point where it came to be recognized as its own sphere of economic activity.

However, it is unlikely that neither this growth process itself, nor the continuity that characterized it, was self-evident at the time. Generally, for a field of economic activities to establish a foothold as an industry, it must satisfy various conditions related to the sustainability of such activities. Viewing the issues from this perspective clarifies the inadequacy of examining an economic activity that has not yet reached the stage of an industry exclusively in terms of its marginal presence in society or its status as peripheral to the core of the economy, and of the resulting discussions of its instability. There is a need to identify the dynamic process of becoming established as an industry, which tends to be overlooked under a static view of core versus peripheral economies. The phrase 'peripheral economy' refers to the initial stage from which the pachinko industry first reached the shores of the island of industry status. Reaching the island requires acclimation to the culture and satisfaction of a wide range of economic conditions (such as certain levels of productivity, tax payments, development, maintenance of employment and sustainable earnings), and failure to do so could lead to deprivation of the sector's 'civil rights', causing it to be cast back into the sea. This sense of starting under such conditions is embodied in the use of the phrase 'from a peripheral economy' in the subtitle of this book, and it signals the approach I will employ to examine a number of stages that had to be overcome in order for pachinko to become a goods and services industry.

At the same time, determining how to ascertain industrial growth and development is no simple task. There are multiple definitions of industrial growth and development, and because general statistics for companies in the pachinko industry and the industry as a whole were not compiled until the 1980s, as noted above, it is difficult to establish the relevant facts. Under a traditional, or economic, approach, indicators such as improving labor productivity, added-value productivity or growth in market size are used to ascertain the growth and development of an industry. Most of these metrics are effective when looking at manufacturing industries, for which quantifiable data are relatively easy to obtain. By contrast, there is room for argument regarding whether or not the application of indicators such as labor productivity to the business of pachinko parlors, which is based mainly on the service of providing amusement, would make it possible to measure growth and development accurately in terms of the actual state of the industry.

This book understands the growth and development of the pachinko industry as a process that began with the resolution of various issues that threatened the business under conditions in which its survival was far from guaranteed and then continued with the development, by manufacturers who developed and produced goods in the form of new amusement machines and pachinko parlors that provided the service of amusement, of a structure for the stable supply of goods and services that satisfied customers, resulting ultimately in sustained market growth. Based on this understanding, this book sees these elements as having been established over the lengthy period from the 1950s through the 1970s. It is likely that the pachinko industry was able, solely through improvements to goods and services that drew out potential demand by satisfying customers, to continue to attract customers as an amusement industry and grow companies' earnings in a stable manner amid long-term market growth. I will discuss the factors behind industry growth and development by elucidating the foundations of legitimacy as a business on the part of pachinko parlors and machine makers, which emerged across this timespan, from the perspective of industrial continuity.

Topics and methodology

The discussion in this book will proceed via two topics. The first concerns elucidation of the foundations of an economic organization consisting of pachinko-parlor businesses, which continually provided services tailored to potential demand for pachinko, and pachinko-machine manufacturers, which developed amusement machines that matched consumers' tastes. Since changes in regulations and the distinctive properties of pachinko machines, with unpredictable levels of popularity, introduce business instability into the pachinko industry, the industry faced a wide range of difficulties until it was able to control such uncertainty through economic organization. Seeing the sustained growth and development of the industry as a process of resolving such challenges is an effective analytical viewpoint. On the subject of pachinko parlors, this book will consider means of competition in addition to the stabilization of revenue foundations and businesses' increasing computability. As to actions of pachinko-machine manufacturers, it will focus on how institutionalization and certain types of regulation, such as discipline and restrictions, led to the restoration of order and competition in the machine market, while adopting the perspective of cartel activities as partial corrections to market functions based on Juro Hashimoto and Haruhito Takeda's approach.[81]

In connection with demand-side factors related to consumers, various issues merit consideration in regard to average customer spending (in terms of the value of balls purchased), for example changes in living conditions including income and lifestyle as well as the attributes of the pachinko-playing population and changes over time. Because it is not possible to consider all such historical changes in customers – i.e., on the demand side – this book will focus on the economic foundations and responses of companies that employed various means to compete under the restrictions imposed by regulations, for example by considering, based on the content of consumer surveys, how the appearance of women customers on the scene was connected to changes in pachinko machines and parlors' locations.

The second topic, which involves a different approach than that described above, concerns how well the processes of the growth and development of the industry and the growth of related businesses can be explained by characterizing the pachinko industry as an ethnic minority business. While this is a somewhat circuitous approach, I will ask which elements of the pachinko industry as an ethnic minority business are essential in order to explain factors of its growth and development and consider what kinds of discoveries can be made in related observations. The view of the industry as an ethnic minority business is related to the high percentage of ethnic minority Koreans involved in operating the industry. In fact, the accumulation of information and provision of funding by their community made it easier for ethnic minority Koreans to open up pachinko parlors, and this combined with the reluctance of those outside the community to enter the industry resulted in a very strong presence of ethnic minority groups in the industry.[82] However, the ethnic element in the industry's development is premised on historical conditions that arose at a particular time. The accumulation of information in the community was not a function specific to that ethnic group but rather was a result of the universal principle that it is easier to start a business from within a dense concentration of information on a certain subject.[83] In light of this understanding, there is also a need to take into consideration the effects that would result from a change in these historical conditions, and while the functions of the community were important at the startup stage, different fundamentals demand attention when considering the growth of individual businesses. This book will reconsider the implications of the pachinko industry for an ethnic enterprise that is deeply related to ethnic minority Koreans in Japan on the growth of individual companies in light of its relation to core elements of the industry's growth and development.

Categorization of industry growth and constructs of this book

In order to examine the process through which the industry was able to secure its long-term survival and prospects for future growth, this book's analysis will focus primarily on the period from the 1950s to the early 1990s. I chose this period because the structure of the pachinko industry is considered to have reached a major turning point in the late 1990s. Developments symbolic of this change include the fact that the pachinko-parlor business came to be reassessed as a 30-trillion-yen industry in 1996, and the Japan Amusement Machine Patent Management Federation (Nihon Yūgiki Tokkyo Unei Renmei, or Nittokuren), which supported interdependence in the machinery market, was dissolved in 1999.

The sense in which this represented the end of an era will be reconsidered in the final chapter. Overall, this book employs a structure based on a consideration of developments according to period. The categorization of these periods will be described below based on a long-term perspective of the pachinko industry's history.

First, see Table 0.3 concerning trends in market size over time. While sales figures presented are based on 1963 levels, it is clear that the market underwent remarkable growth. The table excludes the effects of the increases in ball charges from 2 to 3 yen in 1972, and then to 4 yen in 1978. The pronounced growth since the 1980s is also clear.

Based on trends in the nationwide number of pachinko parlors and machine manufacturers, discussed below, this book divides the postwar history of the growth and development of the pachinko industry into four periods and investigates each (Figure 0.3[84]).

Chapter 1 will cover the 1950s relevant to the initial stage of the industry when the number of pachinko parlors exhibited severe fluctuations. These dramatic ups and downs are related to the development of successive-shot machines involving

Fiscal year	Sales	Multiplier	Fiscal year	Sales	Multiplier
1952	700~800	0.2~0.3	1990	169,460	2,824
1954	2,500	0.8	1991	232,990	7,766
1963	3,000	1	1992	263,240	8,775
1965	3,804	1.27	1993	274,210	9,140
1967	4,140	138	1994	304,780	10,159
1969			1995	309,050	10,302
1970	5,372	179	1996	300,700	10,023
1971	6,016	201	1997	284,160	9,472
1972	6,852	228	1998	280,470	9,349
1973	8,394	187[b]	1999	284,690	9,490
1974	9,930	221	2000	288,680	9,623
1975	10,751	239	2001	292,430	9,748
1976	11,384	253	2002	304,420	10,147
1977	13,499	300	2003	323,900	10,797
1978	14,233	316	2004	339,120	11,304
1979	13,977	233[b]	2005	348,620	11,621
1980	13,678	228	2006	336,420	11,214
1981	22,134	369	2007	301,770	10,059
1982	43,044	717	2008	288,190	9,606
1983	52,503	875	2009	282,420	9,414
1984	64,335	1,072	2010	259,830	8,661
1985	61,247	1,021	2011	254,890	8,496
1986			2012	256,720	8,557
1987	116,020	1,934	2013	250,050	8,335
1988			2014	245,040	8,168
1989	152,710	2,545	2015	232,290	7,743

Table 0.3: Market size of the pachinko industry (unit: hundreds of millions of yen)

Notes:

a. For a list of average exchange rates by year, see JPY-USD exchange rate table on p. xv.

b. Ball fees were 2 yen (about US$0.01) starting in 1948, 3 yen (about US$0.01) in 1972 and 4 yen in 1978 (about US$0.02). Consequently, sales for 1973 through 1979 have been calculated by eliminating the increase of 150 or 200 percent, respectively, based on the 1963 figure.

Source: Asahi Shimbunsha (1953: 255), Economic Planning Agency (1957: 114), Tokei (1964), 'パチンコもうけばなし生産管理と統計学' (A tale of profit in pachinko: Production management and statistics), 16(3), Table 0.1 above, Leisure Development Center (1980: 29; 1983: 51; 1986: 82, 87; 1997) and Japan Productivity Center (2011: 84-85; 2016: 118-19)

a pronounced speculative element and the National Police Agency's enactment of regulations to ban such machines. Through verifying that the regulations had positive effects for the start of the pachinko industry, the investigation will question the one-sided view of the negative relationship between regulation and the development of industries.

While the number of parlors was stable, manufacturers continued to exit the industry during the 1960s (see Figure 0.3). A look at the number of pachinko machines per parlor as shown in Figure 0.4 reveals that the market continued its steady growth during this period. Chapter 2 will explore the context of the exit of manufacturers

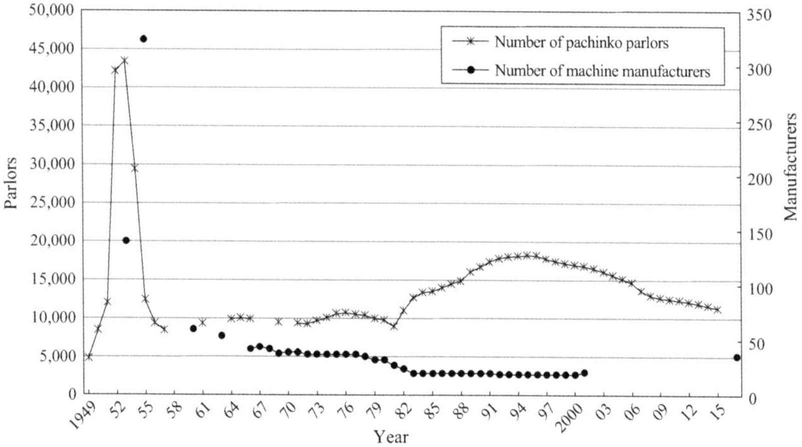

Figure 0.3: Number of pachinko parlors and machine manufacturers (1949 to 2017)
Note: The number of members of the Japan Amusement Machine Industry Association, as provided by that organization, has been used as a proxy for the number of manufacturers.
Source: See Leisure Development Center (1983: 56) as well as (1) and (3) in Table 11, 'Trend in leisure market growth rates', in Leisure Development Center (1983: 58).

from the growing market in the 1960s. What did they identify as problematic in the chaotic machine market? How did the institutionalization of this disordered market affect manufacturers?

In the 1970s, the drop in the number of manufacturers eased until it reemerged toward the end of the same period (see Figure 0.3), and the growth in the size of pachinko parlors was slow (see Figure 0.4). Chapter 3 will analyze the intense R&D competition among manufacturers in the 1970s, focusing on the conditions surrounding the development of pachinko machines. Players were easily bored by machines, whose popularity fluctuated rapidly depending on trends. How did manufacturers accommodate this high-risk characteristic and develop new machines to realize market growth?

The 1980s and 1990s represent a remarkable period of growth in the history of the pachinko industry (see Table 0.3 and Figure 0.4), resulting from the development of Fībā-type machines. Even compared to other leisure sectors, the pronounced growth of the pachinko industry during the 1980s was astonishing. While its growth was not so pronounced through the 1970s as that in other leisure industries such as food service and travel, the pachinko industry exhibited a remarkable upturn beginning in the 1980s (see Table 0.4).[85] Chapters 4 and 5 will focus on the changes during this period. Chapter 4 will analyze how the growing market was brought about by new technology and look at the difficulties faced by traditional management. Chapter 5 examines the management style of big companies in contrast to the traditional model.

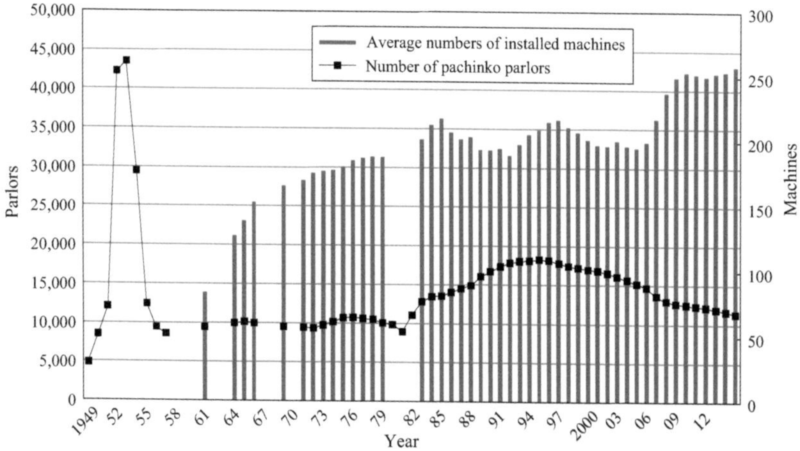

Figure 0.4: Average number of machines installed in pachinko parlors (1949 to 2015)
Note: Average numbers of installed machines were calculated by dividing the total number of installed machines by the number of parlors.
Source: See Leisure Development Center (1983: 56) as well as (1) and (3) in Table 11, 'Trend in leisure market growth rates', in Leisure Development Center (1983: 58). Average numbers of installed machines were calculated based on Federation of Tokyo Amusement Associations / Tokyo Amusement Industry Cooperative Association, p.154, 'パチンコ遊技機備付台数等比較表' ([Comparative table of installed pachinko machine counts], Zenyūren Kōhō, February 15, 1968), and '店舗数·備付台数前年度比較表' ([Comparative table of the number of parlors and installed machines for previous fiscal year], Zenyūren Kōhō, September 15, 1968). After 1990, the total number of installed machines reflects the number pachinko machines alone as of December 31 of each year, excluding pachislot *and other machines (as per the page 'Member parlors and machine counts' on the website of the All-Japan Federation of Pachinko Business Cooperative Associations, http://www.ennichiyuren.or.jp/material/report.html/tenpoindex/tenpo_02.html, accessed on May 8, 2017). The original data was announced by the National Police Agency.*

	1965–75	1975–76	1976–77	1977–78	1978–79	1979–80	1980–81	1981–82
Leisure category	15.9	21.0	9.7	6.1	8.1	14.4	11.7	6.9
Pachinko parlors	10.9	5.9	7.6	5.1	–1.9	–2.4	65.3	20.4

Table 0.4: Comparison of market growth rates (unit: %)
Source: See Leisure Development Center (1983: 56) as well as (1) and (3) in Table 11, 'Trend in leisure market growth rates', in Leisure Development Center (1983: 58).

The main concern of the Essay is to shed light on the connection between ethnic minority Koreans in Japan and the pachinko industry, reviewing the industries in which the ethnic group has played an important role. This chapter will reconsider the significance of this group in the development of the pachinko industry.

Allow me to offer a word on the distinct approach taken in this work. Several general points at issue related to economic phenomena are discussed with regard to the historical details of pachinko, which is a very local topic related to Japan. This structure is not intended to be a mere time-series description of developments. Rather, the challenges that needed to be resolved to ensure the survival of the industry differed from one period to the next, and each chapter's analysis will illuminate initiatives undertaken in light of the status of the industry at the end of the previous period.

Reading through the entire book from the beginning would benefit historical understanding, but it would also be fine to read individual chapters of interest in relation to specific economic and social issues. For example, Chapter 1 focuses on the reinterpretation of regulations for the formation of a new industry in the market. Chapter 2 examines how competition and cooperation are organized and adjusted for economic advantage. Chapter 3 describes functions of the patent pool related to R&D and manufacturing as an industry that is prone to outside influence and instability in a way that is similar to the open innovation system.[86] Chapters 2 and 3 analyze the formation and management of a patent pool. The system's prioritization of economic rationality is suggestive of possibilities for systems to support development and production in the assembly machinery industry, which is subject to dramatic technological innovation. In chapters 4 and 5, the narrative will chart the spread of innovation and dynamic change. One can develop an understanding of the relationship between the Korean minority in Japan and the pachinko industry from an economic perspective by reading the Essay. I hope that this book, which presents detailed historical facts combining economic and social aspects, will also provide a distinctive methodology for business history in Japan.

It must be acknowledged that this book has limitations related to its analytical methods. Due to its approach, it omits an analysis of slot-based amusement machines (known as *pachislot* machines, meaning pachinko-size Japanese slot machines), which have underpinned the popularity of pachinko in recent years. This book does not address the historical background of the rapid increase in the number of such machines installed in pachinko parlors since the 1980s. Their recent popularity, too, compels an analysis of *pachislot* machines as an essential part of any effort to understand today's pachinko industry. However, this book excludes them from consideration because they were not very important during the period it examines.[87] This book, which focuses chiefly on an analysis of the pachinko machine industry, can be considered meaningful as a source of historical background information for understanding the distinguishing features of the *pachislot* machines market.

I hope readers enjoy taking a journey into the world of pachinko and come to ponder the characteristics of Japanese society as well as common attributes that transcend borders by focusing on the history of pachinko as a peripheral sphere in business and society delivered by marginal players in Japan.

1

Inception of the Pachinko Industry: Commercialization of Traditional Festival-day Entertainment

INTRODUCTION

This chapter explores the ten-plus years from the end of the 1940s into the 1950s to explain how the foundations of the pachinko industry were laid during a period characterized by the most dramatic upheaval in the sector's history.

For the purposes of this book, 'the industrialization of pachinko' refers to the establishment of both the foundation that allowed pachinko to be made available to the public and certain conditions necessary for the nascent sector's growth into an industry. Associated developments included the enactment of legal structures and the implementation of machine improvements that facilitated popularization and market formation, as well as the forging of a division of labor between pachinko parlors and machine manufacturers, ultimately leading to the emergence of entities able to provide pachinko machines and services. However, these developments alone were not sufficient to guarantee the sustained production and reproduction of pachinko (that is, its provision as a service). In light of accompanying problems that attracted social criticism in the wake of the sector's growing popularity, including the illegal exchange of prizes for cash and associations with organized crime, the entire process could hardly be described as stable. In fact, the manner in which pachinko businesses operated and various issues arising from the consumption of the service they provided prompted a flurry of regulations that called into question the very viability of the industry. The purpose of this chapter is to test the proposition that a base had been put in place to facilitate stable profits in parlor operations as part of these first steps toward industrialization by examining the relationships among three factors – industry actors, various problems and regulations – through the series of complex incidents that occurred during this time.

On July 10, 1948, the Entertainment Establishment Control Act[1] was promulgated, regulating businesses with pachinko machines. Of the three business categories regulated by the act, parlors[2] qualified as 'businesses with billiard tables, rooms for

Fiscal year	Number of parlors	Increase (▲ decrease)
1949	4,818	
1950	8,450	3,632
1951	12,038	3,588
1952	42,168	30,130
1953	43,452	1,284
1954	29,416	▲ 14,036
1955	12,391	▲ 17,025
1956	9,365	▲ 3,026
1957	8,487	▲ 878
1958	8,792	305

Table 1.1: Number of pachinko parlors
Note: Number of parlors as of June as reported by the National Police Agency.
Source: Compiled based on National Confederation of Amusement Industry Associations (1977: 307).

mahjong or other spaces that encourage customers to participate in a game that could invite a fondness for gambling',[3] with the result that would-be operators were required to seek a license from their prefecture's public safety commission before they could open for business.[4] The act also subjected businesses to government scrutiny to ensure they operated in accordance with certain methods set forth in the legislation. Starting in 1949, with the introduction of the act's licensing scheme, it became possible to determine an official count for the number of parlors (see Table 1.1).

As indicated by the above definition, the text of the 1948 Entertainment Establishment Control Act did not explicitly mention pachinko parlors or *pachinko-ya* (pachinko businesses), as they were called at the time. Its failure to do so indicates that the pachinko industry was less prominent in the minds of regulators than other entertainment (gaming) businesses such as mahjong. It was in 1954 that the phrase *pachinko-ya* was first used.[5] As described in Table 1.1, this change was a reaction to remarkable growth in the number of parlors since 1950.

As reflected in its recognition in applicable laws, the industry embarked on a period of growth from around 1950. From 1949 to 1951, the number of parlors grew by more than 3500 each year, for a total increase of 2.5 times over the two-year period. However, explosive growth in the number of parlors at the beginning of the 1950s was neither welcomed by the police, who had been responsible for regulating the entertainment industry prior to World War II, nor by society as a whole.

Lamenting that students and factory workers were spending their book money – and that housewives were spending their grocery money – on pachinko balls,[6] the daily column 'Tensei Jingo' in the May 26, 1952, edition of the *Asahi Shimbun* criticized pachinko as a decadent pursuit. Speaking at a press conference in 1952, Hayato Ikeda, who had just become Minister of International Trade and Industry, reiterated the view he had voiced in a reply to a question in the Diet six months earlier,[7] saying, 'Bicycle racing and pachinko are both social evils, and my unchanged belief is that they, along with lotteries, should be eliminated as soon as possible'.[8] No doubt made while casting a sidelong glance at the record number of new pachinko businesses, this pronouncement, while not official policy, offers a glimpse of the government's stance on regulating pachinko by treating it as a type of gambling, like bicycle racing, at a time when the direction and prospects of the nation's economic recovery remained uncertain. The concept of enjoying leisure time was not yet established in daily life, and no social consensus on encouraging free personal consumption had developed.

Although sources that give a comprehensive account of the characteristics of the consumers who enjoyed pachinko are limited, the memoir[9] of one *pachinko musume*, as the female attendants who supplied and retrieved balls manually behind the machines were known, paints a picture of parlors' clientele. The location of the parlor where the author worked is unknown, but she describes an array of customers, including workers at a nearby lumberyard, members of the yakuza, intellectuals, housewives, parents and their children, middle-aged ladies, high-school students and a detective who was a regular. However, there was no official move by the government in response to the surging popularity of pachinko, which was attracting a diverse range of customers, on a general consumer level. Notwithstanding the critical view of pachinko that was prevalent in broader society, in 1952 the number of parlors grew by a factor of more than three on the previous year's figure (see Table 1.1). The possibility of statistical issues cannot be excluded, but there is no doubt about pachinko's robust and rapid growth during this period. However, the path taken by the industry during this initial stage was not a smooth and consistent one, evident from the trend's flip to abrupt decline in just five years. The entry into, and subsequent exit from, the industry of large numbers of businesses suggests both the challenges of the environment in which pachinko businesses operated and the fragility of the parlor business's revenue base. It is generally understood that abrupt changes in the number of parlors are due to the debut of popular machines and regulation under the Administrative Order Prohibiting Successive-shot Machines, enacted in 1955.[10] The following description appears in the history of the Japan Amusement Machine Industry Association (Nihon Yūgiki Kōgyō Kumiai; abbreviated as 'Nikkōso'), whose membership consists of machine manufacturers:

> In 1953, the successive-shot boom spurred a surge in the number of pachinko parlors to reach 43,000, and of pachinko machines, to 1.5 million. Concerned about this state of affairs, the National Police Agency banned successive-shot machines, albeit with a one-year grace period, in November 1954. The ban, which ushered in an unprecedented crisis for the pachinko industry, caused the number of parlors

> nationwide to plummet at a stroke to 9000, compared to 50,000 when the prohibition was introduced, and the number of pachinko machines to fall to the 56,000 level, heralding an era of severe tribulation for the industry.[11]

The estimate of 50,000 parlors at the time the prohibition was introduced reflects the author's personal view and cannot be verified from available documentation.[12] An April 1954 amendment of the Entertainment Establishment Control Act introduced a system that made license renewal contingent on the payment of taxes,[13] and so it is possible that this figure may include some businesses that were unable to renew their licenses. I will address the issues of taxation and license renewal later in this chapter, but for now, suffice to say that our understanding that the abrupt decline in the number of parlors was linked to the 1955 ban may need to be partially revised. If we accept the official statistics shown in Table 1.1 at face value, the fact that the peak occurred in 1953 means that the shift to falling numbers cannot be explained solely by the introduction of regulations. If, for the sake of argument, we accept that the number of parlors peaked in 1954 before regulations spurred a broad retreat from the market, the existence of more than 20,000 parlors that do not appear in the statistics needs to be explained. On the other hand, if the shortfall is related to 'invisible' parlors that were unable to renew their operating license for tax reasons, the explanation would need to take into account the reason for their failure to pay taxes and its significance.

In this chapter, I will explain the conditions under which parlors and machine manufacturers operated against the backdrop of these extreme fluctuations and shed light on a number of problems that acted to call the viability of continued operation into question. Although it is not possible to overcome statistical issues and determine the exact moment at which the number of parlors peaked, the actual conditions under which parlors operated suggest the possibility that the decline in their numbers was a matter of appearance only while offering clues that can aid our understanding of tax-related problems. I will demonstrate how the industry gained viability with the discovery of a revenue base for parlor operations, in terms of internal industry trends, by describing management as well as the offensive and defensive maneuvers undertaken in response to regulations that developed in the context of the legal system that governed entertainment businesses. In addition, I will identify the characteristics that shaped the subsequent growth of the industry. Finally, I present a discussion of specific issues and analytical methods.

A consideration of examples from other countries that led to prohibition on the basis of gambling[14] makes it clear that regulation under the Entertainment Establishment Control Act, described above, had a definitive impact on the existence of the pachinko industry. In fact, the pachinko business is subject to licensing by public safety commissions, and a variety of regulations on such aspects as fees charged to redeem balls, upper limits on the value of prizes, game methods and machine inspection standards had a major impact on the industry. However, as noted above, regulations are not a silver bullet that explains every aspect of the industry's history. While it is meaningful to consider the nature of the impact of regulations on the industry for its own sake, it is also necessary to examine the history of the industry from the standpoint of the mutual interactions between those regulations and the various conditions that allowed pachinko to develop into a viable business.

An examination of changes within the industry reveals that pachinko, an amusement offered by pop-up street stalls prior to World War II,[15] transitioned to a brick-and-mortar business that specialized in providing a gaming service from the second half of the 1940s to the early 1950s. Externally, the requirement, imposed by the Entertainment Establishment Control Act, that new pachinko businesses had to occupy a brick-and-mortar facility provided a major opportunity. The important thing from a management perspective was the question of whether locations offering a 'non-productive' activity – pachinko – as their sole amusement could become established businesses during the first half of the 1950s, when consumers lacked confidence as to whether personal income would rise in a sustained manner. To the extent that we rely on Table 1.1, the answer to that question remained unclear in 1955 and 1956.

In this chapter, I will reveal the process by which parlors developed as businesses by shedding light on the instability that characterized the pachinko industry during the early stages of its growth and on the initial challenges that the industry had to overcome in order to establish itself in society. Using the number of parlors, which fluctuated during the early 1950s, I will locate the revenue base on which these businesses were built and consider how it was discovered.

The process that led parlors to secure stable profits signifies that by which they discovered a sustainable business model. In this chapter, I refer to that process as the accumulation of management expertise. Management expertise embodies the ability to control a variety of factors that affect revenue, for example the ability to attract customers in the context of competitive relationships with other parlors in the course of day-to-day operations and secure repeat customers while increasing operating rates. Naturally, the accumulation of such expertise is a precondition for parlors to operate as businesses. Although the selection of machines is also related to the accumulation of such expertise, this chapter will focus on the process of pin adjustment as it was carried out based on a consideration of a variety of factors. Because pachinko machines were initially produced as handicraft products in workers' homes, quality was inconsistent, and techniques for adjusting pins based on the condition of individual machines had a significant effect on each parlor's operations. This book's emphasis on pin adjustment takes into account the period-specific characteristics of machine technology.[16] I will examine the process by which parlors sought to provide long-term stability for

Figure 1.1: Masamura Shōkai's 'kingdom'

Note:

- *M式パチンコ宣伝部: M-style Pachinko Machine Advertising Department*
- *M商会直営パチンコ: M Shōkai Factory Outlet*
- *元祖M式パチンコ: Original M-style Pachinko Machines*
- *○○式パチンコ総本部: Acme Pachinko Machines*
- *パチンコ: PACHINKO*

Source: Ōru Seikatsu *(1952), '変わった町・変わった村パチンコのメッカ名古屋訪問記' (A strange town, a strange village: Account of a visit to Nagoya, the Mecca of pachinko), 7(3), p. 78.*

their businesses based on data describing daily sales and profitability (gross profit margins), which were the result of pin adjustment. I will also demonstrate how, during the second half of the 1950s, when the initial explosion of popularity seems to have been forcibly reined in by regulation, the pachinko business nonetheless managed to establish itself while laying the groundwork for its future development. In doing so, I will draw on the operational track record of Masamura Shōkai, the premier company in the pachinko industry at the time.[17] The restructuring of the company's business expresses the transformation of the pachinko industry in vivid detail.

Figure 1.1 depicts an illustration that featured in the magazine *Ōru Seikatsu*[18] around 1952. Signs advertising 'M-style Pachinko Machine Advertising Department' and ' M Shōkai Factory Outlet' stand out in the image. They refer to Nagoya-based Masamura Shōkai, the subject of this chapter. Masamura Shōkai drove the popularity of pachinko at the time because it understood what kinds of machines consumers wanted.

The company, which was founded in 1951 to 'sell pachinko machines and operate game parlors', was a vertically integrated enterprise whose operations included producing machines on an original equipment manufacturer (OEM) basis. After inventing the Masamura-type pachinko machine,[19] which is considered the 'godfather' of all pachinko machines, founder Takeichi Masamura began selling his product in 1949. Around the middle of the 1950s, Masamura's business experienced a golden age, having established a nationwide market for pachinko machines. In 1955, the *Imperial Bank Company Digest* records Masamura Shōkai as a 'manufacturer and seller of pachinko machines'[20] and one of the six leading companies in the pachinko industry (which included two machine manufacturers, two manufacturers that also operated parlors, one machine sales company and one pachinko ball manufacturer). The company had 400 employees,[21] making it one of the largest manufacturers in the industry, and recorded annual sales of 480 million yen (about US$1.33 million), second only to those of Okumura Sangyō. The growth of Masamura Shōkai as an industry leader, the setbacks posed by the Administrative Order Prohibiting Successive-shot Machines and the subsequent restructuring of the company's management provide ideal material through which to examine the characteristics of the pachinko industry's infancy during the 1950s and the significance of the regulations that consistently governed its development.

THE PACHINKO BOOM

Improvements to machines

The primary force behind the rapid growth in the number of pachinko parlors during the first half of the 1950s (see Table 1.1 above) was the popularity of improved machines.[22] Thanks to the debut of refinements such as the Masamura Gauge (Masamura Gēji) and successive-shot machines, which triggered a series of steps in the industry's development, pachinko transitioned from prewar machines known as *komono* to a generation of postwar machines that were better suited to business. The new technologies that emerged during this period went beyond mere improvements to make a definitive contribution to the industry's development. How was this so?

The Masamura Gauge[23] invented by Masamura Shōkai founder Takeichi Masamura around 1948 ushered in a new era in terms of the design of pin arrangements for machines' display boards and became the de facto standard for some fifty years. That said, numerous attempts were made to differentiate machines dating back to the emergence of the Masamura Gauge. In 1951, just after the debut of Masamura Gauge machines, an industry paper suggested that it was necessary to move away from Masamura-type gauge boards so that new varieties of pachinko could be developed. The paper noted that manufacturers were struggling to respond.[24] The experiences of manufacturer Ōyama Shōten[25] in Nagoya, which ran advertisements offering prize money for anyone who could create a new type of pachinko after it failed to do so internally, speaks to the difficulty of the task. Other companies' efforts to compete with the Masamura Gauge bore little fruit, and related designs failed to gain traction. In short, the Masamura Gauge was backed by customers' full-throated support – which is to say, by the popularity of the machines that used it – and as a result, it squeezed out competing designs to become the standard.

Pachinko Hyakka Jiten (Encyclopedia of Pachinko),[26] published in 1953, had this to say about 'Masamura-style machines, the godfather of pachinko machines' in its introduction of leading machines: 'Most pachinko machines made by today's manufacturers adopt a Masamura-style gauge, and that design can fairly be described as the standard. In any case, the well-established Masamura design has achieved overwhelming dominance in today's industry, where exceptional new machines appear continuously, and its popularity demonstrates how effectively it has taken the country by storm'. In this way, the Masamura Gauge took hold as the de facto standard in pachinko machine design.

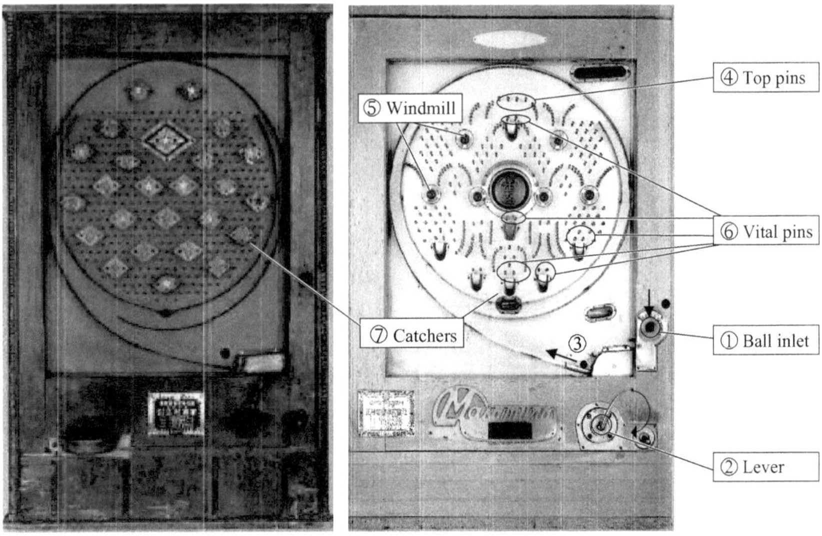

Figure 1.2: A prewar komono machine from 1946 (left) and an 'All 15' machine with Masamura Gauge from 1951 (right)
Note: Labels ① through ⑦ added by the author.
Source: Compiled based on Hyakusu Henshūshitsu (1985: 4, 7).

The most significant factor in its popularity was its injection of gaming technology into the randomness of prewar machines. Additionally, the increase in the speed at which customers could cycle through balls boosted turnover and created the potential for growth in sales. With *komono* machines (Figure 1.2, left), which had about 340 evenly spaced pins, whether any given ball entered one of the twenty-five catchers (⑦) was purely a matter of chance. Since the balls struck the pins at high frequency, it took time for each ball that was launched to either enter a catcher or fall out of the playing field.[27]

By contrast, the Masamura Gauge (Figure 1.2, right) sped up the movement of the balls by eliminating about 100 of the pins found in the typical *komono* machine. One begins playing pachinko by placing balls in the ball inlet (①). If any balls enter catchers (⑦), prize balls will be dispensed into a tray, allowing play to continue. Once all the balls fall out of the playing field, play is over. When playing on the Masamura Gauge, the smaller number of pins reduces the time until the result of play is known (that is, whether any prize balls are won) to about one-half or one-third of the six seconds this process takes on *komono* machines. The designer, Masamura, sought to increase the pleasure of play by introducing a variety of features, for example adding a windmill (⑤) that caused changes in the trajectory of the balls to bring in an element of surprise.[28]

The most noteworthy characteristic of the Masamura Gauge is that it creates an expectation in players that increased skill leads to greater likelihood of winning prize balls. The introduction of technique into gameplay was made possible as follows. Masamura developed pin arrangements on the machine's boards to prompt specific ball trajectories. Pachinko parlors determined the prize-ball percentage by closing pins (by angling pairs of pins so that they face inward, making it less likely that a ball will enter the hole between the pins), primarily the 'vital pins' (⑥) above catchers (⑦).[29] The prize-ball percentage refers to the ratio of the number of prize balls the parlor allows to the number of balls customers launch. On days when a parlor adjusted pins to create a prize-ball percentage of 100 percent or greater, a strategy known as 'opening the pins', customers could gain more balls than they launched. By contrast, on days when the pins were 'closed', customers would win fewer prize balls than they launched. Parlors attracted customers by manipulating the prize-ball percentage. Customers who wanted to increase their winning percentage had to develop two skills: first, learn to read the intentions behind the gauge design and the manner in which the pins had been adjusted so that they could choose the 'right' machine, and second, figure out how to launch balls from the shooting point (③) by operating the lever (②). In short, skilled players were able to determine which of the four top pins (④) (Figure 1.2, right) a ball would strike by modulating the strength with which the ball was launched when they pulled the lever (②). Balls that traveled on certain trajectories were more likely to enter a catcher, and if a player could refine their technique so that they could accurately launch balls such that they would strike certain pins, they could increase their winning percentage.

In this way, for customers, the Masamura Gauge brought an increased likelihood of winning as they increased their skill in reading pins and launching balls; for parlors, it boosted the number of balls that could be launched per unit of time, which affected sales, by accelerating the movement of balls (in other words, it raised the upper limit on machines' real operating time compared to previous designs). Subsequent evolutions in machine design came with 'all-win' models such as the 'All 10' and 'All 15' (in 1951) and additional enhancements in successive-shot machines such as machine-gun (late 1952) and circulating-type designs (1953).[30] Conventional machines had simple designs that yielded from one to three prize balls at a time. These designs reflected mechanical limits that meant machines could only dispense several balls from specific holes, known as 'jackpot' holes. The 'All 10' and 'All 15' machines developed by Kazuo Nagasaki took advantage of technological progress that allowed them to supply up to ten balls (hence the 10 in 'All 10') for each catcher.[31] The ability to gain at least three to five times more balls for each catcher than was possible with previous machines excited customers at the time. The more balls customers received, the more prizes for which they could exchange those balls. This new reality fueled customers' expectations of winning and stimulated their fondness for gambling.

Machines combining successive-shot capability with the dispensation mechanism so that balls were automatically launched one after the next from a pool fed by the customer into the ball tray were developed by Tokuharu Kikuyama of the Hōkoku Yūgiki Seisakusho (Amusement Machine Works). The new design enabled customers to launch a stream of balls successively, any of which could enter a catcher on the machine's pin board.[32] Technological developments[33] played an essential role in improvements to ball feed and dispensation mechanisms that allowed more balls to be launched and to enter catchers in successive-shot machines. As this was accompanied by the progressive introduction of ball-circulating designs (such as the circulating-type 'flurry of blows' pachinko machine invented by Kohei Takeuchi of Takeya Shōkai[34]) and then motorized pachinko machines,[35] there was dramatic growth in the number of balls that could be launched in a given amount of time.[36] The new machines were capable of launching as many as 160 to 180 balls per minute, and the resulting boost in speculative appeal knew no bounds.

Mechanical improvements made around 1950 not only afforded a certain amount of control over the element of chance, but also increased the speed of the game. As a result, these enhancements broadened the appeal of play for customers and the business potential for parlors. In this way, such improvements put in place the conditions necessary for the transition from a festival-day entertainment industry, which depended solely on keeping prize ball percentages low by adjusting the pins on machines' boards and by imposing a high discount rate on prize redemptions in order to maintain its viability, to an industry that could operate brick-and-mortar service spaces. Combined with technological progress in pachinko machines' ball-launching and dispensation mechanisms and mechanical elements that increased the speed at which balls could be launched, these improvements allowed customers to pursue winnings – and parlors, increased sales – without limit.

Appearance of specialized services

The counterfeit machine incident involving Masamura Shōkai in 1952 offers a glimpse of the dark side of the popularity of the Masamura Gauge.[37] In 1953, Masamura Shōkai nameplates were being bought and sold for 100 yen (about US$0.28) in the company's hometown of Nagoya as well as in more distant locales where its machines were overwhelmingly popular, for example Kobe and Miyazaki.[38] The differences between Masamura Gauge machines and previous designs were clear, as illustrated by Figure 1.2 above, and it is not difficult to imagine how customers flocked to parlors with Masamura Gauge machines once their appeal became a topic of conversation. Imitation is a phenomenon that highlights the innovative nature of the product copied, and this episode points to parlors' desire for Masamura Shōkai's machines due their superior ability to attract customers.

The popularity of pachinko spurred by the Masamura Gauge and 'all-win' machines found direct expression in the reaction of customers, who formed long lines to use them. Entrepreneurs were enticed to enter the parlor business by people who saw opportunity in this popularity and by acquaintances who had profited from it in the past.[39] The sheer number of newly opened parlors was striking. Even in Tokyo, where the industry was more strictly regulated, the number of parlors exceeded expectations. According to game parlor statistics compiled by the Metropolitan Police Department, as of September 10, 1951, pachinko, with 1294 establishments, had surpassed billiards (155 locations), a Japanese-style pinball game known as '*smāto bōru*' (smart ball) (142 locations) and even mahjong (1147 locations).[40] Authorities were receiving close to thirty applications for new businesses every day around that time, and that trend showed no sign of declining. The number of pachinko businesses, which accounted for some 80 percent of all gaming establishments, was predicted to approach 3000 by the end of the year. In the end, even that prediction proved to be far too low, and the number of newly established businesses reached 4231 as 416 parlors closed, with the result that the number of pachinko businesses grew abruptly by a factor of about ten compared to the previous year, when there were 385 such businesses. The literature indicates that many parlors had, surprisingly for the time, around 100 machines.[41]

There is little in the way of governmental research or accurate statistical data to determine the economic impact of pachinko's newfound popularity. However, there are a number of accounts from observers at the time who reacted perceptively to the unusual popularity of the pastime, and they offer a glimpse of the size of the market. According to one estimate by the country's monopoly retailer of tobacco products, Nippon Senbai Kōsha (Japan Tobacco and Salt Public Corporation), based on growth in sales of cigarettes, which were used as prizes by pachinko parlors, sales totaled from 70 (about US$194 million) to 80 billion yen (about US$222 million) during the 1952 business year.[42] This figure is about 1.2 to 1.5 times the 57 billion yen (about US$158 million) in annual sales generated by bicycle racing, the most popular type of state-controlled gambling at the time.[43] Machine manufacturers, which were concentrated in the city of Nagoya, received a rush of orders. One source notes that an examination of cargo handling records from JR Sasajima Freight Station in Aichi Prefecture, where Nagoya is located, indicated that pachinko machines were included at the top of the list for 1952.[44] Pachinko grew into the largest entertainment industry that included an element of gambling during the postwar reconstruction period between about 1945 and 1955.

GROWTH OF MASAMURA SHŌKAI

As clarified in the previous section, machines incorporating a pin board featuring the Masamura Gauge, as well as Masamura Shōkai as the design's creator, occupied a central position in the popularity of pachinko during this period. Masamura Shōkai was organized into separate manufacturing, sales and parlor departments, with manufacturing drawing on contractor-operated factories, while sales and parlor operations were independently run by relatives and others. These organizational divisions were linked by a series of close personal relationships culminating in Masamura at the pinnacle of the company's management, forming a group whose operations extended from the manufacture of machines to the provision of entertainment services. That said, the arrangement was not preplanned, but rather took shape as officials, who had not anticipated the popularity of the Masamura Gauge, reacted to the pachinko boom. The organizational makeup of the company and the way it pursued manufacturing and sales offer a glimpse of the foundations on which the pachinko industry rested at the time.

Organizational base

Before World War II, company founder Takeichi Masamura ran a pachinko side business inside his glass store.[45] Pachinko was banned during the war, but once it was revived after the end of the conflict, Masamura focused on prototyping a new kind of machine.[46] From 1947 until the completion of the Masamura Gauge and the Masamura manual 'all-win' design in 1949, Masamura opened two parlors that he operated himself along with two jointly run parlors (which his business partners later transferred to him) as part of the prototyping process. Because one of his business partners had no experience with pachinko operation, Masamura cooperated from an operational technology standpoint with one of the jointly operated parlors, for example by helping with pin adjustment. In 1950, he opened his fifth personally managed parlor, and in 1951, after overcoming issues with his manually operated design to perfect the Masamura 'all-win' machine, he established Masamura Shōkai Co., Ltd., with an investment of 1.5 million yen (about US$4167).[46] The manufacturing department was spun off as the No. 1 Factory as part of the organization of the company, and Masamura Shōkai began selling pachinko machines in earnest while operating four parlors.[48]

Parlors run by Masamura Shōkai and equipped with its machines attracted large numbers of customers on a daily basis. Their popularity served as an advertisement for the company's machines, and the company was visited by many who were interested in operating their own parlor. Starting around 1951, the enterprise began instructing the customers purchasing its machines to keep statistical records of ball payouts, and

Masamura issued guidance concerning how pins should be 'opened' and 'closed' based on those records.[49] Some 'disciple' parlors that received technical instruction on pin adjustment acted as distributors for Masamura Shōkai's machines.[50] It goes without saying that these parlors also served as an advertising team for Masamura machines.[51]

Although Masamura Shōkai held training sessions concerning pins in various locations,[52] one can focus on the role of these distributor 'disciples' in offering training that helped entrepreneurs open new parlors. They led the Chūō Line Group (from the city of Nagoya to Nagano Prefecture) and the Kintetsu Line Group (from the city of Nagoya to Mie Prefecture), groups of parlors located near train stations on rail lines that comprised sub-groups of the Masamura Association, which consisted of parlors that exclusively used Masamura Shōkai machines.[53] In light of the fact that the Masamura name was being used without the founder's knowledge by businesses with names like Masamura Gaming, Masamura Parlor and Pachinko Masamura,[54] it was presumably advantageous for parlors to join the Masamura Association, which gave them the right to use the Masamura name officially. For their part, distributors were better able to maintain and grow their customer lists. Although disciples taught directly by Masamura seem to have had close personal relationships, their supervision of parlors, while offered via loose connections, provided a realistic and broad basis for transforming the popularity of pachinko into a business. Examining this operational structure provides an understanding of the route by which pin adjustment technology, which was essential in opening and operating parlors, spread out from the creator of the machines and of the roles played by the manufacturer and distributors.

Market base

How did the arrangement described above impact the manner in which Masamura Shōkai sold its products? According to a biography of Masamura, Masamura Shōkai machines started to sell surprisingly well during the summer of 1950,[55] after which the company established seventeen sales offices and satellite sales offices throughout Japan.[56] However, it is not possible to reproduce the sales network described in that work using available documentation. It is only possible to review sales for individual business partners starting in August 1954, and information that would be valuable in understanding the characteristics of the market is limited to a period of about one year since the company's sales began to fall significantly during the second half of 1955. Customer ledgers for business partners outline customer surnames and locations (for example, 'Imanishi in Tokyo'), numbers of machines sold, unit prices and transaction amounts.

The information is limited in this way, but it provides sufficient data to identify the regional distribution that distinguished the company's sales – that is, the broad

(Units: parlors, %)

Area	Number of customers (parlors)[a]	Of which, customers with transactions (fiscal year average)		Sales[b]	
		Second half of 1954–First half of 1955	Second half of 1955–First half of 1957	Second half of 1954–First half of 1955	Second half of 1955–First half of 1957
Hokkaido/ Tohoku	16	4.6	4.7	2.7	2.3
Kanto	19	4.7	2.2	39.7	3.6
Koshinetsu/ Hokuriku	19	7.2	5.0	3.0	1.0
Tokai	111	43.1	48.3	32.0	44.2
Kinki	34	11.1	11.3	5.5	7.2
Chugoku	20	4.8	7.0	1.3	28.5
Shikoku	15	7.8	8.7	3.8	6.5
Kyushu	18	5.4	6.2	2.0	3.1
Unknown	35	11.3	6.5	7.2	3.6
Total[c]	287	100.0	100.0	97.2	100.0

Table 1.2: Masamura Shōkai's sales network

Notes:

a. Number of customers (including distributors) as recorded in accounting ledgers.

b. Regional sales as an average percentage of total sales over multiple fiscal years (see Note 3) before and after the second half of 1955, when the trend clearly changes.

c. General trend, since the total sales listed in the accounting ledgers do not match the figures in the year-end statements of account.

*Source: Compiled based on Masamura Shōkai's accounts receivable ledger (*tokuisaki motochō*) for 1954 through 1957.*

geographical characteristics of its principal markets. Table 1.2 summarizes the sales network to clarify the extent to which Masamura Shōkai machines were being sold (i.e., the market base).

With regard to the regional distribution of business partners, more than 40 percent of those customers – far more than other regions – were located in the Tokai region, which includes Aichi Prefecture where Masamura Shōkai was based. The Kinki region (which consists of six prefectures including Osaka and Kyoto in western Japan) and Shikoku accounted for slightly more than 10 percent and 7.8 percent of all customers, respectively, less than about one-quarter of the number of customers found in Aichi Prefecture. The Kanto region, home to Tokyo, accounted for less than 5 percent, and a cursory examination of the data suggests that transactions with parlors located near the company accounted for most of its business. However, customer counts are skewed by the fact that parlors located nearby, for example in Aichi Prefecture, dealt directly with the company, while more distant parlors worked through distributors. Consequently, it can be inferred that the results in the table contain more of the former and less of the latter. In that sense, there would have been a certain number of customers nationwide, including in Kyushu and Hokkaido, and it is intriguing that products manufactured in the manner of a household-based handicraft industry spread so widely. This fact likely reflects Masamura Shōkai's reputation.

Based on the above, we can derive a more accurate picture of regional characteristics from the ratio of sales presented in the table. The Kanto region accounted for about 40 percent of all sales, and the central base formed by this region, which includes the largest market, Tokyo, tells the story of the popularity of Masamura Shōkai's machines. The company recorded sales in excess of 60 million yen (about US$166,700) in Tokyo over about one year starting in August 1954, making the city the company's largest core market. An examination of sales figures reveals that the regions that included Hokkaido and Kyushu accounted for about 2 to 3 percent of all sales, with the percentage falling as one moved further afield from the country's representative major cities – Tokyo, the Tokai region and the Kinki region. However, the figures also show that the company enjoyed a market base in a broad range of regions.

Incidentally, the company's high level of sales in the Tokyo market, its largest, likely provided the background against which counterfeit machines emerged, as described above. Attempts to imitate machines that earned praise in Tokyo[57] can be seen as regional efforts to accommodate popular models. Masamura Shōkai's lopsided sales structure drew attention to the fact that local manufacturers were producing machines in regions where the company had not yet managed to provide a sufficient supply. It is unclear whether this absence in certain markets resulted from the priority given by Masamura Shōkai to the Tokyo market or from other factors – for example, regional characteristics – that prevented its entry into regional markets. One conclusion can be reached when demand for similar products is taken into consideration. Demand in certain regions depended on the ability of purchasers (parlors) to shoulder prices that included the distribution costs befitting the distances over which machines were shipped and on Masamura Shōkai's production capacity as a machine manufacturer. Here I will examine the latter. How did Masamura Shōkai structure its manufacturing operations to accommodate the abrupt boom in the popularity of pachinko?

Production system

Unable to keep pace with the rush of orders by producing machines solely at its head-office factory, Masamura Shōkai sought the cooperation of six subcontractors in its manufacturing operations. The company managed the entire process, including order processing, the placement of manufacturing orders with its seven factories and the delivery of machines to distributors.[58] The subcontractors were located in Nagoya's Nishi Ward,[59] where the company was headquartered, in order to keep them close at hand so that Masamura Shōkai could provide thorough manufacturing technical guidance. Meticulous attention characterized manufacturing operations, right down to components that affected the quality of the plants' final products. For example, the company paid close attention to ensuring flippers[60] were pliant enough to keep customers' hands from developing blisters during long play, and its exhaustive quality control system included inspections of all delivered plywood boards, with non-compliant items returned to suppliers.[61] Compared to other companies' products, Masamura Shōkai excelled most in terms of special-order pins and technology for fixing pins on boards that could only be explained by the company's unique intuition.[62] One account records how Yamaki Plywood Works had to overcome a series of difficulties before reaching the manufacturing stage in response to Masamura Shōkai's request that its products conform to a special standard.[63] In this way, the company's effort to differentiate itself in ways that could not be ascertained visually and to manage the quality of individual components served to underpin its positive reputation.

This dedication to quality answered the doubts of observers at the time who wondered, 'What is so great about Masamura's machines, and why do they sell so well [...] when all manufacturers seem to use the same pin technologies; what is different about Masamura?'[64] It was impossible to differentiate the company's machines from those of competitors at a glance, prompting some to complain about machine prices, which stood at 7000 yen (about US$19.4) around October 1952. However, parlor operators were in fact satisfied, remarking, 'Masamura machines were expensive but upon use proved to be cheap in the end' while pointing to their favorable track record and noting that 'customers love them, so they're very profitable'.[65] This praise presumably reflects the thorough quality control practiced by Masamura Shōkai during the manufacturing process. Even in December 1953, when the most expensive machines were selling for 7000–8000 yen (around US$22.2),[66] wholesale prices for machines from Masamura Shōkai held steady at the 7000-yen level (see Table 1.7 below), highlighting the strength of the brand's reputation.

Factors including the guidance offered by Masamura Shōkai to its subcontractors concerning technology for installing pins (by hammering them into the pin board), which depended on experience-based intuition, and the company's use of special-order plywood sheets highlighted the characteristics of the machines of the time, as well as the limits of manufacturing. In short, the prize-ball percentage, which affected customers' winning percentages, was affected by not only pin adjustment, but also pin installation technology and plywood sheet properties. Masamura's demanding approach to manufacturing can be seen as an attempt to minimize the effects of factors that caused prize-ball percentages to vary through thorough quality control.[67] Such efforts allowed the company to earn a solid reputation in representative urban

	Business unit profit (thousands of yen)				Percentage of business unit profit of total			Business profitability (business profit/ business sales) (%)	
	Machine sales	Pachinko parlors	Traditional Japanese-style inns (*ryokan*)	Total	Machine sales	Pachinko parlors	Traditional Japanese-style inns (*ryokan*)	Machine sales	Pachinko parlors
Old company									
1952·8–53·7	99,291	5,745		105,036	88.6	11.4		29.9	13.4
1953·8–54·7	179,198	-5,151		174,047	88.1	11.6		32.1	-7.0
1954·8–55·7	63,757	714		64,471	82.6	16.6		21.2	1.2
1955·8–56·7	118	0		118					
New company									
1955·9–56·7	19,994	9,535		29,529				34.3	10.3
1956·8–57·7	19,144	15,964	1,987	37,094	25.3	71.1	2.5	36.6	10.9
1957·8–58·7	14,131	17,853	10,952	42,935	18.2	72.2	8.5	36.5	11.6
1958·8–59·7	11,488	15,735	19,151	46,374	15.9	69.8	13.4	33.3	10.4
1959·8–60·7	8,705	13,641	23,531	45,877	21.8	56.7	20.5	23.3	14.0
1960·8–61·7	10,812	16,849	25,379	53,040	24.2	51.3	23.4	26.3	19.3
1961·8–62·7	16,715	19,224	33,457	69,396	20.0	52.6	27.2	43.8	19.1
1962·8–63·7	11,282	21,549	36,082	68,913	16.4	31.3	52.4	36.3	20.2
1963·8–64·7	9,711	19,546	43,663	72,920	13.3	26.8	59.9	40.5	20.1
1964·8–65·7	6,125	13,377	43,968	63,470	10.4	46.0	43.7	41.8	20.6
1965·8–66·7	4,614	11,643	45,070	61,328	8.9	43.4	47.7	39.8	20.6

Table 1.3: Masamura Shōkai's profit structure

Note: The exchange rate during the years in question was fixed to about US$1 = ¥360.

Source: Balance sheets and profit-and-loss statements from Masamura Shōkai's year-end statements of accounts (fiscal years 2 [August 1952] through 5 for the former company, and fiscal years 1 [September 1955] through 11 for the new company).

markets. However, because management was carried out in a way that depended on resources brought together by Masamura, for example intuition and dedication, production capacity was likely governed by these individual characteristics. It is probable that the blank in regional markets caused by the limits on Masamura Shōkai's production capacity was filled by similar but comparatively inexpensively priced products from local manufacturers.

This period marked the peak of the company's operations at a time when the surging popularity of pachinko spurred growth in the number of parlors, which sought out Masamura Shōkai machines as the ultimate products of their kind. Machine manufacture and sales, which accounted for more than 80 percent of the company's revenue, lay at the heart of its operations at the time (see Table 1.3). This segment boasted profitability beyond 20 percent, far in excess of the parlor business, which fluctuated wildly from 1952 to 1954 (but averaged less than 3 percent).

WERE MACHINES WITH A STRONGER SPECULATIVE NATURE MORE PROFITABLE?

Disappearance of 14,000 parlors

Was operating a pachinko parlor actually a profitable business?

With regard to parlors changing or discontinuing their business, a trend that was particularly pronounced during the 1950s as illustrated in Table 1.1 above, the pachinko industry had until that point mainly focused on developments after the ban on successive-shot machines went into effect in April 1955. In 1955, there were a total of 12,391 parlors operating as of June 30, a decline of about half compared to June 1954. The reduction in the number of manufacturers during that year was also dramatic, as 386 of 466 manufacturers went out of business after the ban, leaving just eighty (the date of the survey is unknown).[67] The extent of the ban's impact is clear at a glance. It is also evident that the grave situation faced by the industry was related to the ban.

However, focusing exclusively on conditions after the ban was implemented in an attempt to link them to the ban as external factors makes it more difficult to discern the internal state of parlor management. It also makes it impossible to understand why some 14,000 parlors had vanished between 1953 and 1954. Why did these parlors go out of business?

A straightforward reading of Table 1.1 suggests that the number of parlors peaked at the end of June 1953 and that a downward trend had already developed the year before the ban was announced in 1954. A careful examination of events during the first half of the 1950s is in order. To be precise, it was during the first half of 1953 that growth in the number of parlors turned into a decline as the number of parlors going out of business (including temporarily) exceeded the number of newly opened parlors (December 1952: 45,317 parlors; June 1953: 43,452 parlors).[69] Consequently, it is appropriate to interpret the ban as having exacerbated a downward trend in the number of parlors that began in 1953, thrusting the industry into a period of recession. The decline, which predates the ban, is worthy of consideration, along with the factors that prompted it. This will make it possible to identify the conditions necessary for the industry to establish itself based on the internal problems it faced.

However, the task is not so simple. It remains a mystery why the commonly accepted view does not pay attention to conditions in the industry prior to the ban's implementation, and why the slump following the ban has not been reinterpreted in light of that existing downward trend. Any judgment that the pachinko industry fell on hard times as a result of the ban on successive-shot machines must be founded on the supposition that the industry had been growing steadily prior to its implementation. Although there are no statistics available offering an accurate assessment of the size of the pachinko market, there are observations that provide indirect support for the idea that the market was growing. Parlor sales during 1954 were estimated to have reached 250 billion yen (about US$690 million), three times the level two years prior and six times the sales in the bicycle racing sector, the most popular type of state-controlled gambling at the time.[70] If we examine the total value of pachinko machine shipments under the 'gaming devices and vending machines [pachinko, etc.]' category, which includes pachinko machines, since it is impossible to ascertain the number of pachinko machines that were shipped, statistics indicate shipments valued at 921.75 million yen (about US$2.56 million) in 1953 and twice that figure in 1954.[71] According to a study by the National Tax Agency, the number of pachinko machines increased in 1954, along with sales, despite a year-on-year decline in the number of pachinko businesses.[72] Masamura Shōkai recorded year-on-year growth of 60 percent in the number machines sold during 1954, and machine prices rose by slightly less than 10 percent (see Table 1.7 below). Based on the fact that the number of parlors was declining even as the number of machines sold was rising, the industry grew during this period, along with the size of the average parlor.

It is worth noting here that large parlors did not immediately enjoy competitive advantages. It should also be noted, against the backdrop of the growth in parlors during 1952 and 1953, that parlor operations were not necessarily stable.[73] The number of parlors operating in Tokyo as of 1952 had increased by 1107 from the previous year to 5126, but just 988 of these establishments had been in operation the year prior. Moreover, the number of parlors being pushed toward closure, 3225, exceeded that of newly opened businesses, 3075.[74] As some rushed to exit the industry, others hurried to enter it. In considering the manner in which the number of parlors peaked in 1953 only to reverse course and embark on a rapid decline, we must take into account how the increase was accompanied by operational instability. The culling of parlors is likely to have been the result of the impact of a certain characteristic of machines with a strong gambling element, which had penetrated the market, on parlor operations.

A rush to open new parlors

Daily pin adjustment played an essential role in determining the success of parlors as businesses. The manner in which parlors set prize-ball percentages, which were determined by the adjustment of techniques for opening and closing pins such as the 'vital pins' near the catchers (see ⑥ of Figure 1.1 above), impacted their customer headcount and profitability. The prize-ball percentage, defined as the ratio of the number of balls returned by parlors to the number of balls borrowed by customers, was the result of pin adjustment, a practical action carried out in the parlors themselves. Since customers naturally gravitated toward parlors that had high prize-ball percentages – that is, parlors whose pins were 'open' – the metric provided a means for parlors to attract customers. Although parlors were under pressure to keep the prize-ball percentage high so that they did not lose customers to other nearby parlors, it was also important to set the percentage appropriately so that they continued to operate profitably.

The importance of pin adjustment grew with increased technological involvement in the game due to the Masamura Gauge and with the number of machines in operation. There was no single technique for adjusting pins. The business owner, or pin adjuster, was required to possess general business acumen in several key areas. First, the individual responsible for pin adjustment had to determine the balance between open and closed pins for each machine to realize the parlor's overall prize-ball percentage (that is, the ratio of 'open' to 'closed' machines) and then readjust those settings after interpreting data describing customers' play as a reaction to pin adjustment. They also had to take into account a variety of factors that influenced the parlor's business performance, for example by considering the parlor's relationships with competing parlors and strategic elements for building its reputation.[75] In the event of a discrepancy between per-machine sales figures, which varied according to the extent to which machines were chosen by customers, and pin adjustment, the individual then had to apply that result to the next day's adjustments. In this way, this book treats pin adjustment as parlors' daily response to customer play, which is to say, as a process in which pins were fine-tuned in the context of an ongoing, two-way interaction.

Were parlors, whose numbers grew rapidly until the beginning of the 1950s, able to obtain sufficient management expertise to integrate pin adjustment into their operations while focusing on the task as a technical aspect of their business? For example, Kenkichi Nakajima, the founder of Heiwa, which became a representative manufacturer of pachinko machines from the mid-1950s, entered the parlor business in 1948 during the pachinko boom but subsequently sustained enormous losses due to his failure to understand the necessity of pin adjustment.[76] Masao Sadoshima, a leader in the pachinko parlor industry in Fukuoka, had opened a pachinko parlor around 1949. He had previous experience in the black-market street-stall business, but was new to pachinko. His business partner, a gentleman named Taniguchi, was knowledgeable about pachinko operations. The method by which they operated their business, as observed by Sadoshima, illustrates why Nakajima failed. Sadoshima was surprised by what he called 'Taniguchi's method of management, which consists of giving away prizes worth twice what the parlor took in in sales during the first two weeks'. Sadoshima describes how the experience left him with great concern about his new business, in which the scale of losses was 'so great that I could hardly avoid questioning him [Taniguchi] about what had gone wrong'.[77] Customers left 'clutching their prizes and beaming like Cheshire cats', but the business broke even in the fourth week. By the tenth week, he was 'laughing all the way to the bank'.[78] The episode demonstrates how the parlor business required unique strategies that differed from other sectors and points to the danger of opening an establishment after being enticed by the surface appeal of a cash business popular enough to draw crowds.

The guidance on pin adjustment offered by Masamura Shōkai and its disciples, as described above, can be reinterpreted in this context. That the business demanded, on a fundamental level, mechanical expertise whose transmission depended upon the experience of manufacturers and parlor operators suggests that it may not have been possible to keep up with demand for such expertise when large numbers of businesses opened up in a short period of time. In other words, it is safe to assume that the rapid growth in parlors during the first half of the 1950s included a large number of new establishments that lacked both an understanding of the business's unique outlook and the expertise needed to adjust pins in order to control it. It would not be unusual for entrepreneurs without the necessary operational skills who entered the industry after being enticed by the popularity of pachinko to end up closing their doors soon after opening them.[79]

Having made this prediction, let us examine the actual conditions under which these businesses operated. From August 1954 to April 1957, Masamura Shōkai recorded sales, prize sales (value of balls redeemed for prizes) and the difference between the two for each parlor it operated in a document known as 'sales statistics tables' (*eigyō tōkeihyō*).[80] Using that source, I will examine the results of pin adjustment at Masamura Shōkai parlors from the standpoint of the accumulation of management expertise and revenue stabilization.

Element of speculation in the revenue base

An examination of sales and profitability figures for each of Masamura Shōkai's businesses (see Table 1.3 above) indicates that parlor profitability actually deteriorated starting in 1953 before lurching into the red in 1954, despite the intense popularity of successive-shot machines such as machine-gun and circulating-type designs. Sales following the installation of successive-shot machines rose by a factor of 30 percent due to the increase in the number of balls launched per unit of time compared to single-shot machines. Consequently, the deterioration in earnings likely reflects the fact that a shift towards emphasizing the number of balls dispensed as a proportion of the number of balls launched (the winning percentage) resulted in more prize redemptions. The fact that such challenges faced even parlors operated by Masamura, who was regarded as the 'god of pin adjustment',[81] suggests the difficulty of controlling the prize-ball percentages of successive-shot machines.

The difficulty of pin adjustment is likely to have been related to the characteristics of parlors' customers as well. Although the characteristics of Masamura Shōkai's customer demographic cannot be pinpointed with any degree of certainty, a number of observations can be made with regard to its customers in 1954. One source observes as follows:

> The industry had changed completely from the time it was billed as good, clean fun. Customers turned pro and semi-pro. Customers who went looking for a short spell during their lunch breaks or after a bath were rare. Most "pachinko men" found themselves driven by the need to recoup losses incurred from what had begun as mere curiosity or amusement, reinforced by prizes dangling carrot-like in front of them, spurring everyone to take great care in how they play.[82]

Rephrased in today's language, customers including 'heavy users' who spent a lot of time at parlors and some whose skill verged on the semi-professional stood out. Such customers presumably played a key role in wildly fluctuating prize-ball percentages.

However, the situation improved significantly as profitability returned during the next year, if only in the order of 1.2 percent. The changes experienced by Masamura Shōkai over the two-year period from 1953 to 1955 tell the story of how a transition in the type of machines used disturbed parlors' profit structure and of how the parlors reacted by struggling to stabilize their operations. Let us examine the characteristics of a single parlor's revenue base using pin adjustment and trends in sales and gross profit margin as clues. Figure 1.3 provides a graph of daily sales and gross profit margins[83] from August 1954 to April 1955, before the ban on successive-shot machines took effect. (I will refer to trends in the sales and gross profit margin graph as 'profit structure' below.) Based on the business-specific profitability figures in Table 1.3, operations returned to profitability after falling into the red during the previous year. Figure 1.3 illustrates the profit structure that triggered improvements during this time, allowing us to infer the direction of the improvements. Since the four parlors operated by Masamura Shōkai mostly exhibit the same trends, I will examine the Main Branch as a representative example.

First, allow me to offer a technical explanation concerning Figure 1.3. Sales, also known as 'ball fees' and shown here on the horizontal axis, was calculated by multiplying the number of balls purchased by customers by the then-current ball price of 2 yen (about US$0.01) (explained below). Sales were governed by the number of customers visiting the parlor and by the amount spent by each. Gross profit margin, shown here on the vertical axis, was calculated by subtracting prize sales from gross sales and dividing the result by gross sales. This figure expresses how parlors used prize-ball percentages to allow customers to win while continuing to generate a profit.

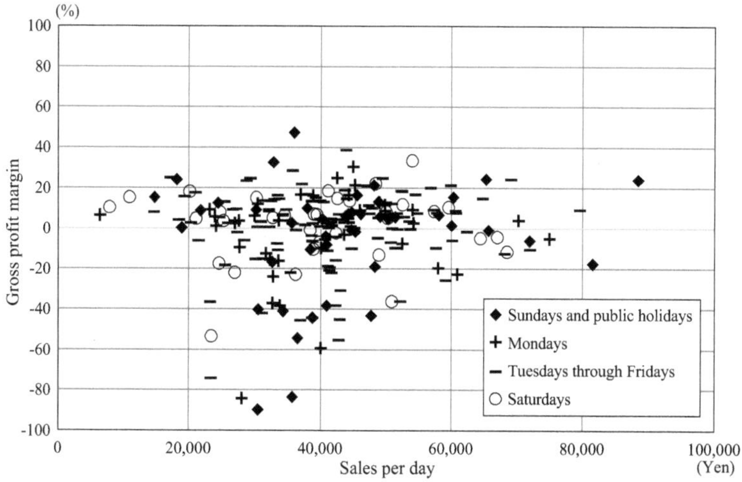

Figure 1.3: Sales and profitability for Masamura Shōkai's main parlor before implementation of the successive-shot ban (August 1954 to April 1955)

Notes:

a. Gross profit margin = (Sales minus prize sales) / sales × 100 (%).

b. The graph shows daily sales and gross profit margin. The same applies to Figures 1.4, 1.5 and 1.7.

c. Daily differences from Tuesday through Friday are unclear, so figures for those days have been grouped together.

*Source: Compiled based on the Main Branch sales statistics tables (*eigyō tōkeihyō *Honten).*

Although the gross profit margin varies with the prize-ball percentage, which in turn is determined by pin adjustment, positive values can be understood as indicating days on which the parlor 'closed' pins, while negative values can be understood as indicating days on which the parlor 'opened' pins.[84] The more the positive gross profit margin values are concentrated on the right side of the graph, and the more the negative values are concentrated on the left side of the graph, the greater the total net parlor profit during the period in question.

Examining Figure 1.3, it becomes clear that areas where the gross profit margin is positive are characterized by a broad horizontal distribution at or below about 30 percent. Areas where the gross profit margin is negative exhibit a greater range of values, including some points where the margin was as low as minus 100 percent. This upside-down triangle-shaped distribution produced profitable performance immediately before the ban on successive-shot machines. Since the 'closing' and 'opening' of pins (to generate positive and negative gross profit margins, respectively) can be seen as the product of intentional adjustments by the parlor, the intentions of the parlor can be compared to the resulting distribution to highlight the characteristics of parlor operations at the time.

Seen in this light, the top left and lower areas represent problematic domains of operation. In the top left area, sales failed to keep pace with the parlor's expectations. The graph in this area is the result of low customer headcount or per-capita customer spending. Examining the distribution of sales by day of the week offers no clear trend. The area contains a number of holidays, including Sundays, when customer counts are likely to have been high, but high traffic did not necessarily result in high sales. We can fairly conclude that differences in sales were more impacted by per-capita customer spending than the overall number of customers. Consequently, the distribution of sales on the left on days when the parlor 'closed' pins (of course, customers did not know that in advance) indicates that per-capita customer spending was lower than expected. Although the fact that profit was positive suggests on cursory examination that these conditions posed no particular problem for the parlor, they were not desirable insofar as they could lead to the loss of customers over time. Not only was profit lower in absolute terms than figures corresponding to points on the top right, but customer traffic would fall if the parlor developed a reputation as having a poor prize-ball percentage, lowering machine utilization and pushing the parlor into gradual decline.

On the other hand, gross profit margin on days when the pins were 'open' ranged widely, including figures as low as minus 100 percent. The breadth of this range causes the average gross profit margin to fall. Intentionally allowing customers to win had a promotional effect, so parlors embraced the tactic. However, the amount parlors could dedicate to such advertising was limited by their revenue. The ability to set the prize-ball percentage so as to maximize the promotional effect by allowing customers to win 'just enough' to attract them constituted operational expertise. When compared to parlor intentions in this way, it becomes clear that pin adjustment during this time had the effect of creating an enormous range of sometimes unintended results.

Incidentally, calculating the number of days with gross profit margins of less than minus 30 percent reveals that eight were Sundays or other holidays, three were Mondays, eight were weekdays from Tuesday to Friday (an average of two) and two were Saturdays. Some parlors reportedly 'loosened up' pins on Sundays and other holidays when customer traffic was expected to increase, and they accepted the resulting – and significant – downward effect on their profits. It is not possible to make any further assessment concerning the question of whether such negative profit days were the result of intentional, tactical decisions made by parlors to attract customers or compete with other nearby parlors, or were instead unanticipated failures. However, the evidence does support a few, provisional conclusions. Excessively large losses (negative margins) indicate a situation that diverges from the parlors' expectations regarding pin adjustment. Such situations suggest the presence of a factor that interfered with attempts at control.

In conclusion, we can observe that the profit structure of the Main Branch during this period was characterized by limits on per-customer spending and profit variability. Based on the assessment that these results flew in the face of parlors' intentions with regard to pin adjustment, I hypothesize that the adjustment expertise that had been accumulated to date was incapable of accommodating the introduction of machines with a more pronounced speculative element.

When contrasted with the effects of incorporating technical elements related to ball dispensation in the Masamura Gauge into machines, we may presume that these more speculative machines instead increased randomness and introduced elements of uncertainty to customers and parlors alike. The successive-shot functionality of these machines itself physically introduced effects that served to destabilize prize-ball percentages. All of the steel balls that were launched flew around between pins. Due to properties unique to lumber, the plywood display boards were affected by atmospheric humidity, causing minuscule changes in the extent to which pins were 'closed'. The condition of pins adjusted before the parlor opened would change over time depending on how the pins were struck, with effects that fell outside the scope of parlors' expectations.[85] The likely result was that the number of balls dispensed exceeded the parlor's expectations, increasing the range of negative gross profit margin figures. For customers, greater speculative appetite (i.e., a desire to play successive-shot machines) meant additional spending, but the associated reduction in their expected winning percentage could also provoke hesitancy to keep pouring money into machines. The economic boom touched off by the Korean War (1950–1953) was short-lived,[86] and income levels during the first half of the 1950s meant that there was a low limit on the amount of money that households could budget for amusement. The distribution of positive gross profit margin figures on the left side of the graph is explained by people who hesitated to consume the service, while the distribution of negative profit figures on the bottom is explained by the skill of semi-professional and better customers and the element of chance introduced by the condition of machines.

Incidentally, Figure 1.3 illustrates an improvement in profitability compared to the significant losses of the previous fiscal year (1953). The fact that even Masamura Shōkai, which employed pin adjusters of the highest caliber, barely managed to escape operating losses from 1953 to 1954 suggests that instability in the operations of other parlors that lacked such resources could only have increased. Based on the above examination, it is clear that there were limits to how much parlors were willing to invest in light of customers' reluctance to spend more money, and that parlors – even those owned by Masamura Shōkai – continued to face difficulty in controlling large swings in gross profit margin from the second half of 1954 to the beginning of 1955, when profits were improving. It is evident that operators were under pressure to offer the pleasure of gambling at reasonable prices as a way to reassure customers that they would not sustain major losses and entice them to spend more than they originally anticipated. Parlors found themselves facing the need to master management expertise and control the physical fluctuations that characterized their machines so that they could secure a sustained and stable revenue base that would allow for their continued operation.

In this way, the decline in the number of parlors starting in 1953 signifies a selection process as the characteristics of machines – the manner in which various factors influenced the physical condition of machines – exacerbated the difficulty of achieving stable management through pin adjustment. That said, the impact of the entertainment tax on this parlor decline cannot be ignored.

Entertainment tax

To understand the entertainment tax, we must go back in time to 1948. Before the outbreak of World War II, a national admission tax levied on movie theaters and game parlors was transferred to local municipalities, which then applied it to pachinko parlors as well.[87] Local tax reforms in 1950 classified pachinko as a Type 3 industry and imposed a 100 percent admission tax on usage fees paid by customers while making parlor operators responsible for collecting and remitting the tax.[88] This taxation method was replete with collection issues. For parlors, which did not require customers to purchase admission tickets in the manner of movie theaters, the tax would have had to be based on ball fees, interpreted as usage fees. However, if ball fees were indeed equivalent to usage fees, 100 percent of parlors' sales would be subject to the tax, and the entire amount would be collected as tax based on the imposed tax rate. Naturally, this approach to taxation was unacceptable to parlors. Reports indicate, for example, that parlors in Hiroshima Prefecture instead based their tax collections on the amount calculated by deducting the value of prizes, which were returned to customers at a rate of 70–80 percent, from ball fees.[89]

However, even this method would not be realistic unless the conditions under which parlors were operating could be ascertained. In fact, collection results were less than stellar since it was no simple task to ascertain those conditions. Accurate information was unavailable despite regional surveys[90] suggesting that tax assessment was a difficult process. Frequent changes in parlor ownership also served to complicate tax collection.[91] In the case of Hiroshima Prefecture, described above, only about one seventeenth of expected taxes on usage fees (ball fees) as noted in the government's official gazette of June 30, 1952, was collected, an amount that failed even to reach that of anticipated taxes once the value of prizes returned to customers was deducted (about 20 to 30 percent of the usage fees). In reality, the 20 to 30 percent of usage fees that ought to have been taxed was gradually declining as the percentage of earnings returned to customers grew amidst intensifying competition among parlors, and some regulators have explained the under-taxation of the industry as having resulted from these characteristics.

The revised Local Tax Act of June 1952, which was enacted to address these tax issues, introduced a pro forma tax based on external criteria designed to capture the scale of the business in question and the extent of its activity, including square footage, machine count, employee headcount and usage fees. This size-based business tax imposed a series of grade-based taxes according to predetermined criteria. For example, in Hiroshima the system included fifteen grades based on the number of machines a parlor had, with a tax of 1800 yen (about US$5) per machine per grade, while Hokkaido's system incorporated ten grades with a tax of 750 yen.[92] While this pro forma tax offered clarity with regard to collection since it eliminated the need to ascertain each parlor's business revenue, it made it difficult for parlors to avoid the tax burden. The changes caused the forecast tax burden to grow by a factor of four to twelve and represented an extreme blow to management. It is estimated that the number of parlors shrank by more than half between the time the new tax was introduced and March 1953.[93]

However, the introduction of external criteria failed to bring different regions into line with each other. The fact that the example cited above for Hiroshima Prefecture came after the introduction of the pro forma tax in other regions suggests that there was confusion in various regions' collection methods and in the establishment of the pro forma tax itself.

Local governments worked to strengthen collection while filling in the gaps between the taxation system and the characteristics of the pachinko business, which often diverged from what was envisioned in regulations. It is difficult to verify the actual effects of this effort based on parlors' operational conditions. At a minimum, it is likely that subsequent administrative measures made late payment of taxes a contributing factor to the decline in the number of parlors. The admission tax was replaced by a usage tax levied on entertainment facilities just as revisions to the Entertainment Establishment Control Act required parlors to renew their business license *every month*.[94] Enforcement was strict, and late payment of the usage tax, which averaged 150 yen (about US$0.42) nationwide, served as a basis for disqualifying parlors from renewing their license (in June). An excerpt from the act is as follows.

Entertainment Establishment Control Act (enacted July 10, 1948, and revised May 13, 1954)[95]

> Business licensing: Article 2 (3) Pachinko and similar businesses as specified by prefectural ordinance must renew their business license every month, [...] which in the absence of renewal [...] shall lapse. (4) In processing business license renewals as described in the preceding paragraph, public safety commissions shall not issue a renewal [...] if the requesting business has unpaid entertainment taxes.

It is useful to make several observations about the admission tax described above with regard to parlor operations from the standpoint of the focus of this chapter, which is dedicated to shedding light on parlor operations. Following the 1955 ban on successive-shot machines, Saburo Nakamura, who managed Wakayama Prefecture's Taxation Section, addressed the reason that the initial self-assessment approach under the special collection system was augmented with the introduction of a pro forma tax while reflecting on the past system of taxation, pointing out that pachinko's unique method of operating influenced the decision.[96] For example, some parlors opted to operate in the red for a month in order to attract customers, as illustrated by the experience of Sadoshima earlier in the chapter. The timing and duration of methods for allowing customers to win were themselves trade secrets,[97] and parlor operators were forced to embrace these methods intentionally. Parlors also attempted to give away more prizes than nearby competitors. These efforts were presumably constrained by the need to operate in the black, but parlors sometimes neglected to set aside money for tax payments as intense competition pushed up the percentage of earnings returned to customers, leading some to 'give greater priority to pursuing profit than to any sense of ethics with regard to tax rules'.[98] Nakamura, who understands the characteristics of parlor operations, offers an insightful analysis, asserting that the pro forma tax system was introduced to augment the self-assessment approach under the special collection system.

These back-and-forth changes to the taxation system point to the challenges faced by government officials, but those difficulties likely reflect the fact that they saw the problem of lower-than-anticipated collections as entirely the result of a lack of morals. The initial tax system, which was based on sales, was in the first place characterized by extremely high collection costs. It was only a matter of time before its limits would become apparent. Setting aside the defects of the system, it may be that the collection of an admission tax that was calculated on a monthly basis was a poor fit for the unique circumstances of pachinko operations, where managers had to undertake loss-generating tactics founded on the medium- and long-term outlook. More critically, there were differences in tax rates and collection ability caused by local governments' various financial situations, and Nakamura acknowledges that the inability to implement a nationally consistent policy itself hindered efforts to smooth the collection process.[99] In this way, the introduction of a tax on pachinko operations, followed by changes to, and then the strengthening of, the system lays bare the poorly developed nature of the taxation strategy of the time.

It remains unclear to what extent the strengthening of collection efforts under the entertainment tax affected parlor operations. However, it is possible that stepped-up collection during a time of management instability temporarily made it more difficult to renew business licenses. If so, the number of registrations for 1954 shown in Table 1.1 above may understate the actual figure since it does not include parlors that had continued to operate after June despite not having renewed their licenses.

Against this backdrop, the ban on the manufacture and installation of successive-shot machines that took effect in April 1955 cast a long shadow over the development of the pachinko industry and triggered qualitative changes.

PACHINKO'S SPECULATIVE ELEMENT AND REGULATIONS

Order prohibiting successive-shot machines

With the enactment of the Entertainment Establishment Control Act in 1948, new game parlors were prohibited from relocating; limited to permanent, brick-and-mortar operations; and required to obtain a license from their local public safety commission in accordance with prefectural ordinances. Following the introduction of these measures, parlors were placed under the management of the local police as businesses 'that could invite a fondness for gambling'. For example, under limits imposed by Tokyo, parlors could charge only 1 yen (about US$0.003) per ball (in 1949, 2 yen) and 20 yen (about US$0.05) per pachinko session, and they could offer prizes worth no more than five times those amounts; prize redemptions included candy worth 3 yen (about US$0.008) for three balls or one Hikari cigarette (which typically sold for 5 yen, or about US$0.013) for six balls.[100] In this way, parlors operated within regulatory frameworks as individual prefectures regulated the fees associated with gaming services.[101]

Tasked with managing the establishment and operation of new businesses in the industry, as the number of parlors grew rapidly around 1950, the police could hardly sit back and watch since they saw these businesses as a substitute for gambling. In fact, in 1951, as the number of parlors surged from 385 to 5200, Tokyo's Metropolitan Police Department 'stepped up enforcement [of pachinko parlors] along with other game parlors in response to criticism of their speculative character as well as of their psychological effects on children'.[102] However, regulation sought not to prohibit the establishment of new parlors per se, but rather emphasized the need to eliminate offenders and therefore targeted the manner in which parlors operated. From the standpoint of parlors, switching to a similar industry was not such a simple task in light of pronouncements such as that of one official, who noted, 'We're receiving applications for the new "Z" games [a type of group game] as an alternative to pachinko, but right now we have no plans to issue licenses [...] due to the dominance of the element of chance'.[103] It is unclear exactly what these 'group games' were, although in some cases the phrase referred to games known as 'bingo', 'dirigibles' or 'hit' that encompassed gambling-like transactions between parlor operators and groups of customers.[104] An only slightly exaggerated interpretation of the nature of 'chance' as a reason for refusing to license group games suggests the presence of pachinko operations in the regulation of that element. This concept of 'chance' and of 'inviting a fondness for gambling' as set forth in the Entertainment Establishment Control Act comprised a vague standard, but the question of how to narrow and control those elements was an important one for the management of a variety of game parlors, including pachinko businesses, and for the development of the industry as a whole. It is necessary to bear in mind that the subsequent disappearance of group games derived from not only demand-side factors such as regulation and declining popularity among customers, but also supply-side problems related to 'chance'.

With the Tokyo Public Safety Commission's announcement on November 16, 1954 of the Administrative Order Prohibiting Successive-shot Machines, which went into effect in April 1955,[105] and a nationwide ban on successive-shot machines the following year,[106] the pachinko industry, which had seemed to be growing smoothly, was overcome by a sense of despair amid fears that the industry would be regulated out of existence. Enforcement was motivated by the conclusion that pachinko had 'invited a fondness for gambling and taken on an increasingly pronounced speculative character',[107] with the result that it qualified as gambling-like behavior as defined by the city's Entertainment Control Act Enforcement Ordinance. The ban touched off fears of serious repercussions since 95 percent of the 200,000 machines installed at the capital's roughly 3400 parlors were successive-shot machines.[108] At that point in time, no substitute for the successive-shot machine, which was the primary factor in the pachinko boom, had been discovered.

Incidentally, it seems apparent that the purpose of the ban was not limited to weakening the speculative character of pachinko by regulating machine structure in the form of a ban on machines with a pronounced gambling element. It posed a unique challenge that pachinko would have to overcome in order to develop as an industry. The customers who enjoyed pachinko were not motivated solely by its gaming element. Aspects related to the prizes that customers took home were also a source of motivation, and the lack of associated structures, as well as dark elements explained in the next section that evolved in response, became problematic.

Photo 1.1: A buyer (1952)
Source: See Yūgitsūshin (2001: 23).

Fanning the speculative flames: the cash exchange problem

As the rising popularity of pachinko drove up the amounts of money involved, a variety of issues arose with regard to prize redemption and associated processes. An examination of records of arrests made for game parlor violations in Tokyo in 1951 totaling 1663 reveals that while unlawful entry by minors accounted for most of the 1383 pachinko-related violations, prize violations were the next most common offense, with 263 arrests.[109] Although the details of these violations are unclear, the phenomenon of prize purchases was first raised as a problem in 1951.[110] Photo 1.1 depicts a woman known at the time as a 'buyer', someone who would approach customers who had won prizes outside parlors to encourage them to sell (exchange) their prizes for cash, around 1952. Buyers played a role in raising awareness of the growing speculative element in pachinko in a way that touched on the legal definition of pachinko businesses.

As successive-shot machines boosted the number of balls launched per unit of time and competition among parlors pushed up prize-ball percentages to a high of 80 or 90 percent, growth in the volume of prize redemptions led to the phenomenon. Prize types and the maximum value of each were regulated by each region's public safety commission. While it is not possible to paint a picture of nationwide practices, prizes in Hiroshima Prefecture, for example, were limited to nine items with a maximum value of 360 yen (about US$1) as of 1954.[111] Practices in other regions are unlikely to have differed significantly. Cigarettes were used as prizes (at a cost of 35 yen, or about US$0.10 in 1954), as were chewing gum (30 yen, or about US$0.08) and razor blades (90 yen, about US$0.25).[112] A donut-like snack known as *anpan* cost about 10 yen (about US$0.03) at the time. There was not much diversity in the selection of items, and prices were capped. It was a regulatory environment in which customers had to content themselves with the quantity of low-cost prizes they received. A new problem emerged in the form of buyers who took advantage of customers' dissatisfaction by offering to exchange prizes for cash.

This activity by buyers such as the woman shown in Photo 1.1 became problematic[113] because it was seen as qualifying as gambling – essentially, spending money to make money. Based on predictions that customers would become excessively absorbed in the ability to exchange prizes for cash if that possibility were available, the implications of the situation from the standpoint of encouraging gambling were seen as serious. In fact, stepped-up enforcement in various regions was reported at an executive meeting of the National Confederation of Amusement Industry Associations (Zen'yūren) held just prior to the announcement of the ban on successive-shot machines in November 1954.[114] According to records of arrests in the Kanto region (eastern Japan), there were forty-five violations likely to have been related to problems with prize purchases and cash exchanges in Tokyo, fifty-three in Gunma prefecture, forty-six in Saitama prefecture and thirty-six in Ibaraki prefecture.[115]

The existence of buyers must be considered in light of latent demand on the part of customers for cash exchanges as well as the parlor business itself. Prizes purchased by buyers as part of this redemption process were subsequently sold back to parlors, where they were offered once more as prizes. From the standpoint of the parlors, any reduction in the price they paid for prizes from ordinary suppliers by paying lower prices to buyers contributed to their bottom line. Suppose that the price paid by the parlor for a prize redeemed for 100 yen (about US$0.28) worth of balls was 80 yen (about US$0.22). If a customer sold the prize to a buyer for 70 yen (about US$0.19), and the buyer then turned around and sold the prize back to the parlor for 75 yen (about US$0.21), that was the equivalent of a saving of 5 yen (about US$0.01) on the price the parlor paid for the prize. If the prize bought by the parlor for 75 yen went on to be redeemed for 100 yen (about US$0.28) of balls, the ball and prize redemption rate for the parlor would improve from 5:4 to 4:3. As a result of this mechanism, some parlors were exposed for hiring buyers themselves and repeatedly engaging in prohibited conduct.

Moreover, as the number of parlors surged after 1952, as shown in Table 1.1 above, and successive-shot machines spurred more intense competition in terms of prize-ball percentages, 'pachinko parlors that had been able to return only about 80,000 yen [about US$222] in prizes on daily ball sales of 100,000 yen [about US$278]' in 1954 found themselves able to 'offer 100,000 yen in prizes on 100,000 yen of ball sales'.[116] Since 'in fact the parlors were purchasing those prizes for 90,000 yen [about US$250] from buyers, they did a good business even if they weren't able to generate profit from pachinko',[117] and the managerial focus shifted from pin adjustment to methods for purchasing prizes at a low cost.

Although it occurred later down the track, the case of Mitsui Shōten is instructive.[118] Authorities charged the business with 'colluding with branch managers and a number of prize buyers to take advantage of customers' fondness for gambling in order to attract customers and advance its own interests by buying back prizes, specifically by having buyers buy up socks, hair cream sticks, Hakugen products [items such as insect repellent and deodorant according to the speaker], caramel candies and food seasonings behind parlors from about May 1, 1957, until arrests were made on August 13 of the same year'. The scale of the operation was extensive, involving buybacks of a total of '2,354,234 prizes worth 16,189,000 yen (about US$44,969)'. Prizes were 'stored in the business's warehouse until a certain quantity accumulated, at which point they were transported to the main branch, sorted and entered into business ledgers, sorted by type and then distributed to its branches'.

Whether direct or indirect, parlors' involvement in the exchange of prizes for cash was illegal, and attracted criminal groups motivated by a desire to tap a source of funds as an organizational substitute for buyers.[119] Growing rapidly due to the widespread popularity of successive-shot machines, the market became a preferred target as a source of black market funds. It goes without saying that developments spurred the police to adopt an even harsher stance toward the cash exchange problem.

The industry could not ignore the targeting of cash exchange routes by criminal groups. In some regions, parlor associations, groups of unemployed individuals and other third-party groups tried purchasing prizes in an effort to exclude organized crime.[120] Against this backdrop, the executive council of Zen'yūren, meeting on November 28, 1954, after the ban on successive-shot machines was announced, adopted a series of 'self-restraint guidelines' that took effect on December 9 as a national initiative.[121] The voluntary initiatives set forth in the document, including a declaration of 'absolute opposition to mechanical limitations on circulating-type designs [successive-shot machines]' and a commitment to 'eliminate individuals buying and selling prizes in order to promote the industry as a healthy type of entertainment', were founded on a certain awareness.

As a member of the executive council put it, 'The relationship between buyers and parlors must be borne in mind [...]. That promotes fondness for gambling [...]. To have the successive-shot ban rescinded, the first step is to cut ties with buyers and turn pachinko into healthy entertainment [...]. The ban doesn't inherently target pachinko, but rather buyers, who invite fondness for speculation and gambling, so the prospects for pachinko will shrink as long as that connection is not severed'.[122] In other words, the ban on successive-shot machines, which had spurred the growth of the industry, was put in place in response to the issue of buyers exchanging prizes for cash and the involvement of organized crime. In this way, the industry believed the regulations to have been prompted by the problem of prize exchanges and the involvement of organized crime and considered the resolution of these issues to be an essential step in having the successive-shot ban rescinded.[123] In fact, regions took the lead in developing their own initiatives. For example, in Tokyo, the Tokyo Pachinko and Pachislot Cooperative Associations (Tōkyōto Yūgigyō Kyōdō Kumiai; abbreviated as Tōyūkyō) issued guidance calling on members, among other things, to 'banish prize buyers, exclude criminal groups, and thoroughly practice self-restraint in their operations' starting in January 1955 based on the belief that 'the popularity of successive-shot machines invited rampant activity on the part of prize buyers'.[124]

The intentions of the Metropolitan Police Department, which led the regulatory drive, can be inferred from its reaction to events following the implementation of the ban. The organization's security section (Hoanka) offered the following bird's-eye perspective:

> It is a fact that the number of greed-crazed customers has fallen dramatically, and that customers can now relax and enjoy themselves for more than twice the time by spending an average of 50 yen [about US$0.14], sometimes 100 yen [about US$0.28]. It looks like the industry has moved closer to being a healthy form of entertainment for the general public. That said, you can still see lots of idle people wandering around inside parlors, and there's been no substantial decrease in the sight of buyers congregating near parlors. Naturally, if this situation continues, we will consider neither the parlors nor the buyers to have exercised self-restraint or exhibited regret, and therefore will strengthen enforcement going forward.[125]

The police recognized that the possibility of cash exchanges offered by buyers served to foster a fondness for gambling, and therefore buyers encouraging customers to exchange their prizes for cash can be seen as the true target of the regulations.

Given the above, the vitally important question on which the continued viability of the industry hinged was whether the crackdown on buyers and efforts to limit the business's speculative element would be successful. While the regulations and industry associations' associated initiatives may have had some effect, they did not provide a fundamental solution to latent demand from customers who had once experienced the cash exchange system or to the involvement of organized crime. One year after the implementation of the ban, one association noted, 'Once again buyers have started to stand out, and they even got into an argument that came to blows in the Jōhoku district. The situation is serious; newspapers are reporting that prize purchases are providing a source of funds for criminal groups, attracting attention from authorities'.[126]

There are reports of a number of arrests related to prize buying,[127] and the parties involved included not only organized crime, but also parlors such as Mitsui Shōten. While these problems continued to surface, defying solution, there can be no doubt that they left the industry with a sense that future uncertainty was only growing more pronounced and that new regulations could appear at any moment, just as the announcement of the ban on successive-shot machines had been sudden and unexpected.

THE BAN'S EFFECTS ON MACHINE MANUFACTURERS

Although it is true that the decline in the number of parlors during the mid-1950s reflected a trend that had already developed prior to the ban on successive-shot machines, the impacts of the ban's implementation in April 1955 proved to be excessive and quickly felt. The number of businesses in the 'other places of gaming or entertainment' category, which included pachinko parlors, had shrunk by more than 40 percent from 1954 to 1957, the years that bracketed the ban (see Table 1.4[128]), while the value of machines produced in 1955 shrank to about one-fourth of the previous year (see Table 1.5). I will examine the impact of the successive-shot ban on manufacturers and then parlors in light of these overall trends.

Sluggish demand for single-shot machines

Table 1.6 describes the condition of parlors in Fukuoka Prefecture, where the ban went into effect on May 1. The data is limited to about one month, but let us focus on the problems that came to light during just that short period of time.

First, I will verify that the number of parlor operators (X) did in fact decline. The cumulative number of operators that closed, seventy-four, accounts for about 10 percent of the total number of parlors as of May 1, illustrating that the effects of the ban were already making themselves felt after just twenty days. Individual manufacturers were facing not only market loss due to parlor closures, but also the shorter-term threat posed to their business by parlors' declining investment appetite. An examination of the trend in the number of temporarily closed parlors and the number of new single-shot machine and modified machine installations suggests that this threat was caused by lower-than-expected demand for new single-shot machines.

As of May 1, when the successive-shot ban went into effect, about 1.7 times the 271 operating parlors were temporarily closed. Although it is possible that some of the parlors that remained closed on the first day of the ban had simply failed to finish replacing their machines on time, about 30 percent of parlors had yet to open as of

	Number of parlors		Number of employees	
	1954	1957	1954	1957
Other gaming and entertainment facilities	23,906	13,671	160,254	84,704
Coefficient of change	100	57.2	100	52.9

Table 1.4: Trend in the number of parlors before and after the successive-shot ban

Source: Compiled based on Statistics Bureau of Japan (1959), わが国事業所の現状—昭和32年度事業所統計調査の解説 (Number of businesses and employees [public- and private-sector] by industry [service industry subcategory]), pp. 240–41.

(Unit: Thousands of yen)

Fiscal year	Value of shipments	Fiscal year	Value of shipments
1950	7,380	1953	921,747
51	236,276	54	1,871,809
52	459,663	55	470,847

Table 1.5: Trend in the value of shipments of 'gaming devices and vending machines [pachinko, etc.]' before and after the successive-shot ban

Note: The exchange rate during the years in question was fixed to about US$1 = ¥360.

Source: Compiled based on Research and Statistics Department, Ministry of Economy, Trade and Industry (1958: 238–39).

May 5.[129] Considering that pachinko is a cash business, a closure of even one day had a materially adverse impact on the operator's bottom line. The not insubstantial number of parlors that remained temporarily closed suggests that there was a problem that made operation difficult. If we posit that there was concentrated demand for single-shot machines in the face of the ban, which took effect at the same time nationwide, it is possible that a supply problem developed due to the dependence of production capacity on household-based handicraft manufacturing techniques. However, the closure of Masamura Shōkai parlors from May 1 to 9, taken with that company's sales volume, makes it unlikely that machine manufacturers' production capacity was causing problems. Supporting this conclusion is the fact that demand representing orders for the company's single-shot machines (based on sales prices) originated in March but had already fallen by about 1000 machines in April and in May did not exceed half the number sold during the previous month.

If there was no problem with the supply of new machines caused by insufficient production capacity, then perhaps the issue lay on the parlor side, in the form of temporary closures. Demand for modified machines, which accounted for more than 30 percent of total demand, explains the situation. Parlors were hesitant to invest in single-shot machines but willing to modify the units they were already operating. That parlors were making do with modifications[130] that cost just 150 yen (about US$0.42) per machine[131] is consistent with the fact that purchasing new single-shot machines

Survey date	May 1	May 5	May 10	May 20
Number of parlor businesses in Fukuoka Prefecture (X)	734	727	715	684
Number of parlor businesses that had closed temporarily (X’)	451	207	143	107
Number of parlor businesses that had submitted a declaration of permanent closure (X”)	12	13	14	35
Number of newly installed single-shot machines (A)	3,639	9,733	13,065	18,258
Percentage of all installed machines (A/Y, %)	6.1	16.6	22.1	31.6
Number of modified machines installed (B)	20,767	32,251	33,559	27,897
Percentage of all installed machines (B/Y, %)	34.7	54.9	56.8	48.3
Number of machines at temporarily closed parlors (C)	34,546	16,732	11,310	8,574
Number of machines at parlors that had submitted a declaration of permanent closure (D)	973	844	1,142	3,076
Total number of machines (Y = A + B + C + D)	59,925	58,716*	59,076	57,805
Average number of machines in operating parlors	90.1	82.8	83.6	85.2
Average number of machines in temporarily closed parlors (C/X’)	76.6	80.8	79.1	80.3
Average number of machines in permanently closed parlors (D/X”)	81.1	64.9	81.6	87.9

Table 1.6: Machine purchases immediately after the successive-shot ban (Fukuoka Prefecture)
Note: *Likely an error for 59,560.
Source: Compiled based on Shiryō Henshū Iinkai (1989), ‘福岡県下における単発式パチンコ業態調査票(福岡県警察庁部調べ)’ (Fukuoka Prefecture single-shot pachinko business survey [by the Fukuoka Prefecture Police Agency Department]), p. 180.

did not necessarily create stable revenue, as described above. In short, if profit margins were low, it is unlikely that parlors would have had the internal reserves needed to replace all machines, and it is likely that they were unable to embrace investments in new machines while earnings remained unstable. If anything, it is natural that parlors would have had second thoughts about such investments in the face of a bleak outlook based on projections that sales would decline due to the transition to single-shot machines. It is likely that such moves by parlors placed manufacturers in the difficult position of needing to accommodate modification demand even as demand for new machines failed to materialize. If we assume that manufacturers had to dedicate some of their production capacity to meeting modification demand, it is possible that problems arose that indirectly affected the supply of new single-shot machines (including the development of such machines).

The relative scarcity of investments by parlors is indicated by the fact that the percentage of modified machines rose even further. At the same time, installations of new single-shot machines began to gradually increase, and the new machines began replacing modified machines from May 10 to 20. Some parlors that had held out by relying on modified machines as they watched how the situation panned out had begun to choose new investment as a viable option.

Although additional analysis is needed,[132] the trend in the average number of machines installed indicates that investment behavior as well as closure status varied according to parlor size. During the five-day period starting on May 1, the size of operating parlors in terms of installed machines shrank from ninety to eighty-two, and it was the relatively large parlors that managed to prepare single-shot machines or modified machines, or that made new investments, in time to open on May 1. The average number of machines operated by parlors that closed first shrank from May 1 to 5 but then grew, indicating that closures of small parlors were concentrated in a small window of time immediately after the implementation of the ban.

Production seasonality: longer replacement intervals

The abrupt post-ban decline in the number of parlors dealt a fatal blow to manufacturers' businesses in the form of market loss and irrecoverable accounts receivable. The impact of the regulation was not limited to the transitional adjustments described above. The ban on successive-shot machines brought long-term changes that imposed on manufactures a new production and development environment.

What is important in this regard is the transition in the types of machines used by the industry from successive-shot to single-shot. Prolonging the service life of machines through external changes was the first step in a series of knock-on effects that lengthened the interval at which parlors replaced machines and ultimately governed the very nature of manufacturers' production systems. Back when one new parlor after another was opening for business, machine production was characterized by a consistently high operating ratio. As the influx of new businesses dwindled, parlors' demand for machines began centering on replacements, and manufacturers were forced to deal with the change. This section examines the process through which this occurred.

When the debut of successive-shot machines at the end of 1952 fueled dramatic growth, parlors faced a problem. One organization's resolution noted, 'Following the emergence of circulating-type designs (successive-shot machines), machine wear and tear became intense. Pachinko parlors that had replaced their machines about every six months in the past found that intensifying competition and wear on machines meant that they couldn't continue to operate if they didn't shorten that interval to four or even three months. Parlors are starting to have difficulty footing the bill for these machines'.[133] The pace of machine replacement had increased, and the associated investment burden was placing unprecedented pressure on parlor management. If high rates of utilization of popular machines were exacerbated by heightened machine damage and wear due to the greater number of balls those machines could launch per unit of time, it is likely that successive-shot designs shortened the service life of machines. At the same time, the switch from single-shot to successive-shot machines was generally associated with an increase in machine prices, reflecting the higher level of technology they incorporated. Conversely, the subsequent transition from successive-shot back to single-shot machines had the potential to lengthen the periods of time over which machines were used and to push down prices.

Let us check that supposition based on sales trends for Masamura Shōkai machines. Although products are not typically manufactured and sold in the same time frames, we can safely assume that machines were generally produced in the same month in which their sale was recorded without being too far off since sales of, and demand for, pachinko machines were influenced by fads, and because as products pachinko machines did not lend themselves to advance manufacture for reasons related to the properties of components such as the plywood sheets used for their display boards (Japan's high humidity could warp the material).[134] A number of differences emerge when the monthly sales figures for the years preceding and following the implementation of the ban are compared. Prior to the ban, the months with the highest sales, December 1953 and October 1954, generated revenue about three times that of the months with the lowest sales, January and August 1954. By contrast, during the year following the ban, from August 1955 to July 1956, the difference between September 1955 and May 1956 widened to about sixteen times. Incidentally, during the year from August 1962 to July 1963, when the industry could be considered to have moved beyond the ban, sales in December 1962 were about eleven times those in May 1963. While somewhat smaller than during the immediate aftermath of the ban, the difference is still greater than during the period when successive-shot machines were in vogue.

The successive-shot ban prompted a flip in overall sales from a positive trend to a negative trend, and Masamura Shōkai's production and sales in particular took an exceedingly severe hit. The increasingly pronounced seasonality of sales (production) mentioned above must be factored into any evaluation, but the following interpretation remains conceivable. Small monthly differences in sales volume before the ban reflected the effects of the service life of circulating-type designs, mentioned in the citation above. Acute wear on machines due to successive-shot designs shortened their service life and prompted parlors to invest in machines in a way that was not governed by any particular replacement season. Furthermore, the steady entry of new businesses into the market served to dampen monthly fluctuations in sales (production) volume for manufacturers, and these factors spurred growth in sales volume and market expansion throughout the year.

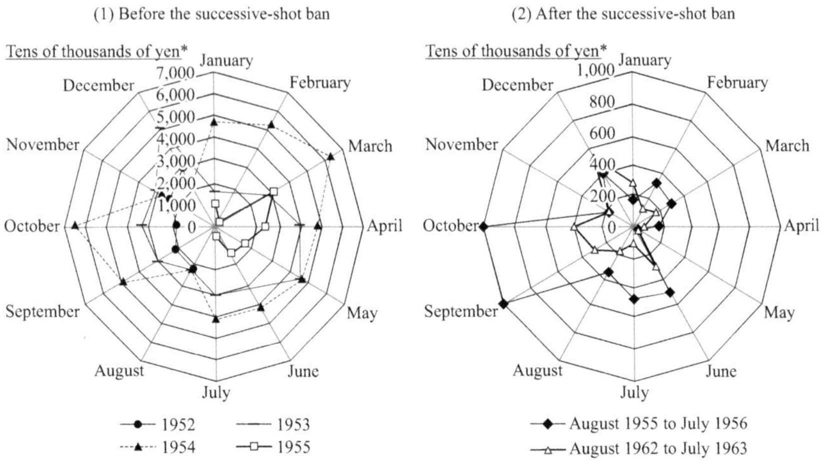

*Note: The exchange rate during the years in question was fixed to about US$1 = ¥360.

Figure 1.4: Seasonality in Masamura Shōkai's production of pachinko machines (August 1952 to July 1963)

Source: Compiled based on Masamura Shōkai statements of accounts for August 1952 to July 1953, August 1953 to July 1954 and August 1955 to July 1956 (for the former company), and September 1955 to July 1956 and August 1962 to July 1963 (for the new company).

Figure 1.4 charts Masamura Shōkai's sales volume throughout the year. The figure depicts monthly sales volumes from August 1952 to August 1956, and from 1962 to 1963, bracketing the announcement of the successive-shot ban. These trends reflect parlors' purchases of machines (newly opened parlors and replacements) and the general extent to which manufacturers concentrated production. Because Figure 1.4 (1), which illustrates sales prior to the ban, covers a period during which the steady entry into the market of new parlors kept sales rising year in, year out, there is no clear difference between figures for months prior to 1953 and those for months after that year, when successive-shot machines began to penetrate the market. Conditions then took a turn for the worse, and seasonality became readily apparent during the downturn that followed the ban, as shown in Figure 1.4 (2).

The 'sales season' (that is, the period during which parlors replaced machines) after the implementation of the ban was considered to include three periods: just prior to early spring, the Obon summer vacation and the New Year's holiday. Although the period of time over which we can verify sales figures for Masamura Shōkai's parlors is limited, we do know that from 1962 to 1963, the Main Branch replaced machines in January and June, and that the Oshikiri Branch did so in July and October.[135] Replacements were generally carried out twice per year, and the service life of each machine is likely to have averaged from six months to one year or more, as it did before successive-shot machines became popular.[136] In contrast to physical service life, which is governed by wear on machines and affected by the characteristics of successive- and single-shot designs, regular machine replacements are related to 'popularity service life'. Parlors' new machine purchases in the run-up to extended public holidays every year can be understood as an effort to overcome waning customer interest.

Following the successive-shot ban, a lengthening of the machine service life led to an extension of the machine replacement interval. As a result, the difference between slow and busy machine production periods became more pronounced. The seasonality of production governed manufacturers' businesses for many years before the development of today's tendency to withdraw machines from service several weeks after they lose popularity. While I will not explore the present topic any further here, the lengthening of service life was more the result of a forcible retrenchment in technology caused by regulations than due to any progress in terms of technological development. How this change would condition the machine market was a key problem for manufacturers insofar as it would come to characterize the competitive environment going forward.

Regulations and structural change in the machine market

How, then, did the ban on successive-shot machines impact Masamura Shōkai's manufacturing business? Data describing orders received by Masamura Shōkai suggests that the market (i.e., parlors) reacted comparatively quickly following the announcement of the ban in November 1954.

According to Table 1.7, monthly sales volume generally outperformed the previous year up until October 1954, with the exception of August 1954, despite individual peaks and troughs. April 1953 set a record for monthly production, after which the company steadily extended its output while setting a series of new monthly records until just before November 1954, when sales volume reached an unprecedented level.

However, after November, when the ban was announced, sales fell below the level of the previous year and failed to recover. The amount of time between orders and deliveries remains unclear, and it may be premature to blame the downturn in November on the announcement. Based on an examination of sales prices, it is likely that demand for single-shot machines dominated the company's sales starting in March. Although it was falling, demand for successive-shot machines continued from November 1954, when the ban was announced, until the following February. Reflecting the successive-shot machine service life of three to four months, it is likely that parlors made purchases based on the assumption that they could install the

(Units: machines, Yen)

Year	Month	Number of machines sold	Sales	Whole-sale price per machine	Year	Month	Number of machines sold	Sales	Whole-sale price per machine
1952	8	711	5,657,400	7,957	1954	2	7,595	53,709,630	7,071
	9	351	1,958,200	5,607		3	8,777	62,638,780	7,137
	10	1,020	6,297,100	6,174		4	6,386	47,880,620	7,498
	11	1,604	11,001,200	6,859		5	6,379	46,962,457	7,362
	12	2,799	17,858,100	6,380		6	5,577	41,815,525	7,498
1953	1	1,193	7,576,100	6,350		7	5,392	41,173,705	7,636
	Subtotal	7,678	50,358,100	6,559		Subtotal	40,107	294,180,717	7,335
	2	1,793	11,899,400	6,637		8	2,991	22,781,500	7,617
	3	2,262	14,857,400	6,568		9	6,580	49,768,850	7,564
	4	3,884	25,187,400	6,485		10	8,720	65,980,300	7,567
	5	4,696	30,840,500	6,567		11	3,847	28,745,000	7,472
	6	2,472	15,311,000	6,194		12	2,924	21,925,500	7,498
	7	3,425	21,595,400	6,305	1955	1	1,464	10,225,400	6,985
	Subtotal	18,532	119,691,100	6,459		Subtotal	26,526	199,426,550	7,518
	8	3,635	23,017,500	6,332		2	306	2,198,400	7,184
	9	4,403	31,511,470	7,157		3	6,889	30,978,800	4,497
	10	5,069	34,260,170	6,759		4	5,520	22,867,870	4,143
	11	4,539	31,959,600	7,041		5	2,942	15,335,600	5,213
	12	7,038	51,042,700	7,252		6	2,484	13,239,500	5,330
1954	1	6,821	47,573,265	6,975		7	849	4,600,500	5,419
	Subtotal	31,505	219,364,705	6,963		Subtotal	18,990	89,220,670	4,698

Table 1.7: Number of machines produced per month and associated sales of Masamura Shōkai
Note: The exchange rate during the years in question was fixed to about US$1 = ¥360.
Source: Compiled based on the Main Branch sales statistics tables (eigyō tōkeihyō Honten).

machines by March, before the ban was to take effect. The decline in sales volume as the ban's implementation approached can be understood as a reflection of this fact. However, it seems that demand for single-shot machines was not sufficient to replace the successive-shot machines. Although rush demand for single-shot machines was expected around April, when the ban went into force, the sales volume for March fell by some 2000 machines from the previous year before continuing a downward trend.

While the ban's implementation was delayed until May in some regions, for example in Fukuoka and Nagoya, it took effect in April in twenty-two of the country's prefectures, about half of the total, including in Tokyo, which was Masamura Shōkai's largest market. The fact that sales stagnated in March and April despite parlors' plans to remove all successive-shot machines under the ban indicates that demand failed to grow in line with expectations. As seen in machine purchase data for Fukuoka (see Table 1.6 above), Masamura Shōkai, one of the era's leading machine manufacturers, was no exception to the problem of falling sales of new single-shot machines, which was the flip side of demand for modified machines. Moreover, demand for new single-shot machines dried up in March and April, and sales during May totaled just half the previous month's figure.[137] Machine sales during April and May were particularly poor in light of the fact that Masamura Shōkai had no small number of customers in Aichi Prefecture, where the successive-shot ban took effect in May.

At the same time, manufacturers' bottom lines faced additional pressure from falling machine prices. According to Table 1.7, prices for machines had fallen about 40 percent by July 1955, when parlors were installing single-shot machines, compared to the record highs set one year prior.

In this way, the challenges confronting Masamura Shōkai after the ban included a decline in total machine sales volume caused by closures of customer parlors, falling unit prices for machines and longer replacement intervals. The company posted a loss for the 1956 fiscal year and sought outside funds for the first time since its establishment.[138]

Of sales booked by Masamura Shōkai's Tokyo distributor, the majority of the 30 million yen (about US$83,333) in accounts receivable dating from February to July 1955 was ultimately unrecoverable. Sales from August 1955 to January 1956 totaled just 45,000 yen (about US$125) (versus about 32 million yen [about US$88,889] for the same period in the previous year). The company lost the Tokyo market, its largest, leaving it with a concentration of customers in Aichi Prefecture and the Chugoku region, where it retained distributors (see Table 1.2 above).[139] A powerful company that tapped a nationwide market had in effect been demoted to a regional player. The transformation left the machine market waiting for someone to seize the initiative by introducing a new type of machine.

PARLORS SEARCH FOR WAYS TO STABILIZE THEIR REVENUE BASE

Effects over time

The ban on successive-shot machines hit parlors' bottom line hard, and its effects were quickly and vividly realized. Let us investigate changes in the profit structure of the four Masamura Shōkai parlors for which documentation remains, before and after the ban took effect. I will examine how the regulation impacted parlors by examining patterns that indicate two general trends.

The first characteristic of the overall impact on parlors manifested itself in a remarkable decline in sales. This decline presumably resulted when customers who were accustomed to successive-shot machines that had a pronounced speculative

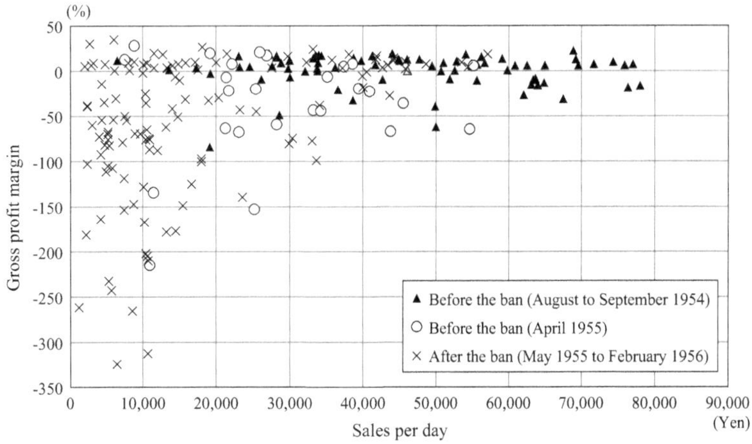

Figure 1.5: Profit structure before and after the successive-shot ban (Endonji Branch; August 1954 to February 1956)

*Source: Compiled based on the Endonji Branch sales statistics tables (*eigyō tōkeihyō *Endonjiten; August 1954 to February 1956).*

element stopped coming to parlors when they became bored with single-shot machines.[140] Even when such effects are taken into consideration, the impact of changes in machines on sales cannot be ignored. Whereas successive-shot machines could semi-automatically launch more than 100 balls per minute, single-shot machines were limited by regulations to a maximum of thirty balls. Customers had to watch to see if the ball they had just launched would foul out or enter a catcher before they could launch the next ball, and the result was a decline in sales per unit of time.[141]

This trend was clear in the case of Masamura Shōkai's four parlors as well. However, there were some differences in terms of profit margin. The first trend is that there were days when the profit margin deteriorated as far as negative 350 percent, as at the Endonji Branch (see Figure 1.5). The Matsubara Branch exhibits the same trend. In the case of the Endonji Branch, we must be careful in blaming the regulations. Data for the period from October 1954 to March 1955, prior to the implementation of the ban, is missing from Figure 1.5. The parlor seems to have been closed during this period. Although it sought to reopen five months later in April, it is clear that sales had fallen and that the gross profit margin had deteriorated. It was under these conditions that the parlor experienced the effects of the ban on successive-shot machines. With the coming of May, when the ban took effect, the parlor closed from the first to the ninth, perhaps to switch over to single-shot machines. Figure 1.5 provides data starting on the tenth, when the parlor finally reopened. However, another period of missing data follows. In short, the parlor seems to have been closed from June to July 7, 1955, as well as from July 15 to 27, from August 16 to 24, from September 5

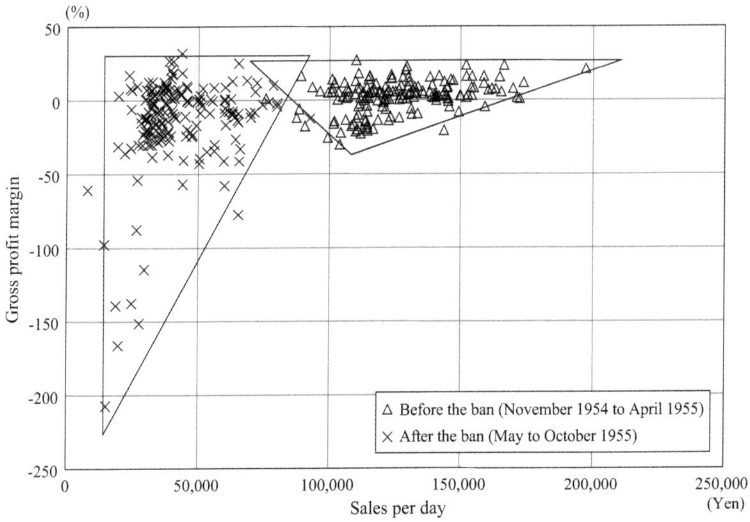

Figure 1.6: Profit structure before and after the successive-shot ban (Oshikiri Branch; November 1954 to October 1955)

*Source: Compiled based on the Oshikiri Branch sales statistics tables (*eigyō tōkeihyō *Oshikiriten; November 1954 to October 1955).*

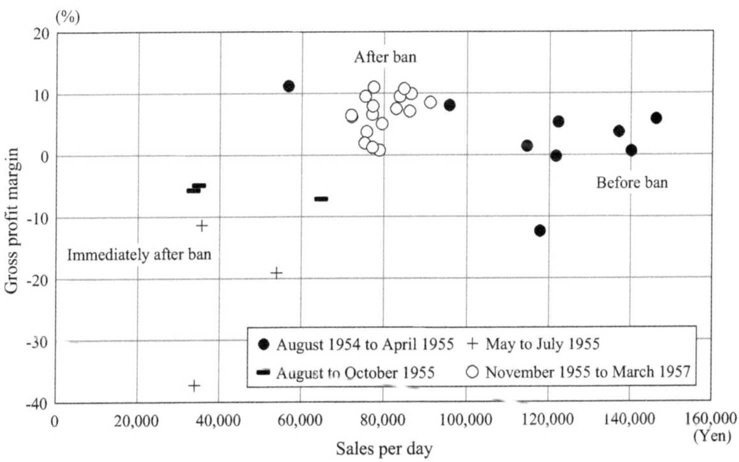

Figure 1.7: Accumulation of management expertise (Oshikiri Branch; August 1954 to March 1957)

*Source: Compiled based on the Oshikiri Branch sales statistics tables (*eigyō tōkeihyō *Oshikiriten; November 1954 to October 1955).*

to November 11 and from December 22 to February 10, 1956. There are no records for March or later months, and there is no related data for the branch after that point.

Compare that to the Oshikiri Branch, detailed in Figure 1.6, which exhibits a different trend. The branch's profit margin hovers around negative 50 percent, with the lowest value about negative 200 percent. Although I will not go into the data here, the Main Branch exhibits a similar trend.

It goes without saying that this assessment is a relative one, but the Oshikiri Branch and Endonji Branch pursued different paths during the subsequent recovery as a result of the differences in the extent to which their profit margins deteriorated. According to Figure 1.7, which depicts changes in profit structure in the form of the monthly average every three months, the average coordinates for the Oshikiri Branch (as well as the Main Branch) began to move upward and to the right from August to October, after the successive-shot ban had taken effect, signaling a trajectory of improvement in profit structure. Sales did not recover to their pre-ban level, but that is likely the result of differences in the type of machine being used.

It seems probable that these two trends emerged due to the scale of operations and external factors such as the characteristics of parlors' physical locations since all four parlors were managed under the same conditions by founder Takeichi Masamura, who drew on the parlors' business expertise and on his skill as a pin adjuster.[142] With regard to the scale of operations, by July 1954 the Endonji Branch had installed ninety-one machines, more than the other parlors, which operated about sixty-one machines.[143] It is possible that the branch failed to see growth in sales due to its poor location, but there are no surviving materials from which subsequent changes in the number of machines it operated can be reviewed, leaving room for additional study of the factors that accounted for differences in the branches' respective recoveries. That said, these operating conditions were consistent with the general manner in which Masamura Shōkai managed its parlors. The company explored its options for closing the Matsubara and Endonji branches, where business was remarkably poor, and ended up restructuring itself to continue operating the Oshikiri and Main branches, which were on the road to recovery.

Discovery of a method for stabilizing the revenue base

Figure 1.8 provides a graph of daily sales and gross profit margin figures after November, when revenue was improving in the wake of the successive-shot ban of May 1955. The revenue base prior to the ban, which was founded on successive-shot machines, was characterized by significant fluctuations in both sales and gross profit, as illustrated by the horizontal breadth of Figure 1.3 above. Interestingly, the profit structure shown in Figure 1.8 is characterized by narrower fluctuations than before

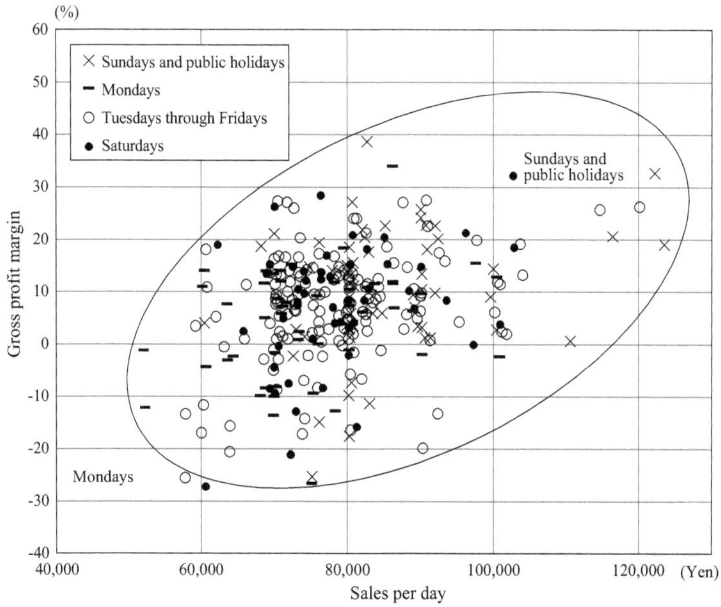

Figure 1.8: Profit structure after the successive-shot ban
(Oshikiri Branch; November 1955 to April 1957)

*Source: Compiled based on the Oshikiri Branch sales statistics tables (*eigyō tōkeihyō *Oshikiriten; November 1954 to October 1955).*

the ban. The reduction in fluctuations can be understood as indicative of the fact that operational control had been simplified. Masamura Shōkai accumulated expertise in pin adjustment in the context of the switchover in machine types.

What must not be overlooked concerning Figure 1.8 is the elliptical, rising pattern of points, which are concentrated at the lower left and upper right. This arrangement suggests that it had become possible to exert control over parlors' overall operations by adjusting prize-ball percentages, allowing them to reliably increase profits. The profit structure seen in the distribution of sales and gross profit margins, which at the time was the result of 'opening' and 'closing' pins as part of the pin adjustment process, can be characterized as having shifted both down and to the left and up and to the right compared to thc structure prior to the ban, which resembled an upside-down triangle. Whereas points in the positive profit zone had been distributed broadly throughout a horizontal band at 0 percent before the ban, they formed a thick vertical column after the ban. Points in the negative profit zone fall within the negative 30 percent range. Overall, this distribution caused the average point to shift up and towards the right.

Figure 1.8 also tells the story of another, deeply significant change. Sundays and public holidays – that is, days characterized by higher sales – are more predominant as we move up and towards the right in the graph. The data indicates that Sundays were characterized by both higher per-capita spending and more customers, even if the pins were 'closed' on those days. Compared to successive-shot machines, where results depended on chance, the return to single-shot machines inspired customers to conclude that they could win more by spending more if they had the requisite level of skill, or conversely that they could limit their losses by minimizing the amount they spent during each visit. The result was that customers did not hesitate to come to parlors and spend money, even on public holidays when the pins were 'closed'.[144] What can be said regarding the negative profit zone is that days with low sales tend to appear on the left. Parlors were presumably able to create a buzz by 'opening' pins on days like Mondays when low attendance was anticipated. In this way, a distribution in which points are concentrated along a rising diagonal line reliably increases the balance of profit. That the average profit margin has moved upwards characterizes the stable operations of this period.

Attempts at organizing prize purchases

In relation to this stable revenue structure, another factor helped indirectly bolster parlors' accumulation of pin adjustment expertise and the increased operational control they enjoyed. Although the change in the way parlors purchased prizes may appear insignificant at first glance, its importance in parlor management's drive to generate profit cannot be overlooked.

In the prize redemption paradigm in place around 1950, the typical approach was for customers to redeem balls for items such as cigarettes and candy. However, latent demand for a means of converting these prizes into cash grew along with the industry's speculative element. I have already examined how the emergence of buyers was emblematic of this need and how they ultimately became the target of a police crackdown. Against the backdrop of a legal framework in which the industry, unlike state-controlled gambling businesses, is not allowed to offer cash prizes, a system known as the 'three-business system' in which parlors are not involved in the conversion of prizes into cash has become established today, with the result that pachinko does not qualify as a type of gambling under Japanese amusement industry regulations.

This system traces its origins back to events in several regions around 1954 that I have described above. For example, a group of unemployed individuals purchased prizes in the city of Kawasaki, while a widows' association in Tochigi Prefecture negotiated with authorities for a license to do the same.[145] The route by which prizes could be redeemed, including the parties responsible for purchasing them, was the subject of a series of trial-and-error experiments, while licensing and other questions remained unresolved.

The three-business system is generally understood to have originated with the Osaka system, which was proposed by Toshie Mizushima, the chairman of the Osaka Prefecture Amusement Industry Cooperative (Ōsakafu Yūgigyō Kyōdō Kumiai), in 1961.[146] To preclude the involvement of organized crime, which was trying to secure ways to convert prizes into cash as a source of funding, the Osaka Prefecture Social Welfare Business Association for Physically Handicapped and Widowed Individuals (Ōsakafu Shinshōsha Mibōjin Fukushi Jigyō Kyōkai) was launched in February that year. The new organization was to obtain a license for antiques and purchase prizes (other than government-controlled monopoly goods such as cigarettes and salt), thereby resolving the problem of organized crime while providing jobs for disabled and widowed individuals.[147] The program received the approval of the Osaka prefecture police,[148] and is likely to have been seen as a pioneering example. Under-the-table transactions by criminal organizations[149] and associated flows of money ought to have been of concern to police, but there were limits on the extent to which they could be regulated. Police were likely seeking to ensure that prize exchange and supply routes were visible and to limit the targets and scope of monitoring. The city of Gifu undertook a similar experiment. The prefectural assembly gathered with people involved with social welfare programs in 1962 and established the City of Gifu Social Welfare Program Cooperative (Gifushi Shakai Fukushi Jigyō Kyōryokukai) with the goal of buying prizes from pachinko customers and donating the profits to social welfare programs.[150] The experiment was conceived to exclude organized crime and restore the healthy image of the industry.[151]

Other efforts were undertaken, likely during roughly the same period of time, to eliminate the influence of organized crime from prize purchase routes. Examples include the 'Mie (prefecture) style system',[152] which through the efforts of a former police chief introduced tickets as a substitute for prizes, and Aichi Prefecture's 'three-party system'.[153] The latter scheme, in which eight candy wholesalers formed a company to purchase prizes at the behest of the chief of their local police force, included a separate entity that supplied prizes to parlors on a wholesale basis.[154] In short, after prizes redeemed by customers at parlors were purchased in an exchange that was independent of those parlors, the prizes underwent sorting and other processing so they could be used as new prizes again. A surcharge was then added, and they were sold back to the parlors by the newly established wholesaler. This system, which enjoyed a status approaching official approval, emerged and became established nationwide during the 1960s.[155]

Prize label	Prize	Number of prize suppliers and suppliers	Total prize value (yen)	Percentage
Standard prizes	Lifestyle (soap,[a] etc.)	4	330,688	0.9
		Fumiya	54.2%	
		Shiseido	24.8	
		Other	4.2	
		Unknown	9.2	
	Cigarettes (Shinsei, Ikoi[a], etc.)	4	11,404,500	31.1
		Itani Shōten	91.8%	
		Other	8.2	
	Food (candy such as caramels and chocolates[a])	8	2,845,097	7.8
		Sakuraya	66.5%	
		Yamamoto	14.4	
		Other	17.2	
Special prizes[b]	Handkerchiefs, candies	35	22,115,953	60.3
		MT	47.1%	
		Sanwa Shōten	22.8	
		Other	28.9	
Total value			36,696,238	100.0

Table 1.8: Prize purchases by Masamura Shōkai (August 1955 to July 1956)

Notes:

a. As recorded in accounting ledgers.

b. Special prize category based on the author's judgment.

*Source: Compiled based on Masamura Shōkai ledger (*motochō*) (August 1955 to July 1956).*

The above signals the development of an organizational basis for the prize supply routes that would spread throughout the industry, but here we must pause to analyze the events that occurred in parlor management with regard to prize exchanges before this system became established, that is, after the successive-shot ban. The willingness of industry associations to undertake related initiatives as described above can be understood in the context of the stabilization of parlors' profit structure as outlined in this chapter. Let us examine data on Masamura Shōkai's prize purchases from the principal perspective of management stabilization. As a result of the spread of the Nagoya three-party system described above, Aisan Shōkai would ultimately become the company's source of special prizes. The process by which that role was narrowed down from several suppliers to a single company bears consideration.

Records of prize purchases in Masamura Shōkai's ledgers do not use explicit terms like 'special prize'; rather, they include frequent entries in which large quantities of prizes such as handkerchiefs and hard candies are purchased. In contrast to consumable treats, for example cigarettes, which were known as typical pachinko prizes, these items were characterized by a mismatch between the size of the lots in which they were purchased and the general utility of the prizes in question.[156]

Month and year	Trend in special prize unit prices (number of orders)				Total
	24 yen	25 yen	26 yen	27 yen	
1955	23	7	11	17	58
August				14	14
September	5	3	2		10
October	1	2		2	5
November	4	1			5
December	13	1	9	1	24
1956	27	1	22	396	446
January	17	1	21	3	42
February	10		1	62	73
March				68	68
April				60	60
May				64	64
June				63	63
July				76	76
Total	50	8	33	413	504

Table 1.9: Unit prices of special prizes purchased by Masamura Shōkai
*Source: Compiled based on Masamura Shōkai ledger (*motochō*) (August 1955 to July 1956).*

It is likely that these products were purchased to function as special prizes, which customers sought out because they could exchange them for cash. Tables 1.8 through 1.10 summarize about one year of data (August 1955 to July 1956) describing purchases of handkerchiefs and other items, which have been classified as special prizes for convenience' sake.

The ratio of the amounts spent on purchasing standard prizes and special prizes in Table 1.8 makes it possible to identify those prizes for which customers preferred to redeem balls. Standard prizes accounted for 40 percent of the total, and special prizes, 60 percent, reflecting customers' preference for the latter. As long as the type and price of each prize were limited by regulations, the prizes for which customers could redeem balls could not increase in value in proportion to the quantity of balls (the total redemption value) they redeemed. Since customers' winnings tended to consist of large numbers of relatively inexpensive items due to limits on the maximum value of individual prizes, it stands to reason that the proportion of prizes purchased by parlors would rise in step with customer preferences for special prizes, which they could expect to exchange for cash. Standard prizes included food, non-food lifestyle items and cigarettes, of which lifestyle items represented only a negligible percentage. Cigarettes accounted for the highest percentage of any single prize at about 30 percent, offering an indirect suggestion that many of the parlors' customers were men.

	Month	Purchases			Prize suppliers	
		Number of orders	Average prize per order (yen)	Monthly total (yen)	Number of suppliers	Percentage of transaction value from principal suppliers (MT, Sanwa Shōten)
1955	8	14	75,141	1,051,974	11	
	9	10	92,826	928,260	9	
	10	5	175,830	879,150	5	
	11	5	221,182	1,105,908	4	Start of transactions with Sanwa Shōten
	12	24	68,760	1,650,232	4	Start of transactions with MT
1956	1	42	73,506	3,087,254	6	84.1
	2	73	31,176	2,275,830	10	82.8
	3	68	32,794	2,229,975	8	84.3
	4	60	32,907	1,974,446	6	90.6
	5	64	31,238	1,999,242	3	92.4
	6	63	31,492	1,983,986	5	91.9
	7	76	38,812	2,949,696	10	63.5
Total		504	75,472	22,115,953	35	

Table 1.10: Methods by which Masamura Shōkai purchased special prizes
*Source: Compiled based on Masamura Shōkai ledger (*motochō*) (August 1955 to July 1956).*

With regard to special prizes, which accounted for about 60 percent of the total, information related to parlor management can be gleaned from Table 1.9, which describes the trend characterizing changes in unit prices for prize items, and Table 1.10, which describes the characteristics of parlors' purchase methods. Total prize purchases by month (see Table 1.10) rose in 1955 through to the year's end before plateauing in 1956. Prize purchases are likely to have been linked to sales, which rose in January and July when machines were replaced, and the figures show how purchases increased throughout the year.[157]

It is the fluctuations in prize prices that demand attention from a management perspective. According to Table 1.9, unit prices rose. At the same time, the field of suppliers narrowed to MT Co., Ltd., and Sanwa Shōten (see Table 1.10). Additionally, the value of the average purchase fell, while the frequency of purchases grew.[158] The increase in unit prices meant higher supply costs for parlors, which translated into downward pressure on profits. Generally speaking, purchasers can push down unit prices in a competitive manner by tapping large numbers of suppliers, but Masamura Shōkai chose the opposite course. What explains this narrowing of business partners and the resulting rise in unit prices, which at first glance seems to place Masamura Shōkai at a disadvantage?

The answer to this puzzle reveals itself when customer preferences are taken into account. In short, customers, in an effort to maximize their return when converting prizes into cash, presumably chose from among multiple exchanges based on which business offered the most advantageous exchange rate. It is possible that Masamura parlors then purchased prizes from wholesalers who obtained them through those exchanges. The fee included in the 24 yen (about US$0.67) per prize was profit for the special prize wholesaler, and customers gained cash income by selling prizes to companies that then sold them on to wholesalers. If we assume that the fees were uniform, then it goes without saying that a unit price of 27 yen (about US$0.75) would be more likely to offer customers an economic gain than a unit price of 24 yen, which suggests that they would seek out companies that offered such advantageous exchange rates. As a result, Masamura parlors probably had no choice but to accept the higher unit price.

It bears keeping in mind that these trends unfolded at a time when parlor revenue was stabilizing. Parlors may have been more willing to accept the 27-yen price point as a result. To put it differently, it seems possible that the increase in the unit prices parlors paid for special prizes was accepted precisely because of parlors' ability to adjust prize-ball percentages, accumulate adjustment expertise and exert overall control over their operations, all of which translated into increased earnings. In this way, the rise in prize unit prices that occurred during this period tells the story of stabilizing management and heightened planning from a different perspective.

That development, along with the narrowing of the field of prize wholesalers, is important when viewed in light of the systemization of the prize exchange routes that were subsequently established. With the organization of the businesses buying special prizes and the wholesalers selling them back to parlors as separate companies under the three-party system described above,[159] the free, unit price-centered competition that we would typically see among multiple wholesalers disappeared. Nonetheless, the three-party system became established because it was able to prevent under-the-table transactions and the funneling of money to criminal groups, both of which were made possible by the recognition of free participation, as described above. The three-party system embodied an organization of the market insofar as parlors locked in prize purchasers and prize wholesalers, but to the extent that they were unable to exert competitive pressure on unit prices, the costs of that effort were borne by the parlors. An analysis of Masamura Shōkai reveals the conditions under which an unusual system that seemed to place parlors at a disadvantage was accepted, as well as how the basis on which the parlors actually chose that system was put in place, allowing those developments to be understood in the context of the operational stabilization that characterized the period.

The reorganization of Masamura Shōkai's business

The revenue recovery experienced by Masamura Shōkai's parlors in fact reflected a broader trend across the entire industry. The ban on successive-shot machines did not place the existence of the business itself in jeopardy, as one parlor manager confirmed: 'It is a fact that the switch to single-shot machines led to a decline in sales, but if we take a sound and steady approach, we ought to be able to make it'.[160] It is unclear exactly what he meant by 'sound and steady', but if parlors could accumulate management expertise based on pin adjustment and establish a more stable profit structure, they could expect to generate a reasonable return, even if their prospects could not quite be described as 'bright'. The industry's own assessment concluded that stability returned after one year.[161]

In December 1955, after the successive-shot ban, Masamura Shōkai reorganized its machine manufacturing operations by consolidating them at its head office factory, which going forward was to become its sole production facility.[162] The move suggests that the impact of the ban, while short-lived, was severe. The impact was probably amplified for Masamura Shōkai due to its status as a leading manufacturer compared to smaller competitors.

Parlor operations were consolidated at two locations: the existing Oshikiri Branch and the Jōshin Branch, which was created by relocating the Main Branch. According to sales statistics (*eigyō tōkeisho*) and statistical tables (*tōkeihyō*), which record daily sales, the Endonji Branch and the Matsubara Branch were listed as 'Closed' after January 1956 and August 1956, respectively, and there are no subsequent records for either location.[163] Both branches had closed repeatedly in the past, which suggests that the reorganization decision to focus on the Oshikiri and Jōshin branches was based on the relatively more serious declines in the profitability of their shuttered counterparts, as analyzed above.[164] The Main Branch retained head office functions,[165] and the parlor was relocated in July 1956 to a more favorable location, where it opened as the Jōshin Branch.[166] The new branch was located about 200 meters away from the former branch at the Jōshin intersection, which was also the location of a streetcar terminal and parking lot and which offered more convenient access to customers than the former location. The closure of the Matsubara Branch came after the relocation of the Main Branch, and ultimately Masamura Shōkai's parlor business came to focus on the Jōshin Branch along with the profitable Oshikiri Branch.

The changes triggered by the successive-shot ban in the revenue structures that characterized Masamura Shōkai's various businesses are obvious at a glance (see Table 1.3 above). Whereas machine sales accounted for more than 80 percent of the company's business prior to the ban, parlor operations represented 70 percent of total sales after the prohibition, signaling a reversal in the position of its businesses. The company's reorganization of those businesses also included an effort to diversify. It purchased land in Niigata Prefecture in August 1955 and completed construction of Akakura Hotel Taiko in December 1956. As the hotel business began to stabilize in 1959, it became a core segment of Masamura Shōkai's operations.

This sweeping reorganization had a number of implications for the company's management from the perspective of the characteristics of its various businesses. The machine sales business, which had enjoyed a profit margin of greater than 30 percent, experienced a striking decline in sales even as the seasonality of its operations became more pronounced, as illustrated in Figure 1.4 (2) above, leading to a weakening of its position as a stable business for the company. At the same time, the parlor business emerged as a core business thanks to improved earnings and became a stable – and seasonally consistent – source of revenue. The hotel business grew into a segment that was second only to the parlor business in terms of sales. It continued to grow even as the parlor business slumped during the 1960s, cementing its position as a linchpin of the company's operations. Masamura Shōkai increasingly strengthened its involvement in the hotel market as a new business.

CONCLUSION: THE INDUSTRY BEGINS TO DEVELOP

The popularity of pachinko around the year 1950 stemmed from a chain of composite, machine-related technological innovations including the Masamura Gauge, 'all-win' machines and successive-shot mechanisms. People reacted to the new industry during a time of postwar reconstruction in sometimes surprising ways, triggering a boom in popularity that saw the numbers of parlors and machine manufacturers soar. However, as symbolized by the expression 'boom and bust', the popularity of pachinko was consistently threatened by the possibility that it might be no more than a passing fad. In fact, that popularity not only contributed directly to the industry's establishment, but also triggered a variety of problems, beyond even regulatory issues.

This chapter has uncovered various issues that threw the very existence of the industry into crisis by focusing on the destabilizing impact of popularity and regulations, the behind-the-scenes reality of parlor operations and the systems that drove its development. The establishment of pachinko as an industry can be understood as a process of overcoming a series of supply-side obstacles.

Challenges that cast doubt on the industry's viability included the instability of parlors' revenue bases caused by successive-shot machines and problems posed by prize exchange systems. Furthermore, environmental changes following the imposition of regulations designed to limit the industry's speculative element led to the development of a serious regulatory element that would affect the subsequent development of parlors and manufacturers. I will summarize the successive-shot ban's impact on, and significance for, the industry from the perspective of solutions to those problems and remaining issues while connecting them to trends in the industry after the 1960s, which will be analyzed in the next chapter.

First, regulations proved to be only temporarily effective in addressing the problems of buyers and the involvement of organized crime in prize exchanges, which was one factor that contributed to the 1955 ban.[167] Ultimately, no solution was found for the root problem of how – or whether – to exchange prizes for cash. Whether the industry would again see regulatory action such as the imposition of the successive-shot ban depended on how the industry dealt with the issue of prize exchanges and the associated problem of organized crime. Signs of a solution appeared as parlor operators deepened their awareness of exchange-related fraud and searched for prize exchange systems that would exclude criminal groups. Initiatives that involved social welfare groups in legal transactions as prize purchasers spread to every region during the 1960s. How successful were such initiatives at systematizing prize exchanges?

An article entitled '風俗営業に関する一問題—ぱちんこ遊技の健全化について' (An issue in the entertainment business: Transforming pachinko into a healthy enterprise) by Kazunari Takita, who served as an assistant to the manager of the Crime Prevention and Youth Section (Bōhan Shōnenka) of the National Police Agency's Security Service (Hoankyoku), offers a glimpse at one aspect of the financial relationship between pachinko and organized crime.[168] One study that examined profits through the pachinko-prize buybacks of 199 parlors in one of Japan's prefectures identified ten parlors that 'arranged to have a criminal group handle purchases of prizes [from customers]', twenty that 'housed prize purchase businesses run by criminal groups' and thirty-four that 'otherwise contracted with a prize purchase business or facilitated the operations of such a business in order to purchase prizes or have prizes purchased'.[169] With regard to the finding that funds flowed to organized crime through thirty parlors, or about 15 percent of the total studied, conditions in other prefectures are unclear, making it difficult to evaluate the results. However, there is no doubt that efforts were underway to build mechanisms such as the Osaka system and other regional analogues. Seen in light of the nationwide spread of such systems starting in the 1960s, the state of affairs in the studied prefecture at that point in time can be understood as a step in a larger process of improvement. As recognized economic organizations that handled secondhand goods, the prize-purchasing companies signaled a progressive narrowing of the path by which organized crime could become involved in the industry. The severing of ties with criminal groups implied that profits from prize exchanges would be plowed back into the industry and that those earnings would provide a basis for investments that would lead to the growth of the industry in line with parlors' accumulation of management expertise and the resulting outlook for stable profits.

Second, the successive-shot ban not only had the negative impact of forcing many businesses to close, but also gave new direction to parlors' businesses by facilitating a more planned and systematic approach to operations. While the Masamura Gauge suppressed machines' element of chance and opened up a way in which parlors could secure profits, highly speculative successive-shot machines destabilized parlor operations, for example by introducing extreme fluctuations in sales that exceeded the range within which control was possible via pin adjustment. This state of affairs created hesitation in customers about making additional investments due to the increasingly speculative nature of the industry. It was also the result of manufacturers' and parlors' limitless pursuit of this aspect of their business in an effort to satisfy the appetite of customers who preferred more speculative gameplay. Regulation of the industry checked this trend. The reversion to single-shot machines eliminated the constraint of profit instability and spurred the emergence of parlors that could secure stable profits under the new conditions. There was no change to the importance of pin adjustment, but these conditions facilitated the accumulation of management expertise and made it realistic for parlors to expect that adding machines – in other words, increasing the scale of their operations – would lead to growth in profit stability. In fact, the most striking expansion in the size of parlors in the history of the pachinko industry occurred during the 1960s. Moreover, this accumulation of management expertise and the still-unresolved problems of buyers and organized crime posed barriers to entry and stemmed the kind of growth in new parlors that the industry experienced during the early 1950s. These conditions developed during the 1950s as a precursor to the industry's experience during the 1960s.

Third, regulation by the police led to major changes in the nature of manufacturer competition. The ban not only reduced Masamura Shōkai, a powerful manufacturer with a nationwide market, to a regional contender, but also brought a challenging level of seasonality to manufacturers' operations. The emergence of Nishijin and Heiwa, which would become powerful industry leaders by the 1970s, was one of the striking developments of this period. The two companies shot to the top of the industry by developing popular products based on their designs of small accessories on display boards known as *yakumono*, given that the Masamura Gauge had become the industry's de facto design. As the speculative aspect of the game declined, it became necessary to keep customers from becoming bored by creating changes, however minor, to spark their interest. Masamura Shōkai's inability to respond to this transformation in the market by creating popular models is a critical part of any understanding of the characteristics of the new machine market that was emerging.

The change in machines brought about by the successive-shot ban and the permit system that governed newly introduced machines posed new questions concerning how regulations would be incorporated into the creation of fads and the associated development of pachinko machines. As individual parlors began operating more machines during the 1960s, it became possible for machine manufacturers to grow if they could secure a stable customer base in the market for regular machine replacements, even as they grappled with the business challenges posed by such seasonality. At the same time, manufacturers were forced to adapt to market instability caused by a stream of counterfeit machines and the problem of unpaid commodity taxes due to the decline in prices and technological retreat caused by the successive-shot ban. Imitation machines made a broad contribution to the formation of the pachinko market in many ways at the time of the Masamura Gauge's emergence. However, as the market shrank, unauthorized copies of machines pushed down prices and made it difficult for manufacturers that were committed to development to reap adequate profits. At the same time, price competition fueled by some parlors' refusal to pay commodity taxes not only sapped manufacturers' interest in developing new machines by exacerbating the downward trend in machine prices, but also led to the stricter regulation of the industry by highlighting its propensity for tax-evasion. The stabilization of manufacturers' businesses so that they could provide new models that offered stronger entertainment appeal to compensate for the less pronounced speculative element was to become the next issue in the industry's sustained development.

As this chapter makes clear, the instability of parlors' businesses during the early 1950s was the first challenge that had to be overcome in order for pachinko to develop as an industry. Ironically, this was accomplished even as an external factor – regulation – limited the speculative character of pachinko gameplay. Pachinko moved beyond festival-day entertainment and took its first step toward becoming an industry even as that element of machines was suppressed and as the amount of money spent by the average customer fell. The next problem facing the industry's development would be the establishment of a basis on which manufacturers could create machines to sell to parlors in a sustained manner. The sharp decline in the number of parlors during a time of technological retrenchment created borderline manufacturers that relied on underselling, and the machine market failed to encourage competition that would enable the accumulation of technology. This state of affairs gained recognition as a problem that threatened the viability of manufacturers, leading to calls for the organization of the machine market.

2

Organization of the Pachinko Industry: Why Did a Patent Pool Evolve?

INTRODUCTION

This chapter reveals the process by which the pachinko machine market, which had undergone severe disruption due to the Administrative Order Prohibiting Successive-shot Machines of 1955, reestablished order. For our present purposes, the market's dysfunctionality can be framed in terms of underselling and the price issues of the time. In their dealings with pachinko machine manufacturers, parlors rejected the addition of commodity taxes and patent fees to the cost of manufacturing in the calculation of machine prices, creating conditions ripe for underselling. Market competition spurred technological progress and productivity increases, and the associated falling prices were both the result of the industry's development and the mechanism by which that development proceeded. However, the prevalence of dumping was considered a factor in the normalization of low prices for pachinko machines from the second half of the 1950s into the 1960s. Because manufacturers were under pressure to sell their products below cost, with the result that commodity taxes and patent fees could not be incorporated into pricing, their very viability as companies was called into doubt. This chapter describes how market order was restored so that the industry could move beyond this situation. What factors led to market confusion, and how were they resolved? By describing these factors, I will outline yet another key condition that underpinned the continued existence of the pachinko industry.

As described in Chapter 1, parlors' discovery of a stable revenue base even as the ban on successive-shot machines dealt their businesses a serious blow provided a path to viability and even growth. In fact, the number of parlors stabilized during the 1960s, and the number of machines operated by the average parlor rose. By contrast, manufacturers continued to exit the industry until the 1970s (see Figure 0.3) as the sector embarked upon a long-term reorganization.

The contrast between the situations in which parlors and manufacturers found themselves, and especially the circumstances surrounding manufacturers' operations, are noteworthy from the standpoint of growth in the size of the industry. Although it is difficult to accurately ascertain the size of the market during this period, increases in the number of machines manufactured and installed leave no doubt that it was in fact expanding (see Figure 0.4).[1] The industry was growing, but it bears noting that this growth occurred after a reorganization in which the number of parlors plummeted briefly after the ban, and that manufacturers' exodus from the market was part of a long process by which excessive machine supply was rectified. If non-competitive businesses went under as a result of that process, the decline in the number of manufacturers may have been the result of a weeding-out process spurred by normal market competition.

That said, if we consider the fact that the market was growing, it would be inappropriate to treat the period of more than twenty years lasting until the 1970s as a single, sustained reorganization spurred by long-term fluctuations. Embracing such an approach would cause us to lose sight of structural problems and key moments of crisis. To dismiss the sequence of events as merely a process by which market competition led to the survival of the fittest is to risk obscuring the reality of how a variety of problems interfered with business operations and posed existential crises for the pachinko industry, along with the significance of the organizational initiatives undertaken to resolve those challenges.

My purpose here is to examine indirect evidence that points to the market's growth during the 1960s and thereby identify the characteristics of the industry's development during this period and clarify the manner in which the machine market grappled with the challenges it faced.

Market growth during the 1960s

The successive-shot ban of 1955 imposed limits on the speculative nature of pachinko gameplay while enhancing its dependence on skill. While the industry had attracted a broad cross-section of consumers up to that time, the 1960s saw the transformation of pachinko into a form of entertainment that was supported, to an overwhelming degree, by men.[2] The penetration of pachinko into society proceeded with the support of 'sararīman' (salarymen, meaning office workers), a new demographic that sprang into existence against the backdrop of Japan's period of rapid economic growth.[3] According to a 1967 survey conducted by the Economic Planning Agency that asked single workers what sort of leisure activities they enjoyed in March, more than half (54.1 percent) of all respondents cited pachinko, making it the most popular response among men.[4] A survey conducted the same year by a private-sector broadcasting company found *shōgi* (Japanese chess) and pachinko to be the first and third most popular forms of entertainment among manager-class employees, respectively, while pachinko was the most popular among white collar workers, artisans and laborers, and agricultural and fishery workers.[5] The category of 'sararīman' encompasses a broad range of industries and positions, and it is clear that pachinko was accepted by a broad cross-section of society, even if its customer base was dominated by young working males.[6] The pachinko-playing population at the time, with male salarymen as a market base, reached 30 million.[7] The comparatively low cost of pachinko was likely the economic reason for which it became part of males' lives. Although there are no systematic sources to back up this presumption, an overwhelming majority of customers resembled the 'nattily dressed gentlemen who quit after just 50 yen [about US$0.14] a pop' at one parlor in Kabukicho, Shinjuku Ward, Tokyo's premier entertainment district.[8] The extent to which average spending was indeed representative remains problematic, but there can be no doubt that patrons spent less on pachinko than they did on other forms of gambling. Years later, one observer remarked of the state of pachinko in 1972, 'Customers risked from 100 yen [about US$0.28] up to 1000 yen [about US$2.80] for from one to forty cigarettes worth around 80 yen [about US$0.22] in prizes. Unlike horse racing and other forms of gambling, there was no need to spend a fortune on a day's action [...] and unlike horse racing and gambling, one could play on a daily basis. In other words, pachinko was awfully petite bourgeoisie in character'.[9]

The game's easily accessible winning percentages also served to keep it well within reach of the daily spending habits of its demographic. A survey of pachinko fans by the pachinko magazine *Ado Sākuru* (AD Circle) in 1968 found that 45.8 percent of 2524 respondents were company employees who won prizes on one out of every 3.8 visits on average, compared to the typical fan, who won a prize on one out of every three visits.[10] Customers could win on their fourth visit, or even on their third visit if they honed their skills, fueling expectations that a win was just around the corner.

By the end of the 1960s, pachinko enthusiasts, drawn by expectations that they could win with a very reasonable investment, were visiting parlors as often as once every two days. At a little less than two hours, a session of pachinko accounted for a reasonably substantial amount of the free time customers had on any given day, a fact that was presumably influenced by the characteristics of those who frequented parlors.[11]

Parlors found a path toward stable management through pin adjustment and focused their hopes for growth on the expansion of the market for male customers, as described above, but the burgeoning economy of the time made improving labor-intensive operations a growing priority. The automated machine shown in Figure 2.1 (on the left), which had a mechanism that allowed balls to be supplied from inside the machine, was an ambitious design that addressed this issue. This machine inspired a chain of knock-on improvements and spurred innovation in the mechanism by which pachinko balls were dispensed and in the layout of parlors' floor space. The series of

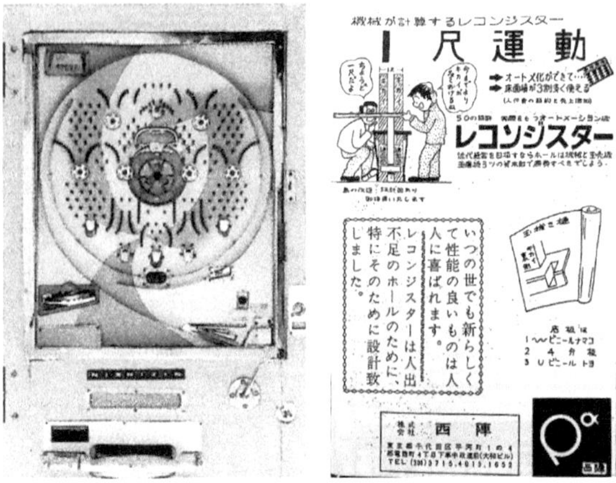

Figure 2.1: Reconjisutā, the first automated pachinko machine (1958; left) and an advertisement claiming the space savings that resulted (right).

Note: The advertisement claims the Reconjisutā will modernize parlors, help them deal with labor shortages and take up less floor space.

Sources: Left, Sōgyō Gojūnen Kinenshi Hensan Iinkai (2001: 39); right, Yūgi Tsūshin *(1961), '広告レコンジスター' (Reconjisutā advertisement), October 15.*

changes associated with the introduction of these innovations to parlors created the growth that characterized the pachinko industry during the 1960s.

Photo 2.1 depicts a parlor around 1955. It is unclear whether the photograph was taken before or after the ban on successive-shot machines, but it shows a busy parlor packed with customers. That the patrons stood instead of sitting, as they do today, suggests that they did not spend too long at the machines. The adoption of 'standing pachinko' in order to improve the profitability per unit of floor space by increasing turnover in confined spaces continued until the introduction of chairs during the 1970s.[12]

Note the women behind the machines. Known as pachinko *musume* (literally, 'girls'), these young female employees[13] stood all day in the cramped, narrow spaces behind machines, where they shuttled back and forth manually replenishing each machine's stock of balls. These women, the numbers of whom grew in direct proportion to the number of machines being operated, represented the most labor-intensive part of the business.

Balls had to be resupplied by hand because the number of balls that could be stored inside a single machine was limited, reflecting the manner in which pachinko was played at the time. Parlors employed two types of balls, each with a distinct function: (a) balls that circulated inside the machine after being purchased by customers and (b) prize balls that were 'paid out' by the machine.[14] Customers were completely absorbed by the prospect of winning, and their greatest area of concern was an error-

Photo 2.1: Manned machines (left, supply of balls before the introduction of automated machines, 1955) and space behind machines (right, 1956)
Source: Left, Hyakusu Henshūshitsu (1985: 23); right, Yūgi Tsūshin Henshūbu (2011: 27).

free and smooth supply of prize balls. Machines and other parlor equipment of the time were frequently not up to the task of making good on this expectation, which was natural enough on the part of patrons. Unlike today's systems, which supply prize balls automatically and without limit, machines in the 1960s drew on a finite supply of balls stored in a tank mounted on top of the machine. This tank had to be replenished once it had been emptied of balls. The frequency of replenishment varied by machine depending on the time of day and the level of use by customers, requiring that balls be added manually based on employees' judgment. Pachinko *musume* moved continually along the narrow aisles behind the machines, supplying prize balls as necessary.

Allowing a machine to run out of balls by botching the timing of replenishment was a sure way to garner customer complaints. For parlors, the manual replenishment process imposed losses from time spent moving around, and adversely affected sales. It also brought cheating on the part of workers, who conspired to sell balls on the black market,[15] among other schemes, creating problems that directly impacted operators' bottom lines. Parlor managers increasingly sought to automate the supply of balls so that this human element could be eliminated, thereby paving the way for higher sales by removing an impediment to continuous play and preventing various problems associated with the manual approach.

These were the circumstances when the machine shown in Figure 2.1 was invented and came into the market. The automated machine developed by Nishijin, a major manufacturer in those days, incorporated an automatic ball replenishment device on the back of the machine.[16] To be precise, the invention did not achieve full automation, but represented rather a more limited improvement that eliminated the work required to replenish balls from behind machines. These automated machines retained balls that fouled out inside the machine so that they could be dispensed as prize balls,[17] limiting the frequency of replenishment. This innovation eliminated the need to have *musume* collect foul balls from behind the machines and made it possible for prize balls to be supplied from the front or side. Without a doubt, automated machines increased the quantity of prize balls that could be dispensed, but there were limits on how efficiently balls could be supplied. Balls were supplied to individual machines, where they circulated until they fouled out; the supply, which was governed by the number of foul balls, was not unlimited.[18] Balls still had to be replenished manually. Nonetheless, the appearance of these machines eliminated the work that had been performed in the narrow aisles behind machines, removing the women shown in Photo 2.1 from parlors and marking the first step toward a fully automatic ball replenishment and recovery system. A series of innovations followed this design as ball replenishment mechanisms evolved towards independence from machines, including in 1963 the Uchū Paipu ('Space Pipe', from Nishijin), which supplied balls from a central repository to all machines in the parlor; in 1965 the Gekkō Rain ('Moonlight Line', also from Nishijin), which improved on the Uchū Paipu; in 1968 the Ōru Maiti ('All Mighty', from Takeya, a manufacturer of pachinko machines and automation equipment), which supplied balls to each island of machines; and in 1968 and 1969 the Sākitto ('Circuit', from Ace Denken, a major manufacturer of automation equipment for parlors), which featured a space-saving design.[19]

The redundancy of *musume* through technological progress even as the scope of the industry was being broadened to encompass computerized ball replenishment and recovery systems had significant effects on parlor management. First, it yielded salary savings by making parlors' operations less labor-intensive. The Japanese economy had been growing at an extremely rapid rate since the second half of the 1950s, prompting a manpower shortage that became more pronounced during the 1960s: 'The strong economy at the time is leading to concerns about employee shortages at parlors nationwide, with the exception of Hokkaido and parts of Kyushu. An increasing number of parlors have prepared to open but are unable to do so due to a shortage of employees'.[20] Nishijin's advertising, which proclaimed that 'a single, scarecrow-like girl can handle 500 machines behind the scenes',[21] targeted managers who were worried about manpower shortages (Figure 2.1, right) with a message that heralded machines as saviors that would resolve the challenges parlors faced, which were not generally seen as a good place to work. Automation of ball replenishment was expected to solve these problems.

Second, it put a stop to complaints from customers about slow replenishment and poor employee service, which were byproducts of handling ball supply manually.

Employees' laxness and associated oversight issues were resolved, and parlors' ability to exert overall control over their operations improved.

Meanwhile, the extra space vacated by *musume* offered an opportunity for growth. With the introduction of automatic machines, space that had been used to replenish and collect balls, as depicted on the right side of Photo 2.1, could be used for other purposes. As explained by the right side of Figure 2.1, the 'islands', as banks of installed pachinko machines were known,[22] shrank in width to approximately one-third of their former size, from about 90.9 centimeters to about 30.0 centimeters. As a result, parlors were able to fill 'about 30 percent more floor space' with islands that were 'exactly 30.3 centimeters', with the result that 'now more machines fit'.[23] In other words, the space taken up by aisles, which had been used for behind-the-scenes tasks, became surplus space, and the number of machines that could be installed in the same amount of parlor floor space increased. More machines meant parlors could expect higher sales. At the same time, indirect expenses such as the cost of land and electricity stayed the same, with the result that the change became one factor behind sustained growth in the parlor business due to the efficiencies gained from the reduction in labor costs spurred by the reduced dependence on labor-intensive processes.

In fact, the average number of machines per parlor increased, as illustrated in Figure 0.4. Growth in the average number of machines during the 1960s, for example the increase from eighty-three machines in 1961 to 166 machines in 1969 and to 188 machines in 1979, was striking compared to growth during the 1970s. During the first half of the 1960s, machines incorporating accessories known as *chūrippu* (tulips) became extremely popular, sparking what became known as the 'second golden age' of the pachinko industry as the number of parlors rose by 1589, from 8487 in 1957 to 10,076 in 1965.

Nature of the problem: pressure to exit the business

However, pachinko machine manufacturers came under pressure from extreme price competition. Over a decade, the number of manufacturers fell by one-third, from some sixty companies in 1960 to forty-two in 1966 and thirty-nine in 1970 (Figure 0.3). The situation didn't necessarily force uncompetitive companies out of business due to market principles. The unstable market environment that resulted from unfair competitive practices such as patent infringements and underselling, as described below, threatened the very existence of the industry's leading manufacturers.

This chapter focuses on manufacturers that suffered due to a challenging machine market environment even as the pachinko industry established itself on a trajectory of growth. It will shed light on problems that threatened to constrain the development of the industry while identifying the most difficult challenges it faced. Organization of machine manufacturers proceeded against the backdrop of market confusion from the second half of the 1950s into the 1960s. Key considerations in assessing this process include why machine manufacturers pursued organization during this period, the general direction and manner in which such organization proceeded, and the results it yielded.

In the process of overcoming the various problems that drove organization, developments centered on the establishment of the Japan Amusement Machine Patent Management Federation (Nihon Yūgiki Tokkyo Un'ei Renmei, or Nittokuren for short), which served as a patent pool, were particularly significant. By analyzing the role and functions that the Nittokuren was expected to fulfill and examining the conditions that the entity imposed on pachinko machine manufacturers, I will verify the validity of the proposition that the 1960s launched the subsequent development of the machine market.

The patent pool

As its name suggests, the patent pool served to 'bring together multiple patents', but the manner in which it is approached has become ambiguous in recent years due to the diverse range of possibilities unlocked by patent use.[24] In the field of law, an interpretation that holds that such pools 'allow multiple rights-holders to exempt one another from infringement liability and to work jointly to invent multiple new patents'[25] has been used in analyzing judicial precedents in the United States. The arrangement places participating companies on a comparatively equal footing. Due to the lack of commonly accepted definitions in areas such as strict rules related to right-holders and licensees, this chapter will limit its understanding of patent pools to the objectives of the Nittokuren and the functions it was expected to serve. In other words, the Nittokuren was an organization that pooled patents related to pachinko machines and managed them through licensing agreements and other means.

First, I will offer some preliminary observations about the relationship between development and patents in terms of the approach taken in this chapter. In the context of pachinko machine manufacturing, 'development' refers to the sequence of corporate activities that comprise the process by which manufacturers create new models that are characterized by a particular narrative concept or distinctive feature in response to seasonal sales. Consequently, development involves every aspect of a pachinko machine. The degree of refinement exhibited by a given machine during this period was significantly influenced by the physical durability of the machine and by manufacturing technology, which depended upon manual production processes.

Patents[26] are granted to mechanisms (parts) that meet a certain standard of novelty, as opposed to being granted to entire machines. Patented parts and mechanisms provide the means by which ideas and specifications take shape during development. Conversely, patents are sometimes created during the development process in order to give shape to the desired narrative concept. Patents are created as the result of the development process carried out by manufacturers day in, day out. To that extent, patents provide an effective means of ensuring that the results of the development process cannot be stolen by virtue of mere imitation.

On the other hand, patents may be used by other companies in the development of their own products since they are related to mechanisms (parts), and as a result, it may be necessary to license rights in the event that a revolutionary patent is developed. In this sense, the relationships between manufacturers concerning patents and development are characterized by dual aspects: competition and mutual dependence. It was only natural that under such circumstances a patent pool would be created. The Nittokuren was established to serve as a patent pool and was tasked with managing patents acquired by manufacturers as a result of development. However, mutually dependent relationships do not arise naturally within industry. Associated methods and manufacturers' expectations toward the Nittokuren took shape against the backdrop of a particular period and were neither uniform in content nor set in stone in advance.

Within research into patent pools, problems concerning the relationship of such structures to the Anti-monopoly Act and effects on innovation attract much interest, but there is little in the way of historical analysis of their formation.[27] In addition to well-known research into patent-related legal disputes in the United States,[28] the historical research of Shigehiro Nishimura in Japan is representative of the literature. Nishimura has described how patent pools in the heavy machinery and light bulb industries, as a pioneering case study in Japan prior to World War II, provided an effective means of coordinating rights with significance for the accumulation of patent and technology management skills.[29] However, such coordination was no simple matter in the pachinko industry, where most stakeholders were small and medium enterprises, and additional study is necessary to assess how the coordination process took shape in the context of the existential crisis facing the industry.

The Nittokuren became the target of an official exclusion recommendation issued by the Japan Fair Trade Commission in 1997 due to the limits it placed on competition among manufacturers and the obstructions it posed to companies wishing to enter the industry.[30] The organization was dissolved two years later in 1999, marking the end of the role it had played for about forty years since its formation in 1959. Although additional study is needed to determine whether the activities and functions of the Nittokuren actually hindered competition during the mid-1990s,[31] it is important to establish how the existence of this patent pool affected competition in the pachinko machine manufacturing industry following its formation. While the literature includes a brief historical explanation of the Nittokuren,[32] the process by which the pool was formed remains unclear. For the purpose of this chapter's analysis, I will remain cognizant of the relationship of these developments to their broader context in terms of such factors as the state of the machine market (i.e., the nature of competition among manufacturers), machine development and the involvement of entities other than patent right-holders such as parlors as I focus not only on the Nittokuren's patent management function, but also on the associated activities of manufacturers.

In this way, I first address the background against which the Nittokuren was established and the expectations it engendered, and then examine the relationship between the organizational process and the establishment of the Nittokuren. I then look at the mechanisms involved in the operation of the Nittokuren, before turning to the functions it carried out. Finally, I will examine the results of the establishment of the Nittokuren.

MARKET IN CHAOS: BACKGROUND TO THE NITTOKUREN'S FORMATION

Pachinko machines had been subject to guidance and licensing by police on a regional basis since before World War II, with the result that the industry was not governed in any clear way in line with systematic standards that cut across regions.[33] After the end of the war, the Entertainment Establishment Control Act of 1948 lacked specific provisions addressing machines, and it was left to police authorities in each region to determine what types of machines would be approved as necessary. It was only with the ban on successive-shot machines in 1955 that machines came under specific regulation, and it was significant that the measure required manufacturers to seek certification from local public safety commissions before machines could be sold.[34] Furthermore, the ban introduced strict and detailed standards on machines, which it classified into three types,[35] and required manufacturers to observe associated rules during the development process. Machines had been subject to standards that emphasized limiting speculative elements since around 1949, before pachinko became popular nationwide,[36] and the period of time until regulations were relaxed in 1969 comprises an ice age in terms of machine diversity insofar as the scope of manufacturers' development programs was tightly constrained.

Patent problems that arose early in the 1950s heralded a set of circumstances that would shake the entire industry at a time when development was subject to strict rules. The connection between pachinko and patents may seem surprising. Although it is not widely known, pachinko machines are assembled from numerous parts that draw on patented technologies. Setting aside parts manufacturers, machine manufacturers alone submit some 8000 patent applications every year, and about 75 percent of those are granted (figures as of 2014).[37] Dividing the number of annual applications by the number of machine manufacturers – thirty-six as of June 2016[38] – suggests that manufacturers developed patents at a rate of about one every two days. As of January 2016, the entire industry held about 40,000 patents.[39] That number attests to manufacturers' active development activities.

The importance of patent development for pachinko machine manufacturers attracted attention comparatively early in the history of the pachinko industry. However, the initial opportunity for manufacturers to actively acquire patents did not derive from their recognition of patents as an obvious method by which to pursue development. Since the business practices of respecting other companies' patent rights and paying technical fees for their use had not become established, manufacturers did not work to develop patents as a way to seek competitive advantage. The attention to patents was a historical product that arose as companies learned through the experience of becoming bogged down in disputes. This section will examine special period-specific issues that formed the background against which the patent pool was created while tracing the lengthy process by which patent rights came to be respected.

As described above, the Nittokuren was formed on June 3, 1959, with the goal of pooling and managing pachinko-related patents and promoting their development.[40] The pool was based on the idea of owning patents, for example by having the Nittokuren purchase patents from participating companies and industries, or by having the organization acquire patent rights by discovering or developing powerful patents itself. However, if we focus exclusively on the organization's patent acquisition and management, we risk losing sight of an important aspect of the pachinko industry during this period. I will examine patent disputes and the problem of underselling as the backdrop to the Nittokuren's formation while making a variety of multifaceted observations on topics such as expectations that a patent pool would encourage development, which facilitated the organization's establishment.

Patent disputes

At the beginning of the 1950s, when the pachinko industry was growing rapidly, patent problems engulfed the entire industry. That said, it is clear that patents did not carry much weight as a tool for protecting the exclusivity of inventions (through the exercise of associated rights). For example, Takeichi Masamura did not patent the Masamura Gauge despite concerns about counterfeit versions, and Kazuo Nagasaki obtained, but did not exercise, patent rights for the 'all-win' machines he developed. If Nagasaki had exercised his patent rights to these technologies, which served to ignite the popularity of pachinko as they spread broadly throughout the industry,

Table 2.1: Patent cases and outcomes (up to the formation of the Nittokuren)

Fiscal year	Case and action	Sequence of events	Patent dispute transitions
1953	Case (1): Infringement of patent and utility model rights by counterfeit versions of the Hōkoku-gō	Plaintiff/defendant: Hōkoku[a] v. Chūō Seisakusho Sequence of events: The plaintiff sought reimbursement for the cost of preserving evidence of patent and utility model right infringement (May to June). Moving to deal with the proliferation of counterfeit versions of a model known as the Hōkoku-gō in early 1953, Hōkoku took a series of actions including sending written notice of patent infringement and preserving evidence at its factory. The company characterized these actions as intended to protect customers who had encountered problems after purchasing counterfeit versions of the Hōkoku-gō machine gun-style pachinko machine. Award sought: Hōkoku sought reimbursement for the 780,000 yen (about US$2,167) it had spent on preserving evidence in addition to several million yen (not less than US$2,778) for utility model registration purposes.	Start
1954	Case (2): Utility model lawsuit targeting a reverse-ball ejection mechanism and an objection to rights held by Hōkoku	Case (2)-1 Plaintiff/defendant: Hōkoku Sangyō Co., Ltd., v. Hōkoku Decision: The case was decided in favor of Hōkoku. The plaintiff's motion was rejected, and the plaintiff was ordered to pay trial expenses (March 24, 1954). Case (2)-2 Plaintiff/defendant: Kansai Yūgi Co., Ltd., v. Hōkoku Decision: The case was decided in favor of Hōkoku. The objection to Hōkoku was found to lack merit, and Kansai Yūgi was ordered to pay expenses associated with the investigation of evidence (May 15, 1954).	
	Case (3): Objection to a countersuit involving rights held by the Tokyo Amusement Machine Manufacturing Industry Association (Tokyo Yūgiki Seizō Kōgyō Kumiai) and Hōkoku	Description: The lawsuit sought to invalidate Hōkoku patent No. 210472 (submitted February 19, 1952 and advertised February 19, 1954), whose scope extended to a recirculating plate mechanism. Sequence of events: Registration of this patent through action by the Tokyo Amusement Machine Manufacturing Industry Association prompted a sense of crisis as it prevented other manufacturers from making recirculating machines at the time. (President Ishihara of the association submitted the objection on April 16, 1954.) → Withdrawn	Intensification
1955	Case (4): Hōkoku v. Suzuki	Plaintiff/defendant: Hōkoku v. Suzuki Shōkai (February 1954) Decision (rendered June 15, 1955): 1. The defendant (Suzuki Shōkai) shall not manufacture, sell or make use of machines or products that infringe on utility model rights or patent rights held by the plaintiff (Hōkoku). 2. The defendant shall immediately dispose of any machines whose design infringes on patent rights. 3. The defendant shall make public apology by placing an ad in the newspaper of the plaintiff's choice. 4. The defendant shall pay damages to the plaintiff in the amount of 3,200 yen per machine manufactured or sold.	
	Case (5): Decision to file an objection in the form of a countersuit by the Zenkōren against Hōkoku (Hōkoku v. Association)	Description: Hōkoku notified industry associations and the industry, published a warning in a daily newspaper (May 27) and published a statement in an industry newspaper (presenting its view of patent problems). The Zenkōren announced its intention to oppose Hōkoku, along with President Takeuchi of the West Nagoya Industry Association, President Nakajima of the Greater Tokyo (Kanto) Industry Association and Nishijin Shōkai. On July 12, the decision was taken to file a suit to invalidate the Shōwa 29-1643 (1954) utility model rights held by Hōkoku. Sequence of events: The Zenkōren expelled Hōkoku. The group issued a joint statement on October 8. Addressing the problem of patent and utility model rights, the statement declared that member associations encouraged inventions and respected associated rights. Nonetheless, the dispute developed into a suit. Plaintiff/defendant: Hōkoku v. Takeya Shōkai (on the Zenkōren side)	

1956	***Problem of underselling***	On March 21, a general meeting of the Zenkōren adopted the practice of affixing member certificates to machines.	Transition (respect for patent rights and recognition of patents as the means of resolving the problem of underselling)
	Result of Case (5): Resolved out of court	On April 24, the suit was withdrawn, and Takeya Shōkai paid compensation for damages to Hōkoku.	
	Patent agreement (1): Hōkoku and Nishijin	On July 5, the parties announced a statement that signaled that respect for patents was gathering momentum.	
	Continued proliferation of counterfeit products	On September 25, products imitating those of Nishijin Shōkai appeared in Tokyo.	
1957	***Problem of underselling*** Patent agreement (2): Formation of the Nishijin Jinmitto Group	On March 26, a general meeting of the Zenkōren resolved to form the Fair Price Support Steering Committee. On June 3, the Jinmitto Association was formed. The official announcement read, 'New Jinmitto models can be purchased from the manufacturers listed to the left. Those companies are parties to Jinmitto technology licensing agreements. Nishijin Komāsharu Co., Ltd.'.	
	Patent agreement (3): Patent and utility model right licensing agreement between Hōkoku and six companies (dated July 5).		
	Problem of underselling and patents	Japan Amusement Machine Research Association: did not recognize Hōkoku patents and consisted primarily of businesses involved with invalidation trials. Japan Amusement Machine Invention Group: formed on September 20 to support prices by means of Hōkoku's patents. Dedicated to respecting inventors' (Hōkoku's) patents, the organization consisted primarily of companies that had entered into rights licensing agreements with Hōkoku, for example Nishijin and Heiwa. Explanation of the reason for the group's founding by its representative: 'Our main purpose is to prevent underselling of crude-quality imitation products in the face of the difficult standards that have been in place since the ban on successive-shot machines. Since the Zenkōren's previous efforts to support prices were not in fact undertaken in a thorough manner, we chose an approach that uses patents as a concrete means of ensuring strict observance of prices'. Members: Hōkoku, Heiwa Shōkai, Nishijin, Takeuchi Shōkai, Masamura Shōkai, Marudai Seisakusho, Tōkai Sangyō, Ōyamashiki Yūgiki Seisakusho, Shin'ei Shōkai, Nagasaki Shōkai (10 companies) On September 29, the Japan Amusement Machine Invention Group and Japan Amusement Machine Research Association agreed to use patents to eradicate price problems and counterfeit machines. On October 25, the Zenkōren Board of Directors resolved to form the Fair Price Promotion Committee.	Formation of the Nittokuren as a means of resolving the problem of underselling
1958	Case (6): Kurada Seru v. Association in a parts-related dispute	On May 15, Kurada Seru issued an evidence preservation notice to Okamura Yūki Co., Ltd. Sequence of events: The company decided to file a lawsuit to invalidate Kurada Seru's utility model in the event talks broke down. The association considered methods for using the rights of Toda, Haga and Uchigashima and tentatively adopted a proposal to affix Zenkōren certificate stamps to machines in order to ensure collection of cooperation fees.	

1958	Patent agreement (4): **Formation of the Heiwa Komikku Group**	'[...] Last year, Heiwa Shōkai launched its *komikku* mechanism [...] which became extremely popular in the industry, earning admiration throughout most of the country. Companies embraced the idea, but licensing fees for the associated rights ended up being significantly lower than initial levels as the result of talks between Chairman Toda of the Zenkōren and President Nakajima of Heiwa Shōkai at a tradeshow last September'. (October) Chairman Toda of the Zenkōren: 'The *komikku* gate invented by Heiwa Shōkai [...] is a revolutionary *yakumono* accessory [...] most manufacturers are moving to respect and confirm *komikku* rights [...]'. President Nakajima of Heiwa Shōkai: 'We'd like to receive 20 yen per machine and affix certificate stamps'. Wishing to 'leave methods and other matters to the Zenkōren, since the purpose of exercising rights is to support pachinko machine prices'[b], the company entrusted operations and other matters to the Zenkōren'. '[...] Mediation involving other companies' patent rights should also be respected. It's unclear how widely technologies will be adopted, but the Zenkōren's policy is to provide mediation services. Adopting this approach [...] will lead directly to growth of new models and development of the industry. Agreement amounts and other terms will vary with the companies involved, but we'd like to enter into agreements covering new models and rights from all manufacturers, if possible'. (November)	Formation of the Nittokuren as a means of resolving the problem of underselling
1959	***Problem of underselling and patents***	Concerning measures to support fair prices: 'Industrial property rights should be put into practice in an appropriate manner! [Takeuchi] It's all about managing industrial property rights in an appropriate manner [...] I think we'll see extremely heavy pressure brought to bear. I think it's a good idea to affix tax payment certificate stamps, but I believe there are loopholes. If we're going to manage industrial property rights in an appropriate manner, I think the approach will be more effective than tax payment certificate stamps. As a measure to accomplish that, we should have all current association members participate in an industrial property rights group and exert aggressive pressure on non-members, which I think will make fair price support an easy matter'.	
	Decision to form the Nittokuren	On April 21, the Zenkōren's annual meeting discussed forming a parent group for the Fair Price Promotion Committee, and it was decided to form the Japan Amusement Machine Patent Management Federation on June 3 (following discussions on May 7 and 15). 'The most important program of the Patent Federation is [...] fair pricing [...]'.	
	Purpose of the Nittokuren	'[...] The greater the motivation for research, the more registered rights such as patents, utility model rights and designs. Our public position was in favor of advance licensing from right-holders, but the inability to come to terms regarding problems of license fees and other issues led to truly miserable disputes among businesses [...]. We established the Japan Amusement Machine Patent Management Federation for the purpose of facilitating continuous exchanges of technologies among businesses involved in manufacturing so they could concentrate responsibility and good conscience in each machine, produce one promising machine after the next and fulfill their mission as suppliers in a satisfactory manner'.	

Notes:

a. Hōkoku = Hōkoku Yūki Seisakusho.

b. Underlined and italicized sections indicate the relationship to the establishment of the Nittokuren as a means of resolving the problem of underselling.

Source: Compiled based on relevant articles published by Yūgi Tsūshin *from 1953 to 1959.*

almost all of the machines installed in parlors at the time would have been covered by the resulting injunction.[41]

When we follow accounts of patent-related cases in industry newspapers of the time, we find that it was only after the popularity of pachinko had made market expansion a sure thing that legal disputes involving patents arose between operators and became increasingly intense. Table 2.1 offers a list of cases that had a pronounced impact on the industry.

The series of patent disputes that roiled the industry began in 1953 with a lawsuit in which Tokuharu Kikuyama of Hōkoku Yūki Seisakusho (an amusement machine manufacturer), the pre-eminent manufacturer of pachinko machines at the time, asserted patents he held on the basic structure of pachinko machines. (The company changed its name to Hōkoku Hanbai in 1961; I use 'Hōkoku' to refer to both below.) Hōkoku developed machines that attracted attention in the industry starting in 1952, including the 'All 20' successive-shot model it launched in 1953, a machine gun-style machine that shocked the industry. The machine was distinguished by a tray on the lower front into which pachinko balls were placed and a mechanism that moved the next ball into the launch position each time a handle was pulled. Customers could lose more money in one turn, with the result that the speculative element of play increased significantly compared to previous models.[42] The machine elicited praise for spurring the rapid growth of the pachinko market and combined technologies so revolutionary that problems stemming from the resulting speculative element prompted the ban on successive-shot machines.[43]

The patent on the circulating mechanism, which was Hōkoku's core technology, related to the basic structure of pachinko machines. The broad scope of the patent meant that it was effectively difficult to manufacture machines without using the technology. Other companies should have obtained Hōkoku's consent before using the technology to manufacture their own machines, but some machine manufacturers produced imitation versions of Hōkoku's new mechanism, as is evidenced by reports describing a market that was 'overrun with counterfeit Hōkoku units'. Case (1) in Table 2.1 likely marked the first time that Hōkoku employed legal means to address a serious patent rights infringement. The details are unknown, but based on the sequence of events that unfolded in other cases, it is likely that the case was decided in Hōkoku's favor. Hōkoku's patent rights were recognized as a result of cases (2) and (3), while the fact that disputes occurred repeatedly, as illustrated by case (5), provides evidence of Hōkoku's victories.

As suggested by the damages awarded as a result of this series of patent disputes, manufacturers on the losing side incurred considerable economic liabilities. For example, Suzuki Shōten, the defendant in the lawsuit described in case (4), *Hōkoku v. Suzuki Shōten*, was ordered not only to cease sales of machines that infringed on the patent rights in question, but also to pay damages of 3200 yen (about US$10.56) for each machine that had already been manufactured and sold. The magnitude of the burden that would have been imposed by such damages is apparent in light of the fact that Masamura Shōkai machines, which were considered a premium brand at the time, sold for an average of around 7500 yen (about US$20.83) (at wholesale; see Chapter 1). Case (5) was resolved when Takeya Shōkai agreed to a settlement.[44]

Incidentally, the industry-wide opposition to Hōkoku hints at the seriousness of the case's impact. In May 1955, when the ban on successive-shot machines took effect, Hōkoku ran ads in various newspapers warning the entire industry not to abuse the patents it held. In response, the National Confederation of Amusement Machine Manufacturing Industry Associations (Zenkoku Yūgi Kikai Seizō Kōgyō Kumiai Rengōkai, or Zenkōren for short)[45] considered using legal means to oppose Hōkoku's broad interpretation of the circulating mechanism. The small number of available articles support the inference that the Zenkōren took an uncompromising stance on the issue, including by forming a committee to discuss countermeasures; sanctioning a lawsuit by Takeya Shōkai, which held similar patents, to invalidate Hōkoku's patent rights; and even expelling Hōkoku from its membership.

A joint statement by both the Zenkōren and Hōkoku issued on October 8, 1955, declared that the parties would respect invention and design rights, suggesting that the problem was moving towards resolution. The acceptance of the concept of respect for patent rights was a major step forward that signaled a new approach with regard to rights. Nonetheless, Hōkoku subsequently filed a lawsuit against Takeya Shōkai. The circumstances remain unclear, but it can be inferred that the views of Hōkoku, the right-holder, were not sufficiently reflected in the new consensus. In this way, confrontations in the form of patent cases enveloped the entire manufacturing industry.

As described above, the Takeya Shōkai lawsuit was settled out of court. Regarding the manner in which this resolution was accomplished, one key takeaway is that the year 1956 signaled a turning point in disputes between manufacturers. It is worth examining a patent agreement between Nishijin and Hōkoku as a development that was emblematic of this change. The actions of Nishijin were definitive in the conclusion of the agreement. Nishijin, one of the industry's leading companies, had represented the Zenkōren's position in negotiations during the disputes with Hōkoku.[46] Nonetheless, the company came to emphasize respect for rights, expressing its wishes to 'stop all imitations and come to terms with Hōkoku' through this agreement.[47] This arrangement came about as follows.

The Hōkoku Type 2, a new model launched by Hōkoku in February 1956, caused a furor nationwide, from the Tohoku region in the north to Kyushu in the south, including in Tokyo.[48] Faced with the growing popularity of the model in Tokyo,

Nishijin, for which the area was a major center of operations, could hardly sit idly by in the face of the market's reaction, so the company sought to license the necessary rights from Hōkoku. Two separate offers were rebuffed by Hōkoku. It is not hard to imagine that Nishijin became impatient as it was unable to endure the strong demand for Hōkoku's machines.

Then came a reversal in the conditions that had seemed favorable from Hōkoku's perspective. Nishjin had sought only to borrow Hōkoku's circulating mechanism while using its own proprietary technologies for the mechanisms responsible for dispensing balls, depositing prize balls and propelling launched balls. However, Hōkoku's lawsuit to invalidate a circulating mechanism developed by the manufacturer Funashita on the grounds that it drew on its own technology was unsuccessful. In response to that verdict, Nishijin acquired rights and thereby gained a means by which it could avoid using Hōkoku's patents.[49] The dispute between the two companies became increasingly acrimonious as Hōkoku signaled its intention to file a lawsuit on the grounds that products that drew on the Funashita patents that Nishijin had acquired nonetheless violated its patent rights.

Incidentally, parlors naturally reacted by hesitating to purchase machines that could become the subject of disputes,[50] and the standoff between the two manufacturers ended up damaging their marketing efforts. This attitude on the part of parlors is interesting insofar as it suggests that long-running disputes about patents that adversely affected transactions with parlors were unwise for manufacturers. It bears remembering that these developments occurred against the backdrop of a market downturn (in the sense that the number of parlors purchasing machines was declining) following the imposition of regulations on successive-shot machines in 1955. The two companies could hardly continue a dispute that was adversely impacting sales. Ultimately, the incident was resolved with the agreement described above about two months after Nishijin's initial request – about half the time until the next slate of new machines was due to appear on the market.

This alliance ushered in a period during which manufacturers actively sought other companies' technologies, a trend that is illustrated by the formation of the Jinmitto Association (Jinmitto Kyōkai) and the Comic Group (Komikku Gurūpu). The move towards such technological alliances was propelled, and accelerated, by not only the need to avoid having patent disputes such as that seen in the *Nishijin v. Hōkoku* agreement process impact on sales to parlors, but also by the need to actively collect information about parlor intentions.

> To accommodate the preferences of our customers [parlors], we [Misono Seisakusho] had to manufacture *jinmitto* accessories ourselves. The only way for us to do that was to enter into a contract with Nishijin, the inventor, which is based in Kiryu,

> Gunma Prefecture, so that we could put our name on machines incorporating those accessories and sell them with pride, confident that we were acting within the law. As a result, we signed a manufacturing agreement to that end. Since some of our customers wanted the new *jinmitto* accessories at the time, we made a commitment to behave in a gentlemanly manner towards each other going forward.[51]

It seems fair to conclude that the manufacturers that chose to participate in the Jinmitto Association did so in response to requests (including latent demand) from parlors that wished to install popular *jinmitto* machines, as was the case with Misono Seisakusho. The term *komikku* ('comic') referred to mechanisms that functioned to move *yakumono* accessories,[52] and newspaper advertisements promoted models such as Tōkai Sangyō's 'Comic Gate' and Shin'ei Seisakusho's 'Comic Super'. The popularity of such mechanisms in the market spurred a stream of announcements of similar products that incorporated *komikku* technology.[53] Okumura Yūki launched a machine known as the 'Comic Gate' in 1957, and Nagoya Ginza launched one known as the 'Comic Center' in 1958. Both models became extremely popular.[54]

The decision-making process of manufacturers, which sought potential solutions to patent problems through trial and error, was likely influenced in a definitive manner by the perspective and reaction of the parlors that purchased their products. Against the backdrop of long-running legal disputes such as lawsuits related to patent rights violations and trials that sought to invalidate the patents in question in response, awareness grew of the need to respect patents (for example, through the regulation of counterfeit products) and advance negotiations so that these issues would not hinder production or sales activities.

The other aspect of Table 2.1 that I would like to emphasize here is changeover in the companies developing technologies and models that attracted attention in the marketplace. In short, there was a shift in development leadership from Hōkoku, which played the lead role from 1953 to 1956 through a series of lawsuits, to Nishijin of the Jinmitto Association, which was formed from 1957 to 1958, and Heiwa of the Komikku Group. Although the table does not include details, Narita Seisakusho, which developed and patented the *chūrippu* (in 1960 and 1962, respectively[55]), a tulip-shaped catcher (holes into which balls fell, signaling a win) that became extremely popular during the 1960s, deserves mention as a business that succeeded in developing new technologies due to the impact it had on the industry. Companies were not necessarily able to maintain their dominant position. Naturally, Hōkoku, which held patents for technologies with a broad range of applications, enjoyed comparatively long-term advantages. The company's patents were such that they could be used continuously as basic technologies for development over the duration of their validity. Such usage was highly likely as long as technologies that could circumvent the patents went undeveloped, or until Hōkoku's patents became obsolete. It may not be appropriate to attempt to characterize the yearlong machine replacement cycle as either long or short. That said, it bears noting that when the industry is assessed as a whole, it becomes apparent that the companies that led development of popular models shifted over time. Moreover, Hōkoku's basic technological patents did not cover popular models exactly. These phenomena signify that patent-based protection did not provide a long-term guarantee of competitive advantage.

Takeya Shōkai's lawsuit targeting Hōkoku marked the start of the industry's response, and the patent agreement between Nishijin and Hōkoku made it possible for Hōkoku, which held patent rights as a powerful outsider, to be drawn once more into the industry as an insider. In the midst of concerns about patent cases involving parts suppliers such as case (6), two groups were formed in 1957: one dedicated to respecting patents and seeking consent for their use in the way Nishijin had with Hōkoku's patents[56] (the Japan Amusement Machine Invention Group [Nihon Yūgiki Hatsumei Jisshi Konwakai, or Konwakai for short], described in Table 2.1) and another that rejected such patents and sought instead to have them invalidated through lawsuits (the Japan Amusement Machine Research Association [Nihon Yūgiki Kenkyū Kyōkai, or Kenkyū Kyōkai for short]). While it is true that industry participants did not necessarily view Hōkoku's patents in the same way or agree on how patents should be managed,[57] they were responding not only through one-on-one negotiation, but also by forming group-based technological alliances even as a trend toward respecting patents developed. As part of this process, the Nittokuren became responsible for organizational coordination, a burden that the entity came to feel quite keenly.

Several things are worth noting about the patent dispute process. First, respect for inventions and underlying motivations were not aligned. The pachinko industry's ability to quickly imitate popular models that incorporated innovations like the Masamura Gauge and 'all-win' designs had helped form the nationwide market. When the time costs of patent development involving associated technologies and transactions are compared to the ever-changing, popularity-based characteristics of pachinko, it is not obvious that respect for inventions would evolve in step with the industry's broader development. In fact, such respect developed not for its own sake, but rather as a result of the need to avoid hindering transactions with parlors and to minimize time losses as much as possible so that market demand for the quick introduction of popular models could be accommodated. Second, disputes were related to regulations. On the one hand, regulations had the potential to precipitate a technical transition in the manner of the 1955 ban on successive-shot machines and to invalidate past manufacturers' accumulated technologies. In this way, they amplified the industry's susceptibility to fads. On the other hand, they narrowed the scope of technological progress and ensured that all manufacturers pursued development in the same general direction. This was the background against which respect for patents developed.

The problem of underselling: price stabilization

The second background factor worth noting with regard to the establishment of the Nittokuren is that a variety of problems, including counterfeit machines, had been exerting downward pressure on machine prices and manufacturer profits. This price problem became more serious as the market contracted in the wake of the 1955 ban on successive-shot machines. A shared awareness finally developed throughout the industry of the need to stabilize machine prices to increase profits. This need was the lynchpin in the historical background that brought about the establishment of the Nittokuren. Solid, accurate evidence of price trends is not available. However, the problem of pricing, which was described as the problem of 'underselling' and which had been occurring since 1956 as shown in Table 2.1, was repeatedly taken up in the industry journals of the time. In this section, I will trace associated developments while paying attention to conditions in the industry at the time and comments related to underselling.

As the number of parlors continued to grow during the 1950s, the supply of pachinko machines failed to keep pace with demand. Some parlors reacted to slow delivery times by resorting to fabricating machines themselves, while other businesses actively entered what was a highly profitable seller's market. Heiwa Shōkai (referred to as 'Heiwa' below), which in 1991 became the first company in the industry to be publicly listed,[58] is an example of the former and a case in which a parlor changed businesses to become a manufacturer.[59] An example of the latter is Nishijin, where Kazuji Shimizu, a graduate of the Faculty of Engineering at Tohoku University, a prestigious national university, began producing machines after becoming aware of pachinko's popularity at the time.[60] It was not unusual for companies to operate both parlor and manufacturing businesses[61] in the manner of Masamura Shōkai, as described in Chapter 1, and Takeya Shōkai, a representative supplier of automatic ball-dispensing systems. That this was possible indicates the dependence of machine manufacturing at the time on household-based handicraft manufacturing, as well as the relatively low technological barriers facing would-be machine makers.

The 1955 ban on successive-shot machines placed a significant burden on manufacturers. Despite a shrinking machine market and falling unit prices,[62] comparatively low technological hurdles made it easy to enter the business, and both parlor-made machines and new manufacturers exerted additional downward pressure on prices.

The commodity tax only exacerbated the situation. The tax, which was introduced in 1952, was initially imposed at a rate of about 20 percent on machine prices. However, the complexity of the industry's production structure made it difficult for the government to accurately assess the actual state of manufacturers' businesses. The passage below, which likely predates the imposition of the commodity tax, describes the high level of frustration felt by officials responsible for tax enforcement in the city of Nagoya, which was home to an increasing proportion of pachinko machine manufacturers and suppliers, as they attempted to assess such conditions and quantify taxes. The citation is a long one, but I include it here because it describes the state of pachinko machine manufacturing, which influenced price-setting, in 1952.

> There are almost no pachinko manufacturers that operate an integrated business that extends from manufacturing to sales. Work is farmed out by subcontractors to more subcontractors, and components are passed around until before you know it, the product is completed and being sold all over the country. It's completely unclear who has done what, or how much money work was sold for. The process is distributed among a varied network of workers who complete their respective tasks according to blueprints – one to cut out the plywood sheets; one to hammer in the pins; one to drill the holes; one to decorate the screens with balls and mitts, flowers and fruit, "All 10" and "All 20"; one to make the fixtures on the back; and one to punch out the nameplates. It's surprising to see – some workers are diligently cranking out piecework at home without any idea that what they're making will be used in pachinko. The situation puts us at a complete loss as to where we should start casting our nets. I just mentioned nameplates, but they're all nonsense. Models come one after the next as if they're just trying to annoy us. Either way, the moment it suits them, companies will change businesses, and new manufacturers spring into existence one after the next, making it extremely difficult to ascertain what's actually going on. That said, starting this year we plan to embark on a thorough survey since these products can't be overlooked as the targets of an important tax. In any case, the people running brick-and-mortar pachinko parlors can't run or hide, but the people making the machines, who operate out of sight behind the scenes, are tricky adversaries. My goal is to identify one and then bring it to an end.[63]

Machine producers were clearly able to launch businesses with extreme flexibility while drawing on Nagoya's extensive base of subcontractors to respond to the rapidly growing popularity of pachinko. From the perspective of the government, which wished to make assessments and levy taxes, the dispersed production structures that underpinned economic actors' ability to respond quickly slipped all too easily through the net of regulatory identification, making them seem like nothing but a hidden nuisance. In light of these conditions, it is likely that neither the rate at which authorities accurately ascertained tax liability nor the rate at which manufacturers paid the assessed amounts was particularly high. Manufacturers reacted strongly to the taxes, and the Tokyo Ball Amusement Machine Manufacturing Industry Association (Tōkyō-to Kyūyūki Seizō Kōgyō Kumiai) and Nishijin filed lawsuits in an effort to have the tax invalidated.[64]

After 1955, the machine market became a buyer's market, and manufacturers found it increasingly difficult to shift the commodity tax onto product prices due to intense price competition. As economic conditions deteriorated, it was only natural that the sector would be rife with illegitimate businesses[65] that dumped products on the market without paying patent fees or commodity taxes and parlors that manufactured their own machines. A newspaper article described conditions in 1956 as follows:

> It is not true everywhere in the country, but in some areas, legitimate factories are wholly unable to compete due to current price competition for single-shot machines. This practice of dumping not only completely fails to cover legitimate factory costs, sales costs, commodity taxes and business taxes, but also entails products being sold at a loss, significantly below cost. This state of affairs did not begin just now, but rather reflects an anomaly that started around last fall [after the 1955 ban on successive-shot machines], and it has been the source of many headaches for manufacturers specializing in single-shot machines.[66]

Dumping spread after the ban, forcing manufacturers into the difficult position of intense, price-based competition that undercut the costs calculated by adding up various expenses and taxes. At the time, one could find phenomena that signaled non-payment of taxes everywhere, for example in the existence of manufacturers that did not declare tax assembling pachinko machines in 'attics' without operating a company or putting up a sign and in the filing of fewer tax returns than there were manufacturers, the latter due in part to anemic sales.[67] 'The number of parlors that were unaware that prices included commodity tax was not insubstantial',[68] with the result that underselling – pricing that barely maintained profitability as long as the manufacturer did not pay taxes – effectively pushed down the tax payment rate even further and created a vicious cycle that made it more difficult to maintain prices.[69]

Some observers noted that a few leading manufacturers were selling machines at normal prices.[70] However, the existence of low-cost manufacturers producing counterfeit products and using 'whatever nameplate you like, including Ginza Shōkai, Okumura Monako, Heiwa and Nishijin'[71] was a factor that threatened the businesses of leading manufacturers over the long term. For example, a machine known as the Half-gauge Circulating Speed Type 2, which Hōkoku launched in March 1955, gained popularity only to have the poor quality of imitations sow doubts among parlors and undermine the model's reputation among customers, with the result that its popularity was short-lived.[72] Since Hōkoku and other leading manufacturers were the companies that developed patents and popular models, the emergence of an endless stream of counterfeit products had the potential to reduce development incentives. In this way, price stability came to be seen as a life-or-death problem by leading manufacturers and the industry as a whole.

Although the issue was addressed by the entire industry, initiatives to standardize prices during the second half of the 1950s were not effective. For example, the Zenkōren began issuing Zenkōren certificates in an effort to support prices in June 1956 and placed ads in industry newspapers asking parlors to 'Talk to responsible Zenkōren members about machine purchases'.

> Recently, the Zenkōren created a certificate to help establish the industry by preventing the underselling of illegitimate machines, which is hindering the industry's development, and distinguishing between fly-by-night manufacturers and legitimate businesses. A certificate like the one shown to the right will be affixed to each machine sold by members of the group on its left side as a symbol of trustworthiness and responsibility. The group is asking parlors to look for the stickers and to talk to responsible members when they need to purchase machines.[73]

In addition to attempting to offer guidance concerning fair price points to insiders (members of the association), the group called on parlors to accept the above initiatives. It also undertook measures such as standardizing selling prices with the purpose of cooperating with tax collection efforts. However, as a result of the intense sales war, Zenkōren's efforts to monitor machine sourcing by affixing certificate stickers went mostly unimplemented[74] before being abandoned the following year.[75]

In light of the existence of parlors that fabricated their own machines and fly-by-night manufacturers, it is likely that the group's guidance on outsider underselling failed to make much of a dent in the problem. As a voluntary group, the organization was unable to treat all manufacturers as members, and its ability to influence the market was limited. The real issue lay with toothless regulations against rule violations and with the discovery and regulation of the illegitimate businesses that were interfering with efforts to maintain prices.

The exercise of patent rights attracted attention as a specific means of regulating the illegitimate businesses that had become the industry's focus. Above I described how associated efforts in the industry took two directions – embraced by the Konwakai and the Kenkyū Kyōkai – even as it respected patents. The two factions agreed to work toward establishing order in the industry, for example by taking advantage of patents to maintain prices, and formed a price support steering committee as a preparatory step on the way to establishing a fair price promotion committee at the Zenkōren in October 1957.[76]

Ensuring support for fair prices was of existential importance to manufacturers, and in fact there was an active push to use patent rights, as had the Komikku Group, as an effective means of controlling manufacturers who tried to engage in outsider behavior that disturbed prices.

> Supporting fair prices is being described as a life-or-death problem for manufacturers, and the Fair Price Support Steering Committee was formed for this reason. There are calls for the elimination of fly-by-night manufacturers as the fastest way to support prices, and the Steering Committee is working to use patent rights for that purpose. The Aichi (prefecture) Amusement Machine Industry Association has entered into a licensing agreement with Heiwa Shōkai covering that company's *komikku* accessories, which are fast becoming a fixture in the industry, in order to ensure respect for rights and price support, and the Tokyo Ball Amusement Machine Manufacturing Industry Association has adopted a similar policy.[77]

Awareness of the need to find an ongoing and organizational solution to the problem of repeated underselling was growing.

That said, each in a series of lawsuits that began in the Tokyo District Court in 1953 seeking to invalidate the commodity tax was dismissed by the Supreme Court in 1958.[78] The rulings resulted in payment of the tax, including unpaid amounts that had accrued, signaling a tightening of regulations concerning tax payment and evasion. The Nittokuren was organized in several stages against the backdrop of growing recognition that resolving patent disputes and tax payment problems was a precondition for maintaining fair prices.

Expectation to promote development

Once it became clear that a new organization centering on the legal regulatory capability of patents was being set in motion in order to resolve the problems of patent disputes and price support, the new organization became the focus of growing expectations that it would also develop new technologies. Expectations that the entity would jump-start development were the third factor encouraging the establishment of the Nittokuren.

This pinning of hopes on invention not only through the hard work of individual companies, but also via organizational initiatives, reflects the fact that machine development was being constrained by the strict regulations of the time. In addition to banning successive-shot machines in 1955, the National Police Agency had announced a series of certification standards for pachinko machines. Development was limited to a framework of detailed standards related to the physical construction of machines, and manufacturers were prohibited from selling machines before they had been certified (see Chapter 1). In light of the problem of underselling described above, it was likely unrealistic for manufacturers, which were mostly small and medium-sized companies, to pursue development on their own within the scope allowed under the regulations, particularly while carrying out basic research related to patents.

As a result, the pachinko machine industry came to recognize the problems being faced by manufacturers, and organizations such as the Konwakai and the Kenkyū Kyōkai, which had been formed in 1957 to address those problems (see Table 2.1 above), were expected to pursue inventions and their use.

It is clear that the Konwakai, whose membership consisted primarily of such leading companies as Hōkoku, Nishijin and Masamura Shōkai, was formed with the intention of revitalizing patents and member companies' ideas and promoting their use in the industry. Representative Kenkichi Nakajima of Heiwa described the situation after 1955 as follows:

> *Regulators' certification standards were extremely narrow and limited, making it extremely difficult to come up with new machines.* [...] Naturally, the ideas and rights of inventors should be respected, and that respect leads to better machines and higher motivation on the part of the inventors. [...] Those of us who think seriously based on those intentions have gathered and tried again and again to argue for things that would bring profit to the industry, but the lack of results has made controlling the situation with legally-backed power unavoidable. As is stipulated in our organization's bylaws, *we also promote the use of new inventions that are not yet protected by right as long as the industry recognizes value in those inventions that will contribute to its development.*[79] (Emphasis added.)

The content for which I've substituted ellipses at the beginning of the quotation emphasized that overcoming the constraints imposed on development by regulations would not be easy. The italicized portion of the quotation describes the group's stance with regard to its operational methods. In light of the industry's characteristics, it is deeply interesting that popular fads changed so drastically – that companies continued to supply different machines by developing new machines every season. In short, the fact that the process of applying for a patent, disclosing the patent and advertising the product after its invention required an indefinite amount of time suggests that manufacturers could expect to stay ahead of the market's changing fads by recognizing one another's inventions before the patent system yielded official results. For example, companies entered into agreements concerning *komikku* mechanisms, which became popular in the market, before they were patented. The industry had identified respect for, and mutual use of, patents as mechanisms that underlaid an environment that encouraged inventions. However, the Konwakai went no further than incentivizing invention in the form of respect for patent rights and references to their mutual use and associated methods, leaving research and development decisions to individual companies.

By contrast, the Kenkyū Kyōkai, whose membership consisted of comparatively smaller manufacturers, emphasized the pursuit of technological research in its role and perspective, and it evaluated exceptional machines and offered prize money to their inventors.[80] While incentives such as evaluation-based prize money had the potential to motivate inventors, the organization's role as a research institution was poorly defined and lacked specificity in terms of systematic activities.

Although they embraced different approaches regarding patent management, the two groups shared a desire to promote development within the industry by encouraging invention. From within the constraints imposed by regulations a desire had emerged amongst manufacturers to develop proprietary models even if that involved using other companies' patents and to produce machines by licensing the patents that protected technologies used in popular machine models. The kind of organized cooperation embodied by such groups attracted high expectations in terms of the ability to discover promising technologies, assist in patenting them and publicize them in order to encourage further machine development.

ORGANIZATION OF MANUFACTURERS AND THE NITTOKUREN'S FORMATION

Even if the commodity tax could be incorporated into machine prices with the consent of parlors under conditions that applied equally to all manufacturers, respect for patented technologies imposed different conditions on different manufacturers as licensees and licensors. Manufacturers that licensed patents were forced to absorb royalties as a cost, placing them at a disadvantage in price competition. Various problems related to methods for resolving patent disputes and price stabilization issues as well as expectations for breakthrough solutions led via a complex path to intense price competition, gradually developing into challenging conditions that exceeded individual companies' ability to respond. Yet because the various initiatives such as collaboration among groups to resolve these problems involved different players, each with its own interests and objectives, they were invariably beset by continual confrontation. For this reason, the organizing process proceeded slowly in fits and starts. Hints of how a substantial solution could be achieved came when patent management was linked to price stabilization measures.

The Fair Price Promotion Committee mentioned above was a concrete example of this trend, and it was formed within the Zenkōren in 1957 to provide price support through the exercise of patent rights. Document 1 below is a proposal outlining a program of activities that would be undertaken by the committee. Using this document as a means of studying the functions that the Fair Price Promotion Committee was expected to perform, we can identify important clues for understanding the mechanisms of the Nittokuren, for which no similar materials remain.

Document 1

Operation Plan[81]

I. In order to achieve the objectives listed below, it is essential that patent rights be applied.
   (a) Underselling must be prevented.
   (b) Parlors that produce their own machines must be eliminated.
   (c) Illegitimate parts businesses must be eliminated. These businesses manufacture parts that infringe on third-party rights and sell them to businesses that go unreported. It is safe to say that these businesses comprise a hotbed of underselling.
   (d) Businesses that imitate the trade names of member companies must be excluded from the market.
   (e) Businesses that violate agreements must be eliminated.
   (f) There is a broad range of other means that can be used to support fair prices. According to Article 273 of the Anti-monopoly Act, the provisions of the act do not apply to the exercise of rights under the Copyright Act, Patent Act, Utility Model Act, Design Act or Trademark Act.

II. The right to license patent rights is limited to members.

III. The practice of affixing certificate stamps must be abandoned because it causes deficiencies in operations.
   (a) It may lead to the proliferation of counterfeit machines.
   (b) When certificate stamps are affixed by **right-holders** [emphasis added], such activity may constitute monopolistic behavior by some manufacturers of pachinko board parts.
   (c) The practice of affixing certificate stamps at one location could invite delays in members' production.
   (d) Affixing certificate stamps forces the disposal of products that are returned or repossessed due to non-payment.

IV. Licensing agreements, production volume assessments and payment of licensing fees.
   (a) Agreements shall be entered into at the time and date chosen by the right-holder.
   (b) The Fair Price Support Committee will form an assessment committee with several members to conduct monthly production volume assessments.
      (i) Members shall submit a production breakdown to the confederation no later than the fifth day of each month and remit licensing fees no later than the tenth day of each month.
      (ii) If the remitted amount is deemed insufficient, the Assessment Committee may request additional payment.
      (iii) The Assessment Committee shall investigate licensees' conditions and exercise care to facilitate smooth operations between licensees and right-holders.

V. In the event of companies acting in violation of fair pricing, the Assessment Committee may request right-holders to cancel agreements. In such cases, the right-holder must accept the request.

VI. The confederation shall carry out public relations campaigns related to the priorities enumerated in (I), and it shall endeavor to increase the rights of members.

VII. Right-holders shall support the goals of the confederation and endeavor to utilize patent rights effectively and to otherwise raise funds. Right-holders shall remit a predetermined percentage of the fees they collect to the confederation.

Fair Price Promotion Committee
November 22, 1957

As is recognized in (I), the document clearly identifies the use of patent rights as a powerful means of establishing order in the market. At the same time, it throws into relief the limits of the initiatives that had been undertaken to date. The first such limit involves the difficulty of the certificate stamp program (described in [III]). The document suggests that the Zenkōren's attempt to use certificate stamps to stabilize prices had experienced a series of setbacks. Difficulties included not only counterfeit certificate stamps, but also a variety of issues involving the location at which such stamps should be affixed and problems related to payment collection.

The second limit revolves around the inadequacy of programs related to the Assessment Committee's activities. Item (b) in (IV) makes a committee consisting of only a few members responsible for assessing production information but leaves the specific procedures associated with this activity undefined. For patent right-holders, the accurate assessment of the number of machines produced and shipped by manufacturers licensing their patents is extremely important. The same is presumably true for the Zenkōren (and its Fair Price Promotion Committee), which wished to extend the legal power of patents to all machines being sold in the market. That was because such assessment has the capability to catch machines shipped by manufacturers seeking to evade monitoring. However, (IV) fails to specify how the accuracy of the production and shipment information provided by factories each month will be assured. The document raises doubts about the suitability of the methods used to secure personnel and conduct assessments and about the committee's investigatory capabilities. Presumably the costs associated with these activities cannot be ignored, but the document avoids addressing the practical methods through which the committee's monitoring mechanisms will operate.

The third limit involves right-holders' motivation for cooperating with the proposed program or accepting the associated structures, which the document leaves unclear, particularly with regard to the benefits that (V) and (VII) offer right-holders. As is made clear by (VII), the operational expenses that are to be incurred by right-holders reflect the Assessment Committee's management costs. For right-holders, the balance of those costs and associated benefits are the key consideration in deciding whether to participate in the initiative. The implementation and success of the proposed program would depend on the degree to which cooperation could be elicited from right-holders.

Subsequent events involving the proposal are unknown. Noteworthy activities in the area cannot be confirmed, and it is likely that the organization was unable to overcome the various problems anticipated above. The long path to the establishment of the Nittokuren led to the coordination of views with right-holders, which was left unclear in the proposed program, and the design of mechanisms that overcame the problems associated with certificate stamps.

The failure of the Fair Price Promotion Committee to undertake noteworthy activities or generate results can also be inferred from the fact that the interests of individual companies with regard to resolving the price support issue were not completely incorporated into activities centering on the Zenkōren, but rather coordinated by other means. The Komikku Group, which I mentioned above, was formed by leading companies in November 1958 to license the *komikku* mechanisms that were popular at the time.[82]

On the other hand, the Nittokuren was formed in June 1959 as a voluntary group dedicated to resolving patent dispute problems, maintaining market order and other conditions to facilitate competitiveness (price stabilization), and jointly developing patent rights with a core membership that overlapped with that of the Kenkyū Kyōkai, which consisted primarily of small and medium-sized businesses.[83]

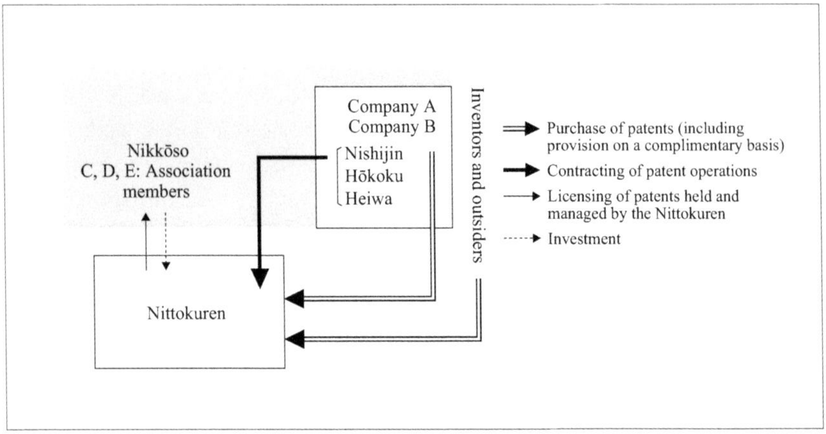

Figure 2.2: Organizational structure of the Nittokuren (1960 to 1972)
Source: Compiled by the author based on related materials, interviews and other sources.

However, the limits imposed by the Nittokuren's Kenkyū Kyōkai-centric membership were thrown into relief at the time of its founding. Critics pointed out that the new group had failed to sufficiently reconcile its views with those of right-holders, calling it a 'league of licensees'.[84] Even at the time of its founding, the right-holders of the time, for example Hōkoku and Narita Seisakusho, which developed *chūrippu* accessories, were not involved. Since leading manufacturers that had already entered into individual patent agreements with Hōkoku were non-cooperative, the practice of affixing certificate stamps issued by the Nittokuren to certify payment of patent fees (i.e., the practice of paying patent fees) was not thoroughly implemented.[85]

Confrontations involving right-holders and licensees, and between leading companies and small and medium-sized businesses, settled down with the gradual inclusion of right-holders as the cooperation of leading manufacturers such as Heiwa was obtained.[86] Driving that process was an industry-wide organization whose principal purpose was to resolve price problems. Specifically, that organization took form in the establishment of the Japan Amusement Machine Industry Association (Nihon Yūgiki Kōgyō Kumiai, or Nikkōso)[87] and the National Confederation of Amusement Machine Merchant Associations (Zenkoku Yūgiki Shōgyō Kumiai Rengōkai, or Zenshōren).[88]

The Nikkōso was formed on February 15, 1960, with the dissolution of the Zenkōren, which had been a voluntary group, and the subsequent establishment of a legal corporation under the Small and Medium-Sized Enterprise Cooperatives Act. In light of the sequence of events that led to the development of a consensus concerning the affixation of tax certificate stamps through discussions with the National Tax

Agency in 1959, the new entity can be thought of as the result of internal industry efforts to address tax evasion undertaken in accordance with the regulatory guidance it received concerning the problem of non-payment of taxes.[89] In short, the industry, reacting to a series of confusing conditions that included the prosecution of multiple manufacturers during 1959 as part of a regulatory crackdown on non-payment of the commodity tax, settled on a solution in the form of a plan that called for the formation of a cooperative with the goal of facilitating tax payments in accordance with guidance provided by the National Tax Agency.[90] The principal activities undertaken by the new group, and its purpose, consisted of managing members' payment of taxes by 'issuing guidance related to cooperation with the commodity tax, issuance of certificate stamps and improvement of tax payment', leading it to embrace a close partnership with the Nittokuren.[91]

The Nikkōso counted thirty-one manufacturers as members when it was formed, and that number had grown to forty by July 1960 and then to fifty-seven by January 1961, when its membership included most of the manufacturers that were actively producing machines at the time.[92] The group, whose principal purpose consisted of administering a joint commodity tax payment program and whose establishment grew out of expectations that such activities would serve to stabilize prices, had manufacturers contribute to a tax reserve fund and offered guidance to members concerning payment of taxes. On July 1, it began issuing and managing cooperative certificate stamps certifying payment of the commodity tax (or more precisely, certifying either that the tax had been paid or that the product in question was a low-cost machine that was exempt from the tax) in order to guarantee that applicable taxes had been paid for members' machines that bore the stamps. In addition to the phrase 'Reported to the National Tax Agency', the issued stamps bore the name of the Nittokuren, with the agency's authorization, in order to integrate the program with the patent certificate stamps that had already been issued by that group.[93] Through the joint management of certificate stamps, the Nikkōso and Nittokuren developed structures to facilitate efficient organizational collaboration.

In response to the establishment of the Nikkōso, the Nittokuren reorganized itself into a joint-stock corporation with capital of 2 million yen (about US$5556) with about fifty members of the Nikkōso as investors.[94] The new entity established programs related to the acquisition, sale and licensing of industrial property rights and undertook operations related to fostering the development of new products and facilitating the manufacture of pachinko machines. The new corporation used invested funds to purchase industry patents to create a basis for its activities. As illustrated in Figure 2.2, entities interested in licensing patent rights owned by the Nittokuren entered into an agreement with a member (the manufacturer) of the Nikkōso to authorize use of the patent and then paid a set patent fee to the Nittokuren.

The Nittokuren also sought to facilitate transactions between patent right-holders and licensees by handling certificate stamps related to rights owned by Hōkoku and Heiwa[95] and by accepting patent-related contract work as necessary.

MECHANISMS OF THE NITTOKUREN

Regulatory mechanisms

The point of departure in achieving a functional organizational process with the objective of price support was a mechanism that centered on certificate stamps that were jointly managed by the Nittokuren and the Nikkōso. These stamps made it possible to efficiently discover illegitimate businesses. However, that capability alone is not sufficient for a functioning mechanism. As was made clear by the proposed program for the Zenkōren, included above as Document 1, it was also necessary to resolve problems associated with patent licensing.

A number of institutional defects account for the failure of price stabilization measures based on the issuance of certificate stamps by the Zenkōren in 1956. In short, non-members were naturally unable to effectively regulate members that violated the rules, even if they failed to affix certificate stamps issued by the Zenkōren, which was a voluntary organization. As was pointed out with regard to the Fair Price Promotion Committee's proposed program, management of certificate stamps required the development of a consensus through the harmonization of various interested parties in relation to the problem of counterfeit machines, the method by which stamps were to be affixed to machines and the setting of patent fees.

The first step was to ensure that members were bound by regulations by incorporating the Nikkōso and making membership mandatory for companies wishing to join the Nittokuren. As I mentioned above, the Nikkōso was a legal group with the goal of managing members' payment of national taxes. The group was able to impose predetermined penalties on members who violated its rules, for example by expunging them from its rolls. These regulations were made materially effective by linking the ability to use patents managed by the Nittokuren with legally binding punitive measures. Tax payment certificate stamps were in the process of being reborn as a program that signified the strengthening of such organizational management. Before these developments, the Nittokuren regulated the behavior of insider businesses by means of contractual terms; afterwards, it became the subject of expectations that it would function as an organization that could wield powerful regulatory authority through legal means such as lawsuits, including over outsider businesses. In this way, institutional limits were improved in a comprehensive manner. The following describes an instance in which a warning from the Nittokuren served just this regulatory purpose:

> Starting on July 1 [1960], the Japan Amusement Machine Patent Management Federation [the Nittokuren] began treating pachinko machines not bearing commodity tax cooperation certificates as a sign of non-support for its objectives and of the violation of the industrial property rights of various types managed and administered by the federation. As a result, the federation began, without delay, "reluctantly taking civil and criminal legal measures to halt the manufacture and use of machines" that did not bear the certificates.[96]

The Nittokuren was incorporated in 1961 with roughly the same membership as the Nikkōso as shareholders, as illustrated in Figure 2.2 above. The organization limited the licensing of patents to investors and contractually required licensee manufacturers to affix certificate stamps. In short, Article 4 of its licensing agreement, 'Principle of affixing certificate stamps', defined the methods by which stamps certifying the payment of royalties had to be affixed to machines along with other obligations.[97] When selling machines, manufacturers were required to purchase certificate stamps and attach them to machines before they could be shipped.[98] The specific methods by which the Nikkōso collected patent fees and issued certificate stamps remain unclear. Only a template for the agreement remains, including Article 5, 'Purchase method and payment of license fees', which notes, 'The licensee shall remit the licensing fees set forth in Article 3 to the right-holder by exchanging funds in the amount of ___ yen for certificate stamps'.[99] The amount is not specified. A published machine manufacturing cost sheet included a licensing fee of 300 yen. The fee was broken down into a 100-yen fee that covered miscellaneous expenses and certificate stamp administration (50 yen each for the Nikkōso and Nittokuren) as well as a licensing fee of 200 yen (Hōkoku, others).[100] Use of this method is likely to have continued based on the fact that at the time the Nittokuren was formed in 1959, companies had to submit the agreement they had signed with parlors when purchasing certificate stamps, which typically specified the number of machines being purchased and the price.[101] It is interesting to note that the Nikkōso and the Nittokuren gained an understanding of how many machines each company was manufacturing – information to which other companies were not ordinarily privy – when certificate stamps were purchased, which was also when patent fees were paid.

Article 14, which was added to the agreement at a later date, is noteworthy from the standpoint of price support. According to the surviving template, 'In the event the licensee violates the instructions of the right-holder or is deemed likely to cause excessive disruption to the normal business relationships of the market, for example by selling machines below cost or otherwise engaging in unfair competition, the right-holder may impose limits on the number of licensed machines'.[102] This provision explicitly sets forth controls that use patent rights to address excessive price competition. The central measure discussed at a members' meeting held in November 1966, which included discussion of measures for addressing challenging business conditions facing manufacturers, is articulated below:

> The association [Nikkōso] should take firm action through some sort of regulatory measure to address the sale of machines at prices that undercut previously arranged pricing (for example, in the manner of the hairdressing industry). It is desirable that the sale of machines at prices that undercut fair prices be punished by means of the exercise of the Nittokuren's rights [...]. (Company T)[103]

The exact fiscal year in which Article 14 was added to the agreement after this meeting is not known. In addition to expressing the challenging business conditions resulting from underselling-based competition at the time, the article is important because it singles out the strengthening of regulations that apply particularly to insider businesses.

Regulatory efforts by the Nittokuren were broader insofar as they extended legal regulations to outsider businesses, and they can be understood as strengthening the management and regulatory control of the Nikkōso. In patent management, an original function of the Nittokuren, embracing the Nikkōso's management of national taxes served to reduce the former organization's management workload, for example through the sharing of information about the number of manufactured machines that were subject to patent fees. The strengthening of comprehensive management both before (by sharing information about the volume of manufactured machines) and after (by implementing regulatory measures) machine manufacture as the two organizations' roles complemented each other enabled appropriate regulation of both member and non-member companies.

Monitoring mechanisms

In order to ensure the above regulations would function properly, it was necessary to establish mechanisms that simplified the discovery of illegitimate conduct in attempts to evade them. In terms of the problem of certificate stamp management, the need to detect manufacturers engaging in illegitimate conduct was compounded by the question of whether parlors' cooperation would be forthcoming. Consequently, the Nikkōso found itself facing the need to obtain cooperation from parlors and to strengthen methods of identifying questionable conduct in order to ensure that discovery and regulation mechanisms would function effectively. An agreement on cooperation with commodity tax payment (Document 2) forged on July 1, 1960, by the Nikkōso and the National Confederation of Amusement Industry Associations

(Zenkoku Yūgigyō Kumiai Rengōkai, or Zen'yūren for short), which was reestablished in 1966 as the National Confederation of Amusement Industry Cooperatives (Zenkoku Yūgigyō Kyōdō Kumiai Rengōkai), gave shape to those mechanisms.[104]

Document 2

Agreement

National Confederation of Amusement Industry Cooperatives (Zen'yūren)
Japan Amusement Machine Industry Association (Nikkōso)

The National Confederation of Amusement Industry Cooperatives and Japan Amusement Machine Industry Association hereby agree to the provisions set forth above with the goal of cooperating with regard to the payment of commodity taxes for pachinko machines and pledge to contribute to the development of the industry. The parties have prepared two copies of this agreement, one of which will be retained by each party.

I. Commodity tax cooperation certificates approved as a result of discussions between the National Tax Agency and the Nikkōso shall be affixed to pachinko machines sold on or after July 1, 1960.

II. Reflecting its acknowledgment that payment of the commodity tax is the responsibility of pachinko parlor operators in a nation governed by laws, the National Confederation of Amusement Industry Cooperatives shall communicate this responsibility at every opportunity, for example by offering instruction and guidance on how to pay the tax, both in district conferences throughout Japan and in written documents.

III. Reflecting its acknowledgement that the healthy development of the pachinko industry is the most essential prerequisite for its own prosperity, the Nikkōso shall actively furnish both material and moral support for research into healthy entertainment conducted by the National Confederation of Amusement Industry Cooperatives and for public relations activities and other initiatives that should be undertaken under the aegis of a national organization.

July 1, 1960

On behalf of the National Confederation of Amusement Industry Cooperatives:
Toshie Mizushima
Chairman

On behalf of the Japan Amusement Machine Industry Association:
Kenkichi Nakajima
Director

The significance of this agreement is, first, that it committed the parlors of the Zen'yūren to purchase machines to which certificate stamps had been affixed in accordance with the tax certificate stamp program, signaling their acceptance of a price increase forecast to total around 1000 yen per machine.[105] In this way, the agreement secured parlors' cooperation in the drive to eliminate illegitimate, tax-evading businesses.

Of course, actual transactions between parlors and manufacturers depended on the balance of power struck during negotiations between the two parties, and the possibility of shifting commodity tax and other expenses onto prices was governed by that balance.[106] To the extent that purchases from illegitimate businesses were carried out as price-based market transactions, it was difficult to impose restrictions. Consequently, the significance of this agreement lies also in the manner in which it made it easier to discover uncertified machines by creating structures that allowed parlors and manufacturers to monitor one another. Looking back, the agreement served to create a precondition that was necessary for the smooth implementation of ex post facto regulations. Parlors were obligated to communicate information about uncertified machines to district conferences or the Zen'yūren, while the Nikkōso received reports from parlor associations and investigated instances in which stamps had not been applied.[107] This mutual cooperation embodied an effort to increase tax payment rates and stabilize prices.

Even if the discovery mechanism described above were put in place, and the presence or absence of certificate stamps were used as a signal to discover violators, it was unclear whether this approach would be feasible. The monitoring method also remained problematic. Surveying all the machines at every parlor nationwide would cost an enormous amount of money, and that amount would only grow with the frequency of such surveys.

In fact, such monitoring to check certificate stamps was not undertaken separately; instead, it was incorporated into ordinary sales activities targeting parlors undertaken by manufacturers and the trading companies selling machines.[108] A former Nittokuren official put it this way[109]:

> It's not like we searched throughout Japan for machines [without stamps]. Rather, we received information because manufacturers' sales reps visited parlors and competed for their business. For example, a manufacturer would say, "Company B isn't affixing stamps to its machines". We'd head over there and if the machines didn't carry certificate stamps, we'd take photographs as evidence, because they were supposed to affix the stamps to machines so that they were easy to see. The photographs made it clear [whether the machines bore stamps or not]. Manufacturers felt the need to monitor each other. (Interview conducted by the author on November 15, 2004.)

Manufacturers' sales activities were not limited to existing customers, but rather extended to parlors that had installed competing manufacturers' machines in an effort to attract new customers. Checking for certificate stamps was something manufacturers did as part of their usual observation of machines at the parlors they visited. That a parlor with uncertified machines might become a new customer only added to manufacturers' motivation to discover violations. Since manufacturers were required to affix the stamps such that they were readily visible, it was a simple matter for salespeople to check for the presence of stamps by glancing at machines. Assuming that sales activities surged when parlors switched machines every season, it is likely that most of the machines installed at parlors nationwide ended up being checked in this manner. When a machine without a stamp was discovered, the fact was reported to the Nittokuren either directly or via a merchant association and then investigated by the Nittokuren.

This firsthand account is consistent with a document entitled 'Guidelines on Eliminating Illegitimate Businesses: Principles of Acceptance and Provisional Action',[110] prepared by the Nittokuren in 1960. The document outlines a process in the context of the use of certificate stamps to stabilize order throughout the industry: If warnings and other measures by involved groups to an illegitimate business did not lead to an improvement of the situation in question, the director determined that it was necessary to exercise patent rights, and documents were compiled certifying the background and setting forth a request. The Nittokuren could then investigate, give warnings and issue citations.[111]

In this way, patents were utilized as a method for maintaining order in related industries, and incentives for discovering uncertified machines and the function of mutual monitoring were incorporated into manufacturers' sales activities and machine distribution operations. In short, a cost-saving mechanism took the place of regular inspections by the Nittokuren and Nikkōso.

There was another benefit for the Nittokuren. If information about members could be shared with the Nikkōso, the organization could easily obtain data describing machine counts, which was necessary for patent management. The advantages of being able to ascertain machine counts by means of the Nikkōso's certificate stamp management activities become clear if one imagines what would happen in the absence of such sharing. The Nittokuren would have no choice but to check machine counts for each manufacturer itself. In addition to dedicating person-hours to inspections, the group would have to monitor the accuracy of sales volume data provided by manufacturers. Linking this information to payment of national taxes meant that if roughly 100 percent of all manufacturers could be compelled to pay taxes, thereby eliminating machines produced by illegitimate businesses from the marketplace, it would be a simple matter to accurately determine the number of manufactured machines that were circulating in the market. For the Nittokuren, which carried out contract operations on behalf of patent right-holders, the collection of patent fees (i.e., the management of patents) was an important activity on the basis of which its operational capabilities would be measured. In fact, improvements in management capability allowed the Nikkōso to achieve roughly 100 percent payment of taxes on the part of its members two years after its formation.[112]

Incidentally, expectations centering on the Nittokuren's monitoring mechanisms are likely to have grown in the wake of the failure of an effort to 'standardize sales prices and unify points of contact' that was announced in March 1961 by the Nikkōso.[113] The program sought to stabilize prices by having the Nikkōso centrally manage sales while allocating manufacturing volume to manufacturers. Specifically, this involved establishing a Cooperative Sales Division that gathered information about parlor order volume from sales companies established by manufacturers and conventional distributors (as designated by the Nikkōso) and then sold machines through the organization's headquarters based on production allocations. The program was characterized by a strong regulatory element that limited free competition in the market. The details of the underlying processes do not concern us here but suffice to say that the effort faced intense opposition from parlors and manufacturers, and internally within manufacturers, even as it attracted the regulatory scrutiny of agencies such as the Japan Fair Trade Commission and the police.[114] In the end, the program was scrapped following four-way talks between the manager of the security section of the police and the Zen'yūren, Nikkōso and Nittokuren. In any case, expectations concerning the stabilization of prices through the exclusion of illegitimate businesses came to rest on monitoring functions that depended entirely on the legal regulatory capabilities of the Nittokuren.[115]

In this way, certificate stamps verifying tax payment cooperation assumed the additional function of signifying the collection of patent fees by the Nittokuren. Through the joint issuance and management of stamps by the Nikkōso and Nittokuren, the two organizations' management structures complemented and strengthened one another. Management of certificate stamps by the Assessment Committee, which grappled with the difficulties and institutional inadequacies seen in the proposed program for the Fair Price Promotion Committee above, was transformed with the development of efficient, low-cost mechanisms for certificate stamp-based discovery and regulation through cooperative structures that involved other organizations in associated industries. This approach made it possible to monitor and regulate illegitimate businesses that manufactured uncertified machines for which they did not pay commodity tax or patent fees, and in some cases to exclude those businesses from the market.

ROLE OF THE NITTOKUREN

Monitoring function and machine market stabilization

How, then, did these mechanisms actually function, and what effects did they produce?

In 1960, the Nittokuren, acting at the request of a merchant association in Kyushu, dispatched observers to investigate the extent to which certificate stamp use had penetrated the market. A report of the results indicated that out of a considerable number of requests for investigations, few had identified violations, numbering just fifty-six.[116] It is important to note here that the number of requests exceeded by a large margin the number of instances that were ultimately judged to constitute violations. This fact indicates that a functioning and effective monitoring network had been implemented in a way that encompassed merchant association activities. If one acknowledges the role of such mechanisms, a violation count of fifty-six at one point in time suggests ongoing progress and an eventual resolution of the underlying issues. From the request through to judgement by investigation, those developments were evidence that awareness of certificate stamps had risen and that use of machines bearing such stamps was becoming established.[117]

The Nittokuren's monitoring activities were proving effective precisely because they were supported by legal regulatory capability based on patents; that the market was being filled with machines to which certificate stamps had been affixed was the result of those activities. The process by which actual lawsuits were resolved offers information that will fill in some of the gaps in our picture of how those activities led to the widespread adoption of certificate stamps. Let us examine three cases of rights infringement brought by the Nittokuren from 1960 to 1962 against parlors that had installed machines without commodity tax cooperation certificate stamps and against both member and non-member companies.

In the fall of 1960, the Nittokuren filed a lawsuit against a number of non-member companies considered to be fly-by-night manufacturers and against Kodama Kaikan, a parlor that had installed uncertified machines that had been manufactured by those companies. The incident offers a glimpse at the ramifications for parlors that installed machines without certificate stamps. The Nittokuren won the lawsuit, which ended in a monetary settlement. Under the terms of the settlement, Kodama Kaikan published a pledge in industry newspapers in which it promised not to purchase machines that did not bear certificate stamps issued by the Nittokuren, including used machines.[118] More than just an example of the issue at hand, the case had a significant impact on the entire industry by highlighting the power of certificate stamps.[119] It furnished a warning to parlors that chose to purchase machines without certificate stamps that they would sustain concrete, visible economic losses in the form of monetary settlements as well as invisible economic losses due to lawsuits that had the potential to hinder their business operations. If parlors chose not to do business with illegitimate businesses, both those businesses and the machines they manufactured would disappear from the machine market. This effect signals the development of order in the market whereby only machines that satisfied certain conditions – machines for which commodity tax and patent fees had been paid – would be bought and sold.

The next example is fascinating as a case that involves an insider who was a member of the Nittokuren.[120] The incident, which is likely to have occurred between 1960 and 1961, began with the discovery of machines without certificate stamps at two parlors in Kobe. The company that manufactured the machines, a concern called Takeya Sangyō, was managed by Kiyoshi Takeuchi, who was also the representative of Meiki Sangyō, which had licensed patents managed by the Nittokuren. In the end, the parlors that had installed the machines and Takeuchi, which had sold the units without affixing certificate stamps, were penalized as described below. The two parlors, Mainichi Kaikan and Masachan, were fined 1200 yen (about US$3.3) (for a total of 75,600 yen [about US$15.6]) and 800 yen (about US$2.2) (for a total of 126,700 yen [about US$352]) per uncertified machine, and the court ordered that no certificate stamps be issued to Takeuchi until allowed by resolution of a plenary session of the association. The order made it effectively impossible for Takeuchi to sell its machines in the market. Following this case, the Nittokuren's board of directors put in place a series of punitive actions for licensees that violated the terms of their agreements, including cancelation of licensing rights with notice and legal action against three-time offenders.[121] Three other parlors that had purchased machines from Takeya Sangyō avoided penalty since it was recognized that they had cooperated with commodity tax cooperation certificates.[122] The sales company, which delivered Takeya Sangyō's machines, was also required to issue a statement of 'extreme regret' through the association to which it belonged. This case indicates that the incident affected not only the parlors that had used the machines in question and the manufacturer that had supplied them, but also the trading company responsible for distributing the machines.

A case in 1962 involved penalizing outsider businesses, including some that had manufactured their own machines. It transpired that none of the machines used by four parlors in the cities of Nagano, Kure and Takasaki, which were manufactured either by an outsider company (in the case of one parlor) or by the parlors themselves (in the case of the other three), bore certificate stamps issued by the Nittokuren.[123] The group took temporary measures against the parlors and manufacturer, and in the case of the latter, recommended that it be prohibited from manufacturing pachinko machines using Nittokuren patents and imposed damages.

This case highlighted the potential problem of outsiders manufacturing and selling machines. Certainly, lawsuits and recommendations that companies that were outside of the Nittokuren be prohibited from manufacturing machines were legal. However, such actions were limited in scope to technologies protected by patents managed by the Nittokuren. They did not completely close the door on opportunities to manufacture machines. While there is no solid supporting evidence for assessing the situation in which such companies found themselves, it can be inferred that outsider manufacturers had two options. First, they could join the Nikkōso, enter into an agreement with the Nittokuren and manufacture and sell machines under that agreement, although this option would require them to pay royalties. To do so, a company would first have to be accepted by the two organizations. As an organization that was dedicated to restoring order to the marketplace, the Nikkōso had an incentive to accept such companies, since doing so would mean that the new members would accept their obligation to pay the commodity tax in full and to price their machines accordingly. To ensure its long-term viability, the industry found the prospect of being able to manage such companies preferable to leaving them to operate free of supervision, where they could invite governmental regulation by failing to pay taxes. Nonetheless, it is likely that securing acceptance of a membership application was no simple task for manufacturers that had a history of violations.

The second option open to outsider companies was to remain independent, manufacture machines that avoided use of Nittokuren patents, and sell them in the marketplace at prices that reflected payment of commodity taxes. The patents held by the Nittokuren and their scope posed technological hurdles for any manufacturer considering this second option. A key characteristic of the technologies of the time was that they were of fundamental importance to pachinko machines and were likely covered by Hōkoku patents whose management had been entrusted to the Nittokuren. Whether this option was viable depended on the difficulty of avoiding use of Hōkoku technologies that had a broad range of applications. In any case, the potential for disputes concerning the interpretation of technologies was ever-present, ensuring such manufacturers' relationships with parlors and the Nittokuren would be characterized by tension on an ongoing basis. When parlors dealt with outsider companies, latent potential for disputes enveloped the associated machines. The possibility caused parlors to refrain from purchasing machines from outsider manufacturers unless they could expect considerable benefits from doing so – for example, exceptionally low prices or a very high likelihood that the machine in question would become popular with customers. For these reasons, parlors gradually came to prefer machines bearing certificate stamps that had been issued by the Nittokuren.

In this way, the Nittokuren, through mutually complementary functions undertaken with the Nikkōso, found that the conditions necessary to simplify patent-related monitoring in the industry, for example ascertaining the number of machines being manufactured, had been put in place. These conditions made it possible to eliminate companies that had not been paying the commodity tax as well as non-member manufacturers that had been infringing on patents.

Once it was possible to ascertain the number of machines being manufactured, two problems remained for insider companies: creating mechanisms for joint management that would facilitate the investigation and quantification of the extent to which machines manufactured by various companies used patents owned or managed by the Nittokuren (including patents the group had been entrusted to manage), and collecting patent fees accordingly.

Low patent fees

During this period, not so many patents were managed that the need for investigations became an important issue (see Chapter 3) because monitoring to maintain prices was important, while licensing fees covered all associated patents and costs. Here I would like to focus on the magnitude of patent fees.

In terms of the fee per machine, patent fees received by the Nittokuren rose from 200 yen (about US$0.55) at the time of the group's establishment to 750 yen (about US$2.08) at the time of its dissolution. Table 2.2 paints a more detailed picture. Patent fees as a percentage of machine prices (C) exhibit a number of deeply interesting trends from the standpoint of long-term change. First, invoice levels were limited, as illustrated by the fact that (C) totaled about 7 percent or more during the 1950s before being set at about 6 percent, including fees, at the time of the Nittokuren's establishment. Second, (C) fell over the long term, which had the effect of reducing in a relative sense the economic burden of patent fees. Whereas machine prices during and after the 1980s were twenty-eight to forty times higher than the corresponding prices during the 1960s, patent fees only rose by a factor of a little greater than four. As a result, (C) at the time of the dissolution of the Nittokuren did not exceed about 0.38 percent. In this way, patent expenses as a percentage of machine prices had a hard upper limit during the Nittokuren's reign.

With regard to the first trend, the organization may have sought to expand membership by keeping patent fees low in accordance with its objective of eliminating illegitimate businesses and stabilizing prices.

With regard to the second trend – the absence of a long-term increase in patent fees – it can be inferred that the significance of patent fees as compensation for use of patents shrank as the emphasis fell on their status as payments for the monitoring undertaken by the Nittokuren. For manufacturers that held patents, it was presumably more effective to rely on the organization's monitoring function than to attempt to investigate infringements by competing manufacturers on their own. Right-holders were able to force outsider manufacturers that did not pay patent fees out of the market

Era	Patent fees per machine (A, yen)	Patent management method	Patent fee breakdown	Machine cost (B, yen)	C = A / B (%)
1950s	500 to 700 (US$1.43 to US$2.00) 3200 (about US$8.90)	Monitoring and litigation by individual companies	Hōkoku patents	6500 to 7200 (about US$18 to US$20)	7 to 50
1960 to 1961	200 to 300 (about US$0.56 to US$0.83)		Nittokuren patents + others (Hōkoku patents)	5000 to 7000 (about US$13.90 to US$19.40)	3 to 6
1960s	300 (estimate) (about US$0.83)	Central management and agreement-related operations by the Nittokuren	Nittokuren (100 yen) + contracted services (200 to 290 yen) + other (temporary, 220 to 300 yen)	18,000 (about US$50)	2
1980 to dissolution*	390 to 750			200,000	0.38
2004	10,000 (about US$93)	Mutual agreement			5 (estimate)

Table 2.2: Patent fees

Note: *US dollar equivalents omitted due to the large range of exchange rates during this period.

Source: Patent fees are drawn from Yūgi Tsūshin, *articles about lawsuits in the* Yūgi Keizai Shimbun, *and the Nittokuren's licensing agreement. Estimates for 2004 are based on interviews with an executive from manufacturer S and a former executive from the Nittokuren (conducted on May 6, 2003, and November 5, 2004, respectively). Machine costs are based on Masamura Shōkai's general ledgers for various fiscal years and on materials provided by the Nikkōso.*

while imposing the burden of patent fees, however slight, on insider companies. In short, when the method of using the Nittokuren's monitoring function to reliably collect patent fees is compared to the alternative of manufacturers becoming parties to patent disputes that required them to negotiate and subjected them to lawsuits in which victory was hardly a foregone conclusion, the former approach, even if it meant lower patent fees, was not necessarily unreasonable. Moreover, maintaining and managing patent portfolios became more expensive as they grew, and a short development cycle imposed time limits on rights (ranging from ten to fifteen years). The result of these realities was that manufacturers could expect to recoup at least a small portion of their development costs by making their rights available while they were still in force. This choice was also reasonable from an economic perspective.

With regard to the second reason, patent fees' shrinking significance as payment for the use of patents can be seen as an indication that manufacturers were not particularly interested in collecting patent fees. The question of how the Nittokuren's monitoring function affected companies' activities merits consideration. From this perspective, let us turn our attention to the incidental effects of the Nittokuren's establishment. The following section examines the Nittokuren's impact on corporate activities and competition.

THE ECONOMIC SIGNIFICANCE OF NOT ELIMINATING COMPETITORS

One motivation for inventing new technologies and developing patents is to secure competitive advantages relative to other companies. On the question of whether to seek exclusivity, recent discussions have offered a variety of observations concerning the meaning of open strategies. In any case, that patents are a means of obtaining favorable conditions relative to competitors is certain. In the pachinko industry, Hōkoku sought significant royalties in lawsuits targeting competitors, and those demands were legitimate insofar as the company was asserting its patent rights. However, the organizational trend was to reduce patent fees, and companies were not excluded from the market as long as they qualified as members. Were low royalties and the failure to exclude competitors merely the result of unique historical circumstances that powerful companies which owned fundamental technologies were forced by the pressure of numerous other companies to accept, or did they constitute irrational economic behavior?

Structural characteristics of machines

A shift in perspective shows that the establishment of the Nittokuren's patent management mechanism, whose preference for low patent fees seems at a glance to be unfavorable for right-holders, offered technical advantages in the form of cross-licensing as a result of the structural characteristics of pachinko machines. Assembled products may incorporate parts covered by powerful patents, but those parts alone do not constitute a machine. Moreover, as described above, there was turnover in the companies developing the patented technologies that lay at the heart of popular models. Realistically, most parts in pachinko machines were protected by patents held by various companies. When patents were licensed, machine prices rose as the patent fees were added to the cost of manufacturing. If patent fees could not be shifted onto machine prices, some manufacturers would incur costs that outstripped sales prices. Cross-licensing provides a method of resolving this problem, which is feasible when there are multiple companies that hold powerful patents.

The passage below describes the structural characteristics of pachinko machines. It records the response of Heiwa's Nakajima, who was serving as the president of the Nikkōso at the time, to the question of whether a patent fee of 300 yen was high.

> If the Japan Amusement Machine Patent Management Federation [the Nittokuren] held all rights related to pachinko machines so that it alone controlled them, there would be no problem, but in fact that is not the case. [...] The difficulty of the patent fee problem lies in the fact that there is no single patent that covers a pachinko machine. The largest portion of the 300 yen is the 100 yen that goes to Company H [Hōkoku]. Apart from Company H, other companies have their own rights. My company, Heiwa, has rights as well, but when one company demands a right, everyone else then wants it, too. [...] When one company demands rights, in an extreme case, patent fees could become more expensive than manufacturing costs. Consequently, I personally would like to assert rights, but I am foregoing collecting patent fees and encouraging other manufacturers to do the same.[124]

Since patents were held by various manufacturers, including part manufacturers, folding them all into the cost of manufacturing, even assuming they were necessary from a manufacturing standpoint, would push up costs to the extent that they could not be shifted onto market prices. For right-holders, offsetting costs by means of cross-licensing has the advantage of limiting market prices. The encouragement of powerful manufacturers to make concessions in the passage cited above occurred in the context of an attempt to create conditions that involved numerous licensees. The principal purpose involved addressing pricing problems, against the backdrop of obtaining the cooperation of powerful manufacturers that licensed such rights.

Regulations and development risk

Another characteristic of the industry is the high level of development risk and the problem of regulations, which exert a significant level of influence on that risk. The pachinko industry is governed by a variety of regulations imposed by the National Police Agency. With regard to the manufacture of machines, the industry has been required since the successive-shot ban of 1955 to have machines inspected and certified before they can be sold in the market, as explained above. If a machine fails the inspection despite the manufacturer's compliance with the certification standards, the company is required to revise the design in order to have it re-inspected. For example, one product developed in 1955 by Hōkoku failed the National Police Agency inspection six times.[125] Its sale was finally authorized after the design was revised and submitted for a seventh inspection. Because pachinko machines are susceptible to the effects of popularity, a long re-inspection delay – even if the process might yield improvements – means that the manufacturer could lose its ability to launch the product during the season in which parlors replace their machines. In some cases, the company might even have to halt development and abandon their effort to commercialize the product. To make matters worse, machines had to be inspected separately by each prefecture as there was no unified set of standards. Sometimes a machine would be certified in one region only to fail the certification process in another.[126]

Two types of constraints imposed by regulations that were incidental to the development process and post-development inspections acted to increase development risk. As a result, when a machine developed using patents acquired by a given manufacturer was certified, use of the patents in question provided a technique for reducing development risk surrounding inspections. If this role were to be apportioned among manufacturers, expectations of risk sharing would likely rise. By using licensed patents to develop machines that resembled those that had proven popular, the risk and cost of development could be reduced. For example, machines that adopted the *chūrippu* accessory for which Narita Seisakusho held the patent became extremely popular during the first half of the 1960s.

The short development cycle also imposed a burden on individual manufacturers. Sales (i.e., replacement) of pachinko machines were concentrated in the period prior to spring and in the lead-up to holidays such as Obon (a festival that honors the spirits of ancestors) and the New Year. Manufacturers' efforts to develop and produce new models were aligned with these three periods over the long term. Manufacturers had to continuously develop new models to launch in accordance with this timeframe. In the short term, fabricating products that resembled popular models from other manufacturers made it possible to lower both development risk and costs.[127]

In fact, driven by the three factors behind the founding of the Nittokuren – in short, the need to promote development – a document entitled 'Internal Rules on Fostering Protection of New Machines' (Nittokuren) was put forward and approved at a Board of Trustees meeting of the National Commerce and Industry Council, a federation consisting of the Nikkōso, Nittokuren, Zenshōren and associations of part manufacturers.[128] Designed to encourage the development of new models, the rules required new models developed by Nittokuren members to undergo inspections by an internal committee of the organization in order to encourage mutual use by manufacturers. The Nittokuren also worked actively to identify new ideas, including by offering financial incentives, and created an initiative for the organizational acquisition of patents. As described above, it took time for patent rights to be recognized, and this initiative sought to facilitate the sharing of development information while postponing the resolution of problems related to licensing until a later date, even as approval remained uncertain. However, because the initiative addressed development information for new products, which for economic actors was a sensitive asset, it remains unclear how these attempts subsequently developed, and I was unable to find any examples in which noteworthy results were reported.

Capital investment risk

Finally, I would like to touch on the inelasticity of capital investment as a characteristic of the manufacture of pachinko machines. Because manufacturing was aligned with the times of year during which parlors replaced machines, the difference between production during quiet and busy periods was pronounced.[129] Due to the unsuitability of producing machines in advance resulting from the high level of development risk (including regulations, a short product cycle, uncertain popularity and the inability to forecast a fad's longevity) and the substantial influence of popularity, manufacturers found it desirable to meet as much demand as possible by adopting a build-to-order approach to production. When a given model came into vogue, parlors worked desperately to get a leg up on their competitors by purchasing that model since popularity and exposure were directly linked to sales and competitiveness. Manufacturers had to meet such demand.

However, two issues arose as they attempted to do so. First, even if a given model sold by a certain manufacturer became popular, the company might not have the production equipment to accommodate that level of demand, because the ability to increase production capacity is inelastic. In such situations, the production of similar products by other manufacturers serves to distribute production capacity. The original manufacturers' lack of production capacity, which is the assumption upon which this scenario rests, derives from the second issue. If the manufacturer maintained a scale of production sufficient to accommodate latent demand for popular models, that equipment would remain idle during times of slow sales, reducing the rate at which the company utilizes its production equipment and casting uncertainty on its prospects for recouping the associated capital investment. Given the impossibility of forecasting how popular any given model would become and for how long, which was directly linked to equipment capacity, it was only natural that companies approached capital investments that could require long periods of time to recoup with great care.[130] The following account describes how the industry's fundamental characteristic of being influenced by popularity colored manufacturers' basic approach to capital investment:

> From the time we began until this April, our factory was usually in a state where production of most machines was running late. [...] We strongly felt that even if we greatly expanded the scale [of our operations], that would become problematic if

> there were a recession. In light of the fact that the life of machines is shorter than in other industries, we didn't expand the scale of production beyond a certain point, even if we received large numbers of orders. Instead, we stuck with the scale we had at the outset and made do with that.[131]

The above account was by Nakajima, who served as president of Heiwa, a representative manufacturer that began its operations during the late 1950s. It dates to the early 1950s, when single-shot machines were typical and successive-shot models had not yet become popular. The description is noteworthy for its expression of a fundamental characteristic of the industry. While production capacity presumably fluctuated in response to the strength of the underlying business in terms of factors such as sales channels and sales, Nakajima adopted a cautious attitude toward expanding his equipment, even though the market was in a stage of growth, and it is clear that this characteristic of the industry impacted corporate behavior. Nakajima later expressed disapproval for this restraint with regard to capital investments[132] and instead sought to strengthen sales capability and expand production to keep pace: 'I think it was not wise to stick to a certain limit by opting not to expand production despite having room to do so. We didn't even try to discover sales routes to target customers in Tokyo or Osaka'. When equipment sat idle, manufacturers also had the option of covering the shortfall through their sales capabilities. Logically, it was possible to expand equipment on an ongoing basis, but it was also essential to enhance sales capabilities. It goes without saying that there was no guarantee a given model would sell out.

Consequently, keeping equipment as lean as possible while accepting the cost of the opportunity when models became popular was also an effective option. The striking difference between slow and busy periods is likely to have strengthened manufacturers' tendency to opt for this latter option. Under such conditions, companies sought to operate existing equipment at full capacity before undertaking new capital investments. The absolute limit on that capacity was defined by the point of equilibrium at which tacit acceptance of competitors' production of similar products balanced the checks on their own capital investments. Here I would like to point out that the way capital investment risk deriving from the seasonality of sales and the vagaries of popularity held production in check was a characteristic that was 'baked into' the manufacture of pachinko machines from the outset.

In this way, certain aspects of development risk caused by the characteristics of pachinko machine manufacturing and of associated products were overcome by the functions of the Nittokuren. Patent licensing fees related to the characteristics of assembled products were offset among the manufacturers holding the patents, necessitating monitoring (investigatory) and licensing operations. For manufacturers, counterparts that licensed their patents were not competitors that ought to be forced out of the market; rather, such arrangements had the potential to facilitate shared development and production, for example by allowing rights to be licensed at low prices so that manufacturers could develop popular models in the future and manufacture similar products.[133] Although it was not the purpose of the Nittokuren to reduce capital investment risk through such arrangements or to influence licensing in an overt way, for example by setting patent fees, the organization's influence on manufacturers through this function should not be overlooked.

CONCLUSION

As this chapter has shown, the Nittokuren, which was established against the backdrop of intensifying patent disputes, guaranteed that manufacturers could make use of one another's rights at low prices by serving as a patent pool. The group also played a significant role in the elimination of counterfeit machines from illegitimate manufacturers, which had been a longstanding and difficult problem for the industry. In that role, the organization helped restore competitive order by organizing machine manufacturers at a time when payment of the commodity tax was an issue in a way that complemented the mechanisms and functions for monitoring machine production made possible with the establishment of the Nikkōso. In closing, I will summarize the results of the establishment of the Nittokuren in line with three key background factors and offer an overview of the significance of the 1960s in the history of the pachinko industry and of that organization's establishment.

First, with regard to the resolution of patent disputes, the effects of the formation of the Nittokuren are captured in a straightforward manner by the fact that incidents revolving around the interpretation of such rights, for example in the form of lawsuits seeking to invalidate patents, disappeared during the 1960s. Incidents spawning such confrontational invalidation lawsuits occurred one after another during the 1950s, leading to the payment of substantial damages. From the standpoint of technology developers, it was only natural to protect these rights. However, the long-running disputes and uncertain outcomes that accompanied lawsuits brought to the surface problems that hindered production and sales activities. Moreover, no single company gained the ability to dominate the market over an extended period of time. The speed with which popular tastes changed and the high levels of uncertainty that surrounded the industry emerged as hard-earned lessons based on participants' experiences, even as regulations and leading companies exhibited a high level of turnover. It was against this backdrop that the role of the patent pool attracted attention. The formation of the Nittokuren brought an intensive and centralized approach to patent management, allowing disputes to be resolved in advance.

Most of the lawsuits filed during the 1960s were intended to control illegitimate businesses in line with the monitoring function of the Nittokuren. The second background factor – fierce price disputes involving machines – was increasingly alleviated through the activities of the Nikkōso and the Nittokuren. For manufacturers, there were limits to how well they could differentiate themselves from competitors through development while complying with the regulations that governed machines, and price competition was a strategic option. However, such competition thrust the industry into an even more dire state of affairs. This was due to the existence of illegitimate businesses that produced unlicensed, counterfeit machines on the one hand and invited excessive price competition by evading the commodity tax on the other. Since the latter was a social obligation, failure on the part of the entire industry to address it threatened the viability of the industry itself, as Nakajima recalled.[134] At a time characterized by pronounced market disorder, it is likely that it would have been difficult to create long-term prospects for stable corporate operations without eliminating such illegitimate businesses. This was likely one reason for the formation of the Nittokuren as an organization that included companies with powerful patents. That said, I would like to emphasize that one must not limit one's evaluation to the legal regulatory capabilities of the Nittokuren. It goes without saying that the effectiveness of the group's regulations with regard to illegitimate businesses was predicated on the functioning of its patent management role – that is, of its role as a patent pool. As symbolized by creative contract terms that controlled fierce price competition, the Nittokuren's monitoring and management functions proved effective with regard to patent use by both members and non-members. The group's role was also deeply significant for right-holders.

At the beginning of this chapter, I asked what factors accounted for the reconstruction of market order backed up by increased payment of the commodity tax. The answer to this question can be summarized as the organization of manufacturers, centering on the functions of the Nittokuren. To put it another way, this reconstruction of order was the result of the imposition of discipline on the machine market by means of a certain type of regulation. This fact highlights the need to closely examine the meaning of regulation. To the extent that the prices forced on manufacturers by the machine market during this period made tax payment difficult and disincentivized invention, they cast the future viability of pachinko into doubt. The system was not one that facilitated competition or effectively stimulated corporate activities, including development, so as to lay the foundation for the industry's development. The wise solution that was needed to escape from the fog into which pachinko had wandered turned out to be restraints – regulations – imposed by the industry itself as it determined what sort of rules to adopt and enforce. That the industry managed to work out a monitoring network that functioned as inexpensively as possible and at a standard that maximized compliance was yet another condition that made possible the future existence of the pachinko industry.

It is hard to conclude that the third factor – the promotion of development – yielded results that lived up to expectations. As I mentioned at the beginning of this chapter, there can be no doubt that out of the pachinko industry's fifty years of history, this period was one of relative stagnation, particularly for manufacturers. That fact indicates that the Nittokuren did not necessarily generate the level of new machine development in line with expectations, and that the initiative undertaken to protect and foster new machines suffered setbacks. Development was likely constrained by the external factor of strict regulation.

In this sense, the revision of the Entertainment Establishment Control Act in 1969 to relax regulations on pachinko machines was significant. With the subsequent announcement in November 1972 that electric machines would be certified (the change took effect in April 1973), the machine market was poised to embark on a new chapter in its history.

Finally, I would like to summarize the significance of the 1960s by presenting a bird's-eye view of the industry's development. After the regulations of 1955 took effect, the pachinko industry shrank markedly as large numbers of both parlor operators and manufacturers were driven out of business. Nonetheless, parlor operators discovered a stable revenue base that would allow them to provide an inexpensive form of entertainment by limiting their product's speculative character and capping the amount of money spent by customers. At the same time, competition in the machine market brought on circumstances that threatened the businesses of powerful, development-driven manufacturers. Starting in 1955, a key issue in the development of the industry became the need to create an environment in which the machine market could supply new machines to parlors in an ongoing manner, primarily by enforcing discipline in terms of tax payments and maintaining prices at levels that would not undermine the incentive to invent new technologies. In this regard, the Nittokuren played a central role in bringing order to the machine market by excluding illegitimate businesses and restricting access to the playing field to manufacturers that could pay the commodity tax and patent fees. From the second half of the 1950s to the 1960s, the market expanded as the size of the average parlor in terms of the number of machines it operated grew at a pace that is significant even in the context of the industry's fifty-year history. The exodus from the market of manufacturers during this time was the result of the exclusion of illegitimate businesses, and the stabilization of the market ushered in a period of growth while bearing fruit for the remaining manufacturers in the form of the industry's development. This machine market ensured the viability of development and signaled that an environment in which pachinko could continue to exist had been put in place.

Just as this stabilization of the market was enabling the Nittokuren to limit fierce price competition, steps taken in 1969 towards deregulation primed manufacturers to embrace development-fueled competition. These developments provide the perspective from which I will analyze the 1970s.

3

Competitive Structure of the Pachinko Machine Market: Promotion of Development-based Competition

INTRODUCTION

With the coming of the 1970s, a broad demographic continued to enjoy playing pachinko. The number of people playing the game at least once per year was estimated at 30,240,000 by a 1975 survey, falling to about 25,000,000 in 1979 due to an economic downturn.[1] While an increase in the number of female customers attracted attention during the decade, the overall demographic centered on men in their twenties to thirties.[2] According to a study conducted by the Nippon Research Center in 1975 entitled 'Study of Gambling by Salarymen', some 90.5 percent of white-collar workers at twenty-four leading companies reported that they had played pachinko (and 70.3 percent that they 'play pachinko currently'), far outpacing the 69.7 percent and 65.5 percent of respondents who reported enjoying mahjong and the lottery, respectively.[3]

The industry continued to offer customers a low-cost consumption expenditure during the 1970s, providing a set of economic terms that allowed most males to enjoy it readily. According to a survey by the pachinko magazine *Ōsama Techō* in 1975, customers spent an average of 540 yen (about US$1.84, equivalent to a little less than 1000 yen [about US$9.27] today) per outing.[4] People were likely able to frequent parlors 11.6 times per month in the survey because pachinko was seen as 'not having a large gambling element [...] people didn't bet a lot, or lose a lot'.[5]

By the 1970s, about one-third of the adult population had been to a pachinko parlor at least once,[6] and the economic scale of the industry (see Table 0.3) had continued to grow. However, the machine manufacturers that ought to have been supporting the industry's growth had grappled with limits placed on development by strict regulations in the run-up to the 1970s and by all appearances did not see themselves as having benefited from opportunities for growth.

As was made clear in Chapter 2, the main issue faced by the pachinko industry during the 1960s was the need to restore order to the market in terms of machine transactions with pachinko parlors and the competitive relationships between manufacturers. The Japan Amusement Machine Patent Management Federation, or Nittokuren, played a role in resolving these problems by eliminating underselling from the market. Once price competition had been limited by the Nittokuren, the next problem became the range of choices available to manufacturers and their viability. In examining this aspect of the industry, the cartel view put forth by Juro Hashimoto and Haruhito Takeda offers an appropriate perspective. The view proposes that after certain constraints are placed on price competition by a monopolistic organization – after partial changes to market mechanisms – companies embark on initiatives to maximize their profits using market prices as data points, spurring competition that involves increases in productivity.[7] This chapter explains the development and technology application mechanisms that supported the sustained growth of the pachinko industry by analyzing the competitive relationships between manufacturers and the nature of competition in the machine market that gives rise to them. By 'competitive structure and nature', I refer to the characteristics that shaped competition between manufacturers of the time and the manner in which that competition developed.

The introduction of this chapter illustrates the emergence of machines with new designs and associated official regulations, painting a picture of an industry poised for long-term growth. After reflecting on the history of the impact of regulations on the industry and clarifying this chapter's approach to the relationship between regulation and development, I will undertake a detailed exploration of the above issues while expanding on the perspective taken in the analysis.

The period that provided the most vivid illustration of the relationship between development and regulation was the 1950s, when the machines that spawned the pachinko boom (the Masamura Gauge, 'all-win' machines, successive-shot machines, etc.) appeared and triggered regulations prohibiting the manufacture and use of successive-shot designs. As I observed in Chapter 1, regulations were imposed on machines' speculative element and parlor operations based on the Entertainment Establishment Control Act enacted in 1948 and were intimately influenced by a variety of social conditions. Targeting models that 'invited a fondness for gambling', standards based on the magnitude of this speculative element so as to judge societal impacts were by nature arbitrary. Further, their interpretation was entrusted to the entities that enforced them, indicating the extent to which details were left to the regulatory authorities' discretion. The Administrative Order Prohibiting Successive-shot Machines of 1955, which was triggered by issues including machines' excessive speculative character, the manner in which prizes were redeemed and exchanged for cash and the involvement of criminal groups, proved to be the first event to express in dramatic style the police's attitude toward pachinko. Numerous companies involved in the industry were forced to close their doors or change businesses as a result, and there can be no doubt that regulation had a decisive impact on the pachinko industry.

Starting in 1955, pachinko machines had to satisfy standards put in place by local public safety commissions before they could be sold.[8] To the extent to which speculative elements would be allowed and the timing of the strengthening of regulations could not be predicted, regulation itself became one aspect of development risk for manufacturers. Although it is difficult to quantify changes in the magnitude of risk since the characteristics of the regulatory regime varied over time, we can note, as an example, that less than half of all pachinko machines that underwent certification in 2016 ended up being licensed.[9] In short, manufacturers were unable to sell about half the machines in whose development they had invested (or that required additional investments to improve them).

At the same time, manufacturers were called upon to take certain steps to satisfy the standards underlying the direction imposed on development by these regulations, specifically by limiting machines' speculative character. In order to broaden our perspective to include changes in regulations, it is necessary to consider not only the passive assumption that development would be constrained by regulations, but also the manner in which manufacturers undertook development while accommodating regulations.

In the case of pachinko, the case study method of observing the development process of particular manufacturers does not provide an adequate approach for answering such questions. Development by other companies sometimes leads to the regulation of an entire industry, and an analysis that focuses on regulations versus individual companies can lose sight of this point. The manner in which successive-shot machines developed by Hōkoku Yūki Seisakusho ('Hōkoku') became popular in the market and prompted the successive-shot prohibition offers a useful example (and is typical of the manner in which such developments played out). Consequently, any analysis must include the development activities of a broad range of manufacturers. In keeping with the perspective that informs this chapter's analysis, which encompasses the relationships between manufacturers, I will discuss how manufacturers bearing development risk took action in response to the conditions they faced and how they pursued development while building competitive relationships with one another.

In clarifying the competitive structure of the pachinko machine market, I will pick up where the previous chapter left off by focusing on the functions of the Nittokuren, a patent pool organization, and on the conditions it imposed on competition among manufacturers. That said, I would like to emphasize that my analysis approaches the patent pool from the standpoint of its relationship with the development of the industry in order to clarify the difference between my approach and other research such as that described below.

Some historical analysis of the functions of patent pools examines the relationship of such organizations to innovation or to monopolistic behavior.[10] Such analysis is meaningful when thinking about the significance of innovation and patent pool organizations as effective (or ineffective) means for bringing it about, or about the administration of anti-monopoly law. However, this approach is prone to treat the functions of patent pools as fixed in nature because an examination of the characteristics of industry does not offer a sufficient platform from which to consider the nature of organizations. Rather than considering the functions of the Nittokuren alone and in isolation, this chapter will place the role of that organization within the broader context of manufacturers' daily development activities and the long-term progress of the industry. This approach will allow us to ascertain changes in the Nittokuren's functions and in the roles it was expected to play while tracing the attendant transformation in the industry's development.

In an industry where it was difficult to predict whether models would be popular and if so, for how long, pachinko machine manufacturers' development activities consisted of creating novel machines for the upcoming season while monitoring how the market received them. Rather than assessing the functions of the Nittokuren based on effects such as innovation, this chapter will direct its interest to how the Nittokuren brought discipline and order to manufacturers' fundamental function – developing machines for the upcoming season. By studying the roles that the Nittokuren was called upon to play, it is possible to identify the historical conditions that made possible the sustained development of machines, which underpinned the long-term development of the pachinko industry.

The issues and method described above are useful in understanding the industry's long-term development for two reasons. The first is related to the significance of the 1970s in the history of the pachinko industry. During the 1960s and 1970s, manufacturers continued to exit the business as the number of parlors failed to rise significantly. From a macro perspective, it was an era of stagnation sandwiched between the 1950s (see Chapter 1), a time of accelerating growth and abrupt slowdowns, and the 1980s, when market growth spurred major changes in the industry's structure. However, the pachinko machine market had continued to expand during the 1960s (see Chapter 2), and for the manufacturers that remained, the period was one of growth as the number of machines operated by existing customers (parlors) increased and as they harnessed new sales to parlors whose suppliers (manufacturers) had exited the business, gaining a foundation on which to grow their own businesses. This state of affairs continued until the 1970s, as illustrated in Figure 0.4, offering the possibility of additional development even as continued competition drove an ongoing weeding out in the industry. Instead of treating the period as a time when manufacturers endured a slowdown caused by the recession that began during the second half of the 1950s and bided their time until the 1980s, it is necessary to view the decade through the lens of the 1980s and beyond, when the structure of the industry changed significantly. In this sense, the seeds of growth were sown during the 1970s. I will examine the historical significance of the 1970s from this perspective.

The second reason that the issues and method I outlined above are useful is that they allow us to reveal the manner in which competition was regulated while focusing on machine development. It goes without saying that a focus on development is a key thread that runs through the approximately forty years of the industry's history covered by this book. However, this thread does not necessarily have the same meaning throughout. This chapter examines the conditions under which development was carried out and the way that environment changed in the course of the pachinko industry's history. In other words, it focuses on the mechanisms that encouraged the hard work by individual companies that formed the soil from which popular models sprung. In my view, this perspective allows us to treat the development of Fībā-type machines, which created an enormous market starting in the 1980s, or rather the mechanism that drove the industry's dynamic development, as a series of historical events rather than as an accidental byproduct. The operative proposition here is this: that developmental mechanisms and relationships among manufacturers stabilized during the 1970s, and that this, more than anything else, accounted for the emergence of the Fībā-type machines of the 1980s.

The first part of this chapter analyzes the role of the Nittokuren during the 1970s, a time of structural change in the development environment, while the second part provides an overview of the competitive structures that defined how manufacturers competed with one another from the 1960s to the 1970s. The final part summarizes the significance of the period in the industry's broader history while describing the relationship between the Nittokuren's functions and the nature of competition among manufacturers.

STRUCTURAL CHANGE AND THE FUNCTIONS OF THE NITTOKUREN

Constrained development and deregulation

Under the standards introduced in 1955, the only machines that were allowed to be manufactured were single-shot models that accepted balls one at a time.[11] As the Masamura Gauge, which debuted around 1950, became the de facto standard for pin boards, a series of detailed regulations extended to the mechanisms behind those boards, including the methods used to launch balls, the number of balls launched and the number of prize balls dispensed when a customer won. For example, regulations required various design specifications, including the diameter of the holes balls entered and the distance from the ball inlet to the opening from which they were launched.

The result was to narrow the scope of development, making significant innovation of internal mechanisms difficult. Development focused on *yakumono* accessories, and machines whose boards featured *jinmitto* (developed by Nishijin in 1956) and *komikku* (developed by Heiwa in 1957) mechanisms became popular. *Chūrippu* ('tulip') accessories, which were patented by Narita Seisakusho, debuted around 1960, and similar *yakumono*, which had initially been limited geographically, became broadly available nationwide in 1966, ushering in a period of nationwide popularity that prompted pachinko's second golden era, after first blossoming during the early 1950s.[12]

However, *yakumono* were transitory in nature, and their diversification triggered production problems. One official – Mr. N, a director of the Japan Amusement Machine Industry Association, or Nikkōso – described parlors' efforts to differentiate their machines in terms of *yakumono* by focusing on diversification as follows: 'As a result of parlor operators struggling with excessive competition and coming up with various countermeasures, seeking machines with such-and-such a new *yakumono* that nearby parlors lacked, the number of types of *yakumono* grew'.[13] The trend demanded measures to address the accompanying rise in production costs.

> We can't keep making lots of different machine models like we do now. Basically, we've got to standardize machines. The top priority is to either eliminate or drastically reduce the number of *yakumono*. In this way [...] excessive costs associated with modulating *yakumono* can be trimmed.[14] (Mr. S, a representative of a machine manufacturer.)

During everyday competition with nearby parlors, some sought *yakumono* with even slight changes in order to secure even short-term advantages. Faced with other development constraints, manufacturers accommodated those wishes, with the result that development focused on the limited scope of differentiated *yakumono*. Efforts to secure growth (see Introduction) looked to the subdivision of the market, and by the end of the 1960s, diversification into multiple models seemed to have gone too far. On the demand side, parlors developed huge expectations regarding the appearance of new machines, while manufacturers became increasingly impatient with the constraints on the scope of development.

It was against this backdrop that the Entertainment and Amusement Establishment Control Act was revised in 1969. The revision introduced a broad deregulation of pachinko machines, inflating expectations that the scope of development could be expanded. Furthermore, electric machines were permitted in November 1972 (as part of changes enacted in April 1973), which had the effect of allowing a certain degree of speculative character.[15]

The revisions to the Entertainment and Amusement Establishment Control Act limited the number of ball launches to 100 per minute and prize balls to fifteen but otherwise imposed no other requirements, in effect lifting the ban on the manufacture of successive-shot machines. A deregulation of this scale presumably ignited manufacturers' appetite for development as they sought to meet parlors' expectations. I will examine that state of affairs in the next part; here I would like to focus first on structural changes and on the Nittokuren's response.

Pitfalls in structures that promote invention

In another noteworthy structural change, the Patent Act was revised in 1971 as part of a series of changes that introduced a public disclosure system.[16] Until that time, only patents that had been assessed and those for which the set patent registration fees had not been paid were publicly disclosed in the *Patent Application Gazette*. Consequently, it took an average of about four years[17] from application to patent disclosure, and the number of applications significantly exceeded the number of disclosed patents.[18] The publication system introduced in 1971 required disclosure of all patents within eighteen months of application.[19] At the same time, a right to demand compensation was introduced (under Article 65 of the Patent Act) allowing right-holders to issue warnings and demand compensation from parties that they deemed likely to have infringed on the disclosed patent rights. That action was taken in advance; right-holders were able to exercise their right to demand compensation once the patent rights had been granted.

On the one hand, the revision was understood as incentivizing development in the pachinko industry, which was characterized by a short development cycle, by improving the standing of right-holders. On the other hand, if the deregulation introduced by the 1969 revisions to the Entertainment and Amusement Establishment Control Act was going to revitalize machine development, the disclosure system would trigger issues involving the need to monitor, manage and deal with disputes involving the resulting increase in patents.

Reacting to the changes in the patent system, manufacturers and officials at the Nittokuren expressed strong misgivings concerning the abuse of rights. A Nittokuren-authored memo entitled 'Concept and Sequence of Events Leading to the Establishment of the National Amusement Machine Right-holders' Association'

(Zenkoku Yūgiki Tokkyo Kenrisha Kyōkai, or Zenkenkyō)[20] proposed the establishment of an organization to prevent the abuse of rights by non-members as follows:

> The Industrial Property Act was also partially revised on January 1 of this year [1971] to introduce changes that strengthen the standing of applicants (right-holders) with a disclosure system [...]. Right-holders can issue warnings to, and demand compensation from, parties that unknowingly use disclosed technologies [...] if, for the sake of argument, we fail to take advantage of this opportunity to discover a way to resolve problems involving industrial property rights and let the situation continue, our industry is certain to enter into a time of patent disputes in the near future, and there will be no hope for companies' stability [...].

The idea took shape, and in 1972, six patent-holding companies that were shareholders of the Nittokuren[21] – Nishijin, Kyōraku Sangyō, Toyomaru Sangyō, Sankyo, Hōkoku and Daiichi Shōkai – came together to form the Zenkenkyō.

An examination of the functions of the Zenkenkyō reveals that it served as a patent pool, just like the Nittokuren. Figure 2.2 (see p. 122) and Figure 3.1, which summarize changes from the 1960s, offer a glimpse of how the group's organizational structure and its relationship with the Nittokuren reflect this functional reality. Before 1972, patents held by the Nittokuren and those the organization had been entrusted to administer by right-holders such as Nishijin and Hōkoku were managed together. In 1972, the Nittokuren entered into an exclusive license with the Zenkenkyō, which had pooled patents, and began managing its patents in bulk (for example, administering non-exclusive licensing agreements with members of the Nikkōso, collecting patent fees, etc.). From the standpoint of non-members, these changes in organizational structure made it seem like right-holding structures had become more complex through the introduction of overlapping licensing routes. It was likely that the changes would lead to increases in research and other costs when pursuing lawsuits concerning technology infringements.

The possibly excessive sense of crisis that can be inferred from the above responses was not caused solely by experience with patent disputes. It was presumably also influenced by technological characteristics that caused development to be conducted outside of machine manufacturers by parlors, part manufacturers and other businesses, as examined in Chapter 2. Without leaving the realm of speculation, it seems reasonable that the industry, having secured its survival by organizing during the 1960s, a time of persistent and sustained concern about outsider involvement, had taken on a defensive posture bordering on the extreme with regard to the possibility of involving non-members that fell outside of the scope of the regulatory framework.

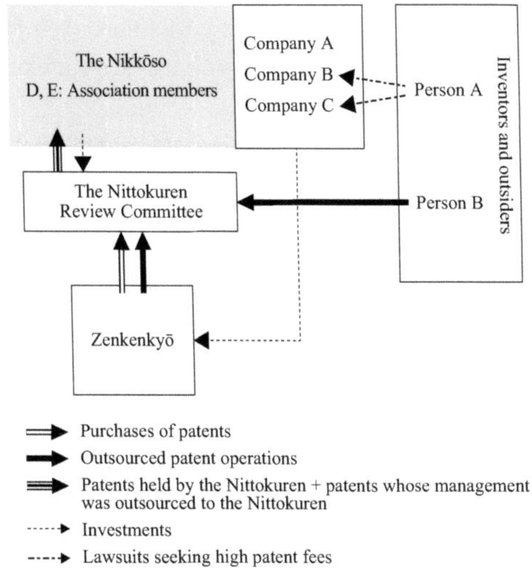

Figure 3.1: Conceptual illustration of the organizational approach to patent management (from 1972)
Source: Compiled by the author based on interviews and the 'Concept and Sequence of Events Leading to the Establishment of the National Amusement Machine Right-holders' Association', which was authored by the Nittokuren (estimated year of compilation: 1971).

Incidentally, a consideration of the formation of the Zenkenkyō that only emphasizes its role in preventing anticipated patent disputes, particularly the abuse of rights by non-members, would yield an overly simplistic understanding of the organization. Although the specific sequence of events leading to the group's formation remains unclear, the concept of 'settling issues involving shareholders, licensees and right-holders'[22] suggests that the founding of the group must also be considered as a measure that was prompted by the legal revisions of the time and designed to deal with right-holders inside the Nittokuren. It goes without saying that the improvements in right-holders' standing that derived from these legal changes applied not only to inventors who were not members of the Nittokuren, but also to members of that group. A consideration of the characteristics of patent ownership up to that point in time is essential if we are to understand the process that led to the formation of the Zenkenkyō.

Patent development by non-members had continued; an executive at Daiichi Shōkai, a member of the Zenkenkyō, observed, 'The pachinko machine manufacturers of the time were in a weak position with regard to patents, and the principal right-holders were companies like manufacturers that had left the business and parts manufacturers'.[23] Although the Nittokuren was initially expected to discover and develop patents as a research institution, the principal sources of patents obtained by the group were ultimately manufacturers exiting the business and non-members.[24]

Patents held by manufacturers that subsequently continued their production activities were retained by those companies, with the result that the Nittokuren was not able to gather up all the patents in the industry.

Inside the organization, the patent right-holders that became the founding members of the Zenkenkyō and other manufacturers found themselves in the same boat despite having opposing interests. Inequality among companies in terms of patent ownership was not in fact reflected in members' voices in the organizations' affairs, which remained equally apportioned in accordance with the fact that all members had made roughly equal investments at the time of the Nittokuren's founding. It is likely that the Patent Act revisions that strengthened right-holders' standing demanded new approaches to the positions of right-holders within the Nittokuren.

As illustrated in Figure 2.2, at this time, manufacturers that were members of the Nikkōso were able to license the patented technologies necessary for development by purchasing a single commodity tax payment certificate stamp in a program managed jointly by that group and the Nittokuren. That single stamp combined patents held by the Nittokuren and those held by other companies. From the perspective of companies holding patents, a route had been provided by which their patents could be used by other manufacturers via the Nittokuren, as illustrated by the example of Hōkoku and Heiwa in Chapter 2. However, under mechanisms designed at a time during the 1960s when the priority was to stabilize prizes, it remained institutionally vague how patents (royalties) were valued within single certificate stamps that consolidated companies' rights, just as it remained unclear how their patents were segregated from those held by the Nittokuren.

Figure 3.1 illustrates the structure through which the shareholders of the Zenkenkyō collectively outsourced patent management to the Nittokuren. This organizational restructuring can be considered to have significant meaning insofar as it marked the institutionalization of outsourced operations between the Nittokuren and the Zenkenkyō. The change created clear differences in the perspectives of right-holders and put in place mechanisms by which they could be evaluated. In another noteworthy development, a review committee was created around 1975 to evaluate patents in a specialized manner. The next part of this chapter introduces this structure, which ended up helping maintain incentives for patent development.

Functional changes at the Nittokuren

For manufacturers, deregulation in 1969 and the Patent Act revisions of 1971 encouraged machine development and at the same time increased their risk of being drawn into patent disputes. Changes in the role of the Nittokuren provide an explanation of the environment in which manufacturers found themselves as a result of these

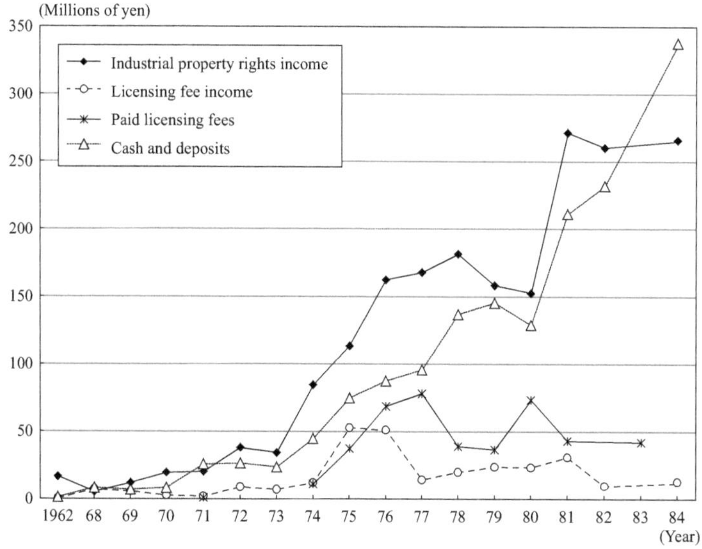

Figure 3.2: Financial structure of the Nittokuren (1962 to 1984)
Source: Compiled based on the Nittokuren's year-end financial statements for 1962 and 1968 through 1984.

conditions. First, let us examine what the Nittokuren's evolving status meant for its revenue base.

Figure 3.2 illustrates major revenue sources, expenditures and assets starting in 1968 based on the Nittokuren's annual financial statements. The organization was primarily supported by two revenue streams – industrial property rights income and licensing fee income – about which two observations can be made.

First, these revenue streams began to grow in 1971, and to grow rapidly from 1973. The revenue growth that began in 1971 was likely the result of the expansion of the scope of patents managed by the Nittokuren after the Zenkenkyō, which was established in 1972, entrusted it with the management of patents previously administered by other companies. In short, this growth in income reflects a strengthening of the rights of companies that owned patents directly and can be understood as the result of the formation of the Zenkenkyō.

The problem involves the nature of these two revenue streams. Although the reason for their separation remains unclear at present, licensing fee income, which was collected separately,[25] was likely still managed and collected by the Nittokuren since it consisted of patent fees set on a per-machine basis and therefore did not require investigation. Two groups of patents generated the industrial property rights revenue stream, a key source of income for the group: (1) patents whose management had been entrusted to the organization and (2) patents held by the Nittokuren itself.

Fiscal year	Patent fee per machine (yen)	Increase relative to 1968
1962	19.9	1.7
1968	11.5	1
1970	16.6	1.4
1972	31.9	2.8
1974	72.2	6.3
1976	155.7	13.5
1978	134.1	11.6
1980	118.3	10.3
1982	111.5	9.7
1984	109.6	9.5
1986	133.8	11.6
1988	141.1	12.2
1993	143.6	12.5
1995	125.3	10.9

Table 3.1: Estimated patent fees per machine

Note: Patent fees = (Industrial property rights income + licensing fee income) / number of machines manufactured during the year in question.

Source: The number of machines manufactured in each year has been calculated based on the year-end financial statements of the Nikkōso, while patent fees have been calculated based on the materials cited in Figure 3.2.

By contrast, the rapid growth in payment derived not from an increase in the number of machines being manufactured, but rather from an increase in the patent fee per machine,[26] as described in Table 3.1.

The second noteworthy point communicated by Figure 3.2 and Table 3.1 is the divergence in the amounts of industrial property rights income and licensing fee payments, which tended nonetheless to move together. Paid licensing fees (see Figure 3.2) were disbursed by the Nittokuren to right-holders (the Zenkenkyō from 1972 and then Chūō Shizai after 1979) after it collected payment for the patents it managed as part of its industrial property rights income and subtracted its management fees. Consequently, it is only natural that the paid licensing fees would track the group's industrial property rights income. What is interesting is their subsequent divergence. That divergence provides a clue for understanding the role that manufacturers expected the Nittokuren to play.

The difference that remained after paid licensing fees were subtracted from industrial property rights income for patent group (1) was the total of fees for patents held by the Nittokuren (2) and management fees charged for patent group (1). If growth in patent fees for group (2) was responsible for the divergence, then that divergence reflected growth in patent rights held by the Nittokuren. However, to the

(Unit: Yen)

Fiscal year	Utility model patent rights	Patent rights
1962	12,029,632	396,000
1963		97,201
1968	4,612,012	
1969	3,571,639	2
1970	2,817,698	2
1971	560,661	2
1972	4,080,420	2
1973	3,285,680	2
1974	2,436,440	
1975	1,578,001	
1976	795,001	
1977	264,169	
1978	161,168	
1979	572,168	
1980	432,168	
1981	292,168	
1982	152,167	
1986		906,251
1987		781,251
1988		656,251
1994	716,000	
1995	582,000	

Table 3.2: Asset value of patents held by the Nittokuren
Note: * For a list of average exchange rates by year, see table on p. xv.
Source: Compiled based on Figure 3.2.

extent that Table 3.2 is accurate, growth in (1) cannot be adequately explained by (2) since the asset value of patents held by the Nittokuren was declining over the long term. For the sake of argument, let us stipulate that (2) stayed constant. In that case, it is likely that the divergence reflects the magnitude of management fees received by the Nittokuren relative to the patent rights it managed.

In other words, the rapid growth exhibited by both reflects the fact that the Nittokuren paid out the patent fees it collected as licensing fees in accordance with the management agreement forged with the Zenkenkyō at the time of that group's founding, which stipulated, 'the contracting party shall bear all costs associated with the outsourced operations, and the Nittokuren shall render payment of collected

Fiscal year	Fiscal-year industrial property rights income per unit (yen)	Fees as a percentage of industrial property rights income per unit (%)	
1968	1		
Average through 1971	3.13		
72~74	9.51		
1975	20.70	90.20	
1976	29.60	77.04	Improving standing of right-holders (1975–1978)
1977	30.53	59.04	
1978	33.04	57.05	
1979	28.79	75.29	
1980	27.78	72.95	
1981	49.39	72.94	
1982	47.36	83.47	
1983			Emphasis on patent management functions (1979–1988)
1984	48.39	84.17	
1985	41.30	97.60	
1986			
1987			
1988	55.99	99.35	

Table 3.3: Operations outsourced to the Nittokuren
Source: Compiled based on Figure 3.1.

licensing fees to the contracting party after subtracting the costs noted above'.[27] Assuming that (2) was constant, the divergence of paid licensing fees from industrial property rights income indicates a rise in management fees.

Management fees were retained by the Nittokuren to cover expenditure associated with the performance of its contractual operations, for example the cost of conducting investigations to determine whether patent rights were being violated and costs associated with the collection of licensing fees.[28] In this sense, increases and decreases can be identified by calculating the management fees retained by the Nittokuren as a percentage of industrial property rights income during different times, as charted in Table 3.3. That figure began to decline from about 90 percent in 1975, when the Review Committee was formed,[29] to less than 60 percent in 1978 before starting to rise again.

The figures illustrate a trend in which the proportion of earnings retained by the Nittokuren declined starting in 1975, pushing up the percentage of income allocated to patent fees, which were returned to right-holders. That tendency reflects the formation of the Review Committee in 1975 and the improvement in right-holders' standing. By contrast, the subsequent sustained divergence of industrial property rights income and patent fee allocations – which is to say, the increase in management fees retained by the group – seems to suggest that right-holders emphasized its management function, expressed as management fees, to a greater degree than the acquisition of patent fees.[30]

In this way, consideration for the interests of right-holders was expressed in the form of changes in payments as a result of the development of an institutional basis for appropriately evaluating patent violations after the establishment of the Zenkenkyō. This point supports the idea that the need to incentivize development was a factor in the establishment of the Zenkenkyō. However, that those increases in payments lagged and faced rigid upward limits indicates that right-holders at the time were restrained in their collection of patent fees and that they put greater emphasis on the Nittokuren's management operations.

As described above, the Nittokuren's financial structure was from the 1970s characterized by consistent growth in revenue from its patent management services (i.e., its monitoring and administration functions) while income from its patent holdings (i.e., its price stabilization function) remained flat. The increase in fees from the organization's patent management services was the result of a rise in its dependence on patent management contracted by manufacturers as well as management operations such as monitoring, investigations and the group's role as a sort of administrative clearinghouse while the patent assets it held increasingly expired. The Nittokuren's management capabilities, which also illustrate changes in its revenue base, were accumulated in the context of the group's experience with resolving actual cases. I will close this section by examining the mechanisms of the Review Committee, which illustrate the strength of the group's monitoring capabilities, along with some specific examples.

Specialized patent management

Following deregulation in 1969 and the revision of the Patent Act in 1971, court cases involving patent infringement arose frequently, as expected. Six major patent disputes occurred during the 1970s.[31] Interestingly, the plaintiffs in all of those cases were individuals who had made inventions, and the defendants were manufacturers involved in production activities. None of them involved the sort of disputes between insider companies that had characterized the 1950s. In the cases, the Nittokuren played the role of a clearinghouse for negotiations. This role, which differed from that played by the group during the 1960s, illustrates how the machine market had changed.

As explained in Chapter 2, most lawsuits filed during the 1960s were intended to regulate outsiders involved in the underselling of machines without paying patent fees or the commodity tax and parlors that had installed those machines. By contrast, disputes during the 1970s involved technological interpretations, for example in relation to patent right infringements. Although the Nittokuren had not initially planned to become actively involved in negotiations, it came to offer such specialized service as disputes accumulated – which is to say, naturally over time.

As an example, consider the Hino incident of 1969, in which a parlor operator named Yoshiyuki Hino who held a patent related to electric machines[32] sued three manufacturers (Daiichi Shōkai, Nishijin and Kyōraku Sangyō) for infringing on that patent. The case took about two years to resolve. The plaintiff asked to consolidate points of contact for the defendants, and the Nittokuren obliged.[33] Negotiations eventually led to a compromise on the part of Hino in return for a lowering of the patent fee from 300 yen to 50 yen and made the Nittokuren responsible for collecting payment. The arrangement continued until 1985. This consolidation of patent dispute resolution became increasingly important as a function of the Nittokuren during the 1970s. While the monitoring and regulation of illegitimate businesses seen during the 1960s moved away from center stage during this period, those functions are likely to have continued as the core infrastructure on which the group's operations were built.

The Review Committee (see Figure 3.1 above) deserves attention as a core function of the Nittokuren that began during this period and served to strengthen patent evaluation and infringement monitoring. I will consider the roles that the committee was expected to play through the lens of the changes that its formation triggered.

The direct reason for the creation of the committee was likely related to the strengthening of the standing of right-holders following the introduction of the public disclosure system in 1971. In short, the ability to review right-holders' assertions and determine their validity emerged as an issue. When patents posed various problems based on the disclosure system, it was no simple matter to determine whether or not actual machine designs constituted infringement. From their experience with legal disputes, manufacturers were well aware of the ambiguity surrounding technological interpretations in decisions about the scope of potential infringements, of the resulting uncertainty in the outcomes of associated lawsuits, and of the extent to which one of their principal functions – production activities – could be impeded until verdicts were handed down (see Chapter 2). At this point in time, the Nittokuren did not have the ability to make judgments about such problems, nor was there any need for it to have that capability. Thus far, the Nittokuren's ability to collect aggregated royalties for the patents it held and managed and its monitoring function for price support had been key. During the industry's existential crisis of the 1960s, patent fees were likely adjusted to reflect levels that could be realistically paid while right-holders made compromises. For that reason, the value of the patents managed by the Nittokuren was not subject to rigorous review.

Consequently, the Review Committee was likely an institutional reflection of the need for patent review capabilities, which became problematic with the onset of the outsourcing arrangement with the Zenkenkyō. While the details of how the committee operated at the time of its formation remain unclear, it can be inferred that it started functioning during the mid-1970s.[34] Reports issued by the Nittokuren in later years offer a picture of the general manner in which the committee operated once it was fully up and running.[35]

The basic membership of the Review Committee consisted of attorneys and individuals with expert knowledge of the patents belonging to the right-holder companies that were members of the Zenkenkyō. The group was chaired by a Nittokuren executive for whom the chairmanship was his principal responsibility.[36] Its corporate membership was not fixed, but rather varied over time as individuals with patent-related knowledge were assigned by companies 'that found themselves filing more potentially valid applications after an employee with experience in patents had joined the company'[37] and manufacturers that were likely to be able to acquire patent rights after establishing a department dedicated to that concern[38] – meaning manufacturers that were actively involved in developing patents.

Comprised of these members, the committee discussed which rights were used (infringed upon) by various manufacturers' machines and examined associated matters. Patents related to basic machine design that the right-holder company had determined were being used by other companies were submitted for review.[39] Representative machines launched each year by all manufacturers were gathered at the Nittokuren in advance[40] so that the Review Committee could examine each to determine whether it infringed on the submitted rights. Following a discussion of whether there were any problems with the proposed interpretations, the committee determined by majority vote whether any infringement had occurred.[41] Based on the results of such votes, the Nittokuren estimated licensing fees in accordance with each company's sales record (from one week to ten days) and drafted agreements.[42]

In this way, it is clear that the expert members of the Review Committee engaged in the rigorous technological interpretation of potential infringements by examining actual machines and ironed out differing interpretations. Submitted (asserted) patents typically excluded transitory designs such as *yakumono* accessories and were instead limited to basic machine design technologies. In this way, the assertion of patent rights remained restrained. What is interesting about this arrangement is that the use of patents came first; review, discussion, payment and contractual agreement only occurred after use. The coordinating role played by the committee can be seen as preventing patent disputes between insider companies while guaranteeing manufacturers' ability to smoothly pursue their primary functions of development and production.

TOWARD DEVELOPMENT-BASED COMPETITION

Rank	1964 Company	Market share (%)	Number of machines sold	1967 Company	Market share (%)	Number of machines sold	1970 Company	Market share (%)	Number of machines sold
1	Nishijin	19.1	156,840	Nishijin	24.2	286,311	Nishijin	20.9	280,332
2	Heiwa	13.4	109,900	Heiwa	14	165,180	Heiwa Kōgyō	11.1	149,625
3	Marushin Kōgyō	9.4	77,008	Marushin Kōgyō	7.4	87,636	Daiichi Shōkai	9.5	127,688
4	Matsuya Sangyō	4.7	38,430	Sanyō Bussan	7	82,939	Maruhon Kōgyō	8.4	112,510
5	Okumura Yūki	4.5	37,166	Daiichi Shōkai	5.3	62,240	Kyōraku Sangyō	8.1	109,150
6	Toyomaru Sangyō	4.3	35,048	Okumura Yūki	4.3	50,578	Sanyō Bussan	7.6	101,543
7	Daiichi Shōkai	3.9	31,963	Sankyo	3.6	42,161	Sankyo	7.3	97,518
8	Daidō Yūki Seisakusho	3.3	26,797	Maruhon Kōgyō	3.2	38,156	Okumura Yūki	5	66,569
9	Kishi Kinzoku Kōgyōsho	2.9	23,823	Toyomaru Sangyō	3.1	37,186	Nyū Gin	4.3	57,832
10	Sanyō Bussan	2.8	23,266	Tōyō Kōgyō Yūki	3	35,369	Toyomaru Sangyō	2.5	33,299
11	Yamato Nishikawa Seisakusho	2.6	21,333	Kyōraku Sangyō	2.9	33,911	Nyū Matsuya Sangyō	1.9	26,193
12	Komura Yūki (Ginza Shōkai)	2.5	20,144	Kokusai Yūki	2.3	27,062	Yamato Seisakusho	1.9	25,130
13	Tōkai Bussan	2.2	18,211	Nyū Purinsu	2.2	26,128	Kyōgoku Seisakusho	1.6	21,058
14	Surī Sutā Kōgyō	1.9	15,721	Yamato Nishikawa Seisakusho	2	24,104	Surī Sutā Kōgyō	1.5	20,723
15	Maruzen Yūki Sankyo Shōkai	1.8	14,792	Tōkai Kōgyō Yūki	1.9	22,938	Takao	1.1	14,965
16	Nyū Purinsu	1.7	14,123	Surī Sutā Kōgyō	1.6	19,084	Mizuho Shōkai	1.1	14,909
17	Hōkoku Kikō	1.6	13,008	Sankō Kōki	1.3	15,267	Matsuya	0.8	11,142
18	Kyōraku Seisakusho	1.6	12,859	Kyōraku Seisakusho	1.3	15,262	Kyōraku Seisakusho	0.8	10,273
19	Kyōraku Sangyō	1.5	12,451	Nyū Matsuya Sangyō	1.2	14,356	Kokusai Yūki	0.7	9,577
20	Sankō Kōki	1.5	12,376	Daidō Kōgyō	0.8	9,612	Daidō Kōgyō	0.6	8,218
21	Naritashiki Seisakusho	1.4	11,521	Isuzu Seisakusho	0.8	9,110	Hōkoku Hanbai (wholesaler of Hōkoku Yūki Seisakusho)	0.5	6,401
22	Tōyō Kōgyō Yūki	1.2	9,626	Nagoya Sangyō	0.7	8,820	Masamura Kikai	0.5	6,189
23	Isuzu Seisakusho	1.2	9,477	Matsumoto Yūki	0.7	8,694	Narita Seisakusho	0.4	4,928
24	Ichigin Kōgyō	1.1	9,440	Giken Kōgyō	0.7	8,009	Nashonaru Yūki	0.4	4,721
25	Monako Shōkai	1.0	8,177	Takeya	0.6	6,908	Takeya	0.3	4,634
26	Matsuya Kikai Seisakusho	1.0	7,842	Hōkoku Kikō	0.6	6,621	Nyū Ichigin	0.3	4,315
27	Toyo Sangyō	0.9	7,099	Narita Seisakusho	0.5	5,506	Monako Shōkai	0.3	4,192
28	Kyōritsu Kikō	0.8	6,467	Marukoshi Kōgyō	0.4	4,256	Isuzu Seisakusho	0.3	4,098
29	Mizuho Shōkai	0.6	4,832	Matsuya Kikai Seisakusho	0.3	4,133	Maruzen Yūki	0.3	3,534
30	Nagoya Ginza Shōkai	0.6	4,683	Maruzen Yūki Sankyo Shōkai	0.3	4,046	Omori Yūki Saisakusho	0.1	812
31	Mitsukoshi Sangyō	0.4	3,494	Mizuho Shōkai	0.3	4,004	Sankō	0.1	757
32	Omori Yūki Saisakusho	0.4	3,456	Monako Shōkai	0.3	3,191	Matsumoto Yūki	0.1	745
33	Shin'ei Sangyō	0.4	3,308	Omori Yūgiki Saisakusho	0.3	3,003	Tamafuku Sangyō	0	447
34	Kyōgoku Seisakusho	0.4	3,196	Takao Seisakusho	0.2	2,631	Shinwa	0	206
35	Masamura Shōkai	0.3	2,787	Masamura Shōkai	0.2	2,002	34 (39)	100.0	1,344,200
36	Takeya	0.3	2,081	Maiami Seisakusho	0.1	1,687			
37	Meiwa Shōten	0.2	1,635	Yutaka Sangyō	0.1	1,302			
38	Kataoka Shōkai	0.2	1,487	Kyōgoku Seisakusho	0.1	1,205			
39	Maiami Seisakusho	0.2	1,487	Meiwa Seisakusho	0.1	1,090			
40	Sanwa Seisakusho	0.1	929	Tamafuku Sangyō	0	300			
41	Nagoya Sangyō	0.1	892	Kataoka Shōkai	0	200			
42	Kansai Yūgi	0.1	818	41 (44)	100.0	1,182,200			
43	Meigin Shōkai	0.1	706						
44	Ani Seisakusho	0.1	706						
45	Chūō Seisakusho	0.1	595						
	45 (47[c)])	100.0	822,000						

1976		
Company	Market share (%)	Number of machines sold
Nishijin	16.3	223,787
Heiwa Kōgyō	14.8	202,302
Sankyo	10.8	147,919
Maruhon Kōgyō	9.2	126,660
Sanyō Bussan	8	109,001
Kyōraku Sangyō	6.3	86,950
Daiichi Shōkai	6	81,616
Mizuho Seisakusho	4	54,290
Nyū Gin	3.9	53,109
Okumura Yūki	3.3	45,200
Surī Sutā Kōgyō	2.9	39,474
Toyomaru Sangyō	2.8	37,833
Takeya	2	27,482
Nashonaru Kikai Kōgyō	1.2	16,381
Daidō	1.1	15,238
Hōkoku Hanbai	1.1	14,821
Nyū Matsuya Sangyō	0.9	11,665
Satomi	0.8	10,730
Matsumoto Yūki	0.7	10,268
Yamato Seisakusho	0.6	8,883
Kyōraku Seisakusho	0.6	7,621
Masamura Kikai	0.5	6,894
Takao	0.5	6,883
Ginza	0.5	6,472
Nyū Ichigin	0.5	6,374
Daikō Monako Yūki Kōgyō	0.3	3,515
Kyōgoku Seisakusho	0.2	3,184
Fuji Shōji	0.2	3,121
Maruzen Bussan	0.2	2,361
Isuzu Seisakusho	0	156
Dōwa Seiki Kōgyō	0	11
Narita Seisakusho	0	0
32	100.0	1,370,200

1982		
Company	Market share (%)	Number of machines sold
Heiwa Kōgyō	27.3	661,237
Sankyo	18.1	436,960
Nishijin	10.9	264,193
Kyōraku Sangyō	10.7	258,493
Sanyō Bussan	8.9	216,437
Daiichi Shōkai	6.2	151,072
Nyū Gin	4.7	113,703
Maruhon Kōgyō	4.1	99,044
Okumura Yūki	3.3	79,463
Toyomaru Sangyō	2.1	50,348
Mizuho Seisakusho	1.2	27,948
Ginza	0.8	18,358
Takao	0.6	15,018
Taiyō Denshi	0.4	10,862
Samī Kōgyō	0.2	5,054
Daidō	0.1	3,045
Fuji Shōji	0.1	2,973
Takeya	0.1	2,154
Maruzen Yūki	0.1	1,531
Mitsuba Sangyō	0	991
Sansei	0	618
Meiyū Sangyō	0	198
22	100.0	2,419,700

1983		
Company	Market share (%)	Number of machines sold
Heiwa Kōgyō	22.4	596,868
Sankyo	20.1	534,019
Kyōraku Sangyō	11.5	306,361
Nishijin	9.8	261,714
Sanyō Bussan	9.7	258,078
Daiichi Shōkai	8.3	220,996
Nyū Gin	4.3	115,085
Okumura Yūki	4.2	111,700
Maruhon Kōgyō	4.1	108,461
Toyomaru Sangyō	2.2	58,206
Mizuho Seisakusho	0.9	24,884
Ginza	0.9	22,637
Takao	0.5	13,241
Taiyō Denshi	0.4	9,447
Masamura Yūki	0.3	8,367
Fuji Shōji	0.1	2,486
Daidō	0.1	2,379
Takeya	0.1	2,126
Samī Kōgyō	0.1	1,343
Sansei	0	552
Meiyū Sangyō	0	50
21	100.0	2,659,000

Fell from rankings or exited business after fiscal year in question

Resumed production

Newly ranked

Paused operations after fiscal year in question

Table 3.4: Manufacturer market share figures

Notes:

a. The Nikkōso administered a program that issued certificate stamps to facilitate manufacturers' payment of the commodity tax. Companies had to purchase the same number of stamps as the number of machines they sold (effectively equal to the number of machines they manufactured) by paying the association.
Since total purchases of certificate stamps became fee income for the organization, the total number of machines manufactured in any given fiscal year can be calculated by dividing total fee income by 30 yen per certificate stamp (from 1960 through 1962) or by 20 yen per stamp (for subsequent years).
The number of machines manufactured by each company was obtained by multiplying the total number of machines manufactured by market share, estimated as described in Note (b) below.

b. Market share figures are estimates. The financial data available for analysis varies with the fiscal year; examples include tax payment reserves, deposit reserves and business volume dividends.
Having concluded that amounts paid by companies are reflected in manufacturing counts (i.e., in each company's rank in the market), I've calculated each company's share of the total amount and used it as a proxy variable for market share.

c. Number of non-members in each fiscal year; unclear after 1970.

Source: Year-end financial statement for the Nikkōso for each fiscal year.

This chapter's ultimate focus is on the effects of the Nittokuren's functions on manufacturers' development behavior and on the relationship between the two. Next, I will examine the characteristics of competition in the machine market in preparation for exploring these issues. Here I would like to address three issues. First, I will offer an overview of competition while paying attention to its relationship with regulation. Second, I will make some observations concerning manufacturer behavior in the context of development-based competition. Third, I will discuss the kinds of machines sought by the market – customers and parlors – based on the general direction of development, which is to say models created in accordance with new standards, and explore how manufacturers had prepared to develop a new generation of technologies.

Let us begin by taking a broad look at competition. Table 3.4 offers estimated market share figures based on the number of machines sold by various manufacturers (see Table 3.4 Notes for more on methodology). Manufacturers' positions in the list fluctuated wildly over time from the 1960s to the 1970s. It is immediately apparent that competition was intense enough to force companies out of business.[42] Two characteristics become clear if we focus on decade-by-decade changes.

Firstly, the 1960s saw cutthroat competition that thrust manufacturers out of the standings or out of the business altogether by the next period in the table (between 1964 and 1967, 1967 and 1970, 1970 and 1976, 1976 and 1982), even companies that enjoyed comparatively high positions in the list. Manufacturers' businesses were presumably unstable. This state of affairs continued until around 1970, when manufacturers that were unable to secure a certain amount of market share exited the industry. It is fair to conclude that the market finally stabilized during the 1970s, although the not insignificant number of companies withdrawing from the machine business indicates that a measure of instability remained. Such withdrawals were concentrated once more among manufacturers with low market share from 1976 to 1982. The causes of exits from the industry during the 1970s, which differ from those in previous periods of the segment's history, and their significance are worth examining from the standpoint taken in this chapter, which anticipates development during the 1980s.

Secondly, I would also like to focus on the degree of concentration. The degree of concentration among the two or three top companies was high, and those manufacturers generally managed to secure a stable position atop the market share rankings over the long term. Against that backdrop, notice how the degree of concentration declined in 1970. The number of companies exiting the industry lagged from 1970 to 1976 compared to other periods, before the top three companies subsequently resumed their former high level of concentration. It is likely that something significant happened between 1970 and 1976.

Year	Number of models	Average	Year	Number of models	Average
1957	3	3.3	1969	9	7
1958	6		1970	7	
1959	4		1971	7	
1960	3		1972	6	
1961	2		1973	7	
1962	2		1974	6	
1963	2		1975	7	
1964	2		1976	6	
1965	6		1977	6	
1966	5		1978	7	
1967	3		1979	9	
1968	2		1980	7	

Table 3.5: Number of models launched by Nishijin
Source: Compiled based on Sōgyō Gojūnen Kinenshi Hensan Iinkai (2001: 73, 87, 109).

Let us examine changes from 1970 to 1976, which cannot be overlooked in any consideration of these two characteristics.

Heightened development: deregulation and development

During the 1970s, the pachinko market's share of the leisure market remained roughly constant, exhibiting little variation: 5.5 percent in 1970, 5.4 percent in 1972, 5.8 percent in 1974, 5.0 percent in 1976 and 5.3 percent in 1978.[44] At a time of stable standings, the pachinko industry did not display the sort of spectacular growth that would allow it to surpass other leisure-related industries, but rather was limited to growing within the context of an expanding leisure market that was being driven by economic growth.[45] When we reexamine the position of manufacturers developing pachinko machines in light of such conditions, we find that while these companies were unable to launch revolutionary machines that would have triggered growth that outpaced the larger economy, they were nonetheless able to consistently supply machines that reliably met consumer demand while keeping pace with the latency of the leisure market's growth. In order to throw the actual conditions surrounding development into relief, it is necessary to examine how regulations constrained development, what sort of changes they precipitated and what sort of relationships were built among manufacturers as development proceeded.

Table 3.5 presents the number of models developed and launched each year by Nishijin, which enjoyed a leading market share from the late 1950s to the mid-1970s, starting in 1955 when the licensing system was introduced. The company had a development-oriented culture and actively registered patents, including its automated machines of 1960 following the launch of *jinmitto* technology in 1957. The company was also known for its pioneering technology for the automatic ball replenishment systems that came into widespread use during the 1960s.

The figures in Table 3.5 are based on products featured in *The 50th Anniversary ROAD* (an account of the company's history), which likely included representative models that had enjoyed a certain level of popularity.[46] The impact of systematic changes in the industry as expressed by means of a consistent criterion such as this one can be treated as a characteristic trend.

Note here the change in the average number of models per year before and after deregulation, which illustrates the effects of the 1969 revision to the Entertainment and Amusement Establishment Control Act. The company launched an average of seven models each year from 1969 to 1980, more than double the annual average of 3.3 models up to 1968. This change reflects the diversification of products in the wake of the relaxation of machine certification standards.

The new machine standards were announced in April 1969 and took effect on June 1. Responding to this systematic change, Nishijin wasted no time in announcing a machine with a 100-shot tray, which satisfied the new regulations, in May.[47] That announcement was likely the first response of any company in the industry. Previously, manufacturers presumably had little difficulty complying with the 1955 regulation since it based its standard on the 1949 single-shot design. However, according to Kinji Konayagi, a former executive of major manufacturer Heiwa, the second top company in terms of market share (see Table 3.4), the new deregulatory changes did not easily lead to machine development.[48] Of the change introduced in 1969, he said:

> When Manager Oda of the PR department took a prototype that had finally been finished after an around-the-clock effort to the National Police Agency, the inspection was exceedingly strict, or rather, they tried things with the machine that we as the manufacturer hadn't even imagined, and if there was ever one ball over 100, the machine was denied. The second, third, fourth and fifth tries were all failures. We were unable to deliver machines when we had promised them, even though we had accepted deposits from customers all over the country [...] we had to travel around apologizing to one [customer] after the next [...] the [development] project team [...] gave up vacation days and focused entirely on satisfying the demanding standards sought by the National Police Agency [...] but [...] we failed to receive approval, even on the eleventh try [...]. It was one dreadful day after the next for fifty days.[49]

In this way, the process of developing machines that complied with the new standards was a trial-and-error affair that demanded strong patience. Although the risks associated with working under these regulations applied to all manufacturers, Nishijin had development capabilities that were second to none, a fact that was highlighted when a later manager of the company's General Affairs Department confidently declared, 'Other companies create one new machine every six months, but we do that in three months [...] our market share just keeps rising'.[50] The diversity of products illustrated in Table 3.5 was a unique accomplishment of Nishijin as a capable manufacturer.

Even granting the difference between Nishijin and its competitors, it would not be far from the mark to conclude, based on the depiction of opportunities provided to individual companies by these systematic changes in Table 3.5, that the deregulation spurred product development at other companies, too, and led to a diversification in their product lines. This general direction was also welcomed by parlors, which had to choose models in line with consumer needs.

A subsequent study undertaken in 1979 offers another perspective on the conditions of this period. The study, administered by the Small Business Information Center (Chūshō Kigyō Jōhō Sentā), an organization dedicated to promoting small and medium-size businesses, was designed to inform proposals about how such entities could respond to 'increasing individuality in consumption and diversity in lifestyles'. According to a questionnaire survey of pachinko fans carried out as part of that study,[51] the most commonly cited request made to parlors by people who played pachinko at least once per week was for 'more winning balls' (67 percent of respondents). That was followed by 'brighter parlors' (at 19 percent) and 'new machines' (at 18 percent).[52] Of the parlors that were supposed to be meeting such demand, 63 percent complained about 'the short machine life cycle and high expense of replacing machines',[53] pointing to concerns about the need to frequently replace machines with new models to attract and retain customers. The findings highlighted manufacturers' efforts to supply numerous types of machines while developing ones that would enable even more frequent updates than in the past.

The study suggested that parlors were in a position to ascertain whether customers preferred gameplay or speculative elements – in short, that they were in the possession of information about customer needs that machines needed to accommodate – and proposed that greater use of such information should be made in development.[54] Diversification can be considered to be the result of manufacturers' efforts to meet demand for new machines on the part of parlors. Seen in this light, wide-ranging product development can be seen throughout the industry, although its extent varied among manufacturers. Companies' product diversification efforts were both the cause of the intensifying competition surrounding development that began in 1969 and its result.

Below I will examine the development activities undertaken by manufacturers as diversification proceeded apace in the wake of deregulation by focusing on two examples. The first is the electric machines that began penetrating the market in 1973, and the second involves manufacturers' responses to Daisangen designs, which became a hot topic the following fall.

Vacuum created by regulations

Electric machines were made possible by a notice describing new requirements for pachinko machines that was issued on November 25, 1972.[55] Yoshiyuki Hino, who operated a parlor in the city of Kure, Hiroshima, applied to have a modified machine to which he had added a motorized ball-launching mechanism certified by the Hiroshima Prefecture Police Headquarters. The machine was approved on September 25, 1972. Electric machine designs spread throughout the industry after the announcement of new requirements in November based on the publication of an opinion piece entitled 'National Police Agency Security Bulletin No. 130 of October 18, 1972: Concerning treatment of the Hino-type 100-launch manual tray amusement machine' by the National Police Agency's Crime Prevention and Youth Section (Bōhan Shōnenka). It was that sequence of events that led to the Hino case, the lawsuit discussed in the first part of this chapter that involved the infringement of three manufacturers' patents.

Pachinko machines had been limited to manual designs since machines with motors were prohibited under the 1955 ban on successive-shot machines (see Chapter 1) on the grounds that they offered an excessively speculative element. Based on this background, there was concern among people calling for the reimposition of the regulation within the industry in response to the effective return of electric machines, about which they noted, 'Electric pachinko machines have become popular recently in many areas [...] [and] phenomena similar to those on the eve of the ban on successive-shot machines [in 1955] call to mind a sense of crisis'.[56] However, the development also exhibited signs of changes that differed from the social conditions during the early 1950s. The state-controlled gambling market was growing, signifying rising social acceptance of gambling. The emergence of a perspective that expected electric machines, too, to penetrate the market was only a natural progression of that trend.[57]

That said, apart from the new machines' relationship to regulations, views concerning their penetration into, and establishment in, the market were not monolithic. Parlors in the Kinki region (which consists of six prefectures including Osaka in western Japan) had made the decision not to use electric machines, and some manufacturers even exhibited a negative attitude toward the development of such machines, a view to which Seiichi Uchigashima, the executive director of the Nikkōso, gave voice when he said, 'We're not putting effort into electric machines because manual machines were mainstream pachinko', which required more skill.[58] However, the manufacturers were all forced to accommodate 'demands to build them, build them'[59] from parlors in Shikoku, Chugoku and Kyushu in southwest Japan with a view toward popularity that could earn customers' enthusiastic support.

When electric machines initially appeared, manufacturers hesitated to develop similar models for regulation-related reasons while adopting a cautious approach that reflected their lack of confidence in the market's reaction. This negative attitude indicates the extent of the risk faced by companies in the sector as they grappled with regulations and the difficulty of predicting popularity, both distinguishing characteristics of the market. At the same time, manufacturers in some regional markets responded positively to the popularity of electric machines. It is likely that companies adopted a variety of attitudes regarding their awareness of the popularity of electric machines and forecasts of new local markets. Although there are no sources that allow a direct investigation of manufacturers' intentions, we can try to detect companies' different approaches by examining ads in an industry magazine for parlors, *Gekkan Yūgi Nihon* ('Japan Amusement Monthly'), to observe disparities in the timing of their development efforts. Working under the assumption that companies ran ads in the same month as they launched products, we can infer the nature of their attitudes toward development from the resulting timeline.[60] We cannot presume that development coincided with the publication of ads, since it had to be completed in advance of the product launch, but we can safely assume that there was only a narrow gap between the two since companies were constrained by the seasons in which parlors replaced machines and by popularity.

Among the first manufacturers reacting to the deregulation were three companies that reportedly announced the first set of new electric machines: Kyōraku Sangyō, Daiichi Shōkai and Toyomaru Sangyō. Hino, who developed the first electric design, used his own machines at a number of parlors he operated, and the results were impressive. In this way, a machine developed by a parlor operator led to the discovery of a new market. The three manufacturers mentioned above were the first to notice the market's reaction and developed their own electric machines with standalone motors.[61]

Based on initiatives like the one described below, Kyoto-based Kyōraku Seisakusho was also likely actively working to develop electric machines at the time. In April 1973, the company launched its first electric machine with a two-page ad featuring the copy, 'Incredible popularity! The Hino-type electric pachinko Star electric mechanism will draw new customers and encourage sales! The Hino-type launch mechanism is amazing – watch it send balls flying as you push on the handle with varying levels of strength! Everyone's talking about this machine, which is attracting attention throughout the Japanese archipelago!'.[62] The company was a month later than the first three of its counterparts, but the move was a bold one since the market remained opaque, and most of the industry was adopting a wait-and-see attitude. Although it is unclear what the label 'Hino-type' actually meant in terms of technology or other characteristics,[63] two-page ads with the same content continued until May. That the company expanded ads that had run on a single page in *Gekkan Yūgi Nihon* during the first half of the 1960s to two pages indicates the extent to which it was focusing on the development of these products.

An examination of operations at the Taigeki Game Center in the city of Kumamoto, which had installed machines from Kyōraku Seisakusho, gives a sense of the solid future potential of electric machines. Reports indicate that the facility, whose electric models accounted for just seventy (11 percent) of the 600 machines it operated, was planning to replace up to half its machines in the near future, signaling that 'the growth of electric models [was] becoming a topic of conversation'.[64]

Such efforts by Kyōraku Seisakusho were recognized as being motivated by a desire to be 'the early bird that gets the worm'.[65] That is, the purchase of the machines by Taigeki Game Center in Kumamoto indicates both that the company was angling to establish its popularity in the city by being one of the first-movers and that it was projecting that electric models would be popular for a fairly long period of time based on its analysis of current conditions and its forecast outlook. The company actively embraced the development risk in an effort to secure the market ahead of competitors because it foresaw that electric machines would become established at parlors.

Spurred perhaps by the active efforts of Kyōraku Seisakusho, other manufacturers attempted – even if in local and gradual ways – to assess reliable changes in markets where electric machines had penetrated starting in May. Using the same catchphrase ('Hino-type') as Kyōraku Seisakusho, Daidō Kōgyō[66] and Surī Sutā launched electric machines as a 'sudden boom in electric designs'[67] was recognized in the industry. In addition to noting the 'great popularity of electric models', observers predicted the entry of Heiwa into the market (in a June ad[68]), and it was reported that middle-ground and higher manufactures like Sanyō Bussan and Nyūmatsuya (see Table 3.4 above) had started making prototypes. Kyōraku Sangyō, which had already announced one of the first electric machines, held a tradeshow that month,[69] and June saw the entry of Nyū Gin and Hōkoku, which had related technologies after achieving popularity during the early 1950s with machines that had automatic, motorized ball launchers.[70]

In August, Sanyō Bussan, which had been working on a prototype, also announced an electric machine.[71] It is interesting to note that leading manufacturer Nishijin was yet to enter the market at this stage.[72] As was made clear by the Small Business Information Center study cited above, electric machines were popular[73] in the Kansai region (western Japan),[74] where Nishijin was considered to enjoy a 70 percent market share. Nishijin seems to have been several steps behind its competitors, although this inference must be qualified by noting that it derives entirely from observations gleaned from ads. It is unlikely that the company, which prided itself on the technological capability that underpinned its consistently growing market share, was encountering technological problems related to a design that had already been discovered during the 1950s.

At the National New Amusement Machine Model Exhibition held on September 9 and 10, 1973, 'most manufacturers exhibited new electric models with a focus on "the popularity of electric"'.[75] Although some observers pointed out that it was 'impossible to clearly predict how popular' electric machines would become when the exhibition was announced in August, reports held that 'the operating popularity [of such models in September] is currently extremely good, and manufacturers are firming up production structures'.[76] In addition to various *yakumono* accessories and fixed gauges that had been developed 'in line with a diversifying era', the exhibition focused on electric machines. This focus on one trend that reflected the character of the times backed up expectations that the models would spread throughout the market. In the event, the exhibition, which with forty-one participants had attracted fewer manufacturers than usual, was a resounding success as reports described unprecedented attendance, including 5000 people with connections to the industry and 10,000 members of the public.[77]

The sequence of events from the debut of the first electric machine to the development and launch of similar models by other manufacturers went as follows: Hino gained certification for its pioneering model in November 1972, four months before another manufacturer developed and launched a similar model in March 1973 (with installations starting in April). About five months later, top manufacturer Nishijin entered the market after a number of other manufacturers began actively working to develop the market. Around this point in time, most other manufacturers began to follow suit by developing electric machines, whose establishment in the market became assured at the September exhibition. If we limit our perspective to manufacturers' development and product announcements, it becomes apparent that there was a lag of about one season.

Manufacturers' different approaches likely reflect the nature of demand in relation to pachinko consumers and parlor operations. That is because manual designs remained doggedly popular, while the popularity of electric machines varied by region.[78] According to the Small Business Information Center study mentioned above, long-time pachinko fans who had skills and who were familiar with manual machines had little positive to say about electric machines,[79] while some parlors cited 'excessive prize balls' as a management-related reason for their decision not to use the new designs.[80]

On the other hand, the appearance of electric machines that allowed customers to hit plenty of balls without a particularly high level of skill attracted a new customer demographic. For example, females drew attention as a new market during the 1970s,[81] and the introduction of electric machines may have contributed to growth in the number of female customers. Due to the presence of such differing needs, markets that exhibited a preference for machines with a more pronounced speculative element did not grow as a result of dramatic change; rather, they formed over time as their contours were thrown into relief.

As manufacturers' adoption of new development programs tended on balance to lag behind new demand, electric machines accounted for no more than 10.4 percent of the 1,369,546 machines manufactured during 1973, when they were first available for purchase.[82] Since the speed at which balls were launched increased significantly compared to single-shot designs, which forced customers to launch one ball at a time with one hand, a customer spending the same amount of money would use up their balls in a shorter period of time. Naturally, the speculative element became more pronounced. If constraints on customer budgets could be relaxed, or if electric machines, which provided lower barriers to entry compared to manual designs in terms of the required level of skill, could attract new customers, the market for electric machines would grow. Electric machines as a percentage of new installations did indeed subsequently grow, reaching 34.0 percent in 1978 and then exceeding 40 percent in 1979.[83] In this way, events ran counter to the initial expectations of parlors and manufacturers that had been pessimistic about the market penetration of electric machines, which became established as the de facto standard.

The switch to electric machines involved changes in machines' basic design, as opposed to technologies shaped by fads in the manner of the *yakumono* accessories on machine boards. The delayed entry into the electric machine market of Nishijin and Hōkoku cannot be explained solely by the diversity of outlooks in individual companies' market forecasts or decision-making. Cautious corporate behavior indicates that regulations can create a certain kind of gap in the development domain, both internally within companies and in the market. Outsider companies are comparatively freer of such constraints, and it is possible that their sensitivity to changes in the social attitude toward speculation and willingness to develop products in response to those changes may have enhanced pachinko's appeal as a game. Manufacturers that had experienced regulation during the 1950s may have felt they had no choice but to remain aware of regulations even after electric machines were certified, leading them to act with caution. A one-track understanding that sees regulation as an obstruction to development and deregulation as a guarantee that manufacturers will launch new machines without constraint provides an insufficient perspective from which to accurately grasp the relationship between development and regulation. While the removal of a regulatory constraint triggered an expansion in the scope of development, some manufacturers continued to be highly aware of regulations. The reintroduction of electric machines and the varied timing of manufacturers' development efforts offer an indirect explanation for how these changes provided development opportunities for outsider companies.

Competition between development and imitation

Another example is provided by a *yakumono* accessory that incorporated elements of mahjong, the Daisangen, which was announced simultaneously by Heiwa, Hōkoku and Yamato Seisakusho at the September 1973 exhibition described above. Although the original inventor is unknown, Heiwa and Hōkoku advertised the new feature,[84] which was introduced as having 'an overwhelmingly positive dynamic design and first impression',[85] at the exhibition.

In October, reports called attention to the popularity of Heiwa machines, citing 'the recent Daisangen boom'.[86] Hōkoku carried out further research after announcing the feature at the September exhibition and then launched it in November. By March 1974, the following year, it had won praise from one parlor manager for its 'miraculous sales record'.[87] Reacting to this high level of popularity, Daiichi Shōkai launched its Daisangen model in November, about two months after the first companies.[88]

In December, Nashonaru Yūki Kōgyō, which had run almost no machine ads, advertised a model featuring the 'explosive popularity of much-talked-about Daisangen'.[89] The company's eagerness to develop Daisangen accessories was palpable. In February 1974, the company again ran an ad for its Daisangen model, but by May information about the feature had disappeared, with ads mentioning only 'a new model with new value'. There is no sign of the promotion of Daisangen accessories by other companies, including Nashonaru Yūki Kōgyō, after that point. The popularity of the feature, which had been strong enough to spur Nashonaru to hop on the bandwagon, lasted only one or two seasons (roughly three to six months).

It is worth noting that three of the companies involved with developing Daisangen accessories behaved in different ways from February through April. Hōkoku advertised the model in March 1974, as described above, and moved to verify its popularity. By contrast, Heiwa announced a new accessory called Saikuron ('Cyclone'), rather than anything Daisangen-related, during the same month.[90] Daiichi Shōkai also advertised a new model, the Hitto Endo Ran ('Hit and Run') the following April.[91] Hōkoku continued to advertise its Daisangen feature, even if the product's actual launch lagged initial development by two months.[92] Heiwa's and Daiichi Shōkai's concerted efforts to develop new models are apparent

The example of the short-lived popularity of Daisangen accessories contrasts with electric machines that became the industry's de facto standard, offering a glimpse of the attitude taken by manufacturers carrying out normal development while grappling with rapid swings in popularity – one of the industry's most noteworthy characteristics. It reveals how companies shaped the development process to take into account elements such as the constant need for novelty (to the extent permitted by regulations) to keep fickle customers from losing interest.[93] For companies following in the footsteps of their competitors, the problem was likely where and how to follow, or discover, the market. One method for minimizing the risk inherent in that process was observing the reactions of parlors, which served as a customer interface, from whom responses could reliably be obtained, along with reactions to other companies' products.

As we saw with both electric machines, which involved changes in the basic mechanical design of machines, and Daisangen accessories, a comparatively more routine part of machine development, manufacturers likely made decisions about whether to develop products and when to enter markets based on a variety of approaches that were in turn based on their own varied market assessments. What did that mean for competition among manufacturers? Let us answer that question briefly.

Table 3.6 lists market share figures for the period from April 1973 to March 1974, when the two models attracted significant attention. While the lack of model-specific sales figures means that it would be hasty to presume that electric machines and Daisangen accessories directly impacted manufacturers' standing in the market, these numbers nonetheless offer some very interesting insights.

Daiichi Shōkai and Toyomaru Sangyō, which launched electric machines comparatively early and embraced the new designs, saw their sales volume and market share rise, and the same applied to Kyōraku Seisakusho, albeit to a much lesser extent. Nishijin, which was one season late to the electric machine market, managed to maintain its ranking at the beginning of the period covered by the table but saw its sales volume shrink substantially due to the trend in total sales volume, losing market share as a result. Kyōraku Sangyō apparently failed to capitalize on its advantage as one of the first to develop electric machines as its sales volume fell (by more than the decline in total sales) along with its market share, albeit by only a small amount in the case of the latter.

Regarding Daisangen accessories, Heiwa and Hōkoku, which contemporary reports indicate gained a high level of popularity, saw their sales volume and market share rise, as did Daiichi Shōkai, which entered the market fast on their heels. By contrast, Yamato Seisakusho, one of the first companies to launch a machine with the

Rank	FY 1973 Company	FY 1973 Number of machines sold	FY 1973 Market share (%)	FY 1974 Company	FY 1974 Number of machines sold	FY 1974 Market share (%)	Increase (▲ decrease) Machines (1973/1974)	Increase (▲ decrease) Market share (1973~74)
1	Nishijin	271,000	18.9	Nishijin	217,523	15.9	0.80	▲ 2.99
2	Sankyo	146,116	10.2	Sankyo	172,342	12.6	1.18	2.40
3	**Heiwa**	141,250	9.8	**Heiwa**	147,000	10.7	1.04	0.89
4	Daiichi Shōkai	131,573	9.2	Daiichi Shōkai	143,127	10.4	1.09	1.29
5	Sanyō Bussan	127,687	8.9	Sanyō Bussan	123,539	9.0	0.97	0.13
6	Maruhon Kōgyō	121,337	8.4	Maruhon Kōgyō	110,870	8.1	0.91	▲ 0.36
7	Kyōraku Sangyō	113,612	7.9	Kyōraku Sangyō	105,056	7.7	0.92	▲ 0.24
8	Nyū Gin	70,519	4.9	Okuamura Yūki	60,144	4.4	0.94	▲ 0.06
9	Okumura Yūki	63,931	4.5	Nyū Gin	58,500	4.3	0.83	▲ 0.64
10	Toyomaru Sangyō	31,038	2.2	Toyomaru Sangyō	39,367	2.9	1.27	0.71
11	Mizuho Seisakusho	27,170	1.9	Takeya	33,198	2.4	1.42	0.80
12	Takeya	23,360	1.6	Mizuho Seisakusho	21,703	1.6	0.80	▲ 0.31
13	Surī Sutā	22,901	1.6	Nyū Matsuya	20,169	1.5	0.98	0.03
14	Nyū Matsuya	20,643	1.4	Daidō Kōgyō	16,581	1.2	1.31	0.33
15	Daishin	19,463	1.4	**Hōkoku**	16,368	1.2	1.44	0.40
16	Masamura Kikai	13,103	0.9	Surī Sutā Kōgyō	15,612	1.1	0.68	▲ 0.46
17	Daidō Kōgyō	12,649	0.9	**Yamato Seisakusho**	11,826	0.9	0.99	▲ 0.03
18	Fuji Shōji	12,038	0.8	Kyōraku Seisakusho	11,502	0.8	1.07	0.09
19	**Yamato Seisakusho**	12,001	0.8	Ginza	9,596	0.7	1.10	0.03
20	**Hōkoku**	11,396	0.8	Masamura Kikai	8,784	0.6	0.67	▲ 0.27
21	Kyōraku Seisakusho	10,711	0.7	Nashonaru Yūki Kōgyō	6,439	0.5	6.29	0.40
22	Ginza	9,579	0.7	Kyōgoku Seisakusho	5,371	0.4	1.15	0.07
23	Sankō Seisakusho	5,482	0.4	Isuzu Seisakusho	4,970	0.4	5.20	0.30
24	Kyōgoku Seisakusho	4,663	0.3	Daitō Kōgyō	4,515	0.3	4.62	0.26
25	Nyū Ichigin	3,815	0.3	Nyū Ichigin	2,381	0.2	0.62	▲ 0.09
26	Monako Shōkai	3,011	0.2	Monako Shōkai	1,915	0.1	0.64	▲ 0.07
27	Narita Seisakusho	2,786	0.2	Narita Seisakusho	1,384	0.1	0.50	▲ 0.09
28	Nashonaru Yūki Kōgyō	1,024	0.1	Fuji Shōji	403	0	0.03	▲ 0.81
29	Daitō	978	0.1	Total machines sold	1,370,185	100.0	0.95	
30	Isuzu Seisakusho	955	0.1					
31	Matsumoto Yūki	293	0					
32	Maruzen Bussan	188	0					
	Total machines sold	1,436,268	100.0					

Table 3.6: Competition involving development of electric machines and Daisangen accessories

Notes:

a. ▒ indicates first-mover to launch electric models, while ☐ indicates second-mover companies.

b. Bold text indicates first-mover to launch Daisangen accessories, while underlined text indicates second-mover companies.

Source: Compiled based on Table 3.5.

new feature, gained almost no increase in market share. The company's sales volume fell by 175 machines, which is equivalent to about one parlor's worth of sales. Total sales for the period in question fell only slightly, so it is safe to assume that the size of the market remained constant. Nashonaru Yūki Kōgyō, which entered the market in 1970 only after carefully gauging its reaction, saw its sales volume rise by a factor of about six as its market share grew. Sales at the company fluctuated between 300 and 550 machines per month until 1972. Since monthly production fell to slightly less than 100 in 1973,[94] it is likely not insignificant that, as it sought to orchestrate a recovery, a lower-ranking manufacturer such as Nashonaru Yūki Kōgyō targeted a segmented popular market despite its limited popularity of one or two seasons. The company later saw monthly production rise to the 2000-machine level, and its market share also grew.

In the case of electric machines, it is likely that the advantages conferred by being early to market faded over time; once the design became an industry trend, most manufacturers launched their own offerings, and even companies like Nishijin that were late to market enjoyed a tenable position. Consequently, a company's maintenance of its market standing progressively came under the influence of transactions based on normal development, even in markets that had been captured through a first-mover strategy. Additionally, companies were not necessarily able to wrest competitive advantages merely by being first. Market share is decided by a number of factors, and it is not possible to make a wholesale determination of whether being first or coming later is advantageous.

Kyōraku Sangyō was unable to turn its early-bird advantage into the results that it expected, while latecomers such as Nishijin risked losing the market. As with Nashonaru Yūki Kōgyō, imitations by latecomers could serve to fuel market growth. The significance here is that during this period, when the price-based competition of the 1960s gave way to true development-based competition, development decisions made by companies on the basis of their own market discoveries and forecasts came to be reflected in market share, even though those decisions progressed along complex pathways. The market had begun to function in relation to development, and this represented a qualitative change from how it had operated previously.

This concludes my analysis of manufacturers' development behavior in terms of electric machines and Daisangen accessories. Next, I would like to expand on the relationship between those two products' characteristics and demand as clarified by this process while focusing on customer expectations, which shaped the development of future products. With regard to *yakumono* accessories, manufacturers pursued minor design changes with an emphasis on introducing novelty to machines' boards in the context of parlors' practice of regularly replacing machines so that customers would not become bored. The 1969 deregulation gave this type of development considerable breadth, and diversity grew as manufacturers that had been stimulated by competitors' development actively entered the fray.

In the case of electric machines with a more pronounced speculative element, the approval of such designs led even manufacturers that had been watching the market cautiously to progressively enter it in earnest. Because machines that raised the bar in terms of speculation imposed harsh constraints on customers' budgets, electric machines were initially only one category of development as manufacturers sought to ensure the continued existence of a diverse range of manual models. However, electric designs lowered the hurdle of pachinko skill compared to manual designs and introduced a greater element of chance, making it possible to attract a new demographic of customers who were pachinko novices. The study of pachinko consumption conducted by the Small Business Information Center that I mentioned above concluded, 'as a result of the widespread adoption of electric machines, the element of chance has become stronger, allowing pachinko to be enjoyed by a comparatively broad demographic', citing 'growth in numbers of middle-age women and young women' as examples.[95] Electric designs eventually became the de facto standard, lending an air of finality to the direction of development. In short, the survey revealed that the preference for electric machines was becoming stronger.[96] If such demand-side expectations were to become the assumption on which development proceeded, the focus of product development would be on further increasing the speculative element to keep the interest of customers who had become accustomed to speed. As it turns out, the foundation for customers' desire for an increasingly pronounced speculative element had already been laid in the formation of the electric machine market.

THE NITTOKUREN AND COMPETITIVE STRUCTURE

This section examines how the functions of the Nittokuren and associated changes described in the first part of this chapter were related to the shifts in competitive structure described in the second part and how they contributed to the development of the pachinko industry. In doing so, I will focus on the significance of companies like Nishijin that carried out development-oriented initiatives. This approach is intended not to paint a portrait of particular companies whose development-oriented outlook earned them success, but rather to throw into relief mechanisms related to the characteristics of the pachinko industry and facilitate an understanding of the significance of the pachinko industry and development in a broader context. I will also focus on the significance of the weeding out of manufacturers at the end of the 1970s, which occurred as a result of the development-based competition that began during the first half of the decade.

Recouping development investments

After the beginning of the 1970s, when development surged (which was one precondition for growth in patents), the Nittokuren strengthened its review function. Having responded with flexibility to changes in the business environment by starting to take on multifaceted functions, where and how did the organization affect manufacturer competition? I will examine the competitive conditions created by the Nittokuren that shaped the strategic options available to manufacturers as competition intensified, with a focus on development expenditure.

As I explained in the first part of this chapter, the establishment of the Zenkenkyō and formation of the Review Committee improved the position of right-holders. Those changes were grounded on the Nittokuren's management functions, which served to keep patent fees relatively low. The decision by manufacturers not to assert their right to collect high patent fees reflected their assumption that they could recoup development investments by other means. It goes without saying that if manufacturers could not do so, they would instead choose to borrow patents as a less expensive alternative due to their desire to limit such expenditure.

Yet the pachinko machine market was not filled with licensees that opted to use low patent fees due to a negative outlook on development. The competitive conditions and surge in development described by Tables 3.4 and 3.5 above show the need to clarify the path that allowed companies like Nishijin that actively pursued development to recoup associated costs.

Particularly at the end of the 1970s, the pachinko industry faced high expectations concerning machine novelty. The Small Business Information Center study cited above indicated that the manner in which consumers enjoyed leisure pursuits diversified during the 1970s and that pachinko was competing against the resurgent popularity of films, automobiles and the arcade game *Space Invaders*, among other activities.[97] Young male customers were particularly likely to become bored with pachinko and switch to other games.[98] Manufacturers needed to launch machines that looked different every season to meet parlors' needs,[99] and from the standpoint of this chapter, which examines the growth of the industry during and after the 1980s as precipitated by the debut of Fībā-type machines (which licensed the design of Sankyo's Fībā ['fever'] model), active development initiatives designed to create novelty need to be explained.

Generally speaking, there are two ways to recoup expenditure on research and product development. One is to raise selling prices, and the other is to collect high patent fees. However, as explained above, pachinko machine manufacturers were precluded from availing themselves of the latter option due to the existence of the Nittokuren. For manufacturers, low patent fees meant that the former option was their only realistic choice.

The amount of patent fees that one company could reasonably expect to collect corroborates the difficulty of the second method. This chapter has assumed that patent fees were low based on relative appraisals of characteristics such as the rigid upper limit on fees. However, in considering development expenditure, we need to make a slightly more concrete assessment of the patent fee income paid to individual companies.

Let us focus on the economic meaning for manufacturers of patent fees paid to the Zenkenkyō and dividends paid to Nittokuren shareholders. It is fair to say that neither payment was sufficiently large for manufacturers to expect it to serve as an ongoing basis for development. The largest patent fee paid to the Zenkenkyō via the Nittokuren was about 80 million yen (about US$410,260), in 1978. That amount was paid to all members of the Zenkenkyō, so each company received an average of about 15 million yen (about US$76,920) if we conservatively limit the number of right-holders to the founding members.[100] Using Nishijin, which actively developed patents and enjoyed top market share in 1976,[101] as an example, that amount would be about 0.2 to 0.3 percent of its sales of 5.9 to 9.4 billion yen (US$20 million to US$32 million)[102] on estimated production of about 224,000 machines (Table 3.4). For its part, the Nittokuren's dividend rate ranged from 50 to 500 percent, which would result in a per-shareholder payment of 420,000 to 1,050,000 yen (US$1433 to US$3584).[103] Either way, the resulting payment was a fairly low percentage of sales,[104] and the example derives from the year with the highest payment. It would be a stretch to characterize such payments as a source of revenue that could fund development on an ongoing basis. Consequently, the only realistic option for recouping development expenditure that was open to manufacturers was to increase sales.

In order to examine the specific way that could be accomplished, we must first focus on the business relationship between parlors and manufacturers. Until the 1970s, parlors generally installed machines from a single manufacturer, and it was typical for transactions to involve one parlor and one manufacturer. The magazine *Gekkan Yūgi Nihon* published articles about the openings of new and renovated parlors. Based on Table 3.7, which summarizes information about sixty-five such openings gleaned from those articles,[105] the trend during the first half of the 1970s – with just one exception – was for parlors to exclusively use machines from a single manufacturer.[106]

The trend continued even after that period; for example, the June 1976 issue of the magazine described a roadside parlor that opened in a suburban district of Fukuoka Prefecture where all 300 machines were sourced from Sankyo.[107] It is not difficult to find similar examples until the end of 1979, and we can conclude that this approach was typical.

Machine manufacturer	Number of parlors with given business relationship	Trend in relationships
Nishijin	16	1 parlor / 1 manufacturer
Heiwa	13	
Sankyo	7	
Kyōraku Seisakusho	5	
Sanyō Bussan	3	
Daiichi Shōkai	3	
Nashonaru Yūki Kōgyō	2	
Nyū Gin	2	
Maruhon	2	
Takeya	2	
Hōkoku	2	
Other	4	
Nishijin/Heiwa	1	1 parlor/2 manufacturers
Unknown	3	Unknown
Total	65	

Table 3.7: Trends in business relationships between parlors and manufacturers
Source: Compiled based on Gekkan Yūgi Nihon *from the 1971 Special New Year's issue to the December 1975 issue. I identified 65 parlor relationships from the 63 articles published from 1971 through 1975 (12 issues over 5 years, missing July 1974 but including four special New Year's issues). Of those 63 articles, I chose 56 that included details about parlor identity and the number of machines they operated, including all reports of renovated parlors for the month in question and news about newly opened parlors as well as articles about interior and design plans, model parlor research, expanded interiors and advertisements placed by pachinko machine manufacturers. I then excluded 2 articles because they lacked sufficient information, leaving 54 articles as the basis of the table.*

There were a number of reasons for the trend. Until the 1970s, machines from different manufacturers lacked clear differences in terms of characteristics such as entertainment value. Parlors set prize-ball percentages[108] by means of pin adjustment based on their management expertise in order to attract customers, and that technique made it possible to differentiate machines from one another. Manufacturers offered an array of services to newly opened parlors, from training pin adjusters (experienced technicians who adjusted how machines yielded prize balls using pins) to looking after employees.[109] Nishijin created a manual titled *Reference Materials for the Opening of New Parlors* (遊技場開設にあたっての参考資料) and offered instruction on topics including prize-ball dispensation, adjustment of pin angles, frequency of days with 'open' pins and daily planning of high and low prize-ball percentages.[110] Manufacturers played a key role in getting parlors up and running, attesting to the close relationship between the two groups. In the course of their normal sales activities, manufacturers' salespeople made the rounds of parlors offering instruction on pin adjustment and advice about parlor operation.[111]

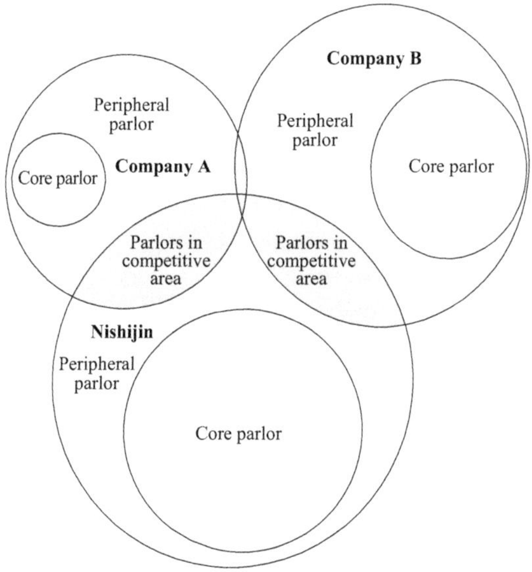

Figure 3.3: Conceptual illustration of transactions between parlors and manufacturers (1960s to 1970s)

Source: Interviews with a former director at Company T with experience in sales (conducted on May 23, 2004).

With physical qualities such as machine robustness an important standard and because pachinko machines were prone to failures and malfunctions, there were few incentives for parlors to switch manufacturers from the perspective of maintenance.[112]

Incidentally, if such long-term transactions were the general rule, one could imagine a static market in which there was no competition among manufacturers. This was not in fact the case, as the shifts in market share depicted in Table 3.4 show. I prepared the conceptual diagram in Figure 3.3 based on interviews in which I questioned manufacturer personnel with a sales background about the business relationship between manufacturers and parlors. From manufacturers' perspectives, trusting relationships between parlor operators and manufacturers' sales representatives meant that the customer base had a stratified structure, with a central zone of stable, long-term customers (core parlors) surrounded by a gray area of customers (peripheral parlors) with a lower level of trust that left room for competitors to get a foot in the door.[113] It is likely that manufacturers' sales representatives made the rounds of parlors in this gray area where sales activities could prompt parlors to switch machine suppliers while taking steps to lock in customers that were stable over the long term, leading to intense competition to capture market share. As a former executive at manufacturer T with sales experience during the 1970s put it,

> Sometimes you'd manage to get machines in there and then fail. A parlor might put in [machines] because it concluded that so-and-so [a manufacturer's sales rep] was good [from the parlor's perspective]. They'd end up getting rid of [machines like that]. Rinse and repeat. As that process repeated, Company T might come out with a good machine itself. If a company delivered good machines, then trust would deepen. And things could grow from there. If those machines were good, then naturally the parlor would place its next order with the same company, right? Sometimes they weren't good, either. It's a matter of luck. [However,] there's no guarantee that the next machines will be good. The difference [between a good machine and a bad one] came down to sales. For example, say a parlor buys our machines [...] and they see a difference of 10 or 20 thousand yen [about US$85.47 or US$170.94 in 2005] per machine. [Because of that difference,] there will naturally be a difference in profit margin. [...] There's a difference between Company T's machines and other machines [...]. Parlors that have been doing business with Company T for a long time don't try other companies' machines, so the managers of those parlors don't realize there's a difference there, but parlors that try various manufacturers' machines, maybe some from Company T, then Sankyo, then Heiwa, say, those parlors know a lot about the numbers. So if they see a decline in those figures, they'll immediately switch machines.[114]

Since sales capability and word of mouth had a large effect,[115] there were cases in which parlors in the gray area would change machine suppliers when it came time to replace their machines if they heard about a machine with a good reputation.[116]

Machine prices, listed in Table 3.8, were significant when it came to recouping the cost of patent development. Prices rose reliably, as was made clear by the transition in models that was triggered by new designs.[117] Since the machine market was generally growing during and after the 1960s, rising prices meant manufacturers could predict that they would be able to recoup development expenditure naturally. They were also able to expect that their revenue would grow as market share expanded.

This path for recouping development investments made it possible for manufacturers that strategically pursued development to exist and grow. That said, we must also assume that the strategic potential that the Nittokuren gave to development allowed for the existence of free-riders who wanted to take advantage of the low patent-fee structure. The next part of the chapter examines the existence of, and the relationships between, companies that embraced two different strategies.

Year	Model	Lowest price (yen)	Highest price (yen)
1929	Single-shot models	3,000	
1952	'All-win' successive-shot models	7,000	8,500
1954	Successive-shot models	8,000	9,000
1957	*Yakumono* models (*Jinmitto*)	14,000	17,000
1960	*Chūrippu* models	18,000	
1969	100-shot models	19,000	21,000
1973	Electric models	45,000	
1980	Fībā-type machines	90,000	
	Manual models	30,000	40,000
1982	Electric models	55,000	100,000
	Pachinko boards	30,000	40,000

Table 3.8: Pachinko machine pricing
Note: Prices for 1929 and 1952 are estimates.
Source: Compiled based on materials provided by the Nikkōso.

Two development strategies: competition

Up until 1980, the pachinko industry's production structures accommodated two to three rounds of machine replacement per year when 'renovated' parlors reopened with new machines.[118] The physical life of machines was three to four months during the first half of the 1950s, but improvements in design and manufacturing technology pushed that figure up to one to two years. The timing of these machine replacements came to vary more in accordance with their 'popularity life' than in the past.[119] Since a majority of parlors' customers were men, popularity fell with the start of the high-school term and professional baseball season in March and April, and then again with vacations in May and trips back home in August. Popularity then rose again, and parlors sought to time their switchover to new machines to coincide with growth in customer numbers. For their part, manufacturers planned development and production to coincide with these replacement periods.

Although there were differences reflecting manufacturers' development and production capabilities, the typical season ranged in length from three or four months to six months, depending on machines' popularity life. At the risk of putting the conclusion first, the Nittokuren's mechanisms had the potential to further strengthen the industry's characteristic tendency toward development-based competition and intense fluctuations in popularity. Here I am referring to the process by which novelty in the market was lost even when manufacturers launched popular models once competitors began supplying imitations (including machines that licensed patents), leading to obsolescence. These characteristics forced manufacturers to recoup development expenditures (including for patent development) more quickly, since similar products tended to appear on the market immediately. Moreover, low patent fees made it even more difficult to recoup those costs. Against this backdrop, the first method for recouping development expenditure – that is, increasing market share – became the most reliable option.

In this case, manufacturers could choose one of two strategies. First, they could develop patents and products more actively than their competitors so that they would be first-movers. It was important to such manufacturers that replacement seasons remain constant so that they were able, at a minimum, to position themselves one step ahead. A manufacturer adopting this strategy would formulate a specific development plan based on this awareness. However, this approach was associated with high development risk.[120] The other strategy was to accept being second to market – that is, following in the footsteps of the 'first-mover' companies by monitoring how their models were received by the market.[121] What I would like to emphasize here is not that either of these approaches was inherently more advantageous than the other, but that they were both options that could be chosen in the context of the mutual regulated relationships enforced by the Nittokuren, just as we saw with the case of Daisangen accessories in the preceding section.

Let us pause to consider why first-mover manufacturers allowed competitors to choose a second-mover strategy through low patent fees. Acceptance of later-to-market rivals was related to limited production capacity, which derived from pachinko manufacturers' capital investment restraint.[122] Aligning production with parlors' replacement seasons created a gap in manufacturers' equipment operation and drove down the average rate at which their equipment was utilized. Due to the high level of uncertainty with regard to machine popularity, operating equipment based on periods of high sales caused low utilization rates when sales slowed. For example, observations describing how the market in 1974 demanded increases in production and fueled expectations of revenue growth bear out this trend: '[...] we've increased production again and again yet still can't keep up with demand. Because we can't undertake such large-scale investment in production equipment based on the past vicissitudes of the pachinko industry, we're unable to increase production as much as we'd like'.[123]

Restrained capital investment was not the only problem. Manufacturers sought to limit latent rivals in the competition for market share to selling the models that lay within the scope of their own development. In the case of Nashonaru Yūki Kōgyō, which rode the coattails of Heiwa, the former was limited to machines that at best matched those of its first-mover competitor, even though it did enjoy dramatic growth in sales volume. As a result, Heiwa was already developing its next run of models when Nashonaru managed to catch up. Meanwhile, manufacturers that encountered difficulties with development could work to maintain market share by 'drafting' behind first-mover competitors.

The first method that comes to mind for realizing business growth in the gray area illustrated in Figure 3.3 above is developing a revolutionary, popular model ahead of other companies. This sort of first-mover strategy would allow a manufacturer to target parlors in the gray area ahead of second-movers biding their time while monitoring the market's reaction. As the former executive from Company T put it above, 'sometimes you'd manage to get machines in there and then fail', but sometimes you might also 'come out with good machines' yourself. Were a company to develop a hit model through this approach, rumors would spread via word of mouth that the machine draws customers, providing an opportunity to gain new customers in the gray area. In this way, it is possible to increase market share until similar models appear.[124]

This approach would allow a company to recoup its development expenditure while utilizing similar products from second-mover competitors to avoid excessive capital investment. However, a company seeking to do so would have to recoup its development costs in the short period of time available until similar products from second-mover companies were launched. A first-mover company following this approach would seek to increase its market share on an ongoing basis during each successive period (until the next model, or until similar models appear) in order to recoup development expenditure. It is likely that the market share growth achieved by Heiwa from 1970 to 1976 in Table 3.4 above and from 1973 to 1974 in Table 3.6 above provides an example of just such a cyclical pattern.

By contrast, companies adopting the second-mover strategy needed only to create popular models on the heels of their first-mover counterparts, which served to reduce development risk and expenditure. They could also create imitation products so long as they paid low patent fees. That said, they ran the risk of losing customers in the gray area to first-mover competitors during the interim. If following this approach, it was essential for manufacturers to shrink the gray area and expand their base of core customers – in other words, to leverage sales capability to shore up their customer base – for the strategy to deliver competitive results.

Additionally, there were technological requirements associated with becoming a second-mover company. Because there was ample room for improvement from a mechanical standpoint, it is likely that competition among second-mover companies involved their technological capacity to imitate successful machines. In other words,

> There were imitations prior to Fībā model, but lower-tier manufacturers didn't do research into glue and plywood quality or pins. Basically, there were variations in quality from product to product and variations due to environmental factors such

> as humidity, so naturally there were differences in product quality and content between upper-tier manufacturers and lower-tier manufacturers. It takes time to eliminate those differences. You have to constantly compare your offerings with other manufacturers and machines that are selling well [...]. You have to analyze how your machines are different from other companies'. I told [employees] to compare and analyze gauges [pin arrangements], *yakumono* accessories, plywood quality, pin quality, Heiwa's pins and our pins, to find out where the differences were. It was clear there were differences when you checked [...] in plywood quality, and in plywood laminate characteristics. If you could do development work to eliminate those gaps, you could reach the same level.[125]

Consequently, the process of following first-mover companies necessitated catch-up competition in terms of content, which involved developing appealing machines, and in terms of manufacturing technologies.

Under such conditions, manufacturers naturally had to price their products lower than those pursuing a first-mover strategy. Chapter 1 described how machines from Masamura Shōkai and Hōkoku, which had premium brand status during the 1950s, commanded higher prices than those from other companies. Although pricing during the 1970s remains unclear, a comparison of pricing for various manufacturers in 1980, which likely reflects the conditions of that period, reveals differences ranging from 1.1 times to 1.6 times.[126] From the standpoint of recouping development expenditure, the conditions were favorable for first-mover companies. That said, it was a given that imitation machines would appear, so those companies embarked on the next series of development in an effort to further increase their market share since the period during which they enjoyed a competitive advantage in the market was short.

In light of the cyclical nature of this process, it becomes clear that the service life of popular models for manufacturers was not an abstract period of time whose end was determined by customer apathy, but rather a period of short-term competition that lasted until the next cycle began, making development of new models a concrete strategic target. What is important here is that the Nittokuren offered two viable strategies and that first-mover and second-mover companies played roles that mutually promoted competition. (First-mover companies could only maintain their advantage until they were copied by second-mover companies, while second-mover companies had to fight first-mover companies for the business of gray-area customers.) Thus, manufacturers had two choices: the first-mover approach of active development, and the second-mover approach of following afterwards. Their strategies were not consistent, but rather varied according to which approach they chose.[127] In the context of this structure, the culling of lower-tier companies that occurred from the late 1970s (see Table 3.4) can be understood as the result of either failing to boost competitive

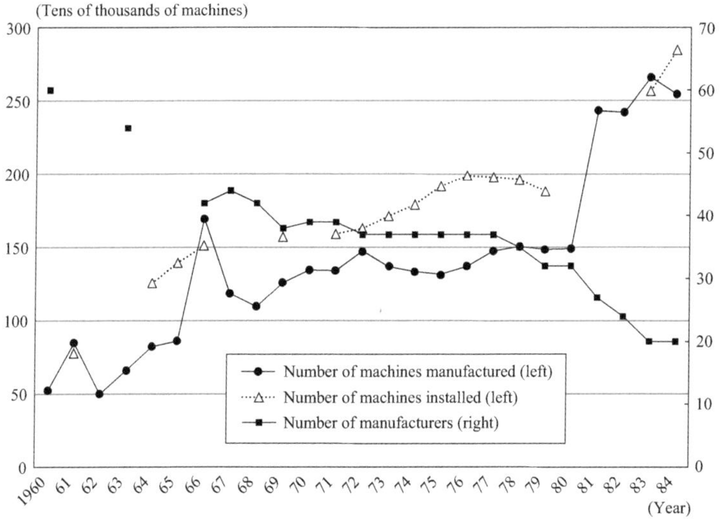

Figure 3.4: Manufacturer competition (1960 to 1984)
Source: Compiled based on materials provided by the Nikkōso.

capability after choosing one of these two approaches, or of not having chosen either of them.

Having discussed these two possibilities, I would like to emphasize once again that the Nittokuren's functions were meaningful not in that they created a group of second-mover companies, but rather in that they led to the continued existence of first-mover companies. This continued existence of development-oriented manufacturers can be understood in the context of two conditions, which resulted from the Nittokuren's monitoring role. First, that role made intense price-based competition impossible and allowed the market to stabilize. This set of circumstances can be considered to have provided an essential basis for manufacturers' ability to raise machine prices. Second, the role made it difficult to directly cover development expenditure with patent fee income. The result was the provision of a path by which development-oriented companies (manufacturers that pursued patent development) could reliably raise machine prices by developing patents in a stabilizing market and thereby recoup development by increasing their market share through a first-mover strategy. It bears remembering that this path incorporated as a condition the Nittokuren's patent-monitoring function, which is to say, the acceptance of imitation products within the scope of monitoring and thus a slight, short-term competitive advantage. In other words, it rested on a developmental mechanism pursued by first-mover companies that was 'baked in' by the Nittokuren.

	Number of manufacturers	Number of machines manufactured	Number of machines installed	Competitive relationship	Nittokuren functions	Significance of Nittokuren functions for competition
1960s	Falling	Rising	Rising	Intense price-based competition	Illegitimate businesses	Clamp-down on illegitimate businesses and limits on intense price-based competition
First half of the 1970s	Stable	Flat	Rising	Start of development-based competition	Development of outsourcing and review structures with the establishment of a patent right-holders organization	Limits on price-based competition = Transition to development-based competition revolving around market share
Second half of the 1970s	Falling	Rising slightly	Falling	Selection process in development capability during economic downturn (withdrawal of companies with low market share) = Intensification of development-based competition	Evolution of outsourcing and review structures	
Start of the 1980s	Falling, then stable	Rising rapidly	Rising rapidly	Structural transition; same as above		

Table 3.9: Functions of the Nittokuren in the competitive structure of the 1960s and 1970s
Source: Compiled based on Figure 3.4.

Competitive structure of the pachinko machine market

In concluding this chapter, I will summarize the overall competitive structure described in Table 3.4, Figure 3.4 and Table 3.9 while focusing on differences between competition during the 1960s and 1970s.

Starting in 1955, the market became the locus of intense, price-based competition created by illegitimate businesses. As described in Table 3.4, the progression of this competition placed even leading companies under pressure to withdraw from the market. Eventually, the Nittokuren developed a monitoring function that laid the foundation for eliminating illegitimate businesses and stabilizing market conditions.

As summarized in Table 3.9, the market stabilization accomplished by the Nittokuren during the 1960s laid the groundwork that would prompt development-based competition during the first half of the 1970s. The start of development as a necessary condition for patent development in the context of institutional changes made the implementation of structures for improving the standing of right-holders and the strengthening of review functions issues for the Nittokuren, prompting experiments such as the establishment of the Zenkenkyō and the formation of the Review Committee. In this way, the function of the Nittokuren during the 1970s served to restrain the intensive, price-based competition of the 1960s, and as those initiatives faded into the background, the emphasis shifted to contractual management of patents. The centralization of oversight functionality in the Nittokuren was only possible due to favorable assessments of its patent management capabilities through the 1960s and expectations that they would continue. This centralization provides evidence that the organization's patent monitoring functions extended not only to outsiders, but to insider manufacturers as well.

As shown in Table 3.4, with the coming of the 1970s, the top two companies lost market share as the next seven companies built on manufacturing volume and market share alike, leading to intensified competition. However, that competition was not price-based, unlike during the 1960s. Instead, companies competed by developing a variety of machines in line with new standards and regulatory liberalization.[128] The decline in the market share of the top manufacturers at the time points to a trial-and-error approach to development in order to preserve competitive advantage in the face of new regulations, and to the potential for other manufacturers to grow. In the pachinko industry, the impossibility of forecasting how machines would be received by the market and the uncertainty of sustained popularity made sudden reversals possible. These developments heralded the start of development-based competition.

Based on the fact that they led to changes in leading companies and to the withdrawal from the business of a group of lower-tier companies during the late 1970s, these experimental efforts had complex implications. With regard to growth against a backdrop of intense, development-based competition, not all leading companies enjoyed advantages, and not all companies attempting to achieve new growth were successful. One result of such competition, which intensified during the 1970s, can be seen from 1976 to 1982.

Even as numerous manufacturers were forced to close their doors despite growth, however slight, in production volume, a bipolar division led to the formation of two concentrated groups of surviving manufacturers (see Figure 3.4 and Table 3.4) and ushered in another period of market stability that began during the 1980s. The historical significance of the industry's development during the second half of the 1970s lies in the evolution of the full-scale development-based competition that would determine the market's structure in the 1980s. More than anything else, it would be the dynamic nature of this competition that explained the appearance of the Fībā model, which was to dramatically alter the market's structure during the 1980s.

CONCLUSION

The Nittokuren was responsible for patent pooling and management, monitoring, review and cross-licensing operations over an extended period of time. Historically, the group's functionality can be described as monitoring price stabilization through patent holdings from its establishment to the 1960s, and as managing patents under contract in the context of changes to the development environment during the 1970s. As I observed at the beginning of this chapter, the significance of the 1970s in the history of the pachinko industry lay in fostering development by ensuring the continuity of those functions, which required the elimination of 'outsider' companies that were disrupting the market during the 1960s, and in providing a foundation for the coming gigantic market.

When we approach the 1970s as a period of preparation for the development of the industry during the 1980s, it becomes important to gauge the extent to which machine development was promoted. Supported by mechanisms such as the Nittokuren, the industry saw the introduction of low patent fees, which served to spur companies to pursue development in order to increase their market share, rather than leading to a dulling of competition. That path was open to it because it was able to lower development risks, even as there was no guarantee that companies would be able to consistently develop hit models. Yet it was only by developing one new machine after another that leading companies could maintain their market share, or that small and less-capable ones could access new markets. Competition progressed in order to recoup development expenditure under those conditions.

Although the 1970s was a period of macro-level stagnation, the industry was able to achieve gradual growth during the decade through intense development-based competition among manufacturers. I would like to emphasize once more that this process prompted the appearance of electric machines; tapped new markets by drawing in a variety of consumer demographics, for example women; continued to capture steady support from its conventional male customer base by regularly providing novel machines; and attracted a broad 'pachinko population'. This sort of development-oriented competition did not evolve as mere competition among companies, but rather presumed relationships among manufacturers, particularly through the Nittokuren, which is to say, relationships that involved the sharing of production capacity after reducing development risk (which were affected by regulations and popularity) and even of development. In this sense, then, the mechanisms that supported development during the 1970s served to stabilize the market, as suggested at the outset of this chapter. It is fair to say that full-bore competitive relationships like these provided the foundation for the debut of Fībā-type machines, which would lead to major innovation during the 1980s.

4

Development of the Pachinko Industry into an Enormous Market

INTRODUCTION

According to a survey of consumer attitudes on pachinko that asked pachinko parlor owners whether the number of 'pachinko customers would increase in the future', conducted in 1979, when loss of customers was considered a serious problem for the industry, about 33 percent of respondents predicted a decline in patronage.[1] Although about half indicated they believed that they would be able to maintain current customer volume, only 7 percent anticipated an increase in attendance.[2] At that point in time, few parlor owners had an optimistic outlook on the future.

However, in the industry's history, the 1980s would turn out to be a period characterized by revolutionary growth. Computerized machines, which would later come to dominate machine designs, emerged during this period, and the market flourished as the speculative element increased markedly. Technological progress-fueled growth in the size of the industry triggered a variety of changes. For example, the increase in parlor owners' socioeconomic position was striking. Individuals earning a living from game parlors and pachinko emerged conspicuously at the top of the National Tax Agency's annual list of top taxpayers during the 1980s. Taking Hokkaido as an example, people on the list from the pachinko industry numbered just one or two during the 1960s and three or four during the 1970s, but that figure grew to twenty-three in 1981 and twenty-five in 1982.[3] Social awareness of pachinko underwent a transformation that began in 1980, drawing other sectors' attention to the parlor business.

This chapter will clarify how the pachinko industry developed during the 1980s, a period of rapid growth, with a focus on how the business changed and in particular on what became of traditional business practices following the transition in machine designs spurred by technological changes.

Market growth during the 1980s

With the coming of the 1980s, the pachinko industry was positioned for growth, having moved rapidly to extricate itself from the difficult circumstances in which it had found itself immediately prior (see Figure 0.3). The number of pachinko parlors fell from 10,734 in 1976 to 10,021 in 1978 and then to 8907 in 1981,[4] a decline of 17 percent over five years, and the number of pachinko machine manufacturers fell from thirty-seven in 1977 to thirty-one in 1979 and then to twenty-four in 1982,[5] a decline of 35 percent. This trend gathered momentum after 1979. The trend then reversed, however, as the number of parlors grew rapidly from 1982, reaching 17,373 in 1991, roughly doubling during the approximately ten years following 1981. Attrition among machine manufacturers slowed and then halted from 1983, a step behind the recovery in parlors, and the number of companies building machines held steady at about twenty until 1990. Both parlors and manufacturers faced situations during the 1980s that differed from those they had encountered before.

The rapid about-face showed every sign of being more than just a short-term recovery from the intense culling the industry had undergone at the end of the 1970s. The number of parlors grew amidst a rush of newly opened businesses, surpassing 12,000 for the first time in the thirty years since the count fell below 10,000 from 1955 to 1956 (see Figure 0.3). The steady decline in the number of manufacturers had also begun during the 1950s. By outward appearances, this change suggests that the 1980s was a period of historic change for the industry, one that is worthy of our attention.

Long-term shifts in the patterns of consumption in Japanese society provided a foundation for the growth of the pachinko industry. Against the backdrop of conspicuous growth in selective preference-driven expenditure relative to outgoings for necessities such as clothing, food and housing from the second half of the 1970s, the growth potential of leisure-related businesses attracted particular attention.[6]

These changes expressed themselves in the form of growth in the size of the pachinko market, which was classified as a leisure or amusement industry. The speed of this growth was remarkable, as a market valued at about 6 trillion yen (about US$36 billion) in August 1986 was estimated to have grown to 10 trillion yen (about US$69 billion) by April 1987.[7] The market's growth spree created quite a stir as it surged in value to 15 trillion yen (about US$118) in 1992[8] and then to 30 trillion yen (about US$276 billion at 1996 rates) by the mid-1990s.

The departure point for this growth was the July 1980 launch of a super-motorized (*chōtokuden*) model[9] known as the Fībā ('fever') by Sankyo.[10] The Fībā triggered a pachinko boom due to its remarkably pronounced speculative element. The rapid rise in the number of parlors due to new companies entering the business points to the nature of Fībā-type machines' popularity. Compared to the analog machines used in parlors up to that time, these models added the characteristics of a slot machine and electronic technology, making them the prototype for today's pachinko machines. Described as innovative at the time, they provided the basis for computerized pachinko, which is distinguished by its use of electronic components such as circuit boards and LCD displays.

A shared consensus in the industry sees the changes it experienced during the 1970s, which can be summarized as a time of striking market growth, as described above, as primarily deriving from the increased speculative element introduced by these machines.[11] In light of the fact that Fībā-type machines' speculative element drove up parlor sales, it would not be unreasonable to conclude that the model's popularity was responsible for the industry's rapid growth.

However, if we recall that machines with a pronounced speculative element not only expanded the market, but also brought instability to parlor operations[12] during the 1950s, as examined in Chapter 1, the conventional explanation of market growth during the 1980s is inadequate for the purpose of understanding the industry's development. There remain numerous questions that demand consideration, including whether the increasingly speculative element destabilized parlor operations, whether those operations continued unchanged as different machine designs – Fībā-type machines – penetrated into parlors (i.e., whether parlors had to make any adjustments), how manufacturers supplied machines (changed their production structures) in response to the sudden and rapid rise in demand, and what reaction the machines triggered in terms of regulations, for example with regard to the response by police.

Identifying issues: a comparison with the 1950s

For customers, a pronounced speculative element signifies a high-risk investment that can be expected to yield a high return. According to the analysis offered in Chapter 1, the more pronounced speculative element that triggered the pachinko boom of the 1950s required parlors to base their businesses on such high-risk investments. Machines with a pronounced speculative element destabilized parlor businesses' efforts to operate profitably by introducing violent swings in daily sales.[13] In this way, the parlor business during the 1950s had to rely on a speculative revenue base, and this requirement made planning and calculation unrealistic.

Generally speaking, parlors could be expected to refrain from making active investments while relying on such an unstable revenue base (for example, replacing their machines with new models or increasing the number of machines they operated), so there was no guarantee that they would be able to attract customers' interest on an ongoing basis. Since the manufacturers that supplied machines to such parlors also had difficulty actively developing new models and making investments in line with long-term prospects, the industry's overall growth was constrained. For the industry to develop in a sustained manner, the parlor business needed to discover managerial expertise that could control the highly pronounced speculative element and to secure a stable revenue base.

During the 1950s, the search for such methods led to the regulation of pachinko machines with a pronounced speculative element. External controls on this element in the form of the prohibition of successive-shot machines in 1955[14] shrank the magnitude of fluctuations in sales and allowed parlors to accumulate expertise in pin adjustment, which offered a means of securing stable profits. The parlor business was thus established as a business whose performance could be calculated, allowing the pachinko industry to take its first step toward development.

In light of the industry's experience during the 1950s, it is not self-evident that the increase in speculative character during the 1980s would serve to fuel its long-term development. The question of how stability was brought to parlor operations is central to any understanding of the factors at work in the industry's development during the 1980s and of that period's historical significance.

Issues and historical materials

This chapter addresses the beginnings of the process by which the penetration of new products into the market led to changes in the industry as a whole while focusing on how the unique characteristics of Fībā-type machines influenced the stability of parlor operations. More specifically, it focuses on the parlor operations of Masamura Shōkai, which introduced Fībā-type machines, in order to clarify the effects of that decision and explicate the following three ways in which new-model development was related to change in the industry.

First, I will focus on parlor sales. The question of how the emergence of Fībā-type machines affected market growth remains insufficiently explored. This chapter offers a fundamental examination of that question while focusing on individual parlors' sales and the role of pin adjustment. Second, I will analyze the manner in which machines were introduced to parlors. The question of how Fībā-type machines were supplied to parlors that were rushing to introduce them in response to their explosive popularity in the market is deeply interesting insofar as it addresses a mechanism that supported the industry's development. Through this analysis, I will examine the changes that the debut of Fībā-type machines prompted in the transactional interactions of manufacturers and parlors in the machine market. Third, I will consider how the intensification of inter-parlor competition, which occurred against the backdrop of new businesses' active entry into the market, affected parlor management and how parlors came under pressure to respond.

As in Chapter 1, I will draw on materials related to parlors operated by Masamura Shōkai, which was founded in 1949 and which exited the business in June 2010. From the time of its founding until the first half of the 1950s, when it served in effect as one of the industry's representative manufacturers, the company's primary businesses were machine sales and parlor operation. Then, after the industry was regulated in 1955, it formed a new company while leaving a large accounts receivable balance at the former company and focused exclusively on its parlor business. Later, the company shifted its focus to the hotel business during the 1960s in an effort to diversify. Although the company did not actively work to expand by rolling out numerous branches, it continued to operate its parlor business for about sixty years in an effort to safeguard the business launched by its founder.

Allow me to offer a brief description of the parlors operated by Masamura Shōkai. As I explained in Chapter 1, Masamura Shōkai Co., Ltd., operated four parlors following its founding in 1951: the Main Branch, the Oshikiri Branch, the Endonji Branch and the Matsubara Branch. However, the company took a number of steps to revamp its operations following the ban on successive-shot machines, including by leaving only head office functions at the Main Branch, relocating the Main Branch to form the Jōshin Branch and closing all other locations except the Oshikiri Branch. The company then consolidated its parlor business into a single location when it expanded the Jōshin Branch at the beginning of the 1970s.[15] It then closed the Jōshin Branch in 1991 when it rebuilt the Main Branch, which had been responsible for head office functions. At that time, the parlor business was relocated to the head office building, where it continued to operate until 2010. The history of Masamura Shōkai's parlor business can be summarized as an effort to maintain a single parlor while working to expand its size but not undertaking any active attempts to operate additional branches.

The existence of parlors operated by the company ('M.S. parlors') over an extended period signifies the extent to which the company accumulated associated knowledge. This chapter's analysis illustrates the significance of the operational expertise accumulated by those parlors against the backdrop of intense growth starting during the 1980s and in response to changes in the industry. In Masamura Shōkai, we have an excellent opportunity to observe the significance of traditional operations in a way that is impossible with companies that took advantage of the business opportunities offered by rapid growth to enter the market. In addition to describing how M.S. parlors took maximum advantage of the opportunity presented by new machine designs, I will examine the difficulties faced by the traditional management techniques that had previously supported the development of the industry.

This chapter's analysis is based on primary resources related to M.S. parlors and on operational materials related to other parlors retained by Masamura Shōkai.

It is difficult to analyze the profitability of the parlor business on a standalone basis because data such as balance sheets and profit-and-loss statements present figures that incorporate the hotel business, an unrelated and multifaceted segment of the company's operations. Reflecting these resource-related constraints, this chapter focuses on explaining the changes in the industry's development around 1980 instead of offering a detailed analysis of Masamura Shōkai's growth as a company. In supplementing that analysis with information about conditions in the parlor business gleaned from sales figures, the cost of prizes purchased by parlors and records, I have limited the resulting discussion to issues related to changes in the industry.

Pachinko parlor profitability and managerial techniques

Chapter 1 addressed parlors' revenue base by analyzing the characteristics of the distribution of sales and gross profit margin (i.e., profit structure). Since the three-business system – that is, the route by which special prizes (prizes such as handkerchiefs offered by parlors based on the assumption that they would be converted by customers into cash) could be exchanged for cash – was subsequently institutionalized, this is a good opportunity to review that mechanism as well as the profitability of the parlor business. As illustrated in Figure 4.1, the three-business system[16] referred to parlors, businesses that bought special prizes from customers and wholesalers of special prizes. This prize-redemption system was the result of regulations that prohibited customers' winnings from being exchanged for cash at parlors.[17] Here I will offer the minimum explanation of parlor profit necessary for our analysis based on the three-business system established during the 1960s.

First, customers would exchange the money they intended to use on pachinko for balls (loaned balls: ① ⇒ ② in Figure 4.1). The ball price around the time of the introduction of Fībā-type machines was 4 yen (about US$0.10) (it had been revised from 2 to 3 yen in 1973, and to 4 yen in 1977). Parlor sales consisted of total receipts for loaned balls.

(A) Daily sales for one parlor (yen) = Number of loaned balls × 4 yen (about US$0.20 in 1977)

The number of (dispensed) balls that a customer could obtain during play on any given day was determined by that day's pin adjustment, and the ratio of the number of prize balls to the number of balls for which the customer had exchanged cash (the number of loan balls) is given by (B), the prize-ball percentage.

(B) Prize-ball percentage (%) = Number of prize balls (A) / Number of loaned balls × 100

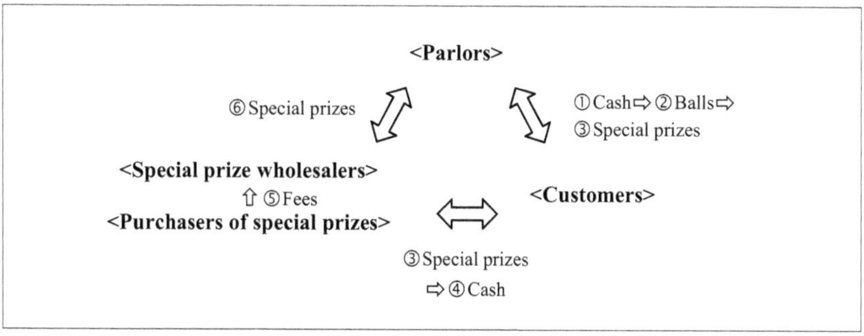

Figure 4.1: Special prize exchange and supply channel
Note: Parlor operators were prohibited from purchasing or wholesaling prizes.
Source: Compiled based on Suzuki (2001: 308–12) and the figure found in Futami (2001: 35).

Prize balls were exchanged for prizes (② ⇒ ③ in Figure 4.1). When thinking about these relationships in terms of parlor profit, the relationship (C: exchange rate) between the amount of prize balls (A × 4 yen) and the exchanged value (that is, the total value of prizes [included as the selling price in M.S. parlor ledgers]) assumes key importance.

(C) Exchange rate (%) = Total value of prizes / (A × 4 yen)

Parlors could increase their profits by lowering the exchange rate. Although a parlor's actual expenditure was determined by the numerical quantity of prizes exchanged (× their cost), the exchange rate could be manipulated to change the conversion value of prize balls. Although no information on this topic survives, it is unlikely that parlors were able to exercise particularly broad discretion regarding such adjustments. The fact that low exchange rates would lead to rumors and customer attrition in the context of competition with other parlors made it undesirable to draw on such adjustments as a sustained source of profit. The likely result was a series of standard regional rates.[18]

The third factor related to parlor profitability was the cost paid by the parlor for standard and special prizes (⑥ in Figure 4.1). Price reductions and downward pressure on overall transaction amounts reflected prices set through negotiations with wholesalers. Prize redemptions at parlors involved either standard prizes such as cigarettes or special prices, which customers could expect to redeem for cash (③ ⇒ ④ in Figure 4.1). The maximum value of prizes was set by regulations at 1500 yen (about US$6.25 in 1977) and later 2500 yen (about US$12.31 in 1980).[19] Consequently, it is likely that customers' tendency to redeem balls for special prizes increased in line with machines' speculative element. Although the effect on profits of the prices parlors paid to suppliers for special prizes intensified, we can conclude that parlors had only a small amount of room within which to make adjustments since those prices were set by pachinko associations in each region.[20]

Based on the above, this chapter's analysis will focus primarily on prize-ball percentages, because it was there that parlors exercised a significant amount of discretion, because those percentages governed the overall extent of profit and because they allowed parlors to control sales in order to attract customers.

ON THE EVE OF THE EMERGENCE OF FĪBĀ-TYPE MACHINES

First, I will provide an overview of the principal M.S. parlor during the period under examination. The business was located at an intersection near Jōshin Station (a subway station that began operating in 1981) in what is now Nagoya's Nishi Ward. In the days when the Nagoya tram ran due north from Nagoya Station, there was a tram garage at the location, which was the northern terminus of the route.[21] At the end of the 1940s, the area around the station comprised one of Nagoya's most prominent shopping arcades.

The number of machines operated by the M.S. parlor grew from about 200 during the 1970s – the period targeted in this analysis – to about 261 in October 1980, just before Fībā-type machines were introduced. Average daily sales in November, after the expansion, were 1,052,341 yen (about US$5183), about twice the August figure (487,336 yen, about US$2400).[22] The number of machines operated by the parlor was relatively static until it was expanded to house about 350 machines and moved to a location around fifty meters away[23] in 1991, when the company built its new head office. We can utilize these facts to cancel out the effects of the relocation and fluctuations in the number of machines from changes in statistical data before and after the introduction of Fībā-type machines.

As the overview at the beginning of this chapter made clear, the pachinko industry was struggling with a recession as the number of parlors and manufacturers fell at the end of the 1970s. In order to ascertain the effects of Fībā-type machines, as described below, let us pause to review the function served by pin adjustment in parlor operations up to that point so that we have a yardstick for comparison. I will then examine the conditions facing parlor operations at the end of the 1970s in connection with the role of pin adjustment.

In 1976, pin adjusters from parlors in leading Tokyo entertainment districts like Shibuya, Ikebukuro, Shinjuku and other areas gathered for a roundtable talk. The descriptions they provided offer hints as to how pin adjustment was related to overall parlor operations.[24]

Paths, known as *michi*, along which balls travel between a pachinko machine's 360 pins,[25] are created by pin adjusters as they adjust the angle of pins by 0.1 or 0.2 millimeters. Just being a pin adjuster[26] did not necessarily mean that one could read those paths, as the task required a substantial amount of skill and experience.[27] It took four or five years for a trainee to become a full-fledged pin adjuster, but even then that person's level of skill was only sufficient to perform the job to a rudimentary standard. More time was required to master the ability to bring business conditions, labor management and product inventory to bear on the pin adjustment process. Consequently, pin adjustment in the context of a parlor with 300 machines referred not only to merely adjusting the pins of each machine, one at a time, but also to the ability to determine how to configure some machines to yield prizes, others to entertain customers and yet others to yield profits for the parlor, all in a well-balanced manner.[28] The prize-ball percentage itself was set by the parlor's owner. However, as one pin adjuster put it, 'For example, a prize percentage of 80 percent means giving customers prizes worth 80 yen [about US$0.27] for every 100 yen [about US$0.34] played. It was our job to set the pins in accordance with that instruction, but when you actually tried to do it, it was maddening...'.[29] That was because actual results would diverge from the set prize-ball percentage depending on the number of customers that came to the parlor: 'Having 100 percent of the machines in use and having just 30 percent of the machines in use are completely different scenarios'.[30] In this way, pin adjusters were required to possess both the ability to set pins in a way that took into account variables in parlor operation and the overall ability to predict results while considering sales and profitability and adjusting how much machines would yield in winnings.

Up until the 1970s, prior to the emergence of Fībā-type machines, the likelihood of customers winning balls was determined by the prize-ball percentage, itself based on daily pin adjustment. Customers would receive a predetermined number of balls, for example ten, when a ball entered a catcher, but it was skill in adjusting pins to open or close them that controlled the prize-ball percentage. There are no surviving records of the prize-ball percentage at the M.S. parlor during this period. As a result, I will examine how pin adjustment was carried out in response to parlors' sales prior to the introduction of Fībā-type machines based on materials describing a different parlor, Parlor B, for which data survives.

Figure 4.2 illustrates average monthly sales for Parlor B, which was located about 100 meters from the M.S. parlor. Around the same distance from Jōshin Station as the M.S. parlor and abutting the same shopping arcade, Parlor B operated in a similar business environment. The parlor was run by the second son of the founder of Masamura Shōkai, and data survives for the period from the end of 1978 to September 1981.[31] Although the M.S. parlor, which I will examine later, introduced Fībā-type machines in April 1981, there is no evidence that Parlor B did so. That conclusion is justified because sales continued according to the trend in place at the end of 1970, and there are no identifiable turning points.

After the end of 1978, Parlor B's sales experienced a decline. Meanwhile, the prize-ball percentage also fell, dragged down by shrinking sales despite evidence of an effort to maintain a figure in the 80-percent range. While raising the prize-ball percentage is an important technique for attracting customers and improving sales, it also exerts a direct, negative impact on short-term profitability. By contrast, the decline in prize-ball percentages, which reflected an effort by Parlor B to operate profitably, is likely to have been a measure intended as short-term compensation for the failure of sales to improve. Consequently, it suggests that the parlor's owner understood that it would drive away customers.

Despite Japan's resounding economic recovery during the second half of the 1970s after the first oil crisis,[32] the pachinko industry remained in recession for several more years, with both the pachinko population and the number of parlors declining after 1976.[33] The industry also faced unique challenges such as a trend on the part of customers to move away from pachinko due to the growing popularity of diversions such as the arcade game *Space Invaders*.[34]

Figure 4.2 examines the period starting in 1980, when Fībā-type machines made their debut. The increase in prize-ball percentages in February, April, November and December 1979 reflect adjustments made to deal with declining sales prior to this period. The measures were effective to a point, for example causing sales to rise during March and April 1979 and from November 1979 to January 1980; however, they did not provide a fundamental resolution to the challenges of long-term recession and customer defections.

By the end of 1980, sales had fallen, but the correlation in terms of rising prize-ball percentages was no longer clearly visible. It is likely that the parlor was forced to reduce prize-ball percentages even as it continued to grapple with the decline in sales. It is clear that the parlor was desperate to secure profits even as it lowered prize-ball percentages, and it was increasingly unable to move decisively to draw in customers by opening up pins. Given that this situation likely only spurred further defections, the parlor seems to have been drawn into a vicious cycle where lower prize-ball percentages and shrinking sales went hand in hand.

Here I would like to emphasize one aspect of the connection between parlor management and pin adjustment. Prior to the introduction of Fībā-type machines, pin adjustment was a method for determining prize-ball percentages, and it functioned to decisively control overall operations, including customer draw and sales. The testimony of Mr. S,[35] who had worked as a pin adjuster since the 1950s, amplifies the testimony of the pin adjusters cited above by providing more details about the

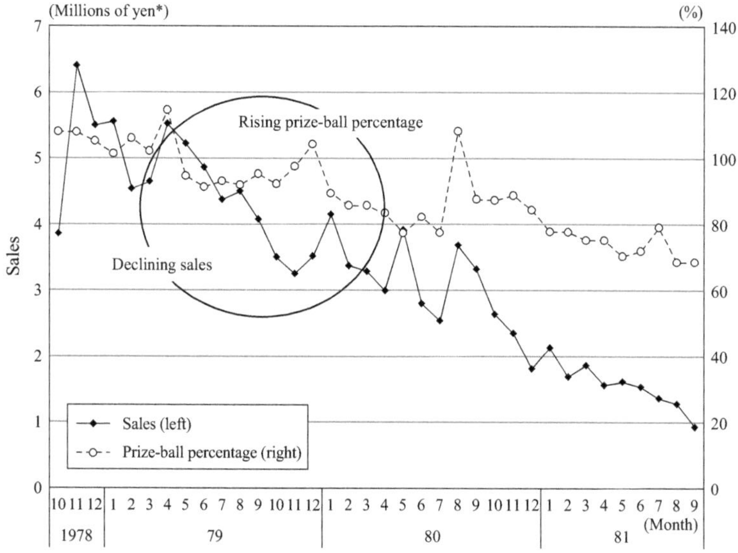

Figure 4.2: Parlor B pachinko sales and prize-ball percentages (prior to the introduction of Fībā-type machines) (October 1978 to September 1981)

Note: *At the average exchange rate for the period of 1978 to 1981, ¥1 million was equivalent to about US$4673.

Source: Compiled based on Parlor B's sales and prize-ball percentage records (uriagedaka / shuttamaritsu kiroku) for October 1978 to September 1981.

division of authority with regard to prize-ball percentages between parlor owners and pin adjusters and about the methods employed. Mr. S described the role played by pin adjustment in parlor operations and the manner in which parlor owners issued instructions as follows:

Question: How did the task of pin adjustment begin? For example, in a parlor with 200 machines, did management show the pin adjuster records detailing profit and loss for each of those machines, from No. 1 to No. 200, to show the status quo and then explain what they wanted, or did they say, here's the status quo, now get things running according to our expectations, or just get things running profitably, tighten up the pins – I imagine there were various ways of offering instructions.

Mr. S: [Pin adjustment] is the key to the business. It [can] bring money in, or let money out. Results were never right on the money, to the nearest 1000 yen, but at a minimum, you couldn't be called a pin adjuster if things didn't run generally according to plan. [For the prize-ball percentage], sometimes instructions come over the phone between individuals [pin adjusters] and parlor owners. Sometimes things

> are left up to the pin adjuster. It depends on the arrangement between the owner and the pin adjuster. Owners don't provide detailed instructions for one machine at a time. How are they thinking [to run] this parlor tomorrow? If they [expect to have] 2 million yen [about US$5555.6] in sales tomorrow, what should be done? Open the pins? Close them? Pachinko parlors gather all the data on nearby parlors, so an owner might say, nearby parlors are attracting customers, increase prize balls some, in which case [the pin adjuster] will say, okay, I understand [and adjust the pins accordingly].

It is possible to predict the prize-ball percentage depending on the extent to which pins are opened and closed. This testimony, like the roundtable discussion held by pin adjusters, suggests that final decisions about prize-ball percentage levels were the purview of parlor owners. However, it was only through the skill of pin adjusters that those decisions could be translated into reality. Sometimes, owners lacked detailed information from the field, for example about conditions at nearby parlors, in which case a pin adjuster might provide decision-making information that could prove decisive in identifying a target prize-ball percentage; in any event, some pin adjusters earned praise for their ability to do so. Working on the basis of past data, an adjustment strategy that loosened up certain machines so that they would generate more winnings or tightened them up to reduce the number of prize balls they generated could ensure the parlor would operate profitably overall while allowing customers a reasonable amount of winnings. Pin adjustment also made it possible to place machines that dispensed balls in an explosive manner at prominent locations in the parlor.[36]

Naturally, pin adjusters relied on a variety of methods to realize the prize-ball percentages that had been ordered by owners (or that they had determined themselves).

> Mr. S: Each pin adjuster had his own approach, but how about starting with a prize-ball percentage of 10 percent? When the parlor closes for the day, the pin notebook comes out [with records of the daily prize-ball percentage for each machine]. If we need to tighten the pins up a certain amount tomorrow, for example, if there are 200 machines installed, I would increase the number of machines I tightened to one-tenth of the total, or twenty machines, to reduce the rate by 10 percent. That would yield a 10 percent reduction. Different people use different yardsticks. Some people use fewer machines than ten. However, using more machines and adjusting them gradually offers a situation in which customers can enjoy gameplay more, even if the pins are closed.

In this way, pin adjusters did their job in order to realize the target prize-ball percentage across an entire parlor of machines, but they used their own unique methods to do so,[37] which affected how customers were drawn in and which as a result affected sales. Naturally, a parlor could not open things up in order to attract more customers when adjusting pins unless it had the financial wherewithal to withstand the anticipated financial losses, so such final decisions depended on the strength of their operations. That said, as long as prize-ball percentages were controlled overall by pin adjusters, there existed a world of skill and experience that lay beyond interference by management.

However, that technique was not sufficient by itself to halt the decline in sales. Observers cited the lack of popular models as another problem,[38] for example by noting that pachinko was less interesting than the arcade game *Space Invaders*, which became popular at the end of the 1970s, and people voiced concerns about the decline of the industry. It was at exactly that point that rumors about the Fībā began to spread.

FĪBĀ-TYPE MACHINES AND REMARKABLE MARKET GROWTH

The Fībā was developed based on a model known as the Burendo ('blend') Akasaka, which had been launched in 1977. That model was the first pachinko machine to incorporate slot machine-like elements. 'There were three push-buttons on the bottom of the machine, which when pushed by the customer at suitable times would stop a rotating drum; when the three pictures on the drum lined up, multiple *chūrippu* [tulips] would open for several seconds'. Additionally, 'It was possible for someone with sharp eyes to "sharpshoot" by pressing buttons while watching the drum rotate'.[39] However, the model was discontinued after it dealt a blow to parlor profits by allowing too much room for customer skill to make a difference.[40] The Fībā, which was launched in July 1980, had improvements that corrected this defect, which had been decisive for parlors, and increased the speculative element of unlimited dispensation, among other enhancements. One anecdote holds that the manufacturer had been looking for ways to develop a machine that would use materials it had purchased for use in producing the Burendo Akasaka, and that customers' joy at seeing broken machines dispense enormous quantities of balls provided a hint for the Fībā's development.[41] The machine's distinguishing characteristic was its pronounced speculative element, as can be seen in the following profile in an industry magazine:

> When balls enter the holes on the left and right above the center of the board and in the chucker [gate] underneath the center, the pictures on the center drum and numbers in the digital display window start to rotate [...]. When the button to the left of the metal frame is pressed, the drum stops from the left side, and the numbers stop as well. Combinations of numbers and drum pictures cause the giant chucker at the bottom of the board to open, providing a chance for winning balls [...]. The giant

> chucker opens for at least two seconds, with other durations including four seconds, six seconds and ten seconds. The greatest chance is afforded when the sun picture and the number seven align, in which case the giant chucker opens continuously for thirty seconds. If a ball enters the V-shaped pocket in the center of the board during this time, the chucker will remain open for another thirty seconds.[42]

The Fībā offered a startlingly pronounced speculative element by continuously dispensing balls until the flow was forcibly stopped – for example until the machine was played out – when the player won a *probability-determined* jackpot.

That said, the model received a poor reaction at tradeshows. This pronounced speculative element led parlor owners to hesitate to purchase the model because they anticipated operating losses – in short, they were concerned that they 'wouldn't be able to balance operations due to the large numbers of balls the machines dispensed at once'.[43] Nonetheless, success came when the owner of a parlor known as Hakuchō Kaikan installed about 100 of the machines at once after noticing how his own employees had become engrossed with about ten Fībā models that had been installed at a nearby parlor.[44] Sankyo is believed to have received orders for around fifteen machines at the time, but *probability considerations* meant that it took at least 100 machines, as at Hakuchō Kaikan, to realize operations that suited the machine's characteristics, as is reflected in the following observation: 'With extreme models like the Fībā, the difference between machines with "open" pins so that they dispensed more prize balls and "closed" pins that dispensed fewer prize balls become too glaringly obvious when only a small number of machines are in use, making them difficult to operate [...] from a business perspective'.[45] In this way, the initial market for the Fībā was discovered through experimentation with customers' actual reactions and then established through the discovery of business methods that suited the machines. A stream of visitors came to Hakuchō Kaikan to view its operation, and the Fībā's popularity spread throughout the industry by word of mouth. After New Year's, production could not keep pace with the rush of orders, and delivery times lengthened to six months.[46]

Sales growth and control

In April 1981, the M.S. parlor also installed Fībā-type machines. It purchased eighteen machines that month and then thirty-six more three months later, and by June, Fībā-type machines accounted for about 20 percent of its total machine base (261 machines). By then, about ten months had passed since Sankyo launched the Fībā. It is likely that the company made its decision after gauging the market's assessment,

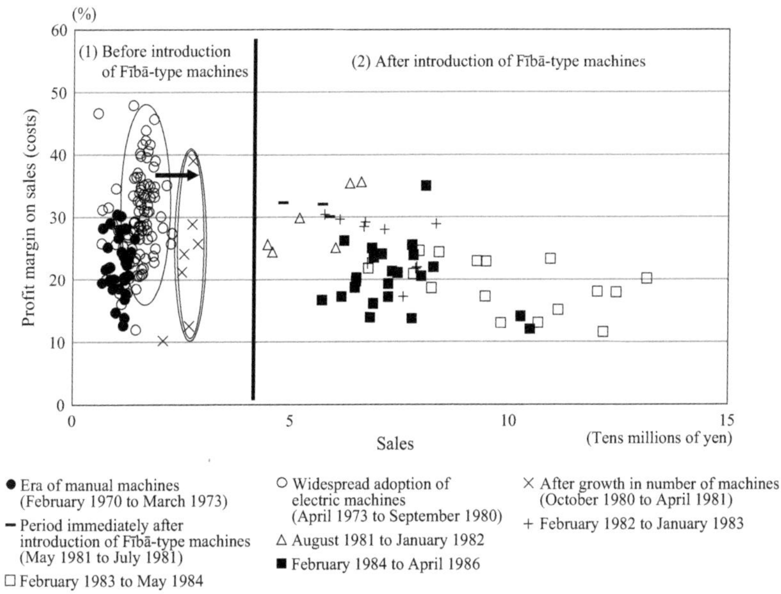

Figure 4.3: Parlor M pachinko sales and profit margin on sales (monthly averages for February 1970 to April 1986)

Note: Profit margin on sales (costs) = (Sales minus cost of prizes) / sales × 100 (%).

*Source: Compiled based on breakdown of daily sales and purchases from prize suppliers from August 1969 to April 1986 as detailed in Parlor M's general ledger (*motochō*).*

despite the machine's popularity on the street. How significantly did that decision affect sales at the M.S. parlor?

Figure 4.3 provides a graph with average monthly sales on the horizontal axis and profitability on the vertical axis (calculated by subtracting the cost of prizes from sales to calculate the amount of profit retained by the parlor after returning winnings to customers, and expressing the resulting value as a percentage of sales). The graph portrays the period from February 1970 to April 1986, so it can be used to compare performance before and after the introduction of Fībā-type machines. As described above, the M.S. parlor increased its 200 machines by 30 percent (to 261 machines) in October 1980, six months before it introduced Fībā-type machines. The effects of that change can be seen in Figure 4.3 in the distribution of results for the second half of 1980, which are shifted to the right from the sales figures for the first half of that year. However, the magnitude of the increase was slight when compared to the change prompted by the introduction of Fībā-type machines.

The effects of installing Fībā-type machines in April 1981 appear as a striking rise in sales starting in May. To measure and evaluate the magnitude of those effects, I assigned daily sales figures to eleven levels and tabulated the results to facilitate a

	Before introduction of Fībā-type machines (October 1973 to September 1980)		After introduction of Fībā-type machines (May 1981 to April 1986)	
	Sales level	No. of business days	Sales level	No. of business days
1	Below 300,000 yen	18	Below 1,250,000 yen	9
2	Below 400,000 yen	143	Below 1,750,000 yen	97
3	Below 500,000 yen	503	Below 2,250,000 yen	320
4	**Below 600,000 yen**	**717**	**Below 2,750,000 yen**	**471**
5	Below 700,000 yen	502	Below 3,250,000 yen	304
6	Below 800,000 yen	145	Below 3,750,000 yen	209
7	Below 900,000 yen	99	Below 4,250,000 yen	112
8	Below 1,000,000 yen	94	Below 4,750,000 yen	74
9	Below 1,100,000 yen	58	Below 5,250,000 yen	23
10	Below 1,200,000 yen	2	Below 5,750,000 yen	21
11	Below 1,300,000 yen	2	Below 6,250,000 yen	5
	Grand total	2,283	Grand total	1,645

Table 4.1: Distribution of Parlor M's daily sales levels (number of business days)

Notes:

a. The following range of dates was used because the number of installed machines in any given fiscal year remains unclear. The period prior to the introduction of Fībā-type machines was defined as beginning in October 1973, when electric machines gained widespread adoption in the industry and sales rose, and ending in September 1980, before the number of machines is seen to grow.

b. Bold text indicates the sales level with the most business days for both periods before and after the introduction of Fībā-type machines.

comparison of sales before and after the introduction of Fībā-type machines (see Table 4.1). Before the introduction (from October 1973 to September 1980), there were 717 business days (31.4 percent of the total of 2283 business days) in the 500,001-yen (about US$1881) to 600,000-yen (about US$2257) level; after the introduction, there were 471 business days (28.6 percent of 1645 business days) with sales in the 2,250,001-yen (about US$10,227) to 2,750,000-yen (about US$12,500) level. (Days were clustered in those levels.) A simple comparison of the 'bands' of sales within which results are clustered reveals an increase by a factor of greater than four.

Let us examine whether the increase in sales went beyond quantitative growth to include qualitative changes. We can measure the degree of variance (standard deviation), which expresses the magnitude of variability in sales per business day, and use it to observe conditions before and after the introduction of Fībā-type machines. Since it is not possible to arrive at an appropriate judgment by comparing the degree of variance figures for an entire year, I will use figures for the relevant months to evaluate the parlor's operating conditions. Since standard deviation typically increases in correlation with increased sales, I have controlled for the effect of sales growth on the degree of variance by dividing by the monthly average. The result serves as a

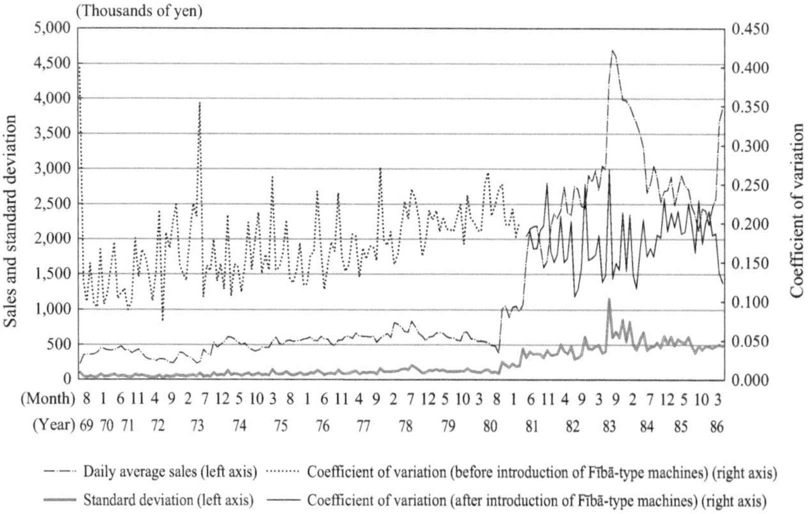

Figure 4.4: Distribution in Parlor M's sales before and after the introduction of Fībā-type machines (August 1969 to March 1986)

Note: Coefficient of variation for daily sales = Standard deviation / average monthly sales

*Source: Compiled based on breakdown of daily sales and purchases from prize suppliers from August 1969 to April 1986 as detailed in Parlor M's general ledger (*motochō*).*

coefficient of variation. This approach allows us to examine the significance of the increase in sales from a different perspective.

Figure 4.4 presents the results of these calculations. The coefficient of variation (defined as the result of dividing the standard deviation by average monthly sales), which had increased through the 1970s, shrank as sales rose after the introduction of Fībā-type machines until mid-1983. Sales were distributed in a narrow band; in other words, the magnitude of variation shrank on an average basis.

To flesh out the knowledge gained by this observation and its interpretation, additional statistical calculations will be provided as further supporting evidence. The tables presented at the end of this chapter[47] provide details on those calculations. Here I will limit myself to a description of the associated data and results. In order to compare how sales were distributed before and after the introduction of Fībā-type machines, I examined the difference in population mean values for coefficients of variation that were calculated from the standard deviation and average values for monthly sales in each of the thirty-one months before the introduction of the new models (September 1, 1978, to March 31, 1981) and in each of the thirty-one months after their introduction (May 1, 1981, to December 31, 1983). The results reveal that coefficients of variation after the introduction of Fībā-type machines were lower than those prior to their introduction, and that the introduction of those models caused variance in pachinko parlor sales to decrease. These results signify that it had become easier for parlors to forecast profits. This change was made possible by probability-controlled jackpots.

It is likely that the reversal that occurred from the second half of 1983 indicates that the effects of Fībā-type machines' characteristics were suppressed due to regulations, as described below, and new businesses' entry into the market. In light of the fact that these machines were to become the long-term standard, it is important not to overlook the characteristics of the sales trend spurred by the machines' probabilistic features.

The significance of the introduction of probabilistic elements to Fībā-type machines lies in the addition of a factor other than pin adjustment that controlled the prize-ball percentage. Given this fact, we must ask how pin adjustment interacted with the new probabilistic element to contribute to the fine-tuning of prize-ball percentages. What role was pin adjustment expected to play, and how did it really function?

Before addressing these questions, we must examine how the introduction of Fībā-type machines changed parlor operations, as illustrated in Figure 4.3. The manifestation of those changes can be divided into three distinct phases based on sales and profitability:

1. an initial phase in which sales and profitability rose abruptly (lasting until the second half of 1982);
2. an intermediate phase in which sales rose but profitability fell (lasting until the second half of 1983); and
3. a final phase in which sales fell as profitability held steady (or increased slightly) (starting during the first half of 1984).

The transition from phase (1) to phase (2), and later to phase (3), was the result of changes in competitive conditions caused by factors including regulations and the entry of new businesses into the market. For example, the industry undertook a voluntary initiative starting in June 1981 that called on parlors to restrain themselves from whipping up speculative fervor, and the installation of Fībā-type machines was limited to 30 percent of all machines that October.[48] However, ascertaining how these factors impacted the M.S. parlor's performance is no simple task. Observers have pointed out that compliance with the 30 percent limit was problematic.[49] Such issues were a factor in creating regional variations.[50] Competition with nearby parlors also impacted parlors' decisions. At the same time, regulations became stricter, and 'attack times', which impacted the number of prize balls dispensed, were limited to half the previous values starting in June 1984. Reports indicate that these changes dealt a blow to the M.S. parlor's profits at a time of intensifying competition, preventing the parlor from even recouping the cost of the machines.[51]

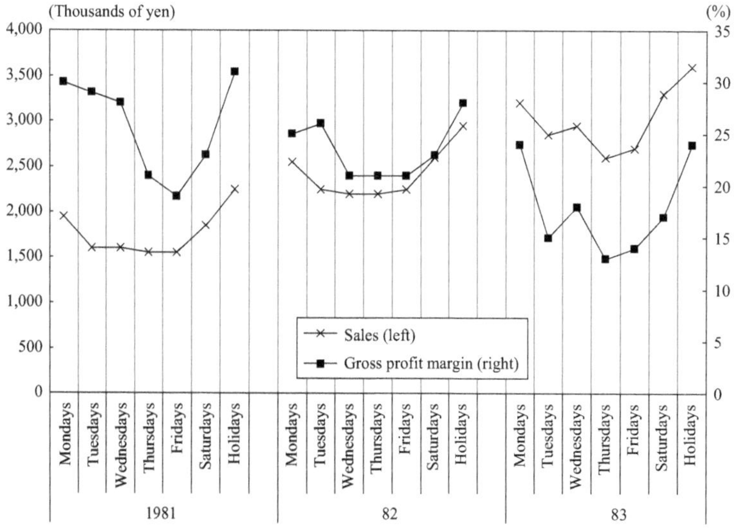

Figure 4.5: Sales and gross profit margin by day of week for Parlor M (1981 to 1983)

Notes:

a. Sales by day are given as average values for one year.

b. Gross profit margin = (Sales minus total prize exchange amount) / sales

*Source: Sales statistics tables (*eigyō tōkeihyō*) for August 1981 to July 1983.*

It is fair to conclude that changing business conditions meant that both sales and profitability were no longer fixed, with the result that parlors needed to take steps to address their changing operating environment in order to pursue stable management. In the next part, I will direct my attention toward how the M.S. parlor chose to respond to these shifts.

Dogged attachment to pin adjustment

Figure 4.5 illustrates the relationship between average sales and gross profit margin by day of the week from 1981 to 1983.[52] This three-year period corresponds to phase (1), the initial phase in which sales and profitability rose abruptly (until the second half of 1982), and phase (2), the intermediate phase in which sales rose as profitability fell (until the second half of 1983), as illustrated in Figure 4.3.

A bit of technical explanation is necessary as we examine the actions of the M.S. parlor based on Figure 4.5. In interpreting the figure, it is necessary to draw a distinction between those elements that could be controlled by the parlor and those that could not. Since sales are determined by customer headcount and customer spending, they represent a factor in parlor operations that cannot be directly manipulated. However, sales that become apparent from long-term observation can be understood in relation to the prize-ball percentages as determined by pin adjustment, a factor that is not represented in the figure. In other words, the prize-ball percentage as set by the parlor based on customer attendance on the previous day (as expressed by sales) and conditions at nearby parlors affects the next day's sales. Consequently, the prize-ball percentage comes back to affect sales even as it is itself the result of corrections that are based on fluctuations in sales. Since the figure provides averages calculated by totaling daily results recorded over a three-year period, it can be seen as an expression of the interrelated nature of prize-ball percentages as the product of intentional adjustments, sales and gross profit margin.

Prize-ball percentages, which were adjusted in response to sales, ultimately affected profits (and profitability). Parlors could raise the prize-ball percentage to draw in more customers on weekdays, for example Tuesdays and Wednesdays, when sales were lower than on holidays. As a result, profitability would fall. By contrast, prize-ball percentages could be lowered on Sundays and holidays since customers would come (i.e., since utilization would be high) even if the parlor chose not to open up the pins. As a result, profitability would be comparatively high. Conditions such as these would support the proposition that parlors were carrying out pin adjustment in line with their intentions. The changes shown in Figure 4.5 across years can be understood as an expression of not only the direction in prize-ball percentages, which the M.S. parlor varied while reviewing its performance, but also the intimate relationship between adjustment technology and its results.

An examination of the figure while comparing performance during those three years based on this perspective indicates that the tendency for sales and profitability to move together increased during 1982 and 1983, compared to 1981. Profitability rose on days when sales were high and fell on days when sales were low. This trend means that the parlor made money by boosting profitability on days that attracted large customer headcounts. Additionally, it is likely that the parlor gained the ability to control operational parameters so that overall profitability rose based on long-term forecasts since the increase in prize-ball percentages on weekdays served as an advertisement that attracted customer support.

Since the trend in prize-ball percentages corresponding to sales on specific days following the introduction of Fībā-type machines exhibits the effects of intentional pin adjustment, we can conclude that pin adjustment was decisive in attracting customers during this period. This conclusion is possible because this sort of adjustment result is not due to the machines' intrinsic performance, which depends on probability. At the M.S. parlor, pin adjustment continued to play a key function as an essential managerial technique after the introduction of Fībā-type machines.

How, then, can the role of pin adjustment as described above be evaluated in light of the probability-based control of prize-ball quantities and gameplay 'personality' that are the unique features of Fībā-type machines? The dispassionate descriptions provided by Mr. S with regard to the scope of pin adjusters' ability to control prize-ball percentages provide a graphic expression of the shrinking role of skill and experience.

> As a result of [Fībā-type machines' built-in] circuit boards, figures no longer move in response to pin adjusters' wishes. Prior to the Sebun-ki [Fībā-type machines],[53] pin adjusters' weight was 80 percent. With the Sebun-ki, now it is 30 percent.

The difference between Fībā-type machines and previous models involved the elements that determine prize-ball percentages. Prior to the Fībā-type machines, prize-ball percentage was determined by the likelihood of balls entering catchers, which changed in response to how pins were opened and closed via the pin adjustment process. By contrast, with Fībā-type machines, the newly introduced jackpot mechanism also affected the quantity of balls dispensed by parlors to customers. For example, in addition to the seven balls received by the customer when a ball entered a catcher, the event caused the drum to start rotating. If it stopped such that the pictures were aligned, an unlimited number of chance-controlled jackpot events, in which balls were dispensed for a certain amount of time (for example thirty seconds), were possible. In the case of Fībā-type machines, pin adjustment only determined the likelihood that balls would enter catchers; jackpot events themselves were unrelated to pin adjustment and were instead controlled by chance. Naturally, the likelihood of a jackpot event was amplified by changes in the frequency at which balls entered catchers, so pin adjustment, which regulated that frequency, indirectly affected jackpots. However, because the prize-ball percentage was now determined by the total number of balls entering catchers and balls dispensed due to jackpot events, the scope within which pin adjustment could control performance was diminished in Fībā-type machines compared to those entirely reliant on that process.

Pin adjustment as carried out by the M.S. parlor after the emergence of Fībā-type machines points to a failure to sufficiently tweak operational protocols to take full advantage of the new type of machine. Additional analysis is necessary based on the long-term trend in prize-ball percentages and the impact of that trend on profitability.[54]

Streamlining of prize purchases

The factors that contributed to increased profitability during the phase in which sales and profitability rose abruptly (until the second half of 1982) following the introduction of Fībā-type machines, as illustrated in Figure 4.3 above, remain obscure.

	Dates	Sales (yen)	Total purchases of prizes (yen)	Prize type as percentage of total prize purchases (%)		Special prize unit cost (yen)
				Special prizes	Standard prizes	
Before introduction of Fībā-type machines (May 1981)	1969/8–70/7	129,087,621	102,331,531	77.6	22.4	206
	70/8–71/7	138,240,229	108,508,216	77.2	22.8	206
	71/8–72/7	124,822,243	95,349,987	77.7	22.3	206
	72/8–73/7	100,657,780	74,022,671	82.0	18.0	206
	73/8–74/7	162,113,700	122,678,872	84.4	15.6	206
	74/8–75/7	157,071,600	119,920,076	80.5	19.5	206
	75/8–76/7	187,141,280	132,540,810	80.5	19.6	206
	76/8–77/7	193,417,020	129,450,546	76.9	23.2	206
	77/8–78/7	216,404,920	141,386,499	79.2	20.8	206
	78/8–79/7	214,715,290	153,112,658	78.9	21.1	206
	79/8–80/7	190,889,340	126,075,397	78.6	21.5	206
After introduction of Fībā-type machines	80/8–81/7	364,845,080	261,121,947	85.0	15.6	205
	81/8–82/7	731,897,210	526,806,311	91.0	9.0	204.5
	82/8–83/7	966,053,930	757,920,792	93.9	6.1	203.5
	83/8–84/7	1,230,267,940	1,001,342,557	95.5	4.5	203.5
	84/8–85/4	2,049,479,740	519,238,420	95.1	4.9	203.5

Table 4.2: Growth in customer preference for special prizes at Parlor M (based on purchases from prize suppliers)

*Source: Compiled based on prize purchases from suppliers from August 1969 to April 1985 as detailed in Masamura Shōkai's general ledgers (*motochō*).*

Taking advantage of the increased speculative element and higher sales, customers sought to extend their winnings by exchanging prizes for cash, and this development fueled parlor profitability.

Table 4.2 provides a summary of prizes purchased by Masamura Shōkai from the 1970s to the first half of the 1980s, grouped into two categories: standard prizes (cigarettes, candy, lifestyle items, etc.) and special prizes, which were recorded with mechanical pencil marks.[55] Customers sought special prizes not for their intrinsic usefulness or value, but rather because they could be exchanged for cash. The question is whether customers exchanged the balls they received for special prizes or standard prizes, and here I have inferred the results of customers' choices based on the M.S. parlor's total prize purchases.

Table 4.2 exhibits a change in purchase trends following the introduction of Fībā-type machines. In terms of the two categories' respective values, special prizes accounted for an average of about 80 percent of all prize purchases until the 1970s. Following the introduction of Fībā-type machines, the category rose above 90 percent and temporarily surpassed 95 percent. The increase in special prizes as a percentage of all prize purchases was the result of a strengthening of customers' tendency to exchange balls for special prizes rather than for standard prizes.

It is difficult to offer a decisive explanation of why customers' preference for exchanging balls for special prizes instead of standard prizes rose along with machines' speculative element, but we can presume that the utility of prizes such as cigarettes fell as the quantity of such prizes received by customers grew. The upper limit on prize value at the time was set at 3500 yen (about US$15.90 in 1981), which meant that customers could not exchange balls for prizes worth more than that. Receiving large numbers of balls presumably gave customers greater incentive to exchange them for a larger quantity of low-cost prizes. Customers faced with this dilemma would presumably opt to exchange balls for special prizes, which could then be exchanged for cash, even if the discount rate was disadvantageous.

Customers' growing latent preference for exchanging balls for special prizes is noteworthy insofar as it exerted a positive effect on parlor profit since those prizes were more profitable for parlors than standard prizes. Calculating prize profitability (by subtracting the purchase price from the exchange price and dividing the result by the exchange price) based on M.S. parlor receipts bearing prize purchase prices and records (entitled 'Prize I') of the prices for which prizes were 'sold' to customers (i.e., exchange prices) yields a figure of 31.8 percent for special prizes. By contrast, the corresponding figure for cigarettes, a representative prize, was lower, at 16.8 percent for all brands (based on books of receipts and 'Prize I'[56]). This fact indicates that the ratio of the (price of the) balls customers received to the (price of the) special prizes for which they exchanged them was lower than for standard prizes,[57] which served to effectively lower the prize-ball percentage and increase parlor profitability.

It is difficult to verify why parlors were able to set prices for special prizes so that they were more profitable than the pricing for standard prizes. Standard prizes were supplied by wholesalers at market value. For standard prices, for which retail prices were known, customers could approximate the exchange rate based on the quantity of balls exchanged. In other words, customers were unlikely to have accepted exchange rate levels that diverged from market prices. By contrast, in the case of special prizes, market value did not provide a basis for comparison, allowing parlors to set prices in the absence of any standards that could be referenced by customers. Customers wishing to exchange prizes for cash likely had to accept terms that were more disadvantageous than those that applied to standard prizes. As a result, parlor profits rose with the percentage of balls that were exchanged for special prizes, as is made clear by parlors' earnings from, and expenditure on, special prizes, which indicate a high level of profitability. Furthermore, it goes without saying that the decline in the prices at which parlors purchased special prizes (see Table 4.2) also improved the profitability of parlor operations.

These two aspects – the increase in the percentage of balls exchanged for special prizes and the decline in the prices parlors paid for them – suggest an interesting difference when compared to how Masamura Shōkai purchased special prizes around the mid-1950s.

As explained in Chapter 1, Masamura Shōkai was forced to accept increases in prize prices as procurement shrank to two special prize wholesalers following the ban on successive-shot machines in 1955. This development is likely to have occurred against the backdrop of customers choosing from among numerous exchanges those businesses that offered the highest exchange rates. Masamura Shōkai drew on its accumulated management expertise to turn the operational burden imposed by higher prize prices into higher profits. Subsequently, customers' ability to choose based on differences in exchange rates is likely to have disappeared when the supply of special prizes shrank to a single company, Aisan Shōkai.[58]

To expand on that change based on some level of conjecture, the pachinko industry took internal steps to narrow the routes by which special prizes were supplied to a smaller number of wholesalers under the guidance of police and other groups so as to exclude organized crime, which had been involved in buying prizes during the industry's early years.[59] From customers' standpoint, such regulatory steps concerning exchanges of special prizes served to create an institutional framework that left no room for choice. Presumably the industry accepted a framework that incorporated a type of social cost in the form of safety by limiting the number of players instead of a competitive market that was open to other participants because it cut off criminal groups' source of funds and because the goal of ensuring the soundness and wholesomeness of pachinko squared with both customers' and society's expectations. In this sense, the three-business system described at the outset functioned as an exclusive business channel that kept organized crime and other groups from inserting themselves into transactions.

Against that backdrop, growth in the speculative character of pachinko during the 1980s caused large numbers of special prizes to circulate from parlors to customers, from customers to special prize wholesalers via prize-buying businesses and from wholesalers back to parlors. Seen from the perspective of special prize wholesalers, the increase in parlors' purchases of special prizes, for which there was no sales risk, can be assumed to have left more room for the wholesale prices at which parlors purchased them to be lowered while leaving the prices for which those prizes were purchased from the businesses that bought prizes from customers unchanged. That is because the margin left for wholesalers should have grown in direct proportion to the quantity of special prizes being distributed. If the prices at which parlors purchased prizes could be lowered for these reasons, the savings would drive up parlor profits.

Naturally, it is not possible to determine how the decline in prices was absorbed by the businesses that bought prizes from customers, or by special prize wholesalers or customers since neither the exchange rate offered to customers for prize balls nor the prices at which special prize wholesalers purchased prizes from the businesses that bought them from customers are known. Certainly, it is possible that the basis for the particularly noteworthy improvement in profitability during the period immediately following the introduction of Fībā-type machines included manipulation of the exchange rates extended to customers for special prizes by parlors so that the terms were somewhat more advantageous as customers began exchanging large quantities of prize balls due to the explosive popularity of the new models.

That said, such manipulation was likely limited to the period immediately following the machines' introduction since intensifying competition among parlors would have made it difficult to orchestrate a sustained, one-sided decrease in the exchange rates extended to customers. Consequently, the decline in the prices at which parlors purchased prizes should be understood to have been created by the transition to large numbers of prize balls as the industry grew rapidly, rather than as the result of disadvantageous exchange rates imposed on customers. While this conclusion remains squarely in the domain of conjecture due to a shortage of material that could be used to verify it, there can be no doubt that lower prize prices fueled growth in the profitability of the parlor business. It is likely that sales and profitability grew in this way during the phase in which sales and profitability rose abruptly (until the second half of 1982) immediately after the introduction of Fībā-type machines.

FISSURES IN BUSINESS PRACTICES

Growth in the number of businesses newly entering the industry combined with rapid growth in demand due to the popularity of Fībā-type machines required a commensurate supply of pachinko machines. How was this increase in supply accomplished?

It would not have been possible to predict the popularity of Fībā-type machines in advance. Similarly, nobody had a firm grasp of how long that popularity would continue. Around 1982, the industry's assessment was that the boom spurred by the new models was a temporary phenomenon in an industry known for dramatic shifts in popularity. For example, Kokuei Takeuchi, director of the Nikkōso (the Japan Amusement Machine Industry Association), observed,

> Industries like this go through a cycle of metabolism that lasts around six months to a year [...]. Instead of continuing the Fībā indefinitely, we'd like to make efforts

> to keep customers from becoming bored while contributing to parlors' operations by launching new models at an interval of six months to a year in order to meet customers' wishes.[60]

Takeuchi is suggesting that because popularity changes, it is not sufficient to simply follow trends, and manufacturers must instead create new trends themselves by launching new models that differ from Fībā-type machines.

Of the fact that manufacturers had to take some action to rapidly increase supply even as they anticipated that the trend would be short-lived, there can be no doubt. If so, then it is possible that the supply methods of machines that accommodated the Fībā boom in the market may have constituted a short-term, temporary effort on the part of manufacturers. That is because the effort hinged not on some special action that introduced major changes to production structures, but rather, at least at first, on conventional production methods that had been utilized in the past.

In the meantime, Fībā-type machines had the potential to change business practices in the machine market. Until that time, only a small number of machines had mustered enough popularity to trigger changes in the overall structure of the industry, including the 'all-win' models that created a nationwide market; the Masamura Gauge (pin arrangement), which became the de facto standard (see Chapter 1); and successive-shot machines such as machine-gun and circulating-type designs, which shortened the machine replacement timeline and smoothed fluctuations in production caused by seasonality (see chapters 1 and 2). If conditions created by Fībā-type machines were to have an impact on transaction practices between parlors and manufacturers and relationships between manufacturers, their popularity would signal more than just a short-term trend. However, the involved parties could not discern whether their efforts were on target at that stage, since it was impossible to predict in advance what changes would occur. This part of the chapter examines the mechanisms of machine supply with special attention on the M.S. parlor's introduction of Fībā-type machines while fleshing out its potential.

M.S. parlor's machine suppliers and introduction of Fībā-type machines

Table 4.3 presents ledger entries from the second half of 1969 to the beginning of 1986 to summarize the number of machines purchased by Masamura Shōkai in each month, along with the manufacturers that supplied them. The monthly machine counts allow us to determine when machines were replaced, while annual counts support an assessment of the average number of replacements carried out and the number of machines affected. Divergence and convergence of machine introduction seasons as made clear by both sets of statistics correspond to changes in the seasonality of production, which affected manufacturers' operations. A breakdown of the manufacturers from which the parlor purchased machines allows us to ascertain the characteristics of the machine market, for example the number of manufacturers with which the parlor did business and whether transactions stabilized (in the form of the bilateral trading arrangement discussed in Chapter 3) or varied over time.

First, let us examine the number of replacements each year (B) as presented on the right side of the table along with the number of machines involved (A / B). While the number of replacements before the introduction of Fībā-type machines varied from one to three per year, that figure rose after the new models were introduced, ranging from four to six. Divergence around the time the new machines were introduced accompanied a decline in the average number of machines purchased as shown below, and changes in the two phenomena were connected. The average number of machines purchased as part of a replacement ranged from about ninety to 150 prior to the introduction of Fībā-type machines. By contrast, that figure shrank to about forty-one to eighty-four, and the number of machines being replaced shrank as a percentage of the total number of installed machines after the new models were introduced, despite the fact that the total number of machines had increased in 1980.

The monthly figures show signs of a trend from consolidation to divergence. Prior to the introduction of Fībā-type machines, replacements tended to take place in November, December and July. After the arrival of the new models, replacement frequency remained high from December to January, corresponding to the New Year's holiday, but there was no discernible trend for other months. I call this tendency 'divergence'. On its surface, this finding indicates that the seasonal element had disappeared from manufacturers' production. Identifying the reason for this divergence requires long-term observation of industry trends, including the circumstances of manufacturers' operations; we must not rush to a conclusion. The following examines this issue with a consideration of the mechanisms by which popular models were supplied.

Table 4.3 offers a number of clues that give an understanding of the business relationships between Masamura Shōkai and manufacturers. One such clue is provided by changes in the companies that supplied machines. From 1969 to 1973, the parlor's principal suppliers were Masamura Kikai ('machine') and Nishijin. Nyū Gin subsequently replaced Masamura Kikai and assumed a central role in transactions. Used machines also made an appearance, along with a one-off deal with Surī Sutā ('three stars') in 1979. Masamura Kikai, which inherited its name from Masamura Shōkai,[61] did not operate during the 1970s.[62] Masamura Shōkai replaced Masamura Kikai with Nyū Gin as a machine supplier against this backdrop, and over the long term, the parlor basically dealt with one or two manufacturers, from Masamura Kikai

	Year	January	February	March	April	May	June	July	August	September	October	November	December
Before introduction of Fībā-type machines	1969					Parlor renewal			191				
	70		70				100					100	2
	71			100				100	1				70
	72							160					136
	73							191				80[e]	
	74			100									
	75				73			282					64
	76					90[e]						70	
	77				98							92	
	78				5				85				
	79				111				10			97	
	80							26	Parlor renewal			262	33
	No. of machine installations by month (C)		1	2	3	1	2	5	3			6	4
After introduction of Fībā-type machines	1981	66					180	36			63	36	85
	82	55			60	90		6					123
	83	18	36		36	65							90
	84			105		46	36			18			96
	85				87			18		72	54	18	
	86	36											
	No. of machine installations by month (C)	4	1	1	3	3	2	3		2	2	2	4

Table 4.3: Introduction of machines at Parlor M

Notes:

a. The number of models includes machines whose model name is clear in the records, for example Nishijin's Shiroi Kamome and Sankyo's Fībā models. Models whose name is not listed were included if the manufacturer was clear and the price was the same.
b. The number of pachinko machines includes entries listing parts, for example front panels.
c. Fībā-type machines were introduced in April 1982 but do not appear until June in accounting ledgers. Sales increased abruptly in May, likely reflecting a discrepancy between the month in which they were installed and the timing of associated accounting entries.
d. The names of manufacturers such as Sankyo reflect record entries.
e. The number of installations includes duplicate entries when the month of installation was unclear.

*Source: Compiled based on Masamura Shōkai's general ledgers (*motochō*).*

or Masamura Kikai and Nishijin, to Nishijin and Nyū Gin. This business practice pattern was a standard in the industry (see Chapter 3). Transactions with Masamura Kikai resumed when that company recommenced production in 1980, replacing Nishijin.

A diversification of suppliers must be identified as one noteworthy characteristic following the introduction of Fībā-type machines in 1981. In addition to Masamura Kikai after the company resumed production, records show purchases from Maruhon

Total number of installed machines (A)	Number of models[a)]	Manufacturers	Number of replacements (B)	Average number of installed machines: A/B (machines)	Average number of installed machines: Left figure as percentage of all installed machines before introduction of Fībā-type machines (%)
191	1	Masamura Kikai			
272	Unknown	Masamura Kikai, Nishijin	3	90.7	47
271	Unknown	Masamura Kikai, Nishijin, unknown	3	90.3	47
296	Unknown	Masamura Kikai, Nishijin, used machines (Masamura Kikai)	2	148.0	77
271	Unknown	Masamura Kikai, used machines	2	135.5	71
100	2+ unknown	Nishijin	1	100.0	52
419	4+ unknown	Nyū Gin, unknown	3	139.7	73
160	7	Nishijin, Nyū Gin, used machines (Nishijin)	2	80.0	42
190	11	Nishijin, Nyū Gin	2	95.0	50
90	9	Nishijin, Nyū Gin	1	90.0	47
218	14	Nishijin, Nyū Gin, Surī Sutā	2	109.0	57
321	11	Masamura Kikai, Nyū Gin, Maruhon Kōgyō	3	107.0	56
466	18	Masamura Kikai, Nyū Gin, Maruhon Kōgyō, Kyōraku Sangyō, used machines (Nishijin)	6	77.7	30
334	19	Nishijin, Nyū Gin, Kyōraku Sangyō, Sankyo[d)]	4	83.5	32
245	12	Nyū Gin, Sankyo	6	40.8	16
301	13	Nyū Gin, Sankyo, Heiwa	5	60.2	23
249	11	Nishijin, Nyū Gin, Sankyo, Heiwa	5	49.8	19
36					

Kōgyō (a new relationship for the company) as well as Sankyo, which developed the Fībā-type machine, and Heiwa. Following its introduction of Fībā-type machines, the parlor tended to add one or two suppliers while purchasing machines primarily from Nyū Gin and Sankyo. In this way, the M.S. parlor began purchasing machines from Sankyo, which developed a popular model, while continuing long-term purchases from Nyū Gin.

Incidentally, the parlor's purchases from Masamura Kikai ended after just two years.[63] Was Masamura Kikai able to smoothly keep up with Fībā-type machines, which required a technological base that differed from previous models in terms of such factors as circuit boards and electronic technologies? The lack of sustained purchases from Masamura Kikai may have been influenced by changes in technological competitiveness related to the new machine designs. In addition to the continuing recession at the time, the shakeout in manufacturers that accompanied the technological transition must be considered as a factor in the continuation of the early 1980s decline in manufacturers (until 1983; see Figure 0.3 and the introduction of this chapter) and in Nishijin's ceding of its long-held market leadership to Heiwa and Sankyo with the coming of the 1980s (see Table 3.4).

In light of these business relationships, several factors require examination with regard to the M.S. parlor's introduction of the suddenly popular Fībā-type machines. Purchase agreements indicate that the M.S. parlor installed Fībā-type machines about five months after December 1980, when Sankyo's Fībā-type machine first generated buzz in the market.[64] At the time, the parlor was purchasing most of its machines from Maruhon Kōgyō, with which it began dealing in 1980, and major supplier Nyū Gin. As a result, it purchased similar models rather than actual Fībā-type machines.[65] I will examine these two facts in the next section.

Flexible production structures

The M.S. parlor introduced new machines one season after it determined that Sankyo's Fībā would become popular. Determining whether these machines were introduced earlier or later by particular parlors is not especially significant. However, it would be useful to direct our interest toward how many manufacturers waited, like Maruhon and Nyū Gin, to develop products that were similar to the Fībā, and the length of the delay. That information offers clues as to how the mechanisms and regulations underpinning the industry's development were related to research and development.

A special certification inspection for 'Fībā-type machines' was carried out in April 1981.[66] It is likely that Fībā-type machines developed by other companies were made available for purchase for the first time after this inspection.[67] Of the seventeen models whose manufacturers applied for certification, one was denied, two were placed on hold, and fourteen were licensed for sale. Since the original Fībā began spreading throughout the country along with associated rumors in February 1981, it took those other companies just two months to respond. Excluding Sankyo, which developed the first Fībā model, ten companies developed certified models: Nishijin (with two models), Heiwa, Sanyō Bussan, Maruhon, Daiichi Shōkai, Okumura Yūki, Toyomaru Sangyō, Kyōraku Sangyō, Maruzen Bussan and Nyū Gin. As of 1981, there were twenty-six manufacturers in the industry,[68] and ten of twenty-five of them (excluding Sankyo) launched models one season later. More than half the industry's manufacturers failed to respond, but the presence and significance of manufacturers that were able to respond quickly is noteworthy from the standpoint of the industry's development.

Other manufacturers began launching their 'Fībā-type machines'[69] as soon as they passed the certification process. The M.S. parlor installed eighteen machines from Maruhon in April and then bought thirty-six machines from Nyū Gin two months later, in June.[70] It was the shortest timeframe within which any parlor that did not have a relationship with Sankyo was able to field the new type of machine.

Despite the seeming continuation of established methods for procuring Fībā-type machines, business practices were beginning to change. Masamura Shōkai's actions throw into relief the fact that supplies of Fībā-type machines were subject to some sort of constraint. The company, which had purchased similar products from Maruhon and Nyū Gin just as in the past, bought Sankyo's Fībā model the following year, in 1982. It is not hard to imagine why Masamura Shōkai might have wanted to purchase the machine that had originally sparked the boom, but the action was an unparalleled exception in the company's long-term business dealings. Here we must also consider the possibility that the company had initially moved to meet customer needs with similar products after it was unable to immediately purchase Sankyo's Fībā model. As one parlor owner put it,

> There were concerns that adding this [Fībā-type machine] would throw [prize-ball] percentages into disarray, and that it would only be possible to operate if parlors were able to generate high percentages. For this reason, it would be risky to add 30 percent of the total machines, so I first added 15 percent at our parlor. Once I switched to Fībā-type machines, I found that the machines were extremely good, but when I realized that, there were no machines, and orders [lead times] were one month out. Thus businesses nationwide competed to purchase the machines.[71]

This phenomenon was partially the result of Fībā-type machines' unusual popularity. But more critically, it was influenced by the characteristics of development and production structures that were intimately related to the interdependent relationships that manufacturers had built since the 1960s and which exerted profound influence on the course of the industry's development (see chapters 2 and 3).

Pachinko machine development was a highly unpredictable enterprise due to regulations and intense swings in popularity, and the attendant risks affected how manufacturers invested in production equipment. Even if a popular model appeared in the market, it was not possible for manufacturers to immediately expand equipment in response to the new demand. Even if, for the sake of argument, manufacturers could expand the scale of production in response to popularity, it would remain difficult to forecast whether they would be able to secure sales at a sufficient level to support the expanded scale of operations. Moreover, a striking divergence between busy and idle periods had become established as a core feature of the industry since the mid-1950s, as explained in Chapter 1. As a result of the seasonality of demand, year-round capacity utilization in the industry's plants was not very high. Machine design was predicated on this seasonality, with the goal being merely to satisfy demand until the next machine replacement cycle began. Even popular models had a service life that would not extend across many years, and there was no assurance that manufacturers would be able to secure sales channels at the time of replacement. For these reasons, pachinko machine manufacturers were hesitant to make capital investments.

However, the actions of manufacturers that were cautious about equipment were disadvantageous for parlors. Fujio Busujima, who served as the manager of Sankyo's New Machine Development Department, perfectly captured the situation for parlor owners when he said,

> Once the product became a hit, there weren't any machines left in the inventory, and deliveries were two to three months out. When deliveries are delayed two or three months, that becomes a delay of in effect five to six months compared to the parlors that purchased the machines first, which for nearby parlors means a loss of customers and declining sales, and in this case, a loss of profits on par with what would be earned in all of 1980.[72]

Due to the difficulty of predicting when a given model might lose popularity, it was desirable from parlors' perspectives to move rapidly to introduce machines while they were still popular so that they could quickly recoup their outlay. To the extent that manufacturers avoided bearing the risk of capital investment, parlors' opportunity cost increased. Cautious capital investment was an important way for individual manufacturers to lower their costs, but the approach prevented those same manufacturers from responding quickly when a machine such as the Fībā became more popular than forecast. Partial optimization does not necessarily lead to overall optimization, and parlors' loss of profit not only translated into loss of future business opportunities for manufacturers, but also obstructed overall industry growth.

In fact, when the Fībā's popularity exploded, the M.S. parlor was able to purchase machines – albeit similar models, not the original Fībā – with a delay of just one season. The mechanism that made it possible to delay capital investment and to respond quickly to demand for popular models hindered by those delays was the acceptance of similar models from other companies.[73]

Sankyo had the option of exercising its legal rights to refuse to allow other companies to manufacture their machines using Fībā patents and instead monopolize the economic opportunities created by the model's popularity. However, management of the patent in question was left to the Nittokuren (Japan Amusement Machine Patent Management Federation), which had been established with investments from the members of the Nikkōso. As a result, it was licensed to other companies in return for low royalties. It was this mechanism that allowed pachinko machine manufacturers that adopted a cautious attitude toward capital investment to respond immediately to demand stemming from the Fībā's popularity. Sankyo's decision to allow other companies to manufacture Fībā-type machines can only be understood in light of certain definitive factors that shaped manufacturers' operations and the broader historical context, as described in the following source.

Historical source: on other manufacturers' production of patented Fībā-type machines

From the testimony of a Sankyo executive on February 17, 1997, as recorded in the Japan Fair Trade Commission Deposition Report (Kōtori Kyōjutsu Hōkokusho[74])

Certainly, we would receive an enormous number of orders if we refused to allow everyone to manufacture the machine. If we made the enormous investments necessary to accommodate those orders, and hired a large number of employees, what would happen afterwards? [...] Products in our industry spark booms as soon as they become popular, but the life cycle is short, so those booms end as soon as they start. When that happens, it becomes impossible to operate while maintaining surplus production equipment and employees. The second reason [...] is that if we monopolized the market, our customers, machine users, would complain vociferously [...]. If we fulfill orders with limited production capability, a substantial difference in sales would emerge between parlors that were able to introduce those machines quickly and parlors that had to wait for delivery for an extended period of time. In that case, we would see a strong backlash from parlors that were unable to obtain the model quickly. Other manufacturers introduced hit models prior to that point in time. We have manufactured machines that are the same as those hit models in the past, and we will presumably continue to manufacture other companies' hit models in the future.

As reflected by the executive's use of the word 'certainly', monopolizing the business opportunities created by the popular model was an option for Sankyo. However, the company also took into account the burden that it would shoulder if it sought to maintain production at a scale suitable to accommodate demand for popular models, and when the Fībā's popularity became apparent, it allowed all machine manufacturers to supply the number of machines they could produce to the market to meet parlors' demand by permitting other companies to manufacture similar products. In this way, the pachinko industry had a unique basis that allowed it to quickly accommodate market expansion.

In light of these facts, caution is warranted before we interpret the changes glimpsed in the M.S. parlor's machine purchases as evidence of a transformation

	January	February	March	April	May	June	July	August	September	October	November	December	Total number of installed machines (A)	Number of models
1987		18		72		18		18	18			18	162	7
1988			18			36			18		36		108	5
1989						18	18				36	39	111	6
1990		18										32	50	3
1991 Old location				18									18	2
New location									237	16			253	8
1992	32		16	80		16	48			16	48	32	288	13
1993			16	32		16	16			32		16	128	8
1994			48	16			16			32		16	128	8
1995		16		32			32			32	16	112[a]	240 (64)[b]	16
1996						16	32		32		16	48	144	8
1997	16		32	16	13		16		32	8[c]		16[c]	149 (16)[b]	12

Table 4.4: Changes in machine installations and supplier relationships at Masamura Shōkai

Notes:

a. Includes 16 pachislot machines (slot-based amusement machines, meaning pachinko-size Japanese slot machines) from Ai Ti Shī. The delivery dates are unclear, so the month has been inferred based on documents whose contents pre- and post-date the period in question.

b. Figures in parentheses in the 'Total' column indicate the number of *pachislot* machines.

c. Number of machines installed per agreement.

*Source: Compiled based on purchase agreements (*baibai keiyakusho*) into which Masamura Shōkai entered from March 1979 to April 1998.*

in the structure of the machine market. The new machines' popularity was abrupt and unanticipated, to the extent that the market could be described as being on fire, and the limited scale of production equipment only spurred demand with which production was unable to keep pace. A certain amount of time is required between the development of imitation products and their stable production. Moreover, the regulatory requirement of certification creates an additional time lag. Parlors had no choice but to purchase machines in small lots from multiple manufacturers. At the M.S. parlor, the implications of that reality can be seen in supplier diversification, purchases of small quantities of machines and the disappearance of seasonality.

However, this phenomenon is not likely to have been a stopgap measure that would give way in favor of the prior arrangements once the problem, which stemmed from the gap between production capacity and the abrupt popularity of the Fībā, was resolved. Going back to Table 4.3, there were about five replacement cycles each year during the five years from 1981 to 1985. Although no continuous data is available from which to observe the subsequent trend, it is possible to survey purchases based on Table 4.4, which summarizes purchase agreements between Masamura Shōkai

Manufacturers	Number of replacements per year	Average number of installed machines per replacement[c)]
4 (Nyū Gin, Heiwa, Nishijin, Taiyō Denshi)	6	23
5 (Sankyo, Daiichi, Taiyō, Mitsuboshi, Heiwa)	4	22
3 (Taiyō Denshi, Kyōraku, Heiwa)	4	22
3 (Nyū Gin, Sankyo, Kyōraku)	2	17
1 (Heiwa)	1	18
7 (Sankyo, Kyōraku, Taiyō Denshi, Heiwa, Daiichi, Ginza, Masamura Yūki)	2	38
7 (Masamura Yūki, Sankyo, Toyomaru Sangyō, Kyōraku Sangyō, Fuji Shōji, Heiwa, Daiichi)	8	18
4 (Heiwa, Daiichi, Nyū Gin, Sankyo)	6	15
4 (Heiwa, Toyomaru, Sankyo, Nishijin)	5	16
5 (Maruhon, Sankyo, San'yō, Daiichi, Masamura Yūki) + 4 (Snappu Bakku, Samī, Ai Ti Shī, Yamasa)	6	15
7 (Nyū Gin, Taiyō, Takeya, San'yō, Sankyo, Daidō, Toyomaru)	5	18
8 (Sanpawā, Maruhon, Fuji Shōji, Kyōraku, Sankyo, Heiwa, Taiyō, Toyomaru) + 2 (Yamasa, Yunibāsaru)	8	13

and manufacturers. Even data tabulated from surviving materials alone exhibits the following trends: the disappearance of seasonality due to an increase in the number of replacements each year,[75] purchases of machines from multiple manufacturers and a decrease in the number of machines purchased at any given time. Temporary actions taken by parlors in response to tightness in the supply of Fībā-type machines became established in parlor operations and continued even after the supply constraints, including on imitation machines, eased as the boom went on. Along with more frequent and less seasonal machine replacements, smaller purchases ended up becoming the norm.

The problem is the cause of such changes, which made a return to the status quo ante impossible. From manufacturers' standpoint, diversification in the number of manufacturers with which parlors did business signified a broadening of the potential for developing new markets, but at the same time, the change made it impossible for them to ensure they would be able to retain previous customers and therefore triggered an intensification of competition among them. Moreover, more frequent replacement cycles and smaller purchase lots served to increase manufacturers' development and production costs. Consequently, it is necessary to examine such changes in light of the factors that led parlors to pursue them. Next, I will examine the problem of rising prize-ball percentages as a result of intensifying competition with nearby parlors, which was triggered by an influx of new businesses into the market. It is against this backdrop that machine purchases became more frequent.

INFLUX OF NEW BUSINESSES AND INTENSIFICATION OF COMPETITION

Renewal reopenings as a means of competition

Shinsōkaiten (renewal reopenings) are a well-known and unique method in Japan employed by parlors to capture customers. In this section, I will examine the effectiveness of this approach by comparing parlor performance before and after such reopenings and verify its role as a competitive technique and method for stabilizing parlor operations by capturing customers.

'Renewal reopening' refers to a parlor's resumption of operations with new models after replacing some of its machines. The origin of the method is unclear, but the practice of replacing machines had already been introduced in the area around Nagoya, historically home to a high concentration of manufacturers, by around 1951.[76] In staging such reopenings, parlors replaced machines while leaving their basic design and layout untouched but used the same promotional decorations as used for new openings. Nonetheless, the expression 'renewal reopenings' was presumably used to distinguish such events from new openings.[77] Although it is impossible to confirm whether renewal reopenings at the beginning of the 1950s followed today's practice of increasing the prize-ball percentage so that machines dispensed large quantities of prize balls, reports indicate that reopenings did attract customers.[78]

The process by which distinctive reopenings in one region later became standard practice in other areas remains unclear. Parlors are faced with the need to replace machines due to their physical service life, which relates to wear sustained in the course of parlor operations, as well as from a 'popularity life' and competitive perspective, which demands that parlors install machines that are popular on the street in order to keep customers from losing interest. If it is true that customers choose parlors that promote new machines by opening up the pins so that customers win more, then renewal reopenings offer not only a means of updating machines, but also a new business practice.

In this case, parlors must determine the timing and frequency of such reopenings based on a consideration of the costs they are able to shoulder, since the associated investment is made in the expectation that it will be recouped in the future (through increased sales and customer headcount).[79] Factors that influence the timing and frequency of renewal reopenings include the physical and popularity service life of machines as well as competitive conditions. During the first half of the 1950s, when successive-shot machines were enjoying their heyday, machine updates related to physical service life were carried out every three or four months due to the severity of wear, as described in Chapter 1. As competition intensified due to successive new openings, higher prize-ball percentages meant shorter mechanical and popularity service lives for machines, making it difficult for parlors to set replacement schedules. However, the ban on successive-shot machines led to an extension of physical service life even as the abrupt decline in the number of operating parlors spurred a relative easing of competition, with the result that the average number of new-machine replacements became established at about two per season.

Here I will treat renewal reopenings as a business practice that was accompanied, as it is today, by increased prize-ball percentages across the board so that customers would win more. Such reopenings served as active sales events conceived to generate new customers in a comprehensive manner, as defensive measures to hold nearby parlors in check and as a passive method for keeping regular customers who had begun to lose interest in the machines installed at the parlor from defecting to other parlors. If the increase in the number of replacements triggered by constraints on machine supply was exacerbated by the debut of Fībā-type machines, as described in the previous part, then the approach of holding renewal reopenings can be considered to have become a competitive technique that became even more accessible during and after the 1980s.

Figure 4.3 above shows a striking decline in sales at the M.S. parlor from the second half of 1983. Nonetheless, profitability held constant and even increased slightly. Seen from the perspective of the business stabilization that enabled the pachinko industry's development and long-term existence, the fact that stalling sales were not accompanied by a decrease in profitability signified that the parlor had in its possession the means to stabilize operations while autonomously safeguarding its business from the impact of the decline in sales caused by factors such as regulation and intensifying competition.

Appendix 1 presents a more detailed analysis of renewal reopenings as a technique for controlling profitability; following is a summary of the results of that analysis.

According to Appendix 1, the 'service' periods of complimentary winnings seen during renewal reopenings had short-term effects. In summary, the parlor that orchestrated renewal reopenings was able to avoid a significant decline in profitability even as it accepted the trend toward falling sales from the second half of 1983 (see Figure 4.3 above). New machines and higher prize-ball percentages kept customers from losing interest. Competition between parlors in terms of 'service' periods of higher winnings, then, offered customers increased choices, which helped prevent the industry from losing its overall appeal.

As the benefits of renewal reopenings were realized and the strategy was promoted as a specific means of competing, the results were presumably expressed in more frequent machine replacements on the part of parlors. It is likely that strong incentives for parlors to choose renewal reopenings accounted for the establishment of the growth trend in the M.S. parlor's machine purchases. At the same time, seen through the lens of standalone (non-chain) parlors such as Parlor C (see Figure App. 1.3), intensifying competition was laying waste to the basis that allowed parlors to offer complimentary increases in the prize-ball percentage, for example in the form of renewal reopenings, by exerting pressure on parlor sales.

Intensifying competition and the M.S. parlor's struggles

As the industry saw a rapid influx of new parlor owners, some parlors, like Parlor C, experienced a long-term decline in customer numbers. The M.S. parlor was similarly unable to resist the trend and consequently faced concerns about stalling sales and declining profits. How did its management change in response?

The striking market growth spurred by Fībā-type machines created a new situation in terms of the industry's development in which both sales and profitability based on parlor purchases fell (see Figure 4.3 above). That situation unfolded against the backdrop of a rapid influx of new businesses into the market in response to its growth with the coming of the 1980s and of regulations on Fībā-type machines (mandating that Fībā-type machines could not exceed one-third of any parlor's installed base of machines and limiting the machine mechanisms that determined the extent of the speculative element). Here I will focus on the influx of new businesses, which imposed new competitive conditions on parlors.

During this period, the entry into the market of businesses from other industries attracted attention.[80] According to accounts at the time, about 90 percent of parlor businesses reported profits to their local tax office at a time when more than 50 percent of all tax returns reported losses.[81] Some companies chose to invest their assets in pachinko to counter a structural recession in their primary business.[82] It was a choice that was expected to deliver higher profitability than other industries. According to a businessman who entered the parlor business at the time in Saitama Prefecture, in about six months he had earned enough profit to pay back the 90-million-yen (about US$409,091 in 1981) startup capital he had borrowed from a local bank.[83] Lease companies funded by banks offered 'ample' capital for investing in the parlor business on relatively easy terms. Such new entrants into the business were widely recognized as promising targets for investment due to the rapid growth of the market, and the ready availability of funding only encouraged the trend.

For existing parlors, the influx of new businesses meant an increase in the number of nearby parlors, which spurred intensifying competition. The M.S. parlor responded by increasing the prize-ball percentage. The prize-ball percentage following the introduction of Fībā-type machines averaged at 96.5 percent during August and September 1981 before rising to a three-month average of 10.7 percent during the fourth quarter of 1981, 106.4 percent during the first quarter of 1982, 107.4 percent during the second quarter of 1982, 108.3 percent during the third quarter of 1982, 113.8 percent during the fourth quarter of 1982, 111.2 percent during the first quarter of 1983 and 110.0 percent during the second quarter of 1983. In this way, the percentage rose about fifteen points during this period, reaching 131.7 percent in July 1983. This trend was the result of an intentional effort to increase the prize-ball percentage: 'Prize-ball percentages rose about 10 percent from the previous period even as the boom in digital [Fībā-type] pachinko machines continued'.[84]

While the influx of new businesses continued, moves such as these were likely unavoidable for the M.S. parlor. Prize-ball percentage figures are not available from the second half of 1983 to 1988. According to a document entitled 'Overview of sales results for the fiscal year under review' ('Tōki no eigyō seiseki no gaiyō') covering May 1988 to April 1989, sales improved after the prize-ball percentage was increased by 8.1 points from 126.1 percent in the previous fiscal year to 134.2 percent at a time when competition with nearby pachinko parlors was intensifying. As a result, sales rose by 15,198,000 yen (about US$110,934 in 1989) from the previous fiscal year.

However, the gross profit margin fell by about 4.1 percent. To compensate for the gross profit margin of 5.4 percent, which had fallen because the prize-ball percentage was increased by 8.1 points, the parlor lowered the prize exchange rate by one point from the previous level of 68 percent. Nonetheless, the increase in gross profit margin was limited to 1.34 percent, and the metric ultimately fell 4.1 points from the previous year.

Although it remains unclear how the parlor calculated gross profit margin, parlor operating profit is typically calculated by subtracting labor costs, utility costs, machine costs (listed as 'consumables' in Masamura Shōkai records) and other expenses from gross profit. The M.S. parlor left some information about gross margin, which was calculated by subtracting these expenses, in its records. Although records describe techniques used to improve operations as mentioned above (tweaking prize-ball percentages and exchange rates), the parlor characterized overall profit for its pachinko business during the year in question as follows, despite robust efforts to implement those policies: 'We posted a gross margin of negative 40,291,000 yen (about US$294,095) for the fiscal year [...] due to factors including increased labor costs and consumable costs associated with machine replacements'.

To reiterate, the M.S. parlor sought to retain customers by increasing prize-ball percentages in an environment of intensifying competition, and those changes drove up sales. The parlor accepted the inevitable decline in profitability as the cost of securing a certain customer headcount (and increased average spending per customer). The reduction in prize exchange rates undertaken to make up for the lower profitability could not serve as a means of sustained competition because it threatened to spur winning customers to defect to other parlors and because the parlor had no choice but to adjust the rate based on competition with nearby parlors. Prize-ball percentages tended to rise after the introduction of Fībā-type machines, but the influx of new businesses into the market pushed percentages even higher and intensified competition. When it came time to close the year's books in April 1989, it presumably became apparent that the parlor was unable to secure a profit due to increases in expenses incurred in connection with machine replacements, which it had embraced as a means of competing with other parlors. It may be that growth in labor costs and other expenses against the backdrop of Japan's bubble economy during the latter half of the 1980s served as an external factor to make Masamura Shōkai's management even more challenging. The parlor had run headlong into the limits on the extent to which conventional operating protocols that depended on adjusting the prize-ball percentage (i.e., on the time-honed techniques of pin adjusters) provided a basis for continuing operations.

The parlor business reaches an impasse

According to the document 'Overview of business results for the fiscal year under review' cited above,[85] Masamura Shōkai's parlor business was operating profitably at the end of the 1970s. Those conditions continued through the first half of the 1980s, until the business started shedding red ink in the first half of fiscal 1985 (May to October). Operations then varied between profits and losses, until the company reported 'losses' and 'substantial losses' after fiscal 1988.

Company records describe the relationship between the parlor business's worsening profit outlook and operations. From 1982 to 1983, the boom in digital pachinko machines drove up the prize-ball percentage by about 10 percent from the previous period. Sales grew steadily until May 1984 thanks to the popularity of the new digital machines that the company purchased in July 1983. Adding to the period's higher prize-ball percentages, increased quantity of prize redemptions and increased profit from prizes, outlays for special prizes fell from 204.50 yen per item in January 1984 to 204 yen (about US$0.86), greatly increasing profits and allowing the company to operate in the black.

However, with observers occasionally pointing to the increases in prize-ball percentages, on one hand the imposition of regulations in June 1984 on the number of Fībā-type machines that could be installed as well as other factors precipitated an abrupt decline in sales, while on the other hand an intensification of competition with nearby parlors led Masamura Shōkai to further boost prize-ball percentages. The combined result of these factors was that it became difficult to secure sufficient revenue to cover expenses. From May 1989 to April 1990, revenue fell despite hikes in prize-ball percentages throughout the year, leading to significant losses during that year and red ink that became chronic after 1988.

As one observer noted at the general shareholders' meeting held in July 1989, as the company was pressed to make some sort of decision, 'Even as gorgeous parlors attract attention in today's pachinko industry, reduced ability to compete with other parlors due to its outdated building and inadequate parking are major factors in the poor performance of the Jōshin Branch [M.S. parlor]'.[86] Masamura Shōkai resolved to open a new parlor nearby as part of the construction of a new head office building in a project that would require a total investment of about 1 billion yen (about US$7.25 million at 1989 rates). In this way, the company expanded its pachinko parlor in its newly built head office in 1991. Nonetheless, challenging business conditions would continue as interest expenses grew and competition intensified.

The conditions encountered by Masamura Shōkai, which were concealed by the brilliant growth in the pachinko market spurred by the introduction of Fībā-type machines, signaled the limits to the traditional parlor business. In short, the business had reached an impasse by focusing exclusively on increasing prize-ball percentages to compete with nearby parlors. That approach dampened the business's gross profit margin and pushed earnings into a gradual decline. By relying entirely on pin adjustment, which depended on the skill and experience of the past, the parlor ended up destroying the stable revenue base promised by the Fībā-type machines. As models that were controlled by probability became the standard machine design, parlors faced the need to establish operating methods that took advantage of the jackpot mechanism, which could not be directly controlled by pin adjustment, in a different sphere than that of the pin adjusters. Tied to traditional methods, Masamura Shōkai was unable to make that breakthrough.

CONCLUSION

There is no need to repeat the results of this chapter's analysis of Masamura Shōkai's parlor. Instead, I will summarize the changes that were occurring throughout the industry based on the case of the M.S. parlor. The factors that drove the rapid development of the pachinko industry during the 1980s can be understood by focusing on changes in parlor operations and manufacturers' machine supply structures.

First, with regard to parlor operations, the key change that occurred during the 1980s was an increase in the stability of the revenue structure on which the parlor business depended as part of a trend that saw an increase in the speculative element of pachinko spur rapid sales growth. That change was realized by two methods that made it possible to introduce Fībā-type machines.

One was the probability-controlled jackpot, which simplified the process of adjusting the magnitude of fluctuations in sales and ushered in the possibility of stabilizing the overall revenue base. During the 1950s, parlors found it difficult to control machines' pronounced speculative element while enhancing their ability to plan their business, giving parlor operations an unstable revenue structure. With the adoption of external regulations that prohibited machines with a strong speculative element, it became possible to stabilize operations by accumulating expertise in pin adjustment. Common to the 1950s and 1980s was increasing operational stability, rather than market growth spurred by an increasingly pronounced speculative element. The 1980s were also significant in that they signaled the possibility of freeing the industry from skill-dependent pin adjustment, enhancing the autonomy of parlor management. That the scope of highly irregular pin adjustment based on intuition narrowed while the dependence of prize-ball percentages (customer winning percentage) on machine designs rose indicates an expansion of the domain in which management could exert control through capital, with the implication that business performance would become more predictable.[87] Another factor that served to stabilize the revenue base was the improvement in parlor profitability, influenced by the higher rate at which customers exchanged balls for special presents.

Second, regarding the structures according to which manufacturers supplied Fībā-type machines in response to the sudden boom in popularity, competitors introduced imitation products in an arrangement that could be characterized as a distribution of the scale of production. Reflecting the striking seasonality of production and the abrupt waxing and waning of popularity, machine manufacturers' production equipment was not capable of quickly supplying models that turned out to be popular. That the patented Fībā-type design was made available at low licensing fees when demand for Fībā-type machines skyrocketed so that other manufacturers could introduce imitation products is likely to have contributed to the rapid growth in demand nationwide. The precondition for that arrangement was the interdependence of manufacturers, which had become established by the 1970s and which served to limit production equipment and minimize development risk.

As a result, parlors were able to replace machines more frequently than in the past, and supply constraints were eased. Once manufacturers were able to accommodate more frequent, smaller-scale machine replacements, it became easier for parlors to make use of the technique of renewal reopenings.

Other developments included a new competitive situation created by an influx of new businesses that were attracted to the market's growth potential. Fībā-type machines and their probability-driven jackpot design ought to have rendered pin adjustment, which relied on individual skills, meaningless. However, one way that parlors such as the M.S. parlor dealt with heightened competition was to increase prize-ball percentages, which relied on pin adjustment. That approach failed to take full advantage of the characteristics of the new Fībā-type machines, which did not necessarily require pin adjustment.[88]

Seen in this light, the fact that the M.S. parlor repeatedly increased prize-ball percentages so as to undermine the business's revenue base following the introduction of Fībā-type machines is suggestive of the future direction of parlor operations.[89] Following the imposition of regulations on Fībā-type machines, the approach may have delayed parlors' ability to enjoy the stability that the probability-driven aspect of the machines ought to have brought to their operations. However, the signs of changes, once they had occurred, may have led to a search for new operating methods as the influx of new businesses progressed.

Faced with chronic financial deficit, the M.S. parlor's expectation of improving profits by expanding its footprint and relocating signifies an attempt to discover a way forward as it encountered the limits of traditional techniques. Attention throughout the industry came to focus on efforts to renew the business through modernizing investments, as was captured by the shareholder in 1989 who noted, 'Even as gorgeous parlors attract attention in today's pachinko industry, reduced ability to compete with other parlors due to its outdated building and inadequate parking are major factors in the poor performance of the Jōshin Branch'.

5

Emergence of Large-scale Operations at Pachinko Parlor Businesses

INTRODUCTION

This chapter examines the 1980s from the standpoint of how the manner in which pachinko parlors operate changed during the period. This task consists of clarifying yet another aspect of the shifts triggered by the emergence of Fībā-type machines, which was analyzed in the previous chapter, but it involves more than just complementing the content of that chapter. My intention is both to discover the origin of a transformation that underpins any understanding of today's parlor operations and to carefully examine its significance.

The effects of the popularity of Fībā-type machines went beyond the superficial phenomenon that drove a conspicuous increase in parlors' sales, as was experienced by Masamura Shōkai. The sustained popularity of machines with a pronounced speculative element created a high growth rate for the industry, attracting a series of new players to the business.[1] Parlors' profits came under pressure due to the effects of new regulations and intensified competition as the appearance of new parlors drove up prize-ball percentages. Just as was the case during the boom in popularity at the time of the industry's creation in the 1950s, sharpened competitive relationships posed a threat to the stable operation of individual parlors. Unlike in the past, when external opportunity in the form of comprehensive limits on the speculative character of pachinko due to official intervention pointed the industry in a new direction, individual parlors would have to cast about for solutions in the context of their corporate activities.[2]

Even as profitability fell, Masamura Shōkai opted to rely on the skill and experience of pin adjusters to fine-tune prize-ball percentages while operating a single parlor without increasing the number of machines in use. Growth in prize-ball percentages sapped profits and brought the parlor to an impasse. Because jackpots on Fībā-type machines were determined by probability, use of such models ought to have reduced dependence on skill and experience compared to machines where the prize-ball percentage was determined solely by means of adjustment by pin adjusters. In the previous chapter, we were unable to discover operational strategies in Masamura Shōkai's management that suited the intrinsic characteristics of the new Fībā-type machines.

In contrast to Masamura Shōkai, a broad survey of the parlor industry reveals that parlors had already launched new experiments in their operations. The number of machines per parlor rose as parlors that had previously been located near train stations and in shopping districts expanded into the suburbs (marking the emergence of the suburban parlor), and the development of chains with large numbers of parlors in multiple prefectures attracted attention. Any assessment of the characteristics of the parlors that stood out during this era and of their operational significance must examine connections to the debut of Fībā-type machines. The proliferation of suburban parlors in locations that one might presume would have been disadvantageous due to low traffic volume also suggests that something about customers had changed. Changes in customer needs manifested themselves gradually because they were related to social mechanisms such as where people lived and worked, indicating the influence of a broader context that lay outside the pachinko industry. Consequently, this chapter, in attempting to track the historical trajectory along which new business formats and operational methods emerged, will also look backwards toward the 1970s as it focuses on demand-side shifts. What potential, then, did operational methods that suited the intrinsic characteristics of Fībā-type machines hold? Before examining the larger questions posed by this chapter, I will look at the fundamental direction that was imposed on parlor operations by the characteristics of the new machines.

The increase in sales that resulted from Fībā-type machines' pronounced speculative element spurred not only industry-wide growth, but also a series of superficial effects that abruptly increased the scale of operations in individual parlors' businesses. Parlor operations came to involve significantly greater flows of funds than in the past. One might observe that the basic conditions for increasing the scale of operations, as necessitated by Fībā-type machines, held the potential to transform small, neighborhood pachinko parlors into large-scale businesses.

Further, the probability-based element of Fībā-type machines had the inherent property of requiring parlors to operate more machines. As was established in Chapter 4, the emergence of probability as a component in the determination of prize-ball percentages for Fībā-type machines reduced variations in sales and made it easier to ascertain the business's outlook. Since such variations decrease gradually in proportion to the number of installed machines, the extent to which individual locations can achieve their overall prize-ball percentage increases with the number of installed machines, up to a certain point. In short, expansion in the number of machines became inevitable as parlors sought to increase their ability to plan their businesses while maintaining a predictable revenue base because it became easier to maintain sales that did not diverge significantly from the level of sales suggested by the set prize-ball percentage as the number of installed machines grew.

However, increasing the number of machines did not mean an automatic increase in the ability to plan. Making a parlor business more amenable to planning meant enhancing the management aspect of operations in terms of factors such as identifying the appropriate number of machines, determining the scale and timing of machine replacements, choosing machines and allocating budgeted funds. In short, the process demanded comprehensive judgment based on a precise analysis of daily business results, requiring parlors to secure human resources with thorough management knowledge and skills and to put in place mechanisms to support them.

Beyond that, parlors had to take steps to compensate for declining profits as entry into the industry by new businesses pushed up prize-ball percentages and intensified competition. One standard response in this scenario is to increase the scale of operations by adding machines in an effort to realize the benefits of narrow-margin, high-turnover operations. However, a single parlor can only increase its operational scale so far. This limit occurs because the area from which service businesses such as parlors draw their business is governed by the size of the local population and the expanse of the area in which people live. It would be out of the question to build a parlor with 10,000 or 20,000 machines and expect to attract customers from throughout the country. The situation suggests an approach analogous not to a convenience store attempting to serve a large geographical area by adopting the scale of a department store, but rather to a business rolling out a large number of small outlets. Consequently, parlors' efforts to expand the scale of their operations took a different approach that in principle promises the same effects for corporate management, for example the development of numerous locations.

In this way, when parlors looked to ascertain the number of machines that suited the probability element or sought ways to overcome reduced profitability so that they could realize the potential for corporate growth promised by Fībā-type machines, they embarked on two simultaneous paths: increasing the number of machines they operated and developing multiple locations. Masamura Shōkai, however, did not actively seek to expand the scale of its operations in this manner.[3]

We also need to examine how the probabilistic character of Fībā-type machines changed the attitudes with which customers approached pachinko. The probability-governed randomness that characterized Fībā-type machines had the potential to expand the business's customer base by lowering the skill barrier that existed in the past.[4] As the element of randomness becomes more important, customers tend to spend more time playing due to heightened expectations of winning. The probability that controls jackpots offers customers the potential to win each time they play, a promise that is inherent in the machine's programming.[5] However, it is possible that probability will more likely manifest as the total number of attempts increases, so customers develop a heightened expectation that wins will increase to a greater extent with longer play than with intermittent play.[6]

Parlors came to emphasize play time in their operations because the more time customers spent in parlors, the more their sales rose, which was good for parlors. Consequently, creating an environment that invited customers to stay longer was one option parlors could choose as a way to tap latent appetite for longer play. Naturally, playing time could not be increased exponentially because customers faced budgetary constraints, and the more pronounced speculative character of Fībā-type machines served to intensify those constraints (since customers tended to run out of balls faster). Business results depended on the specific manner in which parlors reacted while keeping an eye on customers who were reluctant to spend more time in their establishments. It goes without saying that it was essential for parlors to keep prize-ball percentages high in order to maintain customer expectations (requiring them to balance attracting customers with profits as effectively as possible), and that intensifying competition drove up those percentages even further. That situation further boosted customers' expectations based on their own subjective determination that they could win, encouraging dependence on randomness and fueling additional extensions of playing time.

Extended playing time fit in well with operations at suburban parlors, even before the introduction of Fībā-type machines. Parlors in areas with highly fluid movements of people, for example near train stations, adopted comparatively low prize-ball percentages[7] and built their businesses on customers with a certain amount of skill, who were able to win when they stopped by during moments of free time. Since those parlors could expect an increase in turnover, they lacked a strong motivation to encourage longer playing times or accommodate latent demand among customers for such. By contrast, parlors in suburban locations, where there were time costs for customers, found it difficult to increase turnover. Instead, they could expect to increase sales by extending the time each customer spent playing.

When Fībā-type machines were introduced under these conditions, rising expectations concerning the likelihood of winning served to encourage customers to spend more time playing. Reacting to such latent needs, parlors that, for example, found the playing environment characterized by small, smoke-filled rooms that typified parlors near train stations problematic would be motivated to focus on improving the environment in their establishments. Since this type of improvement required additional investment, it is likely that such measures were not necessarily advantageous for parlors located near train stations, which could expect high turnover. In addition to facility-related improvements to create a comfortable environment, demand began to emerge for improvements in customer service. Unlike conventional investment in equipment such as machines that yields profits directly, such measures are more difficult to identify. Additionally, parlors were moving away from the practice of biannual machine replacements, which made related arrangements a management skill issue that depended on corporate decision-making to determine how often, and to what extent, machines should be replaced.

Along with attention on expanding the scale of the parlor business and on extended playing times, the direction of related investments can be thought of as one method for meeting the new demand embodied by Fībā-type machines during this period. It is not that there had been a lack of similar experiments in the past. Fībā-type machines forced the entire industry to contend with actions that had been limited in the past to choices by particular companies. Consequently, the question of how such examples emerged and took hold, and what operational consequences they triggered, must be treated as the establishment of a new approach to operations that suited Fībā-type machines. I will examine the new potential introduced by Fībā-type machines by focusing on operations at Maruhan, a typical parlor business. First, I will explore how changes in the nature of demand that began before the emergence of Fībā-type machines created new operational approaches.

THE HISTORICAL DEVELOPMENT OF SUBURBAN PARLORS

With the coming of the 1970s, suburban parlors began to attract attention as a new trend. The National Confederation of Amusement Industry Cooperatives (Zenkoku Yūgigyō Kyōdō Kumiai Rengōkai, or Zen'yūkyō) surveyed pachinko parlor unions nationwide about suburban parlors. That such a survey was carried out is itself a sign of new developments during the period.

Until that time, areas with high fluidity in terms of people's movements were seen as favorable locations for pachinko parlors, which came to be clustered near train stations and in shopping districts. For example, location was the most emphasized characteristic in handbooks given to those who wanted to open a pachinko business in 1951. Sales depended on a parlor's location, of which favorable examples included 'areas where people gather near locations such as train stations and movie theaters and other areas with high traffic'.[8] That outlook remained fundamentally unchanged over the course of the industry's history, and at the beginning of the 1960s, it was thought that 'areas near train stations have always been places where there were large buildings and ample movement of people, making them the best locations for pachinko businesses'.[9] During the 1970s, however, phenomena that diverged from this outlook, which had long comprised the conventional wisdom in the industry, and that shifted from the traditional neighborhood and urban landscape near train stations began to stand out.

The definition of 'suburban parlor' is not clear. For example, one could establish a standard related to site differences, for example in terms of distance from a train station, compared to parlors in neighborhood and urban locations, which are the conceptual opposite of their suburban counterparts. One could also focus on associated facilities such as parking lots, which make access by car possible. Suburban parlors can also be differentiated from neighborhood and urban parlors by emphasizing the population density of the surrounding community.

This chapter will offer an overview of parlors based on the survey carried out by the Zen'yūkyō, which defined suburban parlors 'without regard to facilities or location as [businesses] with extensive facilities including large parking lots with dozens of spaces'.[10] I will focus on the emergence of suburban parlors during a particular period of time based on this survey, which was carried out in a sustained manner by a single organization. Parlors sited differently than their conventional counterparts tell us a story of changes in lifestyle, values and other social conditions that made such locations possible – that is, changes in society that impacted demand.

Social changes and the emergence of suburban parlors

Discovery of a suburban market

Table 5.1 summarizes the results of a survey about suburban parlors conducted by the Zen'yūkyō from January 1973 to August 1974. The distinction between new and existing businesses evident in the table is interesting, but the underlying intention can be ascertained from the fact that the survey results were summarized in an article entitled 'Issues with measures for preventing excessive competition'.[11] The entry into the parlor business of companies from other industries was attracting attention at the time, prompting a sense of concern that new pachinko businesses adopting approaches classified as suburban, particularly instances in which parlors were established alongside bowling alleys, shopping centers and motels, were encouraging competition.[12] Setting aside the question of the survey's intentions, what I would like to emphasize here is that suburban parlors identified a new customer need. First, let us examine how far this progressed based on the survey results.

Growing attention on suburban parlors can be discerned in how parlors closed and how new businesses opened in particular regions. Although the larger picture remains unclear, in Aichi Prefecture, which had the most parlors after Tokyo and Osaka, reports indicated that ten existing parlors had closed as of October 1973 and that as many new suburban parlors were planning to open as the number of existing

District	New businesses		New openings by existing operators		Total
	Suburban	Neighborhood and urban	Suburban	Neighborhood and urban	
Nationwide* A	259	233	125	169	786
Total of new and existing B	492		294		
Ratio (%)	33.0	29.6	15.9	21.5	100.0
A / B (%)	52.6	47.4	42.5	57.5	

Table 5.1: Development of suburban parlors – results of a survey by the Zen'yūkyō (January 1973 to August 1974)

Note: *Except Tokyo, where results are unclear.

Source: Compiled based on Zenyūren Kōhō *(1975) '過当競争防止対策の問題点' (Issues with measures for preventing excessive competition), September 15, p. 3.*

parlors that anticipated closing by the end of the year.[13] In the city of Ichinomiya, located fifteen kilometers from Nagoya, seven of thirty-nine parlors closed, and eight suburban parlors opened. A company that I will call 'Branch P' in Hamamatsu, a city located between Tokyo and Osaka with a concentration of small and medium-size enterprises in the machinery and parts industries, which opened a suburban parlor as part of an effort to diversify in the face of a decline in its bowling business, asked, 'Can we possibly expect to profit by opening a pachinko parlor in such a remote location?' That concern turned out to be groundless, and the new business 'once opened, attracted more customers than expected'.[14] Such success is likely to be characterized in retrospect as reflecting a 'revolution in siting'[15] and drawing on foresight, but in this case, the experiment was not driven from the outset by high expectations. As a result, overall performance was met with surprise. In the case of Ichinomiya, reports indicated that sales per machine for suburban parlors (ranging from 2000 [about US$7.52 in 1973] to 3000 yen [about US$11.29]) outpaced similar figures for parlors in neighborhoods and urban areas (1500 [about US$5.64] to 2000 yen) by a factor of about 1.5.

Looking at conditions nationwide (see Table 5.1), suburban parlors accounted for almost half – 48.9 percent – of 786 newly opened parlors. The breakdown of those figures makes it clear that close to 60 percent of existing businesses opted for neighborhoods and urban locations, while more than half of parlors that were new to the business, which accounted for about 60 percent of new openings, preferred to establish their operations in a suburban setting. In short, businessmen who were new to the parlor industry believed the suburban approach was promising. The results provide a glimpse of how new parlor businesses offered the parlor industry an experiment that leveraged new demand and the discovery of a new market to create a novel business format. Following is a description of the background that led to the emergence of suburban parlors, conceived to foster an understanding of this fact against the broader backdrop of the era. Specifically, a number of changes served to ease disadvantageous characteristics that affected neighborhood and urban parlors' ability to attract customers.

Widespread adoption of automobiles and suburbanization of consumption

The first factor was a broadening of trade areas due to motorization, which triggered changes in the movements of people. In Japan, purchases of durable consumer goods such as automobiles surged during the period of high economic growth that lasted from the latter half of the 1950s until the beginning of the 1970s as average income rose (the automobile segment in particular grew at a high rate from the latter half of the 1960s).[16] As a result, car ownership, which was limited to 22.1 percent in 1970, rose to 41.2 percent in 1975 and surpassed 50 percent in 1978 before rising to 57.2 percent in 1980,[17] when the population per passenger car reached 4.9 people.[18]

The proliferation of automobiles spurred a new lifestyle. For example, according to the Consumer Behavior Survey conducted by the Economic Planning Agency in September 1973, the leisure activity in which unmarried office workers 'engaged' that grew at the highest year-on-year percentage was driving.[19] Widespread car ownership gave direct rise to new forms of play while indirectly creating different markets by expanding the geographic area in which consumers were active and decentralizing movements of people. Branch P in Hamamatsu, which I mentioned above, concluded, 'If we build a free parking lot, people will be able to come, even from distant areas. For example, cars enabled people to make a ten-kilometer road trip in less than fifteen minutes. Even if we target people living seven or eight minutes away, cars yield a radius of five kilometers. It may be a suburban area, but we're not talking about some isolated mountain village, so there's plenty of population within that zone'.[20] Pachinko's customer base had shifted away from the fluid population in areas near train stations to consumers living within areas located a medium or long distance from the parlor. In this way, suburban parlors can be understood as having emerged in the context of new business formats that appeared in response to the activity of a mobile population.

At the same time, reorganization of trade areas due to changes in the living environment became a variable in parlor siting conditions. As the suburban population grew, its need for various services in support of consumer life held the potential for new markets to form. This comprehensive phenomenon was the suburbanization of various types of consumption due to population movements. Although the following applies only to population fluidity in the Kinki region (which consists of six prefectures including Osaka in western Japan), an industry magazine's report of the 1970 national census results indicated that populations in the urban cores of the cities of Osaka, Kobe and Kyoto were declining every year.[21] In the case of Osaka, the population concentration in the area twenty to forty kilometers from the center of the city was striking, whereas the population in the area within ten kilometers of the center was stagnating, signaling an outflow to suburban areas. Population increases were forecast to move from the twenty-kilometer zone to the thirty-kilometer zone. The formation of an expanding urban area in this manner prompted a trend toward the decentralization of residential areas, which governed the size of the nighttime and weekend population, even as the daytime population in the city rose. At the same time, development of new commercial areas progressed as old shopping districts declined.[22] These changes in trade areas likely influenced the rise and fall of parlors in urban areas[23] as well as the emergence of suburban parlors.

Indicators that capture these trade area changes are easy to find. For example, the percentage of large retail stores such as supermarkets that were located in suburban areas almost doubled across all cities, rising from 20.6 percent to 37.7 percent between 1974 and 1979.[24] The location disadvantages and uniqueness of large, suburban retail businesses relative to urban shopping districts and supermarkets hint at the geographic relationship of suburban parlors to neighborhoods and urban locations.

For parlors, the consumers who enjoyed the benefits of motorization and accomplished the expansion and decentralization of the areas in which they lived represented a latent market ripe for development. An article in a trade magazine claiming that drive-in parlors embodied a new direction in the siting of such businesses offered an explanation of this shift.[25] In short, the saturation of neighborhoods and urban areas and the difficulty of securing customers eliminated the space needed for new businesses, such that targeting automobile owners had potential as an operational approach for the new era, as was the case with bowling alleys.[26] Expectations centered on the growth potential of that approach, fueled by instances where the outlook proved correct.[27]

In the article, Mr. M, who worked as a consultant at the time, offered the following advice:

> The era in which pachinko parlors had to be located right in the middle of busy downtown districts is over. There are two or three pachinko parlors in agricultural areas of suburban Nagoya, thirty to forty minutes by car from the city. They're all deluxe establishments with large parking lots, and they're always completely full [...]. *Customers are going out of their way to come enjoy themselves by car [despite the comparative inconvenience of doing so]* [...]. One characteristic of these parlors is that compared to customers at parlors in busy downtown districts, their customers spend not 200 or 300 yen [about US$0.67 or US$1.00], but – without exception – more than *1,000 yen* [about US$3.32 in 1972].[28] (Emphasis added.)

Customers at the new parlors spent more than those at neighborhoods and urban parlors, suggesting the growth potential of targeting wealthy consumers who owned cars. Another survey found average consumer spending of 800 (about US$2.66 in 1972) to 1000 yen at suburban parlors, about twice the approximately 430 yen (about US$1.43) at parlors located in busy downtown districts.[29] Moreover, young customers aged thirty-four and younger accounted for about 67 percent of all patrons at suburban parlors, but only about 38 percent at downtown parlors. Urban parlors' core demographic was middle-aged customers aged thirty-five and over, who accounted for 45 percent of all patrons. Suburban parlors emerged at this time after identifying the needs of a new generation of customers who enjoyed driving.

In this way, societal changes such as rising incomes were a necessary precondition for the emergence and establishment of suburban parlors, but that outcome was neither self-evident nor assured. Urban parlors were not merely transplanted; the transition to suburban locations demanded creative approaches to attract dispersed, mobile customers compared to parlors located near train stations. Incidental services comprised one such creative approach. An analysis of one parlor in the city of Atsugi, Kanagawa Prefecture, which is part of the greater Tokyo metropolitan area, that opened with about 300 machines in a renovated bowling alley found that its target customer base was economically well-off[30] and therefore proposed that it was necessary to furnish the business's interior in a way that would please that demographic.[31] The thinking went that incorporating not only obvious features such as large parking lots and adjacent facilities like coffee shops and restaurants where customers could eat and drink, but also non-pachinko attractions such as saunas and billiards, could serve to attract interest, along with flamboyant interior designs.[32] It is also likely that suburban parlors actively incorporated seating, a feature that became more common during this period. Seats were an enhancement to the playing environment that suburban parlors, with their surfeit of space,[33] were uniquely able to make as they sought to improve their service in a way that took into account customer fatigue, and from a business perspective, the addition of seating served to facilitate longer playing times. In total, the proposed approach diverged from urban parlors, which called to mind a stereotypically negative image of a 'certain type of dark unwholesomeness that was characteristic of pachinko parlors'.[34]

Time-use, consumption and pachinko

Another social change that deserves attention for providing a basis for suburban parlors was growth in the amount of free time consumers enjoyed. This trend also affected changes in consumption habits. The percentage of consumption that involved things, for example durable consumer goods, which had been driven up by growth in income until the period of high growth, began to decline during the 1970s, which was described as a period of stable growth. Instead, consumer behavior related to service-driven leisure – for example educational and recreational services – eating out and automobile-related expenses became progressively more conspicuous.[35] It is likely that the five-day workweek,[36] which began to become increasingly common during the first half of the 1970s, had a direct impact on this trend.

Growth in free time due to reduction in working hours was expected to translate into more time for recreation, a fact that attracted significant attention in the parlor industry. The change had the potential to exert both positive and negative effects on the entire pachinko industry. Some believed that more free time could be expected to drive up footfall in locations such as busy downtown districts that were likely to be crowded on weekends[37]; others took the pessimistic view that pachinko would be negatively impacted as the extra free time would be spent on travel and other pursuits[38]; and still others, the optimistic view that existing budgetary and time constraints would lead to increased spending not on travel, but rather on pachinko as an everyday amusement with which consumers were familiar.[39] This diversity of views indicates that the increase in free time was not uniform, but rather influenced by the extent and speed with which the five-day workweek progressively permeated society, starting with the large companies that first introduced it, and that parlors in different types of locations had different expectations regarding such customers. Let us pause here to examine the nature of new customer needs as they related to the establishment of suburban parlors.

For parlors located in urban areas or near train stations, office workers utilized moments of free time or stopped by pachinko parlors on their way home, enjoying short intervals of play that fit into their lifestyle. If consumers gained more free time on weekends, they would be able to spend comparatively more time at pachinko parlors. Parlors located in urban areas or near train stations were unable to accommodate that use of time in an appropriate manner because high land prices and other factors led them to value high turnover while giving priority to profitability and establishing low prize-ball percentages. In the context of growing adoption of the automobile, needs that conventional parlors were unable to meet in an appropriate manner presented a business opportunity to suburban parlors in locations that could be easily accessed by car from residential areas.[40]

That said, too much should not be made of the actual impact of the five-day workweek, since it has been pointed out that its adoption leveled out during the second half of the 1970s.[41] While the impact of the five-day workweek was limited, for our purposes here it is sufficient to examine whether it was possible that demand created by the new system was better satisfied by the business format embraced by suburban parlors.

From other businesses to suburban parlors

Some of the factors that spurred the emergence of suburban parlors lay outside the pachinko industry. As indicated by the results of a survey of new urban worker consumption trends announced at the end of 1972, articles describing how businesses had been switching from bowling alleys to pachinko parlors[42] until the mid-1970s after the peak in the number of people enjoying bowling frequently attracted attention. (The popularity of bowling exploded during the 1960s, fueling a boom in the construction of new alleys, before evaporating just as quickly.) Nobody expected the sudden decline, which explains why (for example) bowling alley bankruptcies in several regions where such closures had the potential to profoundly influence the local economy during 1972 were reported as shocking events.[43] Robust performance that had continued up to the previous year reversed, and in the space of a month, three companies shuttered their operations in a chain reaction.[44]

It is likely that, due to the nature of the sites they had occupied, the trend toward bowling alley operators switching businesses as prospects for their industry's growth faded during a transition period[45] attracted attention as an increase in the number of suburban parlors. As a string of parlor bankruptcies created a lingering sense of recession in the early 1970s, the prospect of intensified competition[46] spurred trepidation in the industry.[47] Since the decline progressed quickly in a short period of time, the pachinko industry saw the influx of new parlors operated by former bowling alleys as an intense, short-term change, prompting a tendency for the industry to overreact in its assessment that the increase in bowling alley operators switching to, or additionally operating, pachinko businesses was likely to encourage competition among parlors.[48]

Certainly, the characteristics of the suburban bowling alley business made it easy to accommodate, or entirely transition to, a parlor business. Drawing on their experience operating bowling alleys, these companies presumably expected to be able to secure customers in their parlor businesses on the basis of the expansion in trade area made possible by motorization. They also had plenty of land, which gave them space to offer parking lots and other services.[49] From a manager's perspective, a declining business losing money provides motivation to search for other businesses, and it is likely that the promise of being able to make effective use of large real-estate assets was one reason that these companies came to focus on the parlor business.

The case of Maruhan, a major pachinko chain, illustrates how companies switched from the bowling alley business to the suburban parlor business and established themselves in their new industry. The company made substantial investments in the bowling alley business from the end of the 1960s to the first half of the 1970s but ended up shouldering enormous losses as it faced the industry's decline. Maruhan's three existing bowling alleys and a new alley that had opened in December 1972 saw their customer counts begin to decline early the following year.[50] This investment failure forced Maruhan to take on a debt of about 6.0 billion yen (about US$20.4 million in 1974, equivalent to about US$75 million in 2015 terms), enough to threaten its existence.[51] The company opted to restructure its business around its pachinko parlors, of which it operated just two at the time. Developing a business centering on pachinko parlors with parking lots as one of a number of businesses that utilized the large spaces and parking lots of bowling alleys proved to be a forerunner of suburban parlors, which were recognized as unprofitable, for the company[52] and provided it with the opportunity to restructure. Looking back, founder Chang-woo Han recalls that 'good locations for bowling alleys were also good locations for pachinko parlors', describing how the experience of traveling around the country in search of good locations in an effort to become 'the king of bowling in Japan' provided expertise that allowed him to find good locations for suburban parlors.[53] This success led to the discovery of the suburban parlor market and subsequently to the development of Maruhan's chain business centering on suburban parlors.[54]

Emergence of a female clientele

Having observed that companies entering the pachinko industry from other businesses were particularly energetic in their efforts to accommodate new customer needs, we must note that suburban parlors represented only a small percentage of all parlors during the 1970s and that they had not yet become a replacement for those in neighborhood and urban locations. While it is impossible to accurately ascertain the nationwide trend, a survey conducted by the Zen'yūkyō[55] (from January 1975 to May 1976) found 1136 suburban parlors outside Hokkaido, Tokyo and Okinawa, or 12.8 percent of the nationwide total of 8879 parlors (as of May 31, 1976, excluding all parlors in Hokkaido, Tokyo and Okinawa). Nationwide, suburban parlors had barely surpassed 10 percent.[56] This slow growth presumably reflects the fact that the customer demographic that underpinned suburban parlors' operations would not be created rapidly without abrupt changes in social conditions, whether in terms of adoption of the automobile, growth in leisure time or take-up of the lifestyle affected by those changes. For this reason, rather than merely wait for far-reaching changes in their customer base, suburban parlors, which had to contend with the disadvantage of a population with low mobility, attempted in various ways to discover new customer demographics on their own. In that sense, the industry was primed with expectations that new demographics would be developed, and it was sensitive to trends concerning female participation.

Until the 1970s, men made up most of the pachinko-playing population. Although there is no systematic indicator that provides a direct expression of this fact, the rate at which male office workers and blue-collar workers participated in the pachinko industry offers indirect support. According to a survey of the consumption habits of single workers conducted by the Economic Planning Agency, just 15.6 percent of female workers responded that they had played pachinko in March 1973, compared to 57.9 percent of men.[57] There can be no doubt that the principal demographic group characterized by high participation was men. However, that the same survey had in March 1967 yielded a figure of 7.3 percent for female workers makes clear that their numbers had doubled in about five years. The same survey, administered again in February 1977, found that 20.7 percent of women had played pachinko, indicating that participation was continuing to rise, although results for February 1978 fell 4.3 points to 16.4 percent.[58] However, there can be no doubt that the number of female customers rose compared to the 1960s, and their numbers showed signs of increasing even further from the mid-1970s. The promise of a robust response from female customers was tempered by inability to gauge where those figures would end up, but the net result was presumably a positive sense of expectation regarding the future in terms of new-market development.[59]

In light of this trend, low female participation suggested a latent market begging for development to suburban parlors just as they were emerging. That female consumption growth in 1973 compared to the previous year attracted concerted interest throughout the industry[60] was a result of the strength of associated expectations. Initiatives intended to boost female customer participation appeared. Parlors were encouraged to create an atmosphere that would make it easy for female customers to visit without hesitation, to train employees to provide service with a smile, to provide locker and cloak rooms for women and to offer female-only restrooms, female prize redemption areas and sitting areas with seats.[61] Active efforts to provide an atmosphere and prizes that women would find desirable can be understood as signs of parlors' desire to develop female customers as a new market. It is likely that these improvements combined with the widespread adoption of electric machines during the first half of the 1970s – which broadened the customer base by lowering barriers to entry in the form of the required level of playing skill[62] – and the introduction of seats were designed to exert a positive effect on female customer numbers.

With the coming of the 1980s, the emergence of Fībā-type machines, which is to say, of machines characterized by an increased element of randomness fueled by probability, allowed parlors to attract housewives and customers over the age of sixty who seemed to have no special pachinko technique,[63] with the result that growth in the number of female customers became even more visible.[64]

There is no decisive evidence that indicates that women became a principal demographic on par with men, or that the changes were enough to erase the gender bias in pachinko customers. There is no systematic data concerning the female demographic, but we can glean some information about the rise of that group from fragmentary data.

Although some observers recalled during the 1980s that female customers accounted for 40 percent of all customers at the end of the 1970s,[65] the number of females who played pachinko as a percentage of the total female population rose just over two points, from 14 percent in 1976 to 16.3 percent in 1984.[66] According to a questionnaire survey of sixty-seven parlors conducted at the end of the 1980s, when Fībā-type machines became a major trend, about 90 percent of parlors (fifty-six parlors) responded that female customers accounted for 30 percent or less of their patrons.[67] While just 10 percent of the sixty-two parlors that responded to the questionnaire indicated that female customers accounted for more than 30 percent of their customer base, one parlor reported a high of about 40 percent.[68] Changes in the trends characterizing female participation were limited, and although it is impossible to identify an overall trend, there can be no doubt that various initiatives such as efforts to improve parlors' interiors that were undertaken during the 1970s targeted a growing number of female customers and were inspired by parlors' expectations regarding that demographic group.

DAILY LIFE AND PACHINKO CONSUMPTION

Considering the examination undertaken in the previous part, let us turn our attention to the people who consumed pachinko as we search for factors behind the changes that progressed during the 1980s. To that end, I will draw on a consumer survey conducted in 1979 to examine how consumers saw pachinko and parlor operations. The survey was the first serious survey to target pachinko with the intention of assessing demand trends,[69] and it is especially significant that it was carried out on the edge of the 1980s. Because the industry changed remarkably at precisely that point in time, the survey provides a useful source for ascertaining the structural characteristics of demand if we identify the period from the second half of the 1950s to the end of the 1970s as a major period of the industry's history. Furthermore, we can use it to retrospectively illuminate hints of new demand based on trends that began during or after the 1980s. Based on this perspective, I will examine how people approached pachinko in their everyday lives, what they sought from pachinko parlors and machines, and how well those tendencies complemented new trends such as the emergence of suburban parlors as outlined above.

Those who consumed pachinko

Of the demographic groups that consumed pachinko, the survey found that men in their twenties and thirties made up the industry's customer base, and that the number of female customers began to increase during the 1970s.[70] Based on another survey by the Leisure Development Center (Yoka Kaihatsu Sentā) that found that about 30 percent of adults (47 percent of men and 14 percent of women) played pachinko at least once per year, the total pachinko-playing population as of 1976 can be calculated as about 30 million people.

People's choice of pachinko indicated their favorable evaluation of its effectiveness as a way to spend their free time compared to other forms of amusement (*go* and *shogi* [a Japanese game similar to chess], mahjong, video games and sailboat, horse and bicycle racing, either as games or for gambling purposes). Another reason cited was its low cost, indicating that respondents took part due to its relatively low financial cost compared to other forms of amusement.

For our purposes here, the results of parlor location are particularly interesting. Insofar as the survey's respondents mentioned the ease with which they could play as one aspect of pachinko's appeal, it seems that convenient access to parlors was a key advantage. With regard to how they made use of parlors, men cited parlors located near their homes or at train stations at which they changed trains on their way home from work, while women cited parlors located in shopping districts on the way to their grocery shopping. The survey offers a glimpse of pachinko not as a leisure activity that customers turned to for unusual experiences, but rather as a pursuit that fit closely into their everyday lives.

Related to this point, visits lasting from thirty minutes to about an hour accounted for 30 percent of respondents' average visit times, while a comparatively larger percentage of women reported visits of thirty minutes or less.[71] Many respondents chose 'ability to play alone' as part of pachinko's appeal, which was related to its viability as a way to spend one's free time as well as its convenience, both cited above. Men and women described average monthly spending on pachinko of 4000 yen (about US$16.74)[72] and 1400 yen (about US$58.60), respectively, and the figure for men was lower than for mahjong or state-controlled gambling.

Many respondents to a survey targeting people who played pachinko at least once per month[73] cited motivations including the ability 'to pass time with a small amount of money', 'win prizes' and 'enjoy the pastime with ease [in terms of access, cost, time, etc.]', and those responses do not diverge significantly from the overall trends described above. Concerning prizes, respondents evaluated pachinko's superior appeal in comparison to other games due to their ability to win cigarettes (men) and snacks/candy (women). By contrast, 'winning money' was comparatively less a priority than the focus on prizes,[74] ranking higher only for men aged twenty or lower and for frequent users. The appeal of pachinko can be understood based not on the sole element of financial reward, but rather on a comprehensive evaluation that incorporates factors including viability as a way to pass time, convenience, low investment cost and prizes.

Subsurface changes

From a historical perspective, pachinko attracted a diverse range of customers during the first half of the 1950s, but once Japan's period of rapid economic growth began after regulations were enacted in 1955, the industry earned the overwhelming support of male white- and blue-collar workers. As explored in Chapter 1, regulations strictly limited the speculative character of play that depended on randomness and created more room for customers' skill and ability to impact results, but the population that constituted demand for pachinko was subsequently narrowed down to male customers, marking the start of an era when the pachinko-playing population numbered 30 million. When electric machines debuted during the 1970s and reduced the level of requisite skill compared to previous models, the number of female customers – as consumers with different preferences and desires – grew. This change served to maintain the character of pachinko as a diversion in which the general public could participate by ever so slightly easing the imbalance that had existed between men and women.

The survey results described above, including descriptions of reasonable customer spending, playing times of around one hour and use of parlors with convenient locations, make it seem as though the far-reaching social changes cataloged in the first part of this chapter did not have such a significant effect on consumption. That is because those changes embodied continuity with the prior characteristics of pachinko. It is also true that the 'leading-edge' experiment with locating parlors in suburban settings depended on a partial market that had not yet become mainstream at the time. Let us look for hints of the evolution of this marginal existence into something beyond the traditional mode of parlor operations as clarified in Chapter 4 by closely and carefully observing small changes signaled by the survey. In this regard, I will focus on a survey of people ('fans') who played pachinko more than once a month. My interest is motivated by the belief that, on both an experiential and theoretical level, new products and services that trigger changes in consumption gain widespread adoption through the behavior of adventurous, risk-taking people.[75]

The survey found that fans spent the most time playing pachinko when they had free time in the evening and at night on holidays and weekdays (in that order). For male fans, the most commonly cited criterion according to which they chose parlors was the 'ease with which machines yielded prize balls', but this response was analyzed as 'signifying not that they would make money, but that the parlors offered a place where they could spend a suitable amount of time'.[76] The next most commonly cited criterion for choosing parlors was convenience of access, and location was also important. By contrast, more than half of all female fans cited 'parlor ambiance' as a key factor.

For male fans, holidays had higher priority than weekdays, which accounted for the majority of daily life, and they cited the ease with which machines yielded prize balls and the ability to spend time at the parlor as key factors. If suburban parlors could maintain comparatively high prize-ball percentages and hold events and special programs that attracted 'holiday customers' as the number of national holidays rose in society, they would presumably see more male customers using their facilities at times when they were comparatively free.

For female fans, the pachinko environment was the key consideration when choosing a parlor. By putting in place the sort of environment that female fans valued, parlors could presumably unearth a latent female market. Suburban parlors would discover potential for surviving business competition through such means as investing in creating an ambiance designed so that female fans could win more readily thanks to higher prize-ball percentages and making prizes that would please female customers available. In this light, women continued to account for a low percentage of pachinko parlor customers, but their emergence lent additional support to new changes in parlor siting requirements.

In fact, the survey also yielded findings that speak to the establishment of suburban parlors. Even as customer counts were declining throughout the industry due to the effects of a recession, suburban parlors were supported by customers who came by car, and more suburban parlors reported increases in such customers than decreases. For parlors located near train stations and in busy downtown locations, however, the opposite was true.[77] This finding suggests that the trend towards restrained consumption due to the recession was comparatively less pronounced on the part of those who frequented suburban parlors. We can understand these findings as indicating that broad changes sweeping society (changes in lifestyle, the living environment and social systems) created the consumption pattern of extended play by customers with some level of economic wherewithal, and that it was suburban parlors that played the lead role in taking advantage of the associated new business opportunities brought by those changes.

INTRODUCTION OF FĪBĀ-TYPE MACHINES AND SHIFT TO LARGE-SCALE OPERATIONS

New development of suburban parlors

The trend towards opening new parlors that could be classified as suburban gathered pace as the popularity of the Fībā that emerged in 1980 became apparent and as the number of parlors began to grow (see Figure 0.3). According to survey results for newly opened parlors from 1981 to 1982 (see Table 5.2), suburban parlors accounted for about 60 percent of all new parlors, exceeding the figure for neighborhood and urban parlors. Although the trend favoring suburban parlors grew even stronger (at 64.3 percent in the 1983 survey), the figure fell to 43.4 percent in the 1987 survey.[78]

	Number of parlors	Ratio (%)
Suburban parlors	394	58.1
Neighborhood and urban parlors	284	41.9
Total	678	100

Table 5.2: Locations of newly opened parlors – Zen'yūkyō survey results (November 1981 to July 1982)
Source: Compiled based on Zenyūren Kōhō *(1982), '新規開店と廃業状況益々大型店が進出の傾向全遊協調べ' (New and closed parlors: Trend towards ever-larger parlors / Zen'yūkyō study), October 15, p. 4.*

The trend toward new suburban parlors did not progress in a unidirectional manner, but there is no doubt that suburban locations became established as a powerful option. The question that demands examination here is what was the nature of the overall changes wrought by parlors' choice of such locations? I reviewed parlor locations recorded in the membership rolls of the Tokyo Pachinko and Pachislot Cooperative Associations (Tokyo-to Yūgigyō Kyōdō Kumiai, or Toyūkyō) to assess changes in location before and after the period during which Fībā-type machines made their debut. It is difficult to define the term 'suburban' in the context of Tokyo, which is characterized by high building density and an extensive rail network with innumerable stations; furthermore, the presence of parking areas, which was assumed in this chapter's discussion up to this point, is unclear. That said, a clue is provided by reports of a trend toward suburban parlors in locations outside the metropolitan area, for example in the Kanto (eastern Japan) region.[79] If some sort of shift can be perceived in siting trends in Tokyo, then we can presume that it represented an overall trend. Here I will consider the relationship of this trend to market conditions during and after the 1980s – in short, how the intensification of competition unleashed by Fībā-type machines affected siting conditions – and to suburban parlors during the 1970s.

Let us compare location information for 1975 and 1993, using information from the membership rolls of the Toyūkyō from those years.[80] Figure 5.1 (1) plots the locations of 1018 parlors out of a total of 1026 parlors in 1975 (excluding parlors

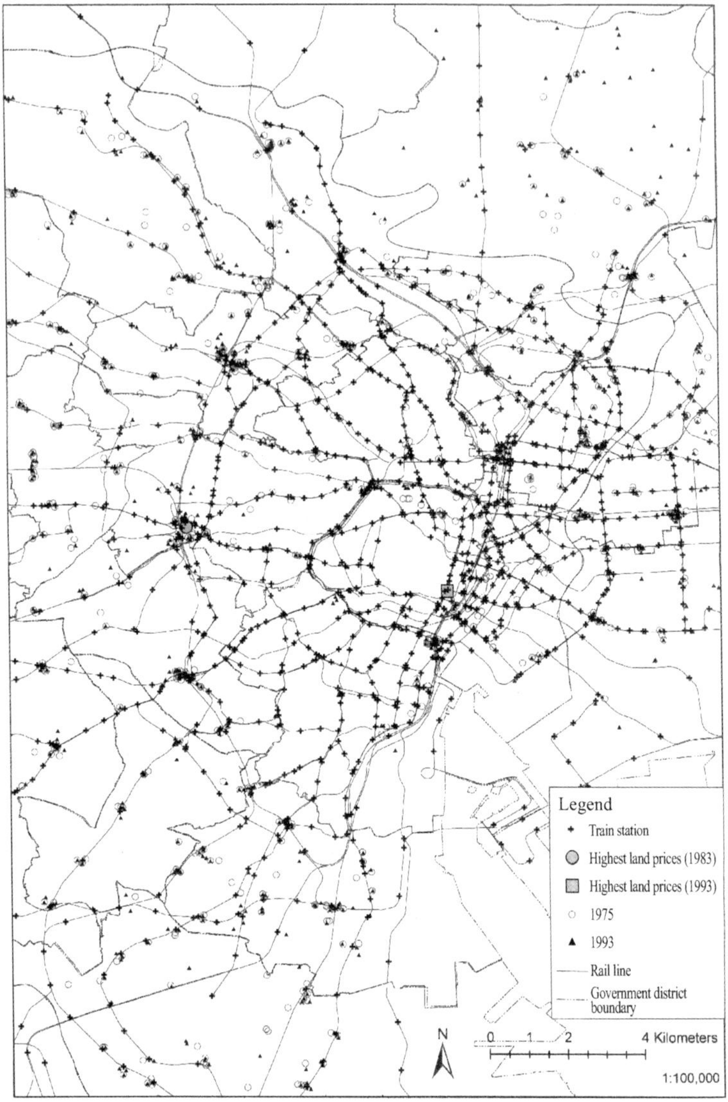

Figure 5.1 (1): Siting changes (1975 and 1993)

Source: Data for rail lines and train stations were drawn from the Statistics Map of Japan (Statistics GIS, time-series data for rail lines in FY2011 from http://nlftp.mlit.go.jp/ksj/gml/datalist/KsjTmplt-N05-v1_3.html, accessed on September 17, 2017). Address data for pachinko parlors was drawn from the 1975 and 1993 membership rolls for the Tokyo Amusement Industry Cooperative and the Tokyo Confederation of Amusement Associations.

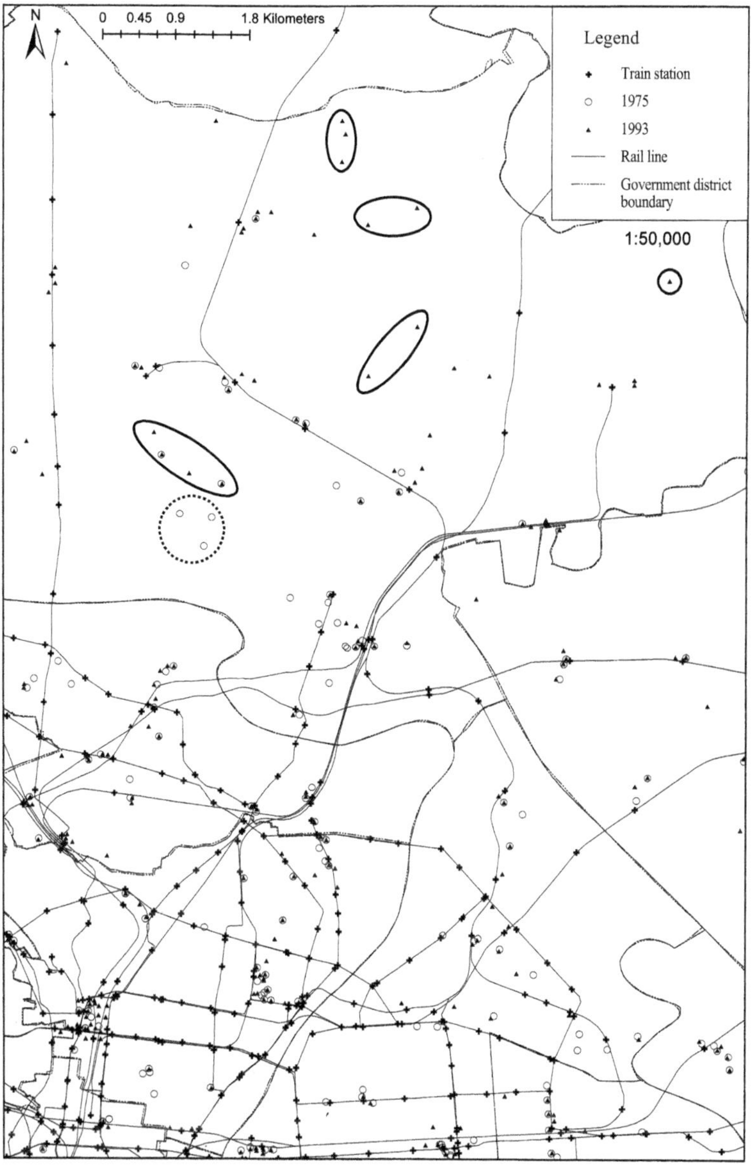

Figure 5.1 (2): Enlarged view

Note: Parlors located at least 1 kilometer from the nearest train station are enclosed by dashed (as of 1975) and solid (as of 1993) lines.

whose locations were unclear) alongside 1508 parlors out of a total of 1509 parlors in 1993 (chosen using the same criterion) on a map of Tokyo. Let us assess that map to gauge the change in siting conditions.

First, there was no change between 1975 and 1993 in the prevalence of parlors near train stations; overall, parlors track train lines. Information for train lines and stations is from fiscal 2001, making it impossible to conduct our analysis while tracing the effects of changes over the twenty-year period due to factors such as new lines and facilities installed between 1975 and 1993. Changes over that period can be summarized, with some degree, as an increase in the number of parlors near stations where there was already one or more parlors in 1975 and a proliferation of parlors at stations where there was no parlor before (setting aside for the moment the question of whether those parlors opened between 1974 and 1993).

However, it is not simply the case that new parlors opened; in some cases, several parlors from 1975 (○) closed while new parlors opened in nearby locations (▲○○). We can surmise that there was a lively turnover in parlors during this period of close to twenty years. In fact, 563 of the 1025 parlors operating in 1975, or 54.9 percent, had shuttered their businesses by 1993. Only 461 parlors continued to operate.[81] Moreover, seventy-nine of the surviving parlors, or about 17 percent, changed ownership, indicating that these figures include a large number of parlors that had difficulty continuing to operate. Such cases indicate that for some reason the locations of parlors exiting the business were perceived as good locations by different operators. As mentioned above, the industry was experiencing an overall recession at the end of the 1970s (see Figure 0.2 and the first part of Chapter 4), and it is clear that 57.0 percent of the 563 parlors that closed did so between 1975 and 1982, when the effects of that recession were hardest felt. What is noteworthy is that 1048 new parlors, an increase due to the popularity of Fībā-type machines, chose different locations than those that closed, unlike the seventy-nine parlors that changed ownership (but not location). What tendencies did those locations suggest?

The change in parlor locations seen between 1975 and 1993 represents a move from urban to more distant locations, which were likely characterized by lower real estate costs. This conclusion can be verified using a number of different data sources. First, Figure 5.1 (2) offers a broad overview. So far, this analysis has defined suburban parlors as those with parking areas, and while it is not possible to ascertain directly whether a given parlor indeed had space for parking based on that map, it is likely that parlors in locations that offered convenient access by car based on their distance from train stations had such space. Based on this inference, an examination of Figure 5.1 (2) tells us there were more parlors with site conditions that differed from parlors near train stations (parlors that were more than one kilometer, or about fifteen minutes on foot, from a train station, enclosed by broken lines for 1975 and by solid lines for

1993) in 1993 (▲) than there were in 1975 (○). We can discern a trend toward new suburban parlors that required parking areas in Tokyo between 1975 and 1993.

The trend can be established through statistical analysis. At my request, Fei Carnes, a GIS specialist at Harvard University's Center for Geographic Analysis as of 2017, and using the shortest-distance function provided by ArcGIS (which calculates the shortest distance between two points), calculated the shortest distances between parlors and train stations based on the addresses for the parlors shown in Figure 5.1 and train station locations as of 2014.[82] Ideally, rail distances from train stations to parlors would be calculated based on actual road routes, but I asked Carnes to calculate the shortest distance on the map for the sake of convenience. If the average distance in 1993 is greater than the corresponding figure for 1975, we can conclude that the trend toward suburban parlors envisioning customers traveling by car accelerated between 1975 and 1993. An opposite result would indicate that the emergence of suburban parlors was a partial phenomenon. Calculating the average distances for the 1018 parlors and 1506 parlors for which the figure can be calculated in 1975 and 1993, respectively, indicates that parlors were located about sixty-one meters (or 31 percent) further from train stations in 1993 (at 259.395 meters) than they were in 1975 (at 198.065 meters). Given that those results include numerous parlors located near train stations, of which there were plenty even in 1993, there is no doubt that the number of suburban parlors, which presumably influenced the increase in average distance, grew.

How did the fact that newly established parlors chose different locations than older parlors manifest itself overall in 1993 locations? To gauge that effect, we must turn to another indicator: suburbanization. I calculated the prevalence of parlors in a band defined by its distance from the area with the highest land prices, which is symbolic of urban locations. I used a band 'width' of three kilometers, the commonly accepted diameter of a parlor's trade area, and, since I was not able to obtain land prices for 1975, I measured from 2-24-3 Shinjuku, Shinjuku ward (the most expensive location in 1983) and 6-9-5 Ginza, Chuo ward (the most expensive location in 1993). I then calculated the number of parlors in that band in 1975 and in 1993 as a percentage of the total. Figure 5.2 presents the results of that calculation. Although the tendency of most parlors to be distributed close to the area with the highest land prices was the same for both years, there was a clear trend for parlors to be located further from those areas in 1993 than in 1975.

This trend means more parlors were choosing cheaper locations, since land prices fall as distance increases from the priciest locations in Tokyo. The development of suburban parlors locationally expresses the spatial reallocation of daily life and consumption that accompanied the sweeping social changes surveyed in the first part of this chapter. At the same time, the phenomenon of overall spatial expansion to the

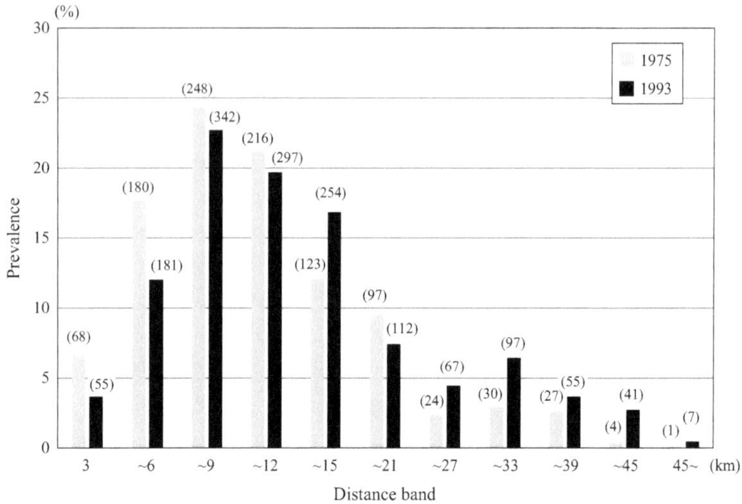

Figure 5.2: Parlor prevalence by distance from the location with the highest land prices (1975 and 1993)

Notes:

a. The location with the highest land prices in 1975 was 3-24-3 Shinjuku, Shinjuku-ku, Tokyo. The location with the highest land prices in 1993 was 6-9-5 Ginza, Chuo-ku, Tokyo. I've used information for 1983 since there is no publicly available data charting land prices in 1975.

b. Distance bands in excess of 21 kilometers have been recalculated using a 6-kilometer width. This change produced no visible difference in the changes seen between 1975 and 1993.

c. Figures in parentheses indicate the number of parlors.

Source: Land prices were compiled based on publicly available data for 1983 and 1993 as from the National Quantitative Data Download Service section of the Ministry of Land, Infrastructure, Transport and Tourism's website (http://nlftp.mlit.go.jp/ksj/gml/datalist/KsjTmplt-L01-v2_3.html, accessed on September 12, 2017). Data for pachinko parlors was compiled as described in Figure 5.1.

suburbs, including locations that envisioned access that differed from parlors near train stations, as seen in Figure 5.1 (2), was also the result of an active effort on the part of the pachinko industry to align its growth to changes in residential areas.

In this way, market growth driven by the emergence of Fībā-type machines motivated parlors to open near train stations in an effort to capture the large mobile population that frequented those areas, even as it simultaneously triggered growth in the number of parlors situated to capture other customer demographics. Nationwide, as we have seen, newly opened parlors actively chose suburban or increasingly suburbanized locations.

In order to understand the change in the distribution of locations in Tokyo, we must take into account the fact that the city, along with the greater Osaka area, has the most densely populated rail transport network in Japan. In that sense, Tokyo saw not only an increase in truly suburban parlors, but also a general trend toward

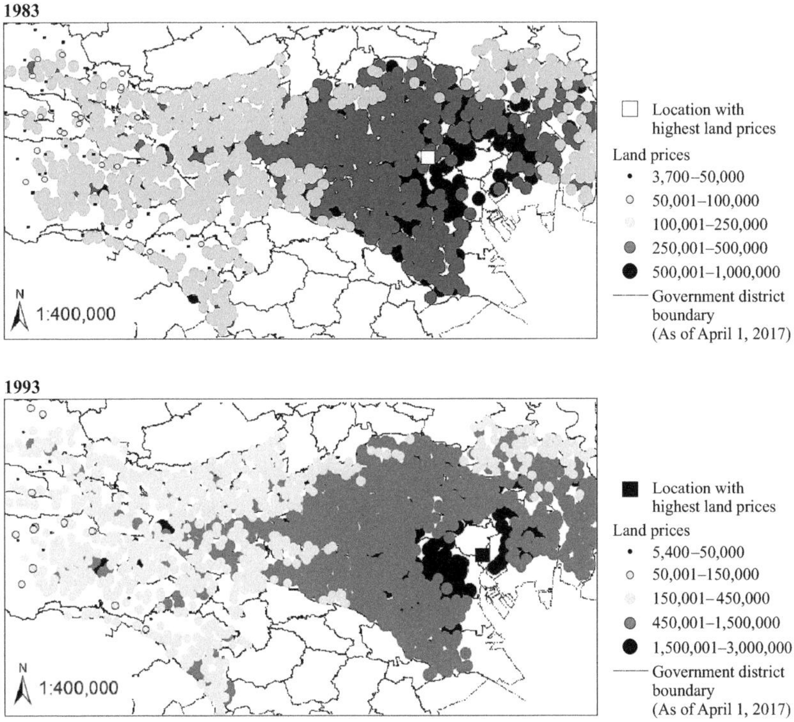

Figure 5.3: Distribution of land prices in Tokyo (1983 and 1993)
Source: Compiled based on publicly available land price data for 1983 and 1993 from the National Quantitative Data Download Service section of the Ministry of Land, Infrastructure, Transport and Tourism's website (http://nlftp.mlit.go.jp/ksj/gml/datalist/KsjTmplt-L01-v2_3.html, accessed on September 13, 2017).

suburbanization as areas near train stations remained central to business development in the city, with parlor operators identifying new business opportunities arising from subway extensions and the construction of new suburban commuter lines. Consequently, suburbanized locations and suburban parlors may have represented a certain type of marginal business format predicated on the assumption of market growth and spurred on by a decreasing amount of space for new parlors in the areas around urban stations. That said, it is likely that the phenomenon of the 1980s was not merely an extension of the trend towards suburban parlor development that had already begun developing during the 1970s.

Suburban parlors were able to grow by accommodating social changes outside the pachinko industry as well as the new needs created by those changes during the 1970s, prior to the introduction of Fībā-type machines, as we saw in the first part of this chapter. By contrast, in examining the trajectory of suburban parlors after the introduction of those models, it is necessary to consider its relationship to changes that occurred inside the industry, as analyzed in Chapter 4. Could we not characterize the aggressive pursuit of a transition to suburban parlors as a way to expand the scale of operations in the face of market growth by accommodating demand from customers who preferred a much more pronounced speculative element? This aspect also provided a means of leveraging the advantages of the new type of machine even as the significance of pin adjustment played a decreasing role in parlor management. To explore the parlor business during this period from the standpoint of this interpretation, we must first examine the way the scale of parlor operations grew.

Expansion in scale during the 1980s

As corporate growth became possible thanks to the rapid development of the industry, the drive to expand the scale of parlor operations gathered momentum as a way to realize such growth. Parlors located in neighborhoods and urban areas ran into limits on the number of machines they could operate. It is likely that as parlors built on changes in their trade area stemming from motorization and the decentralization and expansion of residential areas and developed expectations of capturing a new customer demographic by attracting women, they actively embraced the benefits of relocating to suburban areas or, in the case of new parlors, opening suburban-style businesses. Table 5.3 summarizes how the drive to expand the scale of parlor operations progressed against this background.

Suburban parlors adopted a larger footprint by utilizing lower land costs from the outset. Although the extent of savings presumably varied with geographic area, some parlors' land costs were just one-third of what they would have paid in an urban setting.[83] Even as the number of parlors remained more or less flat after 1965, the number of installed machines rose from 1.57 million in 1970 to an estimated 2.00 million in 1978, and the average number of machines per parlor rose from 165 to 190.[84] In the survey conducted from 1975 to 1976, introduced above, 1136 new parlors, close to half of which were suburban, installed 578,580 machines, an average of 245 machines per parlor, exceeding the overall average (of 190.1 machines[85]) by more than fifty machines.

Parlor size was steadily increasing in Tokyo, too, although the city was not included in the survey. Table 5.3, which was compiled using the membership rolls of the Toyūkyō, lists the number of parlors for each of several size groups based on the number of installed machines as a percentage of the total as well as the average annual number of machines for 1975; 1982, immediately after the introduction of Fībā-type machines; 1988, which reflected the effects of the 1980s; and 1993. That the transition to larger parlors bracketed the emergence of Fībā-type machines is

Parlor size (number of machines)	1975		1982		1988[a]		1993	
100 or less	184	17.9%	145	16.1%	154	13.6%	224	14.8%
101 to 150	238	23.2%	183	20.4%	161	14.2%	179	11.9%
151 to 200	203	19.8%	182	**20.2%**	216	19.0%	251	16.6%
201 to 250	176	17.2%	147	16.4%	229	**20.2%**	298	**19.7%**
251 to 300	91	8.9%	103	**11.5%**	188	**16.6%**	269	**17.8%**
301 to 350	61	5.9%	61	**6.8%**	100	**8.8%**	153	**10.1%**
351 to 400	28	2.7%	26	**2.9%**	40	**3.5%**	52	**3.4%**
401 to 500	36	3.5%	28	3.1%	47	**4.1%**	65	**4.3%**
500 or more							17	**1.1%**
Missing	9	0.9%	24	2.7%		0.0%	1	0.1%
Grand total	1,026	100.0%	899	100.0%	1,135	100.0%	1,509	100.0%
Average parlor size (number of machines)	188.0		193.2		211.6		219.6	

Table 5.3: Size of parlors in terms of number of machines before and after the introduction of Fībā-type machines (Tokyo)

Notes:

a. Since parlors belonging to the Senju Area Association, the Shakujiōen Association and the Mejiro Area Association were not included, information for those was supplemented with the 1991 membership roll.

b. Figures enclosed in solid lines indicate the two groups with the highest percentages, while figures in bold indicate groups exhibiting growth relative to 1975.

Source: Compiled based on membership rolls for the Tokyo Amusement Industry Cooperative and the Tokyo Confederation of Pachinko Associations for 1975, 1982, 1988, 1991 and 1993.

indicated by the fact that average parlor size increased and that the figures enclosed in solid lines (denoting the size groups to which the largest percentages of parlors belonged) moved progressively towards larger groups with each passing year.

A number of changes over time demand our attention. First, the decrease of more than 100 parlors between 1975 and 1982 reflects the effects of the recession at the end of the 1970s, which was precipitated by the second oil crisis (see the first part of Chapter 4). Whereas the 195 new parlors that entered the industry during this period operated an average of 202.2 machines in 1982, the 322 parlors that went out of business operated 151.6 machines in 1975, indicating that parlors closing up shop were disproportionately smaller ones. As a result, the percentages of parlors belonging to the top groups were higher in 1982 than in 1975, and the average parlor size in the former was about 193 machines, an increase of about three points from 1975.

The number of parlors grew by 238 between 1982 and 1988, reflecting a surge in new openings. Average parlor size also increased by a remarkable twenty machines, reaching about 212. The 207 parlors that went out of business in 1982 operated about the same number of machines on average (149.7) as the parlors that went out of business in 1975, whereas the 443 new parlors that year operated 211 machines, indicating that it was smaller parlors that were closing their doors. Even so, the size group that contained the parlors that went out of business (101 to 150 machines) declined even as other groups reversed that trend and grew.

The trend toward new parlors and larger establishments continued until 1993. At that point, all groups exhibited growth. This change can presumably be attributed to the fact that small parlors remained viable in favorable locations near train stations, since there were limits on how well such sites could accommodate large parlors. We can conclude that overall market growth during and after the 1980s offered a certain amount of opportunity to a diverse range of parlor sizes. However, an examination of prevalence by size group indicates that small groups had embarked on a long-term decline, while large groups were increasingly making their presence felt.

EXPECTATIONS TOWARD PARLOR CHAINS

Development of chains

How did the development of chains of parlors progress as another aspect of the increase in size prompted by Fībā-type machines? Although I was unable to find sources that establish a nationwide trend, we can use the Toyūkyō's membership rolls to focus on changes during the 1980s in order to learn as much as possible about trends in the market.

The membership rolls do not classify chains as such, which makes it difficult to develop a systematic understanding of which parlors were operated by the same company. To address this challenge, I identified parlors with the same managers based on information about managers in the membership rolls and compiled a list based on the number of parlors operated by those chains. Table 5.4 presents the results of that effort. However, the data is limited to Tokyo – since it is not possible to track which companies established parlors in other prefectures, the list does not reflect those operations and as a result understates the actual number of chains. It may overstate reality in other ways, since it is possible that the same name appearing in records may in fact refer to different individuals. In this section, I will attempt to discern how the industry evolved during the 1980s based on the broad trend that emerges from data about pachinko chains for each of several fiscal years.

I will focus on changes in businesses that operated two or more parlors as the threshold that constitutes a 'chain'. As Table 5.4 indicates, companies operating a single parlor accounted for 70 percent of all pachinko companies as of 1975, and the

Number of locations	1975		1982		1988		1993	
	Instances	Total number of locations	Instances	Total number of locations	Instances	Total number of locations	Instances	Total number of locations
21							1	21
15					1	15	2	30
14							1	14
11					1	11	1	11
10					2	20	1	10
9					1	9	4	36
8			2	16	3	24	1	8
7					2	14	2	14
6	3	18	2	12			3	18
5	1	5	4	20	2	10	6	30
4	5	20	7	28	7	28	16	64
3	22	66	15	45	28	84	57	171
2	94	188	88	176	127	254	145	290
1	729	729	600	600	666	666	790	790
Missing			2	2			2	2
Total number of parlors		1,026		899		1,135		1,509
				Ratio (%)				
20 or more								1.4
10 to 19						4.1		4.3
5 to 10		2.2		5.3		5.0		7.0
2 to 4		26.7		27.7		32.2		34.8
1		71.1		66.7		58.7		52.4
Missing				0.2				0.1

Table 5.4: Trend in chain development (Tokyo)
Source: Compiled based on Table 5.3.

typical 'neighborhood pachinko parlor' had an average of about 190 machines (see Table 5.3) at the time.[86]

Although the number of parlors fell in absolute terms in 1982, following a period of recession, the number of companies operating four, five or eight parlors grew. Looking at the percentage of parlors operated by chain businesses, the percentage of single parlors fell 4.4 points, but that of parlors operated by businesses with two or more parlors rose. That said, businesses with a single location accounted for about 67 percent of all parlors, indicating that chain businesses had not become an overwhelming presence.

As the number of parlors grew in 1988, the downward trend for the percentage of businesses with a single location continued. At the same time, the number of businesses operating two or more parlors rose 8.4 points. Businesses operating ten to nineteen parlors in particular had been unknown in the past. Their emergence suggests that some new development leading to large-scale operations was at play.

The above trends did not change substantially in 1993. Single-parlor management fell an additional 8.6 points from 1988. Insofar as that arrangement accounted for about 50 percent of all parlors, it can be seen as a business format that cannot be ignored. However, the direction of change in Tokyo, where the distribution of businesses was weighted in favor of single locations, merits our attention, and the development of chains can be discerned in the fact that the trend toward operating two or more parlors grew stronger as well as in the fact that close to 50 percent of all parlors had adopted that approach.

Chain development and its expected functions

The development of pachinko parlor chains became more noticeable during the second half of the 1980s and then in the 1990s. This trend stands out in a survey conducted in 1989 of companies seen as major players in the industry entitled 'Strategies of Major Pachinko Parlor Businesses', which targeted parlors in twenty-two prefectures nationwide.[87] Although the method by which 'major' businesses were chosen remains unclear, and despite the fact that the survey's sample size was just sixty-seven, it allows us to assess how parlors saw the development of chains. The term 'chain' is used but not precisely defined in the survey, but it refers to arrangements in which one company operated multiple parlors. Table 5.5, which summarizes the survey's findings, indicates that about 80 percent of the companies that responded operated two or more parlors. While it is true that operation of a single parlor, as we saw with Masamura Shōkai in Chapter 4, continued to account for 20 percent of respondents, there can be no question that, at a minimum, that was not the typical approach for major companies.

Additionally, we must note with care that close to 30 percent of the survey's respondents recognized the operation of two or three parlors as a true chain. Although there were ten companies that operated eleven or more parlors, such cases accounted for just 15 percent of all respondents. However, in terms of the trend toward chains, the number of parlors operated by those companies weighed heavily on the overall statistics, as indicated by ratio (C), and we can conclude that the influence of parlors operated by companies with chains grew in a readily visible manner in the context of corporate competition. Such results trigger interest in the actual influence, which is to say the economic function, of chain development. Let us, then, examine the functions that representative companies expected chain development to play as a forerunner of the changes that would lead to the characteristics of today's parlor operations.

In fact, the survey found that of the thirty parlors that indicated they had not pursued chain operations, fourteen were 'interested' in the future potential of such an approach, which exceeded the nine parlors that described themselves as 'not interested'

Number of parlors (A)	Number of operators (B)	Percentage of operators (%)	Total number of parlors (A × B)	Percentage of total (%)
1 parlor	14	**20.9**	14	3.5
2 to 3 parlors	18	**26.9**	41	10.4
4 to 5 parlors	14	**20.9**	63	**15.9**
6 to 10 parlors	7	10.4	78	**19.7**
11 to 15 parlors	4	6.0	52	13.2
16 to 20 parlors	2	3.0	33	8.4
20 or more parlors	4	6.0	114	**28.9**
Grand total	67	100.0	395	100.0

Table 5.5: Chain development by major parlor operators (1989)
Note: Bold figures indicate the groups representing the highest percentages of the total.
Source: Compiled based on 'Strategies of Major Pachinko Parlor Operators' in Yano Research Institute (1989: 313–80).

(seven parlors did not reply), indicating overall interest in chain development. Of the twenty-nine parlors with chain operations,[88] ten reported that they were 'interested' and planned to continue with that approach (while one indicated it was 'not interested' and eighteen declined to reply). These results are a testament to parlor expectations based on the economic advantages offered by chain development.

Regarding the economic benefits of chain operations, the responses of the thirty-one parlors that replied can be classified into five categories, as shown in Table 5.6. These include 'scale advantages' that allowed operational streamlining; 'human resources' benefits whose precise nature remains unclear; 'stabilization of management related to profit, etc.' through a companywide leveling of inter-location differences; benefits of 'competition among parlors run by the same company' through the introduction of the principle of competition based on the comparison of operating results for parlors managed by the same company; and 'other' benefits. 'Scale advantages' attracted a high level of expectation, with twenty-six respondents exhibiting a shared recognition that chain development made efficient information acquisition operations possible (indicated by ● in Table 5.6) and reduced purchase-related expenses (indicated by ◉).

We can catch a glimpse of chain development, which had attracted the interest of these representative parlors, in the tracks left by individual companies. Table 5.7 summarizes information gleaned from companies that responded to the survey and whose online histories included information about parlor locations as of August 2013. The table also includes information about two companies (Aizen Kōgyō and Kinbasha) chosen at random using the same method.

The companies can be divided into groups as described below if we trace the manner in which their new parlors opened on the time axis.

Advantages of becoming a chain
It makes fund management more convenient.
It helps companies save on taxes while contributing to corporate health.
It allows follow-up when a parlor is competing with nearby parlors.
It reduces purchasing costs by increasing order quantities.
It takes advantage of machinery, appliances and related products sold by affiliated companies.
It allows operators to move machines among locations and to obtain information about new machines.
It allows operators to take advantage of their expertise. It streamlines profit-making. It makes it easier to deal with competition with other parlors.
It serves to aggregate information. It streamlines management and enhances the company's base.
It allows operators to capture regional demographic flows.
It allows operators to develop a sales strategy for each location in the region.
It fosters corporate prosperity. It contributes to parlor recognition.
It burnishes the operator's image.
It offers synergistic advantages. It diversifies contacts. It allows operators to adapt to their times.
It increases internal awareness through regional information and competition with other parlors.
It allows operators to secure larger and more stable sales and profits by working to increase their market share.
Pros and cons for particular site conditions serve to further strengthen the basis of management through related chain development.
It allows total control.
It levels out parlor performance. It expands the scale of operations.
It allows the operator to make up for differences in parlor performance through its profits/losses and overall capabilities, thereby strengthening the basis of its operations.
It allows parlors to make up for losses by cooperating with other locations when customer counts are low. It keeps employees from becoming bored with their jobs.
It reduces management costs. It increases management information. It fosters personnel exchanges. It boosts employee motivation.
It aids in model selection, purchasing, recruiting and streamlining.
It allows operators to make effective use of machines as assets. It allows operators to utilize personnel.
It motivates employees. It offers advantages of scale.
It makes available research by other locations and fosters employee exchanges.
It allows operators to retain personnel and save money.
It offers advantages related to personnel.
It allows locations' sales to be compared.
It stimulates competition within the company and enhances companies' strength.
It suits the family-run nature of the business.
Grand total

Table 5.6: Effects of chain development

Note: Solid circles indicate the accumulation of regional information, while concentric circles indicate operator expectations of cost savings in purchasing.

Source: Compiled based on 'Strategies of Major Pachinko Parlor Operators' in Yano Research Institute (1989: 313–80).

	Reasons				
Number of instances	Streamlining of management due to advantages of scale (information, purchasing of equipment, expenditure, etc.)	Human resources	Stabilization of management due to profit, etc.	Competition between parlors run by same operator	Other
1	○				
1	○				
1	○				
1	⦿				
2	⦿				
1	●⦿				
1	●				
1	●				
1	●				
1	●				
1	○				
1	○				
1	○			○	
1	●			○	
1	○		○		
1	○		○		
1	○		○		
1	○		○		
1	○		○		
1	○	○	○		
1	⦿	○			
1	⦿	○			
1	○	○			
1	○	○			
1	●	○			
1		○			
1		○			
1				○	
1				○	
1					○
36					
67	26	8	6	4	1

Data no.	Company	Head office	Capitalization (tens of thousands of yen)	Number of employees (number of part-time workers, if known)
①	Miyazaki Shōten	Morioka, Iwate Prefecture	700	228
②	Nissin Kankō	Naka-ku, Nagoya	10,000	420 (Including 244 part-time employees)
③	Aizen Kōgyō	Takamatsu, Kagawa Prefecture	4,000	600
④	Ohkiya	Toyohashi, Aichi Prefecture	10,000	1,033
⑤	Harimaya	Sumiyoshi-ku, Osaka	10,000	300 (160)
⑥	Ichifuji Kōgyō	Fukuyama, Hiroshima Prefecture	9,000	337
⑦	Yūkō	Kurume, Fukuoka Prefecture	100,000	2,355 (Including affiliates and part-time employees)
⑧	Amenities	Tomi, Nagano Prefecture	9,000	540
⑨	Kinbasya[c]	Hitachi, Ibaraki Prefecture	10,000	833

①
②
③
④
⑤
⑥
⑦
⑧
⑨

Table 5.7: Meaning of the 1980s for chain operators

Notes

a. Shaded cells indicate periods when the company in question opened a large number of locations.
b. The Amenities Group includes 2 parlor companies. The table provides information for parlors for which the operator's first year in business can be ascertained. Another 14 parlors were operated by other companies.
c. Kinbasya obtained approval for a reorganization plan in September 2015. The information in the table is based on the company's website and is current as of August 2013.

First, companies ② and ⑤ opened between the establishment of their companies and 1980 (group 1). However, company ②, which was established in 1949, opened just two new parlors in thirty years. The company may have resumed opening locations during the 1990s, but it hardly seems to have actively embraced the chain idea. Company ⑤ opened a new location on average every two or three years during the 1970s after it was established in 1971. Then, after a temporary lull during the

Year of establishment (year of entry into pachinko parlor business)	Number of new locations				Cumulative number of parlors (current count as of May 2016 based on website)
	From entry into market until 1980	From 1981 to 1990	From 1991 to 2000	From 2001 to 2016	
1937 (1974)	1	5	2	1	9 (8)
1949 (1949)	3	0	2	1	6 (5)
1945 (1951)	5	6	2	5	18 (16)
1945 (1952)	3	9	4	6	22 (19)
1971 (1971)	5	1	5	3	14 (13)
1966 (1948)	6	10	6	4	26 (22)
1948 (1974)	2	6	10	19	37 (29)
1953 (1974)	1	6	4	6	17 (14[b)])
1957 (1954)	2	4	5	7	18 (21)
	11.1	55.6	22.2	11.1	100%
	50.0	0	33.3	16.7	100
	27.8	33.3	11.1	27.8	100
	13.6	40.9	18.2	27.3	100
	35.7	7.1	35.7	21.4	100
	23.1	38.5	23.1	15.4	100
	5.4	16.2	27	51.4	100
	5.9	35.3	23.5	35.3	100
	11.1	22.2	27.8	38.9	100

1980s, it continued opening new locations during and after the 1990s. It is clear that companies ② and ⑤ both hesitated to invest in new parlors during the 1980s.

In contrast to group 1, companies ①, ③, ④ and ⑥ (group 2) opened new locations primarily during the 1980s. These companies had already adopted the chain approach, and they embraced it even more enthusiastically during the 1980s. In this way, they took timely advantage of the opportunities posed by market growth during that decade. Efforts by companies ⑦, ⑧ and ⑨ (group 3) to open new locations were concentrated during the 2000s, but it was during the 1980s that their approach gathered momentum.

In this way, behavior exhibited during the 1980s varied slightly from company to company. These differences tell us that the companies' understanding of the timing and nature of market growth was diverse, and that the intensity of their embrace of chain development was not uniform, reflecting differences in prospects they perceived in, and in their expectations toward, the industry. That said, it is clear that with the exception of companies ② and ⑤, companies chose to develop chains during the 1980s, even if there were differences in when they most actively did so.

POTENTIAL OF LARGE-SCALE OPERATIONS: *Maruhan's Chain*

Finally, I will add a simple examination of the economic benefits of suburban parlors and chain development as expressed through operating income. I will use Maruhan Co., Ltd., which had the highest sales in 2020 at about 1.46 trillion yen (about US$13.50 billion), as an example. After being founded as a coffee shop in Kyoto Prefecture in 1957, the business switched to operating a pachinko parlor in April 1958 (it was incorporated as a joint-stock corporation in 1972). During the 1970s, the company opened a series of parlors in multiple prefectures, including Shizuoka Prefecture,[89] before evolving into a representative business with a nationwide chain including (as of March 31, 2017) 320 pachinko and *pachislot* parlors, bowling alleys, amusement facilities (karaoke, etc.) and other holdings (golf courses, etc.).[90] Parlors that could be characterized as suburban make up the core of its operations, and 292 of the 316 pachinko and *pachislot* parlors it operated as of January 2016 had parking areas, while twenty-four did not (of which ten were located in Tokyo and six in Osaka).

Origins of chain development: 1980s

Table 5.8 summarizes the number of new parlors opened by the company by decade. The table includes only locations that were operating as of August 2013[91] and therefore does not include parlors that opened and closed in the past. That said, it is clear that the trend observed for other companies so far, wherein changes occurred in chain development during the 1980s, clearly applies to Maruhan as well. Parlors established during the 2000s account for 70 percent of the total; certainly, the company embarked wholeheartedly on a course of expansion, and it was during that decade that it pursued those plans at an altogether different speed than in the past. However, to trace the origin of that program of development, we must go back to the 1980s.

After tracing Maruhan's parlor development program while supplementing the story with information about parlor openings and closings from the company history,[92]

Period		Number of new locations	Ratio (%)
1970s	1975 to 1979	3	1.0
1980s	1980 to 1984	4	1.4
	1985 to 1989	9	3.1
1990s	1990 to 1994	5	1.7
	1995 to 1999	15	5.2
2000s	2000 to 2004	100	34.6
	2005 to 2009	107	37.0
2010s	2010 to 2014	46	15.9
Other (bowling, game centers)		9	
Total parlors (including other)		289 (298)	100.0

Table 5.8: Years in which Maruhan opened new locations (as of August 2013)
Source: Maruhan's homepage (http://www.maruhan.co.jp/parlor/index.html, accessed August 2013). The table tabulates the years in which parlors opened based on a search for parlors as of August 2013.

I will pinpoint the point at which its approach changed. Maruhan operated two parlors in 1965, three in 1973 and seven in 1975, after which a series of openings and closings left seven parlors in operation at the end of the 1970s, before the emergence of Fībā-type machines. During the 1980s, the number of locations grew to eight in 1982, eleven in 1984, twelve in 1986, eighteen in 1988 and twenty-four in 1989. What is noteworthy here is the trend between 1986 and 1989. Until that period, the company opened at most two new locations per year, and it never opened new parlors during two consecutive years. That the company launched twelve new parlors during the four-year period starting in 1986 means it opened an average of three parlors per year in a sustained effort.

The evolution of chain development at Maruhan into an active program during the second half of the 1980s occurred against the backdrop of special circumstances: the enormous debt being shouldered by the company. The failure of Maruhan's bowling business during the 1970s left it with a total debt of 6.0 billion yen (about US$20.4 million in 1974). Pressed to repay its loans, the company continually contended with funding pressure.[93] The popularity of Fībā-type machines during the 1980s allowed it to accelerate its repayment, and accounts describe how it finished doing so in 1986.[94] Although it bears noting that Maruhan's active program of chain development overlapped in time with an improvement in the company's financial position, the move can also be understood in connection with the emergence of Fībā-type machines during the 1980s, a development that went beyond Maruhan's unique circumstances.

Let us pause to examine Maruhan's actions as an expansion in operational scale that occurred in the context of the rapid growth and qualitative changes that followed the debut of Fībā-type machines – for example, the narrowing scope of skill and pin

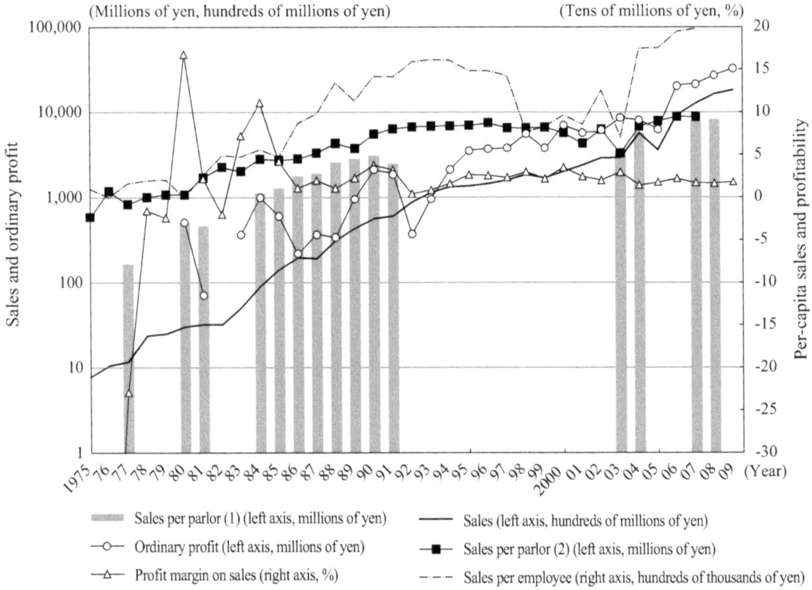

Figure 5.4: Maruhan's performance (1975 to 2009)

Notes:

a. Sales per parlor (1) was calculated by dividing sales by the cumulative number of parlors based on information about openings listed on the timeline in the company's history, while sales per parlor (2) was calculated by dividing sales by the number of parlors based on information about the openings of parlors listed on the website as operating as of August 2013. The number used to calculate sales per parlor (2) understates the actual number of parlors since information about closed parlors is unavailable, resulting in a higher figure than sales per parlor (1).

b. Sales per employee was calculated as follows: Sales / (number of employees + number of part-time employees). The number of part-time employees can be ascertained starting in 1998.

c. Profit margin on sales = Ordinary profit / sales × 100.

Source: Sales, ordinary profit and the number of parlors used for sales per parlor (1) were calculated based on Maruhan (2008), while the number of parlors used for sales per parlor (2) was calculated based on Maruhan's website (http://www.maruhan.co.jp/hall/index.html, accessed August 2013).

adjustment experience. In the case of Masamura Shōkai, as examined in Chapter 4, after experiencing the high profitability brought on by the introduction of Fībā-type machines, the company was forced to take difficult steps as profits came under pressure due to intensifying competition caused by regulations and a series of new entrants into the industry. In Figure 5.4, which illustrates operating conditions at Maruhan during and after 1975, the company – like Masamura Shōkai – experienced a rapid improvement in ordinary profit as a percentage of sales ('profit margin on sales'), followed by a rapid decline, during the first half of the 1980s. It is likely that these conditions forced the company to make choices concerning parlor locations and management policies, and that chain development was one answer to the quandary in which it found itself.

However, if we pay attention to the *rapidity* with which the company acted after 1986, we cannot simply dismiss it as solely a response to declining profitability. Rather than treating chain development as a passive response to intensifying competition, we ought to emphasize it as an action taken by a company responding actively to market growth spurred by Fībā-type machines. As was the case with Masamura Shōkai, parlors in traditional locations near train stations and shopping districts were susceptible to intense competition from new entrants to the business within a confined area. Because the suburban parlor market being pursued by Maruhan was new and only gradually spreading during the 1970s, its development had only just begun. When Fībā-type machines caused the speed of market growth to accelerate, Maruhan found room to develop new locations while distancing itself in relative terms from the sort of intense competition encountered in urban settings.

Seen in this light, the fluctuations in profit margin on sales that occurred during the first half of the 1980s at Maruhan as shown in Figure 5.4 indicate that it was facing the same conditions as were being experienced by the entire industry, but it is worth noting that they did not lead to a further decline after 1986. That this indicator only rose after 1989 following a period of stability[95] was likely the result of the company's active pursuit of a growth strategy. We must consider this fact in light of how Maruhan went about developing its chain and of the actual benefits that approach delivered. Below I will examine the specific economic function played by the company's chain development approach.

I would like to pay special attention to how the tactical operating methods that individual parlors were forced to adopt vis-à-vis their competitors and the companywide parlor development strategy differed fundamentally in terms of their objectives and effects. The advantages that any given parlor enjoyed when competing directly with other parlors were related to daily operating methods including its selection of machines that suited the preferences of the area's customers; the timing with which it replaced machines (the timing of renewal reopenings); the level of service it offered, for example in terms of customer service; and its adjustment of prize-ball percentages. It is unclear how the companywide development of a chain would contribute directly to the ability of single parlors, which were operating while putting down roots in their communities and competing with other parlors, to gain competitive strength.

I examined the effects of chain development by Maruhan in Appendix 3 while bearing the above points in mind. Below I have summarized the results of that analysis.

Effects of chain development by Maruhan

First, in the initial stage of the chain development, Maruhan developed its parlors in a concentrated manner (in a specific region), rather than uniformly throughout Japan. There are a number of potential explanations for that approach. Regional concentration could provide a rational basis for dealing with the institutional frameworks related to machine permits, which varied from region to region, and allowed for the accumulation of expertise related to understanding regional-specific consumption trends. Situating parlors in a particular region could also be efficient from a management perspective, simplifying the management of new parlors from the perspective of supervision by keeping them close together.

Second, their operating conditions were nothing if not diverse, and that variety influenced the accumulation of information as a resource. For companywide management, such disparities in operating results both signaled potential problems and served as a valuable resource insofar as they presented opportunities for improving performance. They provided a motivation to analyze the underlying causes and take corrective action to rectify differences, encouraging improvement in the challenges faced by parlors that performed relatively poorly.

I examined some relevant factors that caused these disparities, including the number of machines; the prize-sale rate, which is related to the probability that customers will win; and utilization, meaning the extent to which a parlor's installed base of machines were being used by customers.

Third, operating at a larger scale offered pachinko businesses a potential means of improving their profit margin ratio on sales, up to a parlor size of 399 machines.

Fourth, higher prize-sale rates, signaling the potential for customers to win more, and utilization both resulted in higher performance as measured by metrics such as profit margin ratio on sales. However, interestingly, prize-sale rates and utilization exhibited a moderately inverse correlation, suggesting that winning was not the sole motivation of pachinko consumption (see Figure App.3.7). Ordinarily, higher prize-sale rates and utilization would be expected to exhibit a direct correlation; that they did not in this case meant that parlors' intentions of attracting more customers by higher prize-sale rates did not lead to increased profitability due to high utilization.

It may be that high prize-sale rates and low utilization were inevitable due to regional characteristics and competition with nearby parlors. These different relationships between the prize-sale rate and utilization, which varied from parlor to parlor, signaled various possibilities related to better operations. It goes without saying that uniform operating methods and top-down instructions are not necessarily effective in situations where operations are influenced by diverse regional demand, as in the service industry. However, the judgment that a given parlor's utilization is lower than average is a results-based evaluation that can be made on a head office level based on data that facilitates comparison. Setting aside the question of whether the discovery of differences led to a reaction that sought to rectify utilization and other parameters, it is important, at a minimum, that information about parlors with good performance and the reasons for that performance accumulate at the head office.

Fifth, services offered by Maruhan during special events and renewal reopenings when parlors changed machines deserve attention, especially from the perspective of the declining significance of pin adjustment. Suburban parlors had to advertise their presence in order to raise recognition, orchestrate renewal reopenings and provide other associated services in order to make it worthwhile for patrons to make the trip to their doors. This task – attracting customers – proved to be particularly challenging for suburban parlors. The key point is that suburban parlors were called upon to plan such events on a sustained basis. Unlike a business approach that relied exclusively on the skill of experienced pin adjusters to attract customers by adjusting the prize-ball percentage, the planning and orchestration of ongoing events signaled the growing importance of the organizational ability to continuously generate new ideas.

Sixth, it is particularly noteworthy that the redecorations, which included both renewal openings and renewal reopenings, actively carried out at existing parlors during this period were accompanied by efforts to modernize facilities under a companywide initiative at Maruhan. In general, redecorations brought business improvements to Maruhan's parlors.

In short, chain development brought expertise to parlor managers through the accumulation of various lessons in the course of comparing and analyzing parlors' operating results and the stabilization of structures capable of absorbing on a companywide level investments borne for a certain period of time, for example when new parlors or parlors opening after renovations (such as an expansion) offer a jackpot service.

Chain development and management

Finally, let us examine companywide business conditions at Maruhan over the course of about two years based on the status of individual parlors' operations.

Figures 5.5 (1) and 5.5 (2) indicate total and per-machine increases and improvements in metrics such as profitability and sales to create an overall picture of Maruhan's business conditions by adding the results for thirty-six parlors. Although total sales fluctuated due to factors including monthly variations, new openings and closures for redecorations, as examined in Appendix 3, performance rose gradually over these two years, as illustrated by the approximation lines. While the gross profit margin ratio failed to keep pace with the speed of sales growth, it can be seen to improve thanks to growth in the scale of operations. This improvement was

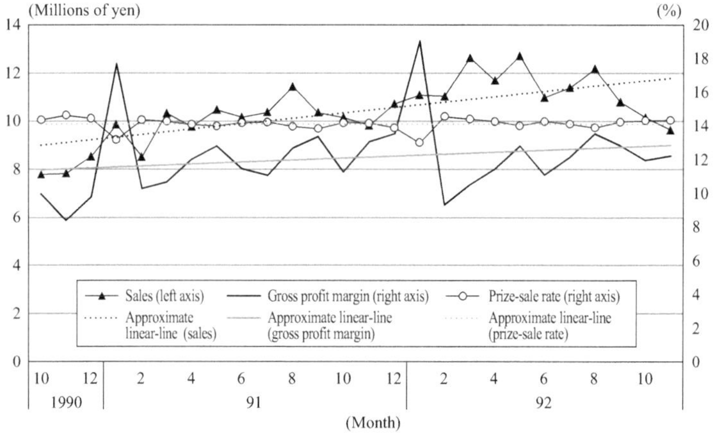

Figure 5.5 (1): Total sales and gross profit margin (October 1990 to November 1992)

Source: Compiled based on tables for October 1990 through November 1992 a list of sales by location provided by Maruhan.

inseparably related to the gradual, companywide decline in the average prize-sale rate. Sales and gross margin both also improved on a per-machine basis.

Let us consider these trends in relation to Maruhan's chain development and business performance as illustrated in Figure 5.4 above. While the factors responsible for destabilizing profit margin ratio on sales and ordinary profit ratio, which fluctuated violently during the 1970s, remain unclear, the analysis described in Chapter 4 suggests that behavior was likely the result of the economic recession faced by the entire industry prior to the debut of Fībā-type machines. After the second half of the 1970s, sales grew steadily, without showing any serious fall-off until 2000. That the company's expansion was not driven by groundbreaking new developments is a testament to the stability of its management. The company grew faster from 1981, after the appearance of Fībā-type machines, to 1984 than it did at any other time, adding four locations and posting sales that grew at a year-on-year rate of about 40 to 77 percent. The extent of that growth is also illustrated by sales per parlor, which grew about 30 to 70 percent. However, the growth did not last long as regulations strengthened (see Chapter 4), leading to negative year-on-year growth in overall sales in 1985 and in sales per parlor in 1984. Although profit margin ratio on sales improved in 1980 with the appearance of Fībā-type machines, performance fell to the 1 percent level after 1983. The backdrop against which this deterioration occurred included the effects of the regulation of Fībā-type machines and intensified competition in the form of rising prize-ball percentages due to new entrants into the industry, as examined in Chapter 4.

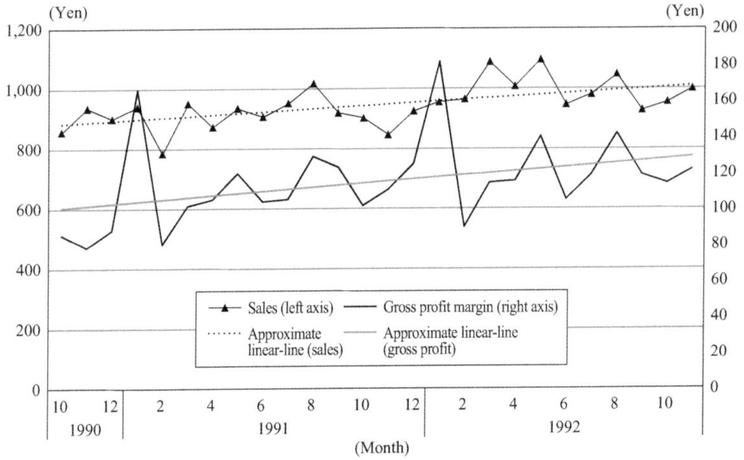

Figure 5.5 (2): Sales and gross profit margin per machine (October 1990 to November 1992)
Note: Sales per machine = total sal es for all parlors / total number of machines; gross profit margin per machine = total gross profit margin / total number of machines. The total number of machines excludes machines operated by all parlors that were closed for the month. If the date on which a parlor opened was unclear, figures for the month were included in the calculations. For example, if the date of a renewal opening fell during the last third of January, the parlor's sales and gross profit margin would be less than average due to the smaller number of business days. When that figure is divided by the number of machines, sales and gross profit margin per machine will be lower than average. Consequently, the overall sales and gross profit margin per machine will be underestimated.
Source: Same as Figure 5.5(1).

In the midst of these conditions, growth in the number of parlors starting in 1986 allowed Maruhan to realize steady growth in sales (including on a per-parlor basis) as well as improvements in profit margin ratio on sales. Based on these business results, we can see the company's opening of new locations from the second half of the 1980s as active, or intentional, development. Profit margin ratio on sales deteriorated, and ordinary profit fell significantly, starting in the 1990s, as if presaging the end of the bubble economy, but the drop-off lasted just two years. The company continued to launch new locations from the first half of the 1990s, albeit at a slower pace, before embarking on a rush to open new parlors during the second half of the decade (see Table 5.8 above), when the pachinko industry began attracting attention as a 30-tillion-yen market (about UD$275 billion in 1996). That sales per parlor exhibited stability from 1992 until the end of the 1990s suggests that chain development contributed to growth in the number of parlors as well as in sales and ordinary profit as the number of parlors increased and average profit margin ratio on sales held steady at 2.67 percent. At a minimum, we can conclude that chain development did not lead to a worsening of profitability since Maruhan shows no evidence of the sort of occasional periods of red ink exhibited by Masamura Shōkai during the second half of the 1980s. The strategy offers a glimpse of a new path that differs from the approach predicated on the adjustment of prize-ball percentages by pin adjusters and unavoidable profit pressure as management is forced to raise them for competitive reasons.

Although the question of why and how chain development helped secure a stable revenue base is best addressed as part of a future comprehensive examination of the topic,[96] it is possible to draw on the analysis presented in this part of the chapter and Maruhan's operating results to offer hypothetical observations concerning a new approach to measurement necessitated by the emergence of Fībā-type machines. In short, it may be that chain development plays a self-reinforcing function by facilitating parlor operations. This effect occurs via two pathways. The first is the approach's impact on the operation of existing parlors. As we saw in the example of the parlor operated by Masamura Shōkai (see Chapter 4), increases in prize-ball percentage and prize-sale rate levels appear in the financial performance of standalone parlors as negative profit. Under such conditions, a period of complimentary ('service') ball dispensation at a high prize-ball percentage – a strategy that serves both as an active method for securing customers and as a competitive tactic – must rely on a company's retained earnings and capital procurement abilities. By contrast, from the viewpoint of the companywide level at which Maruhan's chain development was pursued, the company was able to maintain active sales methods based on redecorations (see Appendix 3) on a sustained basis, even as those efforts were supplemented by normal operations at other parlors, guaranteeing more stable funding conditions. In addition to impacting management in a favorable manner through the active development of multiple locations in a way that drove up company-level sales, the effects of such a companywide approach spread throughout the organization and made renewal reopenings (see Appendices 1 and 3) a more stable operational method for individual parlors.

The second pathway by which the self-reinforcing function operated is likely to have been reductions in the cost of opening new locations. Although I was unable to sufficiently observe the phenomenon in this chapter due to problems with sources, the creation of standardized parlors served to standardize design drawings, and their reuse served to reduce additional design costs, while the potential of using machines with a proven track record at other parlors lowered equipment costs. In addition to the advantages provided by economies of scale, these methods worked to stagger the timing of new openings, allowing the company to repeatedly invest in individual locations. All else being equal, opening large numbers of parlors offered undeniable economies of scale while allowing methods for lowering the cost of new parlors to become more refined with repeated practice and shortening the amount of time required to recoup invested funds compared to single-parlor operations.

CONCLUSION

At the outset of this chapter, I identified its goal as examining noteworthy aspects of the parlor business that appeared during the 1980s. Compared to other chapters that have sought to examine problems that had to be overcome in order for the industry to continue to exist over the long term, this chapter's principal interest lay in exploring those tendencies that led the industry into the next era, defined as what came after the period leading up to the beginning of the 1990s, which it treats as a single period. A concise and provisional answer to the questions posed by that topic would be that experiments in suburbanization, expansion in parlor size and chain development progressed, with the 1980s serving as an inflection point.

However, it proved difficult to identify conspicuous phenomena that combined to define the 1980s as an era. Suburbanization had begun prior to the period, and it would be difficult to argue that chain development emerged fully during those years; one must acknowledge that all of these tendencies, including expansion in parlor size, progressed gradually. It is no new discovery to find a dichotomy between one continuous aspect that follows in the wake of what came before, and another discontinuous aspect that leads definitively to the next era. In light of the subsequent acceleration of expansion in size and chain development, it is likely important to consider continuity with the 1980s. Let us, then, pay close attention to small developments and rethink the nature of this inflection point and new beginning while asking why new directions did not emerge in a more striking manner. Specifically, we can examine the prospects for subsequent large-scale management while supplementing the picture with some developments that lay outside the scope of this chapter's analysis, using Maruhan as an example.

Three clues deserve our attention. The first is that Fībā-type machines had characteristics that made expansion in parlor size a natural choice. One characteristic of probability is that dispersion of outcomes decreases as the number of machines grows, and I have already pointed out that increases in the size of individual parlors made it easier for them to stabilize their management. When probability-governed machines overtake a parlor, progress in machine technologies summons irreversible changes that tend toward growing scale. Intensifying competition only adds to this momentum, moving the logic of management inexorably towards chain development.

The second noteworthy clue is information from parlor locations involved in diverse operational arrangements, as gathered from Maruhan's chains. For Maruhan, the period from its development of a large number of locations to the beginning of the 1990s was an era during which it collected a variety of information related to the direction of parlor management. While the nature of diversity presumably varied by region, machine count, site characteristics and the surrounding environment (competitive conditions), information from individual parlors, which exhibited variations when assessed on a companywide level, was itself a variable resource. However, that only means that the information was accumulated, not necessarily that it was used. To couch the situation in terms of Edith Penrose's concept of 'unused productive services' (resources), which would be the base for the future growth of the firm,[97] this period represented for Maruhan a time during which unused surplus information was discovered.

The third noteworthy tendency at Maruhan, which is closely related to the first two, consists of initiatives to build human resources development and head office functions starting in 1989,[98] as well as the start of college graduate recruitment and the enhancement of human resources development from 1993.[99] As I emphasized in Chapter 4, Fībā-type machines reduced the significance of pin adjusters and their expertise, which lay at the center of traditional operating methods. Consequently, the future opened up by Fībā-type machines brought rising managerial autonomy from the world of skill, while the search for expertise that held the key to operations as an alternative to pin adjustment became an issue that directly impacted sales. When information about distinctive operational methods and differences is found in a company, it raises new questions about how to use or rectify them. It was a new type of manager, rather than conventional pin adjusters or parlor managers, that was expected to take the lead in dealing with these two issues, which is to say, utilizing unused information as a resource to drive the next period of growth. Those managers needed the ability to analyze a variety of information and to harness it in parlor operations. Maruhan began experimenting with training this new type of parlor manager in 1992, and two years later the company began replacing 'old-style parlor managers'[100] at all of its parlors, some twenty locations, in Shizuoka Prefecture. This development spurred human resources development: by the 2000s, Maruhan had established a career path that allowed employees who had graduated from college to become parlor managers with at least eight years of experience, and employees with more experience to become area managers in charge of multiple parlors.[101] Even as Maruhan's example embodied the larger trend throughout the industry, the development of pioneering experiments led Hiroyuki Kaji[102] to characterize the 1990s as an era in which companies operating parlors transformed their image and worked actively to hire college graduates.

Thomson offers an interesting suggestion with regard to the meaning of these developments. His research into the sewing machine industry during the nineteenth century found a strong correlation between learning through distributorships and other sales companies and secondary inventions.[103] The importance of sales in terms of its impact on research and development was not self-evident in the parlor industry as a service industry, particularly in the traditional approach to operations. Perhaps performance that varied from parlor to parlor at Maruhan, as described in the last section of this chapter, encouraged the company to move beyond conventional service that merely offered a space in which customers could play, while simultaneously demanding analysis to facilitate improvements. In addition to the head office's ability to systematically analyze how its chain of parlors should operate, it was likely the development of operational capabilities at parlor locations that could accept feedback from above and the creation of mechanisms that could sustain autonomous operational planning, for example of programs and events, on an organizational basis facilitated that effective process.

Installation of Fībā-type machines was limited until the emergence of regulations and of other highly speculative gaming machines after the imposition of new requirements in 1985, and the trend towards large-scale management was not conspicuous from the 1980s until the beginning of the 1990s, due in part to general social conditions including high land prices and labor shortages during the economic bubble of the late 1980s. When this era is surveyed from the standpoint of changes in the industry, it seems that companies' ability to secure parlor managers was the first bottleneck in chain development. The position required not the skill of the pin adjusters of the past, but rather a new type of employee as a human resource, one who could use a diverse range of information and make comprehensive judgments. The external market, where 'itinerant' pin adjustment experts were typical until the 1970s,[104] could hardly be expected to serve as a source of such employees. Internal human resources development was a problem that could only be resolved over time. Upon reexamination, the various experiments upon which Maruhan embarked during this period can be characterized as an exploratory process focusing on discovering accumulated but unutilized information and training parlor managers in an effort to realize the growth potential of Fībā-type machines.

The period from the 1980s to the beginning of the 1990s was an era of discovering resources, and it marked the start of new trends that through human resources development exhibited continuity with the next era. Maruhan's institutional and organizational development gathered pace with the coming of the 2000s.[105] These trends signal an attempt to deal with the broadening of the domain of administrative control that I pointed out in connection with 'operational methods that suited the intrinsic characteristics of Fībā-type machines' at the beginning of the chapter, and it is significant that the development of parlor staff and managers had begun in advance of that broadening. The period leading up to the beginning of the 1990s can be characterized as a time of pre-dawn preparation. In this way, Maruhan's approach to chain development entered a different stage during the 2000s based on what it accomplished during the 1990s, when human resource development progressed and organization-building began, as seen in Table 5.8 above.

In the context of the industry as a whole, the significance of Maruhan's approach is not that large-scale management progressed linearly from its beginnings in the 1980s, but rather that Maruhan's chosen strategy – human resources development combined with organization- and mechanism-building – became an important element in the drive to secure a competitive advantage over rivals, and that approach itself served to lay the groundwork for a new era. A full-bore analysis of the experience of the 1990s and the industry's development during and after the 2000s falls outside the scope of this work, but I look forward to the topic being more deeply explored at some point in the future.

Essay: Pachinko and Ethnic Minority Koreans in Japan

INTRODUCTION

> Pachinko is the largest ethnic industry in Japan built and developed by a non-Japanese ethnic minority consisting primarily of resident foreigners. Pachinko parlors nationwide number 18,244 (as of December 1995, according to a study by the National Police Agency's Community Safety Bureau) [...]. In many cases, individual businesses are managed using multiple corporations and individuals, and the pachinko industry is estimated to include a total of 6000 to 7000 businesses. Of those, Japanese businesses account for around 25 percent, and the remaining 70 percent are said to be run by resident foreigners, for example ethnic minority Koreans and Chinese in Japan.[1]

This account is in close alignment with the general awareness that the pachinko industry is run primarily by ethnic minority Koreans in Japan, even if it diverges slightly in terms of details. While it is impossible to marshal accurate supporting statistical sources, the relationship between ethnic minority Koreans in Japan and the pachinko industry has been a consistent topic of discussion over time, as indicated in this work's introduction. That said, no account has ever addressed the changes in the pachinko industry's relationship with ethnic minority Koreans in Japan that have occurred over the course of its development.

As I explained in my book published in 2010,「在日企業」の産業経済史——その社会的基盤とダイナミズム (An Industry and Economic History of Companies Operated by Ethnic Minority Koreans in Japan: Their Social Base and Dynamic Change), the strong relationship between the pachinko industry and ethnic minority Koreans in Japan was the result of historical factors. Consequently, the ethnic character of the pachinko industry, which is to say its connections to a particular ethnic group, could vary with changes in those factors and associated conditions. My book examined the pachinko industry primarily from the perspective of the role played in business activities by ethnic minority Koreans in Japan. Here I will focus instead on changes in the industry's relationship with that group based on the industry's history as presented in this work. Due to the lack of historical sources suitable for use in an empirical analysis of this topic, I will offer a bird's-eye view of ethnic businesses in the industry by superimposing the areas in which businesses were run by ethnic minority Koreans and the periods during which those businesses grew onto the history of the pachinko industry's development, while making maximum use of the analysis presented so far in this work.

THE PEOPLE WHO CHOSE PACHINKO AS A LIVELIHOOD[2]

First, I will advance my line of thinking by offering two observations that serve as evidence of the link between the pachinko industry and ethnic minority Koreans in Japan. The first is that with regard to the business activities of ethnic minority Koreans in Japan, the pachinko industry – particularly the pachinko parlor business (as explained in more detail below) – not only occupied a central position in the structure of industries in which ethnic groups were involved, but also exhibited increasing significance over time, for example by serving as a historical driver of transformation of relative importance in terms of the industries in which the community was involved.[3] The second is that although it is difficult to calculate what percentage of the pachinko industry was made up of businesses run by ethnic minority Koreans, companies like Maruhan (a parlor operator) and Heiwa (a machine manufacturer) which had Korean founders, grew into leading companies that marked an epoch in the industry's development.[4] Let us consider how the factors underlying these two characteristics of the industry differed from one another.

How and when did ethnic minority Koreans in Japan come to be involved with the pachinko industry? The boom in pachinko during the first half of the 1950s provided the opportunity for that involvement. Among the various people who turned to pachinko, which was rumored to be highly profitable, for a livelihood were ethnic minority Koreans in Japan. Although it is impossible to determine nationwide trends characterizing ethnic minority Koreans in Japan during the 1950s, fragmentary information remains about Korean-heritage businessmen in Hiroshima Prefecture. A group known as the Liaison Conference of Amusement Operators (Yūgigyōsha Renraku Kyōgi) in Hiroshima, which was formed by ethnic minority Koreans,[5] had 100 members as of March 1955.[6] While the total number of parlors in Hiroshima Prefecture that year remains unknown, there were 729 parlors in 1954, and 186 in 1956.[7] This was just before the Administrative Order Prohibiting Successive-shot Machines took effect in April 1955, a time characterized by an abrupt decline in the number of parlors (see Chapter 1), making it likely that the overall parlor count, including Japanese operators, fluctuated from day to day, along with the number of ethnic minority Korean operators. Those changing conditions make it difficult to nail down the percentage of parlors run by ethnic minority Koreans, but the number of parlors in the prefecture the previous year, 1954, before the impact of the 1955 regulations was fully felt, suggests a figure of about 14 percent, while the intermediate parlor count for 1954 and 1956 – 459 parlors – yields a figure of about 25 percent.

Rather than determining the percentage of parlors run by Koreans in Japan and assessing whether the figure was high or low, the important thing is that ethnic minority Koreans in Japan had experience in the parlor business at this point in time.[8] In the business activities of ethnic minority Koreans, information about specific industries accumulated within the community as one member's experience in a certain industry, whether pachinko or another sector, propagated in the form of information that was useful for other members and then influenced their selection of businesses in which to become involved. Through such mechanisms, the business activities of ethnic minority Koreans in Japan came to be centralized in a number of fields. That there were a large number of ethnic minority Korean businessmen involved with the parlor business in 1955, which was to become a key turning point in the pachinko industry's development, signifies that there was already an accumulation of information resources in the community and that there was the possibility that those resources would be updated. That said, it is important to bear in mind that it was unclear how the industry would develop going forward, even at the turning point of 1955. In other words, it was not self-evident that the information resources would continue to accumulate; the future of those resources depended on whether ethnic minority Koreans in Japan would continue to choose that business, and a variety of factors influenced their choices. I will examine that point next.

In order to facilitate a deeper examination of the connections between the pachinko industry and ethnic minority Koreans in Japan, it is worth noting the following three facts concerning the group's involvement in the pachinko industry.[9] An examination of the respective involvement of ethnic minority Koreans in Japan with parlors and manufacturers during key periods in the industry's history[10] reveals, first, that while Koreans participated in both the parlor and manufacturing businesses from the end of the 1940s until the first half of the 1950s, when the industry was growing rapidly, their point of entry into the industry was limited to the parlor business following the 1955 regulations. Factors that potentially account for this characteristic include the discovery of a stable profit structure for the parlor business (see Chapter 1) as well as machine market disruption and business instability (see Chapter 2). The pachinko machine market experienced an exodus of manufacturers until the 1980s, and it attracted few new entrants during that period (see Figure 0.4 and Chapter 3). There is no evidence to suggest that ethnic minority Koreans in Japan went against this trend.

The action of participating in a given business after securing information and resources that had accumulated in the community, which shaped the business activities of ethnic minority Koreans in Japan, was related to fundamentally *profitable* businesses. Additionally, in instances where clusters of businesses formed, as they did with pachinko machines in Nagoya, information accumulated in certain locations. Even in the pachinko industry, which was a growth industry for an extended period of time after 1955, the search for a business by would-be entrepreneurs who were looking to draw on community resources was directed not to the pachinko machine manufacturing sector, but rather to the parlor business, which existed nationwide.

Second, the social environment that influenced Japanese people's motivations for entering the pachinko industry is likely to have changed around the time of the 1955 ban on successive-shot machines, with the result that ethnic minority Koreans in Japan became primarily responsible for the industry. This transition must be understood in the context of the period in which it occurred, when the pachinko industry was flourishing during Japan's postwar reconstruction. Prior to World War II, pachinko was seen as a business run by *yashi* (travelling street vendors and merchants who were often associated with festivals starting during the Edo period),[11] presumably creating the impression that it was a job properly pursued by people from other regions. That said, the period of postwar reconstruction was hardly a time of economic stability: a variety of people searched for work in a highly fluid manner, and pachinko was one option open to them. As pachinko shifted from a portable format to a brick-and-mortar business and the market expanded nationwide, a variety of people entered the parlor business and improved pachinko machines as part of the industry's boom (see chapters 1 and 2). Ethnic minority Koreans in Japan were just one of a diverse range of groups involved in that endeavor. However, a growing speculative (gambling) element and the involvement of criminal groups led to the 1955 regulations, tainting the pachinko industry's image. Coming as it did in the midst of a recession, this negative image combined with uncertainty about the industry's future direction to prompt Japanese people to exit the business, and the pachinko business came to be avoided by Japanese who had other, more stable options during the subsequent period of high economic growth.

By contrast, ethnic minority Koreans in Japan did not enjoy the same freedom in terms of occupational choices as did their Japanese counterparts.[12] For the group, the parlor business stood out from a number of options as a valuable opportunity that was backed by actual evidence in the form of business experience. Labor market-related factors were not the only elements that motivated ethnic minority Koreans in Japan to enter the pachinko industry. Among the manufacturing industry sectors that had served as the principal businesses in which ethnic minority Koreans in Japan were involved, some – for example, textiles – had been facing decline since the 1950s. As a result, people with business experience switched occupations to enter the growing parlor business. Additionally, people who had already found success in other fields such as construction and civil engineering entered the growing parlor business as part of an effort to diversify. Spurred by such composite motivations, ethnic minority

Koreans in Japan continued to choose the pachinko industry. In this way, the presence of ethnic minority Koreans in Japan as key figures in the pachinko industry grew, even as involvement by Japanese fell.

Despite these composite incentives, it would be premature to conclude that ethnic minority Koreans' ongoing selection of, and entry into, the pachinko industry was the natural result. Launching a business is generally more difficult than participating in the labor market, and leveraging experience in another industry to invest in the pachinko business was not a simple matter. On what basis was it possible for ethnic minority Koreans in Japan to enter the industry? The third fact in terms of this group's involvement in the pachinko industry relates to the accumulation of resources from several industries in the community. Their effects stimulated ethnic minority Koreans in Japan to enter the industry, and the group continued to launch parlor businesses that were increasingly amenable to planning (calculation). It was this community function[13] that provided the basis for implementing those businesses.

'Community function' here refers to the procurement of information influencing the discovery or selection of businesses, funding and other resources via the community when ethnic minority Koreans in Japan set out to launch or enter particular businesses. Information accumulated in connection with occupations and industries was disseminated through the relationships between Koreans in Japan, for example through participation in the activities of their ethnic group, including economic transactions, everyday interactions, folk events and educational institutions, and funds that had been built up both formally and informally were supplied through both informal financial arrangements and institutional programs (organizations) within the community such as ethnic credit unions. As a result of the effects of this community function, ethnic minority Koreans in Japan developed businesses with a focus on parlors in addition to principal industries such as certain manufacturing sectors, construction and civil engineering. Resources accumulated over time while those principal industries grew, creating an environment that made it increasingly easy for members of the ethnic group to enter the business.

This sort of community function was not limited to the parlor business, nor was it unique to Koreans in Japan. Other ethnic groups and associations of Japanese people from the same parts of the country exhibit similar phenomena.[14] People universally choose occupations and businesses not as isolated individuals, but in the context of relationships with primary groups to which they belong and with other people. For example, there were many Japanese-style baths (*sentō*) in Osaka managed by people who had come from Ishikawa Prefecture after obtaining information related to the bath business and financial aid from an association of Japanese people originally from that prefecture but living in Osaka. In this case, it was Japanese who made up the community in question, indicating that their gravitation towards the bath business was not the result of ethnic discrimination; rather, they enjoyed additional opportunities by accessing resources accumulated in the community. As is clear from this case, the operation of the community function of ethnic minority Koreans in Japan does not necessarily signify that they shunned relationships with people outside the community; instead, it provided a means of utilizing resources obtained from the external environment – human resources, information and funds – as fully as possible.

An examination of information related to the pachinko industry reveals that experiences up to 1955 comprised a set of initial conditions,[15] that related information was successively 'overwritten' through its use in ethnic minority Koreans' selection of businesses and that such information was accumulated asymmetrically within the community as a non-Japanese space at a time when the industry was avoided by Japanese. As a result, ethnic minority Koreans in Japan, for whom information lay within easy reach, became a sort of reserve force of businesspeople who were prepared to carry on the pachinko industry.

From the first half of the 1950s, ethnic credit unions established by Koreans in Japan[16] played a central role in the accumulation of funds and their supply to the pachinko industry. After its establishment in 1952, the first Dōwa Credit Association (*dōwa* means harmonizing; the association later changed its name to Chōgin Tōkyō) became a nationwide operation during the 1960s, and as of 1983, seventy-seven credit associations had been established as ethnic credit unions servicing all forty-four prefectures. Because they had an autonomous financial infrastructure, ethnic minority Koreans in Japan, who became latent entrepreneurs through exposure to community information related to the pachinko industry, reacted to business conditions in the industry and launched businesses at *great speed*. It is also important that ethnic credit unions actively sought to do business with the pachinko industry. Among industry-based transactions undertaken by ethnic credit unions, there was a stronger tendency toward transactions with the parlor business than toward those with the other principal industries in which ethnic minority Koreans were involved, for example manufacturing, construction and civil engineering. Viewed from a different perspective, this characteristic indicates the difficulty that the pachinko industry faced in procuring funds in the broader financial market, and it tells the story of how the community of ethnic minority Koreans in Japan made up for that defect in industrial finance.

In this way, the deep involvement of the ethnic minority Korean community in Japan with the pachinko industry, and especially the parlor business, began in 1955. That involvement was influenced by the varying viability of the business choices available to Japanese and ethnic minority Koreans in Japan in the context of a Japanese society that was undergoing a major transition from the reconstruction period to the period of high economic growth as well as changes in the nature of the industry itself and business. In the meantime, ethnic minority Koreans in Japan came into early contact with information based on the community function against the backdrop of composite motivations to enter the business, and they enjoyed the support of credit unions that actively provided funding. As a result, they managed to enter the business quickly under favorable business conditions, leading them to become more deeply and proactively involved with the parlor business following the successive-shot ban of 1955.

In this way, the community function provided a specific basis for deepening the involvement of the ethnic group with the pachinko industry. Among people outside the community, who had difficulty acquiring the information that was readily available within the community, the environment surrounding the pachinko industry was seen as high risk. While they were unwilling to shoulder high risks, the parlor business presumably did not register as a business opportunity.

INDUSTRY DEVELOPMENT AND ETHNIC MINORITY KOREANS' BUSINESSES[17]

As businesses run by ethnic minority Koreans in Japan who had experienced some degree of success after entering the business grew into leading companies, the community function receded into the background. Further growth required that companies procure funds on their own.[18] In other words, the accumulation of resources related to technology, expertise, funding and human resources by leading companies such as Maruhan and Heiwa as economic organizations was not made available to the community. Sharing among members of the group, a practice of considerable importance early on when entering the business, faded in significance as information was increasingly hidden behind the walls of individual companies. From a different standpoint, that the incorporation of pachinko machine manufacturers such as Heiwa into an ordered system, as examined in Chapter 2, was devoid of noteworthy ethnic elements, and that the search for market order transcended ethnic boundaries, indicate the fact that these companies did not absorb the community function as a necessary element of their operations. The additional resources that were necessary for growth were procured through broader relationships with markets and society that went beyond the ethnic minority Korean community. A concrete example of funding follows.

As described above, ethnic credit unions existed in a complementary relationship with general financial markets outside the community in terms of industrial finance. What did this arrangement signify? Ethnic credit unions played a financial infrastructure role for the pachinko industry, which was likely to be shunned by regular financial institutions including banks. However, the complementary function revealed the limits in accommodating the growing demand for funding that accompanied the growth of individual companies and the pachinko industry. Regular banks became key funders of the development of the pachinko industry. For example, *shinkin* banks, which generally are larger and serve a more varied range of businesses than credit unions, along with mutual banks serviced the demand for funding by ethnic minority Koreans in Japan operating large businesses and seeking to expand, for example through chain development, during the 1970s. The role of mutual banks in particular went beyond examples of those that dealt with individual companies run by ethnic minority Koreans in Japan,[19] and that role was more important than the role of other credit unions throughout Japan based on lending balances (in 1968 statistics) for the 'film and entertainment' category, which included the parlor business.[20]

This fact must be seen from two perspectives. The first asks how ethnic minority Koreans in Japan, who were seen as disadvantageous in the financial markets, began dealing with regular banks, and the second asks why regular banks dealt with the pachinko industry.

The development of transactions with regular banks by ethnic minority Koreans in Japan was predicated on securing creditworthiness. One route for doing so was to launch a business by borrowing the requisite funds from an ethnic credit union and then gaining the ability to do business with a regular financial institution after establishing a successful track record (instances in which regular leading banks determined that a given company was a capable business and therefore offered to lend it money provide an eloquent account of this approach). The important thing is that this route was made viable by ethnic credit unions that essentially played the role of angel investors, offering a guaranteed period during which the startup was supported. If businesses run by ethnic minority Koreans in Japan were able to take advantage of this period and establish a track record of success, it was possible that regular credit unions might recognize them as exceptional businesses. The second route was to enter the parlor business as part of a diversification or business change that drew on creditworthiness established in another industry. In this case, the company would have already been doing business with local and mutual banks. It is likely that even if a financial institution was cautious about the prospect of taking on the risk of lending funds to a pachinko parlor, they would provide funding to a parlor business as a new enterprise if it already enjoyed a relationship of trust with the ethnic minority owner or company involved. For example, the construction and civil engineering business, which completed a large number of public works projects, was a stable business that was highly likely to be able to repay loans, and as a result, local banks extended loans to ethnic minority Koreans in Japan who had an established record in this field.[21] In the manufacturing business, for example, if a company had been able to maintain a business relationship over the long term with a creditworthy Japanese individual or company, regular credit unions saw such relationships as a basis for extending credit to ethnic minority Koreans.[22] It is likely that companies were able to obtain business loans based on such track records in the regular financial markets.

The background against which mutual banks, as regular credit unions, took notice of the parlor business is unclear, but the large-scale circulation of cash in the business may have been a factor. For credit unions that had difficulty attracting deposits, which provided the basis for lending, parlors' daily cash revenue may have made transactions with them an appealing prospect. In fact, transactions with parlor businesses were a valuable means of locking down such deposits for ethnic credit unions, which dealt with the same problem. Since the savings of ethnic minority Koreans in Japan were insufficient, ethnic credit unions had difficulty accommodating the robust demand for loans as their ability to secure deposits faced a bottleneck.[23] Stabilization of deposits was the most pressing issue for ethnic credit unions from the second half of the 1950s to the 1960s, the initial stage of their operations following their establishment. Parlor businesses exhibited lower borrowing demand against deposits than other industries, and as a result they played a key role in ethnic credit unions' ability to secure deposits. It is entirely possible that regular financial institutions, which faced the same problem, saw the appeal in such characteristics. Competition with other credit unions for high-performing companies presumably played a role as well.[24]

This situation suggests that for pachinko parlor businesses operated by ethnic minority Koreans in Japan, transactions with top-tier credit unions, for example commercial banks, were subject to even stricter constraints. With the exception of a small number of large companies that pursued chain development during the 1990s, many ethnic minority parlor owners had trouble procuring funds. Furthermore, the Small Business Finance Corporation and Shōkō Chūkin Bank, which were tasked with offering policy-based finance to small and medium-size businesses, did not offer any lending programs for which the pachinko industry was eligible, and the industry was not on the radar of the Development Bank of Japan.[25] In this sense, we can conclude that parlor operators expanded their range of financial business partners on their own as they grew, even as they were fostered by community resources such as ethnic credit unions.

PACHINKO WINS GROWING RECOGNITION AS A BUSINESS OPPORTUNITY

During and after the 1980s, when the pachinko industry experienced a transition and its high rate of growth came to signal business opportunity, new participants entered the business. These participants triggered a set of circumstances that differed from the conditions of the past, when people who could not be entirely reduced to 'economic men' chose pachinko as an occupation for a diverse range of subjective value-based reasons related to the social condition of Japanese society, even as they learned of the possibility of earning a livelihood thanks to the informal propagation of information in the ethnic minority Korean community in Japan. Once pachinko was recognized as an enormous market, companies that made organizational decisions to invest in a business that was expected to grow even more emerged in a way that transcended the community.[26]

Even as the overall economy was embarking on a period of low growth, a higher rate of growth made the pachinko industry an attractive target for investment.[27] Parlors' high profitability drew the attention of a variety of industries, and the entry into the pachinko business of companies in industries with stagnating sales, for example large supermarkets that could leverage synergistic effects in terms of customer patronage, attracted interest in society.[28] Once the constraint of operational expertise in terms of procuring pin adjusters with the experience and skill to perform pin adjustment was comparatively reduced by the emergence of Fībā-type machines (see chapters 4 and 5), the hurdles to entry must not have seemed high to companies that could resolve the funding problems associated with expanded investment scale, if such investment was recognized as a business opportunity.

Meanwhile, how did the community function that came into play when ethnic minority Koreans in Japan launched businesses respond during this stage of rapid growth? Let us examine whether growth after the 1980s changed the way ethnic minority Koreans in Japan entered the industry and how the industry's ethnic character was influenced as a result by tracing shifts in the ethnic boundary lines that characterized such entry.

The community function continued to operate as it had in the past.[29] A closer examination of the actions of leading ethnic credit unions reveals that a noteworthy organizational initiative was being pursued more actively. Ethnic credit unions began working to strengthen networks of ethnic minority Korean entrepreneurs in Japan and dedicated resources to building platforms, for example by hosting lectures for businessmen or planning inter-company golf events that would allow members of the community to exchange business information in an autonomous manner. At the same time, such institutions provided information related to opening new businesses to entrepreneurs, including Koreans active in unrelated industries, while conducting business analyses of parlors in terms of location and other characteristics themselves. These efforts served to stimulate appetite for entering the parlor business, which was exploding due to the popularity of Fībā-type machines. Leading ethnic credit unions took information that had been propagated in an informal manner based on relationships between individuals and produced it on an organizational basis, accumulated it and circulated it. It goes without saying that the addition of credit unions into the mechanism of conventional network-based ethnic relationships brought a more systematic approach to the entry of new participants into the parlor business.

However, this approach was only partial in scope when seen from the standpoint of the entire community. The effectiveness of the initiative depended on the organizational capabilities of ethnic credit unions whose growth was driven by the large communities that formed in cities with large concentrations of ethnic minority Korean residents, for example Osaka. Moreover, these ethnic credit unions were all associations with limited funding ability, which meant that they were unable to meet the funding demands of growing companies and a pachinko industry that had become a huge market. As Fībā-type machines drove the business towards an operational format founded on large-scale chain development (see Chapter 5), ethnic credit unions had difficulty accommodating these changes.[30] Seen through the lens of the pachinko industry's size, the importance of the community function declined in terms of the quantity of industrial lending. As the size of initial investments and additional investment demand in the parlor business grew, it became essential for ethnic minority Koreans in Japan who were entering the business to procure financing from regular credit unions capable of providing sufficient funds.

In this way, in contrast to participation by ethnic minority Koreans, who were supported by functioning community resources (albeit ones that were running into limits), it was the high rate of growth exhibited by the pachinko industry that signaled business opportunity to people outside that community (Japanese society in general). That high rate of growth was presumably also the condition that triggered changes in business attitude on the part of the regular credit unions that were the providers of funds. We can speculate about the impact of these changing conditions on the ethnicity of the parlor business by estimating trends in origin from the membership rolls of the Tokyo Amusement Industry Cooperative.

However, the most useful clues from that list are surnames, so allow me to note at the outset that this analysis is subject to significant limits. Generally speaking, many ethnic minority Koreans in Japan adopt Japanese names for use personally or in business, making it difficult to infer accurate information from the member rolls. Moreover, the percentage of ethnic minority Koreans with Japanese names, or aliases that are counted as Japanese, may rise (or fall) over time. Since it is technologically impossible to address the latter issue, I will assume for the purpose of this analysis that the percentage of ethnic minority Koreans in Japan using Japanese names is generally constant.

Although I was unable to find any studies that offered insight into historical changes in the use of Japanese names, the results of a study in Kanagawa Prefecture in 1986 are of interest here as we examine periods on either side of the 1980s. According to that study, 3.5 percent of people used their real name only; 58.9 percent, both their real name and their Japanese name; and 37.0 percent, their Japanese name only.[31] Use of Japanese names reached 95.9 percent. The quality of the data in the cooperative's membership rolls will be affected by which name the roughly 60 percent of people who used both a Japanese name and their real name chose to use in business, specifically in the field of pachinko parlors. People applying for a parlor operating license from the Public Safety Commission had to use their real name, but there were no particular rules concerning the compilation of membership rolls,[32] and which name was used in the list was left up to the discretion of the individuals compiling it.

Since there is currently no way to control for this issue, I would like to focus not on the actual percentage of cooperative members who were of Korean ancestry, but rather on what kind of characteristic changes we can discover during the 1980s in terms of the trend in industry participation by groups with different ethnic origins.

Table Ess.1 summarizes my classification of the member list. I identified names consisting of three Chinese characters, which are often used by groups whose participation in the pachinko industry is discussed, for example ethnic minority Koreans and Chinese living in Japan.[33] I then separated those names into Japanese and non-Japanese groups and classified them as shown in the table. I used two categories (labeled '1' and '2' in the table) in order to minimize distortion in the tabulation when identifying ethnic origin based on surname-related information.

The percentage of non-Japanese based on real names as of 1975 as shown in Table Ess.2 was about 20 percent. It is not possible to detect 'invisible' Koreans who were counted as Japanese members due to their Japanese names.[34] This figure may seem low in contrast to the rumor quoted at the beginning of this essay, which claimed that 70 percent of the industry's parlors were run by non-Japanese, but the fact that a conservative estimate of Koreans' involvement in particular businesses and regions could reach 20 percent merits surprise given that ethnic minority Koreans accounted for about 0.5 percent of Japan's total population (or about 0.7 percent if naturalized individuals are included). That said, it is not possible to delve any further into the issue.

What I would particularly like to note with regard to Table Ess.2 is that both category 1, which overstates the number of Japanese, and category 2, which overstates the number of non-Japanese, fell during the 1980s. While the conclusion must be qualified by noting that we have excluded the common situation in which the trends concerning use of Japanese names change, the percentage of non-Japanese involved in the industry fell during the 1980s.

Classification method	(1) Korean	(2) Korean, Japanese, or Chinese and either Korean or Japanese	(3) Korean or Chinese	(4) Other (Chinese, etc.)
1	剛 Kang; 姜 Kang; 洪 Hong; 咸 Ham; 朴 Park; 全 Jeon; 尹 Yun; 権 Kwon; 權 Kwon; 閔 Min; 盧 Roh; 廖 Lyo; 裵 Bae; 任 Yim; 卞 Byun; 崔 Choi; 申 Shin; 丁 Chung; 金 Kim; 白 Baek	林 Yim in Korean or Hayashi in Japanese or Lin in Chinese (below, follows this order); 南 Nam or Minami or Nan; 柳 Yu or Yanagi or Liu; 張 Chang or Hari or Cheng; 辺 Byun or Hotori or Pien; 池 Chi or Ike or Chi; 元 Won or Gen, Hajime or Yuan; 安An or Yasu or An; 方 Bang or Kata or Fang; 史 Sa or Fuhito or Shih; 西 Seo or Nishi or Seo; 廉 Yeom or Ren or Lien; 梁 Yang or Yana or Liang; 劉 Yu or Ryu or Ryu; 成 Seong or Nari or Cheng; 文 Mun in Korean or Bun in Japanese, 河 Ha or Kawa, 金 Kim or Kon	荘Chang in Korean or Cheng in Chinese (below, follows this order); 馬 Ma; 陳 Jin or Chen; 羅 Na or Luo; 彭 Paeng or Peng; 蔣 Chang or Jiang; 李 Lee or Ly; 魏 Wi or Wei; 王 Wang; 韓 Han; 宋 Song; 孫 Son; 周 Ju or Zhou; 千 Cheon or Chien; 趙 Cho or Cao; 揚 Yang; 高 Ko or Gao; 呉 Oh or Wu; 徐 Seo or Xu; 鄭 Jeong or Zheng; 謝[e] Sa or Sha	顧 Gu; 戴 Dai; 傅 Fu; 詹 Zhan; 何 He; 柯 Ke; 苗 Miao; 繆 Mou; 泰 Tai
2	剛 Kang; 姜 Kang; 洪 Hong; 咸 Ham; 朴 Park; 全 Jeon; 尹 Yun; 権 Kwon; 權 Kwon; 閔 Min; 盧 Roh; 廖 Liao; 裵 Bae; 任 Yim; 卞 Byun; 崔 Choi; 申 Shin; 文 Moon; 元 Won; 方 Bang; 史 Sah; 西 Seo; 廉 Yeom; 劉 Ryu; 成 Sung; 丁 Chung; 金 Kim; 白 Baek; 河 Ha	林 Yim or Hayashi or Lin; 南 Nam or Minami or Nan; 柳 Yu or Yanagi or Liu	荘 Chang or Cheng; 馬 Ma; 陳 Jin or Luo; 羅 Na or Luo; 彭 Pang or Heng; 蔣 Chang or Jiang; 李 Lee or Ly; 魏 Wi or Wei; 王 Wang; 韓 Han; 宋 Song; 孫 Son; 周 Ju or Zhou; 千 Cheon or Chien; 趙 Cho or Cao; 鄭 Jeong or Zheng; 張 Chang or Cheng; 楊 Yang; 辺 Byun or Pien; 池 Chi or Chi; 安 An; 高 Go or Kao; 呉 Oh or Wu; 徐 Seo or Xu; 梁 Yang or Liang; 謝 Sa or Sha	顧 Gu; 戴 Dai; 傅 Fu; 詹 Zhan; 何 He; 柯 Ke; 苗 Miao; 繆 Tai; 泰 Tai

Table Ess.1: Surname classification

Notes:

a. Column (1) lists surnames known to be Korean, while column (2) lists surnames that could be either Korean, Japanese, or Chinese and either Korean or Japanese. Column (3) lists surnames that could be Korean or Chinese, and column (4) lists other surnames, for example those that are likely to be Chinese.

b. First classification method: I identified primarily three-character names that are common in Korea or China and consulted (a) '苗字由来net' (see http://ko.wikipedia.org/wiki/%ED%95%9C%EA%B5%AD%EC%9D%98_%EC%84%B1%EC%94%A8_%EB%AA%A9%EB%A1%9D#. E3. 84.B1" concerning Japanese names and (b) '한국의 성씨 목록' (an index of Korean surnames; see http://myoji-yurai.net/searchResult.htm?myojiKanji=%E6%9F%AF) concerning Korean names. Surnames not registered in (a) but found in (b) I classified as (1) Korean. (These classifications are based on the facts that there are more Koreans than Chinese in Japan and that the pachinko parlor is not necessarily primary business for Chinese. Because of this classification, [1] includes surnames also used in China, for example, 廖 and 任.) Surnames not found in (a) that could belong to East Asians in Japan (Chinese and Koreans), for example 池, I classified in group (2), along with surnames that could belong to Koreans in Japan, for example 文, and surnames that could be verified in both (a) and (b), for example 林 and 河. Surnames that could be verified in (a) but that were in common use by East Asians in Japan (Chinese and Koreans), for example 鄭, I classified as (3). Finally, surnames that were in common use by ethnic minority Koreans in Japan, for example 金, I classified as (1), and surnames that I was unable to find in (a) and (b) I placed in the 'Other' category.

c. Second classification method: Of the surnames assigned to category (2) above, I classified surnames that were in common use by Japanese but also used by ethnic minority Koreans in Japan as (1), while classifying surnames that were likely to belong to East Asians in Japan (Chinese and Koreans) as (3).

d. When a common name was noted, I determined the user to be an ethnic minority Korean and classified the name as (1).

e. I classified '謝' as (4) in the original Japanese edition but corrected it here.

Source: Compiled based on Tokyo Amusement Industry Cooperative Association (1975, 1982, 1988, 1993).

Classification 1		Origin				Total number of parlors
Fiscal year		(1) Korean	(2) Korean, Chinese or Japanese	(3) Korean or Chinese	(4) Chinese	Percentage of foreign operators
1975	The number of parlors	79	68	106	11	1,026
	Percentage of total parlors	7.7	6.6	10.3	1.1	19.1
1982	The number of parlors	64	41	64	9	899
	Percentage of total parlors	7.1	4.6	7.1	1.0	15.2
1988	The number of parlors	72	50	70	10	1,135
	Percentage of total parlors	6.3	4.4	6.2	0.9	13.4
1993	The number of parlors	91	61	86	11	1,509
	Percentage of total parlors	6.0	4.0	5.7	0.7	12.5

Classification 2		Origin				Total number of parlors
Fiscal year		(1) Korean	(2) Korean, Chinese or Japanese	(3) Korean or Chinese	(4) Chinese	Percentage of foreign operators
1975	The number of parlors	94	42	116	11	1,026
	Percentage of total parlors	9.2	4.1	11.3	1.1	21.5
1982	The number of parlors	70	28	68	10	899
	Percentage of total parlors	7.8	3.1	7.6	1.1	16.5
1988	The number of parlors	87	33	70	10	1,135
	Percentage of total parlors	7.7	2.9	6.2	0.9	14.7
1993	The number of parlors	108	48	81	11	1,509
	Percentage of total parlors	7.2	3.2	5.4	0.7	13.3

Table Ess.2: Percentage of foreign-operated parlors

Source: Compiled based on Tokyo Amusement Industry Cooperative Association (1975, 1982, 1988, 1993).

THE CHANGING SOCIAL ENVIRONMENT

The decline in the percentage of non-Japanese described in Table Ess.2 needs to be considered more carefully in light of its timing. Between 1975 and 1982, a recession drove many parlors out of business, and while the exact cause of the relative decline in the percentage of parlors run by non-Japanese remains unclear, numerous comparatively small parlors shuttered their businesses during this period (see Chapter 5). I will not delve any further here into how small parlors can be linked with the real names of ethnic minority Koreans in Japan as that issue demands a separate examination of both correlation and causality. In any case, it is likely that the entry into the market of Japanese (businesses) would only come once the market environment could be established in a more broad-based manner, as described below.

There was little active involvement of Japanese with the pachinko industry for many years due to the sector's 'dirty' image, for example in the form of questions concerning its association with organized crime in connection with the 1955 regulations. Since developments served to make it impossible for criminal groups to become involved as principal operators of businesses due to their exclusion from the licensing process by regional police (see Chapter 1), those groups' involvement with the industry proceeded primarily via protection money.[35] Although industry association-led campaigns to drive out organized crime began in some regions during the 1960s, those efforts did not succeed in completely excluding the groups.[36] We do not have a full picture of how protection money was paid by parlor businesses, but there were reports of changes that were seen as the outcome of such campaigns. According to a 1982 survey by the National Police Agency, criminal organizations nationwide peaked in 1963 before experiencing a decline, with the number of groups and members falling about 39 percent and 36 percent, respectively, from 1965 to 1982.[37] One factor contributing to that decline was anti-violence campaigns, which for example led pachinko associations and others to commit to breaking off relations with criminal groups. A series of incidents in which criminal groups whose source of funds had been cut off harassed parlors during the first half of the 1960s attest to the success of such initiatives.[38]

It was the enactment of the Act on Prevention of Unjust Acts by Organized Crime Group Members in 1992 that provided the opportunity for a nationwide severing of relations between such groups and parlor businesses. Efforts to ensure that unreasonable demands were rejected were undertaken more aggressively after that point, with the parlor industry forming an organization dedicated to driving out organized crime, parlors declaring that they would not pay protection money and posting notices in their businesses that criminal groups were not welcome, and the industry distributing 'compliance marks'.[39] A 1997 survey by the Tokyo Metropolitan Government reported that parlors continued to pay protection money but that those payments averaged a little less than 1 percent of parlor sales[40] suggesting that they were trending down. What these measures signify is that steps to address the industry's relationship with organized crime, which had been one cause of its negative social image and which had depended to that point on efforts by regional parlor associations and individual parlor businesses, were not being pursued in a more concerted manner in conjunction with government and industry entities, facilitating industry-wide improvements. It seems likely that this substantial weakening of the industry's relationship with organized crime operated in tandem with attention on its growth – including in comparison to other businesses – to accelerate the involvement of Japanese people. In this way, the participation during and after the 1990s of Japanese people (businesses) who recognized business opportunity augmented the effects of the sustained growth of businesses run by ethnic entrepreneurs such as Maruhan, which had developed in the midst of the industry's growth to that point. The result was a dilution of the industry's ethnic character.

Change visited the machine market as well. The number of machine manufacturers held steady at twenty (see Table 0.1) until the end of the 1980s. As a number of leading manufacturers began to be listed on the stock exchange at the end of the 1980s following growth during that decade, the Nittokuren, which had played a central role in facilitating mutually interdependent relationships among manufacturers (see chapters 2 and 3), was dissolved in 1999.[41] A series of new companies subsequently entered the machine manufacturing business.

CONCLUSION

Ethnic minority Koreans in Japan had important connections to the pachinko industry compared to other businesses. However, those connections must be understood as the product of an evolving, long-term process that was driven by complex interactions among a variety of elements. A more accurate understanding of the relationship reveals that it was governed by the historicity of environmental conditions and the nature of the ethnic community, and that it had the potential to change in response to conditions.

The intimate relationship between pachinko and ethnic minority Koreans in Japan goes further than the industry being a principal focus of the group's business activities. The relationship with a community function that provided support when members of the group, a key driver of the pachinko industry, entered the business, was also important. The fundamental reason driving ethnic minority Koreans' choice of the pachinko industry was the sector's growth, which served as a market signal, and it was the community that disseminated associated information. In that sense, the origins of the development of the pachinko industry as explored in this work were built into the industry as an internal mechanism, and the fact that the mechanism existed outside the community indicates that it actively responded by taking the industry's development as a given.

For individual parlor businesses run by ethnic minority Koreans, it was already essential during the 1970s to procure the resources (for example, funding) that were needed to drive growth such as chain development from outside the community.[42] This fact made it necessary to understand an increasing portion of the growth of companies involved with the pachinko industry in terms of continuity with regular economic society, rather than in terms of something that could be accomplished solely within a closed community. In light of that reality, we must exercise caution in our tendency to see the pachinko industry in relation to the procurement of resources such as funds as simply an ethnic minority Korean industry. That said, operation of individual parlors remained the core business model in the industry for a long period of time, and the ethnic minority Korean community in Japan served as a key foundation for the industry until factors such as the growth of ethnic credit unions and the associated accumulation of organizational information stimulated entry into the business.

Nonetheless, the rate at which the industry was growing exploded during the 1980s, and it became difficult for the economic growth of the community to keep pace. As noted above, the origins of the pachinko industry's development lay in connections with the technological development of a broad range of industries outside the ethnic minority Korean community. Faced by the burdens imposed by chain development, growth in parlor scale and capital investment, for example in the computerization of information management, parlors operated by ethnic minority Koreans in Japan turned increasingly, and ultimately decisively, to sources outside the community for funding and management resources. These conditions threw into relief the limits on the business creation and participation stage, where the ethnic minority Korean community had played an important role.[43]

The pachinko industry flourished, and the social environment in which pachinko existed changed in response. Market information and industrial finance broadened the range of ordinary companies entering the industry. Positive changes in how the industry was viewed by Japanese society were also a factor. These changes may seem like only unidirectional environmental changes to ethnic minority Koreans in Japan, but in fact they are more complex. The relationship between pachinko and ethnic minority Koreans is also influenced by the transformation of the community function – particularly in the condition of ethnic credit unions[44] – and by the range of choices available to the community in society. The result of that process is the dilution of the ethnic character of the pachinko industry. More than a matter of fate or inevitability, the relationship between that industry and ethnic minority Koreans in Japan evolved as a complex historical encounter.

Conclusion: The Black-box Industry

INTRODUCTION

The process by which pachinko was transformed from a marginal economy into a massive market was driven by the development of mechanisms of autonomy that empowered businesses (and the industry as a whole) to search for a means to achieve sufficient stabilization to continue operating.

In this context, 'stabilization' refers to the elimination of various elements that ran counter to the existence of those businesses (and the industry). It does not mean that the process removed competition, creating a set of static market conditions. Rather, controlling elements of instability consisted of endowing businesses (and the industry) with internal conditions that presumed market competition characterized the development of pachinko machines and the provision of services. In this sense, stabilization, more than anything else, became the foundation that made the long-term existence of the business (and industry) possible, providing the opportunity for dynamic change.

'Autonomy' here does not refer to the construction of a position that is completely free from regulation. Even if businesses accept a regulatory system as a given and with it, the fact that the system's rules impose certain restrictions on the strategic choices available to them, that system presumably offers them just enough space to bring their managerial efforts to bear in an autonomous manner. The enactment of the Entertainment Establishment Control Act after World War II classified the pachinko industry as a regulated industry and subjected it to governmental monitoring. Rather than establishing public regulations[1] deemed necessary to facilitate industrial and economic development, the act sought to improve social welfare by safeguarding youth and transforming entertainment businesses into a sound and wholesome segment of the economy.[2] Consequently, while the law recognized the industry's freedom to operate and the legitimacy of economic activities driven by market competition, the fundamental position of the regulations was presumably that the social problems attendant upon the development of the industry precluded the government from sitting idly by while it turned into a juggernaut. The fact that the pachinko industry continued to exist even as many other forms of entertainment and amusement rose and fell over time suggests that the growth of the industry into an enormous market did not progress in a planned and harmonious manner, but rather was accomplished through the pursuit of market competition within limited bounds. Embracing a perspective that recognizes the central importance of autonomous mechanisms means adopting a focus on the activities of businesses as they pursued market competition in this regulated environment, including the various factors that governed those activities.

In this book, I have sought to offer an internal understanding of the pachinko industry by elucidating mechanisms of autonomy and stabilization. Accounts of the pachinko industry have tended to repeat certain stylized formulations while lacking sufficient insight into actual conditions, leaving the pachinko industry something of a black box. If I have managed to present an account that diverges from those typical formulations on the development of a vaguely conceived pachinko industry, then perhaps this book will have made some small contribution as a work of history.

CHAPTER SUMMARIES

Focusing on the developments that have come to characterize each period in the history of pachinko throws certain issues that the industry has faced over time into sharp relief. Far from unfolding in the context of some master plan in which pachinko developed inexorably into a gigantic market, those problems must have prompted a sense of crisis at the time, even calling into question the industry's day-to-day viability. More than anything else, the instability of the business itself made the establishment of an independent industry a challenging and complicated proposition. What is more, the ease of discovering activities associated with the underground economy, for example the illegal exchange of prizes for cash and the attempted involvement of organized crime, prompted sharp social criticism of pachinko's potential to serve as a source of funds for such groups, putting regulatory authorities in a position where they were unable to ignore activities associated with the industry and their circumstances. The survival of the industry would not have been possible without solutions for these problems, which occurred as a division of labor evolved within the pachinko industry during the earliest phases of its development.

As analyzed in Chapter 1, during the 1950s, the industry's foundation was laid as the prospects for surmounting the initial obstacles that had to be overcome before pachinko could establish itself became clear. First, as it negotiated the requirements imposed by the Administrative Order Prohibiting Successive-shot Machines of 1955, the parlor business eventually arrived at a basis for continued operation that would allow it to escape an unstable revenue structure. Prior to those regulations, competition among businesses had been driven by the battle to develop machines with an ever-more pronounced speculative element as the popularity of successive-shot machines stimulated people's appetite for gambling and impacted both machine developers and the business activities of parlor operators. The actions of customers and businesses, which both demanded an ever-increasing speculative element, as well as the resulting destabilization of the parlor business, ultimately led to the end of that phase of the industry's history with the imposition of the successive-shot ban in 1955. As speculation was restricted by society in this way, parlors turned the accumulation of operational expertise around the practice of pin adjustment into a stable revenue base and brought an element of planning to bear on their operations.

The second opportunity that led to the survival of the industry was the discovery of the potential for institutionalizing the exchange of prizes in a way that precluded the involvement of organized crime. From the middle of the 1950s, the idea that led to the genesis of today's three-business system for prize exchanges was put into practice on an experimental basis around the country. The police, who wanted to exclude organized crime by unearthing flows of funds at risk of disappearing into the black market, offered guidance in some cases, and the new prize exchange system spread throughout the country from the 1960s. This change had two implications for the continued existence and development of pachinko. The first was that parlor owners, who were subject to strict policing of now-illegal prize exchanges, had to seek alternative sources of profit from the accumulation of operational expertise, for example by improving services. The second implication was related to the exclusion of people involved in organized crime and other undesirable groups from the process by which public safety commissions issued the certifications necessary for parlor and prize exchange operations. Those people were not necessarily seeking to operate parlor businesses, which makes it likely that there was little incentive for them to reinvest in profit-making businesses. The introduction of the three-business system may have served as an opportunity for reinvestment-minded individuals to take on responsibility for a key aspect of parlor operations.

However, the 1955 ban forced manufacturers to take a technological step backwards in terms of machine design, triggering significant changes in the competitive conditions under which they operated and bringing the pachinko industry face to face with a new problem. A rush by parlors to exit the business led to a surplus of machines, even as regulations increased development risk and the seasonality of production posed serious challenges for manufacturers. The sustained development of new machines so as to ensure customers would not lose interest was the key to the continued existence of pachinko, but underselling-based competition threatened manufacturers' operations. Shoring up the foundations of manufacturers' businesses would be critical if the nascent industry were to survive.

Following the 1955 regulations, the pachinko machine market, which was in a state of oversupply, saw average manufacturing costs augmented by the commodity tax and patent fees, making transactions difficult and threatening even leading manufacturers with an existential crisis. The industry was faced with the need to ensure that development-oriented manufacturers could operate in a viable manner, spurring the emergence of an institutional basis for restoring the market's competition-promoting function during the 1960s, as examined in Chapter 2. This institutionalization focused on restoring market pricing, and there was an urgent effort to build structures to monitor underselling that disregarded the commodity tax and patent fees as well as illegal imitation products that violated patents. The Japan Amusement Machine Industry Association, or Nikkōso, and the Japan Amusement Machine Patent Management Federation, or Nittokuren, played key roles in the development of rules governing tax and royalty payments as well as associated monitoring structures. The Nittokuren, whose shareholders consisted of Nikkōso members, brought discipline to manufacturers by mediating the licensing of patents while sharing information about machine manufacturing with the Nikkōso, which was responsible for providing guidance on tax payments. Members and non-members that violated the rules faced sanctions in the form of legal measures such as seizures based on patent rights. Order gradually returned to the market, and the conditions necessary for the ongoing creation of new machines were put in place.

Nonetheless, manufacturers had fallen prey to a siege mentality due to the strict limitations imposed on the scope of development by the 1955 regulations. The easing of regulations related to pachinko machine certification and changes to the patent system had the potential to revitalize development. How was that promise realized under the Nittokuren's patent management regime, and was the Nittokuren effective at exerting a moderate influence on manufacturers' development activities? This was the point at issue in Chapter 3. The patent management regime served to curtail patent disputes, royalties and monitoring costs. The resulting market environment fostered competition, which was accompanied by dizzying changes in market share rankings as leading manufacturers developed new machines and others played a game of catch-up by launching imitation models. The imposition of uniform, low-cost royalties did not undermine the motivation of development-oriented manufacturers.

In addition to boosting compliance because of low royalties, the licensing of patents to other companies subjected licensees (including companies that sought to follow in the wake of competitors by launching imitation products) to conditions that were disadvantageous, even if only slightly so. At the same time, they offered security in case the companies' relationship reversed in the future. What is noteworthy is that imitation by other companies served to reduce an equipment burden that was prone to become excessive due to the seasonality of production and the fickle vicissitudes of machine popularity. Active manufacturers could pursue development that stayed a step ahead of competitors in response to seasonal replacement demand while reaping the benefits of savings on equipment costs and then gain market share until other companies imitated them or followed in their footsteps. Manufacturers that bet on market expansion on the basis of the temporal advantages conferred by their lead in development were prone to embrace a development-centric approach. For their part, manufacturers that followed in the tracks of their development-oriented peers were given catch-up opportunities to boost their development and manufacturing technologies through imitation. Both first- and second-movers alleviated development risk and the burdens imposed by production equipment in light of both swings in popularity and regulations through the sharing of development and production with other companies, subject to the conditions imposed by the Nittokuren. The nature of such relationships, which reduced the uncertainty inherent in manufacturer operations, also functioned as flexible mechanisms that supported machine updates so that customers would not become bored (renewal reopenings by parlors), and the resulting fostering of development-based competition led to the appearance of Fībā-type machines during the 1970s.

If we take the establishment of a suitable business environment through the stabilization of parlors' and manufacturers' businesses and the institutionalization of prize exchanges as the yardstick against which the development of the pachinko industry ought to be measured, then the reproduction structures that allowed the pachinko industry to continue to exist had taken shape by the end of the long journey that lasted from the second half of the 1950s to the 1970s. Although the basis for the industry's development would be shaken by Fībā-type machines and subsequently fall behind the times, the new machine designs exploded onto the scene by fueling marked growth in the speculative element of play, transforming the structure of pachinko in society.

With the coming of the 1980s, what had passed as managerial expertise in the parlor business up until that time was pushed towards fundamental changes by the emergence of Fībā-type machines as verified in Chapter 4. In what sense, then, did conventional operational protocols stall?

Fībā-type machines spurred rapid market growth by bolstering the speculative element of play, making winning percentages more dependent on chance (as controlled by probability programmed into the machines) than on customers' skill. Although the reduction in the amount of requisite skill bolstered the potential ranks of customers, the increased speculative element provoked predictions that the industry might again experience gambling fever, as had previously occurred during the 1950s. For the parlor business, any return to the conditions of the 1950s threatened a reversion to the instability that had jeopardized the very survival of the industry. Yet Fībā-type machines, which were heavily dependent on probability, ultimately dampened fluctuations in sales and increased parlors' ability to plan their operations while reducing the role of experience-based pin adjustment. It turns out that the industry had achieved conspicuous market growth without hindering parlors' ability to conduct their business in a calculated manner. Some degree of gambling was accepted by society, and the general thrust of the changes brought by Fībā-type machines became well established in the industry.

Underneath the surface of pachinko's growth into an enormous market, the industry was also undergoing a series of irreversible internal changes. The one-to-one business relationships between parlors and manufacturers that governed machine purchases were becoming a thing of the past. Frequent purchases of machines by parlors from multiple makers turned out not to be merely an expedient necessitated by their desire to install Fībā-type machines, but rather became cemented in place as the new normal. Parlor operations that clung to traditional methods dependent on pin adjustment encountered limitations. Parlors began to search for new operational approaches that suited the intrinsic characteristics of Fībā-type machines even as they became more dependent on the machines themselves, which is to say, on the capabilities of capital rather than on pin adjustment, which had built a world where skill was king. The basis for the industry's reproduction structure, which had taken years to establish, ironically began to crumble from its very foundations even as it embarked on an era of dramatic growth thanks to Fībā-type machines, the product of that foundation and a development that might as well have been in answer to the industry's prayers.

How would the new approach that replaced traditional operations be put in place, and what possibilities would it offer the industry? As for this point at issue, as examined in Chapter 5, certainly, suburban parlors, the trend towards larger-scale operations and chain development had already begun to germinate, but from the 1980s these trends developed in new ways. A move toward larger parlors capitalized on the potential for probability-driven operations to make the parlor business more amenable to planning. The intensification of competition by new entrants into the business locked in that new direction. The move toward larger-scale operations also progressed through the development of chains of suburban parlors. First, the trend conferred advantages in terms of the economic benefits of parlors with large bases of installed machines as well as company-level advantages (company-scale economics) as chain development itself made it significantly easier to add locations.[3] Second, the trend towards larger-scale operations made parlors recognize that they needed to embrace information management as distinct from pin adjustment, which had been dominated by the operational expertise of pin adjusters (who inhabited a world where skill was king), leading parlors to accumulate a variety of information. More than anything else, this new type of information management would become the key to establishing competitive advantages in the coming era.

The changes in the machine market finally took center stage as the direction of parlor management (towards large-scale operations) driving the market manifested itself from the 1980s into the 1990s. Manufacturer relationships characterized by development and production-sharing were on the verge of complete collapse.

DISSOLUTION OF THE NITTOKUREN:
The End of an Era

In 1997, the Public Safety Commission applied Article 3 of the Act on Prohibition of Private Monopolization and Maintenance of Fair Trade ('Prohibition of Private Monopolization') as it was written at the time to ten leading manufacturers and the Nittokuren, which had formed a pool of pachinko machine patents, to bar restrictive licensing agreements after finding that 'a policy of excluding would-be competitors through combinations and collusion and restrictive licensing agreements based on the same had effectively limited competition'.[4] Two years after that recommended finding, in 1999, the defendants embarked on a voluntary dissolution of the Nittokuren.[5]

The case, which marked the first application of the Act on Prohibition of Private Monopolization and Maintenance of Fair Trade to a patent pool, has prompted a variety of legal analyses, criticism of the finding and questioning of associated factual findings.[6] The case hinged on developments after the 1980s, and the essential facts of the case as well as critical studies of the finding exceed the scope of the analysis presented in this work. Here I would like to focus on the fact that the Nittokuren ended up *being dissolved* despite the absence of any such recommendation in the Public Safety Commission's finding and place that development in historical context.

The central problem addressed by the finding was whether the defendants leveraged their ability to refuse to license patents as a means of interfering with attempts to enter the machine market by companies that manufactured automatic pachinko ball replenishment machines, which were used to automate parlors, and *pachislot* machines (Japanese-style slot machines about the same size as pachinko machines, as described in the Introduction). The finding went no further than certifying those actions as facts.[7] With the exception of a few cases, including when Sankyo became independent of Heiwa in 1966 (see Table 3.4), the period saw the first robust influx of new companies into the machine market since 1955. With the listing of a series of leading manufacturers on the stock exchange after the market's growth during the 1980s, the emergence of these new companies meant changes in the machine market likely reflected how society viewed pachinko.

First and foremost, the dissolution of the Nittokuren embodied a reassessment of patent management structures in the wake of the Public Safety Commission's recommendations. Documents submitted by people interviewed in the commission's investigation along with associated notes and memos suggest that differences in development capabilities among the ten leading companies addressed in the recommendation and other manufacturers had become conspicuous. Whereas members of the Nikkōso, which is to say, most pachinko machine manufacturers, were permitted to use the patents managed by the Nittokuren, the number of development-oriented manufacturers providing patents was limited (see Chapter 3). Consequently, action was called for to address the opposing interests of a small number of licensing companies and a large number of licensees during the 1970s. In light of the fact that licensing had been coordinated while maintaining existing manufacturer relationships at that point in time (see Chapter 3), one interpretation is that the complementary role played by other companies' production capabilities was emphasized. An empirical examination by Satoru Tanaka and Shuya Hayashi indicates that a structure characterized by unequal development capability continued to be maintained as of 2000.[8] The existence of manufacturers that played an active role in shouldering part of the industry's production capacity by leveraging advantages granted by the Nittokuren to become 'free riders' meant that it was difficult to eliminate differences in patent development capability. At the same time, royalties remained low. The dissolution of the Nittokuren can be seen as an attempt to address this asymmetrical balance of patent development capability.

However, we cannot conclude that there was a direct link between the differences in development capability and the dissolution of the Nittokuren because production structures based on the maintenance of the Nittokuren were found to have meaning under the approach of the 1970s, as described above. We must focus on actual business practices and equipment capacity, both of which impacted manufacturer relationships.

Chapters 2 and 3 described how manufacturers maintained relationships founded on the sharing of development and production work with other manufacturers with the support of the Nittokuren's functions, and during the 1970s, average annual production per manufacturer was about 39,567 machines.[9] This structure offered the incidental benefit of facilitating the monitoring function required by the nature of a regulated industry by placing other companies underneath the umbrella of the Nittokuren (because other companies' actions could invite regulation). Parlors replaced their machines two or three times a year and engaged in long-term transactions with a single (or a small number of) manufacturers in doing so. This approach was adopted because parlors' operational performance was influenced more by their pin adjustment expertise than by use of particular machines from particular manufacturers.

It is likely that the centrality of interdependent relationships in development and production gradually faded as the nature of transactions between parlors and manufacturers and of parlors' purchasing practices changed during the 1980s. Transactions with large numbers of manufacturers became standard, and replacement demand tended towards more frequent purchases of smaller numbers of machines due to parlors' renewal reopenings (see Chapter 4). At the same time, the average number of machines produced annually by manufacturers during the 1980s almost tripled from the level of the 1970s to 117,588 machines (9799 machines per month). Production volume continued to grow, with average annual production in the 1990s (from 1991 to 1997) reaching about 182,637 machines (15,220 machines per month), more than four times the level in the 1970s. Unlike the parlor segment of the industry, which saw a brisk succession of new companies, the number of manufacturers remained stable at twenty (see Figure 0.4), which meant that the rapidly growing market for pachinko machines starting in the 1980s was supplied entirely by increased utilization and expanded production capacity on the part of existing manufacturers.

The type of limited capital investment that prevailed until the 1970s was viable only to the extent that parlors' replacements of pachinko machines occurred *at predictable intervals* and that machine demand did not grow rapidly, and the imitation of other companies' products – industry-wide distribution of production capacity – was accepted within the scope of that approach. The potential for increasing market share until products were imitated by second-movers provided the basis on which development-oriented first-movers existed (see Chapter 3). Certainly, manufacturers were more keenly aware of the problem of tight supply during rapid growth in the 1980s because production capacity had been limited until that time. When parlors' operational methods changed as described below, market growth drove growth in the production capacity of individual companies, sending fissures through manufacturers' relationships.

As parlors expanded the number of machines they operated in order to achieve prize-ball percentages based on Fībā-type machines' probability, they more actively turned to the selection of a variety of machines (including through transactions with a large number of manufacturers) and to renewal reopenings as effective operational tactics. As a result, manufacturers lost some *stable, long-term customers* but gained opportunities for developing new markets, likely forcing them to react as described below.

The first change centered on development structures to accommodate demand for more frequent machine replacement. Acceptance of imitation products from other companies was part of a development strategy that unfolded over a limited period of time lasting only until the next replacement. As parlors' renewal reopenings became less regular (based on managerial objectives at individual parlor locations) and more frequent, the customary seasons on which conventional development structures were based became less well defined. The second change involved production and sales structures that took into account increased production capacity. Increases in production capacity across the industry robbed companies that shouldered part of the industry's production capacity by manufacturing niche imitation products.

Furthermore, as parlors shifted their business to a large number of manufacturers and as machine replacements came to consist of smaller, more frequent purchases, the conventional approach of increasing market share by developing individual parlors as customers must have prompted manufacturers – particularly development-oriented manufacturers – to perceive a lack of freedom across the board, from development to manufacturing and the recouping of costs through sales. Although it is impossible to paint a comprehensive picture of these changes, we can safely infer that, at a minimum, growth in production capacity and the transformation of business practices triggered a reexamination of conventional corporate relationships.

What, then, was the thinking behind the dissolution of the Nittokuren? The number of machines manufactured intensely fluctuated during the 1990s.[10] This upheaval suggests a number of possibilities. The market seemed to exhibit an increase in variables despite the growth in production capacity. Under these conditions, perhaps manufacturers were unable to accept imitation by competitors as they sought to maintain their expanded production equipment. The dissolution of the Nittokuren signaled that relationships with other companies in the market would be governed entirely by competition, and that individual companies would shoulder development risk as well as the burden of borderline-excessive production equipment capacity as two sides of the same coin. In other words, a structure in which competition unfolded in the context of the advantages of coexistence with other companies gave way to one in which competition forced companies to seek to drive competitors from the market. We can speculate that the risk of development targeting a shorter and more vaguely defined season as well as growth in production costs caused by small-scale supply may have pressured individual manufacturers to pursue an even higher level of rationalization.

Framed in light of changes in the nature of manufacturers' production and their business relationships with parlors, the voluntary dissolution of the Nittokuren during the second half of the 1990s can be seen as leading to the end of manufacturer relationships that maintained mutual dependence even as they encouraged competition under fundamental conditions provided by the Nittokuren. Structural changes to the framework that had long underpinned the development of the pachinko industry first emerged in parlor operations due to the declining importance of skill-based pin adjustment, but it was the dissolution of cooperative relationships between manufacturers that sounded the death knell for that arrangement. The dissolution of the Nittokuren can be seen as symbolic of the latter change. In this way, the pachinko industry marked the end of an era and embarked on a new journey that would expose its companies to a new type of competition.[11]

REGULATION AND THE DEVELOPMENT OF INDUSTRY

How should the significance of regulations be understood in the context of the pachinko industry's development into an enormous market? As I explained in the Introduction, in this work I have not limited the entities that drive regulation to public bodies, but rather have adopted a broader concept that includes the development of rules and organizations that govern the behavior of market players. I will offer some thoughts on regulation and the development of industry while focusing on a number of developments in the pachinko industry and their results.

First, regulation in the form of the prohibition order issued by the police in 1955 limited the speculative nature of pachinko, which had caused considerable instability in parlors' revenue bases. While regulation was the starting point in the industry's search for a stable revenue base, it did not directly lead to the industry's development. Rather, the important question to ask is: What difficulty facing the pachinko industry did regulation control? The answer throws into relief essential elements in the industry's formation. Pin adjustment based on skilled techniques was not able to control the factors that triggered instability in the parlor business at the time (inconsistent quality [technological problems] caused by machine materials and household-based handicraft manufacturing, as well as conspicuously speculative play and the competition that encouraged it), and neither customers nor parlors were able to stop the excessive inclination toward speculative play. Although it was an external shock in the form of regulations that eliminated a composite series of unstable elements, the transformation into a business that was amenable to planning through the securement of a stable revenue base was made possible by the accumulation of managerial expertise once the speculative element had been brought under control. Regulation established the preconditions needed to enable the accumulation of expertise for creating profit on a sustained basis in parlor operations. At the same time, regulation subjected the machine market to conditions that differed from the parlor business.

Second, confusion brought on by the underselling of machines – a problem that was prevalent enough that it would be difficult to claim that the market's competition-encouraging function was operating properly – was assuaged by regulation in the broad sense of the term, through manufacturer initiatives, which is to say, through self-regulation and institutionalization on the part of businesses. Pursued against the backdrop of postwar structures that prohibited direct controls on prices through the Act on Prohibition of Private Monopolization and Maintenance of Fair Trade, institutionalization was subject to limits on its attempt to restore appropriate pricing. That said, the Nittokuren enjoyed some measure of success in restoring order to the market by imposing rules that governed underselling through non-payment of the commodity tax and unauthorized duplication, bringing discipline to market players and expelling non-members that violated those rules. The market's competition-promoting functionality was not an unconditional given in the formation and development of the industry. In order to facilitate competition that progresses based on various elements inherent in the business, rather than opportunistic competition that is removed from the actual state of goods and services, it is essential to accumulate management resources related to development capabilities and production technologies. Market order (regulation) had to be achieved once such corporate activity had been realized.

Previously, Juro Hashimoto and Haruhito Takeda used partial adjustment of market mechanisms as an approach for understanding cartels.[12] That approach revealed that limiting price competition through agreements did not usher in a state that brought a halt to competition. Even if the price aspect of competition is limited, businesses can take steps to increase profit while taking pricing as a given by intensively investing resources in a specific arena of competition, for example quality or cost.[13] It is likely that a similar principle was at work in the pachinko machine market. In other words, even if conspicuous price competition was limited by regulation and patents, businesses were able – indeed, all the more so because of those circumstances – to focus their resources on original and ingenious ways to attract customers. Even if we acknowledge the existence of companies that got a free ride, development-based competition among manufacturers was possible precisely as a result of the order and foundation the industry gained.

Insofar as regulations imparted a particular direction to manufacturers' development activities, it is necessary to examine the nature of the order they imposed, which brings me to my third point. The fundamental motivation behind police regulations was to limit the speculative character of play, and there was always the possibility that those regulations would change in sudden and unexpected ways due to tension in the industry's relationship with society. To that extent, such regulations increased development risk and posed obstacles to latent, would-be entrants. Regarding this point, regulations had two contradictory impacts. One made the accumulation of development information by existing manufacturers advantageous. The other prompted changes in the conditions of competition through sudden regulation and deregulation so as to render the advantageous position of existing manufacturers meaningless and offer other companies opportunities to secure new status. This tendency can be seen in the change in Masamura Shōkai's position following the regulations of 1955, in market conditions following deregulation in 1969 and in the emergence of digital pachinko after 1980.

The fourth point that deserves our attention is related to the fact that regulations on machine development clarified particular constraints. Because regulations clarified objectives that had to be overcome, they concentrated the investment of resources in a comparatively narrow range. Following the 1955 ban on successive-shot machines, manufacturers focused all of their abilities on attracting the interest of pachinko-playing customers within a narrowly defined range; as has often been pointed out, the relaxation of regulations on machines led to the elaboration of new technologies and designs, of which the Fībā is the prototypical example. If this aspect is emphasized, we find that regulations do not necessarily restrict the industry in a unilateral manner, but rather also hold the potential to function as a source of breakthroughs in machine development and dynamic technological progress.

BETWEEN MASAMURA SHŌKAI AND MARUHAN

There is no need to directly compare Masamura Shōkai's operation of a single parlor (see Chapter 4) with Maruhan's 300 locations, the most in the industry (see Chapter 5). Chains of large, suburban parlors are not the only option: Masamura Shōkai parlors put down their roots in locations close to subway stations and shopping districts and provided a service more closely connected to customers' lifestyles until 2010. Urban and neighborhood parlors with favorable locations presumably drew on their own, unique base, one that allowed them to exist on a standalone basis for many years. The following example offers useful material for considering the differences between the two alternatives.

Around 1991, at about the same time Masamura Shōkai at last embarked upon a renewal reopening after grappling with the limits of its management approach, a representative of the Garden Group resolved to transform his business from a family-managed enterprise into a corporation, specifically from a single parlor into a chain business.[14] The representative, an ethnic minority Korean in Japan who had graduated from Meiji University, a leading private university in Tokyo, had taken over his parlor from his father and placed it on a sound business trajectory. The turning point came in the form of information indicating that a larger parlor was going to open two new locations in the vicinity of Kita-Urawa Station, which is located in a residential area in the greater Tokyo area, where his parlor as well as four others were located. The owner's decision, itself the result of a struggle to conceive a way to deal with intensifying competition, was the start of a series of reforms to ensure survival by establishing a number of parlors and becoming a leading company in the industry. Considered against the backdrop of developments in the industry, the transformation envisioned by Garden Group's strategy was by no means ahead of its time.

At the time he made the decision to change strategies, the owner did not realize he would have to overcome many obstacles before he could implement the chain approach. His first step was to hire employees who could operate multiple parlors, but it was only later that he realized there was a need to create a philosophy to guide employees' efforts before deciding on that direction. Building an organization whose capabilities included sales and financial functions was an urgent priority for the company, and the strategic shift would require buy-ins from existing employees as well as changes in their relationship to the company, which in turn would require education. Given social conditions at the time, characterized as an aversion toward working in the pachinko industry, it was by no means a simple thing to hire the human resources needed by a parlor operator from the general labor market, and at first the owner relied on a series of persistent attempts to convince prospective hires through his connections. In the absence of key people who would respond favorably to such a challenging initiative, the project could not advance to the next stage. Obtaining funding proved to be particularly difficult. The existing parlor had a successful track record as well as a relationship with a credit union, from which it had primarily borrowed working capital. In order to procure the funds necessary to open a second parlor, it would be essential to obtain financing from financial institutions lying upstream from the credit union, for example *shinkin* banks, which generally are larger and serve a more varied scope of businesses than credit unions, or regional banks. Obtaining financing from powerful financial institutions was no simple task, and the owner had to start doing business with them by utilizing family members' names to open seven accounts, for example accounts for the existing parlor, at regional banks and *shinkin* banks. The list of challenges went on.

The process from the time the Garden Group embraced the chain development approach until it achieved stable operations illustrates just how difficult it was to take advantage of the opportunities posed by market growth after the appearance of Fībā-type machines and how different the businesses that emerged once those obstacles were overcome were. As of December 31, 2016, the Garden Group employed 1150 employees (including part-time workers) at thirty parlors, which generated sales of 110 billion yen (about US$1 billion).

The final question remaining is the link between the narrative about ethnic minority Koreans in Japan and the pachinko industry, as raised in the Introduction of this book. An examination of the industries in which companies run by Koreans in Japan are active reveals that the principal sectors are civil engineering and construction; Kyoto-style *yuzen* dyeing and the manufacture of *nishijin*-style brocade, both used in kimonos; *yakiniku* restaurants; and synthetic footwear manufacturing in Kobe's Shinnagata Ward.[15] That said, with the exception of attention to cultural factors based on *yakiniku* restaurants, almost no sources discuss these businesses from that standpoint. Naturally, companies run by ethnic minority Koreans in Japan have been concentrated in fields that are typically characterized by the involvement of foreigners, for example harsh processes entailing steaming and washing with water in the case of *yuzen* dyeing. However, none is understood with as persistently negative a bias as pachinko parlors, including *yakiniku* restaurants.

The association between the pachinko industry and ethnic minority Koreans in Japan formed against the backdrop of the positions that both historically had to shoulder in Japanese society, and that connection is perhaps best understood as a result of the confluence of respective negative images that developed in different contexts. The strength of the influence of the pachinko industry, which far outpaced other industries in terms of the duration of its growth and the geographic expansion of its market, worked to spread the perception of the link with ethnic minority Koreans in Japan until it permeated every corner of society.

The dilution of the 'ethnicity' of the pachinko industry as examined in the essay does not refer only to the decline in the standing of companies run by ethnic minority Koreans in Japan due to growth in the number of companies run by Japanese, or to an attenuation of that ethnicity. The stabilization that Masamura Shōkai parlors achieved in their business, the transformation of the Garden Group, the nature of Maruhan's growth-oriented management and the historical process that led to the development of an enormous market, which I have attempted to describe in this work, by no means constitute a special story insofar as the same areas of focus explicated here can be applied to the development of other industries and the growth of other companies (for example institutionalization, business stabilization, the nature of market competition and technological innovation). When the growth of pachinko into a huge market is seen not as the result of growth in the underground economy, but rather as a natural development of the activities of businesses that wished to move out of the peripheral economy so that they could continue to operate over the long term, we find a narrative that diverges from twin negative stereotypes about the pachinko industry and ethnic minority Koreans in Japan. The dilution of ethnicity, then, ought to prompt us to question conventional images and move beyond them to examine the true nature of the industry.

Although it lies along the trajectory of this work, an examination of the conditions now faced by this enormous market comprises another tale, and a topic for future examination.

Appendix 1: Effectiveness of Renewal Reopenings

As I mentioned in Chapter 4, *shinsōkaiten* (renewal reopening) is a well-known and unique method in Japan for parlors to prevent customers from getting bored with machines. 'Renewal reopening' refers to a parlor's resumption of operations with new models after replacing some of its machines. Here I will focus on renewal reopenings as a technique that made it possible to control profitability and examine its effectiveness.

Masamura Shōkai has retained data (sales, operating hours, customer headcounts, balls sold, total prize value, sales per machine, gross margin, etc.) for another parlor, which I refer to here as 'Parlor C'. While the name of Parlor C, its location and its relationship with Masamura Shōkai remain unknown, we are fortunate that its more detailed data makes it possible to ascertain valuable information about conditions at the time, for example customer headcounts, and the effectiveness of various measures. Based on the sales per machine and total sales data, the parlor seems to have had 202 machines.

Figure App.1.1 illustrates Parlor C's average monthly sales and gross profit margin from November 1982 to April 1985. The long-term decline in sales as part of the same trend exhibited by the M.S. parlor's financial data can be understood as the effect of changes to machine specifications, regulations such as limits on the number of machines that parlors could operate and an influx of new businesses into the market. That the gross profit margin as shown in Figure App.1.1 grew or held steady illustrates the parlor's concerted effort to maintain profit in the face of gradually declining sales (an average of 10.8 percent in November and December 1982, 24.3 percent from January to June 1983, 29.5 percent from July to December 1983, 29.7 percent from January to June 1984, 28.0 percent from July to December 1984 and 31.1 percent from January to April 1985).

How was this accomplished? Let us focus on the periods when the gross profit margin fell significantly: November 1982, March 1983, October 1983 and October 1984. These periods include closures of the parlor, likely to accommodate machine replacements, and the change in business performance is apparent after a striking increase in prize-ball percentages. It is likely that renewal reopenings occurred at those points in time.

November 1982 differed from the renewal reopenings of 1983 and 1984 in that high prize-ball percentages (negative gross profit margins) imposed losses on the parlor on eleven of the month's twenty-seven business days, and in that those days were distributed throughout the month (including November 1, 2, 5, 6, 7, 10, 11, 13,

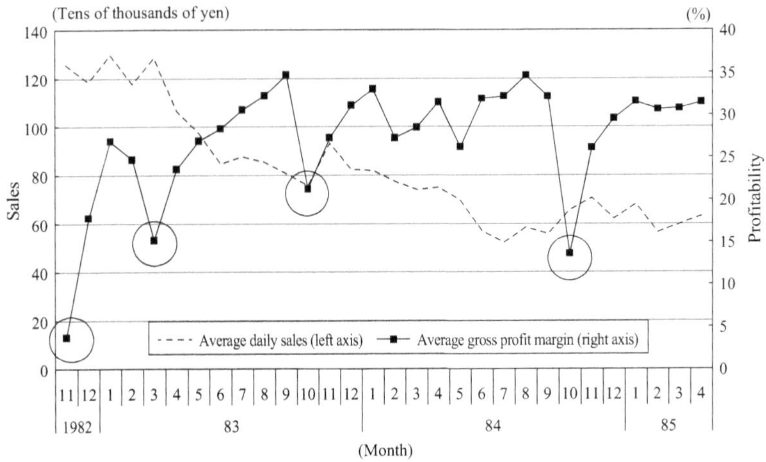

Figure App.1.1: Parlor C sales (monthly average) (November 1982 to April 1985)
Note: Gross profit margin = Gross profit / sales.
*Source: Compiled based on business results statistics tables (*eigyō jisseki tōkeihyō*) for November 1982 to April 1985.*

17, 19 and 23; data for November 1982 is from the parlor's business results statistical tables [*eigyō jisseki tōkeihyō*]). Although it is difficult to directly measure the effects of the increased prize-ball percentages during that month since the trend to that point is unknown, the fact that sales during the period were higher than those after April 1983 suggests that the underlying intention was something other than improving sales. March 1983 can be thought of as an extension of the trajectory established in November, so it makes sense to examine October 1983 and October 1984 first.

Figures App.1.2 and App.1.3 illustrate gross profit margin, prize-ball percentages and hourly sales before and after the service periods for October 1983 and October 1984. Looking at the end of October 1983 (Figure App.1.2), we find that sales from October 1 to 24, a period during which sales had declined from the previous year, averaged 778,955 yen (about US$3280) per day, only about 60 percent of the 1,257,063-yen (about US$5047) sales figure for the corresponding period for November 1982, about one year prior. The gross profit margin ranged from negative 70 percent to 20 percent during the three-day period from October 26 to 28 following the parlor's closure on October 25 as a result of shorter business hours (three, four and 5.4 hours) and of prize-ball percentages around 200 percent. Sales per hour during the period rose by a factor of 1.7 to 105,759 yen (about US$455) from the corresponding figure for October 1 to 24 – 61,822 yen (about US$266). The parlor returned to normal operation at about twelve hours per day from October 29 to 31 but continued to dispense large quantities of balls by leaving

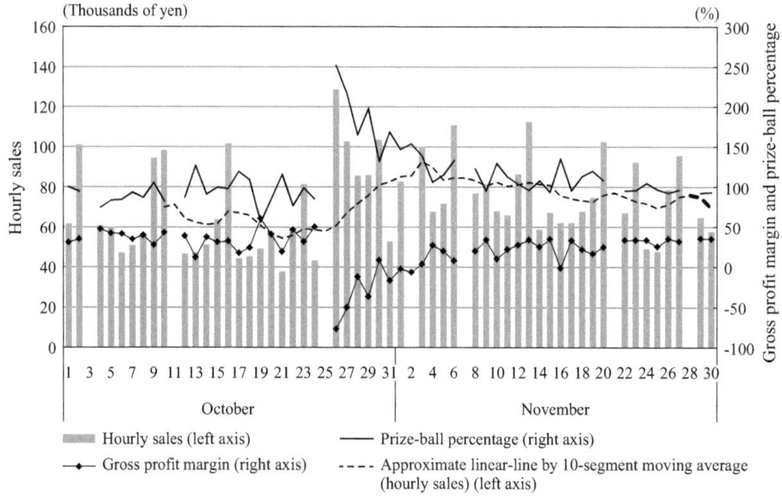

Figure App.1.2: Parlor C renewal reopening (October 1983)
Source: Same as Figure App.1.1.

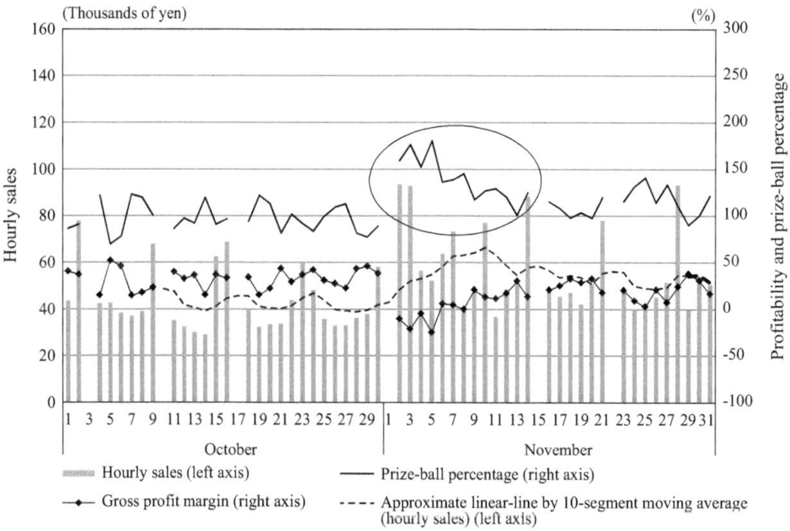

Figure App.1.3: Parlor C renewal reopening (October 1984)
Source: Same as Figure App.1.1.

the prize-ball percentage high at 130 to 190 percent. As a result, the gross profit margins on those days were minus 36.9 percent, 8.5 percent and minus 17.1 percent. As we enter November following this 'service' period from October 26 to 31, sales

	Profitability (%)	Average spending per customer (yen)	Hourly sales (yen)	Prize-ball percentage (%)	Customer headcount per day
March 4, 5 and 7, 1983					
February 1 to March 3	25.0	2,447	94,200	108.0	484.4
During complimentary ball dispensation period	-5.8	2,427	144,236	154.5	Unknown
March 8 to March 31	17.8	2,466	102,105	118.8	519.5
Rate of change	0.71	1.01	1.08	1.10	1.07
October 26 to November 2, 1983					
	Profitability (%)	Average spending per customer (yen)	Hourly sales (yen)	Prize-ball percentage (%)	Customer headcount per day
October 1 to 25	35.5	2,798	61,821	93.5	279.4
During complimentary ball dispensation period	-24.3	1,663	91,800	179.2	Unknown
November 3 to 30	24.9	2,144	75,665	108.0	443.4
Rate of change	0.70	0.77	1.22	1.15	1.59
October 2 to 8, 1984					
	Profitability (%)	Average spending per customer (yen)	Hourly sales (yen)	Prize-ball percentage (%)	Customer headcount per day
September 1 to 30	32.2	1,939	43,397	97.1	291.8
During complimentary ball dispensation period	-7.4	1,731	67,360	155.5	Unknown
October 9 to 31	20.6	1,974	53,511	115.0	347.3
Rate of change	0.64	1.02	1.23	1.18	1.19

Table App.1.1: Effects of Parlor C's renewal reopenings
Source: Same as Figure App.1.1.

per day (which averaged 932,652 yen, about US$4020) and sales per unit time both show improvement. The parlor tried to break out of a period of declining sales, and its efforts delivered results. Roughly similar measures to attract customers, for example significantly raising prize-ball percentages, can be seen in early October 1984, although they differed in degree.

Let us examine the effects of the renewal reopenings of March 1983, October 1983 and October 1984 based on the overview of 'service' periods provided above. Table App.1.1 offers a number of indicators that provide a basis for comparison. The table provides average figures for each indicator during the month before and after each renewal reopening in order to indicate the impact of the machine replacements. Examining the figures requires a degree of caution since the reopening periods differed, as did the magnitudes of the associated prize-ball percentages. That said, the improvement in hourly sales across the renewal reopenings emerges as a common characteristic. The direct cause of that improvement was likely growth in customer headcounts. Complimentary ball dispensation caused by higher prize-ball percentages presumably drove that increase.

However, in the case of March 1983, the difference in prize-ball percentages before and during the renewal reopening was about fifty points, which was less than the approximately eighty-five-point difference the following October and the approximately eighty-seven-point difference in October 1984, suggesting that customer perceptions of a complimentary period of increased winnings were relatively weaker at that time. As a result, the increase in customer headcount was negligible, and the rate of change in other parameters was not particularly clear. Potential factors include a failure in the choice of machines, the effects of competition with nearby parlors and problems that might lead the parlor to hesitate to orchestrate a bold increase in the prize-ball percentage (for example, funding problems). In any case, that particular renewal reopening was comparatively low-key in light of subsequent business conditions and customer headcounts, so it may be that the parlor was primarily concerned with eliminating customer boredom with machines, rather than offering a bold 'service' period of complimentary winnings.

It is likely that the 'service' of March 1983, which suggests a sense of confidence and strength on the part of the parlor, reflects conditions prior to the subsequent decline in sales and ramped-up competition. By contrast, the parlor orchestrated a bold 'service' period at the end of October 1983. The move likely represents an experiment based on the striking decline in sales and the abrupt drop-off in customer headcount compared to about one year prior. Judged in terms of the improvement it yielded in sales per unit time and customer headcount, the measure resulted in substantial business benefits. The growth in customer headcount was particularly prominent, which suggests the aim of the period and indeed the action helped compensate for the decrease in average spending per customer.

Slight differences are apparent in the renewal reopening of October 1984, which was held against the backdrop of a further downturn in sales. Although the parlor had been successful in securing profits through a slight increase in average spending per customer, and while it had benefited from its efforts to increase customer headcount, there were limits to its ability to reverse the trend toward lower sales. The reopening suggests that the unfavorable conditions in which Parlor C was operating, for example the intensification of competition, weighed heavily on its performance, spurring ongoing changes in the nature and effects of renewal reopenings. How the parlor subsequently fared remains unknown.

In any case, we can conclude that the 'service' periods of complimentary winnings seen during renewal reopenings had short-term effects. Adoption of such measures explains how Masamura Shōkai was able to avoid a significant decline in profitability even as it accepted the trend toward falling sales that began during the second half of 1983 (see Figure 4.3 in Chapter 4). It is not difficult to imagine how new machines and higher prize-ball percentages kept customers from becoming bored. Competition in terms of 'service' periods of higher winnings between parlors, then, offered customers increased choices among multiple parlors, which helped prevent the industry from losing its overall appeal.

Appendix 2: Did the Introduction of Fībā-type Machines Increase Parlor Sales Variance?

DATA USED

Drawing daily sales data from a pachinko parlor (over the period from August 1, 1969, to April 30, 1986), I extracted statistics for the thirty-one months before and after the April 1981 switchover to Fībā-type machines (period prior to the introduction of Fībā-type machines: September 1, 1978, to March 31, 1981; period following the introduction of Fībā-type machines: May 1, 1981, to December 31, 1983). I then used the coefficients of variation, which I calculated by dividing the standard deviation for monthly sales by the average monthly sales, to test the proposition (see Tables App.2.3 and App.2.4).

TEST METHOD

If the coefficients of variation after the introduction of Fībā-type machines are smaller than before the introduction, we can conclude that the introduction reduced variance in sales. Consequently, I used the difference in the population mean for coefficients of variation before and after the introduction to test the proposition.

A Shapiro-Wilk test yielded W and p values of 0.976 and 0.701, respectively, prior to the introduction, compared to W and p values of 0.936 and 0.064, respectively, after the introduction, indicating the normality of both distributions. Additionally, an F test of both distributions indicated a significant difference ($p = 0.004 < 0.05$). As a result, I used a Welch t-test.

TEST RESULTS

I performed a one-sided test with a null hypothesis stating that the average coefficient of variation prior to the introduction of Fībā-type machines was equal to the corresponding figure after the introduction. The results indicated a significant difference ($p = 1.113 \times 10 - 5 < 0.001$), as indicated in Table App.2.2. Consequently, because coefficients of variation declined after the introduction, we can conclude that the introduction of Fībā-type machines reduced variance in pachinko parlor sales.

	Before introduction	After introduction
Average	2.086×10–1	1.694×10–1
Unbiased variance	5.925×10–4	1.591×10–3
No. of observations	31	31

Table App.2.1: Coefficients of variation before and after the introduction of Fībā-type machines

t-value	4.679
Degree of freedom	50
p-value	1.113×10–5

Table App.2.2: Result of the Welch t-test

Fiscal year	Month	Average daily sales	Max. value	Min. value	Standard deviation	Coefficient of variation (Standard deviation / average)
1978	9	765,378	1,204,600	497,800	178,032	0.2326
	10	663,825	1,045,700	488,000	138,241	0.2082
	11	621,230	807,500	475,800	98,263	0.1582
	12	560,264	865,100	402,200	99,336	0.1773
1979	1	608,879	851,500	412,700	132,164	0.2171
	2	617,112	896,700	418,900	126,171	0.2045
	3	664,950	1,061,000	432,500	144,092	0.2167
	4	675,841	953,100	490,700	128,110	0.1896
	5	659,204	1,002,400	486,000	137,548	0.2087
	6	613,489	912,200	411,900	118,217	0.1927
	7	593,104	846,700	420,100	113,869	0.1920
	8	597,775	850,800	447,700	113,398	0.1897
	9	563,019	803,400	409,000	118,016	0.2096
	10	558,875	878,100	315,800	125,812	0.2251
	11	684,419	984,300	533,200	118,803	0.1736
	12	673,250	1,067,100	445,900	159,408	0.2368
1980	1	588,379	851,200	397,200	121,443	0.2064
	2	577,077	798,900	432,300	116,136	0.2012
	3	549,989	799,400	424,700	104,827	0.1906
	4	556,493	764,200	418,100	106,015	0.1905
	5	543,946	888,000	392,500	136,545	0.2510
	6	533,267	834,800	332,900	141,710	0.2657
	7	493,336	754,500	357,000	103,786	0.2104
	8	487,004	709,700	299,500	109,233	0.2243
	9	377,940	533,000	220,900	91,861	0.2431
	10	1,008,118	1,497,900	554,800	252,722	0.2507
	11	1,052,341	1,477,600	590,000	209,604	0.1992
	12	891,668	1,264,900	366,500	176,311	0.1977
1981	1	1,034,682	1,436,100	702,500	226,491	0.2189
	2	1,050,300	1,481,700	800,900	192,349	0.1831
	3	978,693	1,384,200	615,100	198,287	0.2026

Table App.2.3: Before the introduction of Fībā-type machines

Fiscal year	Month	Average daily sales	Max. value	Min. value	Standard deviation	Coefficient of variation (Standard deviation / average)
1981	5	1,719,221	2,408,400	1,296,000	316,364	0.1840
	6	2,141,331	3,015,100	1,595,400	408,733	0.1909
	7	2,176,568	2,911,000	1,648,000	364,743	0.1676
	8	2,188,375	2,980,400	1,531,200	368,275	0.1683
	9	1,921,900	2,688,300	1,302,300	368,231	0.1916
	10	1,595,104	2,388,300	1,141,800	315,194	0.1976
	11	1,690,607	2,732,000	728,800	426,155	0.2521
	12	2,152,725	2,770,300	1,729,600	354,571	0.1647
1982	1	2,364,039	3,218,600	1,852,700	355,272	0.1503
	2	2,299,344	2,941,500	1,705,900	369,959	0.1609
	3	2,416,218	3,597,500	958,700	505,092	0.2090
	4	2,746,052	3,582,500	2,001,700	413,524	0.1506
	5	2,385,800	3,059,800	1,826,600	371,023	0.1555
	6	2,337,667	3,218,100	966,100	474,256	0.2029
	7	2,758,264	3,400,300	2,225,400	293,257	0.1063
	8	2,711,396	3,410,700	2,122,000	313,140	0.1155
	9	2,476,496	3,150,500	1,801,500	353,884	0.1429
	10	2,449,864	3,872,700	1,459,000	613,082	0.2503
	11	2,908,448	3,804,600	2,395,000	446,241	0.1534
	12	2,819,182	3,711,200	2,043,200	437,566	0.1552
1983	1	2,978,396	3,948,700	2,301,700	477,113	0.1602
	2	2,711,344	3,453,700	2,096,400	364,234	0.1343
	3	2,706,404	3,918,300	1,245,800	499,975	0.1847
	4	3,045,578	3,916,200	2,332,200	380,153	0.1248
	5	3,001,546	3,835,100	2,433,800	401,830	0.1339
	7	4,279,100	6,051,700	969,400	1,154,119	0.2697
	8	4,691,014	6,140,300	3,581,200	606,982	0.1294
	9	4,605,667	5,931,200	3,605,600	686,223	0.1490
	10	4,288,121	5,348,300	3,059,500	603,903	0.1408
	11	3,980,896	5,599,700	1,605,500	854,506	0.2147
	12	3,969,732	5,182,300	3,050,800	552,489	0.1392

Table App.2.4: After the introduction of Fībā-type machines

*Source: Compiled by Hiroto Suzuki (Josai International University, Faculty of Management and Information Sciences); Compiled based on breakdown of daily sales and purchases from prize suppliers from August 1969 to April 1986 as detailed in Parlor M's general ledger (*motochō*).*

Appendix 3: Effects of Chain Development by Maruhan around the Early 1990s

Let us examine the effects of chain development by surveying operating conditions at all Maruhan parlors at the beginning of the 1990s. Those effects include, in terms of managerial expertise, the accumulation of various lessons in the course of comparing and analyzing parlors' operating results and the stabilization of structures capable on a companywide level of absorbing investments borne for a certain period of time, for example when new parlors or parlors opening after renovations (such as an expansion) offer a jackpot service. These effects are consistent with the expected effects listed in Table 5.6 in Chapter 5: competition among locations, accumulation of information as well as profit stabilization and other measures of performance on a companywide level.

RATIONALITY OF REGIONAL CONCENTRATION

Table App.3.1 summarizes the operating status and opening information for parlors run by Maruhan from October 1990 to November 1992. The sources on which the table is based – lists of sales for all parlors – were compiled by parlors on a monthly basis, for example for October 1990 and November 1992, and sent to head office for tabulation. These sources include the site name, sales, prize value, prize-sale rate, payments (including as a percentage of sales), gross margin (including as a percentage of sales), sales per machine (and rank), gross margin per machine (and rank) and utilization (after February 1992).

Using that data, I calculated the monthly average operating results for twenty-six months by parlor, estimated the number of machines (sales / sales per machine) and calculated the prize discount rate (the rate at which prize balls were exchanged for prizes). Table App.3.1 summarizes the results of those calculations. The rightmost column in the table indicates whether the parlor in question staged a renewal reopening or a new opening. Average values for corresponding parlors are calculated using data after their opening. It is unclear how the information in the table was used, or how it drove feedback regarding each parlor's operations. That said, the underlying intention of comparing parlors is clear given that results are recorded in units, for example sales or gross margin per machine, that allow comparison, and that results are ranked.

First, we can see that Maruhan developed its parlors in a concentrated manner (in a specific region). Table App.3.1 roughly reproduces the categories used in the original sources and summarizes them by region; of the total of thirty-six parlors, more than half (twenty) were located in Shizuoka Prefecture between Tokyo and Osaka. Parlor numbers were based on the year in which each was established. If we trace those numbers back to the beginning, we find that the first parlor opened in Kyoto Prefecture, followed by additional locations in the adjacent prefectures of Osaka and Hyogo, which signaled an expansion but nonetheless stayed within the confines of western Japan. During the active push to open new parlors that began in 1986, parlors after the ninth parlor were concentrated in Shizuoka Prefecture, even as those in western Japan centered on Hyogo Prefecture. Parlors in these two regions account for about 85 percent of the total, and we can conclude that the regional centralization was intentional.

Regarding the aim of this approach to parlor development, the accumulation of region-related information (indicated by a solid circle, ●) stands out among the effects related to managerial streamlining pointed out in Table 5.6 in Chapter 5. A number of factors are likely to have been responsible for this regional concentration. First, there were systematic influences. Until 1985, when the Entertainment Establishment Control Act, which took effect in 1948 (amended to become the Entertainment and Amusement Establishment Control Act in 1959), underwent major changes in the form of the Act on Control and Improvement of the Amusement Business, etc., purchases by parlors differed by region because only machines from manufacturers that had been licensed by each prefecture's public safety commission could be sold in that region.[1] The regional decentralization of parlors undermined the advantages conferred by economies of scale in terms of machine selection and handling expertise. This institutional framework presumably influenced the magnitude of the speculative element preferred by customers based on regional differences, and an understanding of region-specific consumption trends was definitive in parlors' operating methods. Situating parlors in a particular region was only reasonable in the accumulation of operational expertise.

It is likely that the regional concentration of parlors was also efficient from a management perspective. Until the computerized control of parlors, which gradually developed during the 1970s, was adopted across the industry, opening parlors in close proximity where they could be monitored by supervisors presumably simplified management.

District category[a]	Prefecture	Parlor	Year of establish-ment	Sales	Prize value	Prize-sale rate[b]	Gross profit margin	Profit margin on sales[c] (%)	Prize discount rate[d] (%)
Kansai/ Greater Osaka	Kyoto Prefecture	Parlor (1)	1957	206,725	321,403	15.55	2,501	1.2	63.54
	Osaka Prefecture	Parlor (6)	1983	321,280	459,117	14.28	33,007	10.3	62.79
	Hyofo Prefecture	Parlor (7)	1983	501,282	690,378	13.39	75,597	14.6	61.66
		Parlor (2)	1973	167,099	227,911	13.62	23,582	14.2	62.97
		Parlor (3)	1975	388,492	535,421	13.79	54,860	14.0	62.31
		Parlor (9)	1986	186,304	260,552	13.99	23,763	12.7	62.38
		Parlor (35)		258,206	365,923	14.14	27,644	10.8	63.01
		Parlor (4)	1975	420,204	571,282	13.61	59,305	14.0	63.17
		Parlor (30)	1991	312,550	426,886	13.64	43,070	13.9	63.13
		Parlor (10)	1986	264,746	364,129	13.75	37,744	14.3	62.34
		Parlor (15)	1987	278,552	383,501	13.79	37,546	13.4	62.84
		Parlor (18)	1988	258,694	360,633	13.95	31,872	11.9	62.9
			1989	209,103	293,235	14.04	22,359	10.6	63.68
		Parlor (22)	1989	187,700	249,485	13.31	31,626	16.4	62.56
Shizuoka	Shizuoka Prefecture	Parlor (23)	1989	329,092	469,847	14.26	39,754	12.2	61.58
		Parlor (5)	1982	388,501	566,027	14.52	41,048	10.8	61.38
		Parlor (8)	1983	456,279	620,137	13.60	74,727	15.9	61.53
		Parlor (11)	1986	300,135	433,777	14.39	32,825	11.2	61.61
		Parlor (12)	1986	312,826	444,052	14.20	39,250	12.5	61.61
		Parlor (16)	1987	382,435	534,490	13.96	50,612	13.4	62.08
		Parlor (24)	1989	258,137	389,403	15.03	26,500	10.4	59.49
		Parlor (31)	1991	363,482	522,247	14.32	41,966	11.6	61.56
		Parlor (32)	1991	289,232	433,513	15.01	22,757	7.9	61.47
		Parlor (33)	1991	293,053	431,593	14.73	35,013	12.0	59.79
		Parlor (13)	1986	262,832	370,952	14.09	34,284	12.8	61.61
		Parlor (14)	1986	284,150	407,217	14.33	33,806	11.9	61.48
		Parlor (17)	1987	349,255	506,118	14.50	40,814	11.7	60.94
		Parlor (19)	1988	313,824	431,465	13.76	44,391	14.3	62.45
		Parlor (20)	1988	295,531	415,067	14.03	40,166	13.7	61.52
		Parlor (25)	1989	277,796	400,971	14.40	31,164	11.3	61.51
		Parlor (26)	1989	231,529	331,558	14.31	28,841	12.0	61.13
		Parlor (27)	1989	232,541	328,400	14.12	32,072	13.8	61.04
			1989	273,058	387,752	14.18	32,147	11.9	62.13
		Parlor (34)	1991	424,622	590,540	13.91	62,728	14.2	61.28
Kanto/ Greater Tokyo	Kanagawa Prefecture	Parlor (29)	1990	661,377	903,500	13.66	70,456	10.6	65.40
	Ibaraki Prefecture	Parlor (36)	Unknown	233,738	344,363	14.74	14,746	6.2	63.59
	Average[e]			310,399	438,135	14.14	38,182	12.1	62.10

Table App.3.1: Overview of Maruhan's parlors (October 1990 to November 1992)

Notes

a. As classified by Maruhan.

b. Prize-sale rate = prize value / sales × 10. The prize-sale rate indicates the extent to which customers won based on probability and pin adjustment. The metric is similar to prize-ball percentage (number of balls customers won / number of balls customers exchanged), but the calculation is performed on a monetary basis.

c. Profit margin on sales (%) = ordinary profit / sales × 100.

d. Prize discount rate (%) = (sales − ordinary profit) / prize purchase price × 100. The exchange rate is calculated based on the cost of prize balls and the exchange value of prizes. If balls purchased for 4 yen were exchanged for a prize at an exchange rate of 60 percent, the customer would receive 3.4 yen of value per ball.

e. Average values represent monthly averages after redecoration; the month of the redecoration and reopening, as well as the following month, have been excluded.

	Per machine					
Utilization[f] (%)	Sales	Sales rank	Gross profit margin	Gross profit margin rank	Number of machines	Renewal reopenings and new openings[h]
45.68	820.3	27	9.9	36	252	1990: Major redecoration to add machines, June and July; renewal reopening, July
54.42	997.1	14	101.8	26	328	
67.86	1,433.4	2	208.8	1	360	1990: Redecoration, October to December; renewal reopening, December
40.89	759.5	31	106.9	21	220	1990: Redecoration, [unknown date] to December; renewal reopening, December
53.26	1,028.8	12	150.3	5	364	
37.63	844.3	26	82.4	31	275	
53.86	818.2	28	86.9	29	315	1992: Renewal reopening, February; machines added, October[g]
56.96	1,207.5	5	169.5	4	348	1991: Major redecoration to add machines, June to August; renewal reopening, August
54.34	1,459.0	1	140.1	8	293	1991: Major redecoration to add machines, June to August; renewal reopening, August; Officially listed as opening in 1991, but data remains for December 1990 (see Table App.3.2).
46.14	897.4	22	127.6	13	295	
54.48	936.6	20	125.7	15	297	
50.74	852.8	25	104.5	23	303	
39.63	675.6	34	74.7	32	454	
35.08	617.5	36	103.8	25	303	
42.16	921.8	21	111.0	20	357	1992: Renewal reopening, June
52.22	1,067.3	9	112.4	19	364	1992: Renewal reopening, February
53.29	1,254.3	4	205.0	2	364	1990: Major redecoration to add machines, October to December; renewal reopening, December
43.60	956.4	17	104.2	24	314	1992: Closed partway through September; closed as of November[g]
40.78	959.2	16	125.3	16	430	1992: Closed partway through September; closed as of November[g]
39.91	948.1	18	135.6	10	515	1992: Number of machines increased from 354 to 370, February to March; closed partway through September; closed as of November[g]
28.68	639.8	35	67.3	33	516	1990: Redecoration, October to November; renewal reopening
44.26	997.2	13	116.0	18	367	1990: New opening, October
34.04	724.2	33	60.4	34	373	1991: New opening, February 1992: new opening, June
37.70	875.7	23	104.7	22	335	1991: New opening, November
39.47	735.7	32	95.5	27	357	
36.30	782.6	29	87.5	28	363	
52.06	1,174.8	7	123.0	17	297	1992: March to April; renewal reopening, April
41.59	973.8	15	138.4	9	324	
44.62	869.2	24	117.7	16	340	
30.82	762.4	30	85.2	30	364	
49.62	1,052.4	11	130.7	12	220	
45.51	1,057.1	10	145.4	6	220	
56.12	1,137.9	8	133.3	11	240	
51.76	1,179.5	6	173.6	3	360	1991: New opening, April
50.73	1,322.8	3	140.4	7	500	
44.17	937.4	19	54.7	35	249	1990: New opening, October, November (based on negative return on sales for October and November and a prize-sale rate of greater than 15.7 for both months)
45.84	963.3		115.6		338	

f. Utilization rates are given as averages for February through November due to the lack of data through January 1992.
g. There is no data for October through November 1992 for parlors 11, 12 or 16. Since those parlors are likely to have closed for redecorations in September, their average values have been calculated using data from October 1990 through August 1992.
h. Months of closures and reopening have been inferred as follows: parlors 2, 4 and 17 are listed as reopening after a 'closure for redecorations' in the source; parlors 8, 18, 19 and 20 have no data for the months in question; and parlors 16, 27 and 36 have average sales for the month in question that are lower than for the previous month, along with negative return on sales, negative gross margin, etc.

Source: Compiled based on tables for October 1990 through November 1992 from a list of sales by location provided by Maruhan.

INFORMATION RESOURCES CREATED BY PERFORMANCE DIFFERENCES

Parlors may have been concentrated geographically in certain regions, but if we go back to Table App.3.1, we find that their operating conditions were nothing if not diverse. For example, there was considerable breadth in the number of machines, with the smallest parlors operating 220 machines (parlors 26 and 27 in Shizuoka Prefecture and the largest parlor operating 516 machine (parlor 24, also in Shizuoka Prefecture), a spread of 2.3 times. Reflecting the influence of size, the sales and gross margin of parlor 29 in Kanagawa Prefecture (the best-performing) were three to four times better than those of parlor 2 in Osaka Prefecture (the worst-performing). Profit margin on sales, calculated based on gross margin as a percentage of average monthly sales, also exhibited a spread of about ten points, ranging from figures such as 1.2 or 6.2 percent to 15.9 percent. Sales and gross margin per machine, which eliminate the effects of parlor size, were also varied: the best-performing parlor's results were 2.4 times the worst-performing parlor's figures (1459 yen [about US$12] for parlor 30 and 617.5 yen [about US$4.94] for parlor 22, both in Hyogo Prefecture) for the former, and 3.8 (208.8 for parlor 7 in Osaka Prefecture versus 54.7 for parlor 36 in Ibaraki Prefecture)[2] for the latter.

In contrast to the diversity in individual parlors' operating conditions, the exchange rate averaged about 62.1 percent, notwithstanding a certain amount of divergence between the lowest (59.5 percent) and highest (65.4 percent) figures. The exchange rate, calculated by dividing the value of the prize for which the balls were exchanged by the balls' nominal value, expresses the effective value of the balls (prize balls) won by customers, as calculated from prize sales and gross margin. A verification of monthly trends over about two years for each parlor based on the original sources found that the average values shown in Table App.3.1 were maintained. Balls were exchanged for prizes at a discount of about 40 percent, and variations in that rate can be understood as regional differences.

For companywide management, such disparities in operating results signaled potential problems. They provided a motivation to analyze the underlying causes and take corrective action to rectify differences, encouraging improvement in the challenges faced by parlors that performed relatively poorly. Let us examine some of the factors that caused these disparities. Customer preferences in each region and the influence of nearby competitor parlors presumably affected indicator levels. Having recognized that these factors exerted an important effect on parlor-level operations, I will examine effects between the factors seen in Table App.3.1 in the next section in order to infer companywide tendencies.

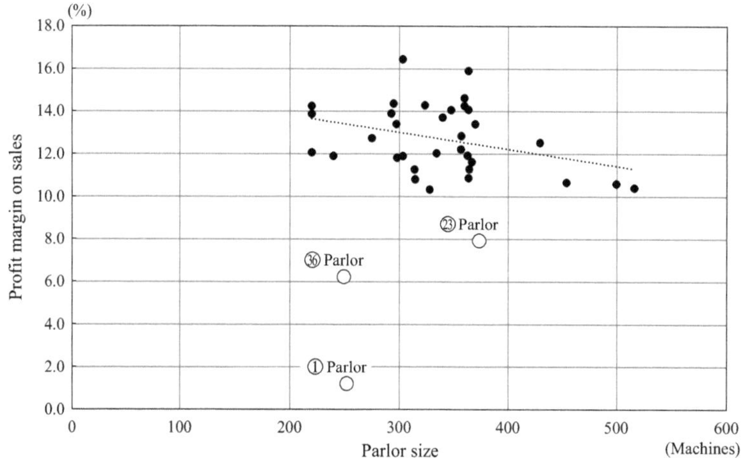

Figure App.3.1: Parlor size (number of machines) and profit margin on sales (October 1990 to November 1992)
Source: Compiled based on Table 3.1.

PARLORS CHOSEN BY CUSTOMERS

First, profit margin ratio on sales fell as size grew, as shown in Figure App.3.1. However, we see a broad distribution of profit margin ratio on sales figures for parlors with about 300 machines, which includes the size of the average Maruhan parlor (338 machines, as per Table App.3.1). If we exclude parlors with 400 or more machines, the inverse correlation is not necessarily clear. We can see increasing size as also holding the potential to lead to increased profitability. Since investments related to parlor size, which refers to the number of machines operated, made by the company that operates the chain did not fall within the purview of individual parlors, results such as those shown in Figure 5.5 can be an effective basis for judgments about expansion. Parlors 1 and 23, which diverge from the overall trend, experienced the effects of renewal reopenings, while the results for parlor 36 indicate poor performance.[3]

The prize-sale rate, or *warisū*, is one factor that exerted a direct influence on profit margin ratio on sales (see Figure App.3.2). The prize-sale rate, which was totaled after the close of business, is calculated as follows: prize sales / sales (loaned ball fees) × 10.[4] Higher prize-sale rates mean customers win, while lower prize-sale rates have the opposite effect. This indicator resembles the prize-ball percentage but has a stronger managerial element.[5] Use of an indicator like prize-sale rate signals an intention to evaluate on a monetary basis how a specific action on the parlor floor (control of the prize-ball percentage through daily pin adjustment) affects parlor management. In light of the nature of the original sources, prize-sale rate offered

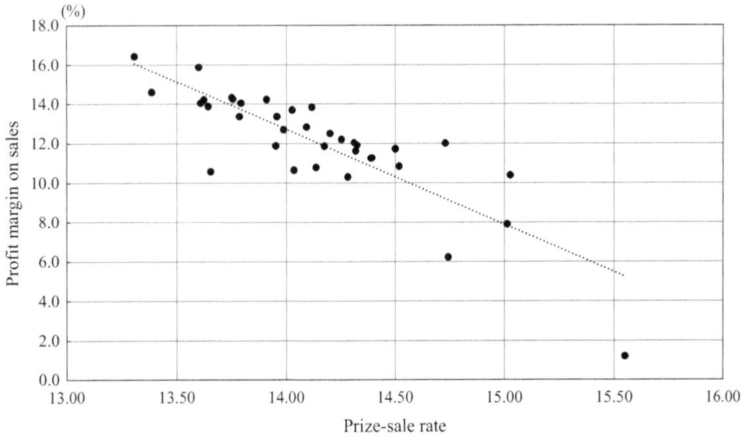

Figure App.3.2: Impact of prize-sale rate on return on sales (October 1990 to November 1992)
Source: Compiled based on Table 3.1.

a more suitable information format, which Maruhan needed so that the head office could determine conditions at individual parlors while searching for companywide managerial directions.

The prize-sale rate was affected by the prize-ball percentage, which in turn was determined by jackpots governed by machine probability, and pin adjustment, which opened and closed pins. The prize-sale rate ultimately moved in response to the results of customer play (customer headcount and play times) relative to such advance adjustments by parlors and affected profit margin ratio on sales. Figure App.3.2 illustrates the inverse correlation between prize-sale rate via the prize-ball percentage and profit margin ratio on sales. In this way, the prize-sale rate, with the exception of probability algorithms that were already programmatically determined, varied with pin adjustment as a parlor-led initiative, and its magnitude can be understood as a proxy variable that indicates the company's intentions with regard to attracting customers. What I would like to note here is that probability itself was not subject to parlors' control. Although they are not directly incorporated into the figure as indicators that can be explained, the methods by which parlors were able to differentiate themselves in terms of attracting customers consisted of which machines they chose and how they adopted unique elements to compensate for the declining role of pin adjustment, which had affected their appeal to customers in the past, for example by offering additional services. I would like to emphasize that Figure App.3.2 expresses the overall results of these efforts.

How, then, were parlors able to control operating conditions by setting prize-sale rates that reflected prize-ball percentages, which in turn directly impacted customer headcount? Customer attendance can be considered from the standpoint of machine utilization. Utilization can be obtained from Maruhan data dating from February 1992 and later. That utilization was added at that time to facilitate comparison of parlors' operations indicates the thinking of management, which had come to emphasize utilization.[6] Figure App.3.3 recalculates each parlor's average prize-sale rate from February to November 1992, when utilization data was available, and summarizes its impact on utilization. (The prize-sale rate figures differ from those shown in Table App.3.1 due to the different date range.)

The average availability for all parlors over the ten months for which utilization data is available was 45.5 percent. That rate provides a yardstick for utilization at Maruhan, which was distinguished by its development of suburban parlors during this period. It is difficult to evaluate the fact that the rate was less than 50 percent. Utilization was calculated twice per day as the percentage of machines in use at the parlor at the time, for example at 2:00 in the afternoon.[7] Data was gathered when parlors were unlikely to be crowded in light of the work schedules of white- and blue-collar workers, who were parlors' principal customers. Rather than indicating operating results during busy hours when utilization figures would rise, the data served as a management barometer that made it easy to discover problems. If addressing those problems drove a bottom-up improvement in results, then focusing on utilization was an effective method for moving overall management in a desirable direction. We can conclude that average utilization, which revealed customer headcount, which in turn directly impacted sales, was sufficient to keep Maruhan's profit margin ratio on sales steady at about 12 percent (the average for all parlors from February to November 1992).

Interestingly, utilization and prize-sale rate exhibit a moderately inverse correlation, suggesting that winning is not the sole motivation of pachinko consumption (see Figure App.3.3). Certainly, the group whose prize-sale rate was higher than the average included numerous parlors that had just staged renewal reopenings, supporting the inference that those parlors offered prize balls in order to attract customers. Additionally, parlors 22 and 2, whose prize-sale rates were the lowest (lower than the average for all parlors) also had low utilization, suggesting that customers drifted away from parlors that did not allow them to win.

That said, parlor 22 seems to have had an issue with attracting customers. The parlor opened at a shopping mall in Seishin New Town, in the city of Kobe, in 1989. New Town was still under development at the time. Observers have pointed out that only about 30 percent of the development was complete as of 1990, making it difficult to draw customers.[8] Parlor 2, which opened in 1973, was located in central Hyogo Prefecture, and it had difficulty attracting customers as it came under intense competitive pressure from seven or eight other parlors.[9] Although customer headcount

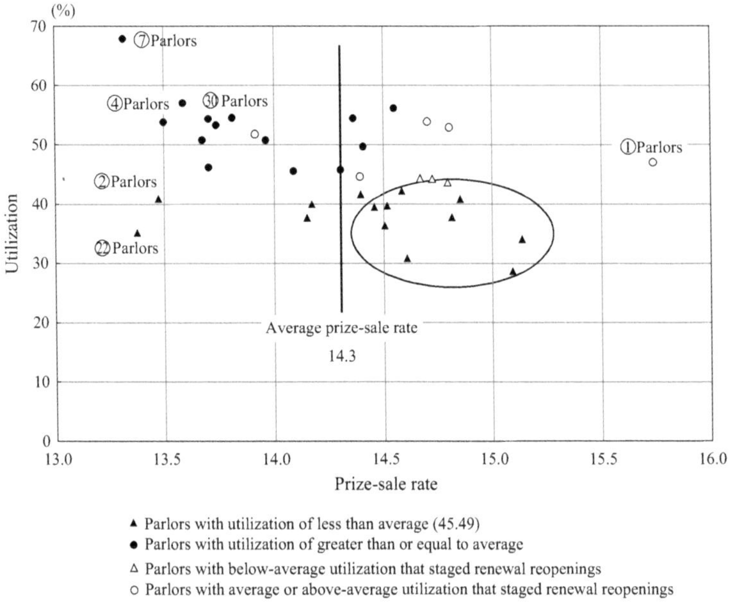

Figure App.3.3: Prize-sale rate and utilization (October 1990 to November 1992)
Source: Compiled based on Table App. 3.1.

rose abruptly following a rebuilding and remodeling project in February 1990,[10] low utilization numbers capture the difficulty of operating in a challenging competitive environment. These two parlors had lower-than-average prize-sale rates, indicating that increasing them could be an effective way of attracting more customers.

Interestingly, for the group with utilization figures that were lower than the average, other than those two parlors, the inversely proportional relationship of utilization and prize-sale rate was stronger than for the group with above-average utilization numbers. That means it is impossible to find a clear relationship in which increasing the prize-ball percentage so that the prize-sale rate rises attracts customers, which pushes up utilization. This result can be characterized as follows: parlors' intention to attract more customers did not lead to increased profitability due to high utilization. It may be that high prize-sale rates and low utilization were inevitable due to regional characteristics and competition with nearby parlors. If so, Figure App.3.3 suggests the possibility that high prize-sale rates alone in the context of competition were not enough to establish a competitive advantage. At a minimum, customers of suburban parlors were not visiting those businesses solely out of a desire to win a jackpot.

For example, parlor 7, which recorded the highest utilization figure, was better at attracting customers than other parlors despite having the lowest prize-sale rate at

13.3 percent. That customers continued to visit parlors despite their low prize-sale rates signifies that they were being attracted by something other than prize-ball percentages. If it is true that unique operational initiatives impacted the performance of parlor 7, then those efforts would constitute Maruhan expertise that could be applied horizontally to other parlors.

Based on high utilization figures that were roughly equivalent as well as low prize-sale rates, parlors 4 and 30 can be understood to have posted some of the best results (good enough to land them within the top ten in terms of sales and gross margin per machine). Both parlors were located in Kobe's Nishi Ward, and they were close enough to one another that we can assume that they competed with each other. Despite the fact that both parlors came under intense competitive pressure when a new, large parlor run by one of the greater Osaka area's foremost parlor chain operators (Takayama Bussan) opened in 1991,[11] the two Maruhan parlors staged a successful counterattack and emerged in an advantageous position,[12] suggesting that chain development offered special techniques for dealing with competition.

It goes without saying that uniform operating methods and top-down instructions are not necessarily effective in situations where operations are influenced by diverse regional demand, as in the service industry. However, the judgment that a given parlor's utilization is lower than average is a results-based evaluation that can be made on a head office level based on data that facilitates comparison. Setting aside the question of whether the discovery of differences led to a reaction that sought to rectify utilization and other parameters, at a minimum, it is important that information about parlors with good performance and the reasons for that performance accumulate at the head office.

EVENTS AND CUSTOMER DRAW:
Decline of Pin Adjusters

Parlors with relatively poor performance faced the question of how to attract customers more effectively and how to encourage them to spend more time at their establishments. It was an easy matter for customers to recognize parlors located near train stations. By contrast, suburban parlors had to advertise their presence in order to raise recognition, orchestrate renewal reopenings and provide other associated services in order to make it worthwhile for patrons to make the trip to their doors. This task – attracting customers – proved to be particularly challenging for suburban parlors.

Prize-sale rates were only one factor in customer appeal: if a parlor's advertisements were ineffective, raising prize-ball percentages would not yield the results they were looking for. In that sense, it was critical to establish stable customer demographics who would become repeat users. Focusing on services other than the prize-sale rate offered one way to make improvements.

This relationship between prize-sale rate and utilization was consistent with services for new customer demographics that emerged during the 1970s. As previously described in Chapter 5, suburban parlors typically attracted customers who were better off economically as well as more women, and those groups placed greater value on ambiance so that they could enjoy their time, signaling a different set of needs than those that characterized customers at parlors near train stations.

Services offered by Maruhan during special events and renewal reopenings when parlors changed machines offer a straightforward expression of these changes in customer demographics and demand. These events were intended both to ensure existing regulars did not lose interest in machines and to bring in new customers. The nature of the services offered on these occasions tells us what sort of customers they were targeting. The vibrant scenery and other practices that came to be associated with renewal reopenings were created in response to attendance by new customers who sought high prize-ball percentages as well as customer demographics that were not technically skilled.[13] In the case of parlor 14, which reopened after installing a slate of new machines from May 12 to 14, 1994, there was no change in service that allowed customers to win by focusing on prize-sale rates.[14] However, the parlor augmented that approach by offering its unique brand of customer service by preparing an even more extensive selection of prizes, including brand-name T-shirts and polo shirts. In this way, the parlor offered a range of creative services that was defined by factors other than the prize-ball percentage.

An examination of a commemorative event staged by parlor 7, which marked the tenth anniversary of its opening on October 23, 1994, reveals changes from past practices. The parlor, having consistently been among Maruhan's top performers,[15] offered brand-name rice, Japanese-harvested *matsutake* mushrooms and Italian-made premium sweaters at 'bargain prices' while working to offer prizes like merchandise for J-League soccer teams, which was difficult to come by in stores,[16] in an effort that can be interpreted as assuming a customer demographic other than men. In accordance with the intention behind the event, the parlor was filled with couples and customers' family members who expressed interest in services that focused on prizes such as premium merchandise offered at bargain prices, for example 'grab bags', as well as 'customers who created the atmosphere of a department store budget floor'. The parlor reported that customers who were drawn to the event exhibited a level of diversity that differed from prior such events. Unlike the 1970s, when parlors assumed that events would be attended by unmarried male office workers and blue-collar workers, customers were accompanied by guests and family members, including fathers and boyfriends. The event offered services that took into consideration such male roles.

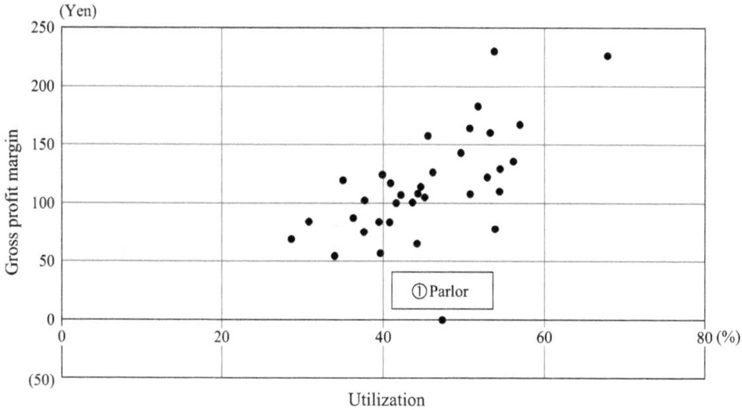

Figure App.3.4: Utilization and gross profit margin per machine (February to November 1992)
Source: Compiled based on Table App. 3.1.

It is difficult to find evidence detailing how successfully parlors were able to leverage such experimental efforts to take advantage of changes in customer demographics to secure new regulars. The key point is that suburban parlors were called upon to plan such events on a sustained basis. Unlike a business approach that relied exclusively on the skill of experienced pin adjusters to attract customers by adjusting the prize-ball percentage, the planning and orchestration of ongoing events signaled the growing importance of the *organizational ability* to continuously generate new ideas.

That Maruhan added utilization as a data point conducive to comparison provides a convincing argument that higher utilization values exerted a positive influence on gross margin per machine, as suggested by Figure App.3.4. They generated a similar result for sales per machine. With the exception of parlor 1, which posted a negative gross margin per machine due to a high prize-sale rate, reflecting the influence of a redecoration in July 1993, most parlors with high utilization also posted a high gross margin. It is clear that utilization governed individual parlors' operating results.

Consequently, it is likely that the question of how to maintain and increase utilization was the definitive problem when parlors sought to expand their operations with additional machines. Since increasing the number of machines also had the potential to improve profit margin ratio on sales up to about 300 machines, attracting more customers was key. A cursory examination of Figure App.3.5 suggests that large size did not, in and of itself, offer a direct motivation for customers to visit a parlor. However, this tendency was strong in groups with an average utilization of about 45.0 or lower, where the inverse correlation was more conspicuous; in groups that recorded

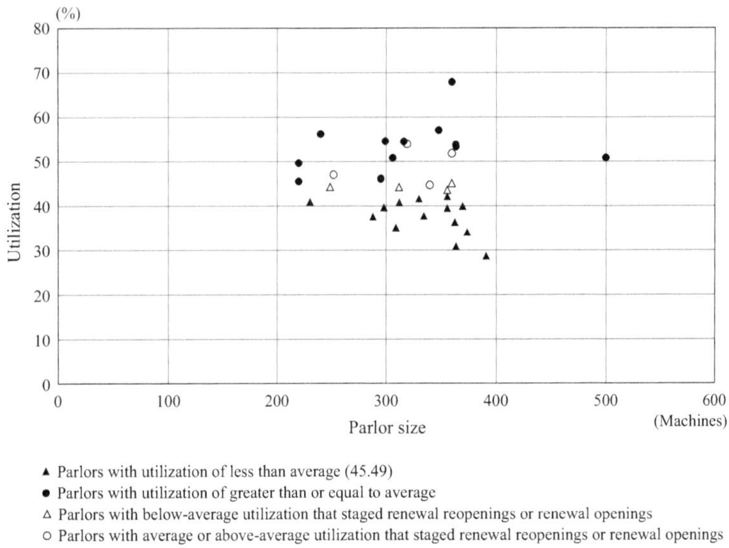

Figure App.3.5: Parlor size (number of machines) and utilization (February to November 1992)
Source: Compiled based on Table App. 3.1.

higher utilization figures, the relationship was not necessarily clear. In fact, it seems that parlors with more machines were able to keep their utilization rates higher. It is likely that there were advantages of scale when it came to customers' selection of machines; for example, diversity of choices would allow customers to discover favored machines or free them from the need to compete with other customers for those machines. Parlors staging renewal reopenings, renewal openings (openings following longer closures to facilitate comprehensive redecoration and changes of all machines) and new openings lie close to the average line, but it is unclear how utilization changed later since those parlors tended to have high prize-sale rates.

REDECORATION AS AN OPERATIONAL TACTIC

Let us analyze business conditions at Maruhan parlors that reopened after a period of closure and newly opened parlors during this period to examine the significance of chain development on a companywide level. Table App.3.2 offers an overview of

(Unit: thousands of yen)

Renewal/ new	Parlor		Month and year	Sales	Prize value	prize-sale rate	Gross profit margin	Gross profit margin on sales (%)	Prize discount rate (%)
Renewal reopenings and renewal openings	Parlor (36)	Month of redecoration	October 1990	224,913	352,434	15.67	−1,052	−0.47	64.12
		Next month	November	256,853	402,305	15.66	−171	−0.07	63.89
	Parlor (24)	Month of redecoration	October 1990	266,319	456,169	17.13	−14,002	−5.26	61.45
		Next month	November	253,384	422,938	16.69	−6,437	−2.54	61.43
	Parlor (7)	Month of redecoration	December 1990	99,930	145,245	14.53	6,992	7.00	63.99
		Next month	January 1991	578,044	767,111	13.27	87,600	15.15	63.93
	Parlor (8)	Month of redecoration	December 1990	186,711	304,930	16.33	−1,142	−0.61	61.61
		Next month	January 1991	437,134	586,101	13.41	76,019	17.39	61.61
	Parlor (4)	Month of redecoration	August 1991	333,279	546,933	16.41	−14,885	−4.47	63.66
		Next month	September	446,545	631,171	14.13	45,152	10.11	63.59
	Parlor (2)	Month of redecoration	December 1991	40,341	65,577	16.26	−1,200	−2.97	63.35
		Next month	January 1992	204,602	278,818	13.63	27,967	13.67	63.35
	Parlor (5)	Month of redecoration	February 1992	359,159	598,744	16.67	−9,161	−2.55	61.52
		Next month	March	510,580	804,353	15.75	15,857	3.11	61.51
	Parlor (17)	Month of redecoration	April 1992	99,748	164,005	16.44	−1,423	−1.43	61.69
		Next month	May	407,609	586,635	14.39	45,840	11.25	61.67
	Parlor (32)	Month of redecoration	June 1992	242,926	401,741	16.54	−5,416	−2.23	61.82
		Next month	July	258,388	410,426	15.88	5,201	2.01	61.69
	Parlor (1)	Month of redecoration	July 1992	6,864	17,693	25.78	−4,225		62.67
		Next month	August	268,117	436,913	16.30	−7,833	−2.92	63.16
	Parlor (35)	Month of redecoration	February 1992	256,539	408,771	15.93	−633	−0.25	62.91
		Next month	March	316,793	477,847	15.08	17,108	5.40	62.72
		Month of increasing the number of machines	October 1992	392,350	533,733	13.60	56,062	14.29	63.01
		Next month	November	339,219	461,065	13.59	47,747	14.08	63.22
	Average	Month of redecoration				17.06 (16.78)	−4,195 (826)	−1.20 (0.087)	
		Next month				14.93 (14.82)	27,846 (29,504)	6.60 (7.22)	
New openings	Parlor (31)	Month of redecoration	October 1990	6,168	20,858	33.82	−7,037	−114.09	63.31
		Next month	November	465,881	811,377	17.42	−33,433	−7.18	61.54
	Parlor (30)	Month of redecoration	December 1990	61,133	98,150	16.06	−668	−1.09	62.97
		Next month	January 1991	311,741	406,626	13.04	54,038	17.33	63.38
	Parlor (32)	Month of redecoration	February 1991	120,388	280,479	23.30	−52,709	−43.78	61.71
		Next month	March	412,884	712,701	17.26	−27,087	−6.56	61.73
	Parlor (34)	Month of redecoration	April 1991	103,662	227,608	21.96	−35,980	−34.71	61.35
		Next month	May	508,121	792,278	15.59	19,182	3.78	61.71
	Parlor (33)	Month of redecoration	November 1991	127,377	223,947	17.58	−14,113	−11.08	63.18
		Next month	December	282,517	438,989	15.54	13,186	4.67	61.35
	Average	Month of redecoration				22.54	−22,101	−40.95	
		Next month				15.77	5,177	2.41	

Table App.3.2: Renewal reopenings, renewal openings, new openings and performance

Note: Average figures for renewal reopenings exclude the results of the expansion of parlor 35, whereas figures in parentheses include those results.

Source: Compiled based on Table App. 3.1.

four newly opened parlors and eleven parlors that reopened following a closure.[17] Before we go any further, let us review an example of the latter.

The fourteen parlors consisting of eleven that reopened following a closure and three that remained closed at the end of the period covered by the data used here (as of November 1992) account for about 44 percent of the total of thirty-one parlors (excluding five parlors that opened for the first time during these twenty-six months).[18] Of those fourteen parlors, parlors 1, 4, 8 and 35 were increasing the number of machines they operated, while seven parlors – parlors 2, 4, 7 and 8 (see Table App.3.2) as well as parlors 10, 12 and 16 (which remained closed as of November 1992; see Table App.3.1 above) – had closures of more than one month.

The purpose of such closures was to stage a renewal reopening. As described in Appendix 1, parlors regularly replaced a certain number of their machines with new models to keep customers from losing interest. Depending on the chosen timing, such reopenings served as an effective tactic for competing with nearby parlors or securing new customers. Many parlors offered complimentary prize ball releases after reopening, and higher prize-sale rates were used to boost the prize-ball percentage. Such closures were typically limited to the number of days needed to replace machines, as was the case with Parlor C in Appendix 1. The data from Maruhan, which is organized by month, does not clarify whether parlors staged renewal reopenings. Based on sales during renewal months for parlors 24, 32, 35 and 36 as shown in Table App.3.2, closures were likely short, making it probable that they were normal renewal reopenings. Other closures presumably involved a different rationale, as suggested by notes recording closure-specific information or a comparatively long duration that was sufficient to impact monthly performance. It is likely that comprehensive renovations, for example involving layout changes or a switchover to all-new machines, were carried out as part of the renewal openings.

Why, then, did Maruhan parlors close for comparatively long periods of time? Renewals at existing parlors were carried out during this period in order to modernize facilities under a companywide initiative.[19] The decision to renovate was not made on the spot at the parlor level, so such closures differed in character from the normal renewal reopenings described above. I will use the term ‘renewal openings’ to indicate reopenings after medium- and long-term closures based on a consideration of how their purpose and character differed from renewal reopenings, which involved much shorter pauses in business operations to facilitate machine switchovers. Renewal openings can presumably produce operational benefits that resemble those of renewal reopenings since they also involve machine replacements and the adjustment of prize-ball percentages, so it is possible to analyze the short-term effects of such initiatives on the operations of individual parlors and on the company as a whole. Below, I will

(Unit: thousands of yen)

Parlor		Sales	Prize value	Gross profit margin	Gross profit margin on sales (%)	Per machine Sales	Rank	Gross profit margin	Rank	Number of machines
Parlor (4)	Average before redecoration	260,322	370,837	30,174	11.6	878.0	16	101.8	17	296
	Average after redecoration	418,323	567,005	60,316	14.3	1,202.1	7	172.3	6	348
	Rate of change	161	153	200	124	137	↑	170	↑	117
Parlor (5)	Average before redecoration	342,545	487,810	42,331	12.5	941.1	14	115.7	17	364
	Average after redecoration	468,821	688,581	47,906	10.2	1,288.0	4	131.6	15	364
	Rate of change	137	141	113	82	137	↑	114	↑	100
Parlor (17)	Average before redecoration	243,927	346,335	30,611	12.5	829.7	22	98.0	20	294
	Average after redecoration	339,529	492,698	39,976	11.8	1,139.6	8	117.5	12	298
	Rate of change	139	142	131	94	137	↑	120	↑	101
Parlor (32)	Average before redecoration	306,530	456,137	25,225	8.3	749.4	25	66.7	30	373
	Average after redecoration	231,975	343,713	26,107	11.2	620.2	31	69.8	29	374
	Rate of change	76	75	103	135	83	↓	105	↑	100
Parlor (35)	Average before redecoration	225,938	311,111	29,177	12.2	724.1	27	92.9	23	312
	Average after redecoration	298,907	442,469	21,938	7.3	958.0	19	70.3	31	312
	Rate of change	132	142	75	59.9	132	↑	75.7	↓	100
	Average number of machines after expansion	365,785	497,399	51,905	14.2	1,051.1	10	149.2	7	348
	Rate of change	122	112	237	194	110	↑	212	↑	112
Parlor (1)	Average before redecoration	119,020	172,948	8,919	7.6	551.0	33	41.0	33	216
	Average after redecoration	206,725	321,403	2,501	1.2	820.3	21	9.9	34	252
	Rate of change	174	186	28	16	149	↑	24	↓	117

Table App.3.3: Benefits of renewal reopenings and renewal openings
Note: Rank reflects share of all parlors.
Source: Compiled based on Table App. 3.1.

use the term ‘redecoration’ to refer generically to both renewal openings and renewal reopenings as I examine their nature and benefits.

Table App.3.2 characterizes business conditions during the month in which redecorated parlors and new parlors opened and in the following month. During months when parlors reopened following redecorations, prize-sale rates were about seventeen, or three points higher than the average of 14.3, and as a result, gross margin and profit margin ratio on sales were both negative. However, since in the following month the prize-sale rate fell to about 14.9, roughly average, parlors’ performance improved, with gross profit and profit margin ratio on sales both flipping from red to black. After reopening in February 1992, parlor 35 added fifty-two machines in October, but the effects of dispensing more prize balls as a result are not clear in terms of monthly prize-sale rates. The changes in operating conditions caused by redecorations were similar to the months in which the four new parlors opened for the first time.

Table App.3.3 summarizes how the redecorations impacted business conditions for the five parlors for which before and after changes can be compared. With the exception of parlor 32, the remaining four parlors' sales rose by a factor of 1.3 to 1.6, and other management indicators improved as well. Parlor 4, which added machines, saw its sales increase at a faster rate than the other parlors. Yet since growth in profit margin ratio on sales, sales per machine, gross margin and other metrics outpaced the 1.2 times increase in the number of machines, it is safe to conclude that the improvements were the result of a renewal reopening or renewal opening.

However, that may not have been the case for all the parlors. Parlor 32 saw gross margin per machine and profit margin ratio on sales rise, but it would be difficult to conclude that business conditions as indicated by metrics such as sales had improved due to growth in customer headcount and playing time, which are related to long-term operating conditions. It may be that the parlor faced problems related to other factors, for example competition with nearby parlors. That said, redecoration in general brought business improvements to Maruhan's parlors.

NOTES

Introduction

1. For an interpretation of whether and how pachinko violates Japan's penal code, see Sibbitt (1997: 569).
2. See *Asahi Shimbun* (2020), '休業応じぬパチンコ店を初公表「裁量権逸脱のおそれ」' (First set of pachinko parlors defying closure requests named, potential for abuse of government authority cited), April 24.
3. Ahead of name-and-shame measures, plenty of information about parlors that had not followed the government's request to shut down was reported by the public to call centers in Kanagawa Prefecture, and about 66 percent of 240 complaints by callers (the total number of calls to a general complaint line between April 11 and 23) were related to pachinko parlors. This shows that pachinko parlors and customers were exposed to strict scrutiny from Japanese society. See Asahi Shimbun, 'First set of pachinko parlors defying closure requests named'.
4. Pachinko parlors objected to the government's policy because it did not reflect the actual reality on the ground. About 98.7 percent of all parlors complied with closure requests, a figure that was higher than that of other businesses. See *Toyokeizai Online* (2020), 'マルハン社長、『パチンコは危険』説への大反論　喫煙対策で換気設備は充実、3密には当たらない' (The president of Maruhan strongly refutes the 'pachinko is dangerous' argument, denies relevance of 3Cs [closed spaces, crowded places, close contact] for pachinko, notes smoking measures serve to increase ventilation), https://toyokeizai.net/articles/-/367220, August 7 (accessed on September 3, 2020).
5. The government has been able to punish businesspeople who are not following its requests since a February 13, 2021, revision to the Act on the Prevention of Infectious Diseases and Medical Care for Patients with Infectious Diseases (the Infectious Diseases Control Act).
6. *Maneposto Web* (2020), 'パチンコ店はいまだ「クラスターなし」、感染リスクが低いワケ' ('No clusters yet' in pachinko parlors, the reason for the low risk of infection), https://www.moneypost.jp/685795, July 31 and August 7 (accessed on September 5, 2021).
7. See Osatake (1925).
8. See '第一二回 国会参議委員予算委員会会議録 第一六号 昭和二六年一一月一五日' (Minutes of the House of Councilors Budget Committee of the 12th Diet, No. 16, November 15, 1951), p. 1. Except as noted otherwise, subsequent references to the debate in the Diet, including quotations, are drawn from this source.
9. After Japan's defeat in World War II, the Japan Racing Association resumed horse racing in Tokyo and Kyoto as early as 1946, and it came under direct government management in 1948 (Moriya 1989: 161). In 1948, as advances were made in laying the legal groundwork, such as the Bicycle Racing Act, the first race was held in the city of Kokura (the present-day city of Kitakyushu). For more on how local governments began to operate bicycle racing as a means of resolving their fiscal issues, see Hasegawa and the Committee on the History of Japan's Trade and Industry Policy (2013: 163–64). Soichi Oya described what he called a 'nation of gamblers' as follows:

   > In the city of Shimonoseki in Yamaguchi Prefecture, […] due to difficult living conditions for residents the amount of residents' tax in arrears is quite large, and

> revenue from bicycle racing just barely fills the gap […] the city of Kawasaki in Kanagawa Prefecture has become the envy of cities nationwide […]. A friend of mine who lives there pays residents' tax much lower than mine, even though his income is much higher than mine […]. The city has fully equipped municipal schools […] and is building numerous public housing complexes in succession, […] and the streets clearly became much better upon crossing the city limits into Kawasaki […]. Residents of Tokyo and the city of Yokohama are jealous of its gas, water and other facilities as well. While this is due in part to the fact that, as an industrial city, Kawasaki was home to numerous leading businesses, it is also due in large part to funding from bicycle racing […]. Under these circumstances, there is a persistent boom in enthusiasm for bicycle racing nationwide. This event has led to plans for the prefectural or municipal operation of horse racing as well. (Oya 1951: 70–71)

10. Public opposition to state-controlled racing, in which gambling took place in the open, persisted over a long period. Cases came to light of improprieties and unlawful operations such as race-fixing and unauthorized bookmaking, and repeated arguments were made in opposition to state-controlled racing or calling for its abolition due to concerns about negative effects on society, such as the involvement of organized crime in the industry. In fact, the issue of the survival or abolition of the racing business was discussed repeatedly. While state-controlled racing was maintained, laws were amended to bolster the industry and prevent foreseeable problems, based on the report of expert deliberations in the Bicycle Racing Management Council (1959–1960), reconsideration of the system by the State-controlled Racing Survey Committee (1960) and a report by the Panel Discussion on Problems in State-controlled Racing (1977). Issues identified as grounds for its continuation in the 1961 report by the State-controlled Racing Survey Committee included the subsidization of related industries through contributions funded by the business, contributions to the budgets of social welfare programs and local public agencies and the need for countermeasures to secure replacement funding, address unemployment among related parties and prevent the spread of informal gambling in the event that state-controlled racing were to be abolished. For more on the series of debates and committee reports related to this process, see Hasegawa and the Committee on the History of Japan's Trade and Industry Policy (2013: 163–92).
11. One issue repeatedly highlighted by those arguing for abolition was its role as a source of funding for organized crime (Hasegawa and the Committee on the History of Japan's Trade and Industry Policy 2013: 163–92).
12. I was unable to find any example that discussed the abolition of pachinko in any formal deliberations related to policymaking decisions. As also evidenced by the fact that Minister of Finance Hayato Ikeda and others at the time believed the amusement businesses of pachinko parlors qualified as gambling, it is conceivable that the view that state-controlled gambling should be abolished and the consideration of policies backed by that view indirectly impacted the forms that pachinko took and its survival. See Note 10 above.
13. See *Mainichi Shimbun* (1951), '是か非か　宝くじ　競輪　パチンコ　本社世論調査過半数が廃止論　卅代は宝くじの愛好者' (Pro or con? Lottery, bicycle racing, pachinko: A majority of respondents to our survey call for abolition, while those in their thirties love the lottery), December 30.

14. See Shinmei (1951: 2313–14). There may be some doubt as to whether the views presented by Shinmei are appropriate as an objective overview of public opinion at the time. My principal purpose here is to examine views both for and against. At the time, Shinmei collected various views from the perspective of the acceptance of pachinko. In light of the fact that no clear point of view can be discerned in Shinmei's 1954 article referenced below (see Note 19), his method of collecting opinions itself may in fact have reflected the atmosphere of the time.
15. See *Shūkan Asahi* (1951), 'パチンコ社会学' (Pachinko sociology), October 14, p. 11.
16. Entry by those under eighteen years of age, like the child in the illustration, was prohibited under the amended Entertainment and Amusement Trades Control Act of 1951, and this ban was strictly enforced thereafter.
17. See Masukawa (1989) and Note 10 above.
18. See Iwanami Shoten (1997), 広辞苑 (6th ed of *Kojien*, the Japanese dictionary), Iwanami Shoten, p. 1194.
19. See Shinmei (1954), '時論要解連発式パチンコの禁止' (Outline of current events: Abolition of self-feeding pachinko machines), *Jiji Press Jiji Kaisetsuban*, 2728, pp. 3129–30.
20. For example, a *Mainichi Shimbun* editorial published on November 19, 1954, titled '健全な社会を作るために' (To build a sound society) and the views of various members of the public as seen in letters to the editors of newspapers (*Mainichi Shimbun* [1954], '国民の声' [Public opinion], November 22; *Tokyo Shimbun* [1954], '声' [Voices], November 23) were in agreement that it should be abolished.
21. This is the term used to refer to these establishments at the time, as used in documents such as police yearbooks and police white papers. It appears that '*pachinko-ya*' and 'pachinko parlors' in this book, which are referred to as *pachinko-hōru* (halls) in statistics and historical materials, were distinguished based on the number of machines in operation, with those with smaller numbers referred to using the former term and those with comparatively larger numbers referred to using the latter (Morita 1953).
22. See *Jitsugyō no Sekai* (1957), 'パチンコ昔と今' (Pachinko then and now), 54(5), p. 1.
23. For example, see cases of entrepreneurs with sufficient capital switching to 'smart ball' (Nakamura 1955: 49) and of Maruhan becoming the largest player in the industry by taking over pachinko parlors from relatives who left the business due to its uncertain future (Han, C. 2008; Han, J. 2014).
24. This view is shared with Nagai (2002), who shows how control of amusement businesses has changed over time; see chapters 2 and 3. In addition, Japanese people's thinking on gambling itself has changed over time. While in the 1951 *Mainichi Shimbun* opinion survey referred to in the text most respondents were opposed to gambling, according to a survey conducted in 1993 by the Leisure Development Center, when asked whether they favored or opposed acts of gambling approximately 71 percent of respondents answered that such acts were 'not bad', while only about 13 percent answered that they were 'not good' (Hasegawa and the Committee on the History of Japan's Trade and Industry Policy 2013: 184). A change in people's thinking on pachinko is also evident. For example, the following was noted in the 1980s:

    > Views of pachinko seem perhaps to have changed too. The recent criticisms of consumer credit call to mind the criticisms once expressed against bicycle

> racing and, even earlier, pachinko. Since both of these were considered to be causes of incidents, some argued for their prohibition or strong regulation. Even though such gambling probably is related to the hellish world of high-interest consumer credit as an impetus, one does not hear such criticism very often. Perhaps opposition to gambling has faded away, or pachinko and similar activities have become firmly established as forms of amusement. (*Nihon Keizai Shimbun* [1983], 'ギャンブルに好・不況——集客努力の差くっきり' [Up and down cycles in gambling: A clear difference based on efforts to attract customers], August 12, evening edition, p. 3)

Pachinko also came to be seen as a subject of investment that could promise synergy effects with other businesses, as seen in the following:

> The introduction of pachinko businesses to shopping centers is one example of how firmly established it has become. Gaps left by stores that have vacated the centers are filled with pachinko outlets, which have the ability to attract customers. They are able to pay high security deposits too, thanks to their high earning potential. What's more, they do not compete with other tenants. They are even considered possible candidates for conversion of unprofitable supermarkets. While despite the presence of such plans there have been few cases of their realization due to inability to reach agreement with pachinko operators, views of pachinko are changing gradually. (*Nihon Keizai Shimbun*, 'Up and down cycles in gambling', p. 3.)

25. This can be seen in the self-regulation of the pachinko parlor industry, an effort to restrain the speculative element of play led by industry associations, as well as in activities to collect and donate funds under the name of contributing to society. For an example of the former, see Chapter 4 of this book. It is easy to find examples of the latter in the history of regional pachinko parlor associations. For example, the Hiroshima Prefecture Amusement Industry Association donated funds to various welfare projects through a 'goodwill box' activity designed to collect excess pachinko balls (annually since 1974; see Sōritsu Sanjū Shūnen Kinen Taikai Kinenshi Bukai 1993: 44–45, 53). Similarly, in Yamaguchi Prefecture, the local association donates funds to activities such as local volunteer programs and crime-prevention programs (Amusement Industry Association 1993: 92–93). These philanthropic activities such as making donations to programs that benefit the public do not differ from corporate activities conducted out of a company's consciousness of its social mission. However, pachinko is distinctive in the way it consciously seeks to secure meaning for its existence through such social activities. Regarding the relationship between society and the gambling industry, see Meich (2008: 458–65), which addresses the thinking on the subject and the related social consensus against a backdrop of the high taxes paid by the industry.
26. For an example, see *Asahi Shimbun* (1996), 'パチンコ店収入三〇兆円九四年調査全サービス業の二六パーセント' (Revenues of pachinko outlets reach 30 trillion yen, or 26 percent of all service industries in a 1994 survey, as the industry escapes the economic downturn to double its revenue over five years), January 26.
27. Ichiro Tanioka critically estimates the size of the pachinko market while comparing it to state-controlled gambling in the form of racing and the gambling industry in the United States (Tanioka 1998: Chapter 1). Tanioka points out the need to make this

calculation, as is carried out for state-controlled gambling and casinos in the United States, by subtracting the amount of winnings converted to cash from the total amount spent by customers – when customers reuse the same balls repeatedly, this refers to the entire amount spent reflecting the number of times they are reused, which should be more than 30 trillion yen – that is, to look at the amount lost by customers (1998: 22–29). However, in the case of pachinko, I have been unable to find any published historical data on the total amounts spent by customers and their win rates.

28. Sales is calculated as sales per machine per day multiplied by the number of business days per year multiplied by the total number of machines installed nationwide. As this method of estimation shows, average sales per machine per day has a major impact on the size of the market nationwide. Average sales varies widely by region, geographical conditions, parlor size and other factors. See Tanioka (1998: Chapter 1) and Mabe (1990: 36–43). Incidentally, estimates of the size of the industry in 1996 show average sales per machine of 20,000 yen and a total of 3.9 million machines installed.

29. Since net spending by customers (A – B) is equal to the amount spent on renting balls (A) – winnings exchanged for prizes and cash (B), there is some doubt about the size of the market based on the sales figure used. Mabe estimates the average winning percentage that determines B at approximately 60 percent as of 1987 (Mabe 1990: 37). However, different authors have different views on this rate of return, and there is no clear evidentiary basis for it. Daikoku Denki Co., Ltd., which supplies computer systems to pachinko parlors, provides high-precision data on this subject. While it does not release clear calculation methods, it claims that the data represent gross earnings calculated by subtracting sales of prizes from sales estimated using data for the parlors that have adopted its systems. Calculation of the average gross profit margin from the figures for the years 2011 through 2015 announced by Daikoku shows a margin of approximately 15 percent (Daikoku Denki Co., Ltd., 'Industry Environment', http://www.daikoku.co.jp/ir/ir_investor/environment/, accessed on May 7, 2017). If this gross profit margin were applied to the market in 1996, then market size calculated based on gross profit would have been approximately 4.52 trillion yen (about US$41 billion). However, this is the result of the calculation of market size in the gambling industry as described in Chapter 1 of Tanioka (1998). It would appear that no consensus has yet formed on an appropriate basis for calculating the size of the pachinko market.

30. See *Mainichi Shimbun* (1989), '桐生の中島さん、金持ち世界二七位パチンコ『タイガー』で' (Kiryu's Nakajima is the 27th richest person in the world, thanks to 'Tiger' pachinko), August 23, Tokyo evening edition.

31. See 'パチンコ屋及び回胴式遊技機等を設置して客に遊技をさせる事業所数' (Number of *pachinko-ya* and businesses in which spinning-drum machines etc. are installed for customer amusement) in National Police Agency (2016).

32. See Yano Research Institute (2016).

33. See Japan Productivity Center (2016).

34. As per the Ministry of Internal Affairs and Communications Statistics Bureau, '平成24年経済センサス—活動調査' (2012 Economic Census for Business Activity), 'Statistical Data', http://www.e-stat.go.jp/SG1/estat/List.do?bid=000001053304&cycode=0, accessed on April 27, 2017.

35. As per the Ministry of Internal Affairs and Communications Statistics Bureau, '平成18年事業所・企業統計調査' (2006 Establishment and Enterprise Census), 'Statistical Data', http://www.e-stat.go.jp/SG1/estat/List.do?bid=000001008300&cycode=0, accessed on April 27, 2017.
36. See Sugiyama (2008).
37. Examples include Sanjūgo nen no Ayumi Henshū Iinkai (1995: 21) and National Confederation of Amusement Industry Cooperatives (1977: 311).
38. Doubts about the theory that it originated in horizontal pinball games are presented in numerous works, including Murofushi (1994), Suzuki (1997), Yamada and Imaizumi (2002) and Jinbo (2007). Kazuo Sugiyama (2008) uses patent data to trace the evolution of pachinko based on technical characteristics and proposes hypotheses on what was imitated in Japan, what kinds of technological changes took place and how pachinko spread in Japan. Sugiyama's hypothesis on pachinko's propagation, and my criticisms of it, are discussed later.
39. See Ado Sākuru Setsuritsu Gojū Nen Henshū Iinkai (2014: 15). This publication argues that the first specialized *pachinko-ya* (see Note 21 above) was the Hirano Pachinko-ten, which obtained a license from the Aichi Prefecture Police Department in 1930.
40. See Ado Sākuru Setsuritsu Gojū Nen Henshū Iinkai (2014: 15).
41. Proposed in 1966 by Vernon, this model was initially used to explain the relationship between the product life cycle and trade structure or the shifting of production facilities overseas, but in recent years it has been adopted proactively in the fields of strategy, marketing and policy (Vernon 1966: 190–207; McGahan and Silverman 2001: 1141–60). An example of a related study in the field of policy can be found in Hanada (2011: 111–37), while an example in the field of strategy can be found in Yamada (1993: 233–40).
42. An example can be found in Higuchi (2006: 19–34), which attempts to analyze the life cycle of the VCR industry by dividing it into six stages.
43. See Mesgena (2006: 211–32).
44. Numerous studies of industrial history have pointed out that various restrictions are faced during the startup and growth stages of an industry. These represent difficulties related to market creation itself and its insufficiency, as well as the procurement of raw materials, production technologies and sales channels. They also vary widely due to the degrees of growth of individual product markets and industries. While there are too many related studies to list here, two particularly effective works that concern the awareness of the issues presented in this book are Hashimoto and Takeda (1985) and Takeda (1995).
45. See Asano (1970: 206–21). Around 1970, the economic scale of fields related to Japanese people's discretionary expenditure, particularly the leisure industry, grew massively, and these came to be seen as new growth industries. To reflect this change in society, administrators became more interested in leisure, and beginning in 1970 there was a full-fledged movement toward conducting various studies concerning discretionary consumption.
46. See *Monthly for Pachinko Management* (1973), '特別レポート 通産省がはじめてまとめた余暇問題レポート我が国余暇の現状と余暇時代への展望パチンコの伸びは低いと分析'(Special report: The first MITI report on leisure issues: The current state of leisure in Japan

and the outlook for the leisure era: Analysis shows low growth for pachinko), April, pp. 56–61. Additionally, the Human Subcommittee was established in the Industrial Structure Council; see Ministry of International Trade and Industry Industrial Structure Council (1973) for a summary of its analysis of the current state of Japanese people's leisure and its future forecasts.

47. It is said that it was funded by profits and subsidies from bicycle racing, other government-related financial institutions, and five private-sector companies. In 2000, the group's name was changed to the Free Time Design Association, and in March 2003 it was dissolved and absorbed by the Japan Productivity Center. Through these organizational changes, publication of the *Leisure White Paper* was continued by the Free Time Design Association and then the Japan Productivity Center.
48. See Asano (1970: 216–17).
49. See Lee, M. J. (2017).
50. For example, see Lee, K. (2017) and Neary (2017). The work was included in a list of novels recommended by BBC.com ('Ten books to read in 2017', http://www.bbc.com/culture/story/20161216-ten-books-to-read-in-2017, accessed on April 3, 2017), and as a recommended new book of the month by the *Chicago Review of Books* ('The 10 Best New Books to Read This February', February 1, 2017, https://chireviewofbooks.com/2017/01/31/the-10-best-new-books-to-read-this-february/, accessed on April 3, 2017), among numerous other accolades. In this way, the book attracted a very high degree of attention from the mass media.
51. See Stacks (2017).
52. See Neary (2017).
53. See Lee, M. J. (2017: 393).
54. See Willis and Lee (2007).
55. For example, see Chapter 5 of Kang (1996).
56. A presentation of this view can be found in Chapter 3 of Han (2010).
57. These surveys were not conducted for research purposes such as for use in this book, but instead primarily to ascertain students' views in order to decide course content and descriptions. For this reason, they were not designed as surveys suited to statistical analysis through means such as extraction of samples with reference to the content of the questions and subjects' ages, genders, etc. They also involve significant issues with regard to generalization in terms of judging whether or not responses are valid. I refer to them nonetheless in order to focus on some highly interesting changes that can be seen in their results.
58. Indeed, there is a need to incorporate regional differences when comparing results for large cities, where ethnic minorities tend to concentrate, with those for provincial cities. However, surveys of university students of around twenty years of age conducted for the same purposes at a university (R) in Tokyo (April 2010) and a university (S) in Shizuoka Prefecture (September 2012) generated results that were substantially the same as those from Hokkaido University. As such, it would not be a significant mistake to consider the differences apparent in the table as reflective of generational differences.
59. I hasten to add that, as pointed out by Kato (2011), in postwar Japan the presence of ethnic minority Koreans had become invisible. This invisibility may have in some

ways weakened younger generations' awareness of the link between the pachinko industry and ethnic minority Koreans, and it should be considered with care. Suffice to note that there is a need to turn our gaze toward changes in the form of industry and that there are limits on how well conventional points of view capture actual industrial conditions and the realities of ethnic minority Koreans' circumstances.

60. For example, see Sakai (2010) and Bessatsu Takarajima Henshūbu (2011). The wording of each of these titles, for example 'Scary tales of a pachinko parlor' ('コワ〜いパチンコ店の話'), seems symbolic of its author's viewpoint.
61. For example, see *Asahi Shimbun* (1975), '脱税王はパチンコ' (Pachinko is the king of tax evasion), April 24.
62. See *Asahi Shimbun* (1976), '病院、いぜん、「脱税王」' (Hospitals remain the kings of tax evasion), May 16.
63. See Kamei (1990).
64. See Tada (1974: 46–47).
65. See Kato (1984).
66. See Ishige (1989).
67. See Tanioka (1998).
68. See Takeuchi (1972: 268–81).
69. Of course, what Takeuchi refers to as the 'underground economy' is a proposed new way of looking at the essence of the Japanese economy from the perspective of peripheral economic activities.
70. See Kaji (2015).
71. See Kawai (1995: 1).
72. See Mabe (1990). Numerous works analyze the economic infrastructure of pachinko service and machine providers and the industry in connection with its economic nature as a massive market; see Murofushi (1994), Kang (1996) and Miyatsuka (1997). These works not only consider the structural characteristics of the pachinko industry, reflecting the fact that it was attracting attention at the time as a massive industry, but also propose future reforms.
73. For an explanation of matters related to subjects such as planning parlor openings, choosing locations and parlor management, see Nakazawa (1995). For some of the many other works on the subject, see Maeda (1991) and Yoshida (1989).
74. See, for example, Kaji (2006; 2007a; 2007b; 2009a; 2009b; 2010). For a distillation of these studies, see Kaji (2015).
75. The evolution of public opinion with regard to gambling seen above in the opinion survey under Note 24 means that restrictions based on the societal view gradually weakened. Tanioka introduces the concept of 'decriminalization' as a way of thinking that supported the acceptance of pachinko and other types of gambling in society. Examples of criminalization of unethical or immoral acts under the penal code during a time in which a certain religion or certain values dominated include the outlawing of alcoholic beverages during the Prohibition era in the United States. In developed countries, diversification of values has led to the removal of material such as pornography that do not cause criminal damage to specific individuals from the definition of crime, based on the belief that they are not actually harmful to legal

protections in a trend known as 'decriminalization' (Tanioka 1998: 150–51). The concept has some commonalities with the debate on whether state-controlled gambling should continue or be abolished in the 1961 report by the State-controlled Racing Survey Committee.

76. See Sugiyama (2008).
77. See Figure 1.2 (left) in Chapter 1 of this book.
78. See *Nihon Keizai Shimbun* (1983), '地方公営ギャンブル寒い冬、「職員ボーナス・手当削れ」—経営改善へ自治省お触れ' (Challenging times for local state-controlled gambling with 'cuts in staff bonuses and allowances': The Ministry of Home Affairs officially announces management reforms), November 24, p. 3, and *Nihon Keizai Shimbun* (1983), '公営ギャンブル青息——岸和田競輪、赤字解消妙案なし' (Distress in state-controlled gambling: No hopeful solution to the losses at bicycle races in the city of Kishiwada), March 10, p. 10.
79. Thirteen revisions have been carried out, with the latest occurring in 2013.
80. See Note 21 above. The name was later changed to '*pachinko hōru*' ('pachinko hall') in the seventh revision in 1972.
81. See Hashimoto and Takeda (1985).
82. See Han (2010). Related statements in this paragraph are also from the analysis in the book referenced here.
83. See Han (2010).
84. For a more detailed account of Figure 0.3, please refer to the original Japanese publication – Han (2018: 30–32). The figure illustrates the unprecedented situation in the pachinko industry brought by the market's extremely rapid growth.
85. Takeuchi identifies three distinguishing properties of the leisure industry in Japan: (1) 'street' leisure, in which people move around from one activity to another instead of taking a rest as in the West; (2) rapid propagation and demise; and (3) everyday leisure centered on transportation terminals (Takeuchi 1983: Chapter 3). Considered in light of his second point, the growth of pachinko until the 1970s did not stand out compared to other types of leisure.
86. Chesbrough (2006) defined open innovation as 'the use of purposive inflows and outflows of knowledge to accelerate internal innovation and expand the market for external use of innovation'.
87. As for the reasons why I did not include an analysis of *pachislot*, please refer to pages 34 and 35 of the original Japanese publication (Han 2018), in which I also confessed that I excluded other areas besides parlors and manufacturers in the pachinko industry.

Chapter 1

1. Prior to World War II, Japan had no comprehensive legal framework governing amusement businesses. Instead, prefectures enacted their own ordinances concerning such businesses in their region through orders issued by the metropolitan police department, for example the Amusement Parlor Regulations (Yūgijō Torishimari Kisoku) issued by the imperial capital of Tokyo. A broad range of entertainment businesses were regulated by police, who yielded considerable authority (Nagai 2002: 22). Nagai observes that the Amusement Establishment Control Act (later amended to the Act on Control and Improvement of the Amusement Business, etc.) was hurriedly

enacted in order to minimize any disorder that the lack of a police structure might invite in entertainment districts as the new postwar constitution took effect following Japan's surrender (Nagai 2002: 76). For more information about the nature of this law, including its attempt to reduce the authority of the police after World War II, see Chapter 2 of Nagai (2002).

2. Various names were applied to pachinko parlors, including 'game parlors', 'amusement parlors' and 'pachinko parlors', including in statistical records. To avoid confusion, this book exclusively uses the term 'pachinko parlors', while the terms 'amusement parlor' and 'pachinko hall' have been used consistently since the March 1972 revision of the principal edition of *Administrative Statistics* published by the Administrative Management Agency (Statistics Bureau 1972).
3. A Type 3 industry. Type 1 industries encompassed 'traditional Japanese restaurants, eateries, cafes and other businesses that entertain customers or serve them food and drink', while Type 2 industries included 'cabarets, dance halls and other businesses that encourage customers to dance'.
4. Nagai observes that as the process of licensing such businesses was entrusted to each prefecture's public safety commission, the range of businesses subjected to such requirements shrank, as did the authority of the police to regulate entertainment businesses following World War II (Nagai 2002: 76–77). Prior to World War II, there were no laws or regulations that applied across the entire amusement industry. Instead, a series of ordinances established for individual industries (by each prefecture) collectively comprised a body of regulation (Nagai 2002: 22–23, 42–45). The Amusement Parlor Regulations offer an example for amusement parlors. The regulations remained in effect after the end of the war. However, they lapsed with the enactment of a law (the Act on the Effect, etc. of Provisions of Orders Effective as of Time of Enforcement of the Constitution of Japan) following the adoption of the new constitution in 1947 (Nagai 2002: 62). The Entertainment Establishment Control Act was enacted in order to address the confusion that occurred once the basis for police regulation was removed. The new law covered the entire entertainment industry, and pachinko was incorporated into its framework. Of the Entertainment Establishment Control Act, Nagai notes that while the law introduced a legal framework to facilitate comprehensive management of amusement businesses, it was rushed through the Diet without sufficient discussion. As a result of factors such as the narrowing of the range of businesses to which the law applied, regulation of the industry was in fact weakened compared to the prewar arrangement in which it was managed under the strong authority of the police (see Chapter 2 of Nagai [2002]).
5. In 1954, the Act on Control and Improvement of the Amusement Business, etc. (previously the Entertainment Establishment Control Act) was amended by the Act to Amend the Local Taxation Act, etc. (as amended by Supplementary Provision 43) (Act No. 95). The revised language cited pachinko businesses as an example of amusement parlors that invite gambling as described in Article 3, Paragraph 3 (Takita 1965: 61).
6. 'The popularity of pachinko is nothing if not disgusting [...]. Money for buying paperback books is used instead to buy balls as the heads of young students and factory workers grow increasingly empty [...]. In residential areas, one often sees housewives who have cast aside their shopping baskets in favor of funding a rattling cascade of

pachinko balls with their grocery money' (*Asahi Shimbun* [1952], '天声人語' [People's voice], June 25).

7. See *Asahi Shimbun* (1952), '池田さん、慎重な第一声生活向上が建前競輪、パチンコは廃止へ' (Minister Ikeda cautiously voices support for improving living standards in first speech, moves toward eliminating bicycle racing and pachinko), October 31.
8. See Introduction of this book.
9. See Yukiko Fushimi (1955), 'パチンコの機械裏から' (From behind the pachinko machine), *Jinsei Techō*, 4(5), pp. 34–39. Fushimi describes how she was forced by a variety of circumstances to work at a parlor for a little over a year around 1954.
10. For example, see the timeline in National Confederation of Amusement Industry Cooperatives (1977: 70–71) as well as the article entitled '業界25年を語る座談会 隆盛時代から連発式禁止前後' (Round-table on twenty-five years in the industry: From peak prosperity to the time of the prohibition on successive-shot machines) (1977: 148–65); see also Takeuchi (1972).
11. See Sanjūnen no Ayumi Henshū Iinkai (1990: 24).
12. It has been noted that there were 10,000 'outsiders', or unlicensed establishments, at the 1953 peak shown in Table 1.1 (Jinbo 2007: 29).
13. See Sanjūnenshi Henshū Iinkai (1981: 337).
14. See Wakamiya (2010).
15. See *Yūgi Tsūshin* (1955), '対談・パチンコ創世記を語る' (Dialog: Discussing the beginnings of pachinko), July 30, and Yūgi Tsūshinsha (2001: 67). Pachinko is believed to have originated in the 1920s before enjoying a 'meteoric rise as it captured the attention of children at street stalls, night-time fairs and similar events' (Nihon Yūgi Shinbunsha 1953: 18).
16. When the role of pin adjustment became comparatively less important as manufacturing and design technologies were improved and new types of machines appeared starting in the 1980s, it is likely that parlors' ability to choose machines from a diverse range of models became more important.
17. For a detailed account of Masamura Shōkai, including a history of its founder, see Suzuki (2001). This chapter relies heavily on Suzuki's work, which draws on internal documents and first-hand accounts from family members who managed pachinko businesses and others who were involved.
18. *Ōru Seikatsu* is believed to have originated with the renaming and relaunch of the amusement magazine *Hōpu* ('hope') as a lifestyle guidance magazine (Jitsugyō no nihonsha 1967: 166).
19. 'Machines designed by Masamura can be held up as the godfathers of the golden age of the industry and the forefather of the transformation of pachinko machines' (Nihon Yūgi Shinbunsha 1953: 40).
20. See Imperial Investigation (1955). The record included in the *Imperial Bank Company Digest* does not align with the description of Masamura Shōkai's operations given above ('sell pachinko machines and operate amusement parlors'), and that publication does not treat Masamura Shōkai as a 'manufacturer that also operates a parlor'. Additionally, its count of 400 employees may include original equipment manufacturer (OEM) employees, and it is unclear whether the annual sales figure of 500 million yen

includes revenue from the parlor business. In this way, boundaries between companies may vary with the entity conducting the research. Certainly, Masamura's management of Masamura Shōkai in fact extended to factories that operated as subcontractors of the company's manufacturing department, and in that sense, the categorization used by the *Imperial Bank Company Digest* is not incorrect. For accounting purposes, as a management entity, Masamura Shōkai Co., Ltd. was limited to machine sales and parlor businesses. My purpose here is not to offer a precise description of the businesses in which the company was involved, but rather to affirm that Masamura Shōkai occupied an important position in the pachinko industry of the time.

21. According to Emiko Suzuki, the company employed from seventy to 100 employees at each of its seven plants, including subcontractor facilities, from 1954 to 1955 (Suzuki 2001: 277).
22. Pachinko industry journals and books unvaryingly cite the importance of improvements to pachinko machines (these accounts include some factual errors, but I will omit the details of their assertions here). Because refinements such as the Masamura Gauge, 'all-win' prize ball dispensation and successive-shot mechanisms, all of which are described later in this book, were invented by different people and companies, subsequent observers have not made a precise assessment of the extent to which each contributed to the growth of the pachinko industry during this period. Due to the difficulty of conducting an empirical analysis of the technologies fielded by small and medium enterprises, I have opted to interpret technologies that are noteworthy from the standpoint of the management of parlor businesses while integrating various associated views.
23. See Suzuki (2001: 135–41).
24. See *Yūgi Tsūshin* (1951), 'ゲージ板の打開に大山商店の新製品' (A new product with a breakthrough gauge board from the manufacturer, Ōyama Shōten), October 25.
25. *Yūgi Tsūshin*, 'A new product'.
26. See Nihon Yūgi Shinbunsha (1953).
27. In the following account of the characteristics of the Masamura Gauge regarding the positioning of pins in *komono* machines, I have drawn on Suzuki (2001: 120–35) unless otherwise noted. Figure 1.1 is based on my own understanding.
28. See Hyakusu Henshūshitsu (1985: 6).
29. The method of controlling customers' winning percentages by adjusting pins near catchers was the same technique used by prewar machines and *komono* machines.
30. The description of machines in this paragraph is based on Nikkōso (Japan Amusement Machine Industry Association) (n.d.), '遊技機の変遷と法的規制' (Game machine transitions and legal regulations), Nihon Yūgi Shinbunsha (1953: 17–40), and Hyakusu Henshūshitsu (1985: 6–18).
31. Whereas '*komono* machines of the time dispensed balls one at a time', the 'all-win' machines, which 'mechanized a stream of ten balls' and which 'embodied the industry's greatest invention', were praised for prompting 'rapid progress in the industry' (*Yūgi Tsūshin* [1951], 'パチンコ隆盛期 (1)' [Pachinko's golden era, part 1], October 5 and *Yūgi Tsūshin* [1951], 'パチンコ隆盛期(2)' [Pachinko's golden era, part 2], October 15).
32. See Yamada and Imaizumi (2002: 14).

33. Improvements in the mechanisms that underpinned this functionality (i.e., in ball replenishment mechanisms) were essential to the industry's long-term development. One factor, as discussed in Chapter 2, was that these improvements addressed the automatic replenishment and management of balls, which were the most labor-intensive aspects of the parlor business. Until the 1950s, people manually replenished balls in narrow spaces between rows of machines (known as 'islands' in industry parlance). From the 1960s, this approach gave way to built-in replenishment systems in machines, which in turn gradually developed into systems that operated separately from machines at all parlors (Higyoku Ehōden: Takeya Gojūnen no Ayumi Hensanshitsu 1996). Another factor was that growth in parlor sales and customer satisfaction depended on increases in the number of game balls played and prize balls won at a time when there was remarkably little increase in the cost of balls, which rose from 3 yen in 1972 to 4 yen in 1978. Improvements in machines that could feed and recover more balls and development of replenishment mechanisms were prerequisites for market growth. These were not likely urgent priorities during the 1960s, when successive-shot machines were banned. However, manufacturers faced pressure to provide such capabilities from the 1970s after those regulations were relaxed, especially when Fībā-type machines (see Chapter 4) that inspired fondness for gambling were introduced.
34. See Higyoku Ehōden: Takeya Gojūnen no Ayumi Hensanshitsu (1996: 24).
35. See Jinbo (2007: 30).
36. The appearance of machines that could launch balls continuously, for example successive-shot and circulating machines, had a number of attendant effects. From before World War II, two types of pachinko machines coexisted: token (alternatively, 'metal') machines, the original type that used 1-sen copper coins (worth about one-hundredth of a yen) and later coins; and steel-ball machines, which appeared when the former type was banned. Two newspaper articles describe an entrepreneur named Seiichi Fujii, who developed the first steel-ball machine and received a business license from the Nagoya police (*Yūgi Tsūshin*, 'Dialog', and *Yūgi Tsūshin* [1956], '特集業界むかしむかし 名古屋市藤井正一氏に聞く' [Special feature: Ask Seiichi Fujii of Nagoya about the industry of old], November 12; see Yūgi Tsūshinsha [2011: 18–20 and 16–17, respectively]). Token pachinko machines made a comeback in the northern Kanto region after World War II, and they came to characterize certain regions, for example Gunma Prefecture, where they were well loved. However, once successive-shot machines gained popularity due to the more exciting speculative experience they offered customers, token machines, which were incapable of matching that appeal, subsequently disappeared (Yūgi Tsūshinsha 2011: 15; Suzuki 2001: 181).
37. See *Yūgi Tsūshin* (1952), '創刊1周年記念特集 ベニヤ1枚にも苦心 M式の本家であるM氏と伊藤主幹との対談' (Special first anniversary commemorative feature: Agonizing over a single sheet of plywood / A conversation between Masamura, creator of the Masamura design, and Editor-in-Chief Ito), October 5.
38. 'If you travel to the area behind the station in Nagoya or to other areas where customers only frequent parlors with Masamura machines, for example Kobe and Miyazaki, you'll find nameplates being bought and sold for 100 yen apiece' (*Yūgi Tsūshin* [1953], '偽物横行に断乎鉄槌を揮ふ' [Crackdown on rampant knockoffs], January 14).

Masamura Shōkai is said to have addressed the problem by calling on parlors to purchase nameplates directly from its sales offices.

39. While it is impossible to synthesize a systematic history of the people involved in the pachinko business during this time, one gets a strong sense from stories recorded in the literature of the period between the late 1940s and the early 1950s as a time of reconstruction and recovery. In these stories, one sees people with experience in a variety of industries entering the business after noticing the profit potential of pachinko as a popular pastime during a time of instability and wildly fluctuating economic fortunes. For example, Saito (1972) introduces the achievements of some of the industry's leading figures, along with the motivations of those who entered the game industry. All of the industry's pioneers were people who entered the business around 1950, and they all had business experience from at least one prior venture. Saito notes that some discovered the market themselves and resolved to enter it, for example after hearing rumors on the street or seeing people playing with steel balls (1972: 61, 123), while others became actively involved as they enjoyed success after initially starting out with some suspicion based on the sales activities of manufacturers that proposed opening a parlor on an experimental basis (1972: 77–78). In many cases, entrepreneurs opened parlors based on word of mouth from acquaintances who knew how to make money. Instances where parlors were jointly run by more than one individual are an example of such cases (Saito 1972: 136). Yoshinobu Tanaka of Sendai, who was unemployed, opened the city's third parlor in 1950 with the encouragement of an acquaintance. He describes how customers were initially skeptical before they got a taste for pachinko, at which point volume grew until the business was full every day (Saito 1972: 153–54). Keizo Matsuo of Osaka opened a parlor in 1949, and Kiyotaka Hirata of Kagawa Prefecture, in 1951, at the urging of acquaintances who described pachinko as 'a pretty promising business' (Saito 1972: 232, 197).
40. See *Yūgi Tsūshin* (1951), '約8割がパチンコ申請 東京3千店を近く突破か' (About 80 percent of applications are for pachinko / number of parlors in Tokyo may reach 3000), October 25. The rest of this paragraph draws on this reference.
41. This trend toward larger establishments was particularly pronounced in Kyoto (*Yūgi Tsūshin*, 'About 80 percent of applications are for pachinko').
42. See Asahi Shimbunsha (1953: 255).
43. That said, different calculation standards were used when determining the size of the state-controlled gambling market and the size of the pachinko industry (Kitahara and Nippon Chōki Shinyō Ginkō Sangyō Kenkyūkai 1970: 168–70). For example, with regard to the size of the leisure industry in 1967, gambling sports-based businesses were estimated to total 215.8 billion yen (about US$600 million) (of which horse racing represented 83.3 billion yen [about US$230 million]), and the size of the pachinko market, which was categorized as a type of commercial entertainment business, was estimated to be 414 billion yen (about US$1.2 billion), about twice as large. Whereas the size of the gambling sports market was estimated by subtracting payouts such as dividends from sales (about 75 percent) and then adding admission fees, the size of the pachinko market was calculated by multiplying the number of pachinko machines nationwide by sales per machine, with the result that the figure included the value of prizes returned to customers.

44. See Asahi Shimbunsha (1953: 255).
45. Unless otherwise noted, the description in this paragraph is drawn from Suzuki (2001).
46. Many parlor operators sought to build and improve machines in the manner of Masamura during this period. Unlike today, there was not significant demand to introduce new machines on a regular basis, as when pachinko parlors reopen after replacing some of their machines with new models, and demand for machines was not consistent enough to provide the basis for specialized manufacturers. Consequently, people who built machines ran pachinko parlor businesses while selling the machines (Saito 1972: 100). From the perspective of parlor operators, the technical hurdles were not particularly significant, and due to the frequency with which mechanical issues occurred, repair service was an essential part of their operation. Moreover, sometimes ideas related to equipment and machines emerged from information obtained through customer contacts (Saito 1972: 100).
47. Documentation related to one of the five parlors cannot be confirmed after the establishment of the company in 1951; only the remaining four are analyzed below (see Note 80 below).
48. See Masamura Shōkai (1954).
49. See Suzuki (2001: 178–99). Pin adjustment required managerial expertise that went beyond the mere technique of changing pin positions. Masao Sadoshima of the city of Fukuoka, who opened a pachinko business around 1950, was reportedly surprised by the managerial technique employed by his business partner that involved operating in the red for a month by dispensing balls so that customers would win (Saito 1972: 136). Because this operational approach was unique to pachinko and differed from that employed in other industries, parlors were reliant upon pin adjustment and a carefully calculated business plan. Masamura is likely to have required customers (parlor operators) to compile a statistical ledger (*tōkeichō*, a record of ball payouts) as a way of offering such guidance.
50. Suzuki observes that the personal connections between the founder and these 'disciples' were closer than the contractual relationships of distributors (Suzuki 2001: 181–83, 225–33). Some parlors opened after receiving funds from Masamura Shōkai. Verifiable documents record four loans in 1953 in amounts ranging from 4 million (about US$11,100) to 8.5 million yen (about US$23,600) (Masamura Shōkai 1954). An account by Masamura's second-oldest daughter, an executive officer at Masamura Shōkai when the interview was conducted, indicated that the purpose of the loans was to provide funds for use in opening new parlors (based on research I conducted on January 18, 2005).
51. See Suzuki (2001: 180–83, 225–33).
52. See *Yūgi Tsūshin* (1952), '経営研究' (Management research), February 15.
53. See Suzuki (2001: 183).
54. See Suzuki (2001: 183).
55. See Suzuki (2001: 227).
56. See Suzuki (2001: 183).
57. Although Masamura Shōkai's market share in Tokyo is unknown, the company enjoyed a solid reputation (see Note 38 above).

58. For more information about the process by which the company established its contract factories, see Suzuki (2001: 174–78, 214–20). Unless otherwise noted, the description in this paragraph is drawn from that source.
59. See Suzuki (2001: 177).
60. 'It's no good if the spring is firm. With customers playing from morning to evening, a firm spring means they'll get blisters on their hands. But our machines don't do that' (see *Yūgi Tsūshin*, 'Special first anniversary commemorative feature').
61. 'We meticulously examine each and every sheet of plywood we receive. If we receive 100 sheets, we check every last one of them. They're made to be rugged, but they must have high quality, too. We send back the sheets we don't like' (see *Yūgi Tsūshin*, 'Special first anniversary commemorative feature'). See also Suzuki (2001: 190–95).
62. See Suzuki (2001: 184–90).
63. See Suzuki (1997: 20).
64. See *Yūgi Tsūshin*, 'Special first anniversary commemorative feature'.
65. See *Yūgi Tsūshin*, 'Special first anniversary commemorative feature'.
66. Circulating machines were selling for 8000 yen (about US$22), and machine gun-style machines, for 7500 yen (about US$21) (Nihon Yūgi Shinbunsha 1953: 315–17).
67. Describing his experience with a management crisis after purchasing defective machines in 1953 or 1954, the former director of the Okayama Prefecture Amusement Industry Cooperative, a gentleman with the surname Chihara whose first name is unclear, said during a roundtable discussion, 'My business almost went under due to the debut of those "machine gun-style" machines. We bought machines that were manufactured poorly' (San'yō Mākettingu Sentā 1991: 107).
68. Sanjūnenshi Henshū Iinkai (1981: 340).
69. See '(表)警察庁調 全国営業許可数推移' ([Table] Trend in nationwide business permits as researched by the National Police Agency), in Shiryō Henshū Iinkai (1989: 181).
70. See Economic Planning Agency (1957: 114).
71. See Research and Statistics Department, Ministry of Economy, Trade and Industry (1958: 238–39).
72. See Asahi Shimbunsha (1955: 526).
73. Certainly, records indicate that the number of parlors fell and that their average size grew in Nagoya during the year that ended in June 1952, and that small parlors were being forced out of business (*Chūō Kōron* [1952], '名古屋とパチンコ' [Nagoya and pachinko], November). However, based on the fact that the number of parlors in operation fell from 649 at the end of 1950 to 539 over the thirteen-month period from January 1951 to March 1952 as the number of closures (756) outpaced the number of new parlors (646), we can conclude that pachinko was an unstable business from which numerous establishments withdrew.
74. While it is necessary to account for the effects of a two-month crackdown on entertainment businesses operating without licenses that began in October of the same year (Planning Division, General Affairs Office, Metropolitan Police Department 1953: 166–67), that campaign is not enough to explain the enormous number of parlor closures. The 5126 figure is likely to be a misrepresentation of the actual figure of 5182 (4019 [the number of parlors operating during the previous year] + 3075 + 988

+ 269 [the number of businesses that changed their category to pachinko from another gaming business] + 56 [the number of parlor businesses undergoing interior and/or machine changes] − 3225 = 5182). Incidentally, there were 4019 parlors as of the end of 1951, and the difference between that figure and the number given in the previous year's yearbook (4200) is too large to ignore. The discrepancy likely reflects the fact that the figures were collected in different months. The details remain unclear, but the tendency for closures to exceed new business openings remains unchanged.

75. A document known as the Masamura Account Book (Masamura Daifukuchō) records information including the number of 'out' balls, 'safe' balls, and the difference between the two for each machine along with the parlor's overall losses and profits and a description of how machines' pins were adjusted (Aida and Akagi 1997: 309–11). For the purposes of this chapter, the accumulation of management expertise includes, in the case of Masamura Shōkai, the ability to analyze such records of business performance, to ascertain the state of competing parlors' operations (Aida and Akagi 1997: 304–09) and to adjust pins accordingly. Incidentally, I was unable to review the Masamura Daifukuchō myself, but the phrase likely refers to the statistical ledger (*tōkeichō*) mentioned in Note 49. The data continues to be used in parlor operations, which have now been computerized (Aida and Akagi 1997: 304–09). Reflecting its focus on a stable revenue base, this chapter uses the sales statistics tables (*eigyō tōkeihyō*) and the statistical tables (*tōkeihyō*), which differ in format but contain the same data.
76. See Nakajima (1997: 25–26).
77. See Saito (1972: 136).
78. See Saito (1972: 136).
79. See *Sandē Mainichi* (1953), 'パチンコ太平記' (Pachinko *taiheiki*: Chronicles of chaotic competition in the pachinko industry), November 8.
80. Sales statistics (*eigyō tōkeisho*) remain for four parlors: the Main Branch, the Oshikiri Branch, the Endonji Branch and the Matsubara Branch. Whereas the Masamura Account Book (Masamura Daifukuchō) described in Note 75 tracked statistics in terms of ball counts, the sales statistics tables (*eigyō tōkeihyō*) used monetary figures.
81. See Suzuki (2001: 202–06).
82. See Yashima (1954: 68). Keizo Matsuo, who opened a parlor in Osaka in 1951, described the period as 'a time when there was no end of parlors that went bust without lasting even a month as a result of how their pin adjusters did their jobs' due to semi-professional and better customers (he was probably referring to the first half of the 1950s) (Saito 1972: 233).
83. In the pachinko industry, gross profit is calculated by subtracting prize sales from gross sales and then adding profit from the prize redemption rate (which is calculated by subtracting the cost of prizes from the value of customer redemptions). Since it is not possible to determine the prize redemption rate or the cost of prizes from Masamura Shōkai documents for this period, I will define gross profit as described in the Notes of Figure 1.3. Chapter 4 of this book calculates the cost of prizes using existing data.
84. This chapter considers the 'opening' and 'closing' of pins to be the principal factors that influence the graph. By focusing on elements that fall under the control of the parlor, we are able to abstract the effects of customers' selection of machines.

85. The extent to which this occurred is likely to have varied greatly based on the quality of the machines. Additionally, because increasing customer skills and competition with other parlors were both important considerations in pin adjustment, as described above, variability in the gross profit margin may have been the result of these factors. In this sense, one must acknowledge that there are limits to how well gross profit margin can be analyzed based on its relationship to pin adjustment. However, this chapter considers pin adjustment as a process that was carried out based on business performance, which in turn was influenced by factors such as the mechanical quality of machines and competition with other parlors, and it seems reasonable to approach data that tracks changes over time as the result of operators' having taken those various elements into account.
86. See Takeda (2007: 55–56).
87. See *Playgraph* (1999), '保存版資料 パチンコ産業五十年史 1945～1998(年表)' (Special issue: 50 years of the pachinko industry, 1945–1998 [a timeline]), September, p. 105.
88. See Nakamura (1955: 49).
89. See Morita (1953: 67–69), who proposed that the value of prizes be deducted when calculating usage fees including taxes and that a pro forma taxation method that takes into account differentials by regional classification (*kyūchi*), which considers disparities in the cost of living and other factors, be introduced based on a consideration of actual operating conditions in order to resolve tax issues. Other information in this paragraph relating to Hiroshima Prefecture is drawn from this source.
90. See *Yūgi Tsūshin* (1953), '各地で起こる不当入場税と斗ふ業界' (An industry grapples with unfair admission taxes in various regions), January 25.
91. See Shiryō Henshū Iinkai (1989).
92. See *Yūgi Tsūshin*, 'An industry grapples with unfair taxes'.
93. See *Yūgi Tsūshin* (1953), '遊技場の外形課税に就いて 自治柴田課長と本社伊藤主幹との対話' (A dialog between Section Manager Murasaki of local government and Yugi Tsūshinsha Editor-in-Chief Ito about the pro forma tax on pachinko parlors), February 25.
94. The renewal period was subsequently extended to three months by a revision to the law in 1964; see Sanjūnenshi Henshū Iinkai (1981: 354).
95. See Shiryō Henshū Iinkai (1989).
96. See Nakamura (1955: 49–50).
97. See Nakamura (1955: 49–50).
98. See Nakamura (1955: 50).
99. See Nakamura (1955: 50).
100. See Sanjūnenshi Henshū Iinkai (1981: 329–30).
101. See National Confederation of Amusement Industry Cooperatives (1977: 127). In light of the fact that amusement regulations such as these were put in place by individual prefectures' ordinances, any analysis must take into account the fact that regulations exhibited regional variations. In fact, there were regional differences in the admission tax rate, and machine gun-style machines with a pronounced speculative element were banned by the cities of Iizuka (in Fukuoka Prefecture) and Ube (in Yamaguchi Prefecture). See *Yūgi Tsūshin* (1953), '機関銃号等の問題近く解決か' (Are we nearing a

solution for machine gun-style machines?), September 5. That said, an examination of the number of parlors approaching June 1955 reveals a common downward trend (see '単発式パチンコ機械制限機順位監視緩和方嘆願の要旨' [Single-shot pachinko machine limiter standings: Summary of a petition to loosen monitoring] of May 13, 1955, in Shiryō Henshū Iinkai [1989]). I would like to emphasize that this chapter addresses nationwide effects and common changes while incorporating a description of how regulations varied from prefecture to prefecture.

102. See Planning Division, General Affairs Office, Metropolitan Police Department (1953: 171–72).
103. See *Yūgi Tsūshin* (1952), '新規開業制限せず 警視庁保安部保安係警部鈴木吉助' (No limits on the establishment of new businesses: Kichisuke Suzuki of the Security Section, Security Department, Metropolitan Police Department), October 5.
104. See Morita (1953: 67).
105. The ban envisioned machines that made it easy to launch balls successively and that invited fondness for gambling by allowing more than 130 balls to be launched per minute (see 'パチンコ取締り措置再検討に関する請願書' [A petition for reconsideration of pachinko controls] in Shiryō Henshū Iinkai [1989]).
106. See 'A petition for reconsideration of pachinko controls', in Shiryō Henshū Iinkai (1989). In some regions, including Aichi Prefecture, the ban took effect in May 1955.
107. See 'A petition for reconsideration of pachinko controls', in Shiryō Henshū Iinkai (1989).
108. See *Gekkan Yūki* (1954), '連発式禁止の波紋' (Repercussions of the successive-shot ban), December.
109. See Planning Division, General Affairs Office, Metropolitan Police Department (1953: 172). According to one industry newspaper, cigarette buyers emerged as a problem in June 1953 (see *Yūgi Tsūshin* [1953], '煙草の買取り屋' [Tobacco buyers], June 15).
110. See Sanjūnenshi Henshū Iinkai (1981: 351).
111. See Shiryō Henshū Iinkai (1989). Starting in November 1954, individual prizes were limited to a maximum value of 100 yen (about US$0.28). (See *Noda Keizai* [1964], '第二の焦点 "パチンコで息抜こう" 大衆のための健全娯楽化図るパチンコ業界' [Focus 2: Let us relax with pachinko! Pachinko industry is trying to transform the industry into healthy entertainment for the masses], 896, p. 81.) These maximum values were based on the recognition of pachinko businesses subject to the constraint that prizes could only 'provide temporary entertainment', as defined in a provision in Article 185 of the Penal Code (Takita 1965: 62–64).
112. See Yashima (1954: 69).
113. In Article 23 of Chapter 6, 'Standards of business conduct', the April 1954 revision of the Entertainment Establishment Control Act explicitly prohibited 'providing cash, securities, etc., as prizes'. Following the enactment of the Act on Control and Improvement of the Amusement Business, etc., in 1985 (revising the Entertainment Establishment Control Act), purchases of prizes by businesses were prohibited.
114. See Shiryō Henshū Iinkai (1989: 76–117). More intense public criticism of pachinko was emphasized at the meeting, against the backdrop of such enforcement actions. In Osaka Prefecture, a petition outlining abuses was submitted by the Council of

Public Welfare Committee Members (Minsei Jōmu Iin Kyōgikai) (Shiryō Henshū Iinkai 1989: 86–87), and it is likely that such criticism was related to the relationships between parlors and buyers, and between parlors and organized crime.

115. Shiryō Henshū Iinkai (1989: 85–86). On November 30, 1954, police in Tokyo ordered seventeen operators to close their businesses for fifteen to thirty-five days for operating without a license or using buyers.
116. See Yashima (1954: 68).
117. See Yashima (1954: 68–69).
118. For more information about the Takei incident, see Planning Division, General Affairs Office, Metropolitan Police Department (1957: 264–65).
119. See the timeline in '景品買いが暴力団の資金源となっていたのは明らか' (It's clear that purchases of prizes were providing a source of funds for organized crime) in National Confederation of Amusement Industry Cooperatives (1977: 70).
120. For a summary of initiatives undertaken by various regions to address the issue of buyers, see Shiryō Henshū Iinkai (1989: 76–128). For example, the city of Kawasaki conducted a trial in which a group of unemployed individuals purchased prizes, and similar efforts were undertaken in Hokkaido and Sendai as well (Shiryō Henshū Iinkai 1989: 94).
121. See *Gekkan Yūki* (1955), '新春の禁止運動をきる' (Breaking off the New Year's prohibition movement), New Year's Special Issue.
122. In the words of a legal advisor of the Amusement Machine Manufacturing Industry Association (*Gekkan Yūki* [1955], '業界はこれでよいのか' [Is the industry OK with this?], May).
123. *Gekkan Yūki*, 'Is the industry OK'.
124. See Sanjūnenshi Henshū Iinkai (1981: 338–40). Although it is difficult to develop a clear, full picture of these efforts, there were initiatives by involved groups in other regions as well that sought to resolve the issue of the involvement of organized crime, including a 'movement to drive out criminal groups' in Hiroshima Prefecture (Saito 1972: 124). It is particularly easy to discover such campaigns during the 1960s. For examples from Tokyo, see *Yūgi Tsūshin* (1956), '東京総連緊急理事会百四十余名追放等を決議す' (Emergency session of the Tokyo Sōren resolves to expel more than 140), July 15, p. 2; for Aichi Prefecture, see *Yūgi Tsūshin* (1963), '暴力団更生資金問題' (Funds for regenerating organized crime seen as problematic), March 5, and *Yūgi Tsūshin* (1963), '盛り上がる暴力団追放運動' (Campaign to expel criminal groups gains momentum), March 25, p. 5; and for Fukuoka Prefecture, see *Yūgi Tsūshin* (1964), '福岡市業者八十名が防犯組織で暴力追放' (80 Fukuoka entrepreneurs expel criminal groups via an anti-crime organization), November 5, p. 19.
125. See *Gekkan Yūki* (1955), '単発式で減ったバイ人達' (Single-shot machines lead to decrease in the number of buyers), May.
126. See Sanjūnenshi Henshū Iinkai (1981: 342–43).
127. See Planning Division, General Affairs Office, Metropolitan Police Department (1957: 264–65).
128. I have already pointed out that the decrease of about 17,000 in the number of parlors (see Table 1.1) from 1953 to 1954 may have included some that were unable to renew their business licenses due to the linkage of such renewals with tax payment.

To the extent that one examines conditions after the ban, it is likely that most of those parlors either switched industries or closed permanently. In Wakayama Prefecture, reports indicate that efforts to strengthen tax collection led to an increase in the rate at which businesses that owed taxes were identified compared to before the ban was implemented (Nakamura 1955: 51–52). In this way, both tax levying and collection systems were improved during the time before and after the implementation of the ban, and regional campaigns promoting tax payment by industry associations were also successful. For example, an association in Niigata Prefecture offered a service in which it collected and paid taxes on behalf of parlors (Saito 1972: 101–02). The process can be seen as forcing the parlor business through a sieve – tax payment – so that the field of participants was narrowed to those with the ability to withstand the tax. The ban offered an even harsher opportunity for parlor operators to orchestrate qualitative changes in their businesses.

129. Installation of new machines was subject to approval by public safety commissions. That the regulation took effect all at once meant that the rush to replace machines could have prevented some parlors from opening.
130. See *Gekkan Yūki* (1955), '改造屋という名の新商売' (Machine modifiers: A new business), April.
131. Demand for modified machines was presumably also due to the inclusion in the ban of a grace period that permitted parlors to use modified machines until they could fully switch to true single-shot machines. Wakayama Prefecture, which implemented the ban in May, required all parlors to have fully switched to true single-shot machines by July 1 (Nakamura 1955: 51). Even taking the grace period into consideration, it is fair to say that the lowering of parlors' appetite for investing in single-shot machines caused by the installation of modified machines and the lack of ample internal reserves, as related above, affected parlors' decisions.
132. Although this chapter focuses, due to problems with available sources, on the parlor-related factors that affected the purchase of single-shot machines after the ban, it goes without saying that various problems involving the supply side of the equation (machine manufacturers) should also be taken into account. As part of the implementation of the ban, public safety commissions imposed a variety of new regulations related to machines. In addition to outlining in a fine-grained manner the specifications of machines that could be used, these regulations required manufacturers to have machines they developed inspected and certified by public safety commissions before they could be sold. The lack of experience on the part of public safety commissions with machine inspections created confusion during the system's implementation, and it is possible that purchases of single-shot machines did not go smoothly for this reason. The details remain unclear, but Chapter 2 of this book includes a brief examination of the subject.
133. See Shiryō Henshū Iinkai (1989), '全遊連東北地区協議会決議 一九五三年五月一三日' (Resolution of the Northeast Japan Regional Council of the National Confederation of Amusement Industry Associations on May 13, 1953).
134. For more on how holding a long-term inventory of machines at the time – manufacturing machines in advance – could lead to quality issues, see Suzuki (2001: 278).
135. See Masamura Shōkai (1963). Parlors operated by Masamura Shōkai also served as 'antenna shops' for the company, which operated as a machine wholesaler. It is

highly likely that these parlors installed machines ahead of other parlors as a way to advertise them.

136. Although Masamura Shōkai's year-end financial statements use a legal depreciable life of two years for machines in all fiscal years, actual use averaged at least one year, with the exception of used machines.

137. In Wakayama Prefecture, the ban took effect on April 1, and the switchover to true single-shot machines began on July 1, but data for May and June from Table 1.7 does not clearly exhibit this sort of regional trend. Additional investigation is needed in order to determine whether Masamura Shōkai lacked orders, or whether demand for single-shot machines from parlors was lower than expected, as is the case for the city of Fukuoka in Table 1.6 above.

138. Result based on the balance sheets and profit and loss statements in Masamura Shōkai (1955) and Masamura Shōkai (1956).

139. Tabulated from data for August 1953 to 1956 in Masamura Shōkai's accounts receivable ledgers (*tokuisaki motochō*).

140. One study in Wakayama Prefecture provided data on the change in customer headcount. Although it is unclear how many parlors were targeted by the survey, it includes parlors with an average of seventy-nine machines in the entertainment district and train terminal in the city of Wakayama. The study, which consisted of observers counting attendance, focused on two full days (Saturday and Tuesday) each in March 1953, before the ban, and in April, after the ban. There are calculation disparities in the tables summarizing the results, and it is unclear which data is correct. I have used only that which can be determined to be free of significant errors. According to the study's results, customer attendance fell from 717 in March to 491 in April (both totals likely represent a total count for two days), a decline of about 30 percent (Nakamura 1955: 49).

141. The study in Wakayama Prefecture found that sales per machine had fallen by about 32 percent, too (Nakamura 1955: 49).

142. Of Osaka Prefecture, one observation made during the same era noted, 'The number of pachinko parlors was in a gradual decline until the summer of the previous year [1956]. While parlors with a poor location or weak economic basis naturally suffered, growth in the number of newly opened parlors and the expansion of existing parlors were conspicuous, and the number of pachinko machines totaled 57,902 at the end of this year, up 7501 (10.7 percent) from the end of last year' (Osaka Prefecture Police Headquarters General Affairs Department Public Relations Section 1958: 179). The source points out various causal factors, including parlors' physical locations, and observes that parlors exhibited different business conditions, some of which may explain the differences among Masamura Shōkai's four parlors. Reflecting on conditions at the time and parlors' physical locations, a deputy chairperson of the National Confederation of Amusement Industry Associations offered an after-the-fact evaluation of the effects of the ban on successive machines: 'I think it's a nationwide phenomenon that the parlors that survived not only worked hard to hone their businesses, but also enjoyed good locations' (see National Confederation of Amusement Industry Cooperatives [1977], '業界二五年を語る座談会　低迷時代だから復興へ' [Roundtable on 25 years in the industry: Towards restoration in a time of stagnation], p. 169).

143. See Masamura Shōkai (1954).
144. Although the possibility that rising incomes exerted an influence on the increase in per-capita spending at parlors during this time cannot be denied, I believe this data reflects the change in machine type because the shift in incomes and spending does not appear in the short term. It is meaningful to consider machine type as a factor that can explain both the extent of customer spending and parlors' accumulation of management expertise.
145. See Shiryō Henshū Iinkai (1989: 93–94).
146. See Yūgi Tsūshinsha (2011: 36).
147. See National Confederation of Amusement Industry Cooperatives (1977), '業界二五年を語る座談会四 "第二次隆盛時代と組織強化"' (Roundtable on 25 years in the industry (4): Towards a second flourishing and organizational strengthening), p. 193; and Yūgi Tsūshinsha (2011: 36).
148. The manager of the prefectural police Crime Prevention Department (Bōhanbu) acknowledged that approving the Osaka system was preferable to having 'profit from prize purchases valued at what is said to total 500 million yen [about US$1.4 million] per year become funding for criminal groups' (Yūgi Tsūshinsha 2011: 36), and it is clear that halting the flow of funds to such groups was an important priority for law enforcement officials.
149. For example, one weekly noted that 'purchases of prizes for cash [by criminal groups] were being conducted in out-of-view places, sometimes under violent conditions' (See *Noda Keizai*, 'Focus 2', p. 82).
150. See *Yūgi Shimbun* (1962), 'パチンコ景品買い取り 岐阜に社会事業団体が誕生' (Pachinko prize purchases: A social program is born in Gifu), December 15.
151. *Yūgi Shimbun*, 'Pachinko prize purchases'.
152. See National Confederation of Amusement Industry Cooperatives (1977: 162–63).
153. 'In Aichi Prefecture, eight candy wholesalers formed a company at the behest of the Naka Police Station chief, a man named Shin'ichi Nagashima, who advised them to carry out a "three-party system" [...] the candy wholesalers did so, since it was the chief who encouraged them, and later reorganized as Kyōritsu Sangyō, which created separate systems for deliveries [with wholesalers delivering prizes to parlors] and pick-up [either exchanging prizes for cash or buying prizes from customers], and which continues to operate today' (National Confederation of Amusement Industry Cooperatives 1977: 163). The quotation above was provided by Kuniei Takeuchi, who served as foreman at one of Masamura Shōkai's contract factories (and who became an executive director of the Nikkōso in 1978). According to Emiko Suzuki's description, Kyōritsu Sangyō, which was formed by candy wholesalers and known as Ichimi Shōji at the time, bought prizes, while Aisan Shōkai was established as a prize wholesaler (Suzuki 2001: 308–12). Masamura Shōkai would later purchase special prizes from Aisan Shōkai (see Chapter 4). This three-party system can be seen as an experimental effort to develop a system for prize exchanges while eliminating the involvement of organized crime within the legal framework that took hold. Like the Osaka system, the guidance of police, who were concerned about the flow of funds to criminal groups, played an important role in the process.
154. See Suzuki (2001: 308–12).

155. See Suzuki (2001: 308–12).

156. For example, entries from January through March 1956 record the purchase of 79,337, 51,077 and 47,952 handkerchiefs, respectively. If these were all exchanged for balls as prizes, customers would need to have received an average of 2559, 1761 and 1547 handkerchiefs every day during those months. Although the number of customers that patronized the company's parlors per day is unknown, Parlor C, which operated 202 machines from 1983 to 1985 and which is described in Chapter 4, drew an average of 313 to 521 customers every day, indicating that each customer would have needed to receive five to eight handkerchiefs per day. This calculation assumes that all customers redeemed all of the balls they won for handkerchiefs, to the exclusion of other prizes. In fact, individual customers would have had to receive even more handkerchiefs. Since growth in the number of handkerchiefs received as a result of the increase in prize exchange value presumably would have lowered the prize's use value, it is likely that the handkerchiefs played a role as a special prize.

157. Purchase prices for prizes increased from 24 to 26–27 yen (about between US$0.07 and 0.08); the upward trend is clear even if that increase is subtracted. (Calculating at a unit price of 24 yen yields the following differences from August 1955 to February 1956: 116,886 yen [about US$324.68], 27,204 yen [about US$75.57], 57,630 yen [about US$160.08], 6502 yen [about US$18.06], 70,284 yen [about US$195.23], 177,596 yen [about US$493.32] and 222,063 yen [about US$616.84].)

158. Although it is unclear what factors are responsible for the decline in the amount per transaction and the rise in the number of transactions, the changes are likely connected to the scale of wholesalers' operations and their ability to procure funding. As the scale of purchases of special prizes from customers grew, wholesalers had to fund their operations accordingly. It is conceivable that when faced with insufficient ability to obtain funding, wholesalers made up for the shortcoming by shrinking delivery lots and increasing transaction frequency (i.e., by increasing the number of times accounts were settled) as they worked to supply special prizes to parlors.

159. See Note 153 above.

160. See *Gekkan Yūki*, 'Single-shot machines lead to decrease'.

161. See National Confederation of Amusement Industry Cooperatives (1977: 27 [timeline]). Another contemporary assessment held that the industry was enjoying a brief period of tranquility (see Shiryō Henshū Iinkai [1989: 246]).

162. This change eliminated its subcontractor relationships (Suzuki 2001: 277–81). Of Masamura Shōkai's former subcontractors, Toshio Ito's factory continued to manufacture machines, receiving permission to use Masamura's name in 1965 (Suzuki 2001: 323), when it changed its name to Masamura Kikai. (The business was incorporated as Masamura Yūki Co., Ltd., in 1983, and changed its name to OK Co., Ltd., in 2011.) Today, it continues to operate as part of the Kyoraku Sangyo Group.

163. According to an account by Masamura Takeichi's second daughter, the Matsubara Branch closed around the end of 1956. An exact date is unavailable for the Endonji Branch, but she described it as having been shut down by 1960. (Both statements were made during an interview conducted on February 17, 2015.)

164. Masamura Shōkai was established as a new company in September 1955, when it inherited principal businesses, including the sales of pachinko machines and the

operation of pachinko parlors, from the former company, which had been established in 1951. This reorganization was necessitated by the company's inability to close its accounts due to a tax-related investigation that began in 1952. This chapter focuses on the process by which individual parlors' operations stabilized, rather than on the operations of the company as a whole. Consequently, I have omitted detailed descriptions of topics such as the financial details of the establishment of the new company and the impact of those details on the management of the new company. My analysis of the statistical tables (*tōkeihyō*) used in this chapter assumes that they provide a continuous glimpse at the business's operations (i.e., that they were not affected by systematic changes such as the establishment of the new company).

165. Based on the account of Masamura Takeichi's second daughter (from an interview conducted on February 17, 2015).
166. According to a modification application (*kaizō shinseisho*) submitted by Masamura Shōkai in June 1962, the new parlor received a business license dated July 6, 1956. According to parlor-specific statistical tables, the Main Branch's sales rose rapidly in July 1956, and that improvement was likely the result of the parlor's relocation as the Jōshin Branch and changes in the number of machines it operated due to its expansion. Based on the growth in sales that the Main Branch experienced, it can be inferred that the impact of its relocation and reorganization as a new branch on its recovery cannot be ignored. That said, it should be emphasized that the Oshikiri and Main Branches had already embarked on a trajectory of short-term recovery in terms of their profitability prior to the closure of the Endonji Branch. Although I did not point out the relocation of the Main Branch parlor as the Jōshin Branch in the article (Han 2006) on which this chapter is based, I have added it to this chapter as the product of subsequent investigation.
167. For example, a 1965 police study found that while there were no major problems after the 1955 successive-shot ban, the problem of pachinko becoming once again a source of funds in the face of a crackdown on organized crime began to attract attention (Takita 1965: 59).
168. See Takita (1965: 59–72).
169. See Takita (1965: 68). There were also twenty-six pachinko businesses that were engaged in 'buying prizes directly', which was illegal.

Chapter 2

1. See also the original Japanese publication of this book, p. 32, Figure Intro.5 (Han 2018: 32).
2. *Chūrippu* (tulip) accessories became so popular around 1965 that observers described a boom second only to that of the early 1950s: 'This boom is primarily supported by salarymen' (*Tōhō Keizei* [1966], '軽バクチ時代とパチンコ' [Pachinko in an era of light gambling], 36[8], p. 54). Of changes in the customer demographic, one observer noted, 'The advance of women, particularly housewives, into this field is striking [...] time was, the only people you'd find in pachinko parlors were questionable-looking toughs'. It is unclear whether the emergence of female customers described here led to a sustained increase in that demographic, but later surveys indicate that it was during the 1970s that the increase in women began to stand out.

3. One source noted, 'Salarymen are great customers for pachinko. Parlors compete with one another to offer the best service so that customers will stop by during their lunch break or on the way home from work' (*Ōru Taishū* [1968], '第二黄金時代を迎えるパチンコ——ブームを支えるマニアの素顔ここにあり' [Pachinko embarks on a second golden age: What's behind the boom?], 21[1], p. 36).
4. See Research Bureau of the Economic Planning Agency (1967: 34–35, Table 9).
5. See Kosugi (1968: 83).
6. The survey targeted unmarried workers and overall is likely to have consisted primarily of young individuals. Age-specific data indicates that pachinko was a favored pastime among the young, with 57.2 percent of respondents aged nineteen and younger frequenting parlors, 58.7 percent of respondents aged twenty to twenty-four, and 49.5 percent of respondents aged twenty-five and older (Research Bureau of the Economic Planning Agency 1967: 34, Table 9).
7. See *Ōru Taishū*, 'Pachinko embarks on a second golden age', p. 36.
8. Parlors 'competed with one another to offer the best service', for example by providing *oshibori* (small, damp towels for customers to clean their hands), color televisions, sumptuous sofas and other accoutrements so that the customer demographic that enjoyed pachinko in this manner would 'stop by during their lunch break or on the way home from work' (*Ōru Taishū*, 'Pachinko embarks on a second golden age', p. 36).
9. See So (1972: 46).
10. See *Ōru Taishū*, 'Pachinko embarks on a second golden age', p. 37.
11. *Ōru Taishū*, 'Pachinko embarks on a second golden age', p. 36. As introduced in the second section of Chapter 4, a large-scale study of pachinko consumption in 1979 found that average times ranging from thirty minutes to one hour accounted for 30 percent of the total (Small Business Information Center 1980: 18).
12. See *Noda Keizai* (1976), '驚異の技術開発力パチンコ産業の不思議' (Amazing technological development capabilities: The mystery of the pachinko industry), 1254, pp. 13–14. The practice of installing seats began in areas where there was extra space, for example in the suburban parlors that emerged during the 1970s, and spread from there (*Gekkan Yūgi Nihon* [1973], '話題を追って"郊外パチンコ"' [Chasing the buzz: 'Suburban pachinko'], December). It is likely to have been motivated by a desire to improve service for customers who preferred to play for comparatively long periods of time (and by a desire on the part of management to encourage customers to do so). See Chapter 5.
13. See Fushimi, Yukiko (1955), 'パチンコの機械裏から' (From behind the pachinko machine), *Jinsei Techō*, 4(5), pp. 34–39.
14. It is worth noting that other balls (c) in the possession of the customer were not classified as either (a) or (b) balls. Those balls were in a 'standby' state as the customer could either be waiting to use them as (a) balls or, as a result of (b) balls, planning to use them again as (a) balls or to exchange them for prizes. I am addressing only the (a) and (b) types here as my focus is on the functional aspect of machine operation.
15. Incidents in which employees embezzled balls were a frequent occurrence at the time. For example, the November 5, 1951, issue of *Yūgi Tsūshin* ('Hōbutsusen' [Parabola], p. 4) reported an incident at a parlor in Tokyo. A newly hired female employee gave 5000

balls to her father, who had visited the parlor as a customer and who then exchanged the balls for 250 cigarettes (worth around 7500 yen [about US$20.83]). The pair were prosecuted for embezzlement and fraud, respectively.

16. The text describes the Reconjisuta Manmosu, a model that was launched in 1960 (Hyakusu Henshūshitsu 1985: 23). It is likely that the model was an improved version of the Reconjisuta, with which it shared the same basic technologies and functions. Similar technology was also proposed in the form of an automated machine developed by Takeya in 1955 on an experimental basis (Higyoku Ehōden: Takeya Gojūnen no Ayumi Hensanshitsu 1996). The approach, in which balls were counted and automatically supplied, dispensed, sent to a polishing machine, polished and then supplied again, provided a prototype for automation (*Noda Keizai*, 'Amazing technological development capabilities', p. 18). However, several years of improvement were necessary before it could be commercialized. According to Suzuki, the initial automated machines did not enter into general use in the area around Nagoya, where Takeya was based (Suzuki 2001: 326).
17. For details, see Suzuki (2001: 314–18).
18. The Uchū Paipu ('Space Pipe'), which was developed by Nishijin and launched in 1963, was the first machine to eliminate this limitation by supplying balls to all machines in the parlor (Sōgyō Gojūnen Kinenshi Hensan Iinkai 2001).
19. Based on information from Nishijin ('開発史 補給機 器･周辺機器の歩み :1960s' [History of Nishijin supply equipment: 1960s], https://www.nishijin.co.jp/supply-system/history.html#chronology1960, accessed on March 4, 2017), Takeya ('会社情報:会社沿革' [Company information: Company history], http://www.p-takeya.co.jp/profile.html, accessed on March 4, 2017) and Ace Denken ('西陣の補給設備の歩み' [Development history: History of supply and peripheral equipment], http://www.ace-denken.com/company/development.html, accessed on March 4, 2017). Initially, automatic replenishment capability was installed on individual machines to automate ball dispensation. Eventually, the technology became independent of machines and developed into a system for connecting and centrally managing all machines. This evolution led to diversification in the entities developing such equipment as specialized replenishment equipment manufacturers like Ace Denken entered the market for such hardware, which had previously consisted solely of pachinko machine manufacturers such as Nishijin. It goes without saying that this change spurred development through competition. This approach to automating ball replenishment reached completion in the 1970s. According to observations dating from 1976, the system in place at the time automatically returned all balls, including non-winning balls. Balls were collected in an underground polishing room from behind the machines, automatically polished at a rate of 150,000 to 200,000 balls per hour, and then transported by means of a vertical lift to, and stored in, a central tank above the machines. Balls were then automatically moved to relay tanks in each island of machines and transported to individual machines or an automatic ball dispenser (Yamaoka 1976: 84). This system allowed the quantity of balls in each machine to be automatically calculated and balls supplied as needed. The approach transformed the type of labor needed in parlor operations, which had relied during the 1950s on pachinko *musume* (girls) to manually replenish and collect balls during operating hours and then wash and polish

them after parlors closed. After about twenty years, one could no longer find people doing this job, which had been the most labor-intensive task at parlors.

20. See *Yūgi Tsūshin* (1960), '広告レコンジスター' (Reconjisutā advertisement), November 25.
21. See *Yūgi Tsūshin* (1960), '広告 レコンジスター' (Reconjisutā advertisement), August 5.
22. As described on the Ace Denken website ('島補給のしくみ' [Island supply mechanism], http://www.acedenken.com/system/, accessed on July 15, 2017).
23. See *Yūgi Tsūshin* (1960), '広告 レコンジスター' (Reconjisutā advertisement), December 5. Other observers have pointed out the revolutionary nature of this model. For example, Suzuki examines this state of affairs from the standpoint of the change in machine design (Suzuki 2001: 318). However, this chapter approaches it from the context of the characteristics of parlor operation and industry growth during the 1960s.
24. See Business IPR Ōpun-gata Tokkyo Pūru Bunkakai (2003: 3).
25. See Miyai (1988: 484).
26. 'Patent' is a category that includes utility model patents, although this chapter will use the word 'patent' in a generic sense to refer to such rights collectively.
27 See Chapter 2 of Business IPR Ōpun-gata Tokkyo Pūru Bunkakai (2003), '特許プールの進化の歴史' (History of the evolution of patent pools). For more information about the relationship between patent pools and innovation, see the analysis of the sewing machine industry as a pioneering example in Lampe and Moser (2010: 898–920).
28. See Miyai (1988; 1989a; 1989b).
29. See Nishimura (2004; 2005).
30. See Japan Fair Trade Commission (1997).
31. Tanaka and Hayashi (2010) offer an economic examination of the Nittokuren's functionality. Judgments related to the conduct of the Nittokuren and related companies have inspired a high level of interest in what they can tell us about the activities of patent pools and their relationship to antitrust law, and several scholars have undertaken legal analyses. See Arai (1997), Tanihara (1998), Eguchi (2002), Murakami (1998a; 1998b) and Suzuki (2003).
32. See Business IPR Ōpun-gata Tokkyo Pūru Bunkakai (2003: 30–34).
33. Although sources that provide a region-by-region picture of how machines were managed prior to World War I are lacking, see Fukuoka Prefectural Police History Compilation Committee (1978) for related information about Fukuoka Prefecture.
34. The Administrative Order Prohibiting Successive-shot Machines was announced in November 1954 by the Tokyo Metropolitan Police Department (it came into force on April 1, 1950, or on May 1, in some regions), and the department finalized machine standards on February 8, 1955 (*Yūgi Tsūshin* [1955], '警察庁警視庁の幹部を囲んで新型機を語る座談会 二月十日本社主催' [Roundtable including the National Police Agency and the Tokyo Metropolitan Police Department to discuss new machine models (held by the paper on February 10)], February 19). Incidentally, the machine standards were finalized by public safety commissions on a region-by-region basis.
35. *Yūgi Tsūshin*, 'Roundtable including the National Police Agency and the Tokyo Metropolitan Police Department', pp. 3–7.
36. *Yūgi Tsūshin*, 'Roundtable including the National Police Agency and the Tokyo Metropolitan Police Department', p. 3.

37. As per the website of the Japan Amusement Machine Patent Association (Nihon Yūgiki Tokkyo Kyōkai) ('会社概要' [Company overview], https://jamp.or.jp/, accessed on June 27, 2016).
38. Number of members of the Nikkōso, an industry association of manufacturers of pachinko and *pachislot* machines, as per the association's website (See '組合員紹介' (Member introductions), http://www.nikkoso.jp/members/index.php, accessed in June 2016.
39. '組合員紹介' (Member introductions), http://www.nikkoso.jp/members/index.php, accessed in June 2016.
40. The organization was incorporated in June 1961.
41. See *Yūgi Tsūshin* (1951), 'オールものも特許が' (Patents for 'all-win' machines, too), December 25. The prohibition of the use of the all-win mechanism by other manufacturers may have negatively affected the development of the pachinko boom of the 1950s.
42. See Hyakusu Henshūshitsu (1985: 12).
43. See Hyakusu Henshūshitsu (1985: 12).
44. The company changed its name to Takeya in 1958, but I refer to it as 'Takeya Shōkai' below.
45. In January 1952, the Aichi Amusement Machine Manufacturing Industry Association (Aichi Yūgiki Seizō Kōgyō Kumiai) merged with the Tokyo Ball Amusement Machine Manufacturing Industry Association (Tokyo-to Kyūyūki Seizō Kōgyō Kumiai) to form the National Confederation of Amusement Machine Manufacturing Industry Associations (Zenkōren). See *Yūgi Tsūshin* (1952), '製作業者も団結 全国遊技機製造工業組合連合会創立総会を終了' (Manufacturers form group: National Confederation of Amusement Machine Manufacturing Industry Associations holds inaugural general meeting), January 25. Later, the Western Japan Amusement Machine Manufacturing Industry Association (Kansai Yūgiki Seizō Kōgyō Kumiai) (1953) and other associations nationwide merged to form the Zenkōren in 1956 (Nijūgonen no Ayumi Henshū Iinkai 1985: 17). Both of these private, voluntary groups were formed to address the commodity tax, which was introduced in 1952, and the regulations that followed the successive-shot ban of 1955. Due to overlap between the memberships of the Aichi Prefecture and Tokyo associations, which consisted of powerful manufacturers, this chapter refers to them collectively as the Zenkōren.
46. See *Yūgi Tsūshin* (1955), '豊国特許問題を重視 全工連総会を開き制度を協議 全工連臨時総会' (National Confederation of Amusement Machine Manufacturing Industry Associations opens general meeting with focus on Hōkoku patent problems: Extraordinary general meeting), and *Yūgi Tsūshin* (1955), '特許問題で緊急招集さる' (Emergency convocation to address patent problems), July 9.
47. See *Yūgi Tsūshin* (1956), '豊国遊機対西陣商会 権利使用と友好的関係結ばる' (Hōkoku Yūki vs. Nishijin Shōkai: Entering a friendly relationship with rights licensing), and *Yūgi Tsūshin* (1956), '声明書' (Public statement), July 5.
48. See 'Type 2 popularity grows not only in Tokyo, but also in Sendai, Niigata, Aizuwakamatsu, Numazu, Kiyomizu, Nagoya, and even distant Shikoku and Kyushu' (*Yūgi Tsūshin* [1956], '二式に湧く北海道' [Hokkaido excited about Type 2], June 5). Unless otherwise noted, information about this incident is drawn from this article.

49. The right was 'finally registered this February [1956] after Hōkoku objected to the registration on the grounds that the technology was only possible by using its rights, at which point a period of confrontation ensued' (*Yūgi Tsūshin*, 'Hokkaido excited about Type 2'). The companies' relationship became confrontational once more when Nishijin acquired the rights.
50. 'It's only natural that pachinko parlors – the ones buying the machines – would balk at the prospect of purchasing machines about which problems could arise' (*Yūgi Tsūshin*, 'Hokkaido excited about Type 2'). For more on why parlors could not sit idly by in the face of patent disputes, see the description of the lawsuit filed against Kodama Kaikan in this chapter.
51. *Nihon Yūkikai* (1957), '御園、銀正も製作協定' (Misono and Ginsei also ink manufacturing agreement), September 25.
52. *Yakumono* accessories are objects affixed to the board to change balls' trajectories apart from catchers and pins.
53. See *Nihon Yūkikai* (1957), '広告' (Advertisement), September 25.
54. See Hyakusu Henshūshitsu (1985: 23).
55. See Hyakusu Henshūshitsu (1985: 29, 60) and Suzuki (2001: 314).
56. See *Nihon Yūkikai* (1957), '業界発展策と価格維持への道' (Measures spurring industry development and the road to price support), September 25.
57. Whereas members of the Japan Amusement Machine Invention Group were paying royalties of 100 yen per machine under the terms of their agreement with Hōkoku, the Amusement Machine Research Association was in favor of 'adopting a system under which manufacturers would pay a gratuity instead of a per-machine fee' (*Nihon Yūkikai*, 'Measures spurring industry development and the road to price support' and *Nihon Yūkikai* [1957], '不良業者撲滅え' [Eliminating fly-by-night businesses], October 5).
58. The business was founded as Heiwa Shōkai in 1949 before splitting into Komikku Shōkai (manufacturing) and Heiwa Kōgyō (sales) in 1956. The two companies merged to become Tōwa Kōgyō in 1960, which then changed its name to Heiwa in 1988.
59. For an account of the founder, see Nakajima (1997).
60. Shimizu Chūkōsho was founded in 1951. After changing its name to Nishijin Shōkai in 1951, the company split into Nishijin (sales) and Sofia (manufacturing) in 1960. I refer to the company as Nishijin below. For an account of founder Kakuji Shimizu's life, see Takizawa (1980).
61. See Higyoku Ehoden: Takeya Gojūnen no Ayumi Hensanshitsu (1996).
62. The prices of Masamura Shōkai machines as described in Chapter 1 were as follows. Selling prices (wholesale and consumer prices) in 1954 ranged from 7000 (about US$19.44) to 8000 yen (about US$22.22) but with the switch to single-shot machines in April 1955 fell to 5500 yen (about US$15.28) and eventually declined as far as 4300 yen (about US$11.9) in 1957 (see Masamura Shōkai [1954 to 1957], 売掛帳 [Accounts receivable]).
63. See *Ōru Seikatsu* (1952), '変わった町・変わった村パチンコのメッカ名古屋訪問記' (A strange town, a strange village: Account of a visit to Nagoya, the Mecca of pachinko), 7(3), p. 79.
64. See *Nihon Yūkikai*, 'Measures spurring industry development and the road to price support'.

65. Such businesses were seen as making price maintenance difficult and came to be labeled as illegitimate. Some were even insider members of the Zenkōren.
66. See *Yūgi Tsūshin*, 'Hōkoku Yūki v. Nishijin Shōkai'.
67. 'Machine-making businesses operating out of attics were having a hard time selling their products and in many cases, collecting payments. As a result, the number of tax returns received fell far below the anticipated number' (*Nihon Yūkikai* [1956], '近いうちに断 めだつ物品税の滞納' [Impending stricter enforcement in response to late payment of commodity tax poised to attract attention], December 15).
68. As Nakajima of Heiwa Shōkai put it, 'It was out of the question to do things like undersell machines while ignoring the commodity tax, but even if we objected due to doubts about the tax on pachinko machines in the past, today things have progressed to the point where the tax must be paid. That said, no small number of parlors remain unaware that the commodity tax is included in prices. The Tokyo Ball Amusement Machine Manufacturing Industry Association, Nishijin, and other manufacturers have filed lawsuits to invalidate the commodity tax, but most of those have ended in failure...' (see *Nihon Yūkikai*, 'Measures spurring industry development and the road to price support').
69. 'Coverage has focused on the commodity tax for many years now. The problem relates to price support. The advent of *yakumono* accessories played a major role in maintaining prices, but underselling emerged again last year, and agreement prices are showing signs of collapse. Moreover, the outsize impact of taxes on the cost sheet [note: the precise meaning is not specified in the article] is causing some businesses to close their doors. Currently, machine prices include the commodity tax, but manufacturers are forced to pay the tax even if they sell machines at a discount' (see *Nihon Yūkikai*, 'Measures spurring industry development and the road to price support').
70. See *Yūgi Tsūshin*, 'Hōkoku Yūki v. Nishijin Shōkai'.
71. For an account of conditions in the industry up to the establishment of the Nittokuren, see *Yūgi Tsūshin* (1960), '日本遊技機特許運営連盟・設立 "戸田構想"実現に一歩前進' (Japan Amusement Machine Patent Management Federation established: One step closer to the Toda idea or plan), June 15.
72. 'Most parlors had doubts about operations using the Type 2 due to issues with counterfeit machines, and the machine's popularity vanished like bubbles on water as parlors rushed to embrace single-shot machines based on the small number of fans' (*Yūgi Tsūshin*, 'Hōkoku Yūki v. Nishijin Shōkai'). Similarly, 'I have heard that in Tokyo, it's really hard to obtain a license from Jinmitto. Then this imitation machine came out and was penalized' (*Nihon Yūkikai* [1957], '機械の適正価格はいかにして維持する メーカー座談会' [Roundtable of manufacturers: How to maintain appropriate machine pricing], May 25).
73. See *Yūgi Tsūshin* (1956), '広告' (Advertisement), June 15.
74. See *Nihon Yūkikai* (1956), '1956年に於ける全工連大ニュース歴史に輝く人々の足跡を見る' (Major news for the National Confederation of Amusement Machine Manufacturing Industry Associations in 1956: Examining the paths of stars in the organization's history), December 15.
75. 'The decision has been made with the goal of preventing fly-by-night businesses and supporting selling prices [...] but its implementation will be truly difficult [...]'

(*Nihon Yūkikai* [1957], '問題の"全工連証"は廃止すると決定' [Decision made to eliminate problematic Zenkōren certificates], April 25).

76. See *Yūgi Tsūshin* (1957), '全工連ニュース 特許問題を中心に懇話会と研究会で論戦' (Zenkōren news: Japan Amusement Machine Invention Group and Amusement Machine Research Association debate centers on patent problems), October 5.
77. See *Yūgi Tsūshin* (1958), '東京工組理事会 権利尊重と価格維持を再確認' (Tokyo Pachinko Industry Association Board of Directors reaffirms respect for rights and price support), December 5.
78. See *Yūgi Tsūshin* (1960), '物品税協力証紙、漸く軌道に……' (Commodity tax cooperation certificate stamp program finally gathers momentum…), August 15. A case seeking to invalidate taxation of pachinko machines was thrown out by the Tokyo District Court in 1953, and the Tokyo High Court and then the Supreme Court of Japan declined to overturn that judgment in 1953 and 1958, respectively (National Tax Agency [1960], '課税部品か否かの認定(パチンコ機械)' [Certification of taxable part status (pachinko machines)] in *Kansetsu Kokuzei Kankei Hanrei Shū* [Digest of Cases Involving Indirect National Taxes], pp. 182–85).
79. *Nihon Yūkikai* (1957), '業界発展策と価格維持への道' (Measures spurring industry development and the road to price support), September 25.
80. 'As a research organization through and through, our group carries out research into technologies for advancing pachinko parlors, and when we develop an exceptional new machine, our association members investigate it and, if it is deemed valuable, we have a mechanism for offering an honorarium to the inventor...' (*Nihon Yūkikai*, 'Eliminating fly-by-night businesses').
81. See *Nihon Yūkikai* (1957), '機械の適正価格具体案' (A concrete proposal for fair machine pricing), December 15.
82. The Zenkōren and Heiwa subsequently entered into an agreement covering such mechanisms.
83. See *Yūgi Tsūshin* (1959), '日本遊技機特許運営連盟・設立' (Japan Amusement Machine Patent Management Federation established), June 15.
84. See *Yūgi Tsūshin* (1959), '日増しに激化しつつある日特連の証紙料問題' (Problems concerning the Nittokuren's certificate stamp fees grow more serious by the day), November 25.
85. *Yūgi Tsūshin*, 'Problems concerning the Nittokuren's certificate stamp fees'.
86. See *Yūgi Tsūshin* (1959), '大同団結の気運濃厚!平和物産を始め各メーカーが日特連運営に加入か?' (Momentum towards unity is building! Will Heiwa Bussan and other manufacturers join the Nittokuren?) and *Yūgi Tsūshin* (1959), '日特連の正常運営を希望する声多し' (Calls grow for normal operation of the Nittokuren), December 5.
87. This organization was established as the 'Japan Amusement Machine Industry Cooperative' (Nihon Yūgiki Kōgyō Kyōdo Kumiai). Following the revision of the Act on the Organization of Small and Medium-sized Enterprise Association in 1962, the group was organized as a commercial association before becoming the Nikkōso in 1963. I used the Japan Amusement Machine Industry Association in this book. See Japan Amusement Machine Industry Association (1963: 4–5).
88. The confederation was formed by commercial associations from Tokyo and the Kansai (western Japan) region on May 22 and later joined by similar groups from

the Kyushu region. It served to facilitate communication among machine sellers and trading companies that sold used machines and parts, but did not include machine manufacturers.

89. 'Through discussions with the National Tax Agency, a consensus formed around the use of tax payment certificate stamps' (*Yūgi Tsūshin* [1960], '東京工組忘年会 組織化への構想発表' [Announcement of an initiative to organize a year-end party for the Tokyo Amusement Machines Manufacturing Association], January 1).

90. According to an interim report delivered by Nakajima of Heiwa, who proposed the group's formation and then represented it, the 'cooperative developed a proposal during talks that included the National Tax Agency' at a time in which 'the pachinko industry [parlors] were doing well, but manufacturers had reached a turning point the previous year [1959] in the commodity tax problem, and there had been several cases of prosecutions' (*Yūgi Tsūshin* [1960], '日本遊技機工業協同組合創立さる' [Japan Amusement Machine Industry Cooperative founded], February 25).

91. See Japan Amusement Machine Industry Association (1961b: 3–4).

92. See *Yūgi Tsūshin* (1961), '広告 使って安心、御店も繁昌!!日本遊技機工業協同組合員メーカー御案内' (Advertisement: Peace of mind for use and prosperous parlors! Information about Japan Amusement Machine Industry Cooperative members), January 1. Incidentally, it is likely that the Nittokuren experienced internal discord, as suggested by reports of 'problems involving licensing of patents held by Hōkoku and incidents involving its withdrawal from the Nikkōso at the time of the former's incorporation' (*Yūgi Tsūshin* [1961], '豊国との交渉を続行中' [Negotiations with Hōkoku continue], September 5). Although the details are unknown, President Shugo Haga of the Nittokuren said, 'Negotiations are ongoing, and I believe they are likely to go smoothly'. The Nittokuren collected patent fees that included fees for rights held by Hōkoku in 1962, and it is likely that the dispute was resolved by placing Hōkoku's patents under the management of the Nittokuren (*Yūgi Shimbun* [1963], '日本遊技機特許運営連盟 昭和三七年度 事業報告書' [Japan Amusement Machine Patent Management Federation FY1962 business report], July 5). Suffice to note that a variety of opposing interests were at play concerning Hōkoku's rights in particular during the two-year period from the Nittokuren's formation in 1959 to its incorporation.

93. See *Yūgi Tsūshin* (1960), '七月一日より協力証紙添付' (Cooperation certificate stamps to be affixed [to machines] starting July 1), June 5.

94. The organization was dedicated to carrying out '1. Programs related to the acquisition, purchase and sale of industrial property rights for pachinko machines and other equipment and to the establishment and authorization of licensing; 2. Programs related to the protection of the industrial property rights described in 1 above, the fostering of new products and the manufacture of pachinko machines; 3. All other programs as incidental to the above' (*Gekkan Nihon Yūgi* [1961], '日本遊技機特許運営連盟定款' [Articles of incorporation of the Japan Amusement Machine Patent Management Federation], June, pp. 60–61).

95. The organization 'handled certificate stamps related to rights held by Hōkoku Yūgiki Hanbai Co., Ltd., and Tōwa Kōgyō Co., Ltd. [which had been established by the merger of Heiwa Bussan's sales operations and Komikku Shōkai's manufacturing operations in 1960], in order to facilitate smooth transactions between right-holders and licensees' (*Yūgi Shimbun*, 'Japan Amusement Machine Patent Management

Federation FY1962 business report'). The specific mechanism remains unknown but can be reasonably inferred from the following statement by Nishijin: 'We hold the patent rights for the automated pachinko machines currently being sold in the market, but we've sent a "Notice to All Parties Interested in Manufacturing Nishijin-type automated Pachinko Machines" dated November 4 of last year to all members through the Nittokuren and instructed them to contact Nishijin by November 7 (in 1961) if interested. At 1:00 in the afternoon on November 8, we held an information gathering about the manufacture of automated pachinko machines with Nishijin at the offices of the Nittokuren, and Manager Umezaki of the Public Relations Section outlined our desired terms under potential licensing agreements. As a result, we entered into agreements with four companies that attended that meeting: Heiwa Bussan Co., Ltd.; Mitaka Kigyō Co., Ltd.; Okumura Yūki Co., Ltd.; and Monako Shōkai Co., Ltd. April 17, 1961: Nishijin Co., Ltd.' (*Yūgi Tsūshin* [1961], '社告' [Statement by Nishijin], April 25). It is likely that the management of Hōkoku's agreements at the time of the Nittokuren's establishment was contracted to the organization.

96. See *Yūgi Tsūshin* (1960), '物品税協力証無貼付機に警告日特連製造／中止の措置' (Warnings for machines not bearing stickers certifying cooperation with the commodity tax: Cessation of manufacture), October 5.
97. Article 4, 'Principle of Affixing Certificate Stamps', read, 'Company A shall affix certificate stamps as designated by Company B to each licensed pachinko machine in the designated location on the pin board on front of the machine' (*Yūgi Tsūshin* [1961], '特連とメーカーとの契約書' [Agreement between the Nittokuren and manufacturers], 15 September).
98. See Article 5, Paragraph 7 (*Yūgi Tsūshin*, 'Agreement between the Nittokuren and manufacturers').
99. See *Yūgi Tsūshin*, 'Agreement between the Nittokuren and manufacturers'.
100. See *Yūgi Tsūshin* (1960), '日本遊技機工業協同組合・全国遊技機商業組合連合会, 原価計算書' (Cost accounts given by the Japan Amusement Machine Industry Association and the National Confederation of Amusement Machine Merchant Associations), November 15.
101. See *Yūgi Tsūshin*, 'Problems concerning the Nittokuren's certificate stamp fees'.
102. See *Yūgi Tsūshin* (1995), '契約書' (Agreement), November 25.
103. See *Yūgi Tsūshin* (1966), '業務機構刷新についての説明会' (Information meeting on reforms to operational mechanisms), November 4.
104. See *Yūgi Tsūshin*, 'Commodity tax cooperation certificate stamp program'.
105. See *Yūgi Tsūshin*, 'Commodity tax cooperation certificate stamp program'. How should parlors' cooperation with price increases be understood? While the details remain unknown, it can be inferred that this cooperation occurred against the backdrop of two factors that parlors had no choice but to accept. First, the Nittokuren took out newspaper ads warning that it would take steps to halt the manufacture and use of machines that did not bear commodity tax cooperation certificates (*Yūgi Tsūshin*, 'Warnings for machines not bearing stickers'). Second, robust legal action directly impacted parlors' operations, for example when a parlor named as a defendant lost its ability to use machines without stamps due to the need to preserve evidence in lawsuits in which the Nittokuren was involved (see below). Incidentally, no discussion about

the institutionalization of the industry or the Nittokuren would be complete without addressing the role of the leadership of parlors' and manufacturers' associations. For more about the achievement of 100 percent payment of the tax and the enlistment of parlors' cooperation with purchasing machines bearing certificate stamps, see the account of the Nikkōso's president in Nakajima (1997: 86–93).

106. A possible prohibition of allowances for traded-in machines as a cause of the collapse of machine prices was raised at a meeting of Nikkōso members in November 1966, but the measure was not officially adopted (*Yūgi Tsūshin*, 'Information meeting on reforms'). This fact indicates that parlors were able to obtain effective discounts through the establishment of prices for machine trade-ins. This sort of transaction became customary for pachinko machines (*Yūgi Tsūshin* [1958], '全工連ニュース' [Zenkōren News], April 14).

107. 'The method by which the tax payment cooperation certificate program was implemented goes to the sale of machines bearing stamps, which was the responsibility of Nikkōso members, but in the event of the discovery of a machine without the stamp, parlors had to report the matter to the district conference or to the Zen'yūren, which in turn reported it to the Nikkōso. Then the Nikkōso would conduct a thorough investigation of the facts' (*Yūgi Tsūshin*, 'Commodity tax cooperation certificate stamp program finally gathers momentum').

108. With regard to the monitoring of certificate stamp labeling, the Nittokuren sought the cooperation of merchant associations, including in Tokyo and western Japan, in connection with the handling of used machines. In addressing 'used pachinko machines being bought and sold by members of your association' as part of its 'efforts to ensure smooth licensing of industrial property rights held by the Nittokuren', the organization described its 'policy to offer licenses to businesses that handle used machines in a responsible manner', and it announced an 'agreement between used machine dealers and the Nittokuren'. The request for cooperation was important in extending the scope of monitoring to include the entire industry since many parlors utilized used machines at the time. Unfortunately for our purposes, it is unknown whether the agreement was actually undertaken (*Nihon Yūgi* [1961], '商業組合への要請書' [Request to merchant associations], September, p. 12).

109. However, at the time of the Nittokuren's formation, the group worked together with the Nikkōso to conduct investigations, including by dividing up responsibility for dispatching investigators by geographic area, for example for the Keihin region (from Tokyo to Yokohama, Kanagawa Prefecture) and the Kinki region (the greater Osaka region) (*Yūgi Tsūshin* [1960], '協組・特連合同理事会' [Joint board meeting of the Nikkōso and the Nittokuren], November 15).

110. See *Yūgi Tsūshin* (1960), '悪質業者排除に伴う要請書受理並びに仮処分の原則' (Guidelines on eliminating illegitimate businesses: Principles of acceptance and provisional action), October 25.

111. The specific results of the process are unclear. We can conclude that if cooperative structures backed by the legal regulatory capabilities of the Nittokuren could be expected to function collectively in the context of other associations' efforts to introduce order and stability, then the fact that discovery mechanisms extended throughout the entire industry can be considered a sign of strengthened management ability on the part of the Nittokuren.

112. See Nakajima (1997: 87–96).
113. See '昭和三六年度事業計画書 窓口1本化の構想について' (FY1961 business plan: About the framework for unifying points of contact for sales of machines), Japan Amusement Machine Industry Cooperative (1960), and *Nihon Yūgi* (1961), '窓口1本化の意味するもの' (What it means to unify points of contact for sales of machines), April, p. 22.
114. See '一 事業報告' (1. Program report), in Japan Amusement Machine Industry Association (1962b), pp. 1–4. See also Nakajima (1997: 87–96).
115. Although one hesitates to draw any definitive conclusions, this process suggests that the Fair Trade Commission had given its tacit approval to the idea that its joint activities to date, for example as the Nittokuren's patent management efforts, fell within the scope of applicable laws.
116. 'The other day at the request of a Kyushu merchant association we dispatched monitor personnel to industry facilities in Kyushu. They received a substantial number of investigation requests, but almost no major violations were found, perhaps due to the thorough manner in which the certificate stamp problem is being dealt with. There were only fifty-six violations [...]' (*Yūgi Tsūshin* [1960], '全商工協議会 各単位組合の状況報告' [Report on the status of member associations of the National Commerce and Industry Council], October 15).
117. See *Yūgi Tsūshin*, 'Report on the status of member associations'.
118. 'We pledge to use products that bear a valid certificate stamp issued by the Japan Amusement Machine Patent Management Federation on their front celluloid panel when purchasing or replacing the pachinko machines at our business, regardless of whether the products in question are new or used' (*Yūgi Tsūshin* [1960], '誓約書 一九六〇年十一月七日' [Pledge (November 7, 1960)], November 15).
119. 'As a result of the case's settlement, the commodity tax cooperation certificate stamps being promoted and advanced by the Nittokuren and the Nikkōso will be even more effective than before, and they played a major role in the resolution of this case' (*Yūgi Tsūshin* [1960], '日特連､協力証紙貼付に勝訴!こだま会館事件が解決' [Nittokuren wins case on affixing cooperation certificate stamps! Kodama Kaikan case resolved], 25 November).
120. See *Yūgi Tsūshin* (1961), '物品税協力証紙貼付に断!神戸地区事件が円滑に解決' (Decision favors affixing commodity tax cooperation certificate stamps! Kobe-region case gets smooth resolution), February 15.
121. See *Yūgi Tsūshin* (1963), July 5. Since this case occurred about two years after 1961, when the Takeuchi case was resolved, it can be inferred that similar cases were still occurring.
122. The details are unclear, but this case involved presenting the agreement for the machine transaction (*Yūgi Tsūshin* [1963], July 5).
123. See *Yūgi Shimbun*, 'Japan Amusement Machine Patent Management Federation FY1962 business report'.
124. See *Yūgi Tsūshin* (1961), 'これからの遊技業界 窓口一本化を主題に' (Focus on creating a single point of contact in the pachinko industry of the future), August 8. As for 'I personally would like to assert rights, but I am foregoing collecting patent fees and encouraging other manufacturers to do the same', the details are unclear, but the patent

fee of 300 yen reflected an increase from the 200-yen fee of November 1960. The certificate stamp fee included the patent fee and operational expenses of 60 yen (for the Nittokuren and the Nikkōso), for a total of 360 yen.

125. 'At the end of December, the seventh research product submitted by Hōkoku finally passed inspection by the Tokyo Metropolitan Police Department' (*Yūgi Tsūshin*, 'Hōkoku Yūki v. Nishijin Shōkai'.). Such inspections remain a fundamental characteristic of the process to the present day. For a similar case, see *Nihon Keizai Shimbun* (2005), 'アルゼの前期経常益80%減 パチンコ不認可響く' (Aruze ordinary profit falls 80 percent for the previous year, reflects pachinko licensing failures), April 12. Of the fall in profit, the report said, 'The company's failure to receive certification for new models prevented their sale, affecting profits'. Particularly problematic in failures to receive machine certification are new regulations on machines resulting from revisions to the Act on Control and Improvement of the Amusement Business, etc. (in this case, the operative revision was made in July 2004). It goes without saying that it is not possible to predict the content or timing of revisions.

126. See *Yūgi Tsūshin*, 'Hōkoku Yūki v. Nishijin Shōkai'.

127. See *Yūgi Tsūshin*, 'Hōkoku Yūki v. Nishijin Shōkai'. That mutually dependent relationships actually worked out in the course of this sort of development is apparent in the account of an executive from Sankyo, a leading manufacturer, as he reflected on the past (see 'Historical source: on other manufacturers' production of patented Fībā-type machines' in Chapter 4 [p. 223]). The reasons for which Sankyo licensed patents related to its Fībā technology to other companies for low royalties during the 1980s include the fickle and unpredictable nature of pachinko machine popularity as well as the company's experience manufacturing popular models from other companies.

128. See *Yūgi Tsūshin*, 'Report on the status of member associations'.

129. These characteristics continued over the course of the pachinko industry's long history. According to an account by a person involved in the industry, around 1999 it was particularly true that 'there was an extremely big gap between busy times and slow times. Some months there's no production at all' (account of a former plant manager for Heiwa, a major manufacturer, from an interview I conducted on October 26, 2004).

130. See also 'Historical source: on other manufacturers' production of patented Fībā-type machines' in Chapter 4 (p. 223).

131. See *Yūgi Tsūshin* (1952), 'メーカー 遊技場との希望座談会 ㈣' (Roundtable on hope with manufacturers and parlors: Part 4), October 24.

132. See *Yūgi Tsūshin*, 'Roundtable on hope'. A similar strategy can be observed in Nishijin's operations.

133. The counterargument would be that this function is only meaningful if participating companies bring an equivalent level of development capability to the table. It is true that the approach is more effective, but it is not a matter of the number of participating companies. Sharing is meaningful even if the scheme is limited to several capable companies. This function must be considered in a comprehensive manner and in the context of the Nittokuren's other functions; it would be hasty to reject the significance of the organization's existence by focusing exclusively on imbalances in members' development capabilities.

134. See Nakajima (1997: 74–96).

Chapter 3

1. See Leisure Development Center (1980: 2–3) and Ito (1979: 34).
2. As per the results of a questionnaire targeting 1034 parlors. Parlors reporting increased attendance by middle-age and young women totaled 45 and 32 percent, respectively (Small Business Information Center 1980: 83). These results suggest that female customers began patronizing pachinko parlors during the 1970s. The trend was particularly pronounced at rural parlors.
3. See Ito (1979: 34).
4. See *Tōhō Keizai* (1976), 'アンテナ' (Antenna), 46(4), p. 145.
5. See *Tōhō Keizai*, 'Antenna', p. 145.
6. See Small Business Information Center (1980: 83).
7. See Hashimoto and Takeda (1985).
8. Although confirmation from the language of the Entertainment Establishment Control Act of the time is not possible, the Act on Control and Improvement of the Amusement Business, etc. (Act No. 122 of July 10, 1948), which was revised in 1984 (the new law took effect in 1985), offers the following explanation: Article 20, Paragraph 3 states, 'The national Public Safety Commission may, in accordance with its rules, establish technological standards for the types of gaming machines set forth by law as necessary for certification by public safety commissions as described in the preceding paragraph, in accordance with its rules'. Paragraph 4 continues, 'In the event standards have been established as described in the preceding paragraph, manufacturers and importers of gaming machines may seek certification from public safety commissions concerning whether the models of entertainment machines they are manufacturing or importing comply with the technological specifications imposed by those standards'.
9. Of 446 applications for which result reports were received, 216 were deemed compliant (Hoan Tsūshin Kyōkai [2016], '統計資料' [Statistical materials], July 4, Table 1. Implementation status on the model examination). According to interviews of Mr. J, who was involved in research and development over about six years starting in 1992 at Okumura Sangyō, a medium-size machine manufacturer, the pass rate varied with the state of regulations (interviews conducted from December 12, 2012, to January 12, 2013). See Note 47 below.
10. For more information about patent pools that do not necessarily stimulate patent development, see Lampe and Moser (2010: 898–920). For more information on the implementation of trust law and other related law, see Miyai (1988; 1989a; 1989b). For more information about the monopolistic behavior of the Nittokuren and related companies, see Business IPR Ōpun-gata Tokkyo Pūru Bunkakai (2003: 30–34), Suzuki (2003: 7–13) and Murakami (1998a: 37–44; 1998b: 54–62).
11. See *Yūgi Tsūshin* (1955), '警察庁 警視庁の幹部を囲んで新型機を語る座談会' (Roundtable including the National Police Agency and the Tokyo Metropolitan Police Department to discuss new machine models), and *Yūgi Tsūshin* (1955), '各地の新型機の基準決定' (Regional standards on new machine models defined), February 19.
12. See Sanjūnen no Ayumi Henshū Iinkai (1990: 62–64).
13. See Japan Amusement Machine Industry Association (1966).
14. See Japan Amusement Machine Industry Association (1966).

15. See *Gekkan Yūgi Nihon* (1973), '警察庁文書通達「パチンコ遊技機の取り扱いについて」' (Written bulletin from the National Police Agency: 'About the treatment of pachinko machines'), Special New Year's Issue.
16. See Yamada (2012).
17. According to Yamada's calculations, the average lag time between patent applications and disclosures each year from 1964 to 1970 grew from 3.4 years in 1964 to 4.3 years in 1970, and the average for the entire period was about four years (2012: 31).
18. See Yamada (2012: 30).
19. The system was intended to address problems such as (a) increased social waste in the form of research and development funds consumed by increased development of redundant technologies as a result of delays in patent reviews due to a sudden increase in patent applications during the second half of the 1960s and (b) growth in companies' patent disclosure costs (Yamada 2012: 25).
20. Although the date on which the Zenkenkyō's 'Concept and Sequence of Events Leading to the Establishment of the National Amusement Machine Right-holders' Association' was authored remains unknown, it was likely created by the Nittokuren in response to the revision of the Patent Act in 1971.
21. These six companies were the founding members, but it is odd that their number did not include Heiwa, which was a leading company, and which later became a member. The omission likely occurred against the backdrop of a dispute within the industry that lasted until the mid-1970s concerning a new machine known as the 'detachable/separable' (*dacchaku/bunri-shiki*) model, which Heiwa launched in 1971. The design separated the machine from the gauge board, allowing the latter part to be replaced separately (*Gekkan Yūgi Nihon* [1971], '緊急新型特報 業界再前進へパターン整う' [New model news flash: Company introduces advanced design standard again in the industry], September, pp. 26–29) in an effort to help parlors save money. Its launch sent waves through the industry because it threatened to reduce manufacturers' sales. Although statistically the manufacture of gauge boards only accounted for about 2 percent of the 1,370,275 machines produced in 1976, that figure rose to 21.8 percent of 1,503,753 machines in 1978 (Japan Amusement Machine Patent Management Federation [c. 1980; the publication was presumably published around 1980 since it includes data for the years 1965 through 1979], 'パチンコ機製造台数の推移' [Trend in pachinko machine production volume]). A document entitled '平成七年度証紙発行数' (Number of certificate stamps issued in 1995), which records Japan Fair Trade Commission reviews and which I used to investigate patent fees in later years, lists the number of machines that were manufactured and sold. Certificate stamps issued for gauge boards represent 24 percent of the total. Although the case is extremely interesting insofar as it touches on pioneering development that would create a new chapter in the industry's history, a detailed analysis is a task we must leave for another time. Those Japan Fair Trade Commission review documents are part of a larger tranche of documents created by the Nittokuren in response to a request from the Japan Fair Trade Commission as part of a 1996 investigation of the Nittokuren and ten manufacturers on suspicion that they had collectively excluded companies from entering the market. As for the documents in detail, see Note 22.
22. As per the 'Concept and Sequence of Events Leading to the Establishment of the National Amusement Machine Right-holders' Association' (see Note 20). The

organizational changes implemented in accordance with the '公取供述報告書' (Japan Fair Trade Commission Deposition Report), which was part of the Japan Fair Trade Commission review documents described in Note 21 above, can be summarized as the formation of the Zenkenkyō as a voluntary group in 1972. The report by manufacturers, referred to as the 'JFTC Report' below, was submitted to the Nittokuren's attorney as a summary of questions posed to manufacturers by the Japan Fair Trade Commission in the course of its investigation and their responses. Although only a portion of the document remains, it reproduces the contents of the Commission's investigation in detail, partially in order to share information. The organization was incorporated in 1975 before reorganizing itself as Chūō Shizai Co., Ltd. in 1979. However, the restructuring of right-holder organizations was not significantly influenced by the organizational chart shown in Figure 3.1 or by the workings of the Review Committee (see below in body text), and the nature of the patent management contracted to the Nittokuren in particular did not change.

23. According to the testimony of Mr. U, a director at Daiichi Shōkai ('JFTC Report') (investigation of February 12, 1997).
24. According to an interview with Mr. K, a former executive of the Nittokuren (conducted on November 5, 2004).
25. According to an interview with Mr. K, a former executive of the Nittokuren (conducted on November 5, 2004).
26. More specifically, patent fees rose as a result of the development of electric machines. I was unable to pinpoint the reasons for the difference in patent fees per machine compared with Table 2.2 (Chapter 2), although they likely include the decline in patent fees, the existence of machines on which no patent fees were levied and other factors such as issues with documentation. That said, most of the patents held by Hōkoku Yūki Seisakusho, with fees collected at the time of the founding of the Nittokuren, were acquired during the mid-1950s and therefore may have no longer been in force. The trend toward lower prices during the second half of the 1960s that is evident in Table 3.1 may also reflect the fact that previously collected patent fees were no longer being collected. In any case, it is the increase in fees starting in 1973 that interests us here.
27. As per Articles 5 and 6 of the '工業所有権運用に関する業務委託契約書' (Contract for outsourcing operations related to industrial property rights). The template is dated January 1996. Outsourcing of these operations began with the establishment of the Zenkenkyō and the formation of the Review Committee in 1972. While no contract dating from the time survives, Mr. K, the former executive of the Nittokuren referenced above, notes that there were no major changes.
28. The above contract includes the following provision: 'Article 1. The Contractor [right-holder] shall entrust the Contractee [Nittokuren] with all decisions concerning possible violations of the industrial property rights listed on the attachment by machines manufactured and sold by members of the Nikkōso'.
29. According to the testimony of Mr. U (see Note 23).
30. Although I will leave the details for another time, the 1990s exhibited a different trend. Allocations toward paid licensing fees were rising, which was likely the result of factors such as growth in patent fees related to *yakumono* accessories, which were

transitory in nature. Additionally, it is possible that there was a change in characteristics based on the fact that the two lines once again exhibited similar trajectories.

31. The figure includes one case that did not develop into a dispute (Nittokuren, '特連で過去に起こった裁判' [Past cases involving the Nittokuren]). Another indicator that corroborates the rise in patent disputes is settlement payments and miscellaneous income, which are included from time to time in year-end financial statements. Those entries likely represent income related to patent disputes.
32. The electric pachinko machine that Hino, who operated a parlor in Hiroshima, created by modifying a conventional machine was licensed by the National Police Agency on November 25, 1972. Electric machines became firmly entrenched in the industry from 1973 (*Gekkan Yūgi Nihon* [1973], '動力発射で新たなファンをつかもう第一陣の三機種、颯爽の登場' [Dashing debut of the first of a new series of three models seeking to capture new fans with electric ball launching], March, pp. 14–15). The next part provides a more detailed introduction.
33. 'Mr. Hino made a special request for the organization to create a single point of contact in order to avoid some of the complexity of administrative processing' (from '日本遊技機工業組合組合員が関係する工業所有権に関する紛争処理業務等' [Concerning processing of disputes related to industrial property rights involving members of the Nikkōso], part of a tranche of documents related to an investigation conducted by the Japan Fair Trade Commission. Information about the Hino incident comes from this source).
34. According to an interview with Mr. K, a former Nittokuren executive who served as chairmen of the Review Committee (conducted on November 5, 2004). See also the Nittokuren's 'JFTC Report' and '決算報告書' (Year-end financial statements for various fiscal years).
35. Unless otherwise noted, explanations related to the Review Committee draw on the 'JFTC Report', authored by Mr. S, an assistant manager in charge of patents at the Nittokuren (investigation of September 10, 1996, October 31, 1996, and November 1, 1996).
36. Mr. K, a former Nittokuren executive, had extensive knowledge of patent-related matters because he was studying to become a patent attorney (as per an interview conducted on November 5, 2004). He continued to serve as the committee's chairperson until the Nittokuren was dissolved in 1999.
37. According to Mr. H, the manager of Sanyō Bussan's Patent Department ('JFTC Report', investigation of February 25, 1997). Examples cited included Okumura Sangyō, Maruhon and Nyū Gin.
38. Although I was not able to confirm that the committee's membership was the same as the Zenkenkyō's due to the lack of detailed information about that organization's shareholders, Zenkenkyō membership required that a company held patents, while new members of the Review Committee were manufacturers 'with a growing numbers of applications that might become valid in the future'. Accordingly, it is likely that the latter requirement was intended to be broader.
39. 'Rights submitted to the Review Committee involved all types of pachinko machines; submissions were not permitted to consist of rights that involved only certain models, which is to say, certain types of pachinko machines' (according to the testimony of Mr. H, an assistant manager in Toyomaru Sangyō's Research and Development Office

as recounted in the 'JFTC Report', investigation of October 1 and November 15, 1996). Among cases in 1996, the Review Committee was requested to investigate only one of the fifty patent rights held by Toyomaru Sangyō based on the above standard. Regarding why all patent rights were not sought in this way, one witness stated, 'Our company uses many rights held by other companies, and it's a give-and-take relationship. [...] If we were to claim other companies were infringing on our rights, we'd be accused of the same thing with regard to our extensive use of other companies' rights, and that would be problematic' (according to the testimony of Mr. H). Another noted, 'The purpose is to ensure we can manufacture and sell our products with peace of mind by protecting them with our own patent rights, which we hold as insurance in a defensive manner' (testimony of Mr. M, the manager of Sankyo's Information Management Office, as recounted in the 'JFTC Report', investigation of February 7, 1997). Manufacturers' approach to patents as examined in Chapter 2, in terms of interdependence in the use of patents and the preferential consideration given to production and sales activities, can be observed here as well.

40. At the time of the compilation of the 'JFTC Report' in 1996, machines were collected in January.
41. According to the testimony of Mr. M.
42. See the description of the testimony of Mr. S, an assistant manager in charge of patents at the Nittokuren, in the 'JFTC Report' and '本遊技機工業組合組合員が関係する工業所有権に関する紛争処理業務等' (Concerning processing of disputes related to industrial property rights involving members of the Nikkōso), part of a tranche of documents related to an investigation conducted by the Japan Fair Trade Commission.
43. I investigated changes in annual market share from 1960 to 1983, with the exception of 1963 (due to insufficient data for major manufacturers), and 1975 and 1977–1981 (due to a lack of data). Table 3.4 reproduces characteristic changes each year during that period.
44. See Small Business Information Center (1980: 57).
45. Striking growth in the leisure market that exceeded other industries during the 1970s is reported in economic white papers (Economic Planning Agency 1983).
46. For example, Nishijin announced five of the six models launched during 1974, which were included in the publication on which Table 3.5 is based (Sōgyō Gojūnen Kinenshi Hensan Iinkai 2001), at the exhibition in September. These models were the Erekkusu Guran Puri (electro grand prix), the Purēn (plain), the Sarukani, the Pawā Piero (power clown) and the Erekkusu Fisshu (electro fish), as well as the Ebira, Burijji Abekku and the Papiyon 11 (*Gekkan Yūgi Nihon* [1974], '西陣 秋を飾る個展催す' [Nishijin lights up the fall by holding an exhibition], September 9, pp. 58–60). These eight models were reported to support twenty-two variations by combining manned and automatic variants and electric *yakumono* accessories. In this way, the number of models announced at this one exhibition exceeds the account in the company's own history. See Sōgyō Gojūnen Kinenshi Hensan Iinkai (2001). In this discussion, our purpose is to ascertain the impact of systematic changes.
47. According to an advertisement that ran in the industry magazine *Gekkan Yūgi Nihon* from January through December 1969.

48. Incidentally, development risk varies with the nature of applicable regulations. According to an interview with Mr. J, who was involved with research and development over about six years from 1992 at Okumura Sangyō, a medium-size machine manufacturer, the pass rate was about 90 percent during the first half of the 1990s and about 65 percent around 2010 (interview conducted between December 12, 2012, and January 12, 2013). With regard to the significance of changes in the pass rate, here I am emphasizing the fact that regulations themselves were recognized as development risk, rather than the effects of strengthened and weakened regulations, since it is impossible to forecast the strength of regulations.
49. See Koyanagi (2000: 134–35).
50. See *Yūgi Tsūshin* (1973), '激烈なる販売合戦ライバル 平和 西陣' (An increasingly fierce sales war: Rivals Heiwa and Nishijin), May 15.
51. See Small Business Information Center (1980). The questionnaire included apparel and residential life and diet products as typical products of small and medium-size companies, followed by leisure products as a fourth category. Pachinko industry consumption is included as part of the latter group (Small Business Information Center 1980: 3). The materials summarize the results of the first full-scale questionnaire of the pachinko industry. The questionnaire targeted 4500 men and women between the ages of fifteen and fifty-nine in four small and medium-size cities (Morioka, Nagano, Matsue and Kumamoto), as well as Tokyo and Osaka.
52. See Small Business Information Center (1980: 48).
53. See Small Business Information Center (1980: 87–88). The results are based on the responses of 847 companies out of 1032 parlors nationwide, about 10 percent of the total.
54. See Small Business Information Center (1980: 104).
55. See Japan Amusement Machine Industry Association (1979), 'パチンコ機の設定基準の取り扱いについての経過報告' (Interim report on the treatment of established standards for pachinko machines), November 30.
56. See *Gekkan Yūgi Nihon* (1973), '業界レーダースタンバイ"適切運営"背景の変化の中に再登場の『電動式』' (Ready the industry's radar: The second debut of electric models against a changing backdrop of 'appropriate management'), August, pp. 12–13.
57. '... Total pachinko sales in 1953 were 273 billion yen [about US$759 million] (with a total volume of 976,000 units), while government-run gambling during the same year [lottery, bicycle racing, horse racing, motorboat racing and automobile racing] totaled 106.7 billion yen [about US$296 million]. […] Estimates of total pachinko sales in 1971 ranged from 680 billion yen [about US$1.89 billion] to 700 billion yen [about US$1.94 billion] […] about the same as bicycle racing among government-run gambling. […] Total sales for government-run gambling were […] 2 trillion yen [about US$5.6 billion] […] a love of speculation has taken hold as part of a Western lifestyle. Pachinko with electric machines […] was a type of model that was appropriate to promote based on this era-specific background […]. In that sense, the government's clear approval can be seen in the introduction of 100-shot machines, the abolition of [regulatory] standards, and the lifting of the ban on electric machines' (*Gekkan Yūgi Nihon*, 'Ready the industry's radar', pp. 12–13).

58. See *Gekkan Yūgi Nihon* (1973), '緊迫の三問題 全遊協が日工組招き接渉' (Three pressing problems: The Zen'yūkyō invites the Nikkōso to participate in direct talks), August, pp. 14–16.
59. *Gekkan Yūgi Nihon*, 'Three pressing problems', pp. 14–16.
60. Development began in advance of advertisements, and the development lead time as relates to development productivity has been abstracted. I should note that nothing is known about manufacturers that did not run advertisements. Additionally, our observations must necessarily be limited since the circulation of *Gekkan Yūgi Nihon* is unknown, making it impossible to clarify how effective advertisements were. Nonetheless, the newspaper covered intense change as it worked to run down stories about hot issues in the industry, popular models and the latest information related to the management and operation of representative parlors. Based on the publication's emphasis of the publisher's own initiatives and the fact that it ran advertisements from representative companies on an ongoing basis, we can conclude that our analysis here is meaningful on some level.
61. See *Gekkan Yūgi Nihon*, 'Three pressing problems', pp. 14–16.
62. See pp. 2–3 of the April 1973 issue of *Gekkan Yūgi Nihon.*
63. The fact that the name 'Hino-type' is used in a National Police Agency bulletin ('警察庁 丁防発第一三〇号 昭和四七年一〇月一八日付 新機種ぱちんこ遊技機「日野式一〇〇発手動皿遊技機」の取り扱いについて' [National Police Agency Security Bulletin No. 130 of October 18, 1972: Concerning treatment of the Hino-type 100-launch manual tray pachinko machine]), it is likely that the document was referring to electric machines and that there was some sort of cooperative relationship with the company that Hino, the machine's inventor, was involved with, although I was not able to confirm either.
64. See *Gekkan Yūgi Nihon* (1973), 'トラトラトラ電動式陽春に咲く ハンドルの微差調整にファン緊張' (Tora tora tora electric model blooms in spring – Fans tense at handle fine-tuning: Report on electric models at Taigeki Game Center in Kumamoto), April, pp. 50–51.
65. See *Gekkan Yūgi Nihon* (1973), 'トピック追跡 Electric Motor 電動式一挙にブームへ' (Topics: The suddenly booming popularity of electric models), May, pp. 12–14.
66. In July, Hino Co., Ltd., and Daidō Kōgyō held a joint exhibition of the Hino-type Daidō model (*Gekkan Yūgi Nihon* [1973], '日野式大同号再び展示会 七月一三日～一五日東京西川口・八州会館で' [Hino-type Daidō model featured in another exhibition: July 13 to 15 at the Hasshū Kaikan in Nishikawaguchi, Tokyo], August, p. 57).
67. See *Gekkan Yūgi Nihon*, 'The suddenly booming popularity of electric models', pp. 12–14.
68. See *Gekkan Yūgi Nihon* (1973), '広告 Electric motor 平和式電動機軽快なグリップ式発射' (Advertisement – Electric motor: Heiwa-type electric machine with light-action grip-style ball launching), June, p. 26.
69. See *Gekkan Yūgi Nihon* (1973), '京楽電動式501 東京の丸越産業が個展' (Tokyo's Marukoshi Sangyō holds exhibition of its Kyōraku electric model 501), May, p. 15.
70. See *Gekkan Yūgi Nihon* (1973), '豊国電発機も戦列へ 完璧の電動メカとスムーズなダイアル式発射スカイベルを電動化' (Hōkoku adds electric models to its line: Company electrifies the Sky Bell with a perfect electric mechanism and smooth dial-type ball launching), June, p. 19 and *Gekkan Yūgi Nihon* (1973), '広告 ニューギン電動機 完璧な電動メカ

本格派遂に登場 ニューギン' (Advertisement – Nyū Gin: Electric models with a perfect electric mechanism: Finally, Nyū Gin machines arrive for true enthusiasts), June, p. 48.

71. See *Gekkan Yūgi Nihon* (1973), '広告 ファンの心を大切にする人気のメカ 電動式三洋号 三洋物産' (Advertisement – Sanyō Bussan: The Sanyō model with a popular electric mechanism that values fans' feelings), August, p. 3.
72. See *Gekkan Yūgi Nihon* (1973), '広告 エレックスロータリー 西陣' (Advertisement – Nishijin: Electronics rotary), August, p. 4.
73. See *Yūgi Tsūshin*, 'An increasingly fierce sales war'.
74. At the end of the 1970s, Hokkaido, the Kanto region and Kyushu were being cited as areas where 'there's a strong customer preference for electric machines' (Small Business Information Center 1980: 92).
75. See *Gekkan Yūgi Nihon* (1973), 'News corner 展示会 '73 new Model show 史上空前のビッグ・スケール・ショウ' (News corner: The 1973 New Model Show, a show of unprecedented size), September, pp. 18–28.
76. See *Gekkan Yūgi Nihon* (1973), '展示会 名古屋で全国新型遊技機展示会 九月九日・一〇日 九時から一八時' (Exhibition of new pachinko machine models from around Japan in Nagoya: 9:00 am to 6:00 pm, September 9–10), August, pp. 10–11.
77. See *Gekkan Yūgi Nihon*, 'News corner: The 1973 New Model Show', pp. 18–28.
78. See Small Business Information Center (1980: 92).
79. 'During the era of manual machines, before electric machines came out, it was possible to launch balls as quickly as you wanted by improving your skill. [...] Then electric machines became popular [...]. If you can't launch balls quickly no matter how great your skill, the pleasure of pachinko will fade' (Small Business Information Center 1980: 86).
80. '[In the case of parlor] A, which has expensive machines, the parlor has to force customers to pay more, and as a result they'll stop coming. Moreover, there's no room for skill with electric machines, so the element of chance is increased. [In the case of parlor] B, which has expensive machines, ultimately the parlor has to lower the prize-ball percentage, giving customers an unpleasant experience. Customers prefer machines where there's some room left for skill. [...] We'll wait to switch to electric machines until we have no other choice' (Small Business Information Center 1980: 85).
81. 'The increase in females has been pointed out by all parlors. Some 45 percent of parlors report "increased numbers of middle-age females"', while 32 percent of parlors report 'increased numbers of young females', and 24 percent of parlors report 'increased numbers of older females'. 'Over the last ten years [during the 1970s], female customers began to come. One is left wondering when it was, exactly, that those numbers started increasing. [...] – A parlor at a shopping arcade in Chiba' (Small Business Information Center 1980: 82–84). See also *Gekkan Yūgi Nihon* (1972), '大手電鉄からデパートまで続々パチンコ経営に乗り出す有名企業の脱・本業' (One famous company after the next, from major railroads to department stores, is leaving its original business to operate pachinko parlors), April, pp. 53–57 and *Gekkan Yūgi Nihon* (1972), '追跡ルポ あれから シリーズ女性専用コーナー' (Then what? Chasing down the story series: Areas just for women), June, pp. 52–53.

82. Manual machines numbered 1,340,843 units that year (85.8 percent), while modified machines numbered 52,546 units (3.8 percent). Numbers of machines manufactured cited in the same paragraph are drawn from Japan Amusement Machine Patent Management Federation (n.d.), 'パチンコ機械製造台数の推移' (Trend in the number of pachinko machines manufactured).
83. See Japan Amusement Machine Patent Management Federation, 'Trend in the number of pachinko machines manufactured'. According to another study conducted during the same period, the preference for electric machines was decisive, with 4 percent of customers preferring manual machines at the end of the 1970s, compared to 58 percent preferring electric machines (Small Business Information Center 1980: 85). The number of manual machines in 1979 had shrunk to about 20 percent of the 1,484,000 machines manufactured that year and 31.1 percent of pachinko machine boards (presumably gauge boards, as opposed to complete machines; see Note 21), for which statistics had been kept since 1976 (Japan Amusement Machine Patent Management Federation, 'Trend in the number of pachinko machines manufactured').
84. See *Gekkan Yūgi Nihon* (1973), '広告 技術の豊国のヤクモノ快作!! New Model 大三元ホールインワン 豊国販売株式会社' (Advertisement – Hōkoku: Masterpiece *yakumono* accessories from Hōkoku, which is known for its technology! Daisangen Hole-in-One, a new model from Hōkoku Hanbai Co., Ltd.), September, pp. 40–41. See also *Gekkan Yūgi Nihon* (1973), '広告 レジャー界を革命する平和……本年度の話題を独占 選択ができる組み合わせ遊技プリンスゲーム スリル満点の組み合わせ遊技パールゲーム お客が泣き狂っちゃうパチンコ大三元 ナウなニューマシン、最高のフィリング電動式パチンコ 平和' (Advertisement – Heiwa: A company that's revolutionizing the world of leisure… Purinsu Gēmu, a combination pachinko game that's monopolizing the buzz this fiscal year; Pāru Gēmu, a combination pachinko game that's full of thrills; Pachinko Daisangen, which makes crazed customers shed tears… Timely new machines and electric pachinko machines that give players the ultimate feeling), September, pp. 40–41.
85. See *Gekkan Yūgi Nihon*, 'News corner: The 1973 New Model Show', pp. 18–28.
86. See *Gekkan Yūgi Nihon* (1973), '平和『大三元』人気爆発 お客が泣き狂っちゃうダイナミック・ゲージ' (Heiwa's Daisangen: A dynamic gauge with explosive popularity, enough to make crazed customers shed a tear), October, pp. 62–63.
87. See *Gekkan Yūgi Nihon* (1974), '豊国大三元稼働ルポ' (Reportage on Hōkoku's Daisangen operation), March, pp. 20–23.
88. See *Gekkan Yūgi Nihon* (1973), '広告……"大三元"のスリルと普通ゲージのアジを巧みにミックスした新ゲージ『東南西北』を注目のうちに発売……"ヒット"と"チューリップ"を計八個混成させてダイナミックな"パワーゲージ"で、そのスリルは、かってない迫力……' (Advertisement – Daisangen: Attention-attracting launch of Tōnanshāpē, a new gauge that skillfully mixes the thrill of Daisangen with the flavor of a normal gauge… Unprecedented power and thrills with a dynamic 'power gauge' that mixes a total of eight 'hits' and 'tulips'), November, p. 19.
89. See *Gekkan Yūgi Nihon* (1973), December issue, p. 69.
90. See *Gekkan Yūgi Nihon* (1974), '広告 八面六臂!着脱分離機SPの威力 ゲージ盤だけの入替で新装開店できます。平和株式会社大阪支社' (Advertisement – Heiwa Co., Ltd., Osaka Branch: A jack of all trades! Open a renovated parlor just by switching capable gauge boards on our detachable/separable SP machine), March, p. 42.

91. See *Gekkan Yūgi Nihon* (1974), '広告 ハラハラ·ドキドキのニューマシン!! ダイイチから『新登場』' (Advertisement – Daiichi: Introducing a new machine filled with suspense and excitement from Daiichi), April, p. 1.
92. See *Gekkan Yūgi Nihon* (1974), '広告 確かな手答!驚異の売上!豊国の技術が生んだヤクモノ·シリーズ……' (Advertisement – Hōkoku: Reliably engaging! Miraculous sales! The *yakumono* series, made possible by Hōkoku's technology…), April, p. 8.
93. 'Twice each year, we replace half our machines. […] We don't replace them because they're old and out of date, but because our customers get bored with them. […] (A parlor in a shopping arcade in Tokyo)' (Small Business Information Center 1980: 88).
94. See Japan Amusement Machine Industry Association (1972; 1973), 決算報告書 (Year-end financial statements).
95. See Small Business Information Center (1980: 19).
96. See Small Business Information Center (1980: 19).
97. See Small Business Information Center (1980: 82–83).
98. See Small Business Information Center (1980: 82–83).
99. See Small Business Information Center (1980: 88).
100. A letter entitled 'Take an interest in patent problems' ('特許問題に関心を') dated January 1, 1980 and sent by the Nittokuren to parlors offers a sense of how companies at the time approached development. The letter observes, 'There are more than 1000 patent and utility model applications every year'. The description indicates how actively manufacturers were developing patents.
101. See Takizawa (1980: 85–86).
102. Calculated based on the minimum (26,200 yen [about US$89.42]) and maximum (42,100 yen [about US$143.69], for an electric model) prices for machines purchased by Masamura Shōkai from Nishijin as described in Chapter 1 as well as the number of machines manufactured (223,787, as per Table 3.4) (Masamura Shōkai [General ledger, August 1976 to July 1977]).
103. The Nittokuren's capital totaled 8.40 million yen (about US$67,200 at 1989 rates) until the 1980s. That figure had risen to 21 million yen (about US$172,716) by the time of the organization's dissolution in 1999.
104. As a general standard drawn from 2007, for which data is available, research and development spending by small and medium-size manufacturing companies totaled about 1.6 percent of sales, as per the website of the Ministry of Economy, Trade and Industry ('平成一〇年商工業実態基本調査報告書総括編 調査結果概要 第9章 中小企業研究開発2. 研究開発費と売上高研究開発費比率' [Report on the basic survey of commerce and industry conditions, summary edition: Overview of survey results Chapter 9 – Research and development by small and medium-size companies – 2. Research and development spending and research and development spending as a percentage of sales], http://www.meti.go.jp/statistics/tyo/syokozi/result-2/h2d5kcaj.html, accessed on July 23, 2017). That amount is equivalent to labor costs of 15 million yen (about US$62,500), and dividing it by the average monthly employment income of a worker's household in 1977 of 273,000 yen (about US$1138) or a household income of 334,000 yen (about US$1392) (Keizai Kikkakuchō 1978: 2–3 [Table 1.1]), yields an average salary of about 4.6 people or 3.7 people per year. Although development

staffing varied by company and time, levels were likely insufficient at companies like Nishijin that focused on patent development. Information about the period remains unclear, but the interview with Mr. J, who was involved in research and development at Okumura Sangyō (see Note 9), suggests that large development departments as established by manufacturers such as Sankyo and Heiwa numbered about twenty people per team during the 2010s, while Okumura Sangyō employed seven or eight people. Incidentally, Nishijin switched from a defensive strategy to a corporate policy of active patent development following the patent disputes of the 1950s (see Chapter 2) (Takizawa 1980: 85–86). In fact, the company consistently competed with Sankyo for leadership in terms of patent applications. For example, Nishijin applied for a total of 1999 patents from 1989 to 1998 (of which sixty-two were utility model patents), about 12.4 percent of all pachinko machine-related patents and the most in the industry (Japan Amusement Machine Patent Management Federation [n.d.] 日本遊技機特許運営連盟, '出願件数' [Number of patent applications]).

105. It is necessary to consider the nature of the sample that yielded these sixty-five instances. The studied regions leaned urban, with a focus on Osaka Prefecture (nineteen notices) and Tokyo (sixteen notices). Other profiled parlors were located in Kanagawa Prefecture, Saitama Prefecture and Yamaguchi Prefecture (four each); Hyogo Prefecture (three); Kyoto Prefecture, Tokushima Prefecture, Fukui Prefecture and Wakayama Prefecture (two each); and Niigata Prefecture, Miyagi Prefecture, Fukuoka Prefecture, Nara Prefecture, Aichi Prefecture and Nagano Prefecture (one each). One parlor's location is unclear. Most of the parlors were comparatively large, with seven operating up to 200 machines, twenty-two operating 201 to 300 machines, twelve operating 301 to 400 machines and fifteen operating 401 to 600 machines. These characteristics are representative of the changing times as illustrated by parlors in large cities.

106. That said, 'Although most parlors in Tokyo only use machines from one manufacturer, parlors located in Nagoya and points further west use machines from various manufacturers' (*Yūgi Tsūshin*, 'An increasingly fierce sales war'). Nothing is known about business transactions with 'various manufacturers'. For our purposes here, it is important to ascertain the era-specific characteristics that defined relationships between manufacturers and parlors until the 1970s. Masamura Shōkai (headquartered in the city of Nagoya), which was covered in Chapter 1, conducted business with primarily one or two of Masamura Kikai, Nyū Gin and Nishijin during the 1970s (based on ledgers from the company during that period). Later, the company dealt with three or more manufacturers during the 1980s (we will examine the situation in the 1980s in Chapter 4).

107. See *Gekkan Yūgi Nihon* (1976), 'OPEN NEWS ボウリング場が併設 バイパス沿いの郊外ホール' (News about newly opened parlors: Suburban parlors opens on bypass next to bowling alley), June, pp. 56–57.

108. For details, see chapters 1 and 4. 'Prize-ball percentage' indicates the percentage of balls bought by customers (when they exchanged money for balls to use at the parlor) that were returned to them. The rate at which customers won prizes was determined by the angles between pins, and in particular by the adjustment of pins near catchers. For parlors, adjusting the prize-ball percentage on a daily basis comprised a type of operational expertise.

109. See *Yūgi Tsūshin*, 'An increasingly fierce sales war'. An interview with a former executive who worked as a salesman for Company T confirmed that manufacturers offered services such as these, including machine maintenance (conducted on May 23, 2004). This role of manufacturers can also be glimpsed in examples of companies entering the business from other industries, which attracted attention as a characteristic of the period. Accounts indicate that when declining movie theaters or railroad affiliates, for example Nikkatsu, Tōei and Keisei Kōgyō, a subsidiary of Keisei Electric Railway, entered the parlor business in an effort to reorganize their businesses or utilize land along train lines, they depended on pachinko machine manufacturers for this key role (*Gekkan Yūgi Nihon*, 'Areas just for women').
110. See Aoki, Sadanobu (1978), 'ギャンブルの研究パチンコ(2) その繁栄のメカニズム(下)' (Research into gambling: Pachinko (2) – Mechanisms of prosperity [Part 2]), *Gekkan Roajīru*, 2(12), p. 31.
111. This approach had the advantage of allowing manufacturers to bring feedback to bear on new machine development by gathering the views of parlors regarding machines as part of their sales activities.
112. As per an interview with a former executive from Company T (May 23, 2004).
113. The number of gray-area parlors as a percentage of all manufacturers varied depending on the market base, which is to say, on regional attributes (large city versus rural areas) and on the volume of business with each parlor (the number of machines each operated). For example, while the figure was overwhelmingly high for Nishijin at about 70 percent in the Kanto region, which includes Tokyo, Heiwa had a uniform nationwide sales network. Therefore, it is likely that the percentage represented by the core customer demographic was determined by customer size and sales capability (*Yūgi Tsūshin*, 'An increasingly fierce sales war'). Another key element in this situation was the tendency for parlors to exit the business (close up shop) and for other companies to enter the business. It is likely that such situation served to broaden the scope of the competitive arena. Unfortunately, the rates at which parlors opened and closed remain unknown.
114. From an interview of a former executive from Company T.
115. 'Most advertisement comes from word of mouth. When a parlor got good machines, for example, "This time the Heiwa machines we got are good". In the past, Heiwa also used a one-parlor, one-manufacturer arrangement, so owners that used Heiwa machines would tell their close friends. "The Heiwa machines we're using now are great, so you should use them too". That sort of word of mouth is how machines were chosen. Managers would tell their friends, "these machines are good", that sort of thing. Depending on performance during use, machines would sell through word of mouth' (From an interview of a former executive from Company T).
116. From an interview of a former executive from Company T.
117. Based solely on models that were announced. The important point here is not the level of actual pricing, but rather the outlook that prices would rise based on an assessment of trends.
118. According to articles based on interviews with parlors, 'Parlors always replaced their machines once or twice a year' (*Noda Keizai* [1976], '驚異の技術開発力 パチンコ産業の不思議' [Miraculous technological development capability: The mysterious pachinko industry], 125, p. 14; Small Business Information Center 1980: 88).

119. As the physical service life of machines had grown thanks to the evolution of manufacturing technology, the relative weight of the popularity life became an increasingly important factor in machine replacements. It is likely that the market underwent a bipolarization as the service life of less popular machines fell below one year to several months while more popular models remained in favor for several years.
120. 'With the opportunity to boost market share at a stroke, new machine development brought the risk of many machines being returned' (*Yūgi Tsūshin*, 'An increasingly fierce sales war').
121. It is difficult to verify the effectiveness of this approach, but conditions in later years offer some degree of corroboration for the situation during the 1970s. A memo entitled 'About rules on the treatment of commercialization of new pachinko models' ('パチンコ機の新機種商品化に関する取扱規定について'), likely drafted by the Nikkōso at the beginning of the 1980s, identified the following problem and described conditions that led to the situation: 'There is a striking trend where, when a manufacturer develops and introduces a model that becomes popular, other manufactures follow in that company's footsteps by making slight changes to the specifications and developing an imitation model'. During the first half of the 1980s, the organization found a problem in speculation-oriented development that ran counter to social norms and that was seen as likely to prompt new regulations (or denial of certification) in relation to imitations of Sankyo's Fībā model (see Chapter 4), which prompted striking market growth at the time. The abovementioned memo was written in response to this problem. Article 3 of the proposed rules states, 'Members seeking to manufacture and sell machines that are equivalent or similar to new models for which another member has already conducted development and received certification must obtain the consent of the original manufacturer for that model in advance'. Although it is unclear whether the rules were ever implemented officially, Tatsuki Shibuya, who analyzed the 1997 investigation by the Japan Fair Trade Commission, believes that they were put into practice from 1983 (Shibuya 1997: 20).
122. For a theoretical explanation, see pp. 139–41 of Chapter 2; for specific evidence, see Chapter 4.
123. See *Rejā Sangyō Shiryō* (1974), 'パチンコ・マージャン 手軽なレジャーとして再び脚光を浴びる' (Pachinko and mahjong: Attracting attention again as an inexpensive leisure pursuit), 7(3), p. 112.
124. 'With the opportunity to boost market share at a stroke, new machine development brought the risk of many machines being returned' (*Yūgi Tsūshin*, 'An increasingly fierce sales war').
125. From an interview of a former executive from Company T.
126. According to lists of various manufacturers' machines created based on Nittokuren-drafted purchase agreements for August, September and October 1980 (wholesale prices that exclude direct sales to parlors), for standard new electric machines, models from Okumura Sangyō were 1.2 times more expensive (at 43,000 yen [about US$211.82]) than those from Takao (estimated at 35,594 yen [about US$175.34]) at the lowest price point, while models from Sankyo were 1.3 times more expensive (at 49,000 yen [about US$241.38]) than those from Takao (estimated at 36,600 yen [about US$180.30]) at the highest price point. The list does not make clear similar data for the top manufacturers of the time. For *tokuden* machines, which were the

most expensive at the time, models from Sankyo were 1.1 times more expensive (at 62,000 yen [about US$305.42]) than those from Company T (at 54,000 yen [about US$266.01]) at the lowest price point, while models from Sankyo were 1.6 times more expensive (at 90,000 yen [about US$443.35]) than those from Takao (at 67,864 yen [about US$334.31]) at the highest price point. Sankyo, which sold the most expensive machines, launched its Fībā model in 1980, propelling it to no. 2 in market share in 1982, as shown in Table 3.4. The company subsequently reigned as a leading manufacturer.

127. Due to the continual presence of development risk, even first-mover companies sometimes failed in their development efforts. While such companies might lose customers in the gray area shown in Figure 3.3 as a result, a manufacturer such as Nishijin, for example, would presumably look to recapture them as part of its next cycle of active development.

128. From the standpoint of development-based competition, the leveling off of manufacturing volume and rise in installed machines during the first half of the 1970s, as shown in Table 3.9, might seem odd. I will leave out the details here, but the increase in installed machines is explained by used machines. Possible causes include the selection of those machines against the backdrop of the recession that followed the first oil embargo and the inability of manufacturers during this period to supply enough machines to fulfill parlors' demand expectations for new models (in terms of either pricing or specifications). The temporary lull in the withdrawal of manufacturers from the industry likely impacted the large-scale withdrawal during the next period.

Chapter 4

1. See Small Business Information Center (1980: 17).
2. See Small Business Information Center (1980: 17).
3. See *Zaikai Sapporo* (1969–1983), '高額所得者番付' (List of high-income taxpayers) and '一千万円以上の高額所得者番付' (List of high-income taxpayers paying more than 10 million yen), 4(6), 5(6), 6(6), 6(7), 7(6), 8(6), 9(6), 10(6), 11(6), 13(6), 16(6) 20(6), 21(6).
4. See National Police Agency (1980; 1993; 2020), *Keisatsu hakusho* (Police white papers); parlor numbers in the rest of this paragraph are also drawn from this source.
5. See year-end financial statement for the Nikkōso (Japan Amusement Machine Industry Association) for each of the fiscal years in question.
6. See Economic Planning Agency (1975; 1980; 1983; 1985b).
7. See Leisure Development Center (1987).
8. See Leisure Development Center (1992).
9. Fībā-type machines were categorized like this model in regulatory orders at the time.
10. The company was established as Chūō Seisakusho Co., Ltd., in 1966 before changing its name to Sankyo Seisakusho Co., Ltd., later that year and then to Sankyo in 1991. Unless otherwise noted, this chapter uses 'Sankyo' to refer to all three entities. As for Fībā, below I will generically refer to this model as well as similar models from other manufacturers that licensed the design of Sankyo's Fībā as 'Fībā-type machines'.
11. See Yano Research Institute (1989: 3). Fībā-driven market growth is noted on most timelines. For example, '1980: Fībā pachinko machines are licensed. 1981: *Yakumono*

accessories that used ICs increase in number. The debut of the Fībā model sparks an explosive super-motorized model boom, and total estimated pachinko sales surpass 3 trillion yen [about US$15 billion]' (Nijūgonen no Ayumi Henshū Iinkai 1985: 26–27). These events also appear in histories of the industry: 'In many ways, pachinko's current [1989] heyday owes much to Sankyo's development of the Fībā in 1980' (Yano Research Institute 1989: 3). A typical description of the Fībā's impact on the pachinko industry is as follows: 'The emergence of the Fībā and subsequent digital pachinko machines even affected the numbers of pachinko machines installed nationwide [...]. In 1981, demand for these machines drove the number of machines up 30,713 to 1,865,735, reversing previous losses, even as the number of parlors fell 249 from the previous year' (Jinbo 2007: 63).

12. In part, this instability in operations reflected the susceptibility of parlor operations to the effects of regulations. In short, 'Because pachinko as an industry received business licenses under the Entertainment and Amusement Establishment Control Act, industry trends are susceptible to changes in laws, regulatory guidance and other official actions; additionally, and as a result, management based on long-term prospects was difficult' (Yano Research Institute 1989: 4). In this way, regulations are understood as one factor that led to the perception of the pachinko industry as a business characterized by difficulty in predicting future performance. For more information on management and regulations, see Chapter 1.
13. During the 1950s, these swings were also affected by factors including machine design and manufacturing technologies that made use of parts made of wood and similar materials. As a subsequent switch to plastic parts progressed, competition among manufacturers drove improvement in manufacturing technologies, as we saw in Chapter 3. At the end of the 1970s, it is likely that the effect of these issues on fluctuations in sales had been ameliorated. For our purposes here, we can think of this change as a given.
14. As we saw in Chapter 1, the Administrative Order Prohibiting Successive-shot Machines of 1955, which prohibited the sale and installation by parlors of successive-shot machines, was not intended to directly regulate the behavior of consumers in line with social rules that outlawed gambling or to eradicate pachinko itself. Arguments in favor of abolishing gambling pursuits such as bicycle racing due to their adverse social impact were becoming prominent at the time, and associated events are instructive regarding the existence of pachinko. Meeting from 1955 to 1956, the Bicycle Racing Administrative Council (which advised the Minister of International Trade and Industry) came to focus on the harmful influence that would result from an outright ban on gambling, for example by triggering abuse by driving the practice underground. Based on the council's report, the Act Revising Portions of the Bicycle Racing Act, which adopted the approach of allowing state-controlled gambling, was approved on June 10, 1956, spurring measures to transform the sport into a wholesome business while diluting its speculative element. The focus of the discussion shifted from the question of whether to abolish the sport to how best to manage it, highlighting the government's stance on allowing state-controlled gambling and implementing policies to manage the manner in which it operated. For details, see Hasegawa and Committee on the History of Japan's Trade and Industry Policy (2013: 164–66).

15. Based on the testimony of the founder's second daughter who was an executive officer at Masamura Shōkai when the interview was conducted. I was unable to find documentation to verify subsequent developments (from an interview conducted on February 17, 2015).
16. For more information about the origins and establishment of this mechanism and of the role of the police, see Chapter 1.
17. According to Article 23 of the Act on Control and Improvement of the Amusement Business, etc., amended from the Entertainment and Amusement Establishment Control Act (Act No. 122 of July 10, 1948), operators of pachinko parlors may not engage in the conduct listed below. In short, pachinko parlor operators were not allowed to '(i) Offer cash or securities as prizes; (ii) Buy prizes that customers had won; (iii) Allow customers to take balls or medals provided for gaming purposes or other similar items off the premises'. The three-business system can be understood as a mechanism that took hold because it allowed the exchange of prizes for cash, which was prohibited under the act, without violating the law's provisions. The prize exchange system described here varied by region because there were prefecture-specific variations in related regulations. This chapter's discussion, while acknowledging those differences, is based on the three-business system that is likely to have been most typical.
18. Although exchange rate levels remain unclear, at least one person with knowledge of the industry describes them as being region-specific (according to testimony from the editor of an industry magazine obtained during an interview on March 31, 2013). Interviews of parlor operators also revealed era-specific differences. Masamura Shōkai records (prize records and ledgers) indicate that total spending on prizes was impacted by fine-tuning of prize exchange rates on an individual basis by management. In any case, it is unlikely that parlors would have been able to differentiate themselves significantly from competing parlors for the reasons described in the text.
19. During the 1980s, the average starting salary per month for college graduates was somewhat higher than 100,000 yen (about US$493 at 1980 rates), while a newspaper subscription cost about 2600 yen (about US$12.81 at 1980 rates).
20. People involved in the industry indicate that this structure has collapsed in recent years, leaving prices to be set by wholesalers through negotiations (according to interviews of a special prize wholesaler involved with the three-business system in Tokyo).
21. See Japan Tramway Society Nagoya Branch (1997: 26).
22. Compiled based on Masamura Shōkai (1980; 1981).
23. According to the purchase agreement ('売買契約書' [Baibai keiyaku sho]) dated November 17, 1997, with Yamasa Sangyō, which delivered machines to the M.S. parlor in 1996, the company's parlors were categorized as being located in an entertainment district (the other categories were defined as being located next to a train station or in a suburban area).
24. See *Hōseki* (1979), '「釘師」座談会 パチンコ台は生き物のように敏感です' (Pachinko roundtable on pin adjusters: Pachinko machines are sensitive, as if they are alive), no. 6, pp. 134–41.
25. See *Hōseki*, 'Pachinko roundtable on pin adjusters', p. 137.
26. According to this article, use of the expression 'pin adjuster' (*kugishi*) was limited primarily to western Japan (Kansai region, especially Osaka) during the 1970s. In that

context, pin adjusters adjusted pins at multiple parlors (*Hōseki*, 'Pachinko roundtable on pin adjusters', p. 134). In eastern Japan (Kanto region, especially Tokyo), where the parlor at which the pin adjuster who appeared in the roundtable was located, pin adjusters held titles such as sales division manager or manager and worked exclusively for a particular parlor, unlike in western Japan. In eastern Japan, the employees who were responsible for pin adjustment also seem to have handled parlor sales, employee labor management and prize purchases, indicating that the scope of their job and responsibilities differed from their counterparts in other areas. Their role was what is today performed by a parlor manager. I use the term 'pin adjuster' to refer to both variations of the job in different regions.

27. See *Hōseki*, 'Pachinko roundtable on pin adjusters', p. 138.
28. See *Hōseki*, 'Pachinko roundtable on pin adjusters', p. 137.
29. See *Hōseki*, 'Pachinko roundtable on pin adjusters', p. 137.
30. See *Hōseki*, 'Pachinko roundtable on pin adjusters', p. 137.
31. Surviving sources from Parlor B record the single-day sales and prize sales figures for the period covered in Figure 4.2. According to the testimony of a family member (from an interview conducted on February 17, 2015), the parlor closed after September 1981.
32. See Economic Planning Agency (1980).
33. See *Gekkan Yūgi Nihon* (1979), '数字が示した減速経済下の実態 経済企画庁『独身勤労者の消費生活』からレジャーの実績 男女ともパチンコが減少率最高示す' (A slowing economy by the numbers: Single workers to men and women who are good at leisure / pachinko posts highest rate of decline ever, from *the consumption lifestyle* by Economic Planning Agency), Special New Year's Issue, pp. 74–77; *Gekkan Yūgi Nihon* (1979), '不況と過当競争の挟み撃ち 店舗数・設備台数ともに減少だが平均台数増えホールは大型化の傾向' (Caught between recession and excessive competition: Parlor and machine counts fall even as average number of machines grows / trend towards larger parlors), April, pp. 20–21; and *Gekkan Yūgi Nihon* (1980), 'レジャー白書にみる様変わりの実態 安上がりに苦心金銭消費型から時間消費型へ' (Changes seen in the *Leisure White Paper*: Struggling with falling prices and shifting from consumption of money to consumption of time), July, pp. 44–46.
34. See Sanjūnen no Ayumi Henshū Iinkai (1990: 66–67). However, the arcade game *Space Invaders*, which started gaining popularity around October 1978, took a downward turn after the next summer, and the boom proved short-lived, lasting only until the end of 1979 (see National Police Agency [1980: 174] and Yūgi Tsūshinsha [2011: 76]).
35. After working for a pachinko parlor in Hiroshima during the 1950s, Mr. S served as a management consultant for manufacturers in the city of Nagoya and pachinko parlors and then as an instructor at a pachinko school (according to an interview conducted on August 4, 2012). Unless otherwise noted, descriptions related to pin adjustment draw on this interview.
36. See Suzuki (2001: 371–72). Such machines, which halted play after dispensing balls in an explosive manner (i.e., by halting ball replenishment to stop play after a certain number of balls had been dispensed), were 'service' units whose pins had been opened. They were set up in advance with the intention of enabling the parlor to control excessive dispensation of prize balls. While they served to advertise to customers the

parlor's willingness to dispense prize balls, they also led to complaints about service. The industry switched over to unlimited dispensation with the coming of the 1980s.

37. Mr. S described how pin adjusters were able to adjust pins so that the average customer would play for twenty minutes, or in the case of parlors in suburban locations, longer at forty minutes, drawing on a tool set of 'warm pin arrangements, urban pin arrangements, suburban pin arrangements and pin arrangements for parlors located near train stations'.
38. According to the results of an interview survey of pachinko fans (*Zen'yūren Kōhō* [1980], '業界最大の課題 若年層ファン離れに歯止めが急務' [The most serious issue facing the industry: The urgent need to halt the loss of young fans], no. 158). Some observers pointed to growth in the number of parlors that were switching to medal-style gaming machines like mahjong (known as *jankyū*) and 'arrange ball' (both types of amusement machine similar to pachinko) or *pachislot* machines as one factor in the decline of locations and machine counts (*Zen'yūren Kōhō* [1981], '遊技機の多様化が影響 前年比三三五軒の減少' [Impact of the diversification of gaming machines: Number of parlors falls 335 from last year], no. 168).
39. See Ado Sākuru Setsuritsu Gojū Nen Henshū Iinkai (2014), 'INTERVIEW 株式会社三共元東京支社長' (Interview: President of the Sankyo Co., Ltd., Tokyo Branch), p. 47.
40. See Ado Sākuru Setsuritsu Gojū Nen Henshū Iinkai, 'Interview', p. 47.
41. See Ado Sākuru Setsuritsu Gojū Nen Henshū Iinkai, 'Interview', p. 47.
42. *Gekkan Yūgi Nihon* (1981) '三共フィーバー人気続伸 セル盤を"宇宙ムード"に' (Sankyo Fībā's popularity continues to grow: Pin board evokes a 'space mood'), February, p. 38.
43. See Yūgi Tsūshinsha (2011), '記事採録 ヒット商品開発秘話(1) 平成一二年二月二三日発行「パチンコ・パチスロ産業フェア二〇〇〇」' (Select article: Unknown episodes in the development of hit products [1], published February 23, 2000: 'Pachinko/*pachislot* industry fair 2000').
44. See Ado Sākuru Setsuritsu Gojū Nen Henshū Iinkai, 'Interview', p. 47. The rest of this paragraph draws on this source.
45. See Yūgi Tsūshinsha, 'Unknown episodes in the development of hit products [1]', p. 79.
46. See Ado Sākuru Setsuritsu Gojū Nen Henshū Iinkai, 'Interview', p. 47.
47. I would like to express my deep gratitude for the across-the-board cooperation and advice of Associate Professor Hiroto Suzuki of the Josai International University, Faculty of Management and Information Sciences, without which I would not have been able to compile this table. Ultimate responsibility for results and their interpretation is mine alone.
48. Another initiative was to limit the number of openings in thirty seconds to ten, whereas it had been unlimited in the past (*Gekkan Yūgi Nihon* [1981], '「超特電」の営業姿勢「超自粛」徹底へ焦点 「自主規制」強く打ち出し 新要件厳しく受け止める' [Super-motorized model operating stance: Focusing on super restraint in the face of robust 'voluntary regulations' / parlors come under strict new requirements], June, p. 16). Subsequently, the Nikkōso announced a plan consisting of voluntary regulations on machine standards that set forth a series of development standards limiting the speculative character of play after negotiating with the National Police Agency (*Gekkan Yūgi Nihon* [1981], '10月1日から「超特電機」新要件実施' [New requirements imposed on super-motorized model starting October 1], July, pp. 17–18).

49. See *Gekkan Yūgi Nihon* (1982), '超特電機の問題を総括「自主規制維持体制」を大きく打ち出す 全遊協三月二九日・非公開理事会' (Summarizing the super-motorized model problem: Zen'yūkyō holds closed-door trustees' meeting on March 29 to outline the self-regulation approach), April, pp. 10–12. Although it is difficult to gauge the direct impact of the 30 percent regulation on the number of installed machines in a climate of intensifying competition, reports following the regulation indicate that conditions in the industry declined by an average of about 30 percent (*Gekkan Yūgi Nihon* [1982], '「新要件」後の機種「認定」に関心集中 一一月二六日・全遊協理事会' [Attention focuses on model certification following 'new requirements': Zen'yūkyō trustees' meeting on November 26], December, pp. 10–11).
50. *Gekkan Yūgi Nihon*, 'Attention focuses on model certification', pp. 10–11.
51. See '当期の営業成績の概要' (Overview of sales results for the fiscal year under review), covering Masamura Shōkai's operating results from August 1984 to July 1985.
52. The standard formula used to calculate gross profit margin in the industry is (1 – prize-ball percentage × prize-cost percentage). In this context, 'prize-cost percentage' refers to the exchange rate (the ratio of the value of the prizes for which customers' balls were exchanged to the value of balls won by customers, always a value of less than 1, which resulted in a discount in favor of the parlor). Since the prize-cost percentage remains unclear, I have calculated figures using the formula described in the text and available data. This approach is limited in that it is impossible to assess either fluctuations in profits caused by fluctuations in the M.S. parlor's prize-cost percentage or daily adjustments in the prize-ball percentage based on those fluctuations. That said, it does allow us to consider major trends in the role of pin adjustment by observing performance over the three-year period.
53. *Sebun-ki* is literally 'Seven-machine', a category of Fībā-type machine incorporating three rotating drums in the manner of a slot machine that yielded a jackpot when three sevens showed.
54. However, there were also factors that preclude the conclusion that the role of pin adjustment was declining in a linear manner. The speculative character of Fībā-type machines was limited by regulations, and other models were mixed in with those machines. However, it is worth reviewing the pure characteristics of Fībā-type machines when those machines started to become popular in order to understand their later dominance in the industry. The question here is whether the methods used by the M.S. parlor changed in response to varying environmental conditions, and if not, what the significance of that inaction was.
55. For more information about the reason for the classification of prizes as special prizes, see Note 156 in Chapter 1.
56. This figure was calculated based on a book of receipts from August 1983 and a list of prizes ('Prize I' from August 1, 1983), the only materials I was able to obtain. It seems unlikely that the tendency of special prizes to yield higher profitability than standard prizes would vary significantly over time.
57. I was unable to discover any sources related to the overall exchange rate for prizes. Reports indicate a figure of around 67 percent during the second half of the 1980s. That figure indicates that 4-yen balls were exchanged for special prizes worth 2.67 yen.
58. As of 1966, Aisan Shōkai did business with 296 parlors in the city of Nagoya and thirty-

eight parlors in the city of Ichinomiya, making it a model company in an industry that consisted of twenty-two companies in Aichi Prefecture (*Chūbu Yūgi Taimusu* [1966], '「景品会社」?という企業の実態は?' [What's the reality of companies known as 'prize companies'?], February 20).

59. For more information about the role of police guidance in prize exchange and the organization of supply routes, see Chapter 1 as well as Zenkoku Yūgigyō Kumiai Rengōkai (1977), '業界二五年を語る座談会 二「隆盛時代から連発禁止前後」' (Roundtable 2 on 25 years in the industry: 'From peak prosperity to the ban on successive-shot machines') and Zenkoku Yūgigyō Kumiai Rengōkai (1977), '業界二五年を語る座談会 四「第二次隆盛時代と組織強化」' (Roundtable 4 on 25 years in the industry: 'A second golden age and organizational strengthening'), p. 163.
60. See 'ビッグ鼎談パチンコ産業業界総展望' (Big three-way conversation: Future prospects for the pachinko industry) in Sogo Unicom (1982), p. 25.
61. See Suzuki (2001: 323).
62. See year-end financial statements for the Nikkōso for each of the fiscal years in question.
63. According to Table 3.4, Masamura Kikai fell out of the rankings between 1976 and 1982. The company was subsequently absorbed by another company in a merger. See Note 162 in Chapter 1.
64. The transaction was recorded in the general ledger in June, as indicated in Table 4.3, for reasons that were presumably related to the parlor's accounting processing. According to a purchase agreement with Maruhon Kōgyō dated April 3, 1982, a model known as the 'Sentā Bikutorī' (center victory) was installed on April 18, spurring sales to increase rapidly from May (see Figure 4.4). (The product was likely a 'Sentā Bikutorī' unit; see *Gekkan Yūgi Nihon* [1981], '「フィーバー・タイプ」を特別検定' ['Fībā-type' machines undergo special certification], April, pp. 13, 15.) Subsequently, the parlor entered into a contract with Nyū Gin that specified delivery on June 1 or 2 (as per a purchase agreement dated May 25, 1981).
65. *Gekkan Yūgi Nihon*, '"Fībā-type" machines undergo special certification', pp. 13, 15.
66. See *Gekkan Yūgi Nihon*, '"Fībā-type" machines undergo special certification', pp. 12–15. The magazine introduced models that were announced each year, along with descriptions of joint industry exhibitions and exclusive exhibitions orchestrated by representative manufacturers. A survey of articles published after July 1980 introducing Sankyo's Fībā model indicates that Fībā-type machines from other companies were first introduced in this article in the April 1981 issue.
67. A special certification for Fībā-type machines alone was carried out by the Kinki district (greater Osaka) conference, which covered six prefectures (*Gekkan Yūgi Nihon*, '"Fībā-type" machines undergo special certification', pp. 12–15.). In this way, machine certifications at the time were carried out in a region-specific manner. Although we need information about certification in the region that includes Nagoya in order to consider the machines' purchase by the M.S. parlor, we can presume that regional markets that included large cities were given high priority, and that the study undertaken in the Kinki region was representative.
68. See year-end financial statements for the Nikkōso for 1981.
69. Note that Okamura Yūki's Fībā-type machine was called the 'Fībā', just like

Sankyo's original model (*Gekkan Yūgi Nihon*, '"Fībā-type" machines undergo special certification', pp. 12–15).

70. See purchase agreements with Maruhon (April 3, 1981) and Nyū Gin (May 25, 1981).
71. See Sogo Unicom (1982: 26).
72. See Sogo Unicom (1982), '運営計画のあり方と収支バランスシート' (Operational planning and the balance sheet), p. 261.
73. As I observed in the analysis described in Chapter 3, not all manufacturers were able to create such imitation models. Development and production of imitation models indicates that the company in question had the requisite capabilities.
74. For more information about this source, see Chapter 3.
75. The company had decided to rebuild its head office building on July 31, 1989 (see the minutes from the 34th Regular General Shareholders' Meeting). The former (Jōshin) branch likely only replaced its machines twice in 1990 and once in 1991 because it was preparing to close and relocate to the head office building.
76. 'In busy entertainment districts, one sees not only new openings, but also renewal reopenings following machine replacements. It's unusual to see in the greater Tokyo area, but it's typical in the area near the city of Nagoya. The practice absorbs plenty of customers [...] and parlors decorate as if they were opening for the first time while replacing just the machines and, naturally, leaving the rest of their layout the same' (*Yūgi Tsūshin* [1951], '地方だより名古屋' [Regional news: Nagoya], November 25).
77. See *Yūgi Tsūshin*, 'Regional news'.
78. See *Yūgi Tsūshin*, 'Regional news'.
79. Whether renewal reopenings occur randomly based on the circumstances of individual parlors or represent a practice that is generally concentrated at specific times across the industry also influences the pachinko machine market, for example through implications for the way manufacturers develop and produce machines.
80. See Sogo Unicom (1982: 38). Entry into the pachinko market by businesses from other industries accelerated during the 1990s. For a more detailed account of the overall trend, see Kaji (2009a) and Kaji (2009b).
81. 'To hear ordinary tax offices tell it right now, 50 percent of returns are in the red [...]. There aren't any pachinko parlors with negative tax returns [...]. Even if there were, it would be about 10 percent of all returns, while 90 percent are in the black [...]. There are plenty [of parlors] filing returns with 100 or 200 million yen [in profits; about US$431,035 or US$862,069]' (Sogo Unicom 1983: 36). Another observer noted, 'Lease companies that are affiliated with banks will lend 500 million or even 1 billion yen [about US$2.16 or US$4.31 million] [...]. Some 70 or 80 percent of new parlors today are borrowing that money' (Sogo Unicom 1983: 31).
82. 'A company in Tokyo is experiencing a structural downturn in its own industry right now [...]. The company has substantial assets [...]. When it conducted market research to identify which industries are currently promising, the answer was "pachinko"' (Sogo Unicom 1983: 38).
83. See Han (2010: 140).
84. See '当期の営業成績の概要' (Overview of sales results for the fiscal year under review), covering Masamura Shōkai's operating results from August 1982 to July 1983.
85. The document is a memo that was submitted when the company settled its yearly

financial statements, along with the balance sheet and profit-and-loss statement. Unless otherwise noted, information about the social environment and operations in this paragraph draw on this source.

86. See the minutes for Masamura Shōkai's 34th Regular General Shareholders' Meeting, held on July 31, 1989.
87. To all appearances, parlors spent less time on pin adjustment in the course of daily sales, as is clear from the following observation: 'Until that time, parlor operations consisted of calculating the rates at which balls were dispensed through careful pin adjustment, one machine at a time, but the appearance of Fība-type machines brought a major shift to "balancing prize-ball percentages across the entire parlor"' (Jinbo 2007: 56–57).
88. There was a general sense that the need for pin adjustment had declined significantly by the second half of the 1990s, and that trend only strengthened as the number of gauges shrank with growing use of LCD components after 2000 (based on the interview with the pin adjustor described in Note 35).
89. With the implementation of the Act on Control and Improvement of the Amusement Business, etc., in 1985, machine certifications were based on a system of three classifications that categorized Fība-type machines as Class 1. The system was abandoned when the law was revised in 2004, with the result that all machines were effectively classified as Fība-type machines.

Chapter 5

1. Kaji (2015) explains the historical development of the pachinko industry with special attention on companies from other industries that entered the business and emphasizes the significance of such 'migration' during the 1980s. See Chapter 10 of his work.
2. Unlike the across-the-board ban on the use of successive-shot machines (Administrative Order Prohibiting Successive-shot Machines) that took effect in 1955, regulations on Fība-type machines implemented in 1981 focused explicitly on limiting the speculative element of their operation. The 1955 regulations were imposed for a complex set of reasons, including the industry's relationship with organized crime, involvement of parlors in illegal operations such as the exchange of prizes for cash, and social criticism of gambling. Although it remains unclear why the nature of regulations changed, the evolution was likely related to the resolution of those problems, as seen in the first part of this chapter, and to changes in social awareness, for example in terms of approval for some level of speculative activity (see Notes 24 and 75 in the Introduction).
3. As noted in Chapter 4, Masamura Shōkai expanded the scale of its parlor when it relocated its head office in 1991. Based on the fact that the company had already experienced declining profitability for a number of years, the move was a passive, reactive measure.
4. 'In the past, the people who won pachinko were those who had the practice to read pins and ball movement […]. After the introduction of Fība-type machines, electronic control gave everyone the same chance of winning or losing […]' (*Asahi Shimbun* [1985], 'ハッピー・ニッポン第二部　人々を覆う気分(5)　パチンコ元年　繁栄を支える身近な技術革命' [Happy Nippon Part 2: People's feelings / (5) Familiar technological innovations

that supported prosperity in the first year of the pachinko era], August 31).

5. 'Whether or not you win a jackpot is entirely a matter of chance. Just because the probability is one in 200 doesn't mean you'll win a jackpot if you feed 200 balls into the hole when the machine starts turning. You might not win a jackpot in 500 balls, or you might win one on your first ball. Either way, it's got nothing to do with skill' (*Asahi Shimbun*, 'Happy Nippon Part 2').
6. This trend was strengthened by the system of fluctuating probability that was recognized in 1990 (making the next jackpot more likely by increasing the probability of a jackpot).
7. Pin adjustment as described by a pin adjuster in Chapter 4 – 'warm pin arrangements, urban pin arrangements, suburban pin arrangements and pin arrangements for parlors located near train stations' (see Note 37 in Chapter 4) – embodied a set of skills that made certain assumptions about customers' playing time. In short, 'suburban pin arrangements' increased the prize-ball percentage so that customers would play longer in order to achieve a target across numerous machines. Such adjustments ran counter to 'urban pin arrangements' and 'pin arrangements for parlors located near train stations'.
8. See Yoshikawa, H. (1951), '常設新規開業手引 私はパチンコ屋を開業したい' (Handbook on new brick-and-mortar businesses: So you want to open a pachinko parlor), *Shōtenkai*, 32(3), pp. 72–73.
9. See *Noda Keizai* (1964), '第二の焦点　パチンコで息抜こう　大衆のための健全娯楽化図るパチンコ業界' (Focus 2: Relaxing with pachinko: The pachinko industry attempts to transform itself into healthy entertainment for the masses), 896, p. 81.
10. See *Zen'yūren Kōhō* (1976), '全国パチンコ店　最近における実態' (Recent conditions at pachinko parlors nationwide), October 1, p. 1. Since there were no standards related to distance from train stations or parking lot size, the count includes neighborhoods and urban parlors with parking areas near train stations. However, the construction of a parking area as a means of attracting customers is more important for suburban parlors than for parlors located near train stations, which leveraged the convenience of access from those train stations. Defining suburban parlors based on the presence of a parking area is a coherent approach. Incidentally, *Zen'yūren Kōhō*, the source referenced above, is the journal of the Zen'yūkyō.
11. See *Zen'yūren Kōhō* (1975), September 15, p. 3.
12. The account is given primarily from the standpoint of existing neighborhoods and urban businesses (*Zen'yūren Kōhō* [1973], '過当競争防止に行政指導群馬県県公委に陳情' [Administrative guidance on preventing excessive competition: Petition to the Gunma Prefecture Public Safety Commission], April 15).
13. See *Rejā Sangyō Shiryō* (1973), 'レジャー特捜班レポート—チェーン化を可能にした立地革命 郊外パチンコの実態' (Leisure special investigation team report: Revolution in siting makes possible chains / What's happening with suburban pachinko), 6(10), p. 249.
14. See *Ōru Seikatsu* (1973), '東に西に話題の商法・儲け比べ・知恵比べ——駐車場が救いの神　はやりにはやる郊外パチンコ　パチンコインター' (Business method buzz everywhere / Comparing profits and know-how: Parking lots as saviors / The exploding popularity and profitability of suburban pachinko and 'pachinko exits'), 28(2), p. 206.
15. See *Rejā Sangyō Shiryō*, 'Leisure special investigation team report', p. 249.

16. The rest of this paragraph draws on Economic Planning Agency (1985a: 185–86). The percentage of consumption that involved durable goods began to decline during the 1970s, which was described as a period of stable growth. Instead, consumer behavior related to service-driven leisure, for example educational and recreational services, eating out and automobile-related expenses, became progressively more conspicuous.
17. See Figure II-2-38, 'Adoption of durable consumer goods', in Economic Planning Agency (1985a: 408–09). At about 65 percent, car ownership was greater than 60 percent in 1984.
18. See Table II-3-1, 'National life: An international comparison', in Economic Planning Agency (1985a: 202–03).
19. The survey targeted 3028 unmarried office workers employed at businesses with at least 100 employees in the cities of Tokyo, Osaka, Sapporo and Kitakyushu (*Gekkan Yūgi Nihon* [1974], 'トップは依然パチンコ' [Pachinko remains in the lead], April, pp. 62–63).
20. See *Ōru Seikatsu*, 'Business method buzz everywhere', p. 206.
21. See *Gekkan Yūgi Nihon* (1971), '不況ムードの近畿圏商業の動向と将来近畿商圏現況レポート' (Report on trends and the future of business in the Kinki region [six prefectures including Osaka in western Japan] in a time of perceived recession), July, pp. 50–54. Population-related information below draws on this source.
22. See *Gekkan Yūgi Nihon*, 'Report on trends and the future of business in the Kinki region', pp. 50–54.
23. One source of information about the influence of changes in trade areas caused by residential suburbanization is Nobuji Sugimura's straightforward, long-running survey. Sugimura describes changes in townscapes through transitions in parlor locations while attempting to compare cities with a focus on the role played by city-based parlors of creating ambiance. See Sugimura (1996).
24. See Table 1 in Motai (1986: 94). The paper defines 'large-scale retail' as businesses with a sales area of at least 1500 square meters and 'suburban' as sites of former plants, agricultural land and similar locations. The change in the tendency for large-scale retail businesses to choose suburban locations favored large regional cities, smaller cities near large regional cities, mid-size regional cities and small regional cities over large metropolitan areas (with the trend growing more pronounced as the size of the city shrank).
25. 'Drive-in style pachinko parlors with large amounts of outside space are extremely popular right now [at the beginning of the 1970s], and one new parlor of this type after another is opening up in the Tokai region [lying between Tokyo and Osaka]' (*Gekkan Yūgi Nihon* [1972], 'ああ新開店!!客もホールも、期待をかけるこの一時!' [Ah, another new opening! A time of high expectations on the part of customers and parlors alike], August, p. 20).
26. 'There are few prospects for new entrants in crowded cities, where there's little appeal. Instead, better to jump on the automobile bandwagon and target affluent customers like suburban bowling alleys […]' (*Gekkan Yūgi Nihon*, 'Ah, another new opening!', p. 20).
27. 'A parlor like a drive-in opened up as a test case. It did remarkably well' (*Gekkan Yūgi*

Nihon, 'Ah, another new opening!', p. 20).

28. See *Nikkan Yūgi Nihon* (1972), '大手電鉄からデパートまで続々パチンコ経営に乗り出す有名企業の脱・本業' [From major rail companies to department stores: One after the next, famous companies move away from their core businesses and into pachinko], April, pp. 53–57.
29. See *Rejā Sangyō Shiryō*, 'Leisure special investigation team report', p. 251.
30. 'Suburban parlors have space that neighborhoods and urban parlors can't imitate [...] as well as unique customer demographics. Most customers are car owners, or can use a car relatively freely [...], are driver's license holders, and their family members and their friends [...] suffice to say, demographics that are economically somewhat well-off' (*Gekkan Yūgi Nihon* [1973], 'また一つ郊外パチンコ誕生' [The birth of another suburban pachinko parlor], July, pp. 10–11).
31. 'More and more fans are focusing on the ambiance of pachinko parlors, rather than on the game itself' (*Gekkan Yūgi Nihon* [1973], '話題を追って「郊外パチンコ」' [Chasing the buzz: 'Suburban pachinko'], December, p. 25).
32. 'Their interiors feature colorful walls and plenty of lighting' (*Gekkan Yūgi Nihon*, 'Chasing the buzz', p. 25).
33. 'The machines have seats, and there's plenty of space around each' (*Gekkan Yūgi Nihon*, 'Chasing the buzz', p. 25). Interior design took a scientific approach to assessing its human occupants in the introduction of chairs, taking into account chair structure and height as well as the most comfortable sitting posture and the position of the wrist when the arms were bent in a comfortable position and designing islands (blocks of about sixteen pachinko machines) so that the wrist would be positioned near the pachinko machine's handle (*Noda Keizai* [1976], '驚異の技術開発力パチンコ産業の不思議' [Miraculous technological development capability: The mysterious pachinko industry], 1254, pp. 13–14).
34. See *Noda Keizai*, 'Miraculous technological development capability', pp. 13–14.
35. The rest of this paragraph draws on *Noda Keizai*, 'Miraculous technological development capability', pp. 185–86.
36. See Economic Planning Agency (1985a: 182). The number of businesses implementing a five-day or five-and-a-half-day workweek more than doubled between 1966 (6.6 percent) and 1970 (15.3 percent) (Economic Planning Agency 1971: 71). It is likely that these improvements were the result of labor policies in response to changes in awareness regarding work and free time on the part of young people, which were described in a 1968 survey, summarized in Table 4.15, 'Attitudes toward the relationship between work and free time' (Economic Planning Agency 1971: 69). In short, it is clear that the people aged thirty and younger at the time valued free time, and reducing working hours was second only to increasing wages as a major demand of labor unions. Companies had to accommodate such demands in order to resolve the problem of securing and retaining young labor (Economic Planning Agency 1971: 69–70).
37. 'If entertainment districts are busy, businesses can expect commensurate customer headcounts' (*Gekkan Yūki* [1973], 'パチンコの伸びに期待もてるか休二日時代にいよいよ突入!企業のレジャー管理が問題点に' [Can pachinko be expected to grow? The era of the five-day workweek is finally upon us! Corporate management of leisure becomes an

issue], March, pp. 18–24).

38. 'If people have more free time, travel and other options become more advantageous [...]. By contrast, pachinko, as an industry that provides short-term amusement, could be adversely affected' (*Gekkan Yūki*, 'Can pachinko be expected to grow?' pp. 18–24).
39. The article went on to predict, 'People can't travel so easily, and in fact, people who wish to travel take steps like saving money, and they avoid wasting money at all times'. Noting that the boost in free time due to the five-day workweek would exert a favorable effect by extending normal consumption, it continues, 'The people who enjoy pachinko day in and day out will have more opportunities to stop by their neighborhood parlors' (*Gekkan Yūki*, 'Can pachinko be expected to grow?' pp. 18–24).
40. See *Gekkan Yūki*, 'Can pachinko be expected to grow?' pp. 18–24.
41. See Economic Planning Agency (1985a: 182).
42. This awareness on the part of the industry is reflected in the Gunma Amusement Industry Cooperative's submission of a petition to the prefecture's public safety commission seeking to have business licensing more strictly enforced (*Gekkan Yūgi Nihon* [1973], '企業対策として『規制陳情』ボーリング場のP店併営に' [Petitioning to regulate bowling alleys with collocated pachinko parlors as a corporate policy], April, pp. 64–65). Observers had concluded that the decline in the popularity of bowling among consumers could not be restored. For example, a survey of consumption trends among single workers conducted by the Economic Planning Agency at the end of 1972 found that among the leisure activities in which respondents engaged, 'bowling has clearly peaked and is declining' (*Gekkan Yūgi Nihon* [1973], '女子のパチンコ党ふえる独身勤労者の消費者動向' [Numbers of female pachinko enthusiasts grow: Consumer trends among single workers], March, pp. 16–17).
43. 'The bowling industry, which was described as experiencing bullish conditions until the year before last [1971] seems to have undergone a rapid and full-scale reversal [...]. Reports indicate that three companies in Ibaraki and Akita Prefectures have already filed for bankruptcy' (*Gekkan Yūgi Nihon* [1972], '峠下ったボウリング場' [Bowling lanes in decline], September).
44. 'Moreover, those three filings surfaced within a single month, prompting no small number of managers to voice pessimism with regard to future conditions and already triggering the formulation of new plans all over the place' (*Gekkan Yūgi Nihon*, 'Bowling lanes in decline').
45. See *Gekkan Yūgi Nihon*, 'The birth of another suburban pachinko', pp. 10–11, and *Gekkan Yūgi Nihon* (1975), 'OPEN NEWS花開く「原田商法」徳山・下松・光・新南陽防南四都市平和パレード' (Open news: Flowering of the Harada business method: A Heiwa parade in the four cities of Tokuyama, Kudamatsu, Hikari and Shinnan'yo), February, pp. 28–30.
46. See *Gekkan Yūgi Nihon*, 'Bowling lanes in decline', p. 51. After the number of parlors fell from 9490 in 1969 to 9393 in 1971 and then to 9304 in 1972, it rose to 9701 in 1973 and then to 10,636 in 1975. The figures illustrate the result of growth in the number of companies entering the business from around 1973. The potential for these conditions to lead to excessive competition was seen as a problem, and bowling alley operators entering the pachinko business were cited as a factor.
47. See for example *Gekkan Yūgi Nihon*, 'Numbers of female pachinko enthusiasts grow',

pp. 16–17.

48. ‘There are examples... of businesses that declined due to bowling alley competition entering the pachinko business or establishing pachinko parlors alongside bowling alleys’ (*Gekkan Yūgi Nihon*, ‘Petitioning to regulate bowling alleys with collocated pachinko parlors as a corporate policy’, p. 64).
49. ‘Since they have land at their discretion that would make neighborhoods and urban parlors jealous, [suburban parlors] can freely create layouts that go beyond the conventional wisdom, not only in terms of parking lots, but also service facilities, and they can embrace the challenges of numerous experiments and possibilities as “experimental amusement facilities”’ (*Gekkan Yūgi Nihon* [1974], ‘今月の新装開店 郊外パチンコトーヨーが誕生 神奈川県大井松田モデル店舗研究’ [Renewal opening this month: Suburban pachinko parlor Tōyō is born / Model parlor research in Oi-Matsuda, Kanagawa Prefecture], March, pp. 68–69). However, observers pointed out that the lack of a fluid population was problematic, and that the parlor would have difficulty increasing utilization if it failed to take steps to improve its service functions.
50. See Chapter 6 in Han (2008) as well as *Maruhan Nyūsu* (1992), ‘ぱちんここぼれ話’ (Pachinko episodes), 7(’92 New Year Edition) in Maruhan (2007), p. 15. Unless otherwise noted, the rest of the notes for this chapter that cite *Maruhan Nyūsu* come from Maruhan (2007). The article consists of the reminiscences of Masayoshi Suzuki, who served as a managing director at the company in 1992.
51. See Maruhan (2008: 64–65, 140–41).
52. See Han (2008: 125).
53. See Āru Ai Shī (2010), ‘会長トップインタビュー’ (Interview with the chairman), July, p. 17.
54. See *Maruhan Nyūsu*, ‘Pachinko episodes’, p. 15.
55. See *Zen’yūren Kōhō*, ‘Recent conditions at pachinko parlors’, pp. 1–3.
56. A study conducted in 1979 by an organization that promotes small and medium-size businesses (Small Business Information Center 1980) administered a questionnaire to about 10 percent of all parlors that were members of the Zen’yūkyō from August 17 to September 17, including parlors in all prefectures (827 parlors provided valid responses, for a response rate of 82.0 percent). The study found that 28 percent of parlors were located near train stations; 17 percent, in entertainment districts; 28 percent, in shopping districts; and 20 percent, in suburban areas (Small Business Information Center 1980: 79). We should not overestimate the significance of the figures since that survey’s methodology differed from that of the Zen’yūkyō survey described in Tables 5.1 and 5.2, but the difference of seven points in five years indicates that there can be no doubt that the number of suburban parlors was growing.
57. See Table 11 in Research Bureau of the Economic Planning Agency (1973: 48). The survey targeted about 3000 of the approximately 3 million unmarried office workers employed at businesses with at least 100 employees in the cities of Tokyo, Osaka, Sapporo, Kitakyushu and Fukuoka.
58. See Table 4 in Research Bureau of the Economic Planning Agency (1978: 6–7). A separate tabulation by the Leisure Development Center found that 46 percent of men played pachinko at least once in 1976, compared to 14 percent of women (Small Business Information Center 1980: 17).
59. See Small Business Information Center (1980: 29, 84).

60. 'What rose compared to the same period of the previous year [1972] was [...] pachinko for women, which is a positive result for an industry that's eagerly awaiting an increase in the number of female fans' (*Gekkan Yūgi Nihon* [1973], '特別レポート改訂前には大きく伸びていた女性ファン経企庁調査にみる独身者のレジャー' [Significant growth in female fans before the revision of the special report: Leisure pursuits of unmarried consumers as seen in Economic Planning Agency surveys], May, p. 16).
61. See *Gekkan Yūgi Nihon* (1975), '女が集まる処には男が集まる敵は本能寺にあり女性客を引き付け 男性客を獲得するWM作戦' (Men gather where women gather: Ulterior motives rule the day / 'WM' strategy to attract female customers and thereby capture male customers), August, pp. 24–25. The headline clarifies the aim of securing male customers, who comprise the key customer base, by attracting female customers.
62. See Chapter 3.
63. See Chapter 3.
64. See *Gekkan Yūgi Nihon* (1982), '新聞折込「チラシ広告」の効果研究 力強い印象を売り込め' (Research into the effectiveness of newspaper inserts as ads: Promote your business by leaving a strong impression), February, p. 23.
65. See 'パチンコファンと女性' (Pachinko fans and women) in Sogo Unicom (1982), p. 63.
66. See Table 6-2 in Leisure Development Center (1985: 35).
67. Tabulated based on 'Strategies of major pachinko parlor operators' in Yano Research Institute (1989).
68. See Yano Research Institute (1989).
69. See Small Business Information Center (1980). After having referred to a number of similar sources, I believe that the consumption-side characteristics that can be gained from this survey are useful in developing an understanding of the period from the 1950s to the 1980s as analyzed in this volume. Although the pachinko industry underwent a major transformation after the introduction of Fībā-type machines during the 1980s, as described in the analysis offered by chapters 4 and 5, there were no results that were observed as major demand-side changes, for example in consumption behavior, during the same era. Rather, it is likely that those changes became clear during and after the 1990s. The topic remains one for future examination.
70. According to the results of a survey targeting 1032 parlors. Parlors reporting increased attendance by middle-age and young women totaled 45 and 32 percent, respectively (Small Business Information Center 1980: 83), and this trend was particularly conspicuous at rural parlors.
71. This duration was shorter than the approximately two hours of average playing time during the 'pachinko mania' at the end of the 1960s as described in the 'Introduction' section of Chapter 2, suggesting that long playing times were not all that common for most people.
72. According to a survey by pachinko magazine *Ōsama Techō* in 1975, customers spent an average of 6000 yen per month (*Tōhō Keizai* [1976], 'アンテナ' [Antenna], 46(4), p. 145). Moreover, the fact that ball fees ranged from 3 yen (about US$0.01) to 4 yen (about US$0.02) starting in 1978 means that the value of the 1979 survey figure of 4000 yen (about US$16.74) would be even less. The *Ōsama Techō* survey likely differed from the 1979 Small Business Information Center survey (Small Business Information Center 1980) in that the former targeted people who played pachinko

comparatively frequently, while the latter targeted a broader range of people.

73. Among men, respondents aged twenty-nine or younger totaled 30 percent; respondents in their thirties, 25 percent; respondents in their forties, 20 percent; and respondents in their fifties or over, just over 10 percent. About 30 percent of all men were single. Among women, half of all respondents were aged twenty-nine or younger, while half were aged thirty or older, and half were single.
74. Some observers have noted that the finding that respondents ranked 'passing time' high and 'making money' low in terms of their purpose in playing pachinko demands careful examination. They assert that for psychological reasons, the people who participated in the survey chose the former response instead of answering honestly with the latter (Ishige 1989: 189).
75. Customer demographics that quickly adopt new goods or services are responsible for the initial market, and they can be seen as playing a key role in product penetration. These are the early adopters of innovation that emerge in the theory of innovation propagation (see chapters 4 and 6 in Rogers [1962]), and the early adopters that form the market for new products in marketing theory (see Moore [2002: 11–18]).
76. See Small Business Information Center (1980: 71).
77. See Small Business Information Center (1980: 81–83).
78. See *Zen'yūren Kōhō* (1983), October 15, p. 3.
79. See Small Business Information Center (1980: 79). The percentage of parlors in suburban locations was high in the Tohoku region (northeastern Japan) as well as in the Chubu region (central Japan) and Hokuriku region (the area to the west of Tokyo on the Sea of Japan side of the country) at 34 percent and 29 percent, respectively, and suburban locations, which were described as 'rising markedly in recent years', were more common in rural areas than in eastern Japan including Tokyo and western Japan including Osaka (at 35 percent and 44 percent, respectively), where many parlors were located near train stations.
80. Membership in associations as of 1973 averaged 95.2 percent nationwide versus 84.4 percent in Tokyo, which was classified in a group with lower membership rates (*Zen'yūren Kōhō*, 'Recent conditions at pachinko parlors', pp. 1–3). Membership rolls also included information about a small number of non-members; it is fair to characterize coverage of greater than 80 percent as an accurate reflection of reality.
81. Of these, three parlors relocated, although in each case their new location was close to the old one.
82. See the following database maintained by the National Land Information Division of the Ministry of Land, Infrastructure, Transport and Tourism's National and Regional Policy Bureau: http://nlftp.mlit.go.jp/ksj-e/gml/datalist/KsjTmplt-N05.html.
83. See *Rejā Sangyō Shiryō*, 'Leisure special investigation team report', p. 251.
84. See Small Business Information Center (1980: 17).
85. Except Hokkaido, Tokyo and Okinawa Prefecture.
86. According to the abovementioned nationwide survey conducted by the Small Business Information Center in 1979, parlors with one location and parlors with multiple locations accounted for 49 percent and 51 percent of the total, respectively (Small Business Information Center 1980: 79). We can conclude that the percentage of parlors with a single location in Tokyo as seen in Table 5.4 was remarkably high. The

preponderance of such parlors was likely related to the geographical characteristics of the Kanto region (eastern Japan), where many parlors are located near train stations (35 percent). Incidentally, of parlors with at least two locations, 26 percent had two locations; 12 percent, three locations; 6 percent, four locations; and 7 percent, five or more locations.

87. See 'Strategies of major pachinko parlor businesses' in Yano Research Institute (1989). The geographical distribution of parlors for targeted companies was as follows: twelve parlors in Tokyo; eleven in Aichi Prefecture; four parlors each in Osaka, Kyoto and Iwate prefectures; three parlors each in Miyagi, Nagano and Aomori prefectures; two parlors each in Akita, Saitama, Hiroshima, Gifu, Fukuoka and Chiba prefectures and Hokkaido; and one parlor each in Yamagata, Niigata, Kanagawa, Shizuoka, Ishikawa and Shimane prefectures.
88. In addition, there were eight parlors that did not respond. It is unclear why the thirty companies that indicated they 'are not pursuing' what the survey termed 'chain development' do not match the fourteen companies operating a single parlor in the tabulation offered by Table 5.5, although the discrepancy may reflect respondents' differing interpretation of the question's reference to 'chain development', or it may be that some respondents were not pursuing 'chain development' at the time of the survey. This chapter's interest lies in companies' policies with regard to parlor development.
89. For more information, see Maruhan (2008).
90. As per the Maruhan CSR Report 2015 (http://www.maruhan.co.jp/csr/pdf/csr_report15_03.pdf, accessed on August 1, 2017) and the 'Company information and IR information company profile' (Kigyō jōhō/IR jōhō kigyō gaiyō) section on Maruhan's website (http://www.maruhan.co.jp/hall/index.html, accessed on August 1, 2017).
91. This is the date at which it can be determined when parlors opened based on Maruhan's website. The year in which parlors opened could not be determined as of August 2017 but subsequently became clear in 2021.
92. See Maruhan (2008).
93. See chapters 6, 7 and 9 in Han (2008).
94. See Maruhan (2008: 74).
95. Naturally, the positive effect on ordinary profit of the full repayment of the debt mentioned above presumably impacted profit margin on sales after 1986. However, since changes in this metric during the first half of the 1980s cannot be explained, the trend exhibited by profit margin on sales after 1986 should as a rule be understood based on operating conditions.
96. Although it falls outside the scope of this book's analysis, the company developed its business nationally in a new manner starting during the 2000s, as described in the text. At the end of the 1990s, sales per location was trending down. It is likely that Maruhan embraced the approach of further chain development in order to overcome some sort of problem.
97. See Penrose (1959: 67–80).
98. See Maruhan (2008: 78–79).
99. See Maruhan (2008: 88).
100. See Āru Ai Shī, 'Interview with the chairman', p. 8 and Chapter 13 in Han (2008).
101. The eight-year minimum experience requirement was calculated based on the careers

of ten parlor and area managers. See Āru Ai Shī (2010) '店長クローズアップ' (Parlor manager close-up) and '「二〇二〇年の躍進」へ 一〇年後を担う九人のリーダー達が描く「マルハン二〇二〇年」の設計図' (Succeeding in 2020: Blueprint for Maruhan in 2020 as envisioned by nine leaders who will be responsible for the next ten years), pp. 116–19.

102. See chapters 5 and 6 of Kaji (2015).

103. See Thomson (1987: 433–45).

104. Around 1975, a pachinko management consultant said, 'It's no exaggeration to say that anyone who wants to start a pachinko parlor in the future has a 100 percent chance of success if he finds a talented manager'. The consultant offered this advice: 'Consult businesses like pachinko machine manufacturers and excellent [successful] pachinko parlors' (Saito 1975: 73). In addition to pin adjustment, their roles included '[managing] the number of balls to dispense each day and product purchasing as well as training and managing parlor employees' (Saito 1975: pp. 73–74), and they had overall responsibility for parlor operations. This observation indicates the extent of parlor managers' responsibility as well as the fact that they were generally hired from external markets. This approach to hiring meant not only that Maruhan's active development of dozens of parlors per year starting in 2000 would be difficult, but also that there was no guarantee that newly hired managers would have new capabilities related to information management required after the 1990s. It is likely that internal human resources development became necessary for both reasons.

105. For example, the sales division created numerous organizational entities and mechanisms to accommodate chain development, including the Amusement Machine Department in 2001, the Sales Strategy Department in 2003 and the New Parlor Preparation Department and Parlor Services Department in 2006 (Āru Ai Shī [2010], '同店の強さを活かしながら「M」のブランドを高める' [Enhancing the 'Maruhan' brand while leveraging its strengths], p. 92; Maruhan 2008: 90–129).

Essay

1. See Kang (1996: 152).
2. Unless otherwise noted, this section draws on Chapter 3 of Han (2010).
3. See Chapter 1 of Han (2010). Businesses run by ethnic minority Koreans in Japan tend to fall within a number of industries, including manufacturing and civil engineering. Parlors were one of those industries. Allow me to emphasize that the concentration of such businesses was relatively higher in other industries than in the parlor business from the 1950s to the 1970s, for example in manufacturing, which encompassed a variety of different sectors, civil engineering and *yakiniku* (Korean barbeque) restaurants.
4. Han (2010: 133–38). The logical connection between the growth of leading companies such as Maruhan and Heiwa in the pachinko industry and the Korean ethnic element remains unclear. What we can say is that both founders were college graduates, and that Japanese individuals with the same academic background would have been able to pursue different paths; the ethnic element presumably had a strong influence on their choice of occupation. That said, the ethnic element helps explain the social environment in which they chose a particular (limited) business, but it did not guarantee the growth of that business.
5. Ethnic minority Koreans in Japan launched a variety of organizations, including

political groups, from the second half of the 1940s to the 1950s. For businessmen involved in commerce and industry in particular, membership in organizations such as associations was essential in order to procure raw materials and continue business operations in the controlled economy that had been established under the allied postwar occupation. Ethnic minority Koreans in Japan in these industries were working to organize autonomously (Park 1989: 113–31). In the case of pachinko, cumulative changes to programs related to the amusement tax led to growth in participation in associations so that members could gather related information and views.

6. See *Yūgi Tsūshin* (1955) '広島朝鮮人業者会合 県連と協力､危機突破へ' (Ethnic minority Korean businessmen in Hiroshima gather: Group to work with prefectural federation to overcome crisis), March 12.
7. See 'Figure: Trend in parlors' in Sōritsu Sanjū Shūnen Kinen Taikai Kinenshi Bukai (1993: 39).
8. The profiling in community newspapers of cases featuring businesses that had grown and succeeded, for example by operating several parlors in multiple prefectures or entering the pachinko machine manufacturing industry, provided an important source of information for those choosing a business (Han 2010: 135–36).
9. It is also possible to consider competitive ability, for example in terms of the performance of businesses after they entered the industry, but any attempt to classify businesses on the basis of whether they were run by ethnic minority Koreans in Japan and then compare them runs into both methodological and source-based difficulties. See Chapter 3 of Han (2010: 150) for a description of how the relationship of ethnic minority Koreans to the community was strong when they entered the business but became comparatively weaker during the subsequent growth stage.
10. Unless otherwise noted, information about the parlor business below is drawn from Han (2010).
11. See Sugiyama (2008).
12. For example, one second-generation ethnic minority Korean who was running a chain of three parlors in Tokyo said, '[...] my father started his pachinko parlor in 1952 while making raw sake [raw sake was also traditionally consumed in Korea; during this period, the beverage was frequently the target of police crackdowns on unauthorized production]. It was a challenging business [smile]. Pachinko enjoyed no social trust, and until ten years ago, banks wouldn't lend money. I inherited that business [...]. Why did I inherit it? Working at a proper company in my era was sheer fantasy [smile]. I had no occupational options other than pachinko' (Kang 1996: 153).
13. See chapters 2 and 3 of Han (2010).
14. Much research has been carried out regarding the former; in Japan, see Higuchi (2012). With regard to the latter, see especially Chapter 2 of Ajisaka (2005).
15. See Han (2010: 133–38).
16. For more information about the process by which ethnic credit unions were established, see Chapter 4 of Han (2010).
17. Unless otherwise noted, the information in this part is drawn from Han (2014).
18. See Han (2010) and Han (2014).
19. See Han (2010: 300–07).
20. See Han (2010: 305, tables 7-7, 7-8).

21. See Han (2010: 140).
22. See Han (2010: 94–95).
23. See Han (2010: 143).
24. From the second half of the 1970s, leading small and medium-size financial institutions were drawn into intense competition with major financial institutions for the business of small and medium-size concerns (Han 2010: 230).
25. According to vol. 17 of the minutes of the Committee on Finance of the 51st Diet, held at 10:51 am on Friday, March 4, 1966, a question was raised in connection with the revision of the Japan Development Bank Act, which addressed the government-affiliated financial institution of the same name. This question concerned whether the bank lent money to businesses in the pachinko industry, and the questioner asked the government delegate to provide an account. Although the example is an unusual one, it is unclear whether in fact the bank had lent money to pachinko businesses, and the government delegate's response was an across-the-board denial. The important element in this question is that both the questioner and the respondent conducted their discussion under the shared assumption that lending to the pachinko industry by the Japan Development Bank would be 'impossible'. That is how distant the pachinko industry was from any sort of policy promotion or support.
26. See Kaji (2009b: 79–109).
27. See *Chūbu Zaikai* (1982), '低成長下、活況続くパチンコ業界' (Pachinko industry booms despite slow growth), 25(22), p. 37.
28. For example, see *Zaikei Fukushim* (1983), 'ピックス パチンコ進出で不況け飛ばす いわきのスーパー藤越、相馬に二店目申請中' (Topics: Banishing recession by entering the pachinko business / Iwaki-based supermarket Fujikoshi applies for second parlor in Soma), 12(3), p. 140. See also Kaji (2015: 314, 318–20) as well as the profile of the parlor operated by Daiei, Inc., a leading operator of supermarket chain stores nationwide at the time, in Chapter 11 of the same work. There was also a far-reaching move by large companies that targeted parlors' standard prize market and other businesses in various fields, for example security equipment, to target pachinko once it grew into an enormous market (*Nihon Ryūtsū Shimbun* [1984] 'フィーバー関連業界五兆円パチンコ産業を狙え' [Fībā-type machine-related businesses strive to become 5-trillion-yen pachinko industry], April 12).
29. See chapters 3 and 7 of Han (2010).
30. See chapters 3 and 7 of Han (2010) as well as Han (2014).
31. See Kimbara et al. (1986).
32. As confirmed via an inquiry emailed to the Tokyo Pachinko and Pachislot Cooperative Associations (October 20 and 23, 2017).
33. Although they are more unusual in the case of South Korea, the country does have a number of two-character surnames, including 南宮 (Nam-goong), 獨孤 (Dokko), 東方 (Dong-bang), 司空 (Sa-gong), 西門 (Sau-moon), 鮮于 (Sun-woo), 小峰 (So-bong), 諸葛 (Je-gal) and 皇甫 (Hwang-bo). I was unable to find any such surnames in the membership list.
34. Incidentally, the 20 percent figure is quite high in light of the 3.5 percent of respondents who indicated that they used only their real name in the Kanagawa Prefecture survey.
35. The long-standing practice of protection money can be seen as a sort of insurance,

for example as the cost of risk management in order to prevent problems that could otherwise occur (see Chapter 4 of Ino [2000]). Since customers' winnings relate directly to the prizes they earn, disputes between customers and parlors as well as the presence of swindlers, known as *gotoshi*, can become problematic from a business standpoint. Competition between criminal groups as they attempt to carve out territory in amusement districts can impact parlor operations, and the payment of protection money served to prevent the emergence of such problems. In the underground economy, where the administrative authority of the police is muted, disputes are an everyday occurrence, and mediation by criminal groups functions to resolve those disputes in a manner that is mutually acceptable to the parties involved (Venkatesh 2009).

36. For example, pachinko parlors and other businesses in the amusement industry gathered in the city of Fukuoka in 1964 to form an anti-crime federation with police support and pursue a campaign to eliminate protection money. Despite accounts claiming that it failed to generate significant results, reports indicate that the active efforts of the parlor industry in particular attracted attention and that the ongoing program was expected to yield results through a liaison with stepped-up enforcement efforts by the Fukuoka Prefectural Police (*Yūgi Shimbun* [1964], '暴力追放の関係記事' [Article about organized crime purge], November 5). During the first half of the 1960s, the *Yūgi Shimbun* ran more articles on campaigns to purge organized crime than during other periods, offering a glimpse of how the issue characterized that time in particular. See Note 121 in Chapter 1.
37. In 1965, there were 3944 such groups with about 196,239 members; in 1982, those numbers had shrunk to 2395 groups and 100,237 members (Ino 2000: 231–32). The rest of this paragraph draws on the same source.
38. See *Yūgi Shimbun* (1963), '暴力団に資金提供' (Funding of criminal groups), and '盛り上がる、暴力団追放運動' (Campaign to eliminate criminal groups gains momentum), March 25.
39. After the Act on Prevention of Unjust Acts by Organized Crime Group Members went into effect, various activities were undertaken in order to root out the activities of organized crime, for example by 'anti-gang roller' programs (efforts by police to visit businesses and other sites in areas to prevent members of criminal groups from obtaining funding through illegal activities). For example, one report notes that in Miyagi Prefecture, anti-gang roller programs combined with the formation of industry organizations dedicated to eliminating organized crime identified protection money payments of more than about 300 million yen (about US$2.70 million at 1993 rates) per year (National Police Agency 1993). According to a 1992 survey of criminal group members by the National Police Agency, 44 percent of businesses refused protection money demands (*Mainichi Shimbun* [1993], '増えた「みかじめ料拒否暴力団新法」の効果じわり——警察庁・組員面接調査' [Effectiveness of new act on criminal syndicates refusing protection money gradually grows: Interview of criminal group members by National Police Agency], February 19).
40. See *Asahi Shimbun* (1996), '東京都内のパチンコ七〇〇店など暴力団に上納年間一一三億円' (700 pachinko parlors in Tokyo and others pay 11.3 billion yen in protection money to organized crime), February 14 (evening edition). The estimated rate was calculated from the number of parlors in 1995 (18,164), the protection money paid

by 700 parlors in Tokyo (11.3 billion yen [about US$143 million at 1996 rates]) and parlor sales (30 trillion yen [about US$380 billion at 1996 rates]).

41. Regarding how the dissolution of the Nittokuren, which served as a patent pool, could have changed the conditions of competition between machine manufacturers, see Tanaka and Hayashi (2010).
42. See Han (2010) and Han (2014).
43. This issue is examined in Chapter 7 of Han (2010). When large investments were required, for example as was the case with parlors in neighborhoods and urban locations, community financial institutions' ability to provide funding was limited.
44. The seventy-seven ethnic credit unions that existed in 1983 underwent a series of mergers starting during the 1990s after the collapse of the bubble economy, before entering upon an across-the-board reorganization that included leading financial institutions from 2000.

Conclusion

1. See Chapter 1 in Uekusa (2000) and Uekusa (1997: 8–14).
2. See Article 1 in Chapter 1 (General Provisions) of the Act on Control and Improvement of the Amusement Business, etc.
3. For more about concepts and empirical analysis of economies of scale in the service industry, see Chapter 3 in Morikawa (2014).
4. See Japan Fair Trade Commission (1997), '(株)三共ほか一〇名に対する件 公正取引委員会平成九年[勧]第五号' (Incident involving ten companies, including Sankyo Co., Ltd. Fair Trade Commission 1997 [recommendation] No. 5) in 平成九年八月六日勧告審決・審決集 (Compilation of recommendations and findings on August 6, 1997), pp. 44, 238; *Nihon Keizai Shimbun* (1997), 'パチンコ機新規参入妨害、製造一〇社に排除勧告——公取委、特許権乱用と認定' (Cease and desist recommendation for ten manufacturers found to obstruct new entrants into the pachinko machine business: Japan Fair Trade Commission acknowledges patent misuse), June 21; and *Economist* (1997), 'パチンコ産業白書 第二部 閉ざされた市場の苦悩 パチンコ機を自由につくれない不可思議' (Pachinko White Paper, Part 2: Anguish in a closed-off market / The absurdity of not being able to manufacture pachinko machines freely), 75(33), pp. 84–87.
5. See Tanaka and Hayashi (2010: 138).
6. See Arai (1997: 63–70), Tanihara (1998: 111–13), Eguchi (2002: 111–13), Murakami (1998a: 37–44), Murakami (1998b: 53–62) and Suzuki (2003: 7–13). In separate works, Onishi and Ito, as well as Tanaka and Hayashi, respectively, reexamine the facts on which the ruling of the Japan Fair Trade Commission was based as well as the verdict and present a series of useful observations concerning the implementation of the Act on Prohibition of Private Monopolization and Maintenance from an economics perspective. Onishi and Ito identify problems involving the political significance of the verdict based on its economic impact, including market conditions after the cease-and-desist order (2009: 251–52). Tanaka and Hayashi gauge the extent to which the patents accumulated and managed by the Nittokuren were utilized and offer a substantive basis for the ruling by concluding that the patents held by the leading companies that were prosecuted had a significant influence on new entries into the industry (2010: 135–62).
7. See Tanaka and Hayashi (2010).

8. See Tanaka and Hayashi (2010: 147–58).
9. Average annual production per manufacturer is calculated based on data in Figure 0.4 in this work and Figure Intro.5 of the original Japanese publication (Han 2018: 32). Unless otherwise noted, all other average annual production per manufacturer cited in this section comes from this source.
10. See Figure Intro.5 and the explanation in the original Japanese publication (Han 2018: 32).
11. After the dissolution of the Nittokuren, the Japan Amusement Machine Patent Association was established in 2008. The group, whose membership consists of thirty-three companies (including one associate member), is dedicated to 'facilitating the development of ball-based amusement machines, the provision of wholesome pachinko machines and the mutual assistance of members with manufacturing businesses' ('Our Purpose' [Honkai no mokuteki] section of the association's website, https://jamp.or.jp/, accessed on October 22, 2017). It seems that after the relationships between members that were linked through the Nittokuren were dissolved, the group was reorganized as a patent pool organization focusing on the licensing and management of patents that were essential to the manufacture of pachinko machines.
12. See Hashimoto and Takeda (1985).
13. See Hashimoto and Takeda (1985) and Takeda (2017: 518–20).
14. See Noji (2016). Other information about the Garden Group below is drawn from this source.
15. See chapters 1 and 2 of Han (2010).

Appendix 3

1. With regard to the licensing of machines after 1985, testing was centralized in the Security Communication Association (Hoan Tsūshin Kyōkai), which was designated to play that role by the national Public Safety Commission. Although the need for regional centralization presumably shrank after that time, the structural framework that had been in place until 1985 was still coloring procedures around 1990.
2. The lowest figure was for parlor 1 in Kyoto Prefecture, at 9.9 yen (about US$0.08 at 1990 rates). This low gross margin is the average figure from September through November after the parlor completed a redecoration in August 1992. That performance was influenced by the parlor's policy of returning a high percentage of earnings to customers after its renewal opening (the average prize-sale rate was 15.55), which I determined to be temporary in nature and so removed parlor 36.
3. The averages for parlor 32 in Shizuoka Prefecture and parlor 1 in Kyoto Prefecture, which staged renewal reopenings in June and July 1992, respectively, have been calculated for July through November and for August through November, respectively, after those events. It is likely that the parlors would offer complimentary service to customers by dispensing more balls so they could win: parlor 32's prize-sale rate (explained later in the text) was 15.01, while parlor 1's was 15.55, both of which were higher than the average of 14.14. As a result, the parlors posted returns on sales figures that were lower than other parlors. Parlor 36 in Ibaraki Prefecture staged a renewal reopening in October 1990, but its utilization (explained later in the text) averaged 44.17 percent, which was lower than the average, and it had little

success escaping conditions of low profitability until November 1992, the last month for which there are records.

4. To be precise, the term used in the industry is 'operating prize-sale rate'. Standing in contrast to that term is the concept of 'machine prize-sale rate', which is calculated from the number of balls played and the number of balls dispensed for each machine, along with the number of balls accumulated by the customer. The operating prize-sale rate is assessed after the parlor closes and represents the business results for that day, while the machine prize-sale rate serves as an indicator for assessing conditions during the day.
5. As indicated by the calculation formula given, the prize-sale rate represents the ratio of loaned ball fees to prize sales as the result of prize balls being exchanged; it serves as a managerial indicator that incorporates other factors such as which prizes customers chose. By contrast, the prize-ball percentage (number of prize balls / number of loaned balls) as a concept relates to the practice of pin adjustment by the parlor on a machine-by-machine basis.
6. According to Maruhan's explanation, the company had collected utilization data prior to that time as well. A variety of information about individual locations was aggregated by the head office, but that information did not immediately become an effective source of managerial data. For our purposes here, I assume that information was used actively from the time that it appeared on charts for the purpose of comparison, which is the timing I have chosen to emphasize.
7. I sent an inquiry about this point to Maruhan by email on March 30, 2016, and received an explanation in reply on April 12, 2016.
8. See *Maruhan Nyūsu* (1990), 'マルハンプレンティ店' (Maruhan Plenty Branch), Inaugural Issue, p. 7.
9. See *Maruhan Nyūsu* (1991), 'マルハン柏原店' (Maruhan Kashiwara Branch), 5, p. 3.
10. See *Maruhan Nyūsu*, 'Maruhan Kashiwara Branch', p. 3.
11. See *Maruhan Nyūsu* (1992), 'マルハン森友店' (Maruhan Moritomo Branch), 7, p. 3.
12. See *Maruhan Nyūsu*, 'Maruhan Moritomo Branch', p. 3. Results like this back up the following benefit that chain development could be expected to play, as noted in Table 5.6 in Chapter 5: 'Affiliated locations could pursue joint initiatives to compete with nearby parlors'. Dispensation of balls so that customers would win during renewal reopenings was subject to budgetary constraints. When locations in the same chain were able to coordinate the times at which individual parlors would dispense balls, that approach served as an effective tactic when competing with other parlors whose efforts to secure customers were subject to such constraints.
13. See *Maruhan Nyūsu* (1994), 'マルハン松原店創業一〇周年イベント' (Event commemorating the tenth anniversary of the opening of the Matsubara Branch), New Year, p. 15.
14. See *Maruhan Nyūsu* (1994), 'マルハン吉原店入れ替えイベント第一弾!' (First in a series of events celebrating the replacement of machines at Maruhan Yoshiwara Branch), 18, p. 12. The remainder of this paragraph draws on this source.
15. In 1992, Maruhan began offering awards based on individual parlors' business results. Criteria for awards included achievement of budgeted sales, budgeted payment receipts and budgeted operating profit; percent and amount of reduction in expenses;

year-on-year growth rate; utilization; and other metrics. Parlor 4 won the grand prize, which was awarded based on an overall evaluation of each indicator, three years in a row, from 1992 to 1994. See *Maruhan Nyūsu* (1994), '九四年度業績表彰式' (Fiscal 1994 performance awards), 19, p. 4.

16. See *Maruhan Nyūsu*, 'Event commemorating the tenth anniversary of the opening of the Matsubara Branch', p. 15. Subsequent information about this event is drawn from this article.
17. Whether the events were renewal reopenings or renewal openings has been inferred based on factors including the magnitude of the month's prize-sale rate, negative profit margin on sales and negative gross margin. However, the expansion of parlor 35 is not included as a factor.
18. Figures for October 1990 through November 1992 are from a list of sales by location provided by Maruhan.
19. See *Maruhan Nyūsu* (1992), 'マルハンニュース " 年頭の辞"' (New Year's address), 7, p. 1.

Afterword

In February 1994, I was in the Immigration Bureau in Osaka to apply to extend my visa for the first time after coming from South Korea to Japan. As the end of my six-month visa, which I had received before arriving, approached, I needed to extend the length of my stay so that I could take a university entrance exam. I didn't know it at the time, but labor shortages during the bubble economy years in the late 1980s had fueled a surge in the number of foreigners living in Japan in the 1990s. The Immigration Bureau was practically teeming with foreigners. People waited in a chaotic line without any clue as to when it might be their turn to make their application.

I recall being nervous. Even now, remembering the experience makes my mouth feel dry. At the time, I knew my application to extend my stay was unlikely to be approved. The Japanese government had recently launched a globalization initiative, but had basically continued to admit a limited foreign population.

Visa applications at the time used a complex format that demanded extensive explanation. My concern was how to convince the immigration authority that my stay would benefit Japanese society, which is essential for having a visa extension approved. I knew my case would have to be extra strong because I did not have any connection to Japan, and could not find anybody to whom I could turn for help in Japan. In the course of renewing my visa before I entered university and extending it every time I reached the end of my stay, an awareness that I had no natural right to be in Japan, and that I wouldn't be allowed to remain in the country without a clear purpose and the ability to explain how I could make a contribution, seared itself into my mind. That situation may have had nothing to do with me as a person, but as long as those extensions were not self-evident, I had no choice but to internalize my status by conflating myself with the meaning of my stay, its purpose and the means by which I would contribute. This was because the ultimate decision about whether I was allowed to remain rested with the Japanese government.

It was when I embarked on the final stage of compiling this work that I realized I could see myself, as a foreigner, projected onto pachinko. Like myself, the pachinko industry would have to evolve to gain recognition in Japanese society.

Over the years, I have met a variety of people who were involved with the pachinko industry. Pachinko parlor companies come in a variety of sizes; there are Japanese and ethnic minority Korean investors, just as there are ethnic minority Korean employees working for Japanese owners. Many of them requested to speak off the record. They expressed hesitancy about describing the inner workings of the industry. Their attitude likely reflected their keen awareness of how they are perceived by Japanese society. In contrast, some aspiring young businessmen saw pachinko parlors as a promising business opportunity.

Each gave me a different impression, but to me, it seemed like they were searching for ways to ensure they would remain in business the next day, asking how an industry whose existence was not obvious on a social level should face society, aware of the need to explain their role. Those stories played out in various ways, but the process by which the pachinko industry established itself seems to me to have been a series of trial-and-error attempts that unfolded against a backdrop of awareness of the industry's social context.

What is the significance of my presence in Japanese society? Am I working hard enough that my ongoing presence will be permitted? I didn't even know to whom I was addressing these fruitless questions, but in time they fostered a stance that led me to repeatedly question the significance of my own research. It may be natural for researchers to ask such questions, but as I asked myself about the implications of this book, whose topic hardly inspires spirited debate in economic history research, I found that forming an answer to that question was beyond what I could accomplish on my own.

One ethnic minority Korean's impression of my research was particularly trying. When I had the opportunity to present my work to the general public, I saw a person in the audience with a dark, stern look on his face as he avoided my gaze. After the presentation, I was able to talk to him. In a quiet, controlled voice, he told me that I knew nothing of the real-life difficulties ethnic minority Koreans face and that there was not a single ethnic minority Korean in Japan who worked in the pachinko industry because they wanted to.

As I explained in the Introduction to this book, the pachinko industry worked as a last resort of employment for ethnic minority Koreans in Japan who sometimes faced discrimination in the job market. They were the ones who shouldered the burden of ethnic minority Korean status, who came to Japan during the colonial period between 1910 and 1945.

My view was that the ethnic minority Koreans embraced the pachinko industry in Japan as an attractive business opportunity in which being a minority Korean was an advantage. Some ethnic minority Korean researchers also agreed with my views and supported my work. I proposed a new historical perspective that positioned ethnic minority Koreans' involvement in the pachinko industry as the result of an autonomous choice in their struggle against discrimination. However, I felt I could not in good faith offer an answer to the criticism of the Korean person in the audience, which left me standing there paralyzed. I saw a gulf between my research and reality. Faced with new questions – and the need to bridge the gap between my work and reality – I set out to write this work.

Perhaps it seems like I have tried too hard to provide internal explanations for the pachinko industry. If so, it is because I have attempted to overcome external preconceptions and pinpoint where the dynamism that has driven the industry's development began, and how far it has come. My hope is that through the pages of the work envisioned in this way I have been able to suggest that the future direction of the pachinko industry cannot be understood merely as a continuation of its historical trajectory, and that there exist multiple possibilities for that future.

On the other hand, I think it is fair to criticize my work for going perhaps too far in throwing off stereotypes and conventional thinking, and for failing to focus on the underground economy. As criminology and journalism alike have pointed out, the enormous size of the pachinko market attracted the attention of organized crime, which saw pachinko parlors as a source of funds. However, in order to understand why this problem has persisted for so long, one must acknowledge that the relationship between criminal groups and the business world, as seen for example in the practice of extracting protection money, is not unique to any particular industry, but rather reflects structural issues within Japanese society. Even if the link between organized crime and pachinko exhibited some degree of economic rationality, I acknowledge that this work, in casting light on those aspects of the connection that have weakened, may attract criticism for glossing over whatever parts of those links remain.

Experiences at the Harvard-Yenching Institute and the Reischauer Institute of Japanese Studies at Harvard University from 2015 to 2016 motivated me to consider publishing my work in English. I was intrigued by the interest researchers had in my work on ethnic minority Koreans in Japan, their history related to the colonization of Korea by Japan, and the pachinko industry, which has become an important business for them.

Researchers in Japan are also interested in the pachinko industry's unique role in providing the livelihood of ethnic minority Koreans in Japan and agree that more research should be done. On the other hand, they are well aware of the politically sensitive nature of the research topic, since it relates to Japan's history of colonialization of Korea and other Asian countries. Those environments have influenced the stereotypical narratives.

Going abroad helped me to free myself from the politically sensitive aspects of the topic and investigate the subject matter with a purely academic interest.

January 8, 2021

Jaehyang Han

PRIMARY SOURCES

Japan Amusement Machine Industry Association (Nikkōso) (1961a) 昭和三五年度 決算報告書 (FY1960 financial statements).

--- (1961b) 昭和三五年度 総会 (The FY1960 general meeting of the Japan Amusement Machine Industry Association).

--- (1962a) 昭和三六年度 決算報告書 (FY1961 financial statements).

--- (1962b) 昭和三六年度 総会 (The FY1961 general meeting of the Japan Amusement Machine Industry Association).

--- (1963) 昭和三七年度 決算報告書 (FY1962 financial statements).

--- (1966) '業務機構刷新についての説明会' (Briefing on operational mechanism reforms). November 4.

--- (1972) 昭和四六年度 決算報告書 (Year-end financial statements 1971–1972).

--- (1973) 昭和四七年度 決算報告書 (Year-end financial statements 1972–1973).

--- (1979) 'パチンコ機の設定基準の取り扱いについての経過報告' (Interim report on the treatment of established standards for pachinko machines). November 30.

Japan Fair Trade Commission (1997) '審決' (Verdict) and '勧告書' (Recommendation). Recommendation No. 5 of 1997.

Masamura Shōkai (1954) 決算報告書 (Year-end financial statements) (August 1953 to July 1954).

--- (1957) 売掛帳 (Accounts receivable) (1954 to 1957).

--- (1963) 決算報告書 (Year-end financial statements) (August 1962 to July 1963).

--- (1977) 総勘定元帳 (General ledger; August 1976 to July 1977).

--- (1980) 総勘定元帳 (General ledger; August 1, 1979, to July 31, 1980).

--- (1981) 総勘定元帳 自昭和五五年八月一日 至昭和五六年七月三一日 (General ledger; August 1, 1980, to July 31, 1981).

Masamura Shōkai (first corporation) (1955) 決算報告書 (Year-end financial statements) (August 1954 to July 1955).

Masamura Shōkai (second corporation) (1956) 決算報告書 (Year-end financial statements) (September 1955 to August 1956).

Tokyo Pachinko and Pachislot Cooperative Associations (ed.) (1975; 1982; 1988; 1993) 都遊協・都遊連組合員名簿 (Membership list of the Tokyo Pachinko and Pachislot Cooperative Associations). Tokyo Pachinko and Pachislot Cooperative Associations.

BIBLIOGRAPHY

Ado Sākuru Setsuritsu Gojū Nen Henshū Iinkai (ed.) (2014) 「グリーンべると」と「王様手帖」が語りかけるパチンコ・パチスロ半世紀1963～2013 株式会社アド・サークル設立五〇周年記念誌 50th anniversary since 1963 (A half-century of pachinko and *pachislot* as told by *GreenBelt* and *Ōsama Techo*, 1963 to 2013: Special issue commemorating the 50th anniversary of the founding of Ado Sākuru Co., Ltd. / 50th anniversary since 1963). Ado Sākuru.

Aida, Y. and Akagi, A. (1997) 新電子立国別巻ソフトウェア・ビジネス (*Shin Denshi Rikkoku* supplement: Software business). NHK Publishing.

Ajisaka, M. (2005) 都市同郷団体の研究 (Research into groups of residents with a common heritage). Horitsu Bunka Sha.

Amusement Industry Association (ed.) (1993) '組合創立四〇周年記念座談会' (40th Association Anniversary Commemorative Conference). 四〇年の回顧——山口県遊協四〇年の足跡 (Looking back over 40 years: 40 years of the Yamaguchi Prefecture Amusement Industry Association). Yamaguchi Prefecture Amusement Industry Association.

Arai, T. (1997) 'ぱちんこ機械製造業者の私的独占事件(事件解説)' (Cases involving private monopolization by pachinko machine manufacturers [case explanations]). *Kōsei Torihiki* (Fair Trade), 564, pp. 63–70.

Āru Ai Shī (ed.) (2010) 販売革新臨時増刊 MARUHANスタディ (Marketing innovation extra edition: Case study of Maruhan Co.). Āru Ai Shī.

Asahi Shimbunsha (ed.) (1953) 朝日年鑑 (Asahi yearbook). Asahi Shimbunsha.

--- (ed.) (1955) 朝日年鑑 (Asahi yearbook). Asahi Shimbunsha.

Asano, Y. (1970) システム産業シリーズ レジャー産業 (Systemic industry series: Leisure industry). Nihon Keizai Shimbun.

Bessatsu Takarajima Henshūbu (ed.) (2011) コワ～い パチンコ店の話 (Scary tales of a pachinko parlor). Takarajimasha.

Business IPR Ōpun-gata Tokkyo Pūru Bunkakai (ed.) (2003) 特許プールの可能性——技術と権利のラビリンスへの挑戦 (The potential of patent pools: The challenges posed by technology and rights). Japan Institute of Invention and Innovation.

Chesbrough, H. (2006) *Open Innovation: The New Imperative for Creating and Profiting from Technology*. Harvard Business Review Press.

Economic Planning Agency (経済企画庁) (ed.) (1957) 国民生活白書 国民生活の現状 (White paper on national life: Conditions of national life). Nihon Keizai Shimbun.

--- (ed.) (1971) 昭和四六年版 国民生活白書 豊かな社会への構図 (White paper on national life 1971: Composition of a prosperous society). Nihon Keizai Shimbun.

--- (ed.) (1975) 昭和五〇年版 経済白書 新しい安定軌道をめざして (Economic white paper 1975: Towards a new trajectory of stability). Nihon Keizai Shimbun.

--- (ed.) (1978) 昭和五三年版 国民生活白書 新しい暮らしと地域のなかの連帯 (White paper on national life 1978: New lifestyles and regional solidarity). Nihon Keizai Shimbun.

--- (ed.) (1980) 昭和五五年版 経済白書 先進国日本の試練と課題 (Economic white paper 1980: Trials and issues facing Japan as an economic superpower). Nihon Keizai Shimbun.

--- (ed.) (1983) 昭和五八年版 経済白書 持続的成長への足固め (Economic white paper 1983: Laying the groundwork for sustained growth). Nihon Keizai Shimbun.

--- (ed.) (1985a) 昭和六〇年版 国民生活白書 戦後四〇年——成熟の時代に向けて (White paper on national life 1985: 40 years after World War II / Towards a mature era). Nihon Keizai Shimbun.

--- (ed.) (1985b). 昭和六〇年版 経済白書 新しい成長とその課題 (Economic white paper 1985: New growth and its challenges). Nihon Keizai Shimbun.

Eguchi, K. (2002) 'ぱちんこ機メーカーの特許プールによる参入の排除' (Pachinko machine manufacturers' use of patent pools to keep competitors out of the market). *Bessatsu Jurisuto* (Another Volume of Jurist), 161, pp. 111–113.

Fukuoka Prefectural Police History Compilation Committee (ed.) (1978) 福岡県警察史 (A history of the Fukuoka Prefectural Police).

Futami, M. (2001) パチンコの経済学 (Economics of pachinko). Ōesu Shuppan.

Gyōsei Kanri Tōkei Shukan (ed.) (1972) 日本標準産業分類——分類項目名、説明及び内容例示、50音索引表 1972年3月改定 (Standard industry categories of Japan – Category names, descriptions, and examples; phonetic index list, March 1972 Rev.). Administrative Management Agency.

Han, C. (2008) 十六歳漂流難民から始まった二兆円企業——パチンコ業で五兆円をめざすマルハンの挑戦 (The two-trillion-yen company that began with a 16-year old boatperson: Maruhan strives to achieve 5-trillion-yen sales in the pachinko industry). Shuppan Bunk Sha.

Han, J. (2006) '縁日娯楽の事業化への道—1950年代におけるパチンコ産業の胎動' (Commercialization of traditional festival-day entertainment: Inception of the pachinko industry). *Keieishigaku* (Japan Business History Review), 41(2), pp. 27–57.

--- (2010)「在日企業」の産業経済史——その社会的基盤とダイナミズム (An industry and economic history of companies operated by ethnic minority Koreans in Japan: Their social base and dynamic change). The University of Nagoya Press.

--- (2014) 'エスニック企業家' (Ethnic entrepreneurs). In Miyamoto, M., Kagono, K. and the Forum for Entrepreneurial Studies (eds.), 企業家学のすすめ (Recommendation of entrepreneurial studies). Yuhikaku, pp. 118–119.

--- (2018) パチンコ産業史—周縁経済から巨大市場へ— (History of the pachinko industry: From a peripheral economy to a huge market). The University of Nagoya Press.

Hanada, S. (2011) '産業サイクルに応じた政策設定の重要性——銭湯産業を事例として' (Importance of the policy response appropriates the industry life cycle: Case from the public bath industry). *Journal of Social Science* (ISS, University of Tokyo), 62(2), pp. 111–37.

Hasegawa, S. and the Committee on the History of Japan's Trade and Industry Policy (eds.) (2013) 1980-2000 通商産業政策史7 機械情報産業政策 (Ministry of International Trade and Industry history of industrial policy 7: Machine and information industry policy, 1980 to 2000). Research Institute of Economy, Trade and Industry.

Hashimoto, J. and Takeda, H. (eds.) (1985) 両大戦間期日本のカルテル (Japanese cartels between the two world wars). Ochanomizu Shobo.

Higuchi, N. (ed.) (2012) 日本のエスニック・ビジネス (Ethnic businesses in Japan). Sekaishisōsha.

Higuchi, T. (2006) 'VTR産業のライフサイクル' (Industrial life cycle in the VCR industry). *Sakushin Policy Studies*, 6, pp. 19–34.

Higyoku Ehōden: Takeya Gojūnen no Ayumi Hensanshitsu (ed.) (1996) 飛玉得宝伝 竹屋 五十年の歩み (A treasure of flying balls: 50 years of Takeya). Takeya.

Hyakusu Henshūshitsu (ed.) (1985) ザ・パチンコ——パチンコ台図鑑 (Pachinko: A pachinko atlas). Riburopōto.

Imperial Investigation (1955) *The Imperial Bank Company Digest*. Imperial Investigation.

Ino, K. (2000) やくざ戦後史 (A postwar history of the yakuza). Chikumashobo.

Ishige, N. (1989) 'パチンコ——遊びの中の仕事' (Pachinko: Work in the midst of play). In Moriya, T. (ed.), 現代日本文化における伝統と変容六日本人と遊び (Tradition and transformation in Japanese culture 6: Japanese and amusement). Domesu Publishers, pp. 173–96.

Itō, M. (1979) '日本人と娯楽第二三回パチンコ——日本を象徴する娯楽の王様' (Japanese and entertainment No. 23, pachinko: The king of entertainment symbolizes Japan). *Rekuriēshon* (Recreation), 230, pp. 32–35.

Japan Productivity Center (ed.) (2011) レジャー白書 進むレジャーの「デジタル」化 (Leisure white paper: The ongoing digitalization of leisure). Japan Productivity Center.

--- (ed.) (2016) レジャー白書 少子化時代のキッズレジャー (Leisure white paper: Kids' leisure in a time of low birth rates). Japan Productivity Center.

--- (ed.) (2020) レジャー白書 人口減少社会への挑戦 (Leisure white paper: Challenge to shrinking population). Japan Productivity Center.

Japan Tramway Society Nagoya Branch (ed.) (1997) 名古屋の市電と街並 (Nagoya's tram and urban landscape). Tonbow Publishing.

Jinbo, M. (2007) パチンコ年代記——銀玉に愛を込めて (Pachinko chronicles: To the silver balls, with love). Basilico.

Jitsugyō no Nihon Sha (1967) 実業之日本社70年史 (Seventy years of Jitsugyō no nihonsha). Jitsugyō no Nihon Sha.

Kaji, H. (2006) 'パチンコホールにおける経営改革の諸要因' (Key factors involved in pachinko-parlor management reforms). *Doshisha Business Review of Graduate Students*, 41(1), pp. 61–90.

--- (2007a) 'パチンコホール業界の現代的課題と対策 (I)' (Present-day problems and measures in the pachinko parlor industry [I]). *Shakai Kagaku* (The Social Science), 78, pp. 23–47.

--- (2007b) 'パチンコホール業界の現代的課題と対策 (II)' (Current issues in the pachinko parlor business, and related measures [II]). *Shakai Kagaku* (The Social Science), 79, pp. 59–82.

--- (2009a) 'ダイエーによるパチンコ業界への参入' (Entry of Daiē into the pachinko industry). *Shakai Kagaku* (The Social Science), 83, pp. 99–125.

--- (2009b) '異業種企業によるパチンコ業界への参入実態' (Status of the entry into the pachinko industry of companies from other industries). *Shakai Kagaku* (The Social Science), 85, pp. 79–109.

--- (2010) 'パチンコホール企業改革の促進要因——二〇〇〇年代の場合' (Factors to reform the pachinko-parlor enterprise: The case of the 2000s). *Doshisha Business Review*, 61(6), pp. 596–624.

--- (2015) パチンコホール企業改革の研究 (Research into innovation by pachinko parlor operators). Bunshindo.

Kamei, S. (ed.) (1990) パチンコけんけん学々 (All about pachinko). Zenponsha.

Kang, S. (1996) 五グラムの攻防戦——パチンコ三〇兆円産業の光と影 (A five-gram struggle for supremacy: Light and darkness in the 3-trillion-yen industry of pachinko). Shueisha.

Kato, C. (2011) '〈周辺〉層と都市社会—川崎のスラム街から' (The 'marginalized' class and urban society: From the slums of Kawasaki). In Okado, M., Otsuki, N., Okada, T., Sato, T., Shindo, H. and Takaoka, H. (eds.), 高度成長の時代Ⅲ 成長と冷戦への問い (The period of rapid economic growth III: An examination of growth and the Cold War). Otsuki Shoten.

Kato, H. (1984) パチンコと日本人 (Pachinko and the Japanese people). Kodansha.

Kawai, H. (1995) パチンコ国富論——二一世紀アミューズメント産業の幕開け (A theory of national wealth based on pachinko: The dawn of the amusement industry of the 21st century). Diamond Inc.

Kimbara, S., Ishida, R., Ozawa, Y., Kajimura, H., Tanaka, H. and Mihashi, O. (1986) 日本のなかの韓国・朝鮮人・中国人——神奈川県内在住外国人実態調査より (South Koreans, North Koreans and Chinese in Japan: From a field survey of foreigners living in Kanagawa Prefecture). Akashi Shoten.

Kitahara, M. and Nippon Chōki Shinyō Ginkō Sangyō Kenkyūkai (eds.) (1970) レジャー産業 (Leisure industry). Toyo Keizai Inc.

Kosugi, T. (1968) 'レジャーと安全10パチンコ' (Leisure and safety 10: Pachinko). *Anzen Eiseino Hiroba* (Safety and Health Plaza), 9(10), pp. 82–85.

Koyanagi, K. (2000) Collaboration——〈生〉 (Collaboration: Life). Ripro.

Lampe, R. and Moser, P. (2010) 'Do patent pools encourage innovation? Evidence from the nineteenth-century sewing machine industry'. *The Journal of Economic History*, 70(4), pp. 898–920.

Lee, K. (2017) 'Home but not home: Four generations of an ethnic minority Korean family in Japan'. *The New York Times*, February 2.

Lee, M. J. (2007) *Free Food for Millionaires*. Grand Central Publishing.

--- (2017) *Pachinko*. Grand Central Publishing.

Leisure Development Center (ed.) (1980) レジャー白書 日本の余暇の現状 (Leisure white paper: Status of leisure in Japan). Leisure Development Center.

--- (ed.) (1983) レジャー白書 生活文化志向を強めるレジャー活動 (Leisure white paper: Leisure activities that are strengthening the focus on lifestyle culture). Leisure Development Center.

--- (ed.) (1985) レジャー白書'85 (Leisure white paper '85). Leisure Development Center.

--- (ed.) (1986) レジャー白書 レジャーも「女性の時代」- (Leisure white paper: Leisure too as an age of the woman). Leisure Development Center.

--- (ed.) (1987) レジャー白書 高まるリゾート需要 (Leisure white paper: Rising demand for resorts). Leisure Development Center.

--- (ed.) (1992) レジャー白書 分散型余暇社会に向けて (Leisure white paper: Towards a decentralized leisure society). Leisure Development Center.

--- (ed.) (1997) レジャー白書 連休新時代 (Leisure white paper: A new era of extended vacations). Leisure Development Center.

Mabe, Y. (1990) 驚異のパチンコ・ビジネス——知られざる一三兆円産業の内幕 (The surprising pachinko business: Behind the scenes of an unknown 13-trillion-yen industry). Sobokusha.

Maeda, S. (1991) パチンコ店経営のすべて (All about managing a pachinko parlor). Management Information Publisher.

Maruhan (ed.) (2007) 縮刷版 社内報マルハンニュース&ルーチェI創刊号から五八号まで (Company newsletter Maruhan news and Luce, pocket edition I: From the inaugural issue to No. 58). Maruhan.

--- (ed.) (2008) マルハン挑戦の五〇 (The first 50 years, 1957–2007: 50 years of Maruhan challenges). Shuppan Bunka Sha.

Masukawa, K. (1989) 賭博の日本史 (History of gambling in Japan). Heibonsha.

McGahan, A. and Silverman, B. (2001) 'How does innovative activity change as industries mature?' *International Journal of Industrial Organization*, 19(7), pp. 1141–60.

Meich, B. (2008) 'The power to destroy: The psychology of gaming taxation'. *Gambling Law Review and Economics*, 12(5), pp. 458–65.

Mesgena, A. (2006) '日本自動車産業のライフサイクル——六つの次元に基づく四つの段階の分析' (Life cycle of the Japanese auto industry: A four stage analysis based on six dimensions). *Ajiya Taiheiyō Kenkyū Ronbunshū* (Journal of the Graduate School of Asia-Pacific Studies), 11, pp. 211–32.

Ministry of International Trade and Industry Industrial Structure Council (ed.) (1973) わが国余暇の現状と余暇時代への展望 (The current state of leisure in Japan and the outlook for the leisure era). MITI Research Council.

Miyai, M. (1988) '特許プールに関するアメリカ判例法の研究(1)' (Study of American legal precedent related to patent pools, Part 1). *Ritsumeikan Hougaku* (Ritsumeikan Law), 200, pp. 475–513.

--- (1989a) '特許プールに関するアメリカ判例法の研究(2)' (Study of American legal precedent related to patent pools, Part 2). *Ritsumeikan Hougaku* (Ritsumeikan Law), 203, pp. 27–55.

--- (1989b) '特許プールに関するアメリカ判例法の研究(3)' (Study of American legal precedent related to patent pools, Part 3). *Ritsumeikan Hougaku* (Ritsumeikan Law), 204, pp. 209–33.

Miyatsuka, T. (1997) パチンコ学講座 (A course in pachinko studies). Kodansha.

Moore, G. (1991) *Crossing the Chasm: Marketing and Selling Disruptive Products to Mainstream Customers.* Harper Business Essentials.

--- (2002) キャズム——ハイテクをブレイクさせる「超」マーケティング理論 (Crossing the chasm: Marketing and selling disruptive products to mainstream customers). Kawamata, M. (trans.). Shōeisha.

Morikawa, M. (2014) サービス産業の生産性分析——ミクロデータによる実証 (Analysis of productivity in the service industry: Verification through micro-data). Nihon Hyōronsha.

Morita, M. (1953) '広島県におけるパチンコ課税の実情と対策' (Pachinko taxation practices and associated countermeasures in Hiroshima Prefecture). *Zei* (Tax), 8-1, pp. 67–69.

Moriya, T. (ed.) (1989) 現代日本文化における伝統と変容六日本人と遊び (Tradition and transformation in Japanese culture 6: Japanese and amusement). Domesu Publishers.

Motai, A. (1986) '大規模小売店立地と商業立地政策——地域経済視点からとらえた商業立地政策の模索' (Large-scale retail siting and business siting policy: Search for business siting policy from a regional economic perspective). *Josai Daigaku Joshi Tankidaigaku Kiyō* (Bulletin, Josai University Junior College for Women), 3(1), pp. 89–103.

Murakami, M. (1998a) 'パチンコ機パテント・プール事件勧告審決をめぐって(上)' (Decisions on official guidance in pachinko machine patent pool cases [Part 1]). *Kousei Torihiki* (Fair Trade), 569, pp. 37–44.

--- (1998b) 'パチンコ機パテント・プール事件勧告審決をめぐって(下)' (Decisions on official guidance in pachinko machine patent pool cases [Part 2]). *Kousei Torihiki* (Fair Trade), 570, pp. 54–62.

Murofushi, T. (1994) 未来産業としてのパチンコ——パチンコからパチーノへ (Pachinko as an industry of the future: From pachinko to pachinko). Niki Shuppan.

Nagai, Y. (2002) 風俗営業取締り (The crackdown on entertainment businesses). Kodansha.

Nakajima, K. (1997) 風雲五十年 (Life and times: 50 years). Saishobō.

Nakamura, S. (1955) '発式禁止後のパチンコ課税の運営' (Taxation of pachinko after the ban on successive-shot machines). *Zei* (Tax), pp. 49–53.

Nakazawa, T. (1995) パチンコビジネスのすべてがわかる本 (All about the pachinko business). Yamashita Shuppan.

National Confederation of Amusement Industry Cooperatives (Zen'yūren) (ed.) (1977) 全遊連(協)二五年史 (25 years of the National Confederation of Amusement Industry Associations). National Confederation of Amusement Industry Cooperatives.

National Police Agency (ed.) (1980) 昭和五五年版 警察白書 (Police white paper 1980). Printing Bureau of the Ministry of Finance.

--- (ed.) (1993) 平成五年版 警察白書 (Police white paper 1993). Printing Bureau of the Ministry of Finance.

--- (ed.) (2016) 平成二八年版 警察白書 (Police white paper 2016). Printing Bureau of the Ministry of Finance.

--- (ed.) (2020) 平成三〇年版 警察白書 (Police white paper 2020). Printing Bureau of the Ministry of Finance. Nikkei Insatsu.

Neary, L. (2017) '*Pachinko* is a family saga of exile, discrimination… And Japanese pinball'. NPR, 'The week's best stories from NPR Books'. http://www.npr.org/2017/02/06/5133046 28/pachinko-is-a-family-saga-of-exile-discrimination-and-japanese-pinball, accessed on April 3, 2017.

Nihon Yūgi Shinbunsha (ed.) (1953) パチンコ百科事典 (Encyclopedia of pachinko). Nihon Yūgi Shinbunsha.

Nijūgonen no Ayumi Henshū Iinkai (ed.) (1985) 二十五年のあゆみ (25 years of history). Japan Amusement Machine Industry Association.

Nishimura, S. (2004) '日本における知的財産管理の形成——重電機器をめぐる特許係争事件を中心に' (Development of intellectual property management in Japan – Patent disputes revolving around heavy equipment). *Keizai Ronsō* (Economic Review Series), 174(3), pp. 234–50.

--- (2005) '特許プールと電球産業統制——東京電気による知的財産管理の展開' (Patent pools and light-bulb industry controls – The development of intellectual property management by Tokyo Electric). *Keizai Ronsō* (Economic Review Series), 175(1), pp. 36–53.

Noji, T. (2016) 北浦和のパチンコ店が一〇〇〇億円企業になった——埼玉・ガーデングループの小さな奇跡 (A pachinko parlor in Kitaurawa became a 100-billion-yen company: The minor miracle of Saitama's Garden Group). President Inc.

Onishi, K. and Ito, T. (2009) 'パテント・プールによる私的独占——パチンコ機／パチスロ機事件' (Private monopolization by means of patent pools: Pachinko and *pachislot* machine incidents). In Okada, Y. and Hayashi, S. (eds.), 独占禁止法の経済学——審判決の事例分析 (Economics of the anti-monopoly act: Analysis of case judgments). University of Tokyo Press, pp. 251–72.

Osaka Prefecture Police Headquarters General Affairs Department Public Relations Section (1958) 大阪府警察年鑑 昭和32年版 (1957 Osaka Prefecture police yearbook).

Osatake, T. (1925) 賭博と掏摸の研究 (Research on gambling and pickpocketing). Sōyōsha Shoten.

Oya, S. (1951) '賭博国家はいつまで続くか' (How long will the nation of gamblers survive?). *Fainansu Daijesuto* (Finance Digest), 5(16), pp. 70–71.

Park, K. (1989) 解放後在日朝鮮人運動史 (History of movements of the Korean minority in Japan after liberation). San-ichi Shobō.

Penrose, E. T. (1959) *The Theory of the Growth of the Firm*. Basil Blackwell.

Planning Division, General Affairs Office, Metropolitan Police Department (ed.) (1953) 昭和二六年 警視庁事務年鑑 (Tokyo Metropolitan Police Department yearbook, 1951).

--- (ed.) (1957) 昭和三一年 警視庁事務年鑑 (Tokyo Metropolitan Police Department yearbook, 1956).

Research and Statistics Department, Ministry of Economy, Trade and Industry (ed.) (1958) 昭和30年 工業統計表品目編 (1955 statistical tables for industry [individual item section]).

Research Bureau of the Economic Planning Agency (経済企画庁調査局) (ed.) (1963) 独身勤労者の消費生活 (Lifestyles of single workers). Printing Bureau of the Ministry of Finance.

--- (ed.) (1965) 独身勤労者の消費生活 昭和四〇年 (Lifestyles of single workers in 1965). Printing Bureau of the Ministry of Finance.

--- (ed.) (1967) 独身勤労者の消費生活 昭和四二年三月 (Lifestyles of single workers in March 1967). Printing Bureau of the Ministry of Finance.

--- (ed.) (1968) 独身勤労者の消費生活 (Lifestyles of single workers). Printing Bureau of the Ministry of Finance.

--- (ed.) (1973) 独身勤労者の消費生活 (Lifestyles of single workers). Printing Bureau of the Ministry of Finance.

--- (ed.) (1978) 独身勤労者の消費生活 第二四回 (Lifestyles of single workers, 24th survey). Printing Bureau of the Ministry of Finance.

Rogers, E. M. (1962) *Diffusion of Innovations*. The Free Press of Glencoe.

Saitō, M. (ed.) (1972) 百年を築いた人びと遊技業界人物伝 (1) (Lives of the people who built the pachinko industry for 100 years, Part 1). Yuhgi Journal.

Saitō, T. (1975) 'いま盛況の商売研究経営安定のパチンコ店' (Research into businesses that are prospering now: Pachinko parlors as consistent performers). *Ōru Seikatsu*, 30(7), pp. 71–74.

Sakai, S. (2010) パチンコ裏物語 (Behind the scenes of pachinko). Saizusha.

San'yō Mākettingu Sentā (ed.) (1991) 三十年の軌跡岡山県遊協の三十年の歩み (Thirty years of the Okayama Prefecture Amusement Industry Cooperative). Okayama Prefecture Amusement Industry Cooperative.

Sanjūgo nen no Ayumi Henshū Iinkai (ed.) (1995) 三十五年のあゆみ (35 years of history). Japan Amusement Machine Industry Association.

Sanjūnen no Ayumi Henshū Iinkai (ed.) (1990) 三十年のあゆみ (Thirty years of history). Japan Amusement Machine Industry Association.

Sanjūnenshi Henshū Iinkai (ed.) (1981) 東京都遊連(協)三十年史 (30 years of the Tokyo Pachinko and Pachislot Cooperative Associations). Tokyo Pachinko and Pachislot Cooperative Associations.

Shibuya, T. (1997) '特許プールと独占禁止法——パチンコ機製造業者事件を中心に' (Patent pools and the Anti-monopoly Act – Pachinko machines: Focusing on manufacturer incidents). *Kōsei Torihiki* (Fair Trade), 566, pp. 20–24.

Shinmei, M. (1951) '時論要解 パチンコの流行 日本文化の象徴' (Outline of current events: The popularity of pachinko, a symbol of Japanese culture). *Jiji Press Jiji Commentary Edition*. Jiji Press, 1835, pp. 2313–14.

--- (1954) '時論要解 連発式パチンコの禁止' (Outline of current events: Abolition of self-feeding pachinko machines). *Jiji Press Jiji Commentary Edition*. Jiji Press, 2728, pp. 3129–30.

Shiryō Henshū Iinkai (ed.) (1989) 全遊協(連)資料昭和篇(I)二八年～三三年 (Documents of the National Confederation of Pachinko Industry Cooperatives, Showa Edition [I] 1953 to 1958). National Confederation of Amusement Industry Associations and Japan Federation of Amusement Business Cooperative Associations.

Sibbitt, E. C. (1997) 'Regulating gambling in the shadow of the law: Form and substance in the regulation of Japan's pachinko industry'. *Harvard International Law Journal*, 38, pp. 569–86.

Small Business Information Center (ed.) (1980) 需要動向調査報告書余暇生活関連品 その四娯楽産業編 (Report on demand trends: Leisure and related, Part 4 – Entertainment industry edition). Small and Medium Enterprise Promotion Corporation.

So, S. (1972) '今月のトピック 葉っぱとパチンコ' (This month's topic: Leaf and pachinko). *Dōmei* (Alliance), 166, p. 46.

Sogo Unicom (1982) パチンコ産業年鑑1983 (Pachinko industry yearbook: 1983). Sogo Unicom.

Sōgyō Gojūnen Kinenshi Hensan Iinkai (2001) 創業五十周年記念誌 (The 50th anniversary road: 50th anniversary issue). Sofia.

Sōritsu Sanjū Shūnen Kinen Taikai Kinenshi Bukai (ed.) (1993) 新たなる健全 娯楽の道をめざして広島県遊技業協同組合創立三〇周年記念誌 (Striving to find a path to a new and healthy amusement industry: Issue commemorating the 30th anniversary of the Hiroshima Prefecture Amusement Industry Cooperative Association). Hiroshima Prefecture Amusement Industry Cooperative Association.

Stacks, L. (2017) 'Why Min Jin Lee's new novel *Pachinko* took 30 years to write'. *Chicago Review of Books*. https://chireviewofbooks.com/2016/05/12/bea-16-why-min-jin-lees-new-novel-took-30-years-to-write/, accessed on April 3, 2017.

Statistics Bureau of Japan, Prime Minister's Office (ed.) (1959) わが国事業所の現状——昭和32年度事業所統計調査の解説 (Businesses in Japan: Explanation of the FY1957 Business Statistical Study).

Sugimura, N. (1996) 都市と遊技場——パチンコ店の地域分析 (Cities and pachinko: A geographic analysis of pachinko parlors). Taimeidō.

Sugiyama, K. (2008) パチンコ誕生——シネマの世紀の大衆娯楽 (Birth of pachinko: Mass amusement in the century of film). Sogensha.

Suzuki, E. (ed.) (1997) 正村竹一資料室 第二章パチンコミュージアム (Takeichi Masamura archives Chapter 2: Pachinko museum). Takeichi Masamura Archives.

--- (2001) 天の釘——現代パチンコを作った男 正村竹一 (Pins of heaven: Takeichi Masamura, the man who created modern pachinko). Banseisha.

Suzuki, M. (2003) 'パテント・プールと独占禁止法——パチンコ機メーカー私的独占事件を中心に' (Patent pools and the Act on Prohibition of Private Monopolization and Maintenance of Fair Trade – Private monopolization cases involving pachinko machine manufacturers). *Tōin Ronsō* (The Toin Review), 10, pp. 7–13.

Tada, M. (1974) 遊びと日本人 (Leisure and the Japanese people). Chikumashobo.

Takeda, H. (1972) 'パチンコ商法の秘密' (Secrets of the pachinko business). *Chūō Kōron Keiei Mondai*, 11(3), pp. 268–81.

--- (1983) 路地裏の経済学 (Back-alley economics). Shinchosha.

--- (ed.) (1995) 日本産業発展のダイナミズム (Dynamisms of Japan's industrial development). University of Tokyo Press.

--- (ed.) (2007) 日本経済の戦後復興——未完の構造転換 (The Japanese postwar economic recovery: An incomplete structural transition). Yuhikaku.

--- (2017) 異端の試み——日本経済史研究を読み解く (Heretical experiments: Deciphering research into Japanese economic history). Nihon Keizai Hyouronsha.

Takita, K. (1965) '風俗営業に関する一問題——ぱちんこ遊技の健全化について' (An issue in the entertainment business: Transforming pachinko into a healthy enterprise). *Keisatsugaku Ronsyu* (Journal of Police Science), 18-6, pp. 59–72.

Takizawa, H. (1980) 明珠照影——パチンコ界の巨星・清水一二の生涯 (An exceptional life: Ichizō Shimizu, shining star in the pachinko universe). Chūō Kōron Jigyō Shuppan.

Tanaka, S. and Hayashi, S. (2010) '『パチンコ機特許プール事件』再考' (Pachinko machine patent pool cases: A reexamination). *Shakai Kagaku Kenkyu* (Social Science Research), 61(2), pp. 136–162.

Tanihara, O. (1998) '経済法判例研究会 ぱちんこ機械製造業者の私的独占事件——公取委勧告審決平成九・六・二十' (Economic Law Judicial Precedent Study Group: Cases involving private monopolization by pachinko machine manufacturers – Decisions of the Fair Trade Commission on June 20, 1997). *Juristo* (Jurist), 1130, pp. 111–13.

Tanioka, I. (1998) 現代パチンコ文化考 (Thinking about pachinko today). Chikuma Shobo.

Thomson, R. (1987) 'Learning by selling and invention: The case of the sewing machine', *Journal of Economic History*, 47(2), pp. 433–45.

Tokyo Pachinko and Pachislot Cooperative Associations (1999) 凌雲 東京都遊技場組合連合会創立50周年記念／東京都遊技業協同組合30周年記念誌 (Commemorative publication of both associations). Tokyo Pachinko and Pachislot Cooperative Associations.

Uekusa, M. (ed.) (1997) 社会的規制の経済学 (Economics of social regulation). NTT Publishing.

--- (2000) 公的規制の経済学 (Economics of public regulation). NTT Publishing.

Venkatesh, S. A. (2009) *Off the Books: The Underground Economy of the Urban Poor*. Harvard University Press.

Vernon, R. (1966) 'International investment and international trade in the product cycle'. *The Quarterly Journal of Economics*, 80(2), pp. 190–207.

Wakamiya, K. (2010) なぜ韓国はパチンコを全廃できたのか (Why was South Korea able to abolish pachinko). Shodensha.

Willis, D. B. and Lee, S. (2007) 'Korean minority entrepreneurs in Japan'. In Dana, L.-P. (ed.), *Handbook of Research on Ethnic Minority Entrepreneurship: A Co-evolutionary View on Resource Management*. Edward Elgar Publishing, pp. 653–68.

Yamada, H. (1993) '製品ライフサイクルから見たOEM戦略' (OEM strategy depending on the product life cycle). *Journal of Science Policy and Research Management*, 7(3), pp. 233–40.

Yamada, S. (2012) '出願公開制度と技術知識のスピルオーバー効果' (Patent disclosure system and the spillover effects of technical knowledge). *Senshū Keizaigaku Ronshū* (Journal of Economics, Senshu University), 47-1, pp. 23–46.

Yamada, S. and Imaizumi, H. (eds.) (2002) ヨーロッパに生まれ日本で育ったパチンコ百年史 (100 years of pachinko: Born in Europe, bred in Japan). Ado Sākuru.

Yamaoka, A. (1976) 'パチンコと技術革新' (Pachinko and technological innovation). *Bungei Shunju*, 540, pp. 83–84.

Yano Research Institute (1989) 一九八九年パチンコ産業白書 (1989 pachinko industry white paper). Yano Research Institute.

--- (2016) 全国パチンコ経営企業数及び店舗数に関する調査結果二〇一五 (Results of a 2015 survey of numbers of pachinko businesses and outlets nationwide). Yano Research Institute.

Yashima, T. (1954) 'パチンコの上前をはねる珍商売買取屋' (The buyers who take a cut of pachinko). *Maru*, 7(10), pp. 68–71.

Yoshida, Y. (1989) 遊技店立て直し屋が語る儲かるパチンコ ちょっといい話 (A specialist in revitalizing amusement parlors tells how to make money from pachinko). Sankei-Shobo.

Yūgi Tsūshinsha (ed.) (2001) 創刊五十年特別記念号 パチンコの八十年 (Special 50th anniversary commemorative issue: 80 years of pachinko). Yūgi Tsūshinsha.

Yūgi Tsūshinsha (ed.) (2011) 遊技通信創刊六〇周年記念号 遊技通信でみるパチンコ業界の六〇年 (Special issue commemorating the 60th anniversary of *Yūgi Tsūshin*'s founding: 60 years of the pachinko industry as seen in *Yūgi Tsūshin*). Yūgi Tsūshinsha.

INDEX